ROMAN STOICISM

T0384924

ROMAN STOICISM

BEING LECTURES ON THE HISTORY OF THE
STOIC PHILOSOPHY WITH SPECIAL
REFERENCE TO ITS DEVELOPMENT
WITHIN THE ROMAN EMPIRE

BY

E. VERNON ARNOLD, Litt.D.

PROFESSOR OF LATIN IN THE UNIVERSITY COLLEGE OF NORTH WALES
AND FORMERLY FELLOW OF TRINITY COLLEGE, CAMBRIDGE

Cambridge :
at the University Press
1911

CAMBRIDGE
UNIVERSITY PRESS

University Printing House, Cambridge CB2 8BS, United Kingdom

Cambridge University Press is part of the University of Cambridge.

It furthers the University's mission by disseminating knowledge in the pursuit of education, learning and research at the highest international levels of excellence.

www.cambridge.org
Information on this title: www.cambridge.org/9781107594135

© Cambridge University Press 1911

This publication is in copyright. Subject to statutory exception and to the provisions of relevant collective licensing agreements, no reproduction of any part may take place without the written permission of Cambridge University Press.

First published 1911
First paperback edition 2015

A catalogue record for this publication is available from the British Library

ISBN 978-1-107-59413-5 Paperback

Cambridge University Press has no responsibility for the persistence or accuracy of URLs for external or third-party internet websites referred to in this publication, and does not guarantee that any content on such websites is, or will remain, accurate or appropriate.

HENRICO JACKSON, Litt.D.

DILECTISSIMO PRAECEPTORI

PREFACE

THIS book is the outcome of a course of lectures delivered by me in successive years to Latin Honours students in accordance with the regulations of the University of Wales. It is therefore primarily intended for the assistance of classical students ; but it may perhaps appeal in its present form to a somewhat wider circle.

At the time that the book was begun the best systematic exposition of the Stoic philosophy available for English readers was to be found in Prof. E. ZELLER'S *Stoics Epicureans and Sceptics*, translated by O. J. REICHEL (Longmans, 1892). This work, admirable in detail, is nevertheless somewhat inadequate to the subject, which appeared to its learned author as a mere sequel to the much more important philosophical systems of Plato and Aristotle. Since its first appearance many qualified writers have been inclined to assign a higher rank to Stoicism, amongst whom L. STEIN, A. SCHMEKEL, and HANS von ARNIM in the German-speaking countries, and A. C. PEARSON, G. H. RENDALL, and R. D. HICKS in our own, are perhaps most conspicuous.

The view taken in this book corresponds generally to that taken by the writers named. Shortly expressed, it regards Stoicism as the bridge between ancient and modern philosophical thought; a position which appears to be accepted by

W. L. DAVIDSON writing on behalf of students of modern philosophy. Mr Hicks and Mr Davidson have recently published works dealing with the Stoic philosophy as a whole; but as neither of these quite covers the ground marked out for this book, I believe that room will be found for a further presentation of the subject.

To the writers named and to many others, my obligations are great, and their extent is generally indicated in the Index. I owe a more intimate debt to Mr A. C. PEARSON and Prof. ALFRED CALDECOTT, who have given me ungrudgingly of their knowledge and counsel during the whole period of the preparation of this book.

The appearance of H. von Arnim's 'Stoicorum veterum fragmenta' made available to me a mass of material from Greek sources, and has (I hope) made this book less imperfect on the side of Greek than it would otherwise have been. For the quotations in the notes from the Greek and the less-known Latin authors I have generally given references to von Arnim's collections, which will doubtless be more accessible to most of my readers than the original writers. These references include those to the fragments of Zeno and Cleanthes, for which von Arnim is in the main indebted to the earlier work of Pearson.

So general a treatment of the subject as is here presented must necessarily leave room for correction and amplification in its various branches, and I trust that I am pointing out to younger students a field in which a rich harvest may yet be gleaned. To such students the appended Bibliography, though necessarily incomplete, may be of use as an introduction to the considerable literature which is available to them.

The concluding chapter makes its appeal not so much to classical students, as such, as to those who are interested in the problem of Christian origins; the further problems of the influence of Stoicism on modern literature and philosophy, though at first included in my programme, I have not ventured to enter upon. But I hope that at least I have been able to show that the interest of classical studies, even as regards Hellenistic philosophy, does not lie wholly in the past.

My sincere thanks are due to the Council of the University College of North Wales for granting me special assistance in my College duties during the Spring term of 1910, in order that I might give more time to this book; to the Syndics of the Cambridge University Press for undertaking its publication; and to Mr Clay and his expert staff for the admirable execution of the printing.

E. VERNON ARNOLD

25 *January* 1911

CORRIGENDA ET NOTANDA

In the text the accentuation of Greek words should be corrected as follows :

P. 117, l. 10, χρεῖαι. P. 239, l. 6, μέρων. P. 423, l. 16, ἀγάπη.

For the quotations in the notes from Greek writers, more precise references will usually be found in the sections named of von Arnim's *Stoicorum veterum fragmenta.* In addition the following amplifications or corrections are needed :

P. 105, n. 44 ; Clem. *Strom.* ii 21, 129. P. 133, n. 38 ; Nem. *nat. hom.* vi 13. P. 142, n. 86 ; Sext. *math.* vii 184. P. 158, n. 17 ; Simp. *Arist. cat.* p. 269, 14 K ; Cens. fr. 1, 1. P. 159, n. 20 ; Simp. *Arist. cat.* p. 350, 16 K. P. 160, n. 30 ; for τόνος the word λόγος is now read, making the quotation inapplicable. P. 161, n. 133 ; add the words τοὺς ἐν ἑαυτῷ λόγους. The reference is to Simpl. *Arist. cat.* p. 306, 23 K. P. 164, n. 45 ; Simp. *Arist. cat.* p. 66, 32 K ; n. 47, *ib.* p. 165, 32 K. P. 166, n. 60 ; *ib.* p. 269, 14 K. P. 168, n. 75 ; *ib.* p. 165, 32 K. P. 173, n. 110 ; Galen *const. art. med.* p. 253 K ; n. 111, *meth. med.* i 2 p. 16 K. P. 185, n. 79 ; for ἀπό read ὑπό. P. 187, n. 86 ; Sext. *math.* viii 271. P. 193, n. 130 ; Nemes. *nat. hom.* xxxviii 95. P. 196, n. 145 ; Galen *de temp.* p. 617 K. P. 222, n. 33 ; Corn. *N. D.* ii. P. 224, n. 47 ; Sext. *math.* vii 93. P. 251, n. 76 ; Galen *plac. Hipp. et Plat.* p. 242 K. P. 255, n. 86 ; for μῖγμα read μίγμα. P. 264, n. 139 ; to the quotation from Comm. *in Luc.* ix 6 add ' et esse sic immortales ut non moriantur sed resolvantur.' P. 298, n. 184 ; Alex. Aph. *de fato* 28, p. 199, 18 B.

CONTENTS

·

CHAPTER I.

THE WORLD-RELIGIONS.

1. THE present work treats of a subject of outstanding
Roman litera- interest in the literature which is associated with
ture. the history of the Roman State, and which is
expressed partly in Hellenistic Greek, partly in Latin. In the
generations preceding our own, classical study has, to a large
extent, attended to form rather than to matter, to expression
rather than to content. To-day it is beginning to take a wider
outlook. We are learning to look on literature as an unveiling
of the human mind in its various stages of development, and as
a key to the true meaning of history. The literature of Greece
proper does not cease to attract us by its originality, charm, and
variety; but the new interest may yet find its fullest satisfaction
in Roman literature; for of all ancient peoples the Romans
achieved most, and their achievements have been the most
enduring. It was the Roman who joined the ends of the world
by his roads and his bridges, poured into crowded towns unfailing supplies of corn and perennial streams of pure water, cleared
the countryside of highwaymen, converted enemies into neighbours, created ideals of brotherhood under which the nations
were united by common laws and unfettered marriage relations,
and so shaped a new religion that if it shattered an empire it
yet became the mother of many nations. We are the inheritors
of Roman civilization; and if we have far surpassed it in
scientific knowledge and material plenty, we are not equally
confident that we possess better mental balance, or more complete social harmony. In this direction the problems of Roman
life are the problems of Western life to-day; and the methods

A. 1

by which they were approached in the Roman world deserve
more than ever to be studied by us. Such a study, if it is to be
in any true sense historical, must break through the convention
by which ancient Greece and Rome have come to be treated as
a world apart; it must seek its starting point in the distant past,
and count that of chief importance which will bear fruit in the
ages that follow.

2. Great achievements are born of strong convictions; and
Beliefs of the   Roman statesmen, jurists, soldiers, and engineers
Romans.   did not learn to 'scorn delights and live laborious
days' without some strong impulse from within. These inner
convictions do not come to the surface everywhere in the Latin
literature with which we are most familiar. The Roman orator
or poet is generally content to express a conventional view of
religion and morals, whilst he conceals his real thoughts in a
spirit of reticence and almost of shame. Yet here and there
every attentive reader will catch the accent of sincerity, sometimes in the less restrained conversation of the lower classes,
sometimes in flights of poetic imagination, or again in instruction
designed for the young. In this way we learn that the Romans
of the last century of the republic and of the first century of the
principate were profoundly concerned, not so much with questions connected with the safety of their empire or the justice
of their form of government, as with problems in which all
mankind has a common interest. What is truth, and how can
it be ascertained? What is this universe in which we dwell,
and by whom and how was it made? What are the beings
called gods, and do they concern themselves with the affairs of
men? What is man's nature, his duty, and his destiny? These
the Romans called the problems of philosophy, and they eagerly
sought for definite and practical solutions to them[1]. Such
solutions when embodied in theoretical systems we still call
'philosophies'; but when such systems are developed in a
practical form and claim the obedience of large bodies of men
they become religions. Stoicism is in the first instance a
philosophy, and amongst its many competitors that one which

---

[1] See below, § 441.

appealed most successfully to the judgment of men who played a leading part in the Roman world; but as its acceptance becomes more general, it begins to assume all the features of a religion. All Latin literature is thickly strewn with allusions to Stoicism and the systems which were its rivals, and thus bears witness to the widespread interest which they excited.

3. The Romans learnt philosophy from Greek teachers; Origin of Philosophy. and they were not free from a sense of shame in thus sitting at the feet of the children of a conquered race. But they acknowledged their obligations in a generous spirit; and from Roman literature an impression has arisen, which is still widespread, that Greece was the birthplace of philosophy, and that its triumphs must be placed to the credit of Hellenic culture. But to the Hellenes themselves philosophy equally appeared as a foreign fashion, assailing their national beliefs and dangerous to their established morality; and of its teachers many of the most distinguished were immigrants from Asia Minor. Thus Greece itself appears only as a halting-place in the movement of philosophy; and we are carried more and more to the East as we seek to discover its origin. Yet at the time with which we are concerned it had also spread to the extreme West. 'The Magi,' says Aristotle, 'taught the Persians philosophy; the Chaldaeans taught it to the Babylonians and Assyrians; the Gymnosophists to the Indians; the Druids and Semnothei to the Gauls and Celts[2].' It was a world-wide stirring of the human intellect, and we must attempt to outline its meaning more completely.

4. Philosophy, in the sense in which Aristotle uses the National and World-Religions. term, appears to be a general name for a great change in man's intellectual attitude towards his environment, corresponding to a definite era in the history of civilization. Before philosophy came nationalism, the habit of thinking according to clan and race; and nationalism remains on record for us in the numerous national religions in which each people does reverence to the deity which lives within its borders and goes forth to fight with its armies. Philosophy

[2] Diog. L. Prooem. 1.

is at once broader in its outlook and more intimate in its appeal. It breaks down the barriers of race, and includes the whole world in its survey; but on the other hand it justifies the individual in asserting his own thoughts and choosing his own way of life. Thus philosophy on its arrival appears in each particular country as a disintegrating force; it strikes at the roots of patriotism and piety, and challenges equally the authority of king and of priest. But everywhere in turn philosophy, as it gains ground, begins to construct a new patriotism and a new piety, and gradually takes concrete shape as a new religion. To us, as we look backwards to the past, the track of philosophy is recorded by a series of religions, all alike marked with the note of world-wide outlook, reverence for reason, and the sentiment of human sympathy. The era of philosophy is the era of the world-religions. It belongs to that millennium when from China to Ireland men of good will and bold spirit realized that they all looked up toward one sky, breathed one air, and travelled on one all-encircling sea; when they dreamed that before long all men should be united in one kingdom, converse in one language, and obey the one unchanging law of reason.

5. The general importance and direction of this movement will best be seen if we select for consideration a certain number of the world-religions in which it was from time to time embodied. Aristotle has

Spread of the World-Religions.

already called our attention to the 'philosophies' of the Chaldaeans, the Persians, and the Indians; amongst these last Buddhism at least was a movement which had shaken off limitations of race and class. To these he has added the Druids, whom we may well keep in mind if only because they are representatives of Western Europe. Stoicism best represents the part played by the Greco-Roman world, and Judaism and Christianity come under consideration as forces with which Stoicism in the course of its history came into close contact. The Greeks little realized that they were being carried along in so mighty a stream. Regarding themselves as isolated and elevated, the sole pioneers of civilization in a 'barbarian' world, the beliefs of neighbouring peoples seemed to them beneath their notice. To this prejudice they clung in spite of the protests of their own men of learning[3]; the Romans inherited it from them ; and though the Europe of the Middle Ages and of to-day professes an Oriental faith, its religious survey is still limited and its critical power impaired by the same assumption of superior wisdom. Our information is however wider than that of the ancient world, and our sympathies are beginning to be quickened ; and we are thus in a position to trace generally the history of these seven religions. In this work we shall use, as far as possible, the classical authorities, supplementing them (where deficient) from other sources.

6. The oldest of these philosophical or religious systems is

Chaldaism.

that of the Chaldaeans, as the Romans termed a pastoral, star-gazing folk[4] presumably identical with the people which, in or about the year 2800 B.C.[5], mapped out the constellations as we now know them, traced the orbits of the planets[6], and predicted their future movements. This work was not carried out entirely in the spirit of modern science ; it was further stimulated by the belief that the skies displayed a written message to mankind. But the nature of that message, of which fragments are possibly embodied in the names of the constellations, was not preserved to the Romans by any tradition. Two principles seem to have survived, those of the inexorable tie between cause and effect called 'fate[7],' and of the interdependence of events in heaven and on earth[8]. Hence arose the hope of prophetic insight into the future ; and the people of Babylon, under Chaldaean influence, are said to have spent

---

[3] Gomperz, *Greek Thinkers*, ii p. 161 ; and below, § 94.

[4] 'principes Chaldaei, qui in patentibus campis colebant, stellarum motus et vias et coetus intuentes, quid ex his efficeretur observaverunt' Gellius, *N. A.* xiv 1, 8.

[5] Sir E. Walter Maunder, in the *Nineteenth Century* for September 1900.

[6] 'quinque stellarum potestates Chaldaeorum observatio excepit' Seneca, *N. Q.* ii 32, 6.

[7] This is well described by Cicero, translating from a Stoic source: 'cum fato omnia fiant, si quis mortalis possit esse, qui colligationem causarum omnium perspiciat animo, nihil eum profecto fallat. qui enim teneat causas rerum futurarum, idem necesse est omnia teneat quae futura sint' *Div.* i 56, 127. It seems reasonable to suppose that this general conception of 'fate' or 'destiny' is deduced from the unchanging movements of the heavenly bodies.

[8] 'videbis quinque sidera diversas agentia vias; ex horum levissimis motibus fortunae populorum dependent' Sen. *Dial.* vi 18, 3.

four hundred and seventy years in collecting observations of the history of boys born under particular combinations of the heavenly bodies[9]. We are not acquainted with the results of these observations; but undoubtedly they established a profession of astrologers, whose craft it was to observe the position of sun, moon and stars at a man's birth or at some other critical hour, and thence to deduce his future character or career. These wanderers, called by the Romans 'Chaldaei' or 'Mathematici,' spread over all Europe, and founded a lucrative trade on men's fears and ambitions. Philosophers studied their methods, and did not always entirely deny their validity[10]. In society the astrologer is a common figure[11]; he found his way to the chambers of princes[12], and was regularly consulted by conspirators. The dramatic scene in Walter Scott's *Betrothed* is as true in character to Roman times as to the Middle Ages. Roman literature is full of allusions to the horoscope[13]. But whether we attribute these practices to fraud or to self-deception, there is every reason to believe that they only form a diseased outgrowth from a system which at an earlier time was of much wider import.

7. The popular expression 'magic' still recalls to us the system of which the Magi of Persia were the professed exponents, and of which the Romans had a knowledge which is to a large extent confirmed from other sources. This system we shall here call 'Persism,' in order to

Persism.

---

[9] 'aiunt quadringenta septuaginta milia annorum in periclitandis experiundisque pueris, quicunque essent nati, Babylonios posuisse' Cic. *Div.* ii 46, 97. I assume that the original tradition named the smaller number suggested above.

[10] 'duo apud Chaldaeos studuisse se dicunt, Epigenes et Apollonius Myndius' Sen. *N. Q.* vii 4, 1; 'Diogenes Stoicus [Chaldaeis] concedit, aliquid ut praedicere possint' Cic. *Div.* ii 43, 90. Seneca concludes against their authority, observing (i) that a proper horoscope should include all the stars in the heaven at the moment of birth, and (ii) that twins should always have the same fortune, which is obviously untrue; see *N. Q.* ii 32, 6 to 8, *Ben.* vii 1, 5.

[11] 'tu ne quaesieris (scire nefas), quem mihi, quem tibi | finem di dederint, Leuconoe, nec Babylonios | temptaris numeros' Hor. *C.* i 11, 1–3.

[12] See the interesting tale of Thrasyllus and Tiberius in Tac. *Ann.* vi 21, to which the author affects to give some credit.

[13] e.g., 'seu Libra seu me Scorpios adspicit | formidulosus, pars violentior | natalis horae, seu tyrannus | Hesperiae Capricornus undae, | utrumque nostrum incredibili modo | consentit astrum' Hor. *C.* ii 17, 17–22.

free ourselves of the popular associations still connected with such terms as Magism, Parsee-ism, and so forth; meaning by 'Persism' the teaching of Zarathustra (the Latin Zoroastres) as it affected the Greek and Latin world. Persism has its roots in the older nationalism, inasmuch as its deity is one who takes sides with his believer and brings him victory in war; but on the other hand it grows into a world-religion because that which begins as a conflict between races gradually changes into a struggle between right and wrong. It is based also on the Chaldaean system, in so far as it looks up to the heaven as the object of human reverence and to the sun, moon and planets as at least the symbols of human destiny; but here again the outlook is transformed, for in the place of impersonal and inexorable forces we find a company of celestial beings, intimately concerned in the affairs of men, and engaged in an ardent struggle for the victory of the better side. The meaning of Persism and its immense influence on the Greco-Roman world are still so little realized that it is necessary here to deal with the subject with some fulness.

8. The Greeks and Romans refer to the teachings of
Zarathustra.
Zarathustra as of immemorial antiquity[14]; whilst on the other hand the direct Persian tradition (existing in a written form from about the year 800 A.D.) ascribes them to a date 258 years before the era of Alexander's invasion of Persia[15]. The best modern authorities incline to the Persian view, thus giving the date of about 600 B.C. to Zarathustra, and making him roughly a contemporary of the Buddha and Confucius[16]. On the other hand considerations, partly of the general history of religion, partly of the linguistic and metrical character of such fragments of Zarathustra's writings as still remain, indicate a date earlier than this by many hundred years[17]. Zarathustra belonged to the tribe of the Magi, who maintained religious practices of which the

[14] 'Eudoxus, qui inter sapientiae sectas clarissimam utilissimamque [artem magicam] intellegi voluit, Zoroastrem hunc sex millibus annorum ante Platonis mortem fuisse prodidit: sic et Aristoteles' Pliny, *N. H.* xxx 2, 1; cf. Diog. L. Prooem. 2 and 8.
[15] Williams-Jackson, *Zoroaster*, p. 161.   [16] *ib.* p. 174.
[17] K. Geldner, *Encycl. Brit.* ed. x, article 'Zoroaster.'

nature can only be inferred from such of them as survived the
prophet's reforms[18]; in their general character they cannot have
differed widely from those recorded in the Rigveda.   In the
midst of this system Zarathustra came forward as a reformer.
He was deeply learned in the doctrines of the Chaldaeans[19], and
was an ardent student of astronomy[20].   In a period of solitary
contemplation in the desert[21], it was revealed to him that a great
and wise being, named Ahura Mazdā, was the creator and ruler
of heaven and earth[22].   Upon him attend Angels who do him
service ; whilst the spirit of Mischief and his attendants cease-
lessly work to oppose his purposes.   Ahura is the light, his
enemy is the darkness[23].   The struggle between them is that
between right and wrong, and in it every man must take one or
the other side.   His soul will survive what men call death, and
receive an everlasting reward according to his deeds.   After
quitting the mortal body, the soul will pass over the Bridge
of Judgment, and will there be turned aside to the right or to
the left; if it has been virtuous, to enter Paradise, but if vicious,
the House of Falsehood.   Full of this doctrine, Zarathustra
enters the court of King Vishtāspa, and converts him and his
court.   The monarch in turn sets out to convert the unbelieving
world by the sword, and the War of Religion begins.

9.   We cannot trace the long history of the War of Religion

Spread of
Persism.
through its whole course, but in the end we find
that the Religion has welded together the great
kingdom of Persia, and its warlike zeal is directed towards
establishing throughout the world the worship of the 'God of
heaven,' and the destruction of all images, whether in the shape

---

[18] Williams-Jackson, p. 7.

[19] 'Magiam...cuius scientiae saeculis priscis multa ex Chaldaeorum arcanis
Bactrianus addidit Zoroastres' Amm. Marc. xxiii 6, 32.

[20] [Zoroastres] 'primus dicitur mundi principia siderumque motus diligentissime
spectasse' Justinus, *Hist. Phil.* i 1, 9 (Williams-Jackson, p. 237): 'astris multum
et frequenter intentus' Clem. Rom. *Recogn.* iv 27.

[21] 'tradunt Zoroastrem in desertis caseo vixisse' Pliny, *N. H.* xi 97.

[22] '[Ahura Mazdā] created the paths of the sun and the stars; he made the moon
to wax and wane' (*Yasna* 43, 3); 'he made the light and the darkness' (*ib.* 5); 'he
is the father of the good' (*ib.* 46, 2).

[23] ' Ζωροάστρης ὁ μάγος...προσαπεφαίνετο, τὸν μὲν ἐοικέναι φωτὶ μάλιστα τῶν αἰσθητῶν, τὸν δ' ἔμπαλιν σκότῳ καὶ ἀγνοίᾳ' Plut. *Isid. et Osir.* 46.

of men or of beasts, as dishonouring to the divine nature. In the sixth century B.C. Babylon opposed the Religion in the east, and Lydia in the west; both fell before Cyrus the Great. The fall of Babylon set free the Jews, who accepted the king's commission to establish the Religion in Jerusalem[24], and (at a rather later date) in Egypt[25]; on the other hand that of Lydia exposed the Hellenes, a people devoted to idol-worship, to the fury of the image-breakers[26]. The battles of Marathon and Salamis checked the warlike advance of Persism, and the victories of Alexander suppressed its outward observance and destroyed its literature and its priesthood. But in this period of apparent depression some at least of its doctrines were winning still wider acceptance than before.

10. The departure of the Persians from Europe was the

Persism in-vades Greece. signal for an outburst of enthusiasm in Greece for the old gods and their worship with the aid of images. Yet, unfavourable as the time might seem, a mono-theistic sentiment developed apace in Hellas, which we shall follow more closely in the next chapter[27]. Even Herodotus, writing as a fair-minded historian, no longer regards the Persians as impious, but realizes that they are actuated by conviction[28].

[24] 'Thus saith Cyrus, king of Persia:—all the kingdoms of the earth hath the Lord, the God of heaven, given me; and he hath charged me to build him an house in Jerusalem' Ezra i 2.

[25] See the interesting papyri records recently discovered in Elephantine, and published by Dr Sachau of Berlin. A general account of them is given by Prof. Driver in the London *Guardian* for Nov. 6, 1907.

[26] Cicero rightly appreciated the religious character of the Persian invasions: 'delubra humanis consecrata simulacris Persae nefaria putaverunt; eamque unam ob causam Xerxes inflammari Atheniensium fana iussisse dicitur, quod deos, quorum domus esset omnis hic mundus, inclusos parietibus contineri nefas esse duceret' *Rep.* iii 9, 14. So Themistocles as represented by Herodotus: 'the gods and heroes grudged that one man should become king both of Asia and of Europe, and he a man unholy and presumptuous, one who made no difference between things sacred and things profane, burning and casting down the images of the gods' *History* viii 109 (Macaulay's translation).

[27] See below, § 41.

[28] 'Images and temples and altars they do not account it lawful to erect, nay, they even charge with folly those who do these things; and this, as it seems to me, because they do not account the gods to be in the likeness of men, as do the Hellenes. But it is their wont to perform sacrifices to Zeus, going up to the most lofty of the mountains, and the whole circle of the heavens they call Zeus: and they sacrifice to the Sun and the Moon and the Earth, to Fire and to Water and to the

Socrates was an outspoken defender of all the main articles of the Religion, to the horror of nationalists like Aristophanes, who not unjustly accused him of corrupting the loyalty of the youth of Athens to the institutions of their mother city. Xenophon, the most intimate of his disciples, translated this bias into action, and joined with the 10,000 Greeks in a vain effort to re-establish the strength of Persia: he did not even hesitate to engage in war against his native land. To him Cyrus the Persian was a greater hero than any Homeric warrior or Greek sage; and from Cyrus he drew the belief in the immortality of the soul which from this time on is one of the chief subjects of philosophic speculation.

11.   The Romans had not the same national motives as the

Persism welcomed in Rome.

Greeks to feel an antipathy to Persism. For the doctrine of monotheism they had probably been prepared by their Etruscan sovereigns, and the temple of Capitoline Jove kept before their eyes a symbol of this sentiment.   But in the Roman period Persian sovereignty had receded to the far distance, and the doctrines of Persism only reached Rome through the Greek language and in Greek form.   Thus of the doctrines of the Evil Spirit, the war between Good and Evil, and the future punishment of the wicked, only faint echoes ever reached the Roman ear.   On the other hand the doctrines of the divine government of the world and of the immortality of the soul made a deep impression; and Cicero in a well-known passage repeats and amplifies the account Xenophon gives in his *Cyropaedia* of the dying words of Cyrus, which is doubtless to some extent coloured by recollections of the death of Socrates:

'We read in Xenophon that Cyrus the elder on his death-bed spoke as follows—" Do not think, my very dear children, that when I quit you I shall no longer be in existence.   So long as I was with you, you never saw my soul, but you realized from my actions that it dwelt in this my body. Believe then that it will still exist, even if you see nothing of it.   Honours would not continue to be paid to great men after death, did not their souls assist us to maintain their memory in freshness.   I have never been able to persuade myself that souls live whilst they are enclosed in mortal bodies,

Winds; these are the only gods to whom they have sacrificed ever from the first' *History* i 131 (Macaulay's translation).

and die when they issue from them ; nor that the soul becomes dull at the moment it leaves this dull body ; I believe that when it has freed itself from all contact with the body and has begun to exist in purity and perfection, then it becomes wise. Further, when the framework of humanity is broken up in death, we see clearly whither each of its parts speeds away, for all go to the elements from which they have sprung ; the soul alone is not seen by us either whilst it is with us or when it departs. Lastly nothing resembles death so closely as sleep. But men's souls, whilst they themselves sleep, most clearly reveal their divine nature ; for then, being set free from their prison house, they often foresee things to come. From this we may gather what their properties will be, when they have utterly freed themselves from the fetters of the body. If then this is so, do reverence to me as a god ; but if the soul is destined to perish with the body, still do reverence to the gods, who guard and rule all this beauteous world, and while so doing keep up the memory of me in loyal and unalterable affection." So spoke Cyrus on his death-bed[29].'

12. The Persian doctrine of the 'Angels' seems to have

The manifold deity.

been very little understood either in Greece or at Rome, but, as we shall see in the course of this book, it profoundly influenced the course of religious history. The 'Angels' or good Spirits of Persism are, from one point of view, identical with the Creator himself, forms under which he manifests himself to men. Their names are all those of abstractions: the Good Mind, the Best Reason, the Desired Kingdom, Holy Humility, Salvation, and Immortality[30]. On the other hand, they gradually assume to the worshipper who contemplates them the appearance of separate personalities, dwelling, like the Creator himself, in an atmosphere of heavenly Glory. Thus a system which is in principle strictly monotheistic gradually developes into one in which the deity is sevenfold, as in the following hymn from the later part of the Avesta:

> 'We praise the heavenly Glory,
> The mighty, the god-given,
> The praiseworthy, the life-giving,
> Healing, strengthening, watching
> High above the other creatures.

[29] Cic. *Sen.* 22, 79 to 81, after Xen. *Cyr.* viii 7.
[30] In the hymns of Zarathustra we can only trace the beginnings of this system, as in the following: 'All-wise Lord, all-powerful one, and thou Piety, and Righteousness, Good Mind and the Kingdom, listen ye to me and prosper my every beginning' *Yasna* 33, 11.

> The Glory that belongs to the Immortal Spirits,
> The rulers, that act by a look alone,
> The lofty, all-powerful ones,
> The strong servants of the All-wise,
> That live for ever, and work justice.

> All seven have the same Thought,
> All seven have the same Word,
> All seven have the same Deed.
> One Thought, one Word, one Deed, one Father and Master
> The All-wise, the Creator[31].'

Of these 'Angels' one was destined to play a considerable part in several of the world-religions; namely that which the Persians called the 'Best Reason,' and which the Greeks knew as Wisdom ($\sigma o \phi i a$) or the Word ($\lambda \acute{o} \gamma o s$). Sometimes an aspect of the Deity, sometimes an emanation from him, and then again a distinguishable personality, this figure is again and again presented to our consideration. The personification of abstractions appealed with special force to the Romans, for from the earliest periods of their history they had raised temples to Faith (*fides*), Concord (*concordia*), and other deified virtues; and its character can perhaps best be appreciated by reference to the personification of Light in Christian hymnology, both ancient and modern:

> 'Hail, gladdening Light, of his pure glory poured
> Who is the immortal Father, heavenly, blest[32]!'
> 'Lead, kindly Light, amid the encircling gloom
> Lead thou me on[33].'

13. Amongst the subsidiary, but still important, doctrines of
Sanctity of the Persism, is that of the sanctity of the four elements.
elements.   Earth, air, fire and water are alike holy. Hence the dead must not be buried, for that would be to defile the earth; nor burned, for that would be to defile fire[34]; nor may any impurity be thrown into the water. This respect for the

---

[31] *Yasht* xix 15, 16. The translation follows Geldner, *Drei Yasht aus dem Zendavesta*, p. 15.

[32] Ancient Greek hymn, $\phi \hat{\omega} s$ $\acute{\iota} \lambda a \rho \grave{o} \nu$ $\acute{a} \gamma \acute{\iota} a s$ $\delta \acute{o} \xi \eta s$, translated by J. Keble.

[33] J. H. Newman.

[34] 'Zoroaster taught the Persians neither to burn their dead, nor otherwise to defile fire.' Xanthos (B.C. 465–425), as quoted by Nicolaus of Damascus (1st century B.C.).

elements often appeared to strangers as worship of them[35]. Between the elements they sometimes discriminated, considering earth and water as more akin to darkness and the evil spirit, but fire and air to light and the good spirit[36]. The element of fire they held in special reverence, so that at all times they have been called fire-worshippers[37]. More careful observers have always recognised them as monotheists, distinguished by a certain rapturous language in their description of the deity which they refused to picture in any concrete shape[38]. They were also zealous that their teaching should find its expression in a healthy social and political life[39]. In the education of the young they laid a special stress on speaking the truth[40].

14. 'The Gymnosophists taught philosophy to the people
Alexander in
the East.
of India[41].' Who are the teachers thus indicated? An answer may be found, though of a later date, in Plutarch's 'Life of Alexander,' where he describes the meeting of Alexander with some eminent gymnosophists, who had stirred up opposition to his rule :—

'[Alexander] captured ten of the Indian philosophers called Gymnoso-phistae[42]; who had been instrumental in causing Sabbas to revolt, and had done much mischief to the Macedonians. These men are renowned for their short, pithy answers, and Alexander put difficult questions to all of them, telling them that he would first put to death the man who answered him worst, and so the rest in order.

[35] See § 10, note 28; Strabo xv 3, 16.

[36] 'Zarathustra said :—the earthly demon is water derived from earth ; the heavenly demon is fire mixed with air' Origen, *contra haereses*, i col. 3025.

[37] 'The Persians first worshipped fire as a god in heaven' Clemens Romanus, *Hom.* ix 4 f.

[38] 'Zoroaster the Magian says :—God is the primal, the incorruptible, the eternal, the unbegotten, the indivisible, the incomparable, the charioteer of all good, he that cannot be bribed, the best of the good, the wisest of the wise ; he is also the father of good laws and justice, the self-taught, the natural, perfect, and wise, the only dis-coverer of the sacred and natural' Euseb. *Praep. ev.* i 10.

[39] 'From the writings of Zoroaster it is inferred that he divided philosophy into three parts, physics, economics, and politics' Schol. on *First Alcibiades*, p. 122 A (Williams-Jackson, p. 231).

[40] 'They educate their children, beginning at five years old and going on till twenty, in three things only; in riding, in shooting, and in speaking the truth' Herod. i 136. [41] See above, § 3.

[42] Alexander had reached the river Hyphasis, the modern Bias.

The first was asked whether he thought the living or the dead to be the more numerous. He answered "The living, for the dead are not."

The second was asked, "Which breeds the largest animals, the sea or the land?" He answered "The land, for the sea is only a part of it."

The third was asked, "Which is the cleverest of beasts?" He answered "That which man has not yet discovered."

The fourth was asked why he made Sabbas rebel. He answered "Because I wished him either to live or to die with honour."

The fifth was asked, which he thought was first, the day or the night. He answered "The day was first, by one day." As he saw that the king was surprised by this answer, he added "Impossible questions require impossible answers."

Alexander now asked the sixth how a man could make himself most beloved. He answered "By being very powerful, and yet not feared by his subjects."

Of the remaining three, the first was asked how a man could become a god. He answered "By doing that which it is impossible for a man to do."

The next was asked which was the stronger, life or death. He answered "Life, because it endures such terrible suffering."

The last, being asked how long it was honourable for a man to live, answered "As long as he thinks it better for him to live than to die."

The king loaded them with presents, and dismissed them[43].'

15. In these 'gymnosophists' it is easy to recognise a type familiar to Indian antiquity. These men, who have

Were the
Gymnoso-
phists
Buddhists?

almost dispensed with clothing and know nothing of the luxuries or even the conveniences of life, are nevertheless influential leaders of the people. They, like the Persians, have broken away from the old religions; they talk lightly of the gods, and do not guide their actions by any decrees supposed divine. The sight of human sorrow fills them with sympathy for the ills of life, and makes them doubt whether death is not the better choice. Their ethical standard is high, and includes both courage and gentleness. That they are Buddhist monks is probable enough, but not certain, because India contained at this time many sects professing similar principles. But the teaching of Gautama, the Buddha or 'enlightened,' represents to us in the most definite form the nature of this propaganda. It implies a revolt against national rivalries, ritualist observances, and polytheistic beliefs; it is severely

[43] Plutarch's *Life of Alexander*, ch. lxiv (translation by Aubrey Stewart and George Long, London, 1892).

practical, and inculcates obedience to reason and universal benevolence ; and it is spread from East to West by devoted bands of ascetic missionaries.

16. The fundamental teachings of Buddhism appear clearly in the traditional account of the *Sermon of Benares* :

'This is the holy truth of Sorrow ; birth is Sorrow, age is Sorrow, disease is Sorrow, death is Sorrow ; to be joined with the unloved is Sorrow, to be parted from the loved is Sorrow ; to lose one's desire is Sorrow ; shortly, the five-fold clinging to existence is Sorrow.

Buddhist teaching.

This is the holy truth of the Origin of Sorrow ; it is the thirst to be, leading from birth to birth, finding its pleasure here and there ; the thirst for pleasure, the thirst to be, the thirst to be prosperous.

This is the holy truth of the Removing of Sorrow ; the removal of the thirst by destroying desire, by letting it go, by cutting oneself off from it, separating from it, giving it no place.

This is the holy truth of the Path to the Removing of Sorrow ; it is the holy Path of eight branches, which is called Right Belief, Right Aspiration, Right Word, Right Act, Right Life, Right Effort, Right Meditation, Right Annihilation of Self[44].'

Specially characteristic of Buddhism is that gentleness of temper, instinctively opposed to all anger and cruelty, which no provocation can turn aside. We read in the Dhammapada :

'Hatred does not cease by hatred at any time; hatred ceases by love ; this is an old rule. Let a man overcome anger by love, let him overcome evil by good ; let him overcome the greedy by liberality, the liar by truth[45].'

17. The doctrines of Buddhism were not inculcated in India alone. From the first it was a missionary religion ; and its emissaries must often have appeared in the Hellenistic world, promising 'to seekers after God eternal communion with his very essence, to the weary pessimist eternal forgetfulness[46].' From contemporary Indian inscriptions we learn of missionaries sent out by Açoka, the first great Buddhist king of India, 'with healing herbs and yet

Buddhists and Cynics.

[44] Mahāvagga i 6, 19 to 22, after H. Oldenberg, *Buddha*, p. 139, and the translation in *S. B. E.* xiii pp. 95, 96.

[45] Dhammapada i 5 and xvii 123 (*S. B. E.* x pp. 5, 58).

[46] Mahaffy, *Empire of the Ptolemies*, p. 164. These alternative interpretations of the doctrine of *Nirvana* must not be accepted as uncontroversial.

more healing doctrine'[47] to Ptolemy II king of Egypt, Antiochus of Syria, and others, before the year 250 B.C. ; and this mission can have been but one out of many. It thus appears very remarkable that we have no record of Buddhist communities established in the Greco-Roman world. But if the name of Gautama remained unknown to the West, and his community had no formal adherents, the manner of life of his apostles did not lack imitators. In the Cynic preacher the Buddhist monk reappears. In Greek literature he is usually an object of ridicule; his uncouth appearance, his pitiable poverty, and his unconventional speech give constant opportunity for the wit of his critics. But the Cynics carried with them not only the out-ward garb of the Buddhist monks, but also their lofty ethical standard, their keen sympathy with human troubles, and their indifference to purely speculative problems[48]. In spite of the contempt heaped upon them (or perhaps in consequence of it) they gradually won respect and admiration as the sincere friends and helpers of the poor. Thus Buddhism at its best is pictured for us in the sketches drawn by Epictetus of Diogenes and the Cynic preachers of his own day, of which the following are examples:

'Did Diogenes love nobody, who was so kind and so much a lover of all that for mankind in general he willingly undertook so much labour and bodily suffering? He did love mankind, but how? As became a minister of God, at the same time caring for men, and being also subject to God. For this reason all the earth was his country, and not one particular place; and when he was taken prisoner he did not regret Athens nor his associates and friends there, but even he became familiar with the pirates and tried to improve them; and being sold afterwards he lived in Corinth as before at Athens. Thus is freedom acquired[49].'

'And how is it possible that a man who has nothing, who is naked, houseless, without a hearth, squalid, without a slave, without a city, can pass a life that flows easily? See, God has sent you a man to shew you it is possible. Look at me, who am without a city, without a house, without possessions, without a slave; I sleep on the ground; I have no wife, no children, no praetorium, but only the earth and heavens, and one poor cloak. And what do I want? Am I not without sorrow? Am I not without fear? Am I not free? When did any of you see me failing in the object of

---

[47] Mahaffy, *Empire of the Ptolemies*, p. 163; V. A. Smith, *Açoka*, p. 174.
[48] See Gomperz, *Greek Thinkers*, ii pp. 155–162, and below, § 52.
[49] Epict. *Disc.* iii 24, 64 to 66 (Long's translation).

my desire, or ever falling into that which I would avoid? did I ever blame God or man? did I ever accuse any man? did any of you ever see me with sorrowful countenance?

This is the language of the Cynics, this their character, this their purpose[50].'

Except that a simple form of theism has replaced the Buddhist atheism, there is hardly a word here that we might not expect from a Buddhist monk.

18. The Stoic philosophy was founded by Zeno of Citium
Stoicism. (350–260 B.C.). Although he lived and taught at Athens, his youth was spent in a city that was half Phoenician, and many of his most distinguished followers had a like association with the Eastern world. The system deals with all the great themes touched upon by Chaldaism, Persism, and Buddhism. Like the first, it insists that there exists an unchanging Destiny, according to which events throughout the universe are predetermined from all eternity. Like the second, it sets up as claiming the worship and allegiance of men a Supreme Deity, who governs the world with boundless power and benevolent will, and is manifested to men as the Logos or 'divine Word.' In its interpretation of the physical universe it accepts as a first principle a living and creative fire, ultimately identical with the deity, and containing the germs of the whole creation. It sees in the will of man an independent and divine power, subject to no compulsion from without, but attaining its highest and best by willing submission to the Supreme Being. In its practical ethics, though it does not advocate the suppression of all desires, it so far agrees with Buddhism as to hold that happiness is only found in the subordination of individual claims to the voice of universal reason. Finally, its teachers are actively engaged in propagating its doctrines and guiding its disciples. Stoicism has, in short, the inward and outward characteristics of the other great movements we have described, and may claim without presumption to be reckoned amongst the world-religions[51].

[50] *ib.* iii 22, 45 to 50.
[51] 'The system that stood to Pagan Rome more nearly than anything else in the place of a religion' Crossley, *M. Aurelius,* iv Pref. p. xii. 'Its history resembles that of a religion rather than a speculative system' Rendall, *M. Aurelius,* Pref. p. xv.

19. If however we reckon Stoicism amongst the world-religions, we must not forget that of all of them

Comprehensiveness of the Stoic view.

it is the most philosophical, and this in a double sense. In the first place the founders of Stoicism are conscious of the problems to which preceding schools of thought have endeavoured to find answers, and attempt to reconcile or at any rate to bring into relation the answers which their predecessors have found. Secondly they are greatly occupied with intellectual problems, and clearness of thought is to them almost equally important with rightness of thought. The theory of Fate which we have attributed to the Chaldaeans is to the plain man irreconcileable with the doctrine of the government of the world by a Supreme Deity; yet the Stoics hold both dogmas. The theory of the freedom of the human will is a limitation equally of the dominion of Fate and of that of the Deity: the Stoics maintain the freedom of the human will and refuse to admit the limitation of either power. The Persians maintained that the power of the principle of Good was balanced by that of the principle of Evil; and from this they drew what seemed to be the legitimate conclusion that man may choose to obey the one or the other, to do good or to do evil. The Stoics omitted the principle of Evil altogether from their scheme, and yet maintained the theory of the moral choice. To understand the Stoic system it is necessary to know exactly in what balance its different elements were maintained, and to avoid identifying it with other systems, ancient or modern, which are more sharply cut. Thus when it is commonly asserted that Stoicism on its religious side is Pantheism, the very brevity of this summary must create suspicion. Certainly the Stoics frequently speak of the universe as divine; but they hold with equal firmness the doctrines that the universe is governed by Providence, and that human perversity may thwart the divine purpose, both being doctrines which in ancient as in modern times are associated with Theism, and held to be inconsistent with pantheistic views.

20. A similar difficulty confronts us when we ask whether

God and the 'Word.'

the deity of the Stoics is to be considered as personal. All the terms commonly used in association with a personal deity are adopted by the Stoics: their god is Lord and Father. But then they use with equal freedom terms commonly associated with materialism: for the Supreme Being is to them body or stuff, a primitive fire which converts itself by natural laws into every form of being. For this reason the Stoics are commonly called materialists, and yet the main body of their teaching is contrary to that usually associated with materialism[52]. Further, beside the personal and the material conceptions of the Deity, they adopted and developed a conception which exercised an extraordinary influence over other systems, when they attributed the exercise of all the powers of deity to the divine Word, which from one point of view is the deity himself, and from another is something which emanates from him and is in some way distinct. Thus the term 'God,' which to children and child-like religions appears so simple, is in the Stoic system extraordinarily complex; and its full content cannot be grasped without a willingness to revise the meaning of many conceptions which seem firmly established, such as those of personality, material, and quality. If we are to suppose that the Stoic conception of the Word arose ultimately from similar conceptions in Hebraism or Persism, by which the voice of a personal God attained to a quasi-independent personality, we must allow that the Stoics made use of this term with a boldness and consistency which from the time of their appearance brought it into the forefront of religious and metaphysical controversy. Through the Stoics the doctrine of the Word passed into the systems of Judaism and Christianity, to perform in each the like service by reconciling doctrines apparently contradictory. Of all the systems we may perhaps say that Stoicism makes the fewest new assertions or negations, but introduces the most numerous interpretations.

21. We have comparatively little means of judging of the
Influence of Stoicism. influence of Stoicism in the world of Asia Minor, but incidentally we may infer that it was very considerable. In Athens the moral earnestness of its teachers found little response in public feeling, whilst it laid the exponents of

[52] See below, § 173.

its tenets open to many a sharp thrust from keen critics whose constructive powers were after all inferior. In Rome itself Stoicism took root rapidly. The brilliant circle that gathered round Scipio Africanus the younger was imbued with its ideals; Cato, the leading republican of the first century B.C., was a living representative of its principles; and Cicero and Brutus, with many others less known to fame, were greatly influenced by it. In the first century of the principate Stoicism imparted a halo of heroism to a political and social opposition which otherwise would evoke little sympathy[53]; in the second century A.D. its influence was thrown on the side of the government; the civilized world was ruled under its flag, and its principles were embodied in successive codes of law which are not yet extinct. Its direct supremacy was not long-lived; for at the very time when a Stoic philosopher sits in the seat of the Caesars its followers seem to be losing their hold on its most important doctrines. It came into sharp conflict with Christianity on matters of outward observance; but in the cores of the two systems there was much likeness[54], and from Stoic homes were drawn the most intelligent advocates of the newer faith.

22. By Judaism we mean here the way of thinking which

Judaism.   was prevalent in the Jewish world from the date of the return from Babylon to that of the destruction of Jerusalem. Judaism was of course by no means restricted to the soil of Palestine; it was carried by the diffusion of the Jewish race to all the coasts of the Mediterranean; besides its national centre at Jerusalem, it included a great centre of learning at Alexandria, and its branches, as we have seen[55], extended to the south of Egypt. The chief external impulse which affected it was the spread of Persism. The two systems agreed

---

[53] 'Patricians, as we call them, only too often fail in natural affection' M. Aurel. *To himself*, i 12 (Rendall's translation). See also below, §§ 442, 443.

[54] 'Dying, [Stoicism] bequeathed no small part of its disciplines, its dogmas, and its phraseology to the Christianity by which it was ingathered' Rendall, *M. Aurelius*, Pref. p. xv. 'The basis of Christian society is not Christian, but Roman and Stoical' Hatch, *Hibbert Lectures*, p. 170. '[The post-Aristotelian period] supplied the scientific mould into which Christianity in the early years of its growth was cast, and bearing the shape of which it has come down to us' O. J. Reichel in his Preface to the translation of Zeller's *Stoics*, etc.

[55] See above, § 9.

in their belief in a God of heaven, and in their dislike to idol-worship; and it can be no matter of wonder if one party at least among the Jews readily accepted the more strictly Persian doctrines of the ministry of angels, the struggle between good and evil, the immortality of the soul, and the reward after death, as well as such observances as the washing of hands[56]. Strong Persian influence has been traced in the book of Daniel[57], and as Jewish speculation developed at Alexandria, it took up the use of the Greek language, and so came into touch with the influences that were moulding thought throughout Asia Minor[58]. The most interesting and elevated production of Alexandrine Judaism is the book known as the *Wisdom of Solomon*, probably composed in the first century B.C.[59]

23. The author of this book, whilst himself a firm adherent 'The Wisdom of Solomon.' of monotheism, shews a not altogether intolerant appreciation of those systems in which either the heavenly bodies or the elements seem to occupy the most important place:—

1. For verily all men by nature were but vain who had no perception of God,
    And from the good things that are seen they gained not power to know him that is,
    Neither by giving heed to the works did they recognise the artificer;
2. But either fire, or wind, or swift air,
    Or circling stars, or raging water, or the luminaries of heaven,
    They thought to be gods that rule the world.
3. And if it was through delight in their beauty that they took them to be the gods,
    Let them know how much better than these is their sovereign Lord:
    For the first author of beauty created them:

[56] It is not admitted by the best authorities that the term 'Pharisee' is in any way connected with the name of 'Persian' or its modern equivalent 'Parsee.' But the resemblance in beliefs and habits is very striking, especially if we contrast the Pharisees with their Sadducee opponents. 'The Sadducees say that there is no resurrection, neither angel, nor spirit; but the Pharisees confess both' Acts xxiii 8.

[57] D. A. Bertholet, 'The value of the history of religions,' *Homiletic Review*, Nov. 1908.

[58] See Fairweather, *Background of the Gospels*, ch. vii (on 'the apocalyptic movement and literature'). [59] *ib.* p. 337.

4. But if it was through astonishment at their power and influence,
     Let them understand from them how much more powerful is he
       that formed them :
5. For from the greatness of the beauty even of created things
     In like proportion does man form the image of their first maker.
6. But yet for these men there is but small blame,
     For they too peradventure do but go astray
     While they are seeking God and desiring to find him.

Wisdom of Solomon, xiii 1–6.

The same author rises to still greater heights when he personifies Wisdom or Philosophy as a Spirit attendant upon, and almost identified with the deity. Here his language resembles that of the Avestic hymns, describing the angels attendant upon Ahura Mazdā[60]:—

22. For there is in Wisdom a spirit quick of understanding, holy,
     Alone in kind, manifold,
     Subtil, freely moving,
     Clear in utterance, unpolluted,
     Distinct, unharmed,
     Loving what is good, keen, unhindered,
23. Beneficent, loving toward man,
     Stedfast, sure, free from care.
     All-powerful, all-surveying,
     And penetrating through all spirits
     That are quick of understanding, pure, most subtil :
24. For wisdom is more mobile than any motion :
     Yea, she pervadeth and penetrateth all things by reason of her
      pureness.
25. For she is a breath of the power of God,
     And a clear effluence of the glory of the Almighty :
     Therefore can nothing defiled find entrance into her.
26. For she is an effulgence from everlasting light,
     And an unspotted mirror of the working of God,
     And an image of his goodness.
27. And she, being one, hath power to do all things :
     And remaining in herself, reneweth all things,
     And from generation to generation passing into holy souls
     She maketh men friends of God, and prophets ;
29. For she is fairer than the sun,
     And above all the constellations of the stars.

Wisdom of Solomon, vii 22–29.

[60] See above, § 12.

24. The fusion of Greek and Judaic modes of thought is most complete in the works of Philo the Jew (c. 20 B.C.—54 A.D.). This writer in commenting upon the books of the Old Testament, finds himself able by way of interpretation to introduce large parts of Greek philosophies. The place of Wisdom in the writer last named is taken in his works by the Logos or 'Word[61]'; and the 'Word' is many times described as an emanation of the deity, after the Persian fashion[62]. Without anticipating the further discussion of this philosophical conception, we may well notice here how characteristic it is of an age which paid boundless homage to reason, and how it supplies a counterpoise to conceptions of the deity which are rigidly personal. But Philo is of still more direct service to the study of Stoicism, because he had so completely absorbed the system that, where other authorities fail us, we may often trust to his expositions for a knowledge of details of the Stoic system.

Philo the Jew.

Another work of about the same period is the *Fourth book of the Maccabees*, in which Stoic ethics, only slightly disguised, are illustrated from Jewish history. In this fusion of Hebraic and Hellenistic thought, unfortunately interrupted by political convulsions, eminent modern Jews have recognised the natural development of the teaching of the Hebrew prophets[63].

25. The foregoing discussions will already have suggested that Christianity is bound by intimate ties to the other world-religions; though it is beyond our present purpose to examine the precise nature of those ties. It is pre-eminently concerned with the breaking down of Jewish nationalism, and its constant appeal to 'the truth' is essentially the same as the appeal of kindred systems to 'wisdom' or 'philosophy.' The Lord's Prayer, addressed to the 'Father in heaven,' and with its further references to 'The Name,' 'The Kingdom,' 'The Will,' 'temptation,' and 'the Evil One,' reflects

Christianity.

---

[61] Heinze, *Lehre vom Logos*, pp. 251, 252.

[62] 'The Logos is related to God as Wisdom, and is the full expression of the Divine mind. He is the sheckinah or glory of God, the first-born Son of God, the second God' Fairweather, *Background of the Gospels*, p. 358.

[63] Friedländer, *Die religiösen Bewegungen innerhalb des Judaïsmus*, 1905.

the principal conceptions of Persism, of which we are again reminded in the Apocalypse by the reference to the 'seven spirits of God[64].' The Sermon on the Mount has been, not without reason, compared to the Buddhist sermon of Benares. With Stoicism Christianity has special ties, both direct and indirect. Its chief apostle was Paul of Tarsus, who was brought up in a city from which more than one eminent Stoic teacher had proceeded[65], and whose ways of thinking are penetrated by Stoic conceptions. The most profound exponent of its theology (the author of the *Gospel according to John*) placed in the forefront of his system the doctrine of the 'Word' which directly or (more probably) indirectly he derived from Stoic sources. The early church writers felt the kinship of thought without perceiving the historical relation. To them Cicero in his Stoic works was 'anima naturaliter Christiana'; and they could only explain the lofty teachings of Seneca by the belief that he was a secret convert of the apostle Paul[66]. Parallelism between Stoic and Christian phraseology is indeed so frequently traced that it may be well to emphasize the need of caution. It is not by single phrases, often reflecting only the general temper of the times, that we can judge the relation of the two systems; it is necessary also to take into account the general framework and the fundamental principles of each.

26. Of the systems named by Aristotle far the least known to us is Druidism. It appeared to Caesar and other Romans to be the national religion of the Gauls and Britons, exactly as Magism appeared to the Greeks to be the national religion of the Persians. But other evidence indicates that Druidism was a reformed religion or philosophy, not unlike Persism in its principles. The training of Druidical students was long and arduous; it claimed to introduce them to a knowledge of heavenly deities denied to the rest of the world,

Druidism.

---

[64] 'There were seven lamps of fire burning before the throne, which are the seven Spirits of God' Revelation iv 5.

[65] Of these Antipater of Tarsus is the best known, for whom see § 110; others are Heraclides, Archedemus, Zeno of Tarsus, Nestor, Athenodorus, etc., for whom see Index of Proper Names.

[66] Winckler, *Der Stoicismus*, p. 2; Lightfoot, *Philippians*, pp. 270, 271.

and to reveal to them the immortality of the soul. Our best authority is the Latin poet Lucan :—

'To you alone it has been granted to know the gods and the powers of heaven; or (it may be) to you alone to know them wrongly. You dwell in deep forests and far-away groves : according to your teaching the shades do not make their way to the still regions of Erebus or the grey realm of Dis below ; the same spirit guides a new body in another world ; if you know well what you say, then death is but an interlude in life. If not, at least the peoples, on whom the northern star gazes directly, are happy in their illusion ; for the greatest of terrors, the fear of death, is nothing to them. Hence it comes that their warriors' hearts are ready to meet the sword, and their souls have a welcome for death, and they scorn to be thrifty with life, in which they can claim a second share[67].'

Druidism, like Stoicism, seems to have prepared its adherents for a specially ready acceptance of Christianity.

27. The story of the world-religions, with their countless prophets, teachers, confessors and martyrs, has its tragic side. We ask what was attained by so much study and self-denial, such courageous defiance of custom and prejudice, such bold strivings after the unattainable, so many hardly spent lives and premature deaths, and feel puzzled to find a reply. To the problems proposed the world-religions gave in turn every possible answer. Some found life sweet, others bitter ; some bowed before the inexorable rule of destiny, others believed in a personal and benevolent government of the universe ; some looked forward to a life after death, others hoped for annihilation. Their theories crystallized into dogmas, and as such became the banners under which national hatreds once more sought outlet in bloodshed. Their adherents sacrificed everything in the hope of reaching certain and scientific truth, and, at the end of all, religion still appears the whole world over to be in conflict with science, and the thousand years during which Wisdom was counted more precious than riches are often looked back upon as a time of human aberration and childishness. It is not to be denied that thousands of noble spirits set out during this period for a goal that they never reached; and those who are inclined to destructive criticism may plausibly characterise their enterprise as vanity.

The goal not reached yet.

[67] Lucan, *Phars.* i 452–462.

28.   It is the task of literary research to pierce through this
limited view, and to trace the real effect of philosophical effort on the life of individuals and nations.
All over the civilized world it raised a race of heroes,
struggling not for power or splendour as in the epoch of barbarism,
but for the good of their fellow-men.   It gave a new value to life,
and trampled under foot the fear of death.   It united the nations,
and spread the reign of law and justice.   Where its influence has
weakened, the world has not changed for the better; so that the
very failures of the world-religions most attest their value.   India
has relapsed from Buddhism, its own noblest work, to its earlier
creeds, and they still bar its path against social progress.   Europe,
no longer united by the sentiment of a catholic religion, and increasingly indifferent to literary sympathies, is falling back into
the slough of frontier impediments and racial hatreds.   From
all this there is no way out except in the old-fashioned quest of
truth and good will.

The path still onward.

29.   Both in ancient and in modern times the importance of
Stoicism has been very variously estimated, according as the critic has set up a purely literary standard,
or has taken into account historical influence.   To
those who look upon philosophy as it is embodied in books, and
forms a subject for mental contemplation and aesthetic enjoyment, the philosophies of Plato and Aristotle have always seemed
of far higher rank.   As contributions to the progress of humanity,
in politics and law, in social order and in the inventive adaptation of material surroundings, they can hardly claim to approach
any one of the systems discussed in this chapter.   But it is with
no wish to depreciate the great masterpieces of Hellenic culture
that we now set against the criticisms of some of its ardent
advocates the maturer judgment of writers who have approached
with greater sympathy the study of the Hellenistic and Roman
worlds.   'In Plato and Aristotle,' says Zeller, 'Greek philosophy
reached its greatest perfection[68].'   'Its bloom was short-lived[69].'
'Greece was brought into contact with the Eastern nations,
whereby it became subject to a back-current of Oriental
thought[70].'   'With the decline of political independence the

Estimates of Stoicism.

---

[68] *Stoics*, etc., p. 1.   [69] *ib.* p. 10.   [70] *ib.* pp. 13, 14.

mental powers of the nation were broken past remedy[71].'
'What could be expected in such an age, but that philosophy
would become practical, if indeed it were studied at all[72]?' To
minds of another temper it does not seem so fatal that 'philosophy should become practical.' 'It should be insisted,' says
Prof. Mahaffy, 'that the greatest practical inheritance the Greeks
left in philosophy was not the splendour of Plato, or the vast
erudition of Aristotle, but the practical systems of Zeno and
Epicurus, and the scepticism of Pyrrho. In our own day every
man is either a Stoic, an Epicurean, or a Sceptic[73].' The greatness of Stoicism in particular was eloquently recognised by a
French writer of the eighteenth century : ' elle seule savait faire
les citoyens, elle seule faisait les grands hommes, elle seule faisait
les grands empereurs[74]!' With these tributes may be compared
that paid by a writer who approaches the subject from the standpoint of modern philosophy and theology. '[Stoicism] has
perennial fascination ; and there are not wanting signs that it
appeals with special attractiveness to cultured minds at the
present day. It has both speculative and practical value ; its
analysis of human nature and its theory of knowledge, no less
than its ethical teaching, giving insight into the problems of the
universe and the right mode of guiding life. As an important
stage in the march of philosophical thought, and as a luminous
chapter in the history of natural theology, it solicits our attention
and will repay our study[75].'

30. Judgments so contradictory reveal the fact that ancient
divergencies of philosophic sympathies have their
Interpretative Stoicism. counterparts to-day; and perhaps in studying and
judging the systems of antiquity a little more is
needed of the sympathy and interpretative elasticity which every
man unconsciously uses in maintaining the political, philosophic
and religious views to which he is attracted by inheritance or
personal conviction. Thus to understand Stoicism fully a man
must himself become for the time being a Stoic. As such he

[71] ib. p. 15.   [72] ib. p. 16.
[73] Greek Life and Thought, Introd., pp. xxxvii, xxxviii.
[74] Montesquieu, Esprit des lois, ii 24.
[75] W. L. Davidson, The Stoic Creed, p. v.

will no longer bind himself by the letter of the school authorities. In many a phrase they use he will recognise an obsolete habit of thought, an exaggerated opposition, a weak compliance in the face of dominant opinions, or a mistaken reliance upon what once seemed logical conclusions. At other points he will see difficulties felt to which an answer can now easily be supplied. At each step he will ask, not so much what the Stoics thought, but what a Stoic must necessarily think. Whilst constantly referring to the original authorities, he will allow much to be forgotten, and in other cases he will draw out more meaning than the writers themselves set in their words. If he can walk, boldly but not without caution, on this path, he will assuredly find that Stoicism throws light on all the great questions to which men still seek answers, and that to some at least it still holds out a beckoning hand.

CHAPTER II.

HERACLITUS AND SOCRATES.

31. WE have seen already that the great problems of which
Stoicism propounds one solution were agitated
Greek thought. during the millennium which preceded the Christian
era alike in India, Persia and Asia Minor on the one hand, and
in Greece, Italy and the Celtic countries on the other. To the
beginnings of this movement we are unable to assign a date;
but the current of thought appears on the whole to have moved
from East to West. But just at the same time the influence of
Greek art and literature spreads from West to East; and it is
to the crossing and interweaving of these two movements that
we owe almost all the light thrown on this part of the history of
human thought. The early history of Stoicism has reached us
entirely through the Greek language, and is bound up with the
history of Greek literature and philosophy[1]. But long before
Stoicism came into existence other movements similar in kind
had reached Greece; and the whole of early Greek literature,
and especially its poetry, is rich in contributions to the discussion of the physical and ethical problems to which Stoicism
addressed itself. From the storehouse of this earlier literature
the Stoics drew many of their arguments and illustrations; the
speculations of Heraclitus and the life of Socrates were especially
rich in suggestions to them. The study of Greek literature and
philosophy as a whole is therefore indispensable for a full
appreciation of Stoicism; and the way has been made easier of

[1] 'Stoicism was the earliest offspring of the union between the religious consciousness of the East and the intellectual culture of the West' Lightfoot, *Philippians*,
p. 274.

late by excellent treatises, happily available in the English
language, dealing with the general development of philosophic
and religious thought in Greece[2]. Here it is only possible to
refer quite shortly to those writers and teachers to whom Stoicism
is most directly indebted.

32. Although the HOMERIC POEMS include representations
of gods and men corresponding to the epoch of
national gods and to other still earlier stages of
human thought, nevertheless they are pervaded by at least the
dawning light of the period of the world-religions. Tales of the
gods that are bloodthirsty or coarse are kept in the background;
and though heroes like Agamemnon, Achilles, and Ajax move
in an atmosphere of greed, bloodshed, and revenge, yet all of
them are restrained both in word and in act by a strong feeling
of self-respect, the αἰδώς or shamefastness which entirely differentiates them from the heroes of folk-lore; in particular, the
typical vices of gluttony, drunkenness, and sexual unrestraint
are amongst the things of which it is a shame to speak without
reserve. The gods are many, and in human shape; yet they
are somewhat fairer than men, and something of the heavenly
brilliance in which the Persian archangels are wrapped seems
to encircle also the heights where the gods dwell on mount
Olympus[3]. Gradually too there comes to light amidst the
picture of the many gods something resembling a supreme
power, sometimes impersonally conceived as Fate (αἶσα, μοῖρα),
sometimes more personally as the Fate of Zeus, most commonly
of all as Zeus himself, elevated in rank above all other gods[4].
Thus Zeus is not only king, but also father of gods and men[5];
he is the dispenser of happiness to men, 'to the good and the
evil, to each one as he will[6],' and the distributor of gracious

Homer.

---

[2] Amongst the most important of these are Th. Gomperz' *Greek Thinkers* (transl.
by L. Magnus and G. G. Berry, London, 1901–5), and J. Adam's *Religious teachers
of Greece* (Gifford Lectures, Edinburgh, 1908).

[3] 'Most clear air is spread about it cloudless, and the white light floats over it'
Hom. *Od.* 6, 46 (Butcher and Lang's transl.). See also Adam, *Religious Teachers*,
p. 31.

[4] 'It is not possible for another god to go beyond, or make void, the purpose of
Zeus' *Od.* 5, 103.

[5] *Il.* 24, 308; *Od.* 14, 404.   [6] *ib.* 6, 188.

gifts[7], unbounded in power[8] and in knowledge[9]. The gods again, in spite of the many tales of violence attached to their names, exercise a moral governance over the world. 'They love not froward deeds, but they reverence justice and the righteous acts of men[10]'; 'in the likeness of strangers from far countries, they put on all manner of shapes, and wander through the cities, beholding the violence and the righteousness of men[11].'

Whilst therefore the philosophers of later times could rightly object to Homer that he told of the gods tales neither true nor worthy of their nature, there was on the other hand much in the *Iliad* and *Odyssey*, and particularly in the latter, which was in harmony with philosophical conceptions. It was not without reason that the Stoics themselves made of Ulysses, who in Homer plays but little part in fighting, an example of the man of wisdom and patience, who knows men and cities, and who through self-restraint and singleness of purpose at last wins his way to the goal[12]. From this starting-point the whole of the *Odyssey* is converted into a 'Pilgrim's Progress'; the enchantress Circe represents the temptations of gluttony, which turns men into swine[13]; the chant of the Sirens is an allegory of the enticements of sensual pleasure.

33. In HESIOD (8th century B.C.) we find the first attempt to construct a history of the universe; his *Theogony* is the forerunner of the Cosmology which later on is a recognised part of philosophy. Here in the company of the personal gods we find not only the personified lights of heaven, Sun and Moon, but also such figures as those of Earth and Ocean, Night and Day, Heaven and Hell, Fate, Sleep, and Death, all bearing witness to the emergence of the spirit of speculation. In Hesiod again we first find the description of the 'watchmen of Jove,' who are no longer the gods themselves as in Homer, but an intermediate class of beings, corresponding to the Persian angels and the δαίμονες of later Greek.

Hesiod.

[7] *Od.* 8, 170.   [8] *ib.* 4, 237.
[9] *ib.* 20, 75.   [10] *ib.* 14, 84.
[11] *ib.* 17, 485.   [12] See below, § 325.
[13] So already Socrates understood it; Xen. *Mem.* i 3, 7.

'Thrice ten thousand are the servants of Zeus, immortal, watchmen over mortal men; these watch deeds of justice and of wickedness, walking all ways up and down the earth, clothed in the mist[14].'

But it is in his ethical standards that Hesiod is more directly a forerunner of the Stoic school: for neither the warlike valour nor the graceful self-control of the hero appeals to him, but the stern sense of justice and the downright hard work of the plain man.

'Full across the way of Virtue the immortal gods have set the sweat of the brow; long and steep is the path that reaches to her, and rough at the beginning; but when you reach the highest point, hard though it is, in the end it becomes easy[15].'

34. Between Epic and Attic literature stands the poetry of The Orphic poems. the 'Orphic' movement, belonging to the sixth century B.C., and exercising a wide influence over various schools of philosophy in the succeeding centuries. For an account of this movement the reader must look elsewhere[16]; here we can only notice that it continued the cosmological speculations of Hesiod's *Theogony*, and in particular developed a strain of pantheism which is echoed in the Stoic poets. According to an Orphic poet

'Zeus is the first and the last, the head and the foot, the male and the female, Earth and Heaven, Night and Day; he is the one force, the one great deity, the creator, the alluring power of love; for all these things are immanent in the person of Zeus[17].'

Here amidst the fusion of poetry and theology we first see the budding principle of philosophic monism, the reaching after a unity which will comprehend all things. To the same school is attributed the doctrine that 'the human soul is originally and essentially divine[18].'

35. To the sixth century B.C. belong also the earliest Greek The Hylo-zoists. philosophers who are known to us by name. In all of these the early polytheism is either abandoned

---

[14] Hesiod, *Works and Days*, 252–255; and see below, § 254.

[15] *ib.* 289–292, quoted Xen. *Mem.* ii 1, 20.

[16] For instance, to Adam, *Religious Teachers*, Lect. v; Gomperz, *Greek Thinkers*, bk. i, ch. ii.

[17] Orphic Fragments, vi 10–12 (fr. 123 Abel).

[18] Adam, p. 114.

or becomes so dim in its outlines that the origin and governing
force of the universe is sought in quite other directions. The
philosophers of Ionia busied themselves with the problem of the
elements. THALES of Miletus was a man of many attainments;
he had travelled both in Egypt and in Babylon, and was an
active political reformer. To him water was the primary substance, from which all others proceeded and to which they
returned[19]. ANAXIMANDER of the same town was the first who
undertook to give the Greeks a map of the whole known world.
To him it seemed that the primary matter could not be the
same as any visible substance, but must be a protoplasm of
undefined character (ἄπειρον), capable of assuming in turn all
shapes[20]. ANAXIMENES (once more of Miletus) assumed air as
the first principle, and derived the other elements from it by
processes of condensation (πύκνωσις) and rarefaction[21]. But on
one point all the Ionian philosophers were agreed: the primary
substance was the cause of its own motion; they were 'hylo-
zoists,' since they hold that matter (ὕλη) is a living thing
(ζῷον). They are from the standpoint of physics 'monists,' as
opposed to those who hold matter and life, or matter and force,
to be two things eternally distinct, and are therefore 'dualists'
in their theory[22].

36. To the same sixth century belong two other notable
philosophers. PYTHAGORAS, born in Samos about
575 B.C., and like Thales, one who had travelled
widely, left his native land rather than submit to the rule of a
tyrant, and founded in Croton in Lower Italy a community half
religious and half political, which in its original form was not
long-lived. But a widespread tradition remained as to his

Pythagoras.

[19] Gomperz, *Greek Thinkers*, i pp. 46–48.
[20] *ib.* 48–56.   [21] *ib.* 56–59.
[22] The terms 'monism' and 'dualism' have recently become the watchwords of
opposing armies of popular philosophers, especially in Germany. In this book they
stand for two aspects of philosophical thought which are not necessarily irreconcileable.
For without such contrasts as life and matter, universe and individual, right and wrong,
thought is impossible; so far we are all 'dualists.' Yet as soon as we fix our
attention on these contrasts, we find that they are not final, but point towards some
kind of ultimate reconciliation; and to this extent all diligent thinkers tend to become
'monists.' Similarly the broad monistic principle 'all things are one' is meaningless
apart from some kind of interpretation in dualistic language.

doctrines, in which the theory of Numbers held a leading position. Pythagoras appears to have been a good mathematician and astronomer, and followers of his school were at an early date led to the doctrines of the rotation of the earth on its axis and the central position of the sun in the planetary system[23]. His name is also connected with the theory of the transmigration of souls, which we may suppose him to have derived ultimately from some Indian source; and to the same country we must look as having suggested to him and his followers the practice of abstaining from animal food[24].

37. If we looked merely to the theories of the philosophers,
Xenophanes. it might seem as if the old mythologies and theogonies were already dead. But in fact the battle was yet to come. XENOPHANES of Colophon (born circ. 580 B.C.) witnessed in his youth the fall of Ionia before the conquering progress of Cyrus king of Persia. Rather than submit to the power of the invader he adopted the life of a wandering minstrel, and finally settled in Elea, in Lower Italy, where he became the founder of the Eleatic school. But in his religious convictions he was whole-heartedly on the Persian side. 'There is one God, greatest amongst gods[25] and men, not like mortal men in bodily shape or in mind[26].' Thus the worship of many gods and that of images of the deity are alike condemned; and it is probable that in this false worship he found the cause of his country's fall. With the lack of historic sense which is characteristic of the zealous reformer, he condemned Homer and Hesiod as teachers of immorality, since they 'ascribed to the gods theft, adultery, and deceit, and all acts that are counted shame and blame amongst men[27].' With keen criticism he pointed out that myths as to the birth of the gods dishonoured them just as much as if they related their deaths; for on either supposition there is a time when the gods do not exist[28]. The conception of the deity formed by Xenophanes seems to approach Pantheism or Nature-

[23] See below, §§ 71, 195.   [24] Gomperz, i 127.
[25] This phrase does not express a belief in polytheism, see Adam, p. 204.
[26] Xen. apud Euseb. *Praep. ev.* xiii 13.
[27] Xenophanes apud Sext. *math.* ix 193.
[28] Id. apud Arist. *Rhet.* ii 23.

worship, and so far to foreshadow the Stoic deity; but the
fragments that survive of his works are insufficient to make this
point clear[29]. The successors of Xenophanes did not inherit his
religious zeal, but they emphasized all the more the philosophic
principle of an ultimate Unity in all things.

38. With the opening of the fifth century B.C. we reach
HERACLITUS of Ephesus, a philosopher of the
highest importance to us, since the Stoics afterwards accepted his teaching as the foundation of their own
system of physics. The varied speculations of the sixth century
were all examined by Heraclitus, and all found wanting by him;
his own solutions of the problems of the world are set forth in
a prophetic strain, impressive by its dignity, obscure in its form,
and lending itself to much variety of interpretation. For the
opinions of the crowd, who are misled by their senses, he had no
respect[30]; but even learning does not ensure intelligence[31],
unless men are willing to be guided by the 'Word,' the universal
reason[32]. The senses shew us in the universe a perpetual flowing:
fire changes to water (sky to cloud), water to earth (in rainfall),
which is the downward path; earth changes to water (rising
mist), and water to fire, which is the upward path[33]. Behind
these changes the Word points to that which is one and unchanging[34]. Anaximander did well when he pointed to the
unlimited as the primary stuff, but it is better to describe it as
an 'everliving fire[35].' Out of this fire all things come, and into
it they shall all be resolved[36]. Of this ever-living fire a spark is

Heraclitus.

[29] On Xenophanes see Gomperz, i pp. 155–164; Adam, pp. 198–211.

[30] 'Eyes and ears are bad witnesses to men, unless their souls have wit' Heracl.
Fr. 4 (Bywater), 107 (Diels).

[31] 'Much learning does not teach sense, else it had taught Hesiod and Pythagoras,
Xenophanes and Hecataeus' *Fr.* 16 B, 40 D.

[32] 'The Word is common, yet most men live as if they owned a private understanding' *Fr.* 92 B, 2 D.

[33] 'All things move and nothing remains' Plato *Crat.* 402 A.

[34] 'Listening not to me but to the Word it is reasonable to confess that all things
are one' *Fr.* 1 B, 50 D.

[35] 'All things change with fire and fire with all things, as gold with goods and
goods with gold' *Fr.* 22 B, 90 D; 'neither God nor man created this World-order
(κόσμος), which is the same for all beings: but it has been and shall be an ever-living
fire' *Fr.* 20 B, 30 D.

[36] 'The fire shall one day come, judge all things and condemn them' *Fr.* 26 B, 66 D.

buried in each man's body; whilst the body lives, this spark, the soul, may be said to be dead[37]; but when the body dies it escapes from its prison, and enters again on its proper life. The 'Word' is from everlasting[38]; through the Word all things happen[39]; it is the universal Law which holds good equally in the physical world and in the soul of man. For man's soul there is a moral law, which can be reached only by studying the plan of the world in which we live[40]. But of this law men are continually forgetful; they live as in a dream, un-conscious of it; it calls to them once and again, but they do not hear it[41]. Most of all it is needed in the government of the state; for 'he who speaks with understanding must take his foothold on what is common to all; for all human laws are nourished by the one divine law[42].'

39. The general import of the physical teaching of Heraclitus, and the indebtedness of the Stoics to it, have long been recognised: the bearing of this teaching upon religion, ethics and politics is a more disputable matter. Does Heraclitus by the 'Logos' which he so often names mean merely his own reasoning and message? is he speaking of the common reason of mankind? or does the term suggest to him a metaphysical abstraction, a divine power through which the world is created and governed? For the fuller meaning we have analogies in the beliefs of Persism before Heraclitus, and of Stoics, Judaists, and Christians afterwards. The latest commentator, adopting this explanation, sums it up in three propositions: first, the 'Logos' is eternal, being both pre-existent and everlasting, like the world-god of Xenophanes; secondly, all things both in the material and in the spiritual world happen through the 'Logos'; it is a cosmic principle,

The Word.

[37] 'Whilst we live, our souls are dead and buried in us; but when we die, our souls revive and live' Sext. *Pyrrh. inst.*, iii 230 (*Fr.* 78 B, 88 D).
[38] 'This Word is always existent' *Fr.* 2 B, 1 D. [39] *ib.*
[40] 'There is but one wisdom, to understand the judgment by which all things are steered through all' *Fr.* 19 B, 41 D.
[41] 'Men fail in comprehension before they have heard the Word and at first even after they have heard it....Other men do not observe what they do when they are awake, just as they forget what they do when asleep' *Fr.* 2 B, 1 D.
[42] *Fr.* 91 B, 114 D.

'common' or 'universal'; and in the third place, it is the duty of man to obey this 'Logos,' and so to place himself in harmony with the rest of nature. And accordingly, in agreement with many recent writers, he adopts the translation 'the Word' as on the whole the most adequate[43]. Even the Romans found it impossible to translate λόγος by any single word, and they therefore adopted the phrase *ratio et oratio* (reason and speech); in modern language it seems clearly to include also the broad notion of 'Universal Law' or the 'Laws of Nature.' If we can rightly attribute to Heraclitus all that is thus included in the interpretation of this one word, he certainly stands out as a great creative power in Greek philosophy, harmonizing by bold generalizations such diverse provinces as those of physics, religion, and ethics; 'he was the first [in Greece, we must understand] to build bridges, which have never since been destroyed, between the natural and the spiritual life[44].' It is to the Stoics almost alone that we owe it that teaching so suggestive and so practical was converted into a powerful social and intellectual force.

40. The prominence given to fire in the system of Heraclitus has very naturally suggested that his doctrine is borrowed from that of Zarathustra[45]. The historical circumstances are not unfavourable to this suggestion. Ionia was conquered in turn by Cyrus and Darius, and definitely annexed by Persia about 496 B.C., that is, at the very time at which Heraclitus taught. Moreover the Persian invasion was akin to a religious crusade, and had for a principal aim the stamping out of the idle and superstitious habit of worshipping images, by which (according to the Persians) the true God was dishonoured. The elevated character of the Persian religion could hardly fail to attract learned Greeks, already dissatisfied with the crude mythology of their own people. Further, the resemblance between the teaching of Zarathustra and that of Heraclitus is not restricted to the language used of the divine fire; the doctrines of an all-creating, all-pervading Wisdom, the

Zarathustra and Heraclitus.

[43] Adam, pp. 217-222. [44] Gomperz, i p. 63.
[45] See Gladisch, *Herakleitos und Zoroaster*; Ueberweg, *Grundriss*, p. 39; above, § 13.

λόγος or Word, and of the distinction between the immortal
soul and the corruptible body, are common to both. But the
differences between the two systems are almost equally striking.
Heraclitus is a monist; according to him all existences are
ultimately one. Zarathustra taught a principle of Evil, everywhere opposed to the Good Spirit, and almost equally powerful ;
his system is dualist[45a]. Zarathustra is not free from nationalism,
Heraclitus is cosmopolitan. In the Ephesian system we find
no trace of the belief in Judgment after death, in Heaven, or
in Hell. We may in fact well believe that Heraclitus was
acquainted with Zoroastrianism and influenced by it, but we
have not the means to determine what the extent of that
influence was. It is related of him that he received (but declined)
an invitation to the court of Darius ; and that his dead body was
given up to be torn to pieces by dogs in the Persian fashion[45b].

41. The development of philosophic thought at Athens
was, as we have noticed, much complicated by the
political relations of Greece to Persia. Although
the Persian empire had absorbed Asia Minor, it was decisively
repulsed in its attacks on Greece proper. Athens was the
centre of the resistance to it, and the chief glory of the victories
of Marathon (490 B.C.) and Salamis (480 B.C.) fell to Athenian
statesmen and warriors. By these successes the Hellenes not
only maintained their political independence, but saved the
images of their gods from imminent destruction. A revival of
polytheistic zeal took place, as might have been expected. The
wealth and skill of Greece were ungrudgingly expended in the
achievement of masterpieces of the sculptor's art, and their
housing in magnificent temples. But even so religious doctrines
strikingly similar to those of the Persians gained ground. The
same Aeschylus who (in his *Persae*) celebrates the defeat of the
national enemy, a few years later (in his *Agamemnon*) questions
whether the Supreme Ruler be really pleased with the Greek
title of Zeus, and the Greek method of worshipping him[46].

The tragedians.

[45a] Gladisch traces this dualism in Heraclitus under the names of Zeus and Hades
(see his p. 26, note 39).

[45b] Clem. *Strom.* i 14 ; Suidas, s. v. Herakleitos. (Gladisch, pp. 65, 75).

[46] *Agam.* 155-161, 167-171.

His more conservative successor Sophocles was contented, in the spirit of the Homeric bards, to eliminate from the old myths all that seemed unworthy of the divine nature. Euripides adopts a bolder tone. Reproducing the old mythology with exact fidelity, he 'assails the resulting picture of the gods with scathing censure and flat contradiction[47].' With equal vigour he attacks the privileges of noble birth, and defends the rights of the slave; he has a keen sympathy for all the misfortunes that dog man's life; but his ethical teaching in no way derives its sanction from any theology. The Hellenes have lost confidence in their inherited outlook on the world.

42. The same problems which the poets discussed in the city theatre were during the fifth century B.C. the daily themes of a class of men now becoming so numerous as to form the nucleus of a new profession. These were the 'sophists,' who combined the functions now performed partly by the university professor, partly by the public journalist[48]. Dependent for their livelihood upon the fees of such pupils as they could attract, and therefore sensitive enough to the applause of the moment, they were distinguished from the philosophers by a closer touch with the public opinion of the day, and a keener desire for immediate results. Their contribution to philosophic progress was considerable. Cultivating with particular care the art of words, they created a medium by which philosophic thought could reach the crowd of men of average education; eager advocates of virtue and political progress, they gave new hopes to a people which, in spite of its material successes, was beginning to despair because of the decay of its old moral and civic principles. In PRODICUS of Ceos we find a forerunner of the popular Stoic teachers of the period of the principate[49]:

> 'A profound emotion shook the ranks of his audience when they heard his deep voice, that came with so strange a sound from the frail body that contained it. Now he would describe the hardships of human existence;

The Sophists.

---

[47] Gomperz, ii p. 13.

[48] 'Half professor and half journalist—this is the best formula that we can devise to characterise the sophist of the 5th century B.C.' Gomperz, i p. 414.

[49] See below, §§ 124, 130, and 131.

now he would recount all the ages of man, beginning with the new-born child, who greets his new home with wailing, and tracing his course to the second childhood and the gray hairs of old age. Again he would rail at death as a stony-hearted creditor, wringing his pledges one by one from his tardy debtor, first his hearing, then his sight, next the free movement of his limbs. At another time, anticipating Epicurus, he sought to arm his disciples against the horrors of death by explaining that death concerned neither the living nor the dead. As long as we live, death does not exist; as soon as we die, we ourselves exist no longer[50].'

To Prodicus we owe the well-known tale of Hercules at the parting of the ways, when Virtue on the one hand, and Pleasure on the other, each invite him to join company with her[51]. This tale we shall find to be a favourite with the Roman philosophers. The same Prodicus introduced a doctrine afterwards taken up by the Cynics and the Stoics in succession, that of the 'in-difference' of external advantages as distinct from the use to which they are applied. He also propounded theories as to the origin of the gods of mythology, explaining some of them as personifications of the powers of nature, others as deified benefactors of the human race[52]; theories which later on were adopted with zeal by the Stoic Persaeus[53]. To another sophist, HIPPIAS of Elis, we owe the doctrine of the 'self-sufficiency' of virtue, again adopted both by Cynics and Stoics[54]. ANTIPHON was not only the writer of an 'Art of Consolation,' but also of a treatise of extraordinary eloquence on political concord and the importance of education. 'If a noble disposition be planted in a young mind, it will engender a flower that will endure to the end, and that no rain will destroy, nor will it be withered by drought[55].'

43. Amongst the sophists of Athens was counted ANAXA-GORAS, born at Clazomenae about 500 B.C., and a diligent student of the Ionic philosophers. But in his explanation of nature he broke away from 'hylozoism' and introduced a dualism of mind and matter. 'From eternity all things were together, but Mind stirred and ordered them[56].'

The Materialists.

---

[50] Gomperz, i p. 428.

[52] Gomperz, i p. 430.

[54] Gomperz, i p. 433.

[56] Arist. *Phys.* viii 1; and see below, § 173.

[51] Xen. *Mem.* ii 1, 21 to 34.

[53] See below, § 89.

[55] *ib.* p. 437.

More famous was his contemporary EMPEDOCLES of Agrigentum, whose name is still held in honour by the citizens of that town. In him we first find the list of elements reaching to four, earth, air, fire, and water; and the doctrine that visible objects consist of combinations of the elements in varying proportions, first brought together by Love, then separated by Hatred. Just in so far as Empedocles abandoned the quest after a single origin for all things, his conceptions became fruitful as the basis of the more limited study now known as Chemistry. His work was carried further by LEUCIPPUS and DEMOCRITUS, both of Abdera, who for the four elements substituted invisible atoms, of countless variety, moving by reason of their own weight in an empty space. This simple and powerful analysis is capable of dealing effectively with many natural phenomena, and with comparatively slight alterations is still held to be valid in chemical analysis, and exercises a wide influence over the neighbouring sciences of physics and botany. When however (as has frequently been the case both in ancient and modern times) the attempt is made to build upon it a general philosophical system, its failure to explain the cohesion of matter in masses, the growth of plants and animals, and the phenomena of mind, become painfully apparent. Such attempts roughly correspond to the attitude of mind now called *materialism*, because in them the atoms, endowed with the material properties of solidity, shape, and weight alone, are conceived to be the only true existences, all others being secondary and derivative. This materialism (with some significant qualifications) was a century later the central doctrine of Epicurus, and is of importance to us by reason of its sharp contrast with the Stoic system of physics.

44. The value of these scientific speculations was not for the time being fully recognised at Athens. It was

Socrates.

in the atmosphere of sophistic discussion, not free from intellectual mists, but bracing to the exercise of civic and even of martial virtue that SOCRATES of Athens (circ. 469–399 B.C.) grew to maturity. He set to his fellow-citizens an example of the vigorous performance of duty. As a soldier he was brave almost to rashness, and took an active part in three campaigns.

As a magistrate he discharged his duty unflinchingly. After
the battle of Arginusae the ten Athenian generals were said to
have neglected the duty of succouring certain disabled ships
and the people loudly demanded that all should be condemned
to death by a single vote. Socrates was one of the presiding
senators, and he absolutely refused to concur in any such illegal
procedure[56a]. Again, when Athens was under the rule of the
Thirty, Socrates firmly refused to obey their unjust orders[57].
But when himself condemned to death, he refused to seize an
opportunity for flight which was given him; for this, he said,
would be to disobey the laws of his country[58].

His private life was marked by a firm self-control. Athens
was now wealthy, and its leading citizens frequently gathered
together for festive purposes. Socrates joined them, but showed
the greatest moderation in eating and drinking: such a course,
he said, was the better for health and also produced more real
pleasure. Over the grosser temptations of the senses he had
won a complete victory[59]. His temper was calm and even; he
was not put out by the violences of his wife, nor did he allow
himself to break out into rage with his slaves. His personal
habits, though simple, were careful: he did not approve any
neglect either of bodily cleanliness or of neatness in dress.

Thus Socrates gave an example of a life of activity and self-
control ($i\sigma\chi\dot{v}s$ $\kappa\alpha\grave{\iota}$ $\kappa\rho\acute{\alpha}\tau os$); and by his character, even more than
by his speculation, exercised an influence which extended widely
over many centuries.

45. The teaching of Socrates is not easily reduced to the
His teaching. set formulae of a philosophic school. But clearly
it was focussed upon the life of men in the city
and in the home, and was no longer chiefly concerned with the
phenomena of the sky or the history of the creation of the
universe. So Cicero well says of him that 'Socrates called
philosophy down from the heavens to earth, and introduced it
into the houses and cities of men, compelling men to enquire
concerning life and morals and things good and evil[60]'; and

---

[56a] Xen. *Mem.* i 1, 18.   [57] Plato, *Apol.* p. 32.
[58] Plato, *Crito*, p. 44 sqq.   [59] Gomperz, ii p. 48.
[60] Cic. *Ac.* i 4, 15; *Tusc. disp.* v 4, 10.

Seneca that he 'recalled the whole of philosophy to moral questions, and said that the supreme wisdom was to distinguish between good and evil[61].' He had no higher object than to send out young men, of whose good disposition he was assured, to take an active part in the affairs of the community, and to this course he urged them individually and insistently[62]. But it must not be supposed that he put on one side problems concerned with the acquirement of truth, or with the constitution and government of the universe. His views on these points carried perhaps all the more weight because they were stated by him not as personal opinions, but as points upon which he desired to share the convictions of his neighbours, if only they could assure him that reason was on their side.

46. Socrates more than any other man possessed the art of persuasive reasoning, thereby making his companions wiser and better men. First he asked that terms should be carefully defined, so that each man should know what the nature is of each thing that exists[63], and should examine himself and know well of what he speaks. Next he introduced the practice of induction ($\dot{\epsilon}\pi\alpha\kappa\tau\iota\kappa\omega\dot{\iota}$ $\lambda\acute{o}\gamma o\iota$), by which men make larger the outlook of their minds, understand one thing by comparison with another, and arrange the matter of their thought by classes[64]. By induction we arrive at general truths : not however by any mechanical or mathematical process, but (at least in the higher matters) by the use of Divination, that is, by a kind of divine enlightenment[65]. He who has accustomed himself to think with deliberation, to look on the little in its relation to the great, and to attune himself to the divine will, goes out into the world strengthened in self-restraint, in argumentative power, and in active goodwill to his fellow-men.

Most directly this method appeals to the future statesman. Of those who seek the society of Socrates many intend to

Reason the guide. (margin note)

[61] Sen. *Ep.* 71, 7. [62] Xen. *Mem.* iii 7.
[63] Xen. *Mem.* iv 6, 1 ; Epict. *Disc.* i 7, 11.
[64] Xen. *Mem.* iv 5, 12 ; Arist. *Met.* xiii 4.
[65] Xen. *Mem.* iv 7, 10. The Socratic $\mu\alpha\nu\tau\iota\kappa\dot{\eta}$ must not be taken too seriously; it is only one of many tentative suggestions for explaining the process of reasoning, akin to our modern use of the term 'genius' in connexion with achievements in poetry and art.

become generals or magistrates. Let them consider well what
these words mean. Is not a pilot one who knows how to steer
a ship? a cook one who knows how to prepare food? must we
not then say that a statesman is one who knows how to guide
the state? And how can he know this but by study and
training? Must we not then say generally that all arts depend
on knowledge, and knowledge on study? Do we not reach the
general truths that 'virtue is knowledge' and that 'virtue can be
taught'? We may hesitate as to how to apply these principles
to our individual actions, and Socrates will accuse none on
this point; but for himself he has a divine monitor which never
fails to warn him when his mind is turned towards a course
which the gods disapprove.

47. In the speculations of the Ionian philosophers Socrates
His dualism　could find no satisfaction. But one day he dis-
in physics.　covered with pleasure the words of Anaxagoras:
it is mind that orders the world and is cause of all things[66].'
Thus he was attracted to a dualistic view of the universe, in
which matter and mind are in fundamental contrast. In the
beginning there existed a chaos of unordered dead meaningless matter, and also mind, the principle of life, meaning, and
order. Mind touched matter, and the universe sprang into
being. Mind controls matter, and thus the universe continues
to exist. The proof is found in the providential adaptation of
the world for the life and comfort of mankind: for it is only
consistent to suppose that things that exist for use are the work
of mind[67]. He that made man gave him eyes to see with, ears
to hear with, and a mouth conveniently placed near to the
organs of sight and smell; he implanted in him a love of his
offspring, and in the offspring a love of its parents; and lastly
endowed him with a soul capable of understanding and worshipping his maker. For the divine power Socrates uses quite
indifferently the words 'god' and 'gods': but his belief is
essentially monotheistic. In the gods of the city of Athens he

---

[66] Plato, *Phaedo*, p. 97 c. The passage gives the impression of a real reminiscence;
at the same time its recognition as such implies that Socrates was not consistent in
disregarding all physical speculations.

[67] Xen. *Mem.* i 4, 4.

has ceased to believe, although he still makes sacrifices upon their altars in good-humoured conformity with the law, and even adopts the popular term 'divination[68],' though in a sense very different to that in which the official priesthood used it.

In the analysis of human nature Socrates adopts a similar dualism. Man consists of body and soul: the soul is lord and king over the body, and indeed may rightly be called divine, if anything that has touch with humanity is such[69].

48. The practical teaching of Socrates was entirely domi-
His pietism. nated by his religious principles. The gods, he held, know all things, our words, our deeds, and the secrets of our hearts: they are everywhere present and give counsel to men concerning the whole of life[70]. The first duty of man is therefore to enter into communion with the gods by prayer, asking them to give us the good and deliver us from the evil, but not qualifying the prayer by any instruction to the gods as to what is good or evil; for this the gods themselves know best[71]. In these words then we may pray: 'Zeus our king, give us what is good for us whether we ask for it or not; what is evil, even though we ask for it in prayer, keep far from us[72].'

In this spirit of what we should to-day call 'pietism' we must interpret his principle that 'virtue is knowledge[73].' This not only asserts that no one can rightly practise any art unless he has studied and understands it, but also that no one can rightly understand an art without practising it. We say that there are men who know what is good and right, but do not perform it; but this is not so; for such men in truth think that some other course is good for them. Only the wise and pious man has a right understanding; others cannot do good even if they try[74]; and when they do evil, even that they do without willing it[75].

In its application to politics the teaching of Socrates came into collision with the democratic sentiments prevalent at Athens.

---

[68] *ib.* i 4, 2.   [69] *ib.* i 4, 9, and iv 3, 14 ; Cic. *N. D.* ii 6, 18.
[70] *ib.* i 1, 19.   [71] *ib.*   [72] Plato, *Alc.* ii 143 A.
[73] Xen. *Mem.* iii 9, 4 and 5.   [74] *ib.*
[75] οὐδεὶς ἑκὼν ἁμαρτάνει; see Plato *Prot.* p. 345 D, *Apol.* p. 25, Xen. *Mem.* iv 2, 20. No one is willingly ignorant, and no one does evil for any other reason than that he is ignorant of the good.

To say the least, Socrates had no prejudice against the rule of kings. He distinguished sharply between kingship and tyranny, saying that the rule of one man with the assent of his subjects and in accordance with the laws was kingship, but without such assent and according to the man's arbitrary will was tyranny. But under whatever constitutional form government was carried on, Socrates asserted that those who knew the business of government were alone the true rulers, and that the will of the crowd, if conflicting with that of the wise, was both foolish and impious[76].

49. So teaching and influencing men Socrates lived in Athens till his seventieth year was past, and then died by the hands of the public executioner. This fate he might so easily have avoided that it seemed almost to be self-chosen. His disciple Xenophon expresses amazement that the jurors should have condemned a man so modest and so wise, and so practical a benefactor of the Athenian people[77]. Modern historians, with a wider knowledge of human nature, wonder rather that Socrates was allowed to live so long[78]. The accusers complained that Socrates offended by disbelieving in the gods of the city, introducing new deities, and corrupting the youth of Athens. From the point of view of conservatively-minded Athenians, the charges were amply justified. Clearly Socrates disbelieved, not merely in the official gods of the city, but also in the deities it worshipped most earnestly, democracy and empire. Not only did he introduce new deities, but it might fairly be argued that he was introducing the most essential parts of the religion of the national enemy, Persia. Daily inculcating these heretical doctrines upon young men of the highest families in Athens, he might well be the cause that the Athenian state was less unquestioningly served than

Why Socrates was condemned.

[76] In accepting generally the statements of Xenophon as to the religious and practical teaching of Socrates I am glad to find myself in agreement with Adam; Gomperz on the other hand is more sceptical. It should however always be realized that Socrates himself veiled his positive opinions under the form of suggestions and working hypotheses or 'divinations.'

[77] *Mem.* i 1, 1.

[78] Grote, *History of Greece*, ch. lxviii. Gomperz gives a very dramatic representation of the attitude of an Athenian of the old school; *Greek Thinkers*, ii pp. 94–97.

before. That the heresies of Socrates were soundly founded on wide observation and general truths could not be considered to make them less dangerous. Athens had already passed the time when its political power could be of service to its neighbours; it had not reached that when it could be content with intellectual influence; Socrates, just because he was in harmony with the future of Athens, was a discordant element in its present.

50. It is with difficulty, and not without the risk of error, that we trace even in outline the positive teaching of Socrates. The severe self-repression with which he controlled his senses was exercised by him no less over his intelligence. In his expositions it took the shape of irony (εἰρωνεία), that is, the continual withholding of his personal convictions, and obstetrics (μαιευτική), the readiness to assist others in bringing their speculations to the birth. Thus he was a great educator rather than a great teacher. For whilst he held that virtue alone was worthy of investigation, and that virtue was essentially wisdom, he professed to be entirely at a loss where to find this wisdom for himself; he left it to his pupils to go out and discover the precious cup. Thus whilst men of all classes and with every variety of mental bias listened to his teaching, not one was content with his negative attitude. Of the various suggestions which Socrates threw out, without committing himself to any one, his pupils took up each in turn and endeavoured to construct out of it a system[79]. These systems were in the sharpest possible contrast one with another, but they have certain points in common. All the teachers retained a strong personal affection and loyalty towards their common master; each was convinced that he alone possessed the secret of his real convictions. All of them held aloof from the physical speculations of which the ripe fruit was already being gathered in by the Atomists. The portal of knowledge was to all of them the right use of the reasoning power; the shrine itself was the discipline of virtue, the attainment of happiness, the perfect ordering of social life. Such were the Socratic

The companions of Socrates.

[79] 'ex illius [Socratis] variis et diversis et in omnem partem diffusis disputationibus alius aliud apprehenderat' Cic. *de Orat.* iii 16, 61.

schools, in which philosophy was now somewhat sharply divided
into the two branches of dialectics and ethics. Another century
had yet to elapse before the rejected discipline of physics again
established its importance.

51. Of the Socratic schools three contributed directly to
The Cynics. the Stoic system. Of these the Cynic school,
founded by ANTISTHENES of Athens (circ. 440–
365 B.C.) and developed by DIOGENES of Sinope, is its immediate
precursor. The Cynic masters inherited most completely the
moral earnestness[80] and the direct pietistic teaching of Socrates;
and for this reason Antisthenes appears to have been the
master's favourite pupil. The lives both of these men and of
their successors were marked by simplicity and self-abnegation,
and they devoted themselves with true missionary zeal to the
reformation of moral outcasts. The caricature of the figure of
Diogenes which was promulgated by his opponents and still
lives in literary tradition needs constantly to be corrected by the
picture which Epictetus gives of him; and which (though not
without an element of idealization and hero-worship) shews us
the man as he appeared to his own disciples.

The breach with the state-religion which was latent in
Socrates was displayed without disguise by the Cynics. Antisthenes, following in the track of the ardent Xenophanes,
declared that the popular gods were many, but the god of
nature was one[81]; he denounced the use of images[82]; and he
and his followers naturally acquired the reproach of atheism[83].
Equally offensive to the Athenians was their cosmopolitanism[84],
which treated the pride of Hellenic birth as vain, and poured
contempt on the glorious victories of Marathon and Salamis.
Nor did the Cynics consider the civilization of their times as
merely indifferent; they treated it as the source of all social evils,
and looked for a remedy in the return to a 'natural' life, to
the supposed simplicity and virtue of the savage unspoilt by

---

[80] παρὰ [Σωκράτους] τὸ καρτερικὸν λαβὼν καὶ τὸ ἀπαθὲς ζηλώσας Diog. L. vi 2.

[81] 'Antisthenes...populares deos multos, naturalem unum esse dicens' Cic. *N. D.*
i 13, 32.

[82] οὐδεὶς [θεὸν] εἰδέναι ἐξ εἰκόνος δύναται Clem. Alex. *Protrept.* p. 46 c.

[83] Epict. *Disc.* iii 22, 91.   [84] See below, § 303.

education. Thus they formulated a doctrine which especially appealed to those who felt themselves simple and oppressed, and which has been well described as 'the philosophy of the proletariate of the Greek world[85].'

52. The destructive criticism of the Cynics did not stop

Cynic intui-
tionism.

with its attack upon Greek institutions; it assailed the citadel of reason itself. Socrates had renounced physics; the Cynics considered that dialectic was equally unnecessary[86]. For the doctrine of general concepts and the exercise of classification they saw no use; they were strict Nominalists; horses they could see, but not 'horsiness.' In their ethics they held to the chief doctrines of Socrates, that 'virtue is knowledge,' 'virtue can be taught' and 'no one willingly sins'; and they laid special stress on the 'sufficiency' ($a\mathring{v}\tau\acute{a}\rho\kappa\epsilon\iota a$) of virtue, which to produce happiness needs (according to them) nothing in addition to itself except a Socratic strength of character ($\Sigma\omega\kappa\rho\alpha\tau\iota\kappa\mathring{\eta}$ $\mathring{\iota}\sigma\chi\acute{v}s$)[87]. But in reality they identified virtue with this willpower, and entirely dispensed with knowledge; virtue was to them a matter of instinct, not of scientific investigation. They appear therefore as the real founders of that ethical school which bases knowledge of the good on intuition, and which is at the present time, under ever-varying titles, the most influential of all. In practice, the virtue which specially appealed to the Cynics was that of 'liberty,' the claim of each man at every moment to do and say that which seems to him right, without regard to the will of sovereigns, the conventions of society, or the feelings of his neighbour; the claim made at all times by the governed against their rulers, whether these are just or unjust, reckless or farseeing.

53. Cynism is in morals what Atomism is in physics; a

Limits of
Cynism.

doctrine which exercises a widespread influence because of its extreme simplicity, which is extraordinarily effective within the range of ideas to which it is appropriate, and fatally mischievous outside that range. Nothing

[85] Gomperz, ii p. 148, referring to Göttling's book, *Diogenes der Cyniker oder die Philosophie des griechischen Proletariats* (Halle 1851).
[86] $\mathring{a}\rho\acute{\epsilon}\sigma\kappa\epsilon\iota$ $a\mathring{v}\tauo\mathring{\iota}s$ $\tau\grave{o}\nu$ $\lambda o\gamma\iota\kappa\grave{o}\nu$ $\kappa a\grave{\iota}$ $\tau\grave{o}\nu$ $\phi\upsilon\sigma\iota\kappa\grave{o}\nu$ $\tau\acute{o}\pi o\nu$ $\pi\epsilon\rho\iota\alpha\iota\rho\epsilon\hat{\iota}\nu$ Diog. L. vi 103.
[87] *ib.* vi 11.

A. 4

is more alien from Cynism than what we now call cynicism ; the
Cynics were virtuous, warm-hearted, good-humoured, and pious.
In their willing self-abnegation they equalled or surpassed the
example set by Buddhist monks, but they were probably much
inferior to them in the appreciation of natural beauty and the
simple pleasures of life. As compared with their master Socrates,
they lacked his genial presence, literary taste, and kindly toler-
ance; and they were intensely antipathetic to men of the type of
Plato and Aristotle, whose whole life was bound up with pride
in their country, their birth, and their literary studies[88].

54. The Cynics themselves seem to have made no effective
use of literature to disseminate their views ; but
in the works of XENOPHON of Athens (440–circ.
350 B.C.) we have a picture of Socrates drawn almost exactly
from the Cynic standpoint. Xenophon was a close personal
friend of Antisthenes, and thoroughly shared his dislike for
intellectual subtleties. He was possessed of a taste for military
adventure, and his interpretation of Socratic teaching entirely
relieved him of any scruples which patriotism might have imposed upon him in this direction, leaving him free at one time
to support the Persian prince Cyrus, and at another to join with
the Spartan king Agesilaus against his own countrymen. From
adventure he advanced to romance-writing, and his sketches of
the expedition of the Ten Thousand Greeks (in which he took
part in person) and of the life of Cyrus the Great have an
interest which in no way depends upon their accuracy. The
account which he gives of Socrates in his *Memorabilia* (ἀπομνημονεύματα) is not always to be depended upon; it is at the best
a revelation of one side only of the historic philosopher; but it
is to a large extent confirmed by what we learn from other
sources, and is of special interest to us because of the great
influence it exercised over Latin literature.

Xenophon.

55. In the opposite direction ARISTIPPUS of Cyrene shared
the sympathetic tone of Socrates, but could not adopt
his moral earnestness or his zeal for the good of
others. He refused altogether the earnest appeal of Socrates

The Cyrenaics.

[88] See Plato, *Theaet.* 155 E, *Soph.* 251 B; Aristotle, *Met.* vii 3, 7.

that he should take part in politics. 'It seems to me,' he says, 'to show much folly that a man who has quite enough to do to find the necessities of life for himself, should not be satisfied with this, but should take upon himself to provide his fellow-citizens with all that they want, and to answer for his action in the courts if he is not successful.' Aristippus revolted altogether from the ascetic form in which the Cynics represented his master's teaching, and held that the wise man, by self-restraint and liberal training, attained to the truest pleasure, and that such pleasure was the end of life. The Cyrenaics (as his followers were called) were the precursors in ethics of the school of Epicurus; and the bitter opposition which was later on to rage between Stoics and Epicureans was anticipated by the conflict between the Cynics and the Cyrenaics.

56. The school of EUCLIDES of Megara swerved suddenly
The Me-   from these ethical interests and devoted itself
garians.   mainly to the problems of dialectic. From the
Socratic practice of classification it arrived at the doctrine of the One being, which alone it held to be truly existent, and which it identified with the One God proclaimed by Xenophanes and his followers of the Eleatic school. To the Megaric school we are therefore chiefly indebted for the assertion of the philosophical principle of monism; the same school drew the necessary logical consequence, that evil is not in any real sense existent. From the Eleatics the Megarians further derived an interest in logical speculation of all kinds, and they were greatly occupied with the solution of fallacies: amongst the followers of this school we first meet with the puzzles of 'the heap' (*Sorites*), 'the liar' (*Pseudomenos*), and others upon which in later times Chrysippus and other Stoics sharpened their wits[89]. DIODORUS the Megarian set out certain propositions with regard to the relation of the possible and the necessary which are of critical importance in connexion with the problem of free-will[90]. Finally STILPO, who taught in Athens about 320 B.C., and who made a violent attack upon Plato's theory of ideas, adopted an ethical

---

[89] See below, § 163.
[90] See below, §§ 220 and 221.

standpoint not unlike that of the Cynics[91], and counted amongst his pupils the future founder of Stoicism. Stilpo enjoyed amongst his contemporaries a boundless reputation; princes and peoples vied in doing him honour[92]; but we have scarcely any record of his teaching, and know him almost exclusively as one who contributed to form the mind of Zeno.

57. With the school founded by Phaedo of Elis we are not Advance of concerned; the consideration of Plato and Aristotle Philosophy. and their respective followers we must leave to another chapter. We have already seen philosophy grow from being the interest of isolated theorists into a force which is gathering men in groups, and loosening the inherited bonds of city and class. So far its course has violently oscillated, both as regards its subject-matter and its principles. But its range is now becoming better defined, and in the period that is approaching we shall find determined attempts to reach a comprehensive solution of the problems presented to enquiring minds.

[91] ' hoc inter nos et illos [Stilbonem etc.] interest; noster sapiens vincit quidem incommodum omne, sed sentit ; illorum ne sentit quidem ' Sen. *Ep.* 9, 3.
[92] Gomperz, ii p. 196.

CHAPTER III.

THE ACADEMY AND THE PORCH.

58. BEFORE a hundred years had passed since the death

Political changes of the 4th century.

of Socrates, the face of the Greek world had been completely changed. Athens, Lacedaemon, Corinth, Thebes, which had been great powers, had sunk into comparative insignificance; their preeminence was gone, and even of their independence but little remained. Throughout Greece proper the Macedonian was master. But if the old-fashioned politician suffered a bitter disappointment, and the adherents of the old polytheism despaired of the future, there was rich compensation for the young and the hopeful. Petty wars between neighbouring cities, with their wearisome refrain 'and the men they killed, and the women and children they enslaved[1],' began to be less common; internal and still more murderous strife between bigoted oligarchs or democrats began to be checked from without. For the enlightened Greek a new world of enterprise had been opened up in the East. Alexander the Great had not only conquered Asia Minor, and established everywhere the Greek language and a Greek bureaucracy; he had opened the way to the far East, and pointed out India and even China as fields for the merchant and the colonizer. His work had been partly frustrated by the disorders that followed his death; but if achievement was thus hindered, hopes were not so quickly extinguished. These new hopes were not likely to be accompanied by any lasting regrets for the disappearance of ancient systems of government now regarded as effete or

---

[1] Thucydides, *passim.*

ridiculous, or of inherited mythologies which were at every point in conflict with the moral sense[2].

59. The same historic events which opened the East to
East and Hellenic adventurers also made the way into
West. Europe easy for the Oriental. As the soldier and
the administrator travelled eastward, so the merchant and the philosopher pushed his way to the West. Not merely in Persia had ancient superstitions been swept away by reforming zeal; the Jews were now spreading from town to town the enthusiasm of a universalized religion which was ridding itself of bloody sacrifices; and, for the time at least, the humane philosophy of the Buddha was dominant in India, was being preached far and wide by self-sacrificing monks, and was inspiring the policy of great monarchies. We find it hard to picture the clashing of ideals, enthusiasms, and ambitions which was at this time taking place in all the great cities of the old world; but it is certain that in the universal excitement the old distinctions of Greek and barbarian, Jew and Gentile, rich and poor, free and slave, man and woman were everywhere becoming weakened, and community of thought and temperament were beginning to reunite on a new basis individuals who had broken loose from the ties of ancient society.

60. During this fourth century B.C. the foundations were
New schools laid of the four philosophical schools which were
of philosophy. destined to vie one with another for the allegiance
of the Roman world. The Socratic schools which we have already mentioned, those of the Cynics and Cyrenaics, did not perhaps altogether die out; in particular the Cynic missionaries appear to have been a social force until the second century B.C. But their intellectual basis was too narrow to admit of their effective transplantation to new soil. At the end of the century each gave place to a new school, which preserved the central doctrines of its predecessor. The Socratic paradoxes were handed on from the Cynics to the Stoics; the doctrine that pleasure is the good was accepted by Epicurus. Stoics and Epicureans disputed with a bitterness as yet unequalled, finding

---

[2] Mahaffy, *Greek Life and Thought*, ch. I.

themselves just as much opposed upon the subjects of logic and physics, which they introduced anew into popular philosophy, as upon the questions of ethics on which their antipathies were inherited. Between them stood two schools which had meanwhile established themselves. Plato, himself a companion of Socrates, founded the Academy at Athens about 380 B.C.; and if he did not impress his own teaching upon it with absolute fixity, still the school flourished under a succession of leaders, always proud of the fame of its founder, and rendering him at least a nominal allegiance. From the Academy branched off the school of the Peripatetics, founded by Plato's pupil Aristotle about 350 B.C. After Aristotle's death this school gravitated towards the Academics, and in later centuries there seemed little difference, if any, between the two. If Stoicism may be called the child of Cynism, it largely drew nourishment from these two schools and their founders. Some account of the teaching of Plato and Aristotle is therefore needed here, partly because of the great importance of both in the general history of philosophy, partly because of their direct influence upon the subject of this book. On account of the much greater prominence of the Academy in the later history we shall often use this term to refer to the general teaching of the two allied schools.

61. Of all the companions of Socrates far the most famous is PLATO of Athens (427–347 B.C.), the founder of the philosophical association known as the 'Academy.' In the general judgment of lovers of Greek letters he stands out not merely as a great master of Attic prose style, but also as the ablest exponent of the true mind of Socrates[3], and the most brilliant light of Greek philosophy[4]. On the first point this judgment stands unchallenged; for delicate and good-natured wit, felicity of illustration and suggestiveness of thought the Platonic dialogues are unrivalled. But it is only in his earlier writings that we can accept Plato as a repre-

Plato.

[3] 'Plato combined the various elements, the, so to speak, prismatically broken rays of the Socratic spirit in a new, higher, and richer unity' Ueberweg, Eng. transl. i p. 89.
[4] 'The philosophy of Greece reached its highest point in Plato and Aristotle' Zeller, *Stoics* etc., p. 11. 'The bloom of Greek philosophy was short lived' *ib.* p. 10.

sentative of Socrates; after the death of his master he travelled
for many years in Egypt, Lower Italy, and Sicily, and absorbed
in particular much of the teaching of the Pythagoreans. The
theory of 'ideas,' the special characteristic of Plato's later work,
is not strictly Socratic. Neither, we must add, is it of first-
rate importance in the history of human thought; from our
point of view it lies apart from the main current both of speculation and of practice. It was a still-born theory, not accepted
even by Plato's successors in the control of the Academy[5]. We
are therefore very little concerned with the direct teaching of
Plato; but all the more readily it should be acknowledged that
the Stoics were often indebted to him for help in the treatment
of important details, and that the Platonic attitude remained
for them a factor of which they needed continuously to take
account.

62. A striking feature of the Platonic dialogues is that their

Plato's
realism.

results are usually negative. First the opinions of
the crowd, then those of Socrates' contemporaries
the 'sophists' and of the other Socratic schools are subjected
to a cross-examination, under which they are one and all
shewn to be unreasonable. This cross-examination is quite in
the Socratic spirit, and is before all things a mental gymnastic,
training the dialectician to observe with keener eye and to
discuss with apter tongue than his fellows. Gradually there
emerges from a mass of doubts something like a positive theory
that Plato is prepared to adopt. The true reasoning is that of
induction from the particular to the general, from the individual
to the class. In the class name we come upon the true being of
the individual, and by a right definition of it we discern what
each thing really is. The 'idea,' which corresponds to the class
name, is alone really existent; the individual is a more or less
imperfect imitation of it ($\mu\acute{\iota}\mu\eta\sigma\iota\varsigma$). In this way Plato found
what seemed to him a solution of a difficulty which Socrates
hardly felt, that of explaining the participation ($\mu\acute{\epsilon}\theta\epsilon\xi\iota\varsigma$) of

[5] The phrases 'cum Platone errare,' 'amicus Plato, magis amica veritas' agree
in expressing the general incredulity with which Platonism was received in the ancient
world. In our own days an ill-balanced sympathy for Platonic dogma is often
a serious hindrance to philosophic progress.

the particular in the general (ὑπόθεσις or ἰδέα). Thus where ordinary men see 'horses,' and Antisthenes holds that they are right, Plato sees 'horsiness,' or the idea of 'horse.' In the language of medieval philosophy Plato is a *realist*, that is, one who holds that our Ideas are more than what men mean when they say 'mere ideas'; that they are Realities, and have their being in a truly existing world ; and that in knowing them we know what *is*. But just as Plato holds that general conceptions are alone true and real, so he necessarily maintains that objects perceivable by the senses are only half-real, and that the ordinary man lives in a world of illusions. Thus the thoughts of the philosopher are separated by an abyss from the world in which men live and die.

63. Upon the basis of the individual 'ideas' Plato builds up by a process of classification and induction higher and smaller classes of ideas, until we begin to see the vision of a single idea, a class which includes all classes, a supreme 'being' from which all being is derived. This highest idea is variously suggested by the names 'the Good,' 'the Beautiful,' 'the One.' By a sudden transformation it becomes the Creator (δημιουργός) of the universe. Containing in itself all being, it needs for its operation some kind of formless and inert matter ; for this the name ἄπειρον, 'the unlimited,' is taken from Anaximander. The whole created universe may be considered as the joint production of the 'idea' and the 'unlimited'; and the cosmology of Anaxagoras, 'all things were together, and mind came and ordered them,' is substantially justified. The world thus created is both good and beautiful, for it is made by a good Creator on the best of patterns.

The human soul is of triple nature. The highest part, the rational soul (τὸ λογιστικόν), is seated in the head; the emotional soul (τὸ θυμοειδές) in the heart; the appetitive soul (τὸ ἐπιθυμη-τικόν) in the belly. Over these two lower souls the reasoning part should hold control, as a driver over two unruly steeds[6]. The rational soul has existed before birth, and may hope for immortality, for it is knit up with the idea of 'being.' Ultimately

God and the soul.

[6] See further, § 284.

it may even attain to perfection, if it is purified as by fire from baser elements that have attached themselves to it.

64. Plato himself does not formulate an ethical ideal of the
Ethics and same precision that his successors used, but we infer
Politics. from his works a goal towards which he points
Thus the ethical end for each man is the greatest possible participation in the idea of the good, the closest attainable imitation of the deity. The virtue of each part of the human soul lies in the fit performance of its proper work; that of the reasoning soul is Wisdom (σοφία); of the emotional soul Courage (ἀνδρεία); of the appetitive soul Soberness (σωφρο-σύνη). Over all (it is hinted rather than stated) rules the supreme virtue of Justice (δικαιοσύνη), assigning to each part its proper function. Thus the four cardinal virtues are deduced as a practical application from the Platonic psychology. The high position assigned to Justice leads up to the practical doctrine of Moderation (μετριότης); even the virtues are restricted both in their intensity and in their spheres of work, and if any virtue passes its proper limit it becomes changed into the vice that borders on it. Thus the ideal of practical life is the 'moderate man,' calm, considerate, and self-respecting, touched with a warm flow of feeling, but never carried away into excitement; and even this ideal is strictly subordinate to that of the life of philosophic contemplation.

The ideal State is modelled on the individual man. To the three parts of the soul correspond three classes of citizens; the rulers, whose virtue is Wisdom; the guardians, on whom Courage is incumbent; the labourers and tradesmen, who owe the State Soberness and obedience. Thus the political system to which Plato leans is that of an Aristocracy; for the middle class in his state has only an executive part in the government, and the lower orders are entirely excluded from it.

65. By far the greatest of Plato's pupils was ARISTOTLE of
Aristotle. Stagira (384–322 B.C.), who introduced into philosophy, now convulsed by the disputes of the
disciples of Socrates, a spirit of reconciliation. From his point
of view the various contentions are not so much erroneous as

defective. To attain the truth we need first to collect the various opinions that are commonly held, and then to seek the reconciling formula of which each one is a partial statement.

66. In his investigation Aristotle did not altogether break
The ten . with Plato's theory of ideas, but brought them
categories. from a transcendental world into touch with common
life. He held fast to the method of induction (ἐπαγωγή) from the particular to the general, and agreed that we reach the true nature of each thing when we have determined the class-conception. But the class-conception or idea (ἰδέα), though the most real existence, does not exist independently, but only in and through the particulars, which compose the class. Having thus come to see that there are gradations of existence, we need to inquire what these are; and to classify the various kinds of judgment with regard to which we inquire whether they are true or false. Now by observation we find that judgments or predications have ten different shapes, to which therefore there must correspond ten kinds of existence. These are the well-known 'categories' of Aristotle, and are as follows:

  (i)   'substance,' as when we say 'this is a man,' 'a horse';
  (ii)   'quantity,' as that he is 'six feet high';
  (iii) 'quality,' as 'a grammarian';
  (iv)   'relation,' as 'twice as much';
  (v)   'place,' as 'at Athens';
  (vi)   'time,' as 'last year';
  (vii) 'position,' as 'lying down';
  (viii) 'possession,' as 'with a sword';
  (ix)   'action,' as 'cuts'; and
  (x)   'passion,' as 'is cut' or 'is burned.'

Aristotle thus reinstates the credit of the common man; he it is who possesses the substance of truth and gives it habitual expression by speech, even roughly indicating the various kinds of existence by different forms of words. It is now indicated that a study of grammar is required as the foundation of logic.

Aristotle also greatly advanced the study of that kind of reasoning which proceeds from the general to the particular, and which is best expressed in terms of the 'syllogism' ($\sigma\upsilon\lambda\lambda o$-$\gamma\iota\sigma\mu\acute{o}s$), of which he defined the various forms.

67. In the study of physics Aristotle picks up the thread
The four   which Socrates had dropped deliberately, that is,
causes.   the teaching of the Ionic philosophers. Either
directly from Empedocles, or from a *consensus* of opinion now
fairly established, he accepted the doctrine of the four elements
($\sigma\tau o\iota\chi\epsilon\hat{\iota}a$), earth, water, air, and fire; but to these he added a
fifth ($\pi\epsilon\mu\pi\tau\grave{o}\nu$ $\sigma\tau o\iota\chi\epsilon\hat{\iota}o\nu$, *quinta essentia*), the aether, which fills
the celestial spaces. Behind this analysis lies the more important
problem of cosmology, the question how this world comes to be.
Collecting once more the opinions commonly held, Aristotle
concludes that four questions are usually asked, and that in them
the search is being made for four 'causes,' which will solve the
respective questions. The four causes are:

(i)   the Creator, or 'efficient cause,' answering the question;
      —Who made the world?

(ii) the Substance, or 'material cause';—of what did he
      make it?

(iii) the Plan, or 'modal cause';—according to what design?

(iv)` the End, or 'final cause';—for what purpose?[7]

Reviewing these 'causes' Aristotle concludes that the first, third,
and fourth are ultimately one, the Creator containing in his own
nature both the plan and the purpose of his work[8]. The solution
is therefore dualistic, and agrees substantially with that of Plato;
the ultimate existences are (i) an informing power, and (ii) matter
that has the potentiality of accepting form.

In consequence of this dualism of Aristotle the term 'matter'
($\mathring{\upsilon}\lambda\eta$, *materia*) has ever since possessed associations which did
not belong to it in the time of the hylozoists. Matter now
begins to suggest something lifeless, inert, and unintelligent;
and to be sharply contrasted not only with such conceptions as
'God' and 'mind,' but also with motion and force. For this
reason the Stoics in reintroducing monism preferred a new term,
as we shall see below[9].

---

[7] See below, § 179.   [8] Aristotle, *Physics*, ii 7.   [9] See below, § 173.

68. What God is to the universe, that the soul is to the
The micro-cosm. body, which is a 'little universe[10].' But the reasoning part of the soul only is entirely distinct; this is of divine nature, and has entered the body from without; it is at once its formative principle, its plan, and its end. The lower parts of the soul are knit up with the body, and must perish with it. So far Aristotle's teaching differs little from that of Plato; but a new point of view is introduced when he speaks of the soul as subject to 'diseases' (παθήματα), and thus assigns to the practical philosopher a social function as the comrade of the physician. Amongst the diseases he specially names Pity and Fear, which assail the emotional part of the soul. Their cure is found in 'purging' (κάθαρσις), that is to say in their complete expulsion from the soul, as reason and circumstances may require; but Aristotle by no means considers that the analogy between body and soul is complete, or that the emotions should always be regarded as injurious[11].

69. In setting forth an ideal for human activity Aristotle
Ethics and Politics. conceives that other philosophers have differed more in words than in substance, and he hopes to reconcile them through the new term 'blessedness' (εὐδαιμονία). This blessedness is attained when the soul is actively employed in a virtuous way, and when it is so circumstanced that it commands the instruments of such action, that is, in a life which is adequately furnished. On such activity pleasure must assuredly attend, and it is therefore needless to seek it of set purpose. Further, virtue appears personified in the 'true gentleman' (καλὸς κἀγαθός), who ever avoids vicious extremes, and finds his highest satisfaction in pure contemplation, just as the Creator himself lives to contemplate the world he has produced[12].

[10] εἰ δ' ἐν ζῴῳ τοῦτο δυνατὸν γενέσθαι, τί κωλύει τὸ αὐτὸ συμβῆναι καὶ κατὰ τὸ πᾶν ; εἰ γὰρ ἐν μικρῷ κόσμῳ γίνεται, καὶ ἐν μεγάλῳ Ar. *Phys.* viii 2, 252 b.

[11] See Ueberweg's note, i (Eng. trans., pp. 178–180; tenth German edition, pp. 238–240), and below, § 362.

[12] 'vitae autem degendae ratio maxime quidem illis [Peripateticis] placuit quieta, in contemplatione et cognitione posita rerum ; quae quia deorum erat vitae simillima, sapiente visa est dignissima' Cic. *Fin.* v 4, 11.

In politics Aristotle can find ground for approving in turn of monarchy, oligarchy, and democracy, according to the circumstances of each state. We cannot however but feel that his sympathies point most towards monarchy, and that his personal association with Alexander the Great was in full harmony with his inmost convictions. As a means of government he advocates before all things the education of the young.

70. The philosophies of Plato and Aristotle, comprehen-
Social prepos- sive in their range, brilliant and varied in their
sessions.   colouring, nevertheless appeal effectively only to
a limited circle. Socrates had been the companion of rich and poor alike; Plato and Aristotle addressed themselves to men of wealth, position, and taste. Their sympathies appear clearly in their political systems, in which the sovereign or the aristocracy is considered fit to play a part, whilst the many are practically excluded from the commonwealth, sometimes as a harmless flock which needs kindly shepherding, and at other times as a dangerous crowd which must be deceived or enslaved for its own good. These prepossessions, which we shall find reappearing within the Stoic system, appear to weaken the practical forcefulness of both philosophies. In the ideal character the Socratic 'force' has disappeared, and 'self-restraint' alone is the standard of virtue; the just man moves quietly and conventionally through life, perhaps escaping blame, but hardly achieving distinction. In resuming the study of ontology, which Socrates had treated as a 'mist from Ionia,' bright fancies had been elaborated rather than dominating conceptions; the deity of Aristotle seems but a faint reflex of the god of Socrates and the Cynics, and neither the 'idea' of Plato or the 'matter' of Aristotle is so well fitted for the world's hard work as the atoms of Leucippus and Democritus. The teachers who succeeded to the control of the two schools inclined more and more to engross themselves in special studies, and to leave on one side the great controversial problems.

71. The followers of Plato were known as the 'Academics':
The Aca-   amongst them we must distinguish between the
demics.   members of the 'old Academy,' as Cicero terms

them[13], and those who followed the innovations of Arcesilaus. The old Academy chiefly developed the ethical side of Plato's teaching, finding that the path of virtue is indicated by the natural capacities of the individual. Thus XENOCRATES of Chalcedon (396–314 B.C.) taught that each man's happiness resulted from the virtue proper to him (οἰκεία ἀρετή)[14]; whilst POLEMO of Athens (head of the school 314–270 B.C.) is said by Cicero to have defined it as consisting in 'virtuous living, aided by those advantages to which nature first draws us,' thereby practically adopting the standard of Aristotle[15]. The teaching of Polemo had a direct influence upon that of Zeno the founder of Stoicism.

But with the first successes of Stoicism the Academy revived its dialectical position, in strong opposition to the dogmatism of the new school. ARCESILAUS of Pitane in Aeolia (315–240 B.C.) revived the Socratic cross-examination, always opposing himself to any theory that might be propounded to him, and drawing the conclusion that truth could never be certainly known[16]. Life must therefore be guided by considerations of probability, and the ethical standard is that 'of which a reasonable defence may be made[17].' This sceptical attitude was carried still further by CARNEADES of Cyrene (214–129 B.C.), whose acute criticism told upon the Stoic leaders of his time, and forced them to abandon some of their most important positions. From this time a reconciliation between the two schools set in[18].

72. The members of the Peripatetic school founded by
The Peri-   Aristotle are of less importance to us. The
patetics.   Romans found little difference between their teach-

---

[13] See note 15, below.   [14] Clem. *Strom.* ii p. 419 a.

[15] 'honeste autem vivere, fruentem rebus eis, quas primas homini natura conciliet, et vetus Academia censuit (ut indicant scripta Polemonis), et Aristoteles eiusque amici huc proxime videntur accedere' Cic. *Ac.* ii 42, 131. Here Prof. J. S. Reid suggests that Polemo may merely have used the phrase κατὰ φύσιν ζῆν, as opposed to κατὰ θέσιν (conventionally).

[16] 'quem [*sc.* Arcesilan] ferunt...primum instituisse, non quid ipse sentiret ostendere, sed contra id, quod quisque se sentire dixisset, disputare' Cic. *de Or.* iii 18, 67. 'Arcesilas negabat esse quidquam quod sciri posset, ne illud quidem ipsum, quod Socrates sibi reliquisset' *Ac.* i 12, 45.

[17] '[cuius] ratio probabilis possit reddi' Cic. *Fin.* iii 17, 58. See further below, §§ 105, 332.   [18] See especially §§ 113 and 123.

ing and that of the earlier Academy. Cicero mentions that
the Stoic Panaetius was a keen student of two of the pupils
of Aristotle, THEOPHRASTUS (his successor as head of the
Peripatetic school) and DICAEARCHUS[19]; amongst later teachers
in whose views he is interested he names HIERONYMUS,
who held that the supreme good was freedom from pain[20];
CALLIPHO, who combined virtue with pleasure, and DIODORUS
who combined it with freedom from pain[21]; and amongst his
contemporaries STASEAS of Naples, who stated the same
doctrines in a slightly different form[22], and CRATIPPUS, whom
he selected as a teacher for his own son[23]. It was a common
complaint of these teachers that the Stoics had stolen their
doctrines wholesale, and (as is the way with thieves) had altered
the names only[24]. All these writers however agree in denying
the doctrine which Zeno accepted from the Cynics that 'virtue
is sufficient for happiness,' and lay stress upon the supply of
external goods (χορηγία) as needed to admit of the active
exercise of virtue. They were diligent students of the written
works of their founder, and thus opened the way for the work
of erudition and interpretation which found its centre in
Alexandria in a later period.

73. Amidst the conflict of these schools ZENO grew up.
Zeno. Born in Citium on the island of Cyprus in 336 B.C.,
in the same year in which Alexander became
king of Macedon, he heard as a boy of the Greek conquest of
the East, and was only 13 years of age when its course was
checked by the death of Alexander. Of the town of Citium the
inhabitants were partly Greek, partly Phoenician; and Zeno,
whether or not he was of Phoenician blood, certainly derived

---

[19] Cic. *Fin.* iv 28, 79.

[20] 'non dolere...Hieronymus summum bonum esse dixit' *ib.* v 25, 73.

[21] 'at vero Callipho, et post eum Diodorus, cum alter voluptatem adamavisset,
alter vacuitatem doloris: neuter honestate carere potuit, quae est a nostris laudata
maxime' *ib.*

[22] *ib.* 25, 75. [23] *Off.* i 1, 1.

[24] '[Stoici] quidem non unam aliquam aut alteram a nobis, sed totam ad se
nostram philosophiam transtulerunt. atque, ut reliqui fures, earum rerum, quas
ceperunt, signa commutant, sic illi, ut sententiis nostris pro suis uterentur, nomina,
tanquam rerum notas, mutaverunt' *Fin.* v 25, 74.

from his environment something of the character of the enter-
prising and much-travelled Phoenician nation, and imparted
this trait to the school which he founded. He was nicknamed
by his contemporaries 'the Phoenician,' and the title clung to
his followers[25]. His father was a merchant of purple, and often
travelled in the one direction to Tyre and Sidon, in the other as
far as Athens, whence he brought back a number of 'Socratic
books,' which were eagerly read by the young Zeno, and in
time attracted him to the famous Greek city[26]. We may presume that when he first came to Athens he intended to carry
further his studies without abandoning his calling; but when
news reached him of the wreck of the ship which carried all his
goods, he welcomed it as a call to devote himself entirely to
philosophy[27]. His first step in Athens was to seek out the man
who best represented the character of Socrates, as represented
in Xenophon's Memoirs; and it is said that a bookseller accordingly pointed him to CRATES of Thebes[28], the pupil and (it
would seem) the successor of Diogenes as acknowledged head
of the Cynic school.

74. Our authorities busy themselves chiefly with narrating
the eccentricities of Crates, who wore warm clothing
in summer and rags in winter, entered the theatre
as the audience were coming out, and drank water instead of
wine. But doubtless, like his predecessors in the Cynic school,
he was a man of the true Socratic character, who had trained
himself to bear hunger and thirst, heat and cold, flattery and
abuse. His life and wisdom won him the love of the high-born
Hipparchia, who turned from her wealthy and noble suitors,
choosing instead the poverty of Crates, who had abandoned all
his possessions. In his company she went from house to house,
knocking at all doors in turn, sometimes admonishing the in-
mates of their sins, sometimes sharing with them their meals[29].

Zeno joins the Cynics.

[25] Ζήνωνα τὸν Φοίνικα, Athen. *Deipnos.* xiii 2 ; 'tuus ille Poenulus,' 'e Phoenicia
profecti' Cic. *Fin.* iv 20, 56.

[26] Diog. L. vii 31 and 32.

[27] 'nuntiato naufragio Zeno noster, cum omnia sua audiret submersa: iubet,
inquit, me fortuna expeditius philosophari' Sen. *Dial.* ix 14, 3.

[28] Diog. L. vii 3.

[29] Diog. L. vi 96 and 97.

In such a life Zeno recognised the forcefulness of Socrates, and in the dogmas of the Cynic school he reached the foundation on which that life was built. From that foundation neither Zeno nor his true followers ever departed, and thus Stoicism embodied and spread the fundamental dogmas of Cynism, that the individual alone is really existent, that virtue is the supreme good, and that the wise man, though a beggar, is truly a king.

75. Whilst still an adherent of the Cynic school[30], Zeno

Zeno's Republic.

wrote his Πολιτεία or *Republic*, which is evidently an attack on Plato's work with the same title[31]. If this work does not reveal to us the fully developed philosopher, it at least shews us better than any other evidence what the man Zeno was. His ideal was the establishment of a perfect State, a completion of the work in which Alexander had failed; and he found a starting-point in a treatise by Antisthenes on the same subject. The ideal State must embrace the whole world, so that a man no longer says, 'I am of Athens,' or 'of Sidon,' but 'I am a citizen of the world[32].' Its laws must be those which are prescribed by nature, not by convention. It will have no images or temples, for these are unworthy of the nature of the deity; no sacrifices, because he cannot be pleased by costly gifts; no law-courts, for its citizens will do one another no harm; no statues, for the virtues of its inhabitants will be its adornment[33]; no gymnasia, for its youth must not waste their time in idle exercises[34].

The people will not be divided into classes (and here Plato's *Republic* is contradicted), for all alike will be wise men[35]; nor will men and women be clothed differently, or shamefacedly hide any part of their bodies[36]. No man will speak of a woman as his property, for women will belong to the community only[37]. As for the dead, men will not trouble whether they bury them

---

[30] *ib.* vii 4.

[31] ἀντέγραψε πρὸς τὴν Πλάτωνος Πολιτείαν Plut. *Sto. rep.* 8, 2 (Arnim i 260).

[32] This doctrine can be traced back to Diogenes and even to Socrates: see below, § 303.

[33] τὰς πόλεις κοσμεῖν οὐκ ἀναθήμασιν, ἀλλὰ ταῖς τῶν οἰκούντων ἀρεταῖς Stob. iv 1, 88.

[34] See below, § 305.

[35] παριστάντα πολίτας τοὺς σπουδαίους μόνον Diog. L. vii 33.

[36] See below, § 318.   [37] § 306.

(as the Greeks), burn them (as the Indians), or give them to the birds (as the Persians); for it matters not at all what happens to men's dead bodies[38], but whether their souls shall reach the abodes of the blest, or need hereafter to be purged by fire from the foulness they have contracted through contact with the body[39]. To conclude, Love shall be master throughout the State, being as it were a God cooperating for the good of the whole[40]; and the wise man shall be a citizen in it, not a missionary, and shall be surrounded with wife and children[41].

76. Zeno, after writing his *Republic*, took up a position more
Zeno seeks independent of the Cynics. He could not, perhaps,
knowledge. avoid noticing that the coming of his model Kingdom was hindered by the narrowmindedness of the philosophers, their disagreement one with another, and their lack of clear proofs for their dogmas. He began to realize that the study of dialectics and physics was of more importance than his Cynic teachers would allow; and he seems to have conceived the idea of uniting the Socratic schools. He became eager to learn from all sources, and turned first to Stilpo, who then represented the Megarian school[42]. Crates, we are told, tried to drag him back from Stilpo by force; to which Zeno retorted that argument would be more to the point[43]. From this time he no longer restricted his outlook to force of character, but sought also for argumentative power and well ascertained knowledge. The foundations of his state must be surely laid, not upon the changing tide of opinion, but on the rock of knowledge. That a wise man should hesitate, change his views, withdraw his advice, he felt would be a bitter reproach[44]. If indeed virtue, the supreme good, is knowledge, must it not follow that knowledge is within the reach of man?

[38] § 307. [39] §§ 296, 297. [40] § 304. [41] § 315.
[42] See above, § 56.
[43] He said 'O Crates, the best handle of philosophers is that by the ear; persuade me if you can, and lead me that way; if you use violence, my body will stay with you, but my soul will be with Stilpo' Diog. L. vii 24.
[44] 'errorem autem et temeritatem et ignorantiam et opinationem et suspicionem et uno nomine omnia, quae essent aliena firmae et constantis adsensionis, a virtute sapientiaque [Zeno] removebat' Cic. *Ac.* i 11, 42.

77. The chief cause of error, Zeno found, lay in hasty

Zeno's theory of knowledge. assertion; and this he held was a fault not so much of the intellect as of the will. In the simplest case the senses present to the mind a 'picture' (φαντασία, *visum*), carrying with it the suggestion of a statement (e.g. 'that is a horse'). But it is for the man to consider well whether this suggestion is true, and only to give his 'assent' (συγκατάθεσις, *adsensus*) when he is so assured. Assent is an act of the will, and therefore in our power. Of a picture to which he has given his assent the wise man should retain a firm hold; it then becomes an item of 'comprehension' (φαντασία καταληπτική, *comprehensio*), and may be stored in the memory, thus preparing the way for further acquisitions of knowledge, which in the end combine in 'scientific knowledge' (ἐπιστήμη, *scientia*).

This theory is little more than an exhortation against the prevailing error of hasty thought (δόξα, *opinio*); but it made a very deep impression, especially as enforced by Zeno's gestures. He stretched out his fingers and shewed the open palm, saying 'Such is a picture.' He partially contracted his fingers, and said 'This is assent.' Making a closed fist, he said 'This is comprehension.' Then closing in the left hand over the right he pressed his fist tight, and said 'This is science, and only the wise man can attain to it[45].'

We have no reason to suppose that this theory was in any way suggested by Stilpo, from whom however Zeno probably learnt to attach importance to the formal part of reasoning, such as 'definition' and the use of the syllogism. With Stilpo he shared an aversion to the Platonic theory of ideas, maintaining that ideas are by no means realities but have only a 'kind of existence' in our minds, or (as we should call it to-day) a 'subjective existence[46].'

---

[45] 'hoc quidem Zeno gestu conficiebat. nam cum extensis digitis adversam manum ostenderat, 'visum,' inquiebat, 'huiusmodi est.' deinde cum paulum digitos contraxerat, 'adsensus huiusmodi.' tum cum plane compresserat pugnumque fecerat, comprehensionem illam esse dicebat; cum autem laevam manum admoverat et illum pugnum arte vehementerque compresserat, scientiam talem esse dicebat: cuius compotem nisi sapientem esse neminem' Cic. *Ac.* ii 47, 145.

[46] See below, § 188.

78. In becoming in turn a listener to Polemo, Zeno, we may imagine, entered a new world. He left behind the rough manners, the stinging retorts, and the narrow culture of the Cynics and Eristics[47], to sit with other intelligent students[48] at the feet of a man of cultured manners[49] and wide reading, who to a love for Homer and Sophocles[50] had, we must suppose, added an intimate knowledge of the works of Plato and Aristotle, was himself a great writer[51], and yet consistently taught that not learning, but a natural and healthy life was the end to be attained. That Zeno profited much from his studies under Polemo we may conjecture from Polemo's good-natured complaint, ' I see well what you are after: you break down my garden wall and steal my teaching, which you dress in Phoenician clothes[52].' From this time it became a conventional complaint that Stoic doctrine was stolen from that of the Academics: yet the sharp conflict between the two schools shews that this cannot apply to essentials. But in two important matters at least Zeno must have been indebted to Academic teaching. This school had elaborated the doctrine of Anaxagoras, which so attracted Socrates, that the world began with the working of mind upon unordered matter. So too, according to all our authorities, Zeno taught that there are two beginnings, the active which is identified with the deity or Logos, and the passive which is inert matter, or substance without quality[53]. This doctrine appears to pledge Zeno to a dualistic view of the universe.

Zeno studies under Polemo.

79. On the other hand the Platonic teaching on the soul was reversed by Zeno. He denied the opposition between soul and body. ' Soul is breath[54],' he taught, and ' soul is body[55].' With Plato's threefold division of the soul he would have nothing to do ; rather he maintained

' Soul is body.'

---

[47] So the Megarians were commonly called on account of their disputatious methods.

[48] As for instance Arcesilaus ; Ἀρκεσίλαος ὁ ἐκ τῆς Ἀκαδημίας, Ζήνωνος τοῦ Κιτιέως συσχολαστὴς παρὰ Πολέμωνι Strabo xiii p. 614 (Arnim i 10).

[49] Diog. L. iv 18.   [50] *ib.* 20.   [51] *ib.*

[52] Diog. L. vii 25.   [53] See below, § 189.   [54] See § 268, note 2.

[55] οἱ γε ἀπὸ Χρυσίππου καὶ Ζήνωνος φιλόσοφοι καὶ πάντες ὅσοι σῶμα τὴν ψυχὴν νοοῦσι Iamb. *de an.* (Stob. i 49, 33).

that the soul has eight parts[56], each displaying itself in a distinct power or capacity, whilst all of them are qualities or operations of one soul in various relations[57]. In this part of his philosophy Zeno appears as a strong monist, and his debt to the Platonists is necessarily restricted to details.

80. It would seem then that Zeno after seeking for philo-
Zeno studies   sophic safety for some twenty years in one harbour
Heraclitus.   after another had so far made shipwreck. But
from this shipwreck of his intellectual hopes he could afterwards count the beginning of a fair voyage[58]. As he eagerly discussed with his younger fellow-student Arcesilaus the teaching of their master Polemon, he took courage to point out its weak points[59], and began to quote in his own defence not only his previous teachers Crates and Stilpo, but also the works of Heraclitus[60]. He thus broke down the barrier which Socrates had set up against the Ionic philosophers. From Heraclitus Zeno drew two doctrines of first-rate importance; the first, that of the eternal fire[61] and its mutation into the elements in turn[62]; the second (already referred to) that of the *Logos*[63]. It is evident that the Heraclitean doctrine of fire breaks down the distinction between God and the world, active and passive, soul and body; and is therefore inconsistent with the dualism which Zeno had

[56] Ζήνων ὁ Στωϊκὸς ὀκταμερῆ φησιν εἶναι τὴν ψυχήν Nemes. *nat. hom.* p. 96 (Arnim i 143).

[57] οἱ ἀπὸ Ζήνωνος ὀκταμερῆ τὴν ψυχὴν διαδοξάζουσι, περὶ [ἥν] τὰς δυνάμεις εἶναι πλείονας, ὥσπερ ἐν τῷ ἡγεμονικῷ ἐνυπαρχουσῶν φαντασίας συγκαταθέσεως ὁρμῆς λόγου Iamb. *de an.* (Arnim i 143). See below, § 270.

[58] τῶν προειρημένων ἤκουσεν ἕως ἐτῶν εἴκοσιν· ἵνα καὶ φασιν αὐτὸν εἰπεῖν· νῦν εὐπλόηκα, ὅτε νεναυάγηκα Diog. L. vii 4. It must not however be assumed that Zeno himself used the phrase in this sense: see the other references in Arnim i 277.

[59] 'iam Polemonem audiverant adsidue Zeno et Arcesilas. Sed Zeno cum Arcesilam anteiret aetate, valdeque subtiliter dissereret et peracute moveretur, corrigere conatus est disciplinam' Cic. *Ac.* i 9, 34 and 35.

[60] ἐπεὶ συμφοιτῶντες παρὰ Πολέμωνι ἐφιλοτιμήθησαν ἀλλήλοις, συμπαρέλαβον εἰς τὴν πρὸς ἀλλήλους μάχην ὁ μὲν Ἡράκλειτον καὶ Στίλπωνα ἅμα καὶ Κράτητα Euseb. *Praep. ev.* xiv 5, 11 (quoting Numenius) (Arnim i 11).

[61] Zeno often calls it *aether*: 'Zenon...aethera...interim vult omnium esse principium' Min. Felix xix p. 58 : Cleanthes calls it *spirit*, see below, § 100. 'The fire of Heraclitus becomes aether or πῦρ τεχνικόν—for this distinction is unknown to the Ephesian—and is thereby spiritualised and rarefied' Pearson, *Fragments*, Intr. pp. 22, 23.

[62] See below, § 196.   [63] See above, § 39.

partly borrowed from Plato. It is not clear whether Zeno attained to clearness on this point; but in the general teaching of the Stoics the monistic doctrine prevailed[64]. Hence God is not separate from body, but is himself body in its purest form[65]. The *Logos* or divine reason is the power which pervades and gives shape to the universe[66]; and this Logos is identical with the deity, that is with the primitive and creative Fire[67]. The Logos (ὀρθὸς λόγος, *vera ratio*) brings into harmony the parts of philosophy; for it is also on the one hand the guide to right reasoning[68]; on the other hand the law which prescribes what is right for the State and for the individual[69].

81. When Zeno definitely accepted the teaching of He-
Zeno opens his school. raclitus, he felt bound to break finally with the school of Polemo, and he founded soon after 300 B.C. a school of his own, which was rapidly crowded. His followers were at first called Zenonians, but afterwards Stoics, from the 'picture porch' (so called because it was decorated with paintings by Polygnotus) in which he delivered his lectures. He now applied himself afresh to the problem of ethics. Whilst still adhering to the Cynic views that 'virtue is the only good,' and that 'example is more potent than precept,' he entirely rejected the intuitional basis which the Cynics had accepted, deciding in favour of the claims of reason. He found his ideal in 'consistency' (ὁμολογία, *convenientia*)[70]; as the Logos or Word rules in the universe, so should it also in the individual. Those who live by a single and harmonious principle possess

[64] Stein, *Psychologie*, i 62 sqq.

[65] Χρύσιππος καὶ Ζήνων ὑπέθεντο καὶ αὐτοὶ ἀρχὴν μὲν θεὸν τῶν πάντων, σῶμα ὄντα τὸ καθαρώτατον Hippolyt. *Philos.* 21, 1 (Arnim i 153).

[66] 'rationem quandam per naturam omnem rerum pertinentem vi divina esse affectam putat' Cic. *N. D.* i 14, 36.

[67] 'Zeno [deum nuncupat] naturalem divinamque legem' Lact. *Div. inst.* i 5, 20.

[68] ἄλλοι δέ τινες τῶν ἀρχαιοτέρων Στωϊκῶν τὸν ὀρθὸν λόγον κριτήριον ἀπολείπουσιν, ὡς ὁ Ποσειδώνιος ἐν τῷ περὶ κριτηρίου φησί Diog. L. vii 54 (quoting Diocles Magnes). It is much disputed who the authorities are to which Posidonius here refers.

[69] 'Zeno naturalem legem divinam esse censet eamque vim obtinere recta imperantem prohibentemque contraria' Cic. *N. D.* i 14, 36.

[70] τὸ δὲ τέλος ὁ μὲν Ζήνων οὕτως ἀπέδωκε, τὸ ὁμολογουμένως ζῆν · τοῦτο δ' ἐστὶ καθ' ἕνα λόγον καὶ σύμφωνον ζῆν, ὡς τῶν μαχομένως ζώντων κακοδαιμονούντων Stob. ii 7, 6 a. 'summum bonum, quod cum positum sit in eo, quod ὁμολογίαν Stoici, nos appellemus convenientiam' Cic. *Fin.* iii 6, 21.

divine favour and an even flow of life[71]; those that follow conflicting practices are ill-starred[72]. In this consistency there is
found virtue, and (here again he follows the Cynics) virtue is
sufficient for happiness[73], and has no need of any external
support.

82. But whilst the virtue of the Cynics is something detached and self-contained, and is 'natural' only
His theory
of virtue. in the sense that it is not determined by custom
or authority, that of Zeno is bound up with the whole scheme
of the universe. For the universe puts before men certain
things, which though rightly named 'indifferent' by the Cynics,
and wrongly named 'good' by the Academics, have yet a certain
value (ἀξία, *aestimatio*), and are a natural goal for men's actions[74].
Such are health, prosperity, good name, and other things which
the Academics named 'things according to nature' (τὰ κατὰ
φύσιν). These Zeno took over, not as a part of his theory of
virtue, but as the basis of it[75]; and for things having value
introduced the term 'of high degree' (προηγμένα), and for their
opposites the term 'of low degree' (ἀποπροηγμένα), these terms
being borrowed from court life. Thus virtue alone is queen,
and all things naturally desired are subject to her command[76].
The end of life is therefore to live consistently, keeping in view
the aims set before us by nature, or shortly, to live 'consistently
with nature.' Our authorities do not agree as to whether Zeno
or Cleanthes was the first to use this phrase[77]; but there can be
no doubt that the doctrine is that of Zeno, that it is a fundamental part of the Stoic system, and that it was maintained
unaltered by all orthodox Stoics. On the other hand the

---

[71] εὐδαιμονία δ' ἐστὶν εὔροια βίου Stob. ii 7, 6 e.

[72] See note 70 above. [73] See below, § 322.

[74] For a fuller treatment see below, §§ 319–321.

[75] οὐχὶ καὶ Ζήνων τούτοις (sc. Peripateticis) ἠκολούθησεν ὑποτιθεμένοις στοιχεῖα τῆς
εὐδαιμονίας τὴν φύσιν καὶ τὸ κατὰ φύσιν; Plut. *comm. not.* 23, 1 ; '[a Polemone] quae
essent principia naturae acceperat' Cic. *Fin.* iv 16, 45.

[76] τὰ μὲν [οὖν] πολλὴν ἔχοντα ἀξίαν προηγμένα λέγεσθαι, τὰ δὲ πολλὴν ἀπαξίαν
ἀποπροηγμένα, Ζήνωνος ταύτας τὰς ὀνομασίας θεμένου πρώτου τοῖς πράγμασι Stob. ii
7, 7 g ; see also below, § 320.

[77] Diogenes Laertius says distinctly that Zeno used the phrase, and names the
book in which he found it ; Diog. L. vii 87. On the other hand Stobaeus (ii 7, 6 a)
attributes it to Cleanthes.

Academics and Peripatetics ridiculed these new and barbarous terms προηγμένα and ἀποπροηγμένα, and their view has generally been supported both in ancient and modern times[78]. We cannot however question the right of Zeno to reserve a special term for that which is morally good; he was in fact feeling his way towards the position, still imperfectly recognized, that the language of common life is inadequate to the exact expression of philosophic principles[79].

83. In expounding his system Zeno made much use of the Zeno's syl- syllogism, thereby laying the foundations of a new logisms. style of oratory, consisting of short and pointed clauses, which became a characteristic of his school[80]. He no doubt regarded this form as a sure method of attaining truth; but even at the present day the principle that truth can only be reached from facts and not from words is not everywhere admitted. The syllogisms of Zeno have all their weak points, and as a rule the term which is common to the major and minor premisses suffers a shift of meaning. These syllogisms can no longer convince us, and even in antiquity they were severely criticized. But they are excellent aids to the memory, and so serve the same end as the catechisms of the Reformation period. Amongst the syllogisms attributed to Zeno are these: 'That which has reason is better than that which has not reason; but nothing is better than the universe; therefore the universe has reason[81].' 'No one trusts a secret to a drunken man; but one trusts a secret to a good man; therefore a good man will not be drunken[82].' 'No evil is accompanied by glory; but death is accompanied by glory; therefore death is no evil[83].' Such syllogisms were embedded in the numerous works of Zeno, of

---

[78] 'Zeno Citieus, advena quidam et ignobilis verborum opifex' Cic. *Tusc.* v 12, 34.

[79] See below, § 165.

[80] ' illa vetus Zenonis brevis, et ut tibi videbatur, acuta conclusio ' Cic. *N. D.* iii 9, 22.

[81] τὸ λογικὸν τοῦ μὴ λογικοῦ κρεῖττόν ἐστιν   οὐδὲν δέ γε κόσμου κρεῖττόν ἐστιν· λογικὸν ἄρα ὁ κόσμος Sext. *math.* ix 104 (Arnim i 111); see also below, § 202.

[82] 'ebrio secretum sermonem nemo committit ; viro autem bono committit ; ergo vir bonus ebrius non erit ' Sen. *Ep.* 83, 9 ; for the original see Arnim i 229.

[83] 'nullum malum gloriosum est ; mors autem gloriosa est ; mors ergo non est malum ' Sen. *Ep.* 82, 9.

which many were certainly extant as late as the time of Epictetus[84].

84. At the very time when Zeno was elaborating the
Epicurus and Arcesilaus. doctrines of the Porch, another school of equal eminence was established at Athens by EPICURUS (341–207 B.C.) in his Gardens. Epicurus combined the ethical principle of the Cyrenaics, that pleasure is the end of life, with the atomistic philosophy of Democritus; he had no respect for the study of dialectic, but placed the criterion of truth in the observations of the senses, leaving little room for the participation of mind or will. Thus in every part of philosophy his teaching was opposed to that of Zeno, and the two schools during their whole existence were in the sharpest conflict. We may nevertheless notice some points of contact between them. Both founded, or conceived that they founded their ethical doctrine upon physical proofs; that is, both maintained that the end of life which they put forward was that prescribed by natural law. As a consequence, they agreed in removing the barrier which Socrates had set up against the pursuit of natural science. • Both again were positive teachers, or (in the language of the ancients) propounders of dogmas; and here they came into conflict with the Academic school, which maintained, and was soon about to emphasize, the critical spirit of Socrates and Plato. For in the last years of Zeno's life his old fellow-pupil Arcesilaus became head of the Academic school (270 B.C.), and at once directed his teaching against Zeno's theory of knowledge[85]. Following the practice of Socrates and of Plato's dialogues, he argued against every point of view presented, and concluded that certain truth could not be known by man[86]. He pressed Zeno closely as to his definition of 'comprehension,' and induced him to add a clause which, in the opinion of his opponent, shewed the worthlessness of the whole

[84] 'If you would know, read Zeno's writings, and you will see' Epict. *Disc.* i 20, 14.

[85] 'cum Zenone, ut accepimus, Arcesilas sibi omne certamen instituit' Cic. *Ac.* i 12, 44.

[86] 'Arcesilas primum...ex variis Platonis libris sermonibusque Socraticis hoc maxime arripuit, nihil esse certi quod aut sensibus aut animo percipi possit' Cic. *de Or.* iii 18, 67.

doctrine[87]. Thus was raised the question of the κριτήριον or test of truth, which for at least a century to come sharply divided the schools[88].

85. The conflict between these three schools, which from Zeno at Athens. this time on greatly surpassed all others in importance, did not embitter the political life of Athens. The citizens watched with amusement the competition of the schools for numbers and influence, and drew their profit from the crowds of foreigners who were drawn to Athens by its growing fame as a centre of adult education. To the heads of the schools they were ready to pay every mark of respect. With Zeno they deposited the keys of their gates, and they awarded him during his life-time a gold crown and a bronze statue. His fame spread abroad, and those of his fellow-citizens of Citium who were then resident at Sidon claimed a share in it. In his old age the high-minded Antigonus Gonatas (who occupied the throne of Macedonia with varying fortune from 278 to 239 B.C.) looked to him for advice and help. But no offers of public employment could draw Zeno himself from his simple life and the young companions who surrounded him : like Socrates, he thought that he could best serve the State by sending out others to take part in its duties[89]. He died in the year 264 B.C.[90], having been engaged in teaching for more than 30 years from the time when he 'discovered the truth[91].'

86. The vote which the Athenians passed in honour of Zeno, Honours paid to him. shortly before his death, deserves record by its contrast with that by which their predecessors had condemned Socrates. It ran somewhat as follows :

[87] ' hic Zenonem vidisse acute, nullum esse visum quod percipi posset, si id tale esset ab eo, quod est, ut eiusdem modi ab eo, quod non est, posset esse. recte consensit Arcesilas ; ad definitionem additum [sc. quale non possit esse a falso]. incubuit autem in eas disputationes, ut doceret nullum tale esse visum a vero, ut non eiusdem modi etiam a falso posset esse' Cic. *Ac.* ii 24, 77.

[88] See below, § 157.

[89] 'compositus sequor Zenona Cleanthen Chrysippum, quorum tamen nemo ad rempublicam accessit, et nemo non misit' Sen. *Dial.* ix 1, 10 ; see also viii 6, 4.

[90] Pearson, *Introd.* p. 1.

[91] προσεμαρτύρησ[εν ἑαυτῷ] τὴν εὕρεσιν τῆς ἀληθείας Sext. *math.* vii 321. Pearson, *Introd.* p. 4.

'Whereas Zeno the son of Mnaseas from Citium has spent many years in this city in the pursuit of philosophy; and has been throughout a good man in all respects; and has encouraged the young men who resorted to him in virtue and temperance, and has sped them on the right path; and has made his own life an example to all men, for it has been consistent with the teaching he has set forth;

Now it seems good to the people of Athens to commend Zeno the son of Mnaseas from Citium, and to crown him with a golden crown (in accordance with the law) for his virtue and temperance, and to build him a tomb on the Ceramicus at the public expense. And the people shall elect five Athenian citizens to provide for the making of the crown and the building of the tomb. And the town clerk shall engrave this vote on two pillars, and shall set up one in the Academy, and one in the Lyceum. And the treasurer shall make due allotment of the expense, that all men may see that the people of Athens honours good men both in their life time and after their death[92].'

We have no reason to doubt the sincerity of this tribute. It is true that all the charges brought against Socrates hold even more forcibly as against Zeno. But the spirit of political and religious independence was now dead, and the advantage of the philosophical schools to the fame and business interests of the city had become clearer; so that nothing prevented any longer the open recognition of Zeno's virtues and eminence. Who will may also read in the decree a belated mark of respect to the memory of Socrates.

87. In this sketch of the life of Zeno no attempt has been made to give a complete view of his philosophy; but a few landmarks have been indicated, by which it may be possible to distinguish which parts of it were his own, which were taken over from others, and how all were gradually combined in one whole. Zeno had not the kind of originality which begins by assuming a general principle, and then explains all things human and divine by deductions from it. Instead of this he gathered together (as Aristotle had done before, but with a very different bias) what seemed most sound and illuminating in the teaching of all the schools which surrounded him. He did this in a positive spirit, feeling assured that truth exists and is discernible, and must be consistent in all its parts. We seem unable to say that in his writings he attained to this consistency,

Zeno's breadth of view.

---

[92] Diog. L. vii 10 and 11.

but at least he worked steadily towards it. The effort for consistency led him in the direction of monistic principle, though his points of departure both in physics and in ethics are dualistic. But the teaching of Zeno does not lend itself to that kind of study which assigns all new facts to compartments of thought ready labelled in advance, nor can it be summarized by any of the technical terms which are in use in modern philosophical thought. Enough has perhaps been said to shew that, great as was the debt of Zeno to his predecessors, he was no mere imitator or plagiarist; the history of the following centuries will shew that he had in some sense touched the pulses of human life more truly than any of his contemporaries.

CHAPTER IV.

THE PREACHING OF STOICISM.

88. DURING the later years of his life Zeno gathered round him a number of men of practical and speculative capacity, not unworthy of comparison with the companions of Socrates. His death dissolved the immediate tie between them. Some took an active part in the work of government; others followed their teacher's example, and became the founders of independent schools of thought; a few devoted themselves to strengthening and extending Zeno's system; and many were doubtless engaged in useful employment of which no record has reached us. Zeno's work had not yet been exposed to the test of time, and another century was to pass before it could be seen that the Stoic school was to be of permanent importance. Towards the schools of the Cynics, the Megarians, and the Academics, from which its principles were so largely derived, the attitude of the hearers of Zeno was that of a friendly interchange of opinions, in which sharp controversy stopped short of enmity; the followers of Aristotle (the Peripatetics) continued to be but slightly distinguished from the Academics. But all these schools appear to have united in opposition to the Cyrenaics and Epicureans; the champions of virtue could hold no communings with the advocates of pleasure. Individual teachers who practically reverted to Cynic or Academic teaching still called themselves Stoics: but the only one of Zeno's hearers who adopted Cyrenaic views was contemptuously branded as 'the deserter[1].'

(margin note: The companions of Zeno.)

[1] See below, § 95.

89. The most intimate companion[2] of Zeno was PERSAEUS
of Citium (circ. 300–243 B.C.). He was the fellow-
townsman of Zeno, and, as good authorities assert,
Persaeus.
at first his personal servant (οἰκέτης)[3] and afterwards his fellow-
lodger. On the recommendation of Zeno he took service, together
with Aratus the poet, with Antigonus Gonatas, king of Macedonia[4]. Here he was often twitted as to the Stoic paradoxes.
King Antigonus sent him messengers announcing the loss of his
wife, child, and property, and found that he was not entirely
indifferent to external circumstances[5]. He adapted himself
easily to court life, and is said to have written a treatise on the
theory of the banquet, in which he did not rise above the moral
standard of his neighbours[6]. Nor did he disdain to hoax Aristo
of Chius, who held strongly to the paradox that 'the wise man
never opines'; he first sent him money by one of two twins, and
then sent another to demand it back[7]. Another Socratic paradox, that 'the wise man is sure to be a good general,' he
endeavoured to maintain by his personal example[8]. Antigonus
placed him in command of the acropolis at Corinth, which was
nevertheless taken by Aratus of Sicyon in 243 B.C. According
to one account, Persaeus was wounded in the attack, and afterwards put to death by the conqueror[9]; others relate that he
escaped to Cenchreae[10]. As a philosopher he is of little importance; but Cicero mentions that he not only maintained that
amongst the gods were men raised to the sky for their services
to mankind (which was an accepted Stoic doctrine), but also
that objects useful to man had been deified[11].

[2] μάλιστα μὲν οὖν τῶν μαθητῶν ὑπὸ τοῦ Ζήνωνος ἠγαπᾶτο ὁ Περσαῖος Ind. Sto.
Herc. col. xii 3 (Arnim i 437).

[3] 'Zenonis Stoici servus, qui Persaeus vocatus est' A. Gellius N. A. ii 18, 8.
ἦν γὰρ ὄντως οἰκέτης γεγονὼς τοῦ Ζήνωνος, ὡς Νικίας ὁ Νικαεὺς ἱστορεῖ ἐν τῇ περὶ τῶν
φιλοσόφων ἱστορίᾳ καὶ Σωτίων ὁ Ἀλεξανδρεὺς ἐν ταῖς Διαδοχαῖς Athen. iv 54 (Arnim i
452). On the other hand 'nullum [servum fuisse] Zenoni...satis constat' Sen. Dial.
xii 12, 4.

[4] Arnim i 439, 440.   [5] ib. 449.   [6] Athen. iv 54 (Arnim i 452).
[7] Diog. L. vii 162.   [8] Athen. as above.
[9] Paus. ii 8, 4; vii 8, 3 (Arnim i 442).

[10] Plut. Arat. 23, 3. According to Plutarch he afterwards admitted that he had
been wrongly taught as to the 'good general.'

[11] 'Persaeus eos dicit esse habitos deos, a quibus magna utilitas ad vitae cultum
esset inventa, ipsasque res utiles et salutares deorum esse vocabulis nuncupatas'
Cic. N. D. i 15, 38. Persaeus derived the theory from Prodicus; Philod. de piet. 9
(Arnim i 448), and above, § 42.

90. Two other companions of Zeno also took service under
Antigonus, apparently at the same time. Of these

Aratus.

PHILONIDES of Thebes[12] is otherwise unknown to
us. The other was ARATUS of Soli in Cilicia, author of the well-
known poem *The Phaenomena*, an astronomical treatise afterwards
translated into Latin by Cicero, and largely used by Virgil in his
Georgics. The poems of Aratus had a wide influence, and were
probably the source from which so many Stoic conceptions
reached Virgil. The most interesting part for us is the Introduction, in which he interprets Zeus in Stoic fashion as the deity
who dwells in sea and land, in markets and streets: whose family
is mankind; and whose providence has set the stars in the heaven
to regulate the seasons of the year and to be a guide to the
farmer and the sailor[13]. The spirit of this poem is closely akin
to that of the hymn of Cleanthes.

91. Still another hearer of Zeno took a prominent part
in political life. SPHAERUS from the Bosphorus

Sphaerus.

(circ. 250 B.C.) was attracted to Cleomenes III,
king of Sparta. who under his influence reintroduced the laws
of Lycurgus in his city, and particularly those which referred
to the education of the youth and the taking of meals in common[14].
With these he combined the plan of a monarchy after the Stoic
model, in which the sovereign was to side with the poor against
the rich[15]. But in 221 B.C. Cleomenes suffered a crushing defeat,
and was compelled to take refuge with Ptolemy III (Euergetes),
king of Egypt. Sphaerus found his way to the same court.
The death of Ptolemy III left Cleomenes in the position of a
disregarded suppliant[16]; but Sphaerus appears to have found a
congenial home in Alexandria, now the centre of Hellenistic
learning, and doubtless introduced the Stoic philosophy in the
circle that gathered round the Museum[17]. He gained a special
reputation by the excellence of his definitions[18]. From an anec-

---

[12] Diog. L. vii 9.

[13] ἐκ Διὸς ἀρχώμεσθα, τὸν οὐδέποτ' ἄνδρες ἐῶμεν | ἄρρητον· μεσταὶ δὲ Διὸς πᾶσαι
μὲν ἀγυιαί, | πᾶσαι δ' ἀνθρώπων ἀγοραί, μεστὴ δὲ θάλασσα | καὶ λιμένες· πάντη δὲ
Διὸς κεχρήμεθα πάντες. | τοῦ γὰρ καὶ γένος ἐσμέν· ὁ δ' ἤπιος ἀνθρώποισιν | δεξιὰ
σημαίνει, λαοὺς δ' ἐπὶ ἔργον ἐγείρει | μιμνήσκων βιότοιο: Aratus, *Phaen.* Pref.

[14] Plut. *Cleo.* 11, 2.   [15] Mahaffy, *Empire of the Ptolemies*, p. 222.

[16] *ib.* p. 245.   [17] Zeller, *Stoics* etc., p. 44.

[18] 'Sphaeri, hominis in primis bene definientis, ut putant Stoici' Cic. *Tusc. disp.*
iv 24, 53.

dote related of him we must infer that whilst adhering to Zeno's
doctrine that the wise man will not opine, he accepted reasonable
assurance (τὸ εὔλογον) as a sufficient guide in daily life[19]. He
appears to have laid special stress upon the unity of virtue, maintaining that the separate virtues are but appearances of virtue
or knowledge in different spheres of action[20].

92. HERILLUS of Carthage (circ. 250 B.C.) is frequently
referred to by Cicero as teaching doctrines hardly
Herillus.
distinguishable from those of the Academy, in that
he made knowledge the highest good[21], and taught that separate
from it, yet with claims of their own, there existed inferior ends
of action (ὑποτελίδες)[22]. It does not, however, appear clearly
that he differed much from Zeno. Sphaerus, as we have seen,
had defined the virtues as being 'knowledge displayed in
different spheres of action,' and the aim of Herillus, 'to live
according to the standard of life accompanied by knowledge[23],'
points in the direction of practical rather than of speculative
wisdom. His 'subordinate aims' appear also to correspond
with Zeno's 'things of high degree' (προηγμένα), and are
defined as being the first states to which an animal is attracted
upon birth, as food, life, strength (πρῶτα κατὰ φύσιν)[24]; they
serve only for 'ends' (τέλη) for men who have not yet attained
to wisdom[25]. This doctrine corresponds closely to the Stoic
doctrine as developed somewhat later[26].

[19] See below, § 332.
[20] 'fortitudo est...conservatio stabilis iudici in iis rebus, quae formidolosae
videntur... [haec definitio erat] Sphaeri' Cic. as above. The principle was accepted
by all Stoics, see below, § 323.
[21] 'omitto...Erillum, qui in cognitione et scientia summum bonum ponit; qui cum
Zenonis auditor esset, vides quantum ab eo dissenserit, et quam non multum a Platone'
Cic. *Ac.* ii 42, 129. See also *Fin.* iv 14, 36.
[22] 'sin ea [quae virtus leget quaeque reiciet] non neglegemus neque tamen ad
finem summi boni referemus, non multum ab Erilli levitate aberrabimus; facit enim
ille duo seiuncta ultima bonorum' *Fin.* iv 15, 40.
[23] ζῆν ἀεὶ πάντα ἀναφέροντα πρὸς τὸ μετ' ἐπιστήμης ζῆν Diog. L. vii 165.
[24] ὑποτελὶς δ' ἐστὶ τὸ πρῶτον οἰκεῖον τοῦ ζῴου πάθος, ἀφ' οὗ κατήρξατο συναισ-
θάνεσθαι τὸ ζῷον τῆς συστάσεως αὐτοῦ, οὔπω λογικὸν [ὂν] ἀλλ' ἄλογον Stob. ii 7, 3 c.
[25] διαφέρειν δὲ τέλος καὶ ὑποτελίδα· τῆς μὲν γὰρ καὶ τοὺς μὴ σοφοὺς στοχάζεσθαι,
τοῦ δὲ μόνον τὸν σοφόν Diog. L. vii 165.
[26] The best discussion is by Hirzel, *Untersuchungen*, ii 46 sqq. He considers the
teaching of Herillus to have inclined to Cynism rather than to Platonism, and to
have been substantially identical with that of Aristo.

A. 6

93. ARISTO of Chios (circ. 250 B.C.) departed more decidedly
from Zeno's teaching, falling back generally on
Aristo.
Cynic views. He was no favourite of Zeno, who
called him a chatterbox[27]: and in later life he was accused of
becoming a flatterer of Persaeus when the latter was in power[28],
and of luxury in his personal habits[29]. But his success as a
teacher was great, and he formed a body of followers who called
themselves Aristonians.

He appears to have supported Zeno vigorously as to the
doctrine of 'comprehension'; and if on this subject he was
worsted for the moment by Persaeus[30], he retaliated on some
Academic by asking: 'do you see who is sitting next you?'
The Academic replied 'I do not.' 'Are you blind, then,' said
Aristo; 'where are your eyes[31]?' Still he considered any
systematic study of dialectics to be a mere waste of time; like
spiders' webs, which seem to display much skill, but are of no
use[32]. With regard to physics he was openly agnostic[33]; of the
nature of the gods he thought we could know nothing, not even
whether the deity were animate or no[34]. Ethics alone remained;
but this part of philosophy he reduced by omitting all practical
precepts, as introducing the element of uncertainty[35]. In ethics
proper he rejects the theory of 'things of high degree'
(προηγμένα), observing that this term does not harmonize with
the treatment of advantages as 'indifferent,' but comes danger-
ously near to calling them 'good[36].' Virtue, or rather knowledge, is, as he maintains, the only good; and all that lies
between good and evil is alike indifferent[37]. The highest good

[27] λάλον ἐπέκαλει Diog. L. vii 18.　　[28] Athen. vi 58 (Arnim i 342).
[29] *ib.* vii 14 (Arnim i 341).　　[30] See above, § 89.
[31] Diog. L. vii 163.　　[32] *ib.* vii 161.
[33] 'nihil istorum [physicorum] sciri putat posse' Cic. *Ac.* ii 39, 123.
[34] 'qui neque formam dei intellegi posse censeat, neque in dis sensum esse dicat ;
dubitetque omnino deus animans necne sit' Cic. *N. D.* i 14, 37.
[35] 'Aristo moralem quoque...quam solam reliquerat, circumcidit' Sen. *Ep.* 89, 13.
'hanc partem [quae dat propria cuique personae praecepta] levem existimat, et quae
non descendat in pectus usque' *ib.* 94, 2 : in this letter the whole subject is very fully
discussed.
[36] ἴσον γάρ ἐστι τὸ προηγμένον αὐτὴν λέγειν ἀδιάφορον τῷ ἀγαθὸν ἀξιοῦν, καὶ
σχεδὸν ὀνόματι μόνον διαφέρον Sext. *math.* xi 64 (Arnim i 361).
[37] 'Aristonis...sententia, non esse res ullas praeter virtutes et vitia, inter quas
quicquam omnino interesset' Cic. *Fin.* iv 17, 47.

may therefore be defined as a state of indifference (ἀδιαφορία) towards all such things[38].

Aristo was however once more in agreement with Stoic doctrine when he maintained the unity of virtue. 'The soul,' he said, 'has one power only, that of reasoning; one virtue only, the knowledge of good and evil. When we need to choose the good and avoid the evil, we call this knowledge Soberness; when we need to do good and not evil, we call it Wisdom; Courage, when it is bold and cautious at the right moments; and when it gives every man his due, Justice[39].' But in deciding his action the wise man will be bound by no theories: he can do whatever comes into his head, provided only he keep himself free from distress, fear and greed[40].

The popularity of these views was repressed by the activity of Chrysippus; in Cicero's time they were, in cultivated society, extinct[41]. But from the numerous references to Aristo in literature it is clear that his teaching was by no means forgotten; and when there took place the revival of the Cynic tone which we see illustrated in the writings of Epictetus and M. Aurelius, Aristo is again treated with high respect[42].

94. An eminent pupil of Aristo was ERATOSTHENES of
Eratosthenes.
Cyrene, the grammarian, whom he won over from the Cyrenaic school. Eratosthenes undoubtedly represented the spirit of his teacher and of the Cynic school towards which he inclined, when he vehemently repudiated the prejudice which then divided mankind into Hellenes and barbarians[43]. He was invited by Ptolemy III (Euergetes) to be chief librarian of the Museum at Alexandria, and tutor to the crown-prince, and has left us an epigram in honour of this great

[38] 'huic [sc. Aristoni] summum bonum est, in his rebus neutram in partem moveri, quae ἀδιαφορία ab ipso dicitur' Cic. Ac. ii 42, 130.

[39] Galen, Hipp. et Plat. vii 2 (Arnim i 374). Chrysippus is said to have complained that he made the various virtues σχέσεις or variations of a single virtue (Plut. Sto. rep. vii 3); nevertheless the same doctrine frequently reappears in Stoic writers.

[40] 'vives, inquit Aristo, magnifice atque praeclare, quod erit cunque visum, ages: nunquam angere, nunquam cupies, nunquam timebis' Cic. Fin. iv 25, 69.

[41] 'Aristonis...iampridem explosa sententia est' Off. i 2, 6; cf. Fin. iv 17, 47.

[42] N. Saal, p. 37 sqq. For fuller discussions of Aristo see Hirzel, Untersuchungen, ii p. 44, and Dyroff, Ethik, pp. 43 sqq., 356 sqq.

[43] Gomperz, Greek Thinkers, ii p. 161.

patron of learning and philosophy[44]. Amongst other followers of
Aristo we hear specially of APOLLOPHANES of Antiochia[45].

95. Alone amongst the hearers of Zeno DIONYSIUS of
Dionysius. Heraclea abandoned his principles, and went over
from the camp of virtue to that of pleasure. A
painful disease of the eyes had made him abandon the doctrine
that 'pain is no evil[46].' His secession was used by Antiochus as
an argument against the doctrine of comprehension or certain
knowledge[47]. That his life after he became a Cyrenaic was
openly scandalous[48] we need not too readily believe: such
accusations may easily be mere deductions from his supposed
philosophic principles. Dionysius appears to have been a
particular friend and admirer of the poet Aratus[49].

Of the less important hearers of Zeno we have the names
of, amongst others, ATHENODORUS of Soli[50], CALLIPPUS of
Corinth[50], POSIDONIUS of Alexandria[50], and ZENO of Sidon[50].
The last, if he existed, must be kept distinct from other Zenos,
such as Zeno of Tarsus the pupil of Chrysippus, and Zeno of
Sidon the Epicurean philosopher.

96. We come last amongst Zeno's hearers to CLEANTHES of
Cleanthes. Assos in Asia Minor (331–232 B.C.), who succeeded
Zeno as head of the school when already advanced
in years, and presided over it for a whole generation. In personal
character he was a worthy successor of Socrates, Diogenes, and
Zeno. He was trained in hardship and willing endurance[51];
and if he did not quickly understand, yet all he learnt was
deeply impressed upon him[52]. He studied Zeno's life even more
attentively than his doctrines; lived with him, watched his hours

[44] Mahaffy, *Empire of the Ptolemies*, p. 207.

[45] Athen. vii 14 (Arnim i 408).

[46] 'nobis Heracleotes ille Dionysius flagitiose descivisse videtur a Stoicis propter
oculorum dolorem; quasi vero hoc didicisset a Zenone, non dolere, cum doleret!
illud audierat nec tamen didicerat, malum illud non esse, quia turpe non esset'
Cic. *Fin.* v 31, 94; τέλος εἶπε τὴν ἡδονὴν διὰ περίστασιν ὀφθαλμίας Diog. L. vii 166.

[47] '[quaerebat Antiochus], Dionysius ille Heracleotes utrum comprehendisset,...
honestum quod esset, id solum bonum esse, an...honesti inane nomen esse, voluptatem esse summum bonum' Cic. *Ac.* ii 22, 71.

[48] Diog. L. vii 167; Athen. x 50 (Arnim i 428).

[49] Diog. L. vii 167. [50] Diog. L. vii 38.

[51] He drew water by night that he might study philosophy by day, according to
Diog. L. vii 168. 'Cleanthes aquam traxit et rigando horto locavit manus' Sen.
Ep. 44, 3. [52] Diog. L. vii 37.

of retirement, inquired whether his actions corresponded to his teaching[53]. Himself a man of the people, he ardently desired to spread his convictions amongst the many, and chose verse as the best means to express clearly his meaning and win access to men's ears[54]. He remained constant to Zeno's teaching[55], but he inspired it with a fresh enthusiasm and developed it in more consistent detail. He is before all things the theologian of Stoicism. The belief in the deity, which in the fragments of Zeno's teaching appears merely formal and argumentative, becomes in the verse of Cleanthes ardent and dominating. God is the creator and the director of the world; his Logos gives it order and harmony. In God's designs it is the privilege and duty of man to co-operate; but since he is possessed of free will, it is also within his power to make a futile opposition. In this way the good and the bad stand in definite contrast. Finally, right knowledge and right action are only possible by association with the deity through praise and prayer.

97. It is our good fortune to possess several complete poems of Cleanthes, which are of more value to us towards appreciating his standpoint than a hundred detached sentences would be. The *hymn to Zeus*[56] is the most important, and its likeness to the opening of Aratus' *Phaenomena*[57] will not escape notice.

His poetry.

Hymn to Zeus.

Supreme of gods, by titles manifold
Invoked, o thou who over all dost hold
  Eternal dominance, Nature's author, Zeus,
Guiding a universe by Law controlled;   2

Hail! for 'tis meet that men should call on thee
Whose seed we are; and ours the destiny
  Alone of all that lives and moves on earth,
A mirror of thy deity[58] to be.   5

---

[53] 'Zenonem Cleanthes non expressisset, si tantummodo audisset: vitae enim eius interfuit, secreta perspexit, observavit illum, an ex formula sua viveret' Sen. *Ep.* 6, 6.

[54] 'sensus nostros clariores carminis arta necessitas efficit' Sen. *Ep.* 108, 10.

[55] ἐπὶ τῶν αὐτῶν ἔμεινε δογμάτων Diog. L. vii 168.

[56] Stob. i 1, 12 (Arnim i 537).   [57] See above, § 90.

[58] I follow the reading γενόμεσθα, θεοῦ. The words γένος ἐσμέν in the text are surely a reminiscence of Aratus, *Phaen.* 5 (so Pearson, p. 276), and θεοῦ μίμημα is confirmed by Musonius ap. Stob. *Flor.* 117, 8 (see below, § 419). Mr Pearson now suggests to me that the MS reading ἤχου may represent the correction of a pious scribe, ῑͨ χͨγ, i.e. Ἰησοῦ Χριστοῦ, for θεοῦ. See below, § 244.

Therefore I hymn thee and thy power I praise;
For at thy word, on their appointed ways
   The orbs of heaven in circuit round the earth
Move, and submissive each thy rule obeys,   8

Who holdest in thy hands invincible
So dread a minister to work thy will—
   The eternal bolt of fire, two-edged, whose blast
Thro' all the powers of nature strikes a chill[59]—   11

Whereby thou guid'st the universal force,
Reason, through all things interfused, whose course
   Commingles with the great and lesser[60] lights—
Thyself of all the sovran and the source: 14

For nought is done on earth apart from thee,
Nor in thy vault of heaven, nor in the sea;
   Save for the reckless deeds of sinful men
Whose own hearts lead them to perversity.   17

But skill to make the crookèd straight is thine,
To turn disorder to a fair design;
   Ungracious things are gracious in thy sight,
For ill and good thy power doth so combine   20

That out of all appears in unity
Eternal Reason, which the wicked flee
   And disregard, who long for happiness,
Yet God's great Law can neither hear nor see;   24

Ill-fated folk! for would they but obey
With understanding heart, from day to day
   Their life were full of blessing, but they turn
Each to his sin, by folly led astray.   26

Glory would some thro' bitter strife attain
And some are eager after lawless gain;
   Some lust for sensual delights, but each
Finds that too soon his pleasure turns to pain.   31

But, Zeus all-bountiful! the thunder-flame
And the dark cloud thy majesty proclaim:
   From ignorance deliver us, that leads
The sons of men to sorrow and to shame.   33

---

[59] The translation follows Pearson's ἐρρίγασιν. Arnim reads ἔργα τελεῖται. Even the meaning is quite uncertain here.

[60] μεγάλῳ μικροῖς τε (Diels) seems the nearest reading to the MS, so that the word 'great' above refers to the sun only.

Wherefore dispel it, Father, from the soul
And grant that Wisdom may our life control,
  Wisdom which teaches thee to guide the world
Upon the path of justice to its goal. 35

So winning honour thee shall we requite
With honour, lauding still thy works of might;
  Since gods nor men find worthier meed than this—
The universal Law to praise aright. 39

Translated by W. H. Porter.

98. Another short poem of Cleanthes identifies Zeus with fate, and points the same moral as to human duty:

Lead me, O Zeus, and lead me, Destiny,
  What way soe'er ye have appointed me!
I follow unafraid: yea, though the will
  Turn recreant, I needs must follow still[61].

In other poems characteristic Stoic doctrines are set forth with clearness and emphasis:

'Look not at common opinion, and be not eager to be wise of a sudden; fear not the chatter of the many, in which there is no judgment and no modesty; for the crowd does not possess shrewd just and fair judgment, but amongst the few you may perchance find this[62].'

'Do you ask me of what kind the good is? Listen then. It is orderly, just, innocent, pious, self-controlled, useful, fair, necessary, severe, upright, always of advantage; fearless, painless, profitable, without smart; helpful, pleasing, sure, friendly, honourable, consistent; noble, not puffed up, painstaking, comforting, full of energy, biding its time, blameless, unchanging[63].'

'He who abstains from some disgraceful action yet all the while has desire for it, will some day do it, when he gets opportunity[64].'

In the last of the passages we are introduced to an ethical paradox of the highest importance to Stoicism: that good and evil are set in the will and the intention, and are not dependent upon the action[65].

---

[61] ἄγου δέ μ', ὦ Ζεῦ, καὶ σύ γ' ἡ πεπρωμένη, | ὅποι ποθ' ὑμῖν εἰμὶ διατεταγμένος. ὡς ἕψομαι γ' ἄοκνος· ἢν δέ γε μὴ θέλω | κακὸς γενόμενος, οὐδὲν ἧττον ἕψομαι Epict. *Manual* 53; 'duc, o parens celsique dominator poli, | quocunque placuit; nulla parendi mora est. | adsum impiger. fac nolle, comitabor gemens, | malusque patiar, quod pati licuit bono. | ducunt volentem fata, nolentem trahunt' Sen. *Ep.* 107, 11. The translation given above is by G. H. Rendall (*M. Aurel.* Introd. p. lxvii).

[62] Clem. *Strom.* v 3, 17 (Arnim i 559).

[63] Clem. *Protrept.* vi 72 (Arnim i 557).   [64] Stob. iii 6, 3 (Arnim i 573).

[65] See below, § 317.

99.   To the ancients Cleanthes was the faithful disciple of
Originality   Zeno.   Persaeus, Aratus, and others had turned aside
of Cleanthes.   from the direct pursuit of philosophy, and their
contact with science and politics might easily sully the purity
of their philosophic creed.   Herillus had adopted Academic
doctrine, Aristo had fallen back into Cynism, Dionysius had
actually seceded to the party of pleasure. It might seem that the
far-reaching sweep of Zeno's intellect had no real hold on his
companions.   But Cleanthes at least stood firm by the old landmarks.   We must not suppose from this that he was a man of
no originality[66]; his language and his style at least are his own.
Nor on the other hand can we go all the way with some recent
writers, who attribute to him exclusively large parts of the Stoic
system[67].   Our authorities commonly refer either to Zeno alone,
or to Zeno, Cleanthes, and Chrysippus jointly, as vouching for
accepted Stoic doctrine ; and we are hardly entitled to lay great
stress on the comparatively few fragments of which the authorship is assigned exclusively to Cleanthes, as evidence for the
independence of his teaching; especially as we can in many
instances see that our authorities delight in attributing a difference of meaning to the Stoic masters, when in reality there is
nothing more to be found than a difference of phrasing[68].   It is
however clear that Stoicism did not assume its complete form in
the hands of its first propagator ; and to a limited extent we can
see the directions in which his teaching was amplified by his
successors.

100.   Cleanthes took a special interest in the physical specu-
Physics of   lations of Heraclitus, on whose writings he com-
Cleanthes.   posed four books[69], and in particular in the bearing
of his speculations upon the nature of the deity.   The belief in
the dualism of God and matter, of the Word and the world, is
attributed to Cleanthes as distinctly as to Zeno[70]; but on the
other hand the conception of an overruling unity is much more

---

[66] As, for instance, Zeller does when he writes 'Cleanthes was adapted to uphold
his master's teaching, but he was incapable of expanding it more completely, or of
establishing it on a wider basis' *Stoics*, p. 41.

[67] Hirzel, *Untersuchungen*, ii pp. 134 sqq. ; Stein, *Psychologie der Stoa*, i 65–72,
162–171, ii 316–332.

[68] Sen. *Ep.* 113, 23.   [69] Diog. L. vii 174.   [70] *ib.* 134.

pronounced in the later writer[71]. Hence from the first Cleanthes endeavours to give a wider meaning to the primary fire of Heraclitus, the creative fire of Zeno. For this fire he proposed the new term 'flame' ($\phi\lambda\delta\xi$)[72]; at other times he identified it with the sky[73], with the sun[74], and with the principle of heat[75]; and finally adopted the term 'spirit' ($\pi\nu\epsilon\hat{v}\mu\alpha$, spiritus), which has ever since held its place in the discussion of natural theology. This term appears to have been at first intended to combine the conceptions of the creative fire and of the Logos[76], but it gradually came to have distinctive associations of its own. Like fire, 'spirit' is to the Stoics a substance, stuff, or body akin to the element of air, but associated with warmth and elasticity; it is conceived as immanent in the universe and penetrating it as the deity; immanent in the human body and penetrating it as the soul[77]. The elasticity of spirit is measured by its 'tension' ($\tau\delta\nu\sigma$, intentio), by means of which its creative power pushes forward from the centre to the circumference: as for instance in the human body walking is effected by 'spirit exercising tension towards the feet[78].' The theory of 'tension' has an immediate application to ethics. When the soul has sufficient tension to perform its proper work, it operates according to the virtues of Wisdom, Justice, Courage, and Soberness; but when the tension is relaxed, the soul becomes disordered and is seized upon by the emotions[79].

101. To Cleanthes also it fell to explain more fully the government both of the universe and of the indi-
Theology of Cleanthes. vidual. Zeno indeed is said to have used the term $\dot{\eta}\gamma\epsilon\mu\nu\iota\kappa\delta\nu$ (principale, principatus)[80], which we may translate by

[71] 'Cleanthes ipsum mundum...deum dicit esse' Cic. N. D. i 14, 37.

[72] Arnim i 497, 511.

[73] 'ultimum et altissimum et omnia complexum ardorem, qui aether nominetur' Cic. as in note 71.

[74] Cic. N. D. ii 15, 41.

[75] 'sic res se habet, ut omnia, quae alantur et quae crescant, contineant in se vim caloris, sine qua neque ali possent neque crescere' ib. 9, 23.

[76] 'haec (quae Zeno dixit $\lambda\delta\gamma\sigma\nu$ esse) Cleanthes in spiritum congerit quem permeatorem universitatis affirmat' Tert. Apol. 21 (Arnim i 533).

[77] The substance of this doctrine is attributed to Zeno also: Z$\dot{\eta}\nu\omega\nu$...$\pi\nu\epsilon\hat{v}\mu\alpha$ $\dot{\epsilon}\nu\theta\epsilon\rho\mu\nu$ $\epsilon\tilde{\iota}\nu\alpha\iota$ $\tau\dot{\eta}\nu$ $\psi\nu\chi\dot{\eta}\nu$ Diog. L. vii 157.

[78] See below, § 277. [79] Pearson, Introd. p. 45; below, § 362.

[80] Arnim i 143.

'ruling power,' or shortly (following the Latin) by 'principate[81],'
for the highest power of the human soul; Cleanthes sought a
similar principle in the universe also, and is said to have found
it in the sun[82]. By thus using the term in a double sense he
implies the analogy which is expressed by the correlative terms
'macrocosm' and 'microcosm,' and which leads up to the definition of God as the 'soul of the universe[83].' Cleanthes further
speaks of the universe itself as god[84]; but before describing him
as a pantheist it is well to consider that this is only one form out
of many in which he expresses his creed. He was also the first
to give the four proofs of the existence of the deity upon which
all discussions of the 'evidences of Natural Religion' have been
based down to the present day, and which we shall further
discuss in a later chapter[85].

The pious zeal of Cleanthes was not without a touch of
bigotry, destined to have serious consequences in the final
developments of Stoicism, and to reappear in the history of
the middle ages with distressing intensity; he was bitterly opposed to the novel heliocentric theory of the universe as an
impiety[86].

102. Thus even though we can no longer discriminate
sharply between the teaching of Zeno and that of
Cleanthes, we have every reason to suppose that
the latter was possessed of originality of thought and vigour
and copiousness of expression. We cannot easily believe that
a man of such powers failed to attract hearers or to retain a
hold upon them. But in his extreme old age it seems that the
majority were drawn aside either to the ingenious arguments of
Arcesilaus the Academic, or to the more independent teaching
of Aristo of Chios. The continued existence of Stoicism seemed

(margin note: Weakness of Stoicism.*)*

---

[81] There is a slight inconvenience, but also a real advantage, in using this term
both in its philosophic sense for the governing part of the soul, and historically for
the system of government founded by Augustus. There is a genuine analogy between
the two, though it is not developed by the Latin writers. Seneca uses *principale* only.

[82] ἡγεμονικὸν δὲ τοῦ κόσμου Κλεάνθει μὲν ἤρεσε τὸν ἥλιον εἶναι Euseb. *pr. ev.* xv
15, 7 (Arnim i 499); and see below, § 201.

[83] Κλεάνθης [τὸν θεὸν] τὴν τοῦ κόσμου ψυχήν Aët. i 7, 17 (Arnim i 532); 'totius
naturae menti atque animo tribuit hoc nomen [dei]' Cic. *N. D.* i 14, 37.

[84] 'Cleanthes ipsum mundum deum dicit esse' *ib.*

[85] Cic. *N. D.* ii 5, 13–15; and see below, ch. x.   [86] See below, § 195.

threatened; its critics were not to be contented with rhetoric or poetry, but insistently demanded proofs. In this crisis it was saved and established by a younger man, CHRYSIPPUS of Soli (280–206 B.C.), who was far inferior in original power, but equally zealous and more in harmony with the tastes and demands of the younger generation.

103. Chrysippus was a fellow-townsman of Aratus of Soli,

Chrysippus.

and his appearance is doubtless a sign of the active interest in philosophy which for some centuries marks the neighbourhood of the important town of Tarsus. Born in 280 B.C. he found in his early manhood three prominent teachers at Athens, Arcesilaus, Aristo, and Cleanthes. Of these Aristo seems to have been the most popular, and surprise was expressed that Chrysippus did not join his school. 'Had I followed the many,' he replied, 'I should not have become a philosopher[87].' His convictions drew him to Cleanthes, but he felt much impatience with his methods. This state of mind he must have expressed freely, for in after life he reproached himself that he had not behaved more kindly towards his teacher in his old age[88]. Confident in his own powers, he desired to relieve Cleanthes of the burden of replying to the many attacks made upon his doctrines, especially as to dialectics[89]. It is well known that he asked his master to supply him with his dogmas only, saying that he himself would find the proofs[90]. Chrysippus probably outlived his opponents, and during the time when he was head of the school (232–206 B.C.) only found himself opposed by men of mediocre talents. He devoted his whole energies to strengthening and systematizing Stoic doctrine. He not only gave its proofs, but used every art of the dialectician to recommend it to his hearers[91]. From his facile pen there poured an endless stream of writings, not remarkable either for originality or for style, but of the highest importance as fixing definitely the

[87] εἰ τοῖς πολλοῖς, εἶπε, προσεῖχον, οὐκ ἂν ἐφιλοσόφησα Diog. L. vii 182.
[88] ἐγὼ δὲ τἆλλα μακάριος πέφυκ' ἀνὴρ | πλὴν εἰς Κλεάνθην· τοῦτο δ' οὐκ εὐδαιμονῶ Diog. L. vii 179.
[89] ib. 182.   [90] ib. 179.
[91] 'num contentus est [Chrysippus] docere, rem ostendere, definire, explorare? non est contentus: verum auget in quantum potest, exaggerat, praemunit, iterat, differt, recurrit, interrogat, describit, dividit, personas fingit, orationem suam alii accommodat' Fronto, ep. ad Ant. p. 146 (Arnim ii 27).

standard of Stoic orthodoxy.   He gathered numerous hearers round him, and before his death it could truly be said that he had saved the Stoa[92].

104. In his method of exposition Chrysippus made great

Dialectic of Chrysippus.
use of the syllogism, thus reverting to the practice of Zeno as opposed to the more poetical style of Cleanthes.   As to the value of this syllogistic reasoning very contrary opinions were expressed in antiquity.   By his contemporaries he was greatly admired, so that it was said that 'if the gods had needed a dialectic, they would have taken that of Chrysippus[93].'   On the other hand members of his own school complained that he often stated his opponents' case more forcibly than his own[94].   The Romans mix their praise with censure, and find that he sometimes entangles himself in the threads of his own argument[95]; and we ourselves cannot fail to notice that when his major and minor premisses are compared, the meaning of the common term has usually shifted[96].   But if Chrysippus did not provide a final solution to great problems, he at least adapted the Stoic system to the taste of his age, alike by his use of syllogisms and by the attention he paid to the solution of fallacies[97].

105. Whilst the works of Chrysippus cover the whole range

Opposition of the Academy.
of the Stoic philosophy, their special colour is largely due to the interests of his own time.   The stress laid by Zeno on the certainty of knowledge had produced a

---

[92] ὅθεν φασὶν ἐπ' αὐτοῦ λεχθῆναι, εἰ μὴ γὰρ ἦν Χρύσιππος, οὐκ ἂν ἦν στοά Diog. L. vii 183.

[93] Diog. L. vii 180.

[94] 'de quo queri solent Stoici, dum studiose omnia conquisierit contra sensus et perspicuitatem...ipsum sibi respondentem inferiorem fuisse; itaque ab eo armatum esse Carneaden' Cic. *Ac.* ii 27, 87; cf. Plut. *Sto. rep.* x 3 and 4.

[95] 'ab Chrysippo nihil magnum nec magnificum desideravi, qui suo quodam more loquitur, ut omnia verborum momentis, non rerum ponderibus examinet' Cic. *Rep.* iii 8, 12; 'ad Chrysippi laqueos revertamur' *de Fato* 4, 7; 'Chrysippus, penes quem subtile illud acumen est et in imam penetrans veritatem, qui rei agendae causa loquitur et verbis non ultra quam ad intellectum satis est utitur, totum librum his ineptiis replet' Sen. *Ben.* i 3, 8; 'magnum mehercule virum, sed tamen Graecum, cuius acumen nimis tenue retunditur et in se saepe replicatur' *ib.* 4, 1.

[96] 'quod est bonum, omne laudabile est; quod autem laudabile est, omne est honestum; bonum igitur quod est, honestum est' Cic. *Fin.* iii 8, 27.

[97] See below, §§ 162, 163.

reaction in the Academic school. Arcesilaus, who had succeeded Polemo as its leader, leaving on one side the positive teaching of Plato's later years, reverted to the sceptical attitude which had been one characteristic of Socrates, and which is so prominent in most of the Platonic dialogues[98]. He attacked with the utmost vigour Zeno's doctrine of 'comprehension'; and further argued that certain knowledge is unnecessary for practical life, of which probability, that is, such action as can find reasonable justification, is the sufficient guide[99]. Chrysippus defended with the utmost energy the dogma of the certainty of knowledge, based upon the perspicuity of true mind pictures[100]; but the teaching of Arcesilaus obtained a hold upon him, and (as we shall see) was ultimately allowed by him a place within the Stoic system.

106. Chrysippus meanwhile had a more dangerous enemy
Spread of   to meet than the Academy. During the weakness
Epicureanism.   which befel the Stoic school in the middle of the
third century B.C., the rival school of Epicurus had won an enormous popularity. Yet its ethical standard, which it had inherited from the Cyrenaics, offended not only the followers of Zeno but all sober-minded philosophers. For Epicurus had set up Pleasure as the queen of life, and had converted the virtues into her handmaidens[101]; and so far was he from taking interest in model states, that he advised his hearers to hold aloof altogether from public life. Worst of all, his followers only smiled at the reproofs that were showered upon them. They formed among themselves a cheerful, affectionate, and united society; their simple pleasures created no public scandal, though their entertainments were often enlivened by tales of the moral lapses of their self-righteous rivals. The bracing morality of Cynism seemed to be quite gone out of fashion, and even the Aristonians had ceased to exist.

---

[98] 'Arcesilas primum...ex variis Platonis libris sermonibusque Socraticis hoc maxime arripuit, nihil esse certi quod aut sensibus aut animo percipi possit' Cic. de Orat. iii 18, 67. See above, § 71.

[99] ὁ προσέχων τῷ εὐλόγῳ κατορθώσει καὶ εὐδαιμονήσει Sext. math. vii 158.

[100] 'cum Chrysippus, Academicos refellens, permulto clariora et certiora esse dicat, quae vigilantibus videantur, quam quae somniantibus' Cic. Div. ii 61, 126; see further, § 147.

[101] See below, § 346.

107.   Under these circumstances the remaining schools began
Alliance of the   to look one to another for support, and were even
three schools.   brought into a kind of alliance.   The adherents of
the Academy and the Porch, in particular, began to meet in
friendly discussion, and sometimes defined anew their doctrines
so as to minimize points of difference, sometimes directly modified them by way of concession to opposed arguments.   This
process resulted in a toning down of Stoicism in every part of its
system.   The Stoic teachers began to disregard or push into the
background those characteristic doctrines which had been embodied in the Socratic paradoxes and enforced by the Cynic
propaganda.   Thus their teaching gave less offence to the lax
crowd, and at the same time (it must be admitted) less support
to the striving few ; but its tone was now so modest that men of
gentle and judicious temperament were attracted to Stoicism for
the first time.   Stoicism began now to shew itself receptive of
literary influences, especially as regards the works of Plato and
Aristotle, and even appreciative of artistic ideals.   Such was
the tendency of the system during both the second and the first
centuries B.C.; but it is more difficult to estimate the extent of the
deviation.   Terms like εὐκρασία 'well proportioned mixture[102],'
εὔροια 'even flow[103],' εὐτονία 'due tone[104],' συμφωνία 'harmony[105],'
are attributed even to the earliest masters : whilst it is abundantly clear that the Socratic and Cynic paradoxes formed at
all times part of the generally accepted view of Stoic doctrine.

108.   It is an interesting question, which perhaps needs
Chrysippus   further investigation, to what extent this approxi-
inclines to the   mation between the doctrines of the Academy and
Academy.   the Porch can be traced in the writings of Chrysippus.   On the one hand we must remember that Chrysippus was a
man of distinctly orthodox temperament; he firmly opposed the
Cynizing heresies of Aristo, and strongly defended the Stoic
theory of knowledge against the Academy.   But our knowledge
of the teaching of Chrysippus, abundant in volume, is lacking in
precision.   Our authorities, as we have seen, very imperfectly

[102] See Pearson, *Cle.* fr. 42.
[103] According to Stob. ii 7, 6 e this term was used by all the Stoic teachers.
[104] Used by Chrysippus, see Arnim iii 473.   [105] Diog. L. vii 88.

distinguish, and very inadequately record, the teaching of the two earlier masters ; and the doctrines which are regarded as common to all Stoics must be assumed to be generally stated in the language of Chrysippus, whose works remained for centuries the recognised standard of orthodoxy. Even so there are few distinctive doctrines of Chrysippus which do not seem to be foreshadowed in expressions attributed to some earlier teacher. Yet we may fairly assume that in his ethical teaching there was a substantial sacrifice of the forcefulness of the Socratic character, and a corresponding approach to Academic views. This appears when he defines the supreme good as ' a life according to nature, that is, both general nature and our individual human nature[106],' and adds, ' for our individual natures are parts of the nature of the all[107].' This approaches the doctrine of 'virtue appropriate to the individual' (οἰκεία ἀρετή), as taught by the Academics[108]. A still more striking concession is his permission to men engaged in practical life to describe advantages as 'good things,' provided they are carefully distinguished from the supreme good[109].

109. The weakening hold of the Stoics upon the principles
Successors of of their founder first becomes evident in the depart-
Chrysippus. ment of physics. Thus it is an essential part of the theory which the Stoics borrowed from Heraclitus, that as the whole universe has proceeded from the all-creative fire, so it must in due course be re-absorbed in it, this periodical re-absorption being technically known as the ' conflagration' (ἐκπύρωσις). On the other hand the followers of Aristotle, following dualistic principles, placed God and the universe in eternal contrast, and held both to be immortal. Ingenious con-troversialists now pressed the Stoics to explain how their deity exercised his providence during the periodic intervals in which the universe had no separate existence. This and like arguments had an immediate effect. BOËTHUS of Sidon, a contemporary of Chrysippus, abandoned altogether the Stoic theory on this

---

[106] φύσιν δὲ Χρύσιππος μὲν ἐξακούει, ᾗ ἀκολούθως δεῖ ζῆν, τήν τε κοινὴν καὶ ἰδίως τὴν ἀνθρωπίνην ib. vii 89.

[107] μέρη γάρ εἰσιν αἱ ἡμέτεραι φύσεις τῆς τοῦ ὅλου ib. 87.

[108] See above, § 71.

[109] δίδωσι τοῖς βουλομένοις τὰ προηγμένα καλεῖν ἀγαθά Plut. Sto. rep. 30, 4.

subject[110]; ZENO of Tarsus, who had been with his father
DIOSCORIDES a pupil of Chrysippus, and who succeeded him
as head of the school, discreetly 'suspended his judgment' upon
the point[111]. But whatever its theoretical embarrassments, the
Stoic school continued to prosper. Zeno of Tarsus wrote but
few books, but had more disciples than any other[112]; he was
succeeded by SELEUCUS of the Tigris[113], and he in turn by
Diogenes[114], Antipater, and Panaetius. The last of these maintained Zeno's 'suspense of judgment[115]' on the question of the
conflagration; but after his death the Stoics quietly returned to
the older opinion.

110. DIOGENES of Seleucia (circ. 238-150 B.C.; often called
Diogenes and   'of Babylon,' or simply *Diogenes Stoicus*), and
Antipater.   ANTIPATER of Tarsus (circ. 200-129 B.C.), were
both men of eminence in the history of Stoicism[116], but they
were unequally matched against Carneades (218-128 B.C.), who
was head of the Academic school about the same time, and who
proclaimed the doctrine of a universal suspension of judgment.
The many volumes of Chrysippus gave Carneades ample opportunities for the exercise of his critical powers; and Antipater,
unable or unwilling to meet him in open argument, fell himself
into the evil habit of book-writing[117]. Both these teachers
specially interested themselves in questions of casuistry.
Diogenes, who defined the good as 'reasonableness in the
choice of natural ends[118],' adopted practically that interpretation
of 'reasonableness' in which divine reason has the least part,
and human plausibility the freest play[119]. Thus he discusses
the problems whether the seller of a house ought to inform the

---

[110] Philo, *inc. mund.* 15, p. 248 (Arnim iii Boëth. 7).

[111] τὸν μὲν γὰρ τούτου [sc. Chrysippi] μαθητὴν καὶ διάδοχον τῆς σχολῆς Ζήνωνά φασιν ἐπισχεῖν περὶ τῆς ἐκπυρώσεως τῶν ὅλων Ar. Did. fr. 36 Diels (Arnim iii Z. T. 5).

[112] Diog. L. vii 35.   [113] Ind. Sto. Herc. col. 48 (Arnim iii Z. T. 2).

[114] See Zeller, *Stoics* etc., p. 50.   [115] See below, § 115.

[116] 'aliud Diogeni Babylonio videri solet, magno et gravi Stoico, aliud Antipatro, discipulo eius, homini acutissimo' Cic. *Off.* iii 12, 51; 'Antipater inter magnos [Stoicae] sectae auctores' Sen. *Ep.* 92, 5.

[117] Plut. *de garr.* 23.

[118] τὸ εὐλογιστεῖν ἐν τῇ τῶν κατὰ φύσιν ἐκλογῇ Diog. L. vii 88; for the Academic view see § 71 above.

[119] See below, §§ 159, 332.

purchaser of its defects, and whether a man upon whom false coins have been passed may transfer them to his neighbour[120]. Exactly as Carneades[121], he finds 'reasonable excuse' for the less scrupulous course. Antipater on the other hand holds that a man's duty to his neighbour requires perfect frankness[122]; yet he is said to have abandoned the Socratic doctrine of the self-sufficiency of virtue, and to have held that external goods are a part (though only a small part) of the supreme good[123].

111. We may now shortly mention some less important
Stoic teachers, chiefly of the early part of the
Lesser Stoics.
second century B.C., since their number alone is
an indication of the wide influence of the sect. ARISTOCREON, said to have been the nephew of Chrysippus, set up a statue in his honour, as the man who could cut his way through the knots tied by the Academics[124]. ZENODOTUS was a pupil of Diogenes, and wrote an epigram on Zeno : he at least defended the 'manly doctrine' of the founder, and recalled the principle of the sufficiency of virtue[125]. APOLLODORUS of Seleucia on the Tigris[126] (sometimes called Ephillus[127]), another pupil of Diogenes, leant towards Cynic views; for he declared that 'the wise man will be a Cynic, for this is a short cut to virtue[128]'; an opinion afterwards adopted by the Stoics generally[129]. He also wrote on physics. A third pupil of Diogenes was APOLLODORUS of Athens[130]. Closely associated with Antipater is ARCHEDEMUS of Tarsus; like his fellow-townsman, he was greatly devoted to dialectics[131]; in ethics he appears to have inclined strongly to Academic views, holding that the end of life was the regular

---

[120] Cic. *Off.* iii 13, 54; 23, 91.

[121] *Rep.* iii 20, 30.

[122] 'tu cum hominibus consulere debeas,...celabis homines' *Off.* iii 13, 52.

[123] 'Antipater...aliquid se tribuere dicit externis, sed exiguum admodum' Sen. *Ep.* 92, 5.

[124] Plut. *Sto. rep.* 2, 5.   [125] Diog. L. vii 30.

[126] Arnim iii p. 259; see also Pauly-Wissowa *sub voce.*

[127] So Diog. L. vii 39, where however others read Ἀπολλόδωρος καὶ Σύλλος.

[128] Diog. L. vii 121.   [129] *ib.* vi 104.

[130] Ind. Stoic. Herc. col. 53 : also a pupil of Antipater; to be distinguished from an Apollodorus of Athens who was an Epicurean ; Diog. L. vii 181.

[131] 'duo vel principes dialecticorum, Antipater et Archedemus, opiniosissimi homines' Cic. *Ac.* ii 47, 143.

A.   7

98 ROMAN STOICISM

performance of daily duties[132]. Just about the time we have
now reached (the middle of the second century B.C.) Eumenes II
founded the great library at Pergamus, intended to rival that of
Alexandria. As librarian he installed a Stoic philosopher,
CRATES of Mallos, who devoted much of his time to grammatical inquiries, and endeavoured to bring Homer into accord
with the Stoic views on geography[133]; he is the first Stoic of
whom we hear at Rome, which he visited about 159 B.C. Being
detained there by an accident, he employed his time in giving
lectures on literature[134]; and his pupil Panaetius was destined
to introduce Stoicism to Roman society. Lastly we may mention HERACLIDES of Tarsus, a pupil of Antipater, said to have
broken away from the teaching of the school by denying that
all sins are equal[135]. Athenodorus of Tarsus, who held the
same view, belongs to a later generation[136]. Of uncertain date
are BASILIDES, who pushed his monism so far as to declare that
all things, even statements, are bodies[137]; EUDROMUS, who wrote
on the elements of ethics[138]; and CRINIS, who interested himself
in logic[139].

[132] πάντα τὰ καθήκοντα ἐπιτελοῦντα ζῆν Diog. L. vii 88.
[133] Sandys, *Classical Scholarship*, i pp. 155, 156.   [134] *ib.* p. 157.
[135] Diog. L. vii 121.   [136] See below, §§ 122, 123.
[137] Arnim iii p. 268.   [138] Diog. L. vii 39.   [139] *ib.* 76.

CHAPTER V.

THE STOIC SECT IN ROME.

112. IN the third century B.C. Stoicism won adherents slowly
Growth of the and one by one, as individuals were convinced by
Stoic 'sect.' reasoning and example. In the second century its
progress became more rapid, for it was reinforced by inheritance
and social influence. Fathers handed down its doctrine to their
sons, and teachers to their pupils. Groups of men united by a
common respect for the school and its founders began to associate together, not only at Athens, but also (as we may well infer
from the list of names given at the end of the last chapter) at such
centres as Pergamus, Babylon, Seleucia, Tarsus, Sidon, and even
Alexandria[1]. Thus out of the school there grew up the 'sect'
(*secta*); that is, a society of men drawn from different nations and
ranks, but sharing the same convictions, united by a bond of
brotherhood, and feeling their way towards mutual consolation
and support; a company going through life on the same path,
and prepared to submit to a common authority[2]. The spread of
the sect was rapid though quiet; and as we cannot expect to
trace its history from place to place, we are unable to say when
first it found adherents at Rome. But early in the second
century B.C. Rome entered into close political relations with two
of the most highly civilized states of Asia Minor, Pergamus and
Rhodes; and through the men of learning and taste who were
associated with these communities Stoicism was introduced to

---

[1] Dill, *Roman Society*, p. 340.
[2] 'omnis natura habet quasi viam quandam et sectam quam sequatur' Cic. *N. D.*
ii 22, 57. 'est tuae prudentiae sequi eius auctoritatem, cuius sectam atque imperium
secutus es' *ad Fam.* xiii 4, 2. 'The sense of the word has been obscured by a false
popular etymology which has connected the word with the Latin *secare* 'to cut,'
Skeat, *Etymological Dictionary*, p. 537.

the ruling class at the centre of the new empire, to win there an
easy conquest which proved no slight compensation for the
political subordination of the states from which its emissaries
had sprung.

113. We have already noticed[3] that the Stoic Crates, the
Panaetius. head of the library established at Pergamus, visited
Rome in 159 B.C. and there gave lectures on literature, in which he may perhaps have taken occasion to expound
at least the chief doctrines of the Stoic school. Only a few years
later, in 155 B.C., the celebrated embassy from Athens, which
included the heads of three of the chief philosophical schools
at that time, arrived in Rome. Diogenes of Seleucia represented
the Stoics, Critolaus the Peripatetics, and Carneades the Academic school ; and all three expounded their respective theories
before enormous audiences. We are told that Diogenes made
a good impression by his sober and temperate style[4]. Thus
the way was prepared for the more permanent influence of
PANAETIUS of Rhodes (circ. 189–109 B.C.)[5]. He was a gentleman
of position in the wealthy and well-governed island state, and in
early youth pursued his studies at Pergamus, so that he was
probably attracted to the school by Crates[6]. From Pergamus he
passed to Athens, where he found established the three teachers
already named, and attached himself to Diogenes[7], and after his
death to his successor Antipater[8]. His writings shew that he was
also much influenced by the teaching of Carneades. But more
than any of his predecessors he appreciated philosophy in its
literary form. Plato, the 'Homer of philosophers,' he held in
veneration[9]; from Aristotle, Xenocrates, Theophrastus and
Dicaearchus he constantly quoted[10]. His admiration for these

---

[3] See above, § 111.

[4] 'dicebat modesta Diogenes et sobria' A. Gellius *N. A.* vi (vii) 14, 10.

[5] For a full account of his life and teaching see Schmekel, *Philosophie der
mittleren Stoa*, pp. 1–9.

[6] Strabo xiv 5, 16.   [7] Ind. Stoic. Herc. col. 51.

[8] 'discipulus Antipatri Panaetius' Cic. *Div.* i 3, 6.

[9] 'credamus igitur Panaetio a Platone suo dissentienti? quem omnibus locis
divinum, quem sapientissimum, quem sanctissimum, quem Homerum philosophorum
appellat' *Tusc. disp.* i 32, 79.

[10] *Fin.* iv 28, 79.

philosophers greatly influenced his style, and caused him to reject the stiff and paradoxical form used by his predecessors[11]; it also led to the surrender of some characteristic Stoic doctrines in favour of the teaching of Plato and Aristotle[12]. His studies extended to every branch of philosophy, including astronomy[13] and politics[14]. The latter interest brought him into association with Polybius the historian, with whom he held frequent discussions as to the best form of government; the two learned and experienced Greeks agreed in their admiration for the constitution of Rome[15]. Panaetius visited Rome, and there became the intimate friend of Scipio Africanus minor: this friendship must have begun before the year 140 B.C., when Panaetius accompanied Scipio on a mission to settle the affairs of the East[16]; it lasted till the death of Scipio in 129 B.C. Round Scipio and his Greek friends Polybius and Panaetius there gathered a society of the noblest and most intelligent men of Rome; and in this circle the Latin language as well as Greek philosophy found a new birth. At the time of Scipio's death Panaetius became the head of the Stoic school at Athens, and held this position till his own death twenty years later[17]. Amongst his friends and pupils were men who took a leading part in the government of their native cities[18].

114. Panaetius may well be regarded as the founder of Roman Stoicism, and is of special interest to us as the writer of the treatise ($\pi\epsilon\rho\grave{\iota}$ $\kappa\alpha\theta\acute{\eta}\kappa o\nu\tau o\varsigma$) which Cicero has freely translated in his *de Officiis*. He sets before us

His ethical teaching.

---

[11] 'tristitiam atque asperitatem fugiens Panaetius nec acerbitatem sententiarum nec disserendi spinas probavit' *ib.*

[12] ἦν γὰρ ἰσχυρῶς φιλοπλάτων καὶ φιλοαριστοτέλης, ἀ[λλὰ κ]αὶ παρ[ενέδ]ωκε τῶν Ζηνων[είω]ν τι δι[ὰ τὴ]ν Ἀκαδημίαν καὶ [τὸν Περίπ]ατον. Ind. Herc. col. 61, quoted by Schmekel, p. 379.

[13] 'quam vellem Panaetium nostrum nobiscum haberemus! qui cum cetera, tum haec caelestia vel studiosissime solet quaerere' Cic. *Rep.* i 10, 15.

[14] 'ain' tandem? etiam a Stoicis ista [de optima republica] tractata sunt? non sane, nisi a [Diogene Stoico] et postea a Panaetio' *Leg.* iii 6, 14.

[15] See below, § 310, note 52.

[16] '[accepi] Publi Africani in legatione illa nobili Panaetium unum omnino comitem fuisse' Cic. *Ac.* ii 2, 5.

[17] This date is determined on circumstantial evidence by Schmekel, pp. 2, 3.

[18] 'Scylax Halicarnasseus, familiaris Panaeti, excellens in astrologia, idemque in regenda sua civitate princeps' Cic. *Div.* ii 42, 88.

Stoicism as the school which will train the scholar, the gentleman, and the statesman, whilst he shrinks from those bolder doctrines, borrowed from the Cynic school, which conflict with that which is conventional, or, as their opponents say, with that which is becoming. The central doctrine that virtue is knowledge, and is the sole and sufficient good, he accepts as the plain teaching of nature; and with it the paradox that the wise man never errs[19]. Yet even these maxims are somewhat toned down as he expresses them; and external advantages appear to him worthy of pursuit, not only as giving a meaning to virtue and providing a field for its exercise, but also for their own sake, so long as they do not conflict with virtue[20]; and he perhaps hesitated to assert positively that 'pain is no evil[21].' In his treatises the figure of the wise man is withdrawn to the background; he is practically concerned only with the 'probationer' (ὁ προκόπτων), who is making some advance in the direction of wisdom. This advance is not made by acts of perfect virtue, but by regular performance of 'services' (καθήκοντα, officia), the simple and daily duties which come in the way of the good citizen[22]. Further, scientific investigation must not become the main end of life, as perhaps it seemed to Aristotle; it is permitted only as a recreation in the well-earned intervals between the calls of active life[23].

115. It does not appear that Panaetius devoted much atten-

His views on   tion to logic[24]; on the other hand he was much
physics.   occupied with that part of philosophy which deals

[19] ' omnes enim trahimur et ducimur ad cognitionis et scientiae cupidinem; in qua excellere pulchrum putamus; labi autem, errare, nescire, decipi, et malum et turpe ducimus' *Off.* i 6, 18; 'cum sit is [Panaetius], qui id solum bonum iudicet, quod honestum sit, quae autem huic repugnent specie quaedam utilitatis, eorum neque accessione meliorem vitam fieri, neque decessione peiorem' *ib.* iii 3, 12.

[20] ' quod summum bonum a Stoicis dicitur, id habet hanc, ut opinor, sententiam, cum virtute congruere semper, cetera autem, quae secundum naturam essent, ita legere, si ea virtuti non repugnarent' *Off.* iii 3, 13.

[21] ' Panaetius, cum ad Q. Tuberonem de dolore patiendo scriberet...nusquam posuit non esse malum dolorem' *Fin.* iv 9, 23; see however below, § 322, note 132.

[22] See below, ch. xiii.

[23] ' cuius [veri investigationis] studio a rebus gerendis abduci contra officium est. virtutis enim laus omnis in actione consistit; a qua tamen fit intermissio saepe, multique dantur ad studia reditus' Cic. *Off.* i 6, 19.

[24] He was however a skilled grammarian; see Schmekel, p. 207.

with the history of the universe and its government by divine providence[25]. The Heraclitean theory he appears to have left altogether on one side; for he rejected the theory of the conflagration[26], as Boethus had done before him, accepting the objection of Carneades that 'if everything turned into fire, the fire would go out for lack of fuel[27].' He therefore joined the Peripatetics in holding that the universe is immortal[28]; but since again Carneades has shown that 'no living thing is immortal,' it follows that the world is not an animal, nor is the deity its soul[29]. Upon all these subjects Panaetius ceased to maintain Stoic doctrines; and, alone amongst Stoic teachers, he 'suspended his judgment' as to the reality of divination[30].

116. Similar concessions to his opponents mark his treatment in detail of ethics. Thus he takes from Aristotle the view that 'virtue is a mean between two vices'; and this doctrine, so alien from true Stoic principle, forms the basis of the treatment which we find adopted in the *de Officiis*. The theory of the four 'cardinal virtues,' Wisdom, Justice, Courage, and Soberness, was probably common property at this time; but whereas in Cynism Courage and in the earlier Stoicism Wisdom are the dominant virtues, in the theory of Panaetius Soberness, identified with decorum, far exceeds the rest in practical importance. Thus the triumph won by Panaetius for the name of Stoicism was purchased by the sacrifice not only of its physics, but very largely of its ethics also; and the success of the new system might not unfairly be described as a victory of literature over logic, of reasonableness over reason, and of compromise over consistency. However this may be, Panaetius undoubtedly succeeded in presenting Greek philosophy to his

Concession in ethics.

[25] He wrote a book 'on providence'; how far he or Posidonius is Cicero's authority for the treatment of the subject in *Nat. de.* ii has been much disputed; on this point see Schmekel, p. 8, n. 4.

[26] 'id de quo Panaetium addubitare dicebant, ut ad extremum omnis mundus ignesceret' Cic. *N. D.* ii 46, 118.

[27] Schmekel, p. 309, and below, § 211.

[28] Παναίτιος πιθανωτέραν εἶναι νομίζει καὶ μᾶλλον ἀρέσκουσαν αὐτῷ τὴν ἀϊδιότητα τοῦ κόσμου ἢ τὴν τῶν ὅλων εἰς πῦρ μεταβολήν Ar. Did. fr. 36 (Diels).

[29] Schmekel, p. 309.

[30] 'vim esse divinandi [Panaetius] dubitare se dixit' Cic. *Div.* i 3, 6.

Roman friends in a form in which it recommended itself alike
to their reasoning powers and to their moral sense.

117. The virtual, though not the nominal, successor of
Posidonius. Panaetius was POSIDONIUS of Rhodes[31] (circ. 135–
51 B.C.[32]), who after studying under Panaetius at
Athens travelled widely, finally settling at Rhodes, and there
took an active part in political life. Like his master, he was
a devoted student of Plato, and he wrote a commentary on the
Timaeus. In this commentary he develops a new theory of the
universe, which he asserts to be that which Plato had learnt from
the Pythagoreans, and to be at root the same as that taught by
the Stoics. The starting-point is the μονάς or unit; from this
are evolved the numbers and the elements by a principle of flux,
as in the system of Heraclitus[33]. The unity and the first of the
numbers, the two, differ as force and matter; so that the dualism
of Aristotle is here definitely subordinated to a supreme monism.
This study of Posidonius is therefore incidentally of high importance as a side-light on Stoic metaphysics and cosmology.
In addition he wrote on almost all the principal divisions of
philosophy, thus acquiring a brilliant reputation, particularly in
the eyes of the philosophic nobles of Rome. Cicero made his
acquaintance at Rhodes in 78 B.C., and refers to him more often
in his works than to any other of his instructors[34]. Pompey, in
the midst of his eastern campaigns, put himself to much trouble
to visit him[35]. Amongst his Roman visitors and admirers were
also Velleius, Cotta, and Lucilius[36]. A century later, Seneca
looked back to him as one of those who had made the largest
contribution to philosophy[37].

118. As compared with the more scientific Panaetius, Posi-
His teaching. donius marks a reaction in favour of the religious
side of Stoicism[38]. Thus it comes about that Cicero
bases on his work 'on gods' (περὶ θεῶν) his own statement of the

[31] He came from Apamea in Syria, but is often described as 'of Rhodes,' as the
latter part of his life was spent there.
[32] Schmekel, pp. 9, 10.   [33] *ib.* p. 428.
[34] Reid, *Cic. Acad.* Introd. p. 5.   [35] Cic. *Tusc. disp.* ii 25, 61.
[36] *N. D.* i 44, 123; ii 34, 88.
[37] 'ecce Posidonius, ut mea fert opinio, ex his qui plurimum philosophiae con-
tulerunt' Sen. *Ep.* 90, 20.   [38] See below, § 195.

Stoic theology in the second book of his *de Natura deorum*[39]. Posidonius restores the theory of Divination, as to which Panaetius had held the gravest doubts[40]. He strongly asserts the divine origin of the soul, and accepts the Persian view that in this life it is imprisoned in the body[41]. He affirmed the future conflagration[42], and found this theory not inconsistent with a belief in the pre-existence and the immortality of the individual soul.

In physics and logic alike Posidonius upholds the doctrine of the Logos, and it appears that it passed directly from him to Philo of Alexandria, and so into Judaeo-Christian speculation. In ethics he maintained the sufficiency of virtue[43], and re-defined it in the spirit of Cleanthes rather than of Chrysippus[44]. In the practical application of such doctrines to cases of conscience he disliked the lax views of Diogenes, and sided rather with Antipater and Panaetius[45]. Finally he held that the ideal Republic had already been achieved in the golden age, when the wise had ruled for the protection and happiness of their subjects[46].

119. HECATO of Rhodes was also a pupil of Panaetius:
Hecato.
he wrote books on ethics and casuistry which were largely used by Cicero and by Seneca, both of whom frequently refer to him by name. In laying the foundations of his ethics he distinguishes between the 'theoretic virtues,' such as Wisdom, Justice, Courage and Soberness, which call for the assent of the individual, and are possessed only by the wise man, and the corresponding 'non-theoretic virtues,' which are dispositions of body found also amongst the unwise; as health which corresponds to temperance, and so forth[47]. By this extension of the

[39] Also the *de Divinatione* and the first half of *Tusc. disp.* i; Schmekel, p. 98, etc.

[40] ' de divinatione libros edidit...quinque noster Posidonius ' Cic. *Div.* i 3, 6.

[41] 'animi vitae necessitatibus serviunt, disiunguntque se a societate divina, vinclis corporis impediti ' *ib.* 49, 110.

[42] ' deflagrationem futuram aliquando caeli atque terrarum ' *ib.* 49, 111.

[43] See § 322, note 132.

[44] ὁ Ποσειδώνιος [τὸ τέλος εἶναι εἶπε] τὸ ζῆν θεωροῦντα τὴν τῶν ὅλων ἀλήθειαν καὶ τάξιν Clem. *Strom.* ii p. 416 B (Schmekel, p. 270) ; see also below, § 321, note 125.

[45] Schmekel, p. 62.   [46] See below, § 214.

[47] Diog. L. vii 90 ; Schmekel, pp. 291, 292.

conception of virtue the doctrine of its sufficiency is rendered
easy of acceptance[48]. In the practical application of his theory
he laid great stress on the doctrine of 'relations' (σχέσεις), that
is on duties towards parent, wife, child, slave, country, and so
forth[49]. In order to be in a position to perform these duties a
man is entitled to care for his own life and property[50]. He need
not be too careful to provide for his slaves if provisions are
dear[51]; nor should he too hastily give up for another his chance
of escape from a shipwreck[52]. Hecato therefore seems rather to
side with Diogenes in questions of casuistry, taking a lax view
where Antipater and Panaetius would be inclined to a more
altruistic standpoint.

120. The three teachers of Rhodes appear to us as men of

*The unsec-
tarian philo-
sopher.*

great learning and of wide interests, and not without original force ; on the other hand we cannot say
that they made any very large contributions towards
the discussion of the great problems of philosophy. Apart
from them we find little trace of creative ability in the school
during the first century B.C. There were however numerous
teachers occupied in expounding and defending the doctrines of
the school, and their special interest lay in the controversies
between the Porch and the Academy. From these there resulted a temporary fusion of the two schools. Their respective
names and dogmas remained unaltered ; but attention was no
longer given to the great differences of principle which divided
them. Learning, politics, and social influences alike were at work,
not to solve the great controversies, but to throw a mist over
them. From these circumstances there emerged the type which
we now call the 'eclectic,' but which the Romans called simply
the 'philosopher'; that is, the man who drew practical wisdom
from all sources alike, binding himself to the dogmas of no
school, but winning his way by aptness of discourse and sympathy

---

[48] Diog. L. vii 127.

[49] Schmekel, p. 294.   [50] See below, § 352.

[51] 'plenus est sextus liber de officiis Hecatonis talium quaestionum ; sitne boni
viri in maxima caritate annonae familiam non alere? in utramque partem disputat,
sed tamen ad extremum utilitate officium dirigit magis quam humanitate' Cic. *Off.*
iii 23, 89.

[52] *ib.* 23, 90.

of manner to social importance[53]. We have but a limited interest at the present day in these ephemeral reputations; the type is still with us, both in the preacher whose sympathies are given with equal readiness to half-a-dozen warring denominations, and in the politician who emphasizes his connexion by birth with three or four nationalities and as many grades of society. Nor are we called upon to question the usefulness of this blurring of differences. We must however remark that so far as our immediate subject is concerned, the fusion was equivalent to a defeat of Stoicism by the Academy. That nothing can be definitely proved; that a man may choose his principles at the bidding of his fancy; that an argument may be sufficiently sound for practical purposes even when there exists a counter-argument of almost equal strength; that the problems of dialectics, physics, and ethics may be discussed separately, instead of being treated as parts of one whole; all these are the points for which the Academic contended with as much consistency as his system allowed, and which every philosopher, whether or not he called himself a Stoic, conceded when he began to combine the teachings of diverse systems.

121. After the death of Panaetius the school at Athens appears to have been conducted by DARDANUS and MNESARCHUS, both of Athens, jointly[54]; later we find at its head DIONYSIUS of Cyrene, who enjoyed a great reputation as a mathematician, and was a vigorous opponent of Demetrius the Epicurean[55]. About the same time[56] ATHENODORUS the elder of Tarsus (circ. 130-60 B.C.) became librarian at Pergamus; he made use of his position to erase from Zeno's works those passages (probably from the *Republic*) which were repugnant to the Stoic teaching of his own time; he was however detected and the passages in question were restored[57]. It appears also that he counselled withdrawal from the vexations of public life, a policy by no means consistent with the teaching of

Lesser Stoics.

[53] 'nullius addictus iurare in verba magistri, | quo me cunque rapit tempestas, deferor hospes' Hor. *Ep.* i 1, 14 and 15.
[54] 'qui erant Athenis tum principes Stoicorum' Cic. *Ac.* ii 22, 69; cf. *de Or.* i 11, 45.
[55] Ind. Stoic. Herc. col. 52 (Schmekel, p. 16); but see Pauly-Wissowa s. v.
[56] i.e. the earlier part of the first century B.C.   [57] Diog. L. vii 34.

Zeno, and for which he is rebuked by Seneca[58]. From him we
first hear the practical precept which both Seneca and Juvenal
echo, to ask nothing of the gods that you cannot ask openly[59].
In his old age he left Pergamus and came to reside at Rome
with M. Porcius Cato in B.C. 70. Amongst the younger friends
of Cato were ANTIPATER of Tyre, who wrote on practical ethics,
and died at Athens about 45 B.C.[60]; and APOLLONIDES, with
whom he conversed on the subject of suicide shortly before his
death[61]. From DIODOTUS Cicero received instruction in Stoicism
before 88 B.C.[62]; he conceived a great affection for him, and
invited him to live in his house[63]: he remained there till his
death in 59 B.C., when he left Cicero a considerable property[64].
In his old age he was blind, but he continued his studies, and in
particular that of mathematics, as ardently as ever[65]. APOLLO-
NIUS of Tyre wrote a biography of Zeno, from which Diogenes
Laertius often quotes[66]. To this period perhaps belongs
HIEROCLES, who was bitterly opposed to Epicurus on account
of his choosing pleasure as the end of life, and still more for
his denial of providence[67].

122. We have little reason to regret that only fragments at
most remain to us of the works of these philosophers,
Cicero. since CICERO presents to us a comprehensive view
not only of the doctrines they professed, but also of the criticisms
which their opponents passed upon them, and again of the
replies they made to these criticisms. In carrying out this work
for Stoicism and its rival systems Cicero not only created the
philosophic terminology of the future by his translations of
technical terms from Greek into Latin, but also established a

[58] 'mihi nimis videtur submisisse temporibus se Athenodorus, nimis cito refugisse'
Sen. *Dial.* ix 4, 1.
[59] 'apud Athenodorum inveni:—tunc scito esse te omnibus cupiditatibus solutum
cum eo perveneris, ut nihil deum roges, nisi quod rogare possis palam' *Ep.* 10, 5.
But it is possible that the quotations are from the younger Athenodorus.
[60] Cic. *Off.* ii 24, 86; but some think that Cato's friend was an earlier Antipater.
[61] Plutarch, *Cato minor* 65–67 and 69. [62] Reid, *Academics*, p. 2.
[63] 'Diodoto quid faciam Stoico, quem a puero audivi, qui mecum vivit tot annos,
qui habitat apud me, quem et admiror et diligo?' Cic. *Ac.* ii 36, 115.
[64] *ad Att.* ii 20, 6. [65] *Tusc. disp.* v 39, 113. [66] vii 1, 2, 24 and 28.
[67] 'verba haec Hieroclis Stoici, viri sancti et gravis: ἡδονὴ τέλος, πόρνης δόγμα·
οὐκ ἔστιν πρόνοια, οὐδὲ πόρνης δόγμα' A. Gellius, *N. A.* ix 5, 8.

new style of philosophic discussion. By the friendly tone of his dialogues, placed in the mouths of men whose common interest in Greek studies made the divergencies of the schools to which they belonged a secondary matter; by the amplitude of his style, which gives itself time and space to approach a difficult conception from many points of view; and by the simplicity of his language and illustrations, which assumes that every philosophical contention can be plainly and forcibly put before the average man of letters, he has set an example of the art of exposition which has perhaps not been surpassed since[68]. His most systematic expositions of Stoic doctrine are as follows. In the *Academica* a general view of Zeno's teaching is given by M. Varro (i 10, 35 to 11, 42), and the Stoic logic, as accepted by Antiochus[69], is defended by L. Licinius Lucullus (ii 1, 1 to 19, 63). In the *de Natura deorum* (bk ii) the Stoic physics is explained by Q. Lucilius Balbus; in the *de Finibus* (bk iii) the Stoic ethics by M. Porcius Cato, as the most distinguished Roman who has adopted them as a standard of life. In the *de Officiis* Cicero adopts the form of a letter addressed to his son when studying at Athens, and avowedly adapts the substance of the work of Panaetius already mentioned, supplementing it from a memorandum of the teaching of Posidonius which was specially prepared for him by ATHENODORUS CALVUS[70]; this book deals with ethics mainly in its practical applications. In many of his other works, such as the *de Amicitia, de Senectute, Tusculan disputations, de Fato, de Divinatione,* and *Paradoxa,* Cicero makes use of Stoic material without giving professedly an exposition of the Stoic system.

123. The school to which Cicero finally attached himself was that founded by ANTIOCHUS of Ascalon (circ. 125–50 B.C.)[71],

---

[68] For a fair-minded estimate of Cicero's services to philosophy see Reid, *Academics of Cicero*, pp. 20–28.

[69] See next section.

[70] 'de tertio [cum utile et honestum inter se pugnare videantur] nihil scripsit [Panaetius]. eum locum Posidonius persecutus. ego autem et eius librum arcessivi, et ad Athenodorum Calvum scripsi, ut ad me τὰ κεφάλαια mitteret' Cic. *ad Att.* xvi 11, 4. 'Athenodorum nihil est quod hortere; misit enim satis bellum ὑπόμνημα' *ib.* 14, 4.

[71] He was head of the Academy at Athens, where Cicero heard him in the year 79–78 B.C., and was patronized by Lucullus.

who under the name of the 'old Academy' taught doctrines which were practically indistinguishable from those of the diluted Stoicism which now prevailed, avoiding only the dogmatic temper and a few of the paradoxes of the Stoics[72]. This appears to have been the prevailing tone of philosophical discussion from the fall of the Republic to the death of Augustus. Brutus (the 'tyrannicide'), though family and political associations have linked his name with that of Cato, was in his philosophical opinions a follower of Antiochus[73]. Not very different were probably the views of two teachers, nominally Stoics, who held high positions in the household of Augustus. ATHENODORUS the younger of Tarsus (possibly the same as the Athenodorus Calvus mentioned in the last section) was a pupil of Posidonius, and whilst teaching at Apollonia counted amongst his pupils Julius Caesar's great-nephew Octavius, who was afterwards to become the emperor Augustus. Octavius took his teacher with him to Rome, and he had the credit of exercising a restraining influence on his patron. In B.C. 30 he was sent in his old age to reform the government of his native city Tarsus. He appears to have written chiefly on popular moral subjects[74]. AREIUS DIDYMUS of Alexandria[75], who was
Areius Didymus.   for a longer period installed in the household of Augustus[76], is of interest to us as the first of those who made excerpts from the works of earlier writers, and to him we owe most of the Stoic fragments found in the work of Stobaeus. He probably depended in the first instance on the writings of Antiochus of Ascalon. He was instrumental in saving his native town Alexandria when taken by Augustus in B.C. 30. It is

---

[72] 'eadem dicit quae Stoici' Cic. *Ac.* ii 22, 69.   'erat, si perpauca mutavisset, germanissimus Stoicus' *ib.* 42, 132. See further J. S. Reid, *Academics of Cicero*, Introd. pp. 15–19, and notes to *Ac.* ii 39, 123 and 40, 126.

[73] 'Brutus tuus, auctore Aristo et Antiocho, non sentit hoc [sc. nihil esse, nisi virtutem, bonum]' *Tusc. disp.* v 8, 21. 'si addubitas, ad Brutum transeamus, est enim is quoque Antiochius' *ad Att.* xiii 25, 3. See also below, § 432.

[74] 'tu nihil errabis, si paulo diligentius (ut quid sit εὐγένεια, quid ἐξοχή intelligas), Athenodorus Sandonis filius quid de his rebus dicat, attenderis' *ad Fam.* iii 7, 5.

[75] For the identification of the writer Didymus with Areius the 'philosophus' of Augustus, see Diels, *Proleg.* pp. 80–88.

[76] '[Augustus] eruditione etiam varia repletus per Arei philosophi filiorumque eius Dionysi et Nicanoris contubernium' Suet. *Aug.* 89.

probable enough that his 'Epitome' was prepared for the use of Augustus, and provided the material for philosophical discussions at the banquet, such as those to which Horace so often refers[77]. Seneca tells us that he was acquainted with the inmost thoughts of the family of Augustus, and reports the language in which he consoled Livia upon the death of her son Drusus[78] (B.C. 9). He was succeeded by THEON of Alexandria, also a Stoic, who took a special interest in physiology.

124. We know from Horace that in the time of Augustus Stoic philosophers were found not only at the court, but also in the public lecture-room, and at the street-corners. Such were Stertinius[79], of whom the commentators say that he was the author of 120 books on Stoicism[80]; Crispinus[81], said to have been a bad poet[82]; and Damasippus[83]. In Horace's amusing sketches we find the Stoic as he appeared to the unconverted. He has sore eyes, or else a troublesome cough[84]; he presses his teaching upon his hearers unreasonably and unseasonably. But in the reign of Tiberius we find these popular lecturers held in very high esteem. One of the most eminent was ATTALUS, of whom

Attalus.

Seneca the philosopher gives us a glowing account. Seneca was the first each day to besiege the door of his school, and the last to leave through it. This philosopher must have exercised an extraordinary influence over the young men of his time. In his mouth the paradox 'the wise man is a king' seemed a modest statement; his pupils were half disposed to regard him as a god[85]. When he declaimed on the misery of human life, a deep pity for their fellow-men fell upon them; when he extolled poverty, they felt disposed to renounce their wealth; when he recommended the simple life, they readily abandoned the use of meat and wine, of unguents and of warm

---

[77] *Sat.* ii 6, 73–76.

[78] Sen. *Dial.* vi 4 and 5 ; see below, § 377.

[79] 'Empedocles, an Stertinium deliret acumen' Hor. *Ep.* i 12, 20 ; 'insanis et tu, stultique prope omnes, | si quid Stertinius veri crepat' *Sat.* ii 3, 32 and 33.

[80] Teuffel, *Röm. Lit.* 250, 4.

[81] 'ne me Crispini scrinia lippi | compilasse putes' Hor. *Sat.* i 1, 120 and 121.

[82] Teuffel, as above, 3.   [83] Hor. *Sat.* ii 3.

[84] Hor. *Ep.* i 1, 108.

[85] 'sublimem altioremque humano fastigio [Attalum] credidi' Sen. *Ep.* 108, 13.

baths[86]. Seneca quotes from him in full an address on the vanity of wealth, which shews his teaching to be very similar to that of the more famous Musonius[87]. He attached a special value to the discipline which hardships bring with them[88]. He incurred the dislike of Seianus, who defrauded him of his property and reduced him to the position of a peasant[89].

125. Our attention is next attracted by L. ANNAEUS

Cornutus. CORNUTUS (circ. 20–66 A.D.), who was born in Africa, and entered the house of the Annaei, presumably as a slave. There he received his freedom, and became the teacher of the two poets Persius and Lucan ; of these the former has left us an attractive account of his personality[90]. He wrote in Greek, and one of his works, 'On the Nature of the Gods,' is still extant. This book is a development of the system which we see followed by Cicero in the *de Natura deorum* (based upon Posidonius), by which a reconciliation is effected between the Stoic physics and the popular mythology. By means of etymology and allegory, all that is incredible or offensive in the old legends of the gods is metamorphosed into a rationalistic explanation of the phenomena of the universe. Thus Zeus is the soul of the universe, because he is the cause of life in all living things, Zeus being derived from ζῆν 'live.' Apollo is the sun, and Artemis the moon : Prometheus the providence that rules in the universe. Pan is the universe. Cronos consumes all his offspring except Zeus, for time consumes all except what is eternal. Hera, the air ("Hρα from ἀήρ) is sister and wife of Zeus, because the elements of fire and air are intimately associated. The popularity of such a treatise goes far to explain to us the close connexion now becoming established between the Stoic philosophy and the practices of Roman religion.

[86] Sen. *Ep.* 108, 14–16.

[87] *ib.* 110, 14–20.

[88] 'Attalus Stoicus dicere solebat; malo me fortuna in castris suis quam in deliciis habeat' *ib.* 67, 15.

[89] Sen. Rhet. *Suas.* 2, 12.

[90] 'teneros tu suscipis annos | Socratico, Cornute, sinu...tecum etenim longos memini consumere soles, | et tecum primas epulis decerpere noctes. | unum opus et requiem pariter disponimus ambo, | atque verecunda laxamus seria mensa. | ...nescio quod certe est, quod me tibi temperat, astrum' Pers. *Sat.* v 36–51.

126. Roughly contemporary with Annaeus Cornutus, but perhaps rather older, was the famous Latin writer L. ANNAEUS SENECA (circ. 4 B.C.–65 A.D.). Born in Corduba in Spain, he may have inherited simple tastes from his provincial origin; but it was the eloquence of Attalus which moved him to a deliberate choice of the philosophic life[91]. Under this influence he was at one time tempted to throw away his wealth; whilst the Pythagorean philosopher Sotion induced him to become for a time a vegetarian[92]. To the end of his days he adhered to the 'simple life'; he felt an aversion to wine, oysters, and all luxurious food; he discarded hot baths and soft chairs as debilitating; and of perfumes he would have only the best, that is, none at all[93]. He was an ardent lover of books, and appears to us as the last Roman who made a systematic study of Stoicism in the original authorities, and thus grasped the system in its full extent. He did not however claim, like his teacher Attalus, to be a wise man; far from that, he laments that he is still in the deep waters of wickedness[94]. In an age when a governmental career was freely open to talent, Seneca's powers and industry carried him to high political station, and greatly increased his inherited wealth. He played a part in the court of Claudius, and in time became the tutor, and ultimately the minister, of Nero. He did not possess the zeal of a reformer, and doubtless tolerated many an abuse, and often bowed his head before power even when linked with tyranny[95]. But if he did not imitate the unbending stiffness of Cato, we have still no reason to credit the personal calumnies that pursued him at court. Had his career as a whole been a discredit to his philosophical profession, we may feel sure that Juvenal would never have overlooked so sensational a contrast. For the last few years of his life he resigned political power, that he might devote himself to what he deemed a more important task, the exposition

Seneca.

---

[91] See above, § 124.   [92] Sen. *Ep.* 108, 17.

[93] *ib.* 13–23.

[94] 'sapientem esse me dico? minime' *Dial.* xii 5, 2; 'multum ab homine tolerabili, nedum a perfecto, absum' *Ep.* 57, 3; 'ego in alto vitiorum omnium sum' *Dial.* vii 17, 4.

[95] 'si respublica corruptior est quam ut adiuvari possit,…non nitetur sapiens in supervacuum' *ib.* viii 3, 3.

A.   8

of the practical teaching of Stoicism[96]. Finally he was, or appeared to be, drawn into a plot against the emperor, and was called upon in consequence to put an end to his life.

127. The literary style of Seneca was severely criticized

His style. by critics almost contemporary with him. Gellius tells us that in his time it was by many not thought worth while to read his writings, because the style was found to be vulgar, the matter characteristic of half-educated men, the argument petty and exaggerated[97]. Quintilian finds that much of his work is admirable, but much also is tainted by a striving for cheap effect and a want of solid knowledge[98]; and he thinks him in no way comparable to Cicero[99]. This judgment is generally maintained in the world of modern scholarship, with the result that Seneca's works are not read in our schools and universities, and are little known even to professional scholars.   On the other side we may set the extraordinary popularity of Seneca both in his own times[100] and in those of the Renascence. It is possible to argue that his style represents the true tendency of the Latin language in his day, and that it is in the direct line towards the modern style of French prose, generally considered the best in the world. As regards his matter it is not possible to deny that he repeats the same moral teaching many times in slightly altered form[101], and that he seldom gives us a continuous or thorough treatment of any important subject[102]. His writings may well be compared with articles in our periodical literature and the hebdomadal productions of our pulpits; they aim at immediate effect rather

---

[96] ' in hoc me recondidi et fores clusi, ut prodesse pluribus possem. posterorum negotium ago. illis aliqua, quae possint prodesse, conscribo. salutares admonitiones litteris mando, esse illas efficaces in meis ulceribus expertus. rectum iter, quod sero cognovi et lassus errando, aliis monstro' *Ep.* 8, 1 to 3.

[97] 'cuius libros adtingere nullum pretium operae sit, quod oratio eius vulgaria videatur et protrita, res atque sententiae aut inepto inanique impetu sint aut levi et causidicali argutia, eruditio autem vernacula et plebeia' A. Gellius, *N. A.* xii 2, 1.

[98] Quint. *Inst. Orat.* x 1, 125–158.

[99] 'potioribus praeferri non sinebam' *ib.* 126.

[100] 'tum autem hic solus fere in manibus adulescentium fuit' *ib.* 125.

[101] 'eandem sententiam miliens alio atque alio amictu indutam referunt' Fronto, p. 157.

[102] How capable Seneca was of continuous exposition we may gather from his excellent discussion of the 'causes' of Aristotle and Plato, in *Epistle* 65: see below.

than at the slow building up of ordered knowledge. Just for that reason they admirably illustrate for us Stoicism in its practical application to daily life; and the extraordinary popularity which they enjoyed for many centuries seems to shew that they are in touch with deeply-rooted instincts of humanity.

128. Seneca claims to be an independent thinker, only adopting the views of Stoic masters because their arguments convince him[103]. Still he does not use the liberty he claims to assert any new principles, but only to deviate occasionally in the direction of popular views. Thus he frequently adopts some dogma of Epicurus or some Cynic paradox to point a moral, and appears unconscious of the deep-lying differences which keep these schools apart from Stoicism; and only in reply to some challenge does he state with any care the Stoic position. This is particularly the case with the problem of wealth, which both Epicurean and Cynic disparage, but the true Stoic is called upon to defend as a 'thing of high degree.' Yet when Seneca is called upon to defend his own possession of wealth he states his case with admirable clearness.

His independence.

129. It is perhaps partly due to his style that it appears at times as if Seneca's hold on Stoic doctrine was often weak. He has no real belief in conviction and scientific knowledge: 'if we try to be exact everywhere, we shall need to keep silence; for there is something to be said against most statements[104].' For the detailed Stoic system of logic he feels only contempt[105]. In physics however his interest is keen, probably under the influence of his favourite Posidonius. he sets forth with great clearness the theory of tone (τόνος, *intentio*)[106]: he eloquently maintains the existence of gods,

Weakening of Stoicism.

---

[103] 'non quia mihi legem dixerim nihil contra dictum Zenonis Chrysippive committere, sed quia res ipsa patitur me ire in illorum sententiam' Sen. *Dial.* viii 3, 1; 'nostram [opinionem] accipe. nostram autem cum dico, non adligo me ad unum aliquem ex Stoicis proceribus. est et mihi censendi ius' *ib.* vii 3, 2.

[104] 'si omnia argumenta ad obrussam coeperimus exigere, silentium indicetur; pauca enim admodum sunt sine adversario' Sen. *N. Q.* iv 5, 1.

[105] 'non tempero mihi, quominus omnes nostrorum ineptias proferam' *ib.* iv 6, 1.

[106] See the notes to § 177.

abandoning the traditional proofs, and basing his conviction upon the moral sense in man[107]: he holds firmly to the doctrine of the conflagration[108]. Still we have constant reason to doubt whether these beliefs are linked together in his mind by any consistent principle. His ethics are marked by a similar weakness: the Socratic 'strength and force' is wanting, and is replaced by a spirit of quietism and resignation. The important position which he has filled in Roman politics awakens no enthusiasm in himself, nor does the greatness of the Roman empire excite his admiration. His heart is in his books; to them he gives up entirely his closing years. His wise man will not go out of the way to mix in politics; rather he will carefully consider how he may avoid the dangers of social strife[109]. This enfeebled moral teaching is found also in the successors of Seneca, and in modern literature is constantly quoted as true Stoic doctrine. But though Seneca's philosophy finds him many an excuse for his retirement, he would have been a more faithful disciple of Zeno and Cleanthes if he had borne the burden of public life to the end.

130. To the same period as Seneca belongs C. MUSONIUS RUFUS, in whom however we observe distinctly, what we may conjecture had also been the case with Attalus, that ethical teaching is becoming divorced from philosophical theory, and so the Cynic standpoint approached. Musonius was a preacher with a singular impressiveness of address. Speaking from the heart on matters of direct moral import, he won respect even from those who were least willing to be guided by him. He disdained the applause of his hearers, desiring instead to see each one tremble, blush, exult, or stand bewildered according as the address affected him[110]. 'If you

Musonius.

---

[107] 'si hominem videris interritum periculis, intactum cupiditatibus, inter adversa felicem, in mediis tempestatibus placidum, ex superiore loco homines videntem, ex aequo deos, non subibit te eius veneratio?...non potest res tanta sine adminiculo numinis stare' *Ep.* 41, 4 and 5.

[108] See below, § 209, note 112.

[109] 'idem facit sapiens ; nocituram potentiam vitat, hoc primum cavens, ne cavere videatur' *Ep.* 14, 8 ; 'circumspiciendum ergo nobis est, quomodo a vulgo tuti esse possimus' *ib.* 9.

[110] A. Gellius, *N. A.* v 1, 3 and 4.

have leisure to praise me,' he said to his pupils, 'I am speaking to no purpose.' 'Accordingly,' said one of them, 'he used to speak in such a way that every one who was sitting there supposed that some one had accused him before Rufus: he so touched on what was doing, he so placed before the eyes every man's faults[111].' Amongst his pupils were Aulus Gellius the antiquarian, Epictetus, and a certain Pollio who made a collection of his sayings (ἀπομνημονεύματα Μουσωνίου), of which extracts have been preserved for us by Stobaeus. They consist of moral maxims (χρεῖαι), such as 'Live each day as if your last[112],' 'Nothing is more pleasurable than temperance[113],' and discourses or 'diatribes' (διατριβαί) dealing with subjects such as discipline, endurance, marriage, obedience to parents, and so forth[114]. In elevation of standard these writings stand higher than those of the early Stoics; and the influence of Musonius was so great that we may almost regard him as a third founder of the philosophy.

131. In public life Musonius played a conspicuous part; he was the Cato of his generation, trusted by all parties for his absolute rectitude of character, and respected for his fearlessness; but he was much less out of touch with the real conditions of the Roman world. When in A.D. 62 Rubellius Plautus found himself unable to quiet Nero's suspicions of his loyalty, it was believed that Musonius encouraged him to await his end calmly, rather than attempt rebellion[115]. After the conspiracy of Piso, Musonius was banished from Rome by Nero, together with most of the eminent personalities of the capital[116]. On Nero's death he returned to Rome, and when the armies of Vespasian and Vitellius were fighting in the suburbs of the city, the senate sent delegates to propose terms of peace. Musonius joined them, and ventured to address the common soldiers, expatiating on the blessings of peace, and sternly reproving them for carrying arms. He was roughly handled and forced to

His part in politics.

[111] Epict. *Disc.* iii 23, 29.   [112] Stob. iii 1, 48.   [113] *ib.* 5, 21.
[114] Specimens are given below, especially in ch. xv.
[115] Tac. *Ann.* xiv 59; Henderson, *Nero*, p. 143.
[116] Tac. *Ann.* xv 71.

desist. Tacitus speaks severely of this unseasonable display of philosophy[117]; and certainly Rome would not have been the gainer if the issue had remained undecided[118]. But that such an attempt was possible in defiance of all military discipline speaks much both for the courage of the speaker and for the respect in which his profession was held. Musonius continued to play an honourable part in public life during the reign of Vespasian, and retained the confidence of the emperor even at a time when his advisers secured his assent to a measure for expelling other philosophers from the capital[119].

132. In the reigns of Titus and his successors pupils and Euphrates converts of Musonius played not inconspicuous parts and Dio. in public life. Amongst them was one EUPHRATES, of Tyre or Epiphania (circ. 35–118 A.D.), who in his day won all hearts and convinced all judgments. 'Some persons,' says Epictetus, one of his fellow-pupils, 'having seen a philosopher, and having heard one speak like Euphrates—and yet who can speak like him?—wish to be philosophers themselves[120].' Pliny made his acquaintance in his native land, and was filled with affection for the man. He found his style dignified and sublime; but especially he noticed its sweetness, which attracted even his opponents. His personal appearance was even more charming; he was tall, handsome, and the proprietor of a long and venerable beard. His private life was beyond reproach, and he was devoted to the education of his family of two sons and one daughter[121]. He appears to have completely achieved the reconciliation of philosophy with worldly success.

More ascetic in temper was DIO of Prusa (circ. 40–117 A.D.), who was first an opponent but afterwards a follower of Musonius[122]. A Stoic in theory, a Cynic in practice, he assumed the shabby cloak, and wandered as a physician of souls. His eloquence succeeded in calming a mutiny of soldiers which

---

[117] *Hist.* iii 81.

[118] 'reipublicae haud dubie intererat Vitellium vinci' *ib.* 86.

[119] See below, § 447.   [120] *Disc.* iii 15, 8; *Manual* 29.   [121] Pliny, *Ep.* i 10.

[122] 'quid nostra memoria Euphrates, Dio, Timocrates, Athenodotus? quid horum magister Musonius? nonne summa facundia praediti, neque minus sapientiae quam eloquentiae gloria incluti extiterunt?' Fronto, *Ep. ad Aur.* i 1 (Naber, p. 115).

followed on the death of Domitian, and won for him from a following generation the title of the 'golden-mouthed.' He was held in high honour both by Nerva and by Trajan. A large number of his harangues are still extant.[123].

133. The influence of such teachers was at any rate widespread, and if we suspect that Stoicism was already
Epictetus. losing its intensive force as it extended the sphere
of its influence, in this it did but obey what we shall see to be its own law of creative activity[124]. We still have to consider the two teachers who are of all the most famous and the most familiar; not however because they most truly express the substance of Stoicism, but because they have most deeply touched the feelings of humanity. These are EPICTETUS of Hierapolis (circ. 50–130 A.D.) and Marcus Aurelius, who later succeeded to the principate. The contrast between their positions has often excited comment, since Epictetus was born a slave, and only obtained his freedom in mature years, that is, after the death of Nero in 68 A.D. In reality it is characteristic of the times that so many men of foreign and even servile origin rose to positions of eminence and became the associates and teachers of men of high official rank. In the great slave households, in particular, of imperial Rome unequalled opportunities lay open to talent; the 'educational ladder' was everywhere set up to encourage the youth to make the best of his gifts. Further, just as young nobles were frequently enamoured of slave girls, so far superior to the ladies of their own class in wit, gentleness of manners, and loyalty in the face of all terrors and temptations[125]; so their elders found a delight in the company of the thoughtful and intellectual men who came to the front through the competition of the slave schools. Thus the emperor Claudius chose his ministers amongst his freedmen, provoking thereby the sneers of the Roman aris-tocracy, but greatly advancing the good government of the Roman empire; and it was Epaphroditus, himself a freedman of Nero, who sent the young Epictetus to study at the feet of

[123] See *Leben und Werke Dion's von Prusa*, by H. von Arnim. Berlin, 1898.
[124] See below, § 216.
[125] See the story of Epicharis in connexion with the conspiracy of Piso, in Tac. *Ann.* xv 57.

Musonius Rufus. Epictetus was a man of warm feelings and clear head; his addresses, recorded for us by his hearer Arrian, serve admirably to stimulate the domestic virtues and to keep alive the religious spirit; but his teaching lacks the force which befits the training of a statesman or a king. In logic he inclines too much to suspense of judgment, in ethics to resignation. But he did not altogether miss the Socratic force: in his youth he had gone about inquiring of his neighbours if their souls were in good health, and even when they replied 'What is this to you, my good man? Who are you?' he had persisted in giving trouble. Only when they raised their hands and gave him blows had he recognised that there was something wanting in his method[126]. Other young philosophers, he felt, lacked this energy, and were men of words, not deeds[127]. Like other philosophers, he was expelled from Rome by Domitian in A.D. 89, when he retired to Nicopolis; there he gave lectures till the time of his death[128].

134. Epictetus was a vigorous opponent of the group of young philosophers who delighted to display their talent upon the intricacies of the Stoic logic, and in his early youth he was taken to task by his teacher Musonius for underrating this part of philosophy[129]. He came however to see the great importance of a thorough training in the methods of reasoning, so that in practical life a man should distinguish the false from the true, as he distinguishes good coins from bad. In physics he lays stress chiefly on theology, and the 'will of God' fills a large place in his conception of the government of the world. In his treatment of practical ethics he makes free use of illustrations from the social life of his own day: he finds examples of Socratic strength in the athlete and the gladiator; and he makes it clear that the true philosopher is not (as many believe the Stoics to hold) a man devoid of natural feeling, but on the contrary affectionate and considerate in all the relations

His Cynism.

---

[126] Epict. *Disc.* ii 12, 17 to 25.

[127] 'plerosque istos, qui philosophari viderentur, philosophos esse eiuscemodi "ἄνευ τοῦ πράττειν, μέχρι τοῦ λέγειν"; id significat "factis procul, verbis tenus" A. Gellius, *N. A.* xvii 19, 1.

[128] *ib.* xv 11, 4 and 5.

[129] Epict. *Disc.* i 7, 32 and 33.

of life. He has a special respect for the Cynic, who appears in his lectures not as the representative of a differing philosophical system, but as philanthropist, teacher, comforter, and missionary. There is indeed in the addresses of Epictetus a complete fusion of Stoicism with Cynism; and we trace in them pictures not only of the Cynic system as a whole, but also of individual teachers like Antisthenes and Diogenes, profoundly different from and much more human than the representations of them familiar through other literature; they are in fact pictures of Cynic teachers passed down or idealized by the members of their own sect. By their side stand the pictures of Ulysses the sage and Heracles the purger of the world, as they must have been described from generation to generation by Cynic orators to their hearers amongst the poor and the unhappy.

135. In the second century A.D. the professed teachers of Stoicism must have been very numerous; with the death of Domitian persecution had passed away. The philosophers were everywhere held in high esteem, and in turn their whole influence was used in support of the existing state of society and the official religion. In the early part of the century FLAVIUS ARRIANUS (circ. 90–175 A.D.) is the most eminent of Stoics; and it was noted that his relation to his teacher Epictetus much resembled that of Xenophon to Socrates. To him we owe the publication of the 'discourses' (διατριβαί) which he heard Epictetus deliver. In A.D. 124, when lecturing at Athens, he won the favour of the emperor Hadrian, and was appointed by him to high public offices, in which he shewed himself a wise administrator and a skilful general; in A.D. 130 he received the consulship; and later he withdrew to his native town of Nicomedia in Bithynia, where he filled a local priesthood and devoted himself to the production of works on history and military tactics. To Stoic doctrine he made no direct contribution.

Arrian.

After Arrian had given up the teaching of philosophy for public life Q. JUNIUS RUSTICUS succeeded to the position he left vacant. To him, amongst other teachers belonging to various philosophical schools, was entrusted

Rusticus.

the education of the future emperor M. Aurelius, who gives us
the following picture of the teaching he received :

'From Rusticus, I first conceived the need of moral correction and
amendment ; renounced sophistic ambitions and essays on philosophy,
discourses provocative to virtue, or fancy portraitures of the sage or the
philanthropist ; learned to eschew rhetoric and poetry and fine language ;
not to wear full dress about the house, or other affectations of the kind ; in
my letters to keep to the simplicity of his own, from Sinuessa, to my mother ;
to be encouraging and conciliatory towards any one who was offended or
out of temper, at the first offer of advances upon their side. He taught me
to read accurately, and not to be satisfied with vague general apprehension ;
and not to give hasty assent to chatterers. He introduced me to the memoirs
of Epictetus, presenting me with a copy from his own stores[130].'

In Rusticus we may confidently trace a successor of the school
of Musonius and Epictetus.

136. M. AURELIUS ANTONINUS PIUS (121–180 A.D.) is
Marcus   commonly spoken of as 'the philosopher upon
Aurelius.   the throne,' but this description may be misleading.
Aurelius was in the first instance a Roman prince ; to the
institutions of Rome and to his own position as their chief
representative he owed his chief allegiance.   He was undoubtedly an apt pupil of the courtly philosophers by whom
he was surrounded ; he deliberately chose philosophy in preference to rhetoric, and of the various schools of philosophy
his judgment ranked Stoicism highest.   He was fairly well
instructed, but by no means learned, in its doctrines ; he
adhered with sincerity, but without ardour, to its practical
precepts.   In the leisure hours of a busy life it was his comfort
and his relaxation to express his musings in the form of
philosophic reflections.   But his attitude towards Stoicism is
always that of a judge rather than that of an advocate ; and
much that the school received as convincing reasoning he rejected
as ingenious pleading.   Hence a large part of Stoic doctrine,
and almost the whole of its detailed instruction, disappears from
his view ; but we have the advantage that the last of the Stoic
writers brings out into clearer relief those features of this
philosophy which could still rivet attention in his own time,

---

[130] M. Aurelius, *To himself*, i 7 (Rendall's translation).

and which therefore form part of the last message of the ancient world to the coming generations.

137.   It follows at once from the judicial attitude of Marcus
His belief in   Aurelius that he cannot countenance the Stoic
the cosmos.   claim to certainty of knowledge.   The objection
of opponents that the wise man, who alone (according to Stoic theory) possesses such knowledge, is nowhere to be found, is sustained :

'Things are so wrapped in veils, that to gifted philosophers not a few all certitude seems unattainable.   Nay to the Stoics themselves such attainment seems precarious ; and every act of intellectual assent is fallible ; for where is the infallible man[131]?'

Yet Aurelius does not relapse into scepticism.   One doctrine at least is so convincing that he cannot for a moment doubt it ; it does after all shine forth as true by its own light.   It is that all things are ultimately one, and that man lives not in a chaos, but in a cosmos :

'All things intertwine one with another, in a holy bond; scarce one thing is disconnected from another.   In due coordination they combine for one and the same order.   For the world-order is one made out of all things, and god is one pervading all, and being is one, and law is one, even the common reason of all beings possessed of mind, and truth is one : seeing that truth is the one perfecting of beings one in kind and endowed with the same reason[132].'

From the belief in a cosmos he is led on to a trust in Providence ; theoretically, because the doctrine of the chance clashing of atoms is out of harmony with the belief in ultimate unity ; practically, because in such a conviction only man can find a starting-point for his own activity.   The choice is to him all-important ; either Fortune or Reason is king, and claims allegiance from all.

'Is it the portion assigned to you in the universe, at which you chafe? Recall to mind the alternative—either a foreseeing providence, or blind atoms—and all the abounding proofs that the world is as it were a city[133].'

'The world is either a welter of alternate combination and dispersion, or a unity of order and providence.   If the former, why crave to linger on in such a random medley and confusion? why take thought for anything

[131] *To himself,* v 10.   [132] *ib.* vii 9.   [133] *ib.* iv 3.

except the eventual "dust to dust"? why vex myself? do what I will, dispersion will overtake me. But on the other alternative I reverence, I stand steadfast, I find heart in the power that disposes all[134].'

138. Aurelius makes full use of the Stoic proofs of the existence of the gods, but it soon appears to us that his attachment to the established religion was

His piety.

not in any way founded upon philosophical arguments. In discussing this point he displays a certain heat which we have not yet had occasion to notice:

'If indeed they [the gods] take no thought for anything at all—an impious creed—then let us have done with sacrifice and prayer and oaths, and all other observances by which we own the presence and the nearness of the gods[135].'

Finally, he breaks away altogether from philosophy and rests his convictions on personal experience:

'To those who press the question, "Where have you seen the gods, whence your conviction of their existence, that you worship them as you do?" I reply—first, they are visible even to the bodily eye; secondly, neither have I set eyes upon my soul, and yet I do it reverence. So it is with the gods; from my continual experience of their power, I have the conviction that they exist, and yield respect[136].'

One further argument he held in reserve; the sword, the cross, and the stake for the 'atheists' who refused to be convinced. He was, after all, a king[137].

139. In ethics, Aurelius states the main principles of Stoicism with clearness; but he altogether ignores the Stoic paradoxes, and does not trouble himself

Ethics.

with any detailed theory of the virtues and vices. Firmness of character is to him the supreme good.

'Be like the headland, on which the billows dash themselves continually; but it stands fast, till about its base the boiling breakers are lulled to rest. Say you, "How unfortunate for me that this should have happened"? Nay rather, "How fortunate, that in spite of this, I own no pang, uncrushed by the present, unterrified at the future!" The thing might have happened to any one, but not every one could have endured it without a pang[138].'

---

[134] M. Aurelius, *To himself*, vi 10.   [135] *ib.* vi 44.
[136] See further, §§ 457 and 458.   [137] M. Aurelius, *To himself*, xii 28.
[138] *ib.* iv 49.

But in spite of these doctrines, we trace throughout his pages a tinge of melancholy. Too apt a pupil of Epictetus, he had learnt from him the principles of submission and resignation, but he had not acquired the joyous confidence of an older period, through which the wise man, even if a slave, felt himself a king. Rather, though a king, he felt himself in truth a slave and a subject to the universe that was his master. He would not go against the universal order, but he hardly felt the delight of active cooperation. In this sense he represents to us the decadence of Stoicism, or (to put it more correctly) Stoicism coloured by the decadence of Rome.

140. On the question of continued existence after death Aurelius takes up and emphasizes the teaching of Epictetus, ignoring the fact that other Stoic teachers, from Zeno to Seneca, had taken larger views or at least allowed themselves an ampler language. There had been, indeed, a change in the point of view. The early Stoics, occupied with the question of physics, had insisted upon the indestructibility of substance, and the reuniting of the 'spirit' ($\pi\nu\epsilon\hat{v}\mu a$) with the all-pervading spirit from which it came at the beginning. The Roman school concerned itself more with the question of individuality and personality. Accepting fully the principle that that which is born must die, it comes to the definite conclusion that that which we trace from the mother's womb through infancy and youth, through success and failure in life, through marriage and the family ties onwards to weakness and dotage, must reach its end in death. The 'I' cannot survive the body. The future existence of the soul, if such there be, is no longer (as with Seneca) a matter of joyful expectation, but of complete indifference.

Absorption of the soul.

Epictetus had expressed this with sufficient clearness:

'Death is a change, not from the state which now is to that which is not, but to that which is not now. Shall I then no longer exist? You will not exist, but you will be something else, of which the world now has need ; for you also came into existence, not when you chose, but when the world had need of you[139].'

[139] Epict. *Disc.* iii 24, 93 and 94.

Aurelius constantly repeats the doctrine in varied forms:

'You exist but as a part inherent in a greater whole. You will vanish
into that which gave you being; or rather, you will be re-transmuted into
the seminal and universal reason[140].'

'Death put Alexander of Macedon and his stable boy on a par. Either
they were received into the seminal principles of the universe, or were alike
dispersed into atoms[141].'

141. The saddened outlook of Marcus Aurelius upon life
harmonizes well with the resignation with which
he contemplates a death, which for himself individually will be the end.. Hence it is that his reflections so
often make the thought of death a guiding principle of ethics;
he who has learnt to look forward calmly to his last act has
learnt thereby to abide patiently all the troubles which postpone
it. Thus the last message of the princely philosopher, as of his
predecessor, is that men should 'bear and forbear':

Preparation for death.

'Contemn not death, but give it welcome; is not death too a part of
nature's will? As youth and age, as growth and prime, as the coming of
teeth and beard and grey hairs, as begetting and pregnancy and the bearing
of children, as all other operations of nature, even such is dissolution.
Therefore the rational man should not treat death with impatience or
repugnance or disdain, but wait for it as one of nature's operations[142].'

'O for the soul ready, when the hour of dissolution comes, for extinction
or dispersion or survival! But such readiness must proceed from inward
conviction[143].'

'Serenely you await the end, be it extinction or transmutation. While
the hour yet tarries, what help is there? what, but to reverence and bless
the gods, to do good to men, "to endure and to refrain"? and of all that
lies outside the bounds of flesh and breath, to remember that it is not yours,
nor in your power[144].'

142. Aurelius was no teacher of Stoicism in his time: his
thoughts are addressed to himself alone[145]. But
the happy accident that has preserved this work,
which for nine centuries was lost to sight[146], enables us to obtain
a view of this philosophy from which otherwise we should have

His yearnings.

---

[140] M. Aurelius, *To himself*, iv 14.

[141] *ib.* vi 24.

[143] *ib.* xi 3.

[145] Rendall, *M. Aurelius*, Introd. p. cxii.

[142] *ib.* ix 3.

[144] *ib.* v 33.

[146] *ib.* cxv.

been shut out. We do not go to Aurelius to learn what Stoic doctrine was; this is taken for granted throughout the book; but we can see here how it affected a man in whom the intellectual outlook was after all foreshortened by sympathies and yearnings which had grown up in his nature. The traditional criticism of the school as being harsh, unsympathetic, unfeeling, breaks to pieces as we read these 'thoughts'; rather we find an excess of emotion, a surrender to human weakness. A study of Stoicism based on the works of Aurelius alone would indeed give us but a one-sided picture; but a study in which they were omitted would certainly lack completeness. He is also our last authority. In the centuries which succeeded, other waves of philosophic thought washed over Stoicism, and contended in turn with more than one religion which pressed in from the East. Yet for a long time to come Stoic principles were faithfully inculcated in thousands of Roman homes, and young men taught in childhood to model their behaviour upon the example of Zeno, Cleanthes, and Epictetus formed the salt of the Roman world. If in riper years they joined, in ever increasing numbers, the Christian church, they brought with them something which the world could not afford to lose.

CHAPTER VI.

OF REASON AND SPEECH.

143. THE history of Greek philosophy, even before the time
of Zeno, leads naturally to its division into the
three parts of logic, physics, and ethics[1]. The Ionic
philosophers had chiefly occupied themselves with the nature and
history of the universe, that is, with the problems of physics.
The sophists were greatly concerned with questions as to the
validity of human knowledge, that is, with logic. Socrates
shared this interest, but attached greater importance to the
discussion of moral activities, that is, to ethics. It is however
not clear when a formal division into these three parts was
first made. Cicero attributes it to the immediate followers of
Plato in the Academic school; others assign it definitely to
Xenocrates[2]. The Peripatetics and Stoics both adopted the
division, but whereas the former assigned to Logic an inferior
position, making it an introduction to philosophy, the Stoics
insist that it is a part of philosophy itself[3]; and that of the
three parts it comes first in the order of study, ' as in the mea-
suring of corn we place first the examination of the measure[4].'
It must not however be thought that the three parts of philosophy can be separately treated, for they are intertwined[5]; so
that in treating of Logic we shall constantly have need to
assume a general knowledge of Stoic views both on physics

Parts of philosophy.

---

[1] '[veteres illi Platonis auditores] totam philosophiam tres in partes diviserunt;
quam partitionem a Zenone esse retentam videmus' Cic. *Fin.* iv 2, 4.

[2] Sext. *math.* vii 16 (Arnim ii 38).

[3] οἱ Στωϊκοὶ ἄντικρυς μέρος αὐτὴν ἀπεφαίνοντο Philopon. *ad Anal.* pr. f. 4 a; Stein,
Psychologie ii 93. See also Arnim ii 49 and 49 a.

[4] Epict. *Disc.* i 17, 6.   [5] Diog. L. vii 40.

and ethics. Logic is subdivided into 'dialectic,' which deals
with reasoning, and 'rhetoric,' the art of speech. The relation
between reason and speech was in ancient times, as now, a
matter of perplexity; but it may be taken as a fundamental
position of Stoicism that the two should always be in agreement.

144. Stoicism, as one of the positive and dogmatic schools,
Knowledge assumes that knowledge is attainable. Since this
is attainable. is the very point on which Socrates never reached
assurance, except on the one particular that he himself knew
nothing, it was a matter of primary importance to the Stoics
to make good this position; more especially since they held
(this time in agreement with Socrates) that virtue is but another form of knowledge. Yet the Stoics could not agree with
the Cynics, that true knowledge can be imparted without a
study of its method[6]. Knowledge is, in their view, a high privilege derived by man from his divine ancestry, and shared by
him with the deity alone; and the whole duty of man may
be summed up by saying that he should keep upright his
reason[7]. They therefore devoted themselves with special zeal
to this part of philosophy[8], and were accordingly nicknamed
'the dialecticians[9].' Their aim in this was solely the ascertainment and imparting of truth; but the common view that
their style was in consequence harsh and repellent will be found
to need considerable qualification[10].

145. The chief argument for the certainty of knowledge is
Are the that we assume as much in the practical affairs of
senses true? life[11]; and (as we have already seen) Aristo found
it ridiculous that his Academic neighbour should not even
know who he was[12]. Against it is the fact that men frequently

---

[6] ἀρέσκει οὖν [τοῖς Κυνικοῖς] τὸν λογικὸν τόπον περιαιρεῖν...καὶ τὴν ἀρετὴν διδακτὴν
εἶναι Diog. L. vi 103 and 105.

[7] τίς οὖν ὕλη τοῦ φιλοσόφου; μὴ τρίβων; οὔ, ἀλλὰ ὁ λόγος· τί τέλος; μή τι
φορεῖν τρίβωνα; οὔ, ἀλλὰ τὸ ὀρθὸν ἔχειν τὸν λόγον Epict. *Disc.* iv 8, 12.

[8] 'Stoici...cum vehementer amaverint artem disputandi' Aug. *Civ. De.* viii 7.

[9] Zeller, *Stoics* etc., p. 66.   [10] See below, §§ 164, 165.

[11] 'hi, qui negant quicquam posse comprehendi...totam vitam evertunt funditus'
Cic. *Ac.* ii 10, 31.

[12] See above, § 93.

disagree even as to what they see, and commonly distinguish between what is known to them and what 'seems' to be this or that. Hence Epictetus well defines the function of dialectic as

'a perception of the disagreement of men with one another, and an inquiry into the cause of this disagreement ; a condemnation and distrust of that which only seems, and some kind of investigation of that which seems, as to whether it rightly seems : and the discovery of some rule (κανών)[13].'

Of all kinds of knowledge that which comes through the senses appears to the ordinary man most worthy of confidence, and of the five senses that of sight seems to the philosopher the most divine [14]. In consequence, the whole controversy hinges on the question whether the eyes can be trusted. The positivist argues that the evidence of sight is so plain and unmistakeable that man, if he had the choice, could wish for no better informant. The sceptic replies that nevertheless, if a straight oar be placed partly in the water, it appears to the eyes to be bent ; and that the feathers on a dove's neck, though really alike, appear to the eyes as many-coloured [15]. To deal with such questions we must examine closely the nature of sensation.

146. The Stoics fancifully derive the word αἴσθησις ('sensation') from εἴσθεσις ('storage') ; it is therefore, strictly speaking, the process by which the mind is stored [16]; but it is also, from an opposite point of view, the process by which the mind reaches out towards an external object [17]. From the object (αἰσθητόν) proceed waves which strike upon the sense-organ (αἰσθητήριον); this impact is called a 'sensation' in a narrower sense. At the same time there proceeds from the mind (which is the ruling part or 'principate' of the soul), a 'spirit' or thrill which goes out to meet

Process of sensation.

[13] Epict. *Disc.* ii 11, 13.

[14] 'Stoici deum visum vocantes, quod optimum putabant' Chalc. *in Tim.* 266 (Arnim ii 863).

[15] Cic. *Ac.* ii 7, 19. [16] Arnim ii 458.

[17] 'mens enim ipsa, quae sensuum fons est atque etiam ipsa sensus est, naturalem vim habet, quam intendit ad ea, quibus movetur' Cic. *Ac.* ii 10, 30. On the other hand the Epicureans treat the senses as bodily, and sensation as automatic.

this impact; and this spirit and its operation are also called 'sensation[18].' As a result of the contact of these two waves, and simultaneously with it, there is produced in the soul an effect like the imprint of a seal[19], and this imprint is the φαντασία or 'mind-picture.' That the process may be sound, it is necessary that the intellect be in a healthy state, and further that the organ of sense be healthy, the object really there, and the place and the manner in accord[20]. But we must carefully distinguish between the single sensation and the mind-picture. A flash of light, a cry, a touch, a smell, a thrill of pleasure or pain, is always that which the senses declare it to be[21]; here there is no possibility of error; so understood 'the sensations are always true[22].' But if we go in each case a step further; if we say 'that is white,' 'this is sweet,' 'this is musical,' 'this is fragrant,' 'that is rough,' we are now dealing with mind-pictures, not with 'sensations' in the strict sense[23]. And as to the mind-pictures we agree with the Academics that things are not always what they seem; 'of the mind-pictures some are true, some are false[24].'

147. In order then that we may distinguish the true mind-picture from the false, we have need of a 'rule' (κανών) or 'criterion' (κριτήριον). The true mind-picture is a stirring of the soul, which reveals both what is taking

The criterion of clearness.

---

[18] αἴσθησις δὲ λέγεται κατὰ τοὺς Στωϊκοὺς τό τε ἀφ' ἡγεμονικοῦ πνεῦμα ἐπὶ τὰς αἰσθήσεις διῆκον, καὶ ἡ δι' αὐτῶν κατάληψις...καὶ ἡ ἐνέργεια δὲ αἴσθησις‚καλεῖται Diog. L. vii 52.

[19] Cleanthes called it 'imprint' (τύπωσις); Chrysippus, lest the word imprint should be interpreted too mechanically, called it 'alteration' (ἀλλοίωσις) Sext. math. vii 227, 372 (Arnim ii 56); 'visum obiectum imprimet illud quidem et quasi signabit in animo suam speciem' Cic. de Fato 19, 43.

[20] Sext. math. vii 424 (Arnim ii 68); 'ita est maxima in sensibus veritas, si et sani sunt ac valentes, et omnia removentur quae obstant et impediunt' Cic. Ac. ii 7, 19.

[21] 'idem fit in vocibus, in odore, in sapore, ut nemo sit nostrum qui in sensibus sui cuiusque generis iudicium requirat acrius' ib.

[22] οἱ Στωϊκοὶ τὰς μὲν αἰσθήσεις ἀληθεῖς Aët. plac. iv 9, 4; '[sensuum] clara iudicia et certa sunt' Cic. Ac. ii 7, 19.

[23] 'sequuntur ea, quae non sensibus ipsis percipi dicuntur, sed quodam modo sensibus, ut haec : "illud est album, hoc dulce, canorum illud, hoc bene olens, hoc asperum." animo iam haec tenemus comprehensa, non sensibus' ib. 7, 21.

[24] οἱ Στωϊκοὶ τὰς μὲν αἰσθήσεις ἀληθεῖς, τῶν δὲ φαντασιῶν τὰς μὲν ἀληθεῖς, τὰς δὲ ψευδεῖς Aët. plac. iv 9, 4 (Arnim ii 78); 'Zeno nonnulla visa esse falsa, non omnia [dixit]' Cic. N. D. i 25, 70.

place in the soul and the object which has caused this: just as light reveals both itself and the objects that lie within its range[25]. On the other hand the false mind-picture is an empty twitching of a soul which is not in a healthy condition[26]; no real object corresponds to it, but to that which appears to be an object corresponding to it we give the name 'phantasm[27].' When Orestes thinks he sees the Furies leaping upon him, though his sister assures him that in real truth he sees nothing, the vision of the Furies is a phantasm. The appearances of dreams are equally phantasms[28]. Now a true mind-picture differs from that of a phantasm by being clearer; or, in other words, the distinctive note of a true mind-picture is its 'clearness' (ἐνάργεια, *perspicuitas*)[29]. Clearness then is a quality which attaches itself to a true vision in a way in which it can never attach itself to a work of phantasy[30]. To this clearness the mind cannot but bow[31]; it is therefore (so far as our study has proceeded) the criterion of truth[32].

148. The mind-picture as such is not within a man's control;

Assent.

but it rests with him to decide whether he will give it his 'assent' (συγκατάθεσις, *adsensio* or *adsensus*)[33]. This assent is therefore an act of the soul, in its capacity as will; and can only be rightly exercised by a soul properly

---

[25] φαντασία μὲν οὖν ἐστι πάθος ἐν τῇ ψυχῇ γιγνόμενον, ἐνδεικνύμενον ἐν αὐτῷ καὶ τὸ πεποιηκός·...καθάπερ γὰρ τὸ φῶς αὐτὸ δείκνυσι καὶ τὰ ἄλλα τὰ ἐν αὐτῷ περιεχόμενα, καὶ ἡ φαντασία ‚δείκνυσιν ἑαυτὴν καὶ τὸ πεποιηκὸς αὐτήν Aët. *plac.* iv 12, 1 (Arnim ii 54). The object which causes the φαντασία is technically called the φανταστόν, but also ὑπάρχον Sext. *math.* vii 426.

[26] διάκενος ἑλκυσμὸς Aëtius *plac.* iv 12, 4.   [27] *ib.* 12, 5.

[28] φάντασμα μὲν γάρ ἐστι δόκησις διανοίας, οἵα γίνεται κατὰ τοὺς ὕπνους Diog. L. vii 50.

[29] 'visis [Zeno] non omnibus adiungebat fidem, sed iis solum quae propriam quandam haberent declarationem earum rerum quae viderentur' Cic. *Ac.* i 11, 41; cf. § 105.

[30] On this point the controversy between Arcesilaus and Zeno hinged; see above, § 84.

[31] 'necesse est animum perspicuis cedere' Cic. *Ac.* ii 12, 38.

[32] 'perspicuitas illa, quam diximus, satis magnam habet vim ut ipsa per sese ea quae sint nobis, ita ut sunt, indicet' *ib.* 14, 45.

[33] 'adsensio nostra erit in potestate' Cic. *Fat.* 19, 43; 'adsensio non [potest] fieri nisi commota viso; tamen id visum proximam causam [habet], non principalem' *ib.* 18, 42; '[Zeno] adsensionem adiungit animorum, quam esse vult in nobis positam et voluntariam' Cic. *Ac.* i 11, 40.

strung, that is, possessed of due tension. Assent wrongly given leads to 'opinion' (δόξα, *opinio*), and all wrong assent is error or 'sin' (ἁμαρτία, *peccatum*). This error may take place in two directions, either by a hasty movement of the will (προπίπτειν), giving assent to a picture which is not really clear; or by feebleness of will, which leads to assent in a false direction (διαψεύδεσθαι)[34]. Even haste however is a form of weakness, so that we may say that all opining is a weak form of assent[35]. To ensure a right assent due attention should be given to each of its parts; it includes (i) the intention of mastering the object (πρόθεσις); (ii) careful attention directed to the object, or 'application' (ἐπιβολή); and (iii) assent in the narrower sense[36]. Apart from assent, three courses remain open: these are (i) 'quiescence' (ἡσυχάζειν, *quiescere*): (ii) 'suspense of judgment' (ἐπέχειν, *adsensum sustinere*), which is a settled quiescence; and (iii) negation[37].

149. Close upon assent follows 'comprehension' (κατάληψις, *comprehensio*): this is the ratification of the assent given, the fixing irrevocably in the mind of the picture approved. This picture now becomes a 'comprehension-picture' (καταληπτικὴ φαντασία), and as such a unit of knowledge. We may understand thereby that the mind has grasped the external object[38], and this is the plain meaning of Zeno's simile; or we may say that the object has gained a hold upon the mind, and has left its stamp upon it. Both interpretations are consistent with Stoic doctrine: but the former view, which represents the soul as active and masterful, undoubtedly expresses the more adequately the meaning of the school[39].

Comprehension.

[34] διττὰς γὰρ εἶναι δόξας, τὴν μὲν ἀκαταλήπτῳ συγκαταθέσιν, τὴν δὲ ὑπόληψιν ἀσθενῆ Stob. ii 7, 11 m (Pearson, Z. fr. 15): cf. Plut. *Sto. rep.* 47, 10.
[35] 'opinionem autem volunt esse imbecillam adsensionem' Cic. *Tusc. disp.* iv 7, 15; 'opinio quae [est] imbecilla et cum falso incognitoque communis' Cic. *Ac.* i 11, 41; so Sext. *math.* vii 151 (Arnim ii 90).
[36] Epict. *Disc.* i 21, 2.   [37] *ib.* i 18, 1; Sext. *math.* vii 416.
[38] ἔστι δὲ αἴσθησις ἀντίληψις τῶν αἰσθητῶν Nem. *nat. hom.* vii p. 175 M (Stein, *Psych.* ii 135).
[39] Cicero's point of view appears to be that the mind-picture grasps the object: '[visum] cum acceptum iam et adprobatum esset, [Zeno] comprehensionem appellabat, similem eis rebus quae manu prehenderentur' Cic. *Ac.* i 11, 41. See further Stein, *Psych.* ii 174, and R. D. Hicks, *Stoic and Epicurean*, p. 71.

From this mutual grasp there follows an important physical deduction. Since only like can grasp like, the soul must be like the object, and the popular dualism of mind and matter is (to this extent) at an end [40]. Still this likeness is not complete; and the soul in sensation does not grasp the object from every point of view, but only so far as its own nature permits in each case [41]. For this reason the trained observer and the artist grasp far more of the object than the ordinary man [42].

150. The soul, having grasped single mind-pictures, retains
From sensa- its hold upon them by memory [43]; the frequent
tion to reason. exercise of which keeps each picture fresh and
complete [44]. As the air, when an orchestra is performing, receives the impression of many sounds at the same time, and yet retains the distinctive tone of each [45], so the soul by concurrent alterations of its texture preserves its hold on the separate pictures it has once grasped. Fresh operations of soul now supervene. First, from the comparison of many like pictures, comes 'experience' (ἐμπειρία, *experientia*) [46]; out of other comparisons, 'similitude' (ὁμοιότης), as 'Socrates' from his portrait; and 'analogy' (ἀναλογία, *proportio*), as 'the centre of the earth' from that of other spheres; 'transference' (μετάθεσις, *translatio*), as 'eyes in the heart'; 'composition' (σύνθεσις, *compositio*), as 'a Hippocentaur'; 'opposition' (ἐναντίωσις, *transitio*), as 'death' from life; 'deprivation' (κατὰ στέρησιν), as 'a cripple [47].' All

---

[40] This view is expressed by Posidonius, who bases it on Plato's *Timaeus*: ὡς τὸ μὲν φῶς ὑπὸ τῆς φωτοειδοῦς ὄψεως καταλαμβάνεται, ἡ δὲ φωνὴ ὑπὸ τῆς ἀεροειδοῦς ἀκοῆς, οὕτως ἡ τῶν ὅλων φύσις ὑπὸ συγγενοῦς ὀφείλει καταλαμβάνεσθαι τοῦ λόγου Sext. Emp. *math.* vii 93. See also below, § 266.

[41] 'comprehensio facta sensibus et vera esse [Zenoni] et fidelis videbatur; non quod omnia, quae essent in re, comprehenderet, sed quia nihil quod cadere in eam posset relinqueret' Cic. *Ac.* i 11, 42.

[42] Diog. L. vii 51; 'quam multa vident pictores in umbris et in eminentia, quae nos non videmus!' Cic. *Ac.* ii 7, 20.

[43] μνήμη θησαυρισμὸς οὖσα φαντασιῶν Sext. *math.* vii 373 (Arnim i 64); '[mens] alia visa sic arripit, ut his statim utatur; alia quasi recondit, e quibus memoria oritur' Cic. *Ac.* ii 10, 30.

[44] 'quicquid frequens cogitatio exercet et renovat, memoriae nunquam subducitur; quae nihil perdit, nisi ad quod non saepe respexit' Sen. *Ben.* iii 2, 3.

[45] So substantially Chrysippus argued. See Sext. *math.* vii 231.

[46] ὅταν δὲ ὁμοειδεῖς πολλαὶ μνῆμαι γένωνται, τότε φαμὲν ἔχειν ἐμπειρίαν Aët. *plac.* iv 11, 2.

[47] Diog. L. vii 52.

these are based on the general principle of likeness and unlike-
ness, and may be summed up under the general heading of
'reason's work of comparison' (*collatio rationis*)[48], or shortly,
of reason (λόγος)[49]. Sensation shews us the present only; but
reason brings the past and the future within our view, and points
out to us the workings of cause and effect[50].

151. With the mind-pictures (φαντασίαι, *visa*) which are
derived from sensation we may now contrast the
'notions' (ἔννοιαι, *notiones* or *intellegentiae*) which
are derived from the combination of sensation and
reasoning; the former correspond generally to 'perceptions,' the
latter to 'conceptions' in the language of modern philosophy[51].
But each of the Stoic terms is also used in a wider sense which
includes the other. The sensory pictures are inscribed upon
the mind as upon a blank sheet from birth upwards; in this
sense they may well be called 'entries on the mind' (ἔννοια
from ἐν νῷ)[52] On the other hand the conceptions may be called
'rational mind-pictures'[53]; quite as much as the sensory mind-
pictures they need the prudent assent of the will before they
become 'comprehensions,' when they are once more units capable of entering into further combinations and becoming part
of scientific knowledge. If then for the sake of clearness we
use the modern terms, we may say that perceptions correspond

*Perceptions
and Con-
ceptions.*

[48] The details of this list are variously given: e.g. 'cum rerum notiones in animo
fiant, si aut usu aliquid cognitum sit, aut coniunctione, aut similitudine, aut collatione
rationis' Cic. *Fin.* iii 10, 33.

[49] Diog. L. vii 52.

[50] 'homo autem, quod rationis est particeps, per quam consequentia cernit, causas
rerum videt, earumque progressus et quasi antecessiones non ignorat, similitudines
comparat, et rebus praesentibus adiungit atque adnectit futuras ; facile totius vitae
cursum videt' Cic. *Off.* i 4, 11.

[51] So Zeller, *Stoics* etc., p. 79.

[52] ὅταν γεννηθῇ ὁ ἄνθρωπος, ἔχει τὸ ἡγεμονικὸν μέρος τῆς ψυχῆς ὥσπερ χάρτην· εἰς
τοῦτο μίαν ἑκάστην τῶν ἐννοιῶν ἐναπογράφεται Aët. *plac.* iv 11, 1. The metaphor
of the *tabula rasa* can be traced back to Plato and Aristotle, but in this application
was first used by Cleanthes. Locke presumably borrowed it from the Stoics. It
must not be thought that this metaphor implies passivity on the part of the soul ;
as the Stoics use it, the soul is from the beginning actively cooperating in obtaining
impressions. See Stein, *Psych.* ii pp. 112 sqq., note 230.

[53] τῶν δὲ φαντασιῶν...οὐκ αἰσθητικαί αἱ διὰ τῆς διανοίας, καθάπερ αἱ ἐπὶ τῶν
ἀσωμάτων Diog. L. vii 51.

generally to individual objects which have a real existence, whilst conceptions correspond to classes of things, which (according to the Stoics) have no real existence in themselves, but only a sort of existence in our minds. Thus the 'ideas' of Plato are all conceptions, subjectively but not objectively existent[54]. So far as our study has gone, all conceptions are based on perceptions : therefore all the elements of knowledge either come from sense and experience solely, or from sense and experience combined with reasoning[55]; and the most important reasoning process is that comparison of like perceptions which in this philosophy takes the place of induction[56].

152. But even if all 'conceptions' are ultimately derived
Preconcep-   from 'perceptions,' it does not follow that in each
tions.   particular case the mind commences *de novo* to
collect and shape its material. On the contrary, it is clear that not only all practical life, but also all philosophy, takes for granted a great many matters which are either allowed by general consent, or at least assumed by the thinker; and these matters are mostly of the nature of class-conceptions. If it is stated that 'the consul entered Rome in a chariot drawn by four horses,' we assume that the ideas expressed by 'consul,' 'chariot,' 'four,' 'horses,' are matters of general consent, and we may go on to assume that the person of the consul and the locality called 'Rome' are also already known to the speaker and his hearers. The general term in the post-Aristotelian writers for such legitimate assumptions is 'preconception' (πρόληψις, *anticipatio* or *praesumptio*). The precise meaning of this term (of which the invention is ascribed to Epicurus[57]) appears not to be always the same. Most commonly the 'preconception' is a general term or conception, and therefore to the Stoics it is one variety of the ἔννοια; it is 'a mental shaping, in accordance with

---

[54] οἱ ἀπὸ Ζήνωνος Στωϊκοὶ ἐννοήματα ἡμέτερα τὰς ἰδέας ἔφασαν Aët. *plac.* i 10, 5 (Arnim i 65) ; cf. Diog. L. vii 61.

[55] πᾶσα γὰρ νόησις ἀπὸ αἰσθήσεως γίνεται ἢ οὐ χωρὶς αἰσθήσεως, καὶ ἢ ἀπὸ περιπτώσεως ἢ οὐκ ἄνευ περιπτώσεως Sext. *math.* viii 56 (Arnim ii 88) ; cf. Diog. L. vii 52 and 53.

[56] 'cetera autem similitudinibus [mens] constituit' Cic. *Ac.* ii 10, 30.

[57] Cic. *N. D.* i 17, 44.

man's nature, of things general'[58]. All such preconceptions are foreshadowings of truth, especially in so far as they correspond to the common judgment of mankind[59]; and the art of life consists in correctly applying these presumptions to the particular circumstances with which each individual man has to deal[60]. If the preconceptions are rightly applied, they become clearer by use, and thus attain the rank of true knowledge by a process of development or 'unravelling' (enodatio)[61].

As to the nature of a preconception, there is a great difference between Epicurus and the Stoics. Epicurus identifies all the terms 'preconception,' 'comprehension,' 'right opinion,' 'conception,' and 'general notion,' and maintains that each of these is nothing but memory of a sensation frequently repeated[62]; the Stoics however hold that preconceptions are established by the mind[63], and (so far as they are common to all men) by the universal reason. This difference is fundamental. Epicurus, as a materialist in the modern sense, explains perception as a bodily function, and 'conceptions' of every kind as mere echoes of such bodily functions. The Stoics on the other hand recognise at each stage the activity of mind, and this in increasing degree as we proceed to the higher levels of thought.

153. We now approach the most critical point in the Stoic theory of knowledge. Is it possible for man to possess knowledge which is not derived, either directly or indirectly, through the organs of sense? Such a

Notions of inner growth.

---

[58] ἔστι δ' ἡ πρόληψις ἔννοια φυσικὴ τῶν καθόλου Diog. L. vii 54; 'notionem appello quam Graeci tum ἔννοιαν tum πρόληψιν; ea est insita et praecepta cuiusque formae cognitio, enodationis indigens' Cic. *Top.* 7, 31; 'nobis notitiae rerum imprimuntur, sine quibus nec intellegi quicquam nec quaeri disputarive potest' *Ac.* ii 7, 21. See also Aët. *plac.* iv 11, 3. If the concept can only be reached by special training, it must not be called πρόληψις.

[59] 'There are certain things which men who are not altogether perverted see by the common notions which all possess. Such a constitution of the mind is named common sense (κοινὸς νοῦς)' Epict. *Disc.* iii 6, 8. See also below, § 158.

[60] 'We need discipline, in order to learn how to adapt the preconception of what is reasonable or unreasonable to the several things conformably with nature' Epict. *Disc.* i 2, 6.

[61] See Cic. *Top.* above, note 58.   [62] Diog. L. x 33.

[63] 'cetera autem similitudinibus [mens] constituit; ex quibus efficiuntur notitiae rerum, quas Graeci tum ἐννοίας tum προλήψεις vocant' Cic. *Ac.* ii 10, 30. As to the possibility of distinguishing the two terms see Prof. Reid's note.

question cannot be answered by any appeal to single Stoic
texts; it needs an appreciation of the whole philosophic outlook, and upon it depend the most vital principles of the system.
Let us then first consider, on the supposition that such knowledge exists, what its nature is, what its content, and how it is
attained by individual men. Knowledge cut off from the sense-
organs is cut off from all human individuality; it is therefore
the expression of the common reason (κοινὸς λόγος), and its
parts are 'common notions' (κοιναὶ ἔννοιαι or προλήψεις), shared
by gods and men, but by men only so far as they are partakers
of the divine nature. The principal content of such knowledge
is also clear; it includes the conception of what is morally good,
and the beliefs that gods exist and that the world is governed
by their providence⁶⁴. Lastly, as of all general conceptions, the
rudiments or rough outlines only of these beliefs are inborn in
men, by virtue of their divine ancestry; whence they are called
'innate notions' (ἔμφυτοι ἔννοιαι, insitae notiones)⁶⁵. These
notions in their full development are not attainable by children
at all, nor by men till they attain to reason, that is, till they
become wise men⁶⁶.

154. The Stoics are naturally reluctant to admit that doc-
'Proofs' of in-   trines which it is impious to deny are nevertheless
born notions.   unattainable except by perfect wisdom; but their
whole system points inevitably to this conclusion. But there
are intermediate stages between the rough inborn outlines of
these truths and their ripe completeness. As man grows in
reason, he becomes increasingly able to appreciate contributory
truths, derived from the combination of perception and reasoning, that is, by processes such as 'analogy' and 'comparison,'
which point in the direction of the supreme beliefs. In this

⁶⁴ See notes to the next section.

⁶⁵ 'rerum plurimarum obscuras necessarias intelligentias enudavit [qu. incohavit?],
quasi fundamenta quaedam scientiae' Cic. *Leg.* i 9, 26; 'quae in animis imprimuntur,
de quibus ante dixi, incohatae intelligentiae, similiter in omnibus imprimuntur' *ib.* i
10, 30; 'As to good and evil, beautiful and ugly...and what we ought to do and
what we ought not to do, who ever came into the world without having an innate
idea of them?' Epict. *Disc.* ii 11, 3.

⁶⁶ ὁ δὲ λόγος...ἐκ τῶν προλήψεων συμπληροῦσθαι λέγεται κατὰ τὴν πρώτην ἑβδομάδα
Aet. *plac.* iv 11, 4; περὶ δὲ τὴν δευτέραν ἑβδομάδα ἔννοια γίνεται καλοῦ τε καὶ κακοῦ
ib. v 23, 1.

sense, and (it is here suggested) in this sense only, can there be 'proofs' (ἀποδείξεις) of these[67]. Only in the crowning moment of that probation which is described later on, at the moment of conversion, these truths finally flash forth, stirred up indeed by secondary evidence, but really rooted in the man's deepest nature[68]; they then reveal themselves to the soul with an illuminating power which is all their own, but which carries with it the most complete conviction. Ordinary men must meanwhile somehow make shift with reflections or pale copies of this knowledge, to which however the name of common or inborn notions can also be applied.

155. The list of 'common notions' is doubtless not limited
The inward touch. to the high philosophical principles which we have mentioned; for instance it must include such mathematical principles as 'two and two make four,' 'a straight line is the shortest distance between two points,' 'a three-sided figure has three angles,' and so forth. With these however we have little direct concern. Of more interest to us is another kind of perception[69] recognised by the Stoics as well as by other schools of philosophy, that called the 'inward touch' (ἐντὸς ἀφή)[70]. By this the soul becomes aware of its own workings, most obviously of its pleasure and pain. The doctrine of the 'inward touch' is of great philosophical importance, for it breaks down the dualism

[67] ἡ δὲ κατάληψις γίνεται...λόγῳ τῶν δι' ἀποδείξεως συναγομένων, ὥσπερ τὸ θεοὺς εἶναι καὶ προνοεῖν τούτους Diog. L. vii 52; 'collatione rationis boni notio facta est; cum enim ab iis rebus, quae sunt secundum naturam, ascendit animus collatione rationis, tum ad notionem boni pervenit' Cic. *Fin.* iii 10, 33; 'nobis videtur observatio collegisse et rerum saepe factarum inter se collatio: per analogian nostri intellectum et honestum et bonum iudicant. noveramus corporis sanitatem; ex hac cogitavimus esse aliquam et animi. noveramus corporis vires; ex his collegimus esse et animi robur' Sen. *Ep.* 120, 4; 'de bonis ac malis sensus non iudicat; quid utile sit, quid inutile, ignorat. non potest ferre sententiam, nisi in rem praesentem perductus est; ratio ergo arbitra est bonorum ac malorum' *ib.* 66, 35.

[68] φυσικῶς δὲ νοεῖται δίκαιόν τι καὶ ἀγαθόν Diog. L. vii 53.

[69] For the classification as a sensation see above, § 146.

[70] οἱ Στωϊκοὶ τῇδε (sc. Aristotelis) τὴν κοινὴν αἴσθησιν 'ἐντὸς ἀφὴν' προσαγορεύουσι, καθ' ἣν καὶ ἡμῶν αὐτῶν ἀντιλαμβανόμεθα Aët. *plac.* iv 8, 7; 'quid de tactu, et eo quidem quem philosophi interiorem vocant aut doloris aut voluptatis?' Cic. *Ac.* ii 7, 20. This feeling, if mistaken for the perception of an external object, is an 'empty twitching': φαντασία τῶν ἐν ἡμῖν παθῶν· ὃ δὴ κυριώτερον διάκενος ἑλκυσμὸς παρ' αὐτοῖς καλεῖται Sext. *math.* vii 241 (Arnim ii 64). See further Hicks, *Stoic and Epicurean*, p. 110.

of subject and object, the barrier between the knowing and the known. Since these are the same in the specific cases named, the door is open to the conclusion that everywhere there is a kinship between the two, and that without this knowledge would be without firm foundation. By this kinship we may also explain the fact that direct communications are made by the deity to man, as by dreams, oracles and augury[71].

156. Thus it appears that the elements of knowledge, according to the Stoics, are sensations, perceptions, conceptions or notions, and general or inborn notions. As in the other parts of the Stoic philosophy, we shall regard this fourfold division as indicating generally the ground covered, and not as setting up definite lines of demarcation. The same material may be analyzed from other points of view, as for instance in the study of words, in which we shall find a division into objects, statements, conditional statements, and syllogisms. The elements may also be combined in various ways. A combination or 'system' (σύστημα) which is directed towards a useful or pleasurable object, such as music or grammar, is called an 'art' (τέχνη, ars)[72]; and arts are attainable by ordinary men. The wise man, on the other hand, is not necessarily acquainted with the several arts; his practice is to 'keep quiet' when matters are discussed which require such special knowledge. The combination of all knowledge in one all-embracing system is 'science' (ἐπιστήμη, scientia); the only science in the full sense is philosophy[73]; and in this system no part can be at variance with any other part[74]. The elements of knowledge also acquire the character of science, when they are found to be parts of this compacted system, and therefore incapable of coming into conflict with any other part[75]; and in

Knowledge; the parts and the whole.

[71] 'visa quaedam mitti a deo, velut ea quae in somnis videantur, quaeque oraculis auspiciis extis declarentur' Cic. *Ac.* ii 15, 47.

[72] Arnim ii 93 and 95; 'ars vero quae potest esse nisi quae non ex una aut duabus, sed ex multis animi perceptionibus constat?' Cic. *Ac.* ii 7, 22; 'ex quibus [perceptis] collatis inter se et comparatis artes quoque efficimus, partim ad usum vitae, partim ad oblectationem necessariis' *N. D.* ii 59, 148.

[73] Arnim ii 95.   [74] πρόληψις προλήψει οὐ μάχεται Epict. *Disc.* i 22, 1.

[75] εἶναι δὲ τὴν ἐπιστήμην κατάληψιν ἀσφαλῆ καὶ ἀμετάπτωτον ὑπὸ λόγου · ἑτέραν δὲ ἐπιστήμην σύστημα ἐξ ἐπιστημῶν τοιούτων Stob. ii 7, 5 l (see also Wachsmuth's crit. note).

particular we find the term 'science' predicated of comprehensions which are firmly established and cannot be refuted by any argument[76]. In the language of Zeno's simile, over the closed fist that grasps the object is placed the other hand, keeping it with firmness and assurance in its place[77]; or, to use a comparison first suggested in ridicule of Stoicism, but which by the progress of architectural skill has since then been made less damaging, science is like a firm and immoveable building constructed upon a shifting foundation[78]. Finally ordinary men can reach comprehension, but only the wise man can attain to science[79].

157. We revert to the difficult problem of the criterion of truth, that is, the discovery of a rule by which the true can be separated from the false. Our authorities differ greatly as to what the Stoic criterion is; and this vacillation must have placed the Stoics at a great disadvantage in their controversy with the Academics, who maintain that there is no criterion. The most usual statement is that the 'comprehensive mind-picture' ($\kappa\alpha\tau\alpha\lambda\eta\pi\tau\iota\kappa\dot{\eta}$ $\phi\alpha\nu\tau\alpha\sigma\dot{\iota}\alpha$) is the criterion; this view is expressly attributed to Chrysippus, Antipater, and Apollodorus[80]. As we have seen, the meaning of this is that a true mind-picture can be distinguished from one that is false by the note of clearness, and this general doctrine can be traced back to Zeno[81]. It appears at first sight to provide a criterion which can be applied by the percipient at the moment when it is needed, and it was doubtless intended to be a practical tool in this sense; but under the pressure of criticism the Stoics were frequently compelled to modify it. They could not but admit that in the case of dreams and drunken visions it is only at

The criterion reviewed.

[76] 'scientiam...quam nos non comprehensionem modo rerum, sed eam stabilem quoque atque immutabilem esse censemus' Cic. *Ac.* ii 8, 23; 'quod erat sensu comprehensum...si ita erat comprehensum ut convelli ratione non posset, scientiam [Zeno] nominabat' *ib.* i 11, 41; 'quamcunque vero sententiam probaverit [sapiens], eam sic animo comprensam habebit, ut ea quae sensibus' *ib.* ii 37, 119.

[77] See above, § 77.

[78] Plut. *comm. not.* 47, 4.

[79] Sext. *math.* vii 151 (Arnim ii 90); 'scientiam, cuius compotem nisi sapientem esse neminem' Cic. *Ac.* ii 47, 145.

[80] Diog. L. vii 54, as in note 84 below.

[81] See especially Pearson, Zeno fr. 11; and above, § 84.

a later moment that the lack of clearness can be appreciated[82];
whereas on the other hand a picture may be perfectly clear, and
yet the percipient, because of some prepossession, may not realize
this. Such was the case when Hercules brought Alcestis from
the world below; her husband Admetus received a true mind-
picture of her, but put no confidence in it, because he knew her
to be dead. It follows that no mind-picture can be implicitly
trusted for itself; for our sense organs may be clouded, or our
previous experience in conflict with it. If the Academics
urged that the sure note of clearness is not to be found in the
senses[83], the Stoics admitted as much when they now said that
a true comprehensive picture must come from a real object[84],
when they added the words that 'no objection must arise[85]';
thus really admitting that it must be not only persuasive, but
also such as no reasoning process can shake, and such as has
been examined from all sides[86]. Thus they shifted the centre
of certainty from the single comprehension to the general field
of science; they still held to it in theory, but no longer maintained its practical application. For this too they had the
authority of the older masters. For we learn on the authority
of Posidonius that 'some of the older Stoics' held the true
criterion to be 'right reason' (ὀρθὸς λόγος)[87], and this is equivalent to saying that only the deity and the wise man possess
the secret[88]. In a loose sense any important part of the Stoic

---

[82] 'omnium deinde inanium visorum una depulsio est, sive illa cogitatione in-
formantur,...sive in quiete, sive per vinum, sive per insaniam. nam ab omnibus
eiusmodi visis perspicuitatem, quam mordicus tenere debemus, abesse dicemus....
itaque, simul ut experrecti sumus [ex somno], visa illa contemnimus neque ita
habemus, ut ea quae in foro gessimus' Cic. Ac. ii 17, 51.

[83] '[ab Academia disputatum est], non inesse [in sensibus] propriam, quae
nusquam alibi esset, veri et certi notam' ib. ii 32, 103; 'dicunt [Academici] hoc
se unum tollere, ut quicquam possit ita videri, ut non eodem modo falsum etiam
possit videri' ib. ii 11, 33.

[84] κριτήριον δὲ τῆς ἀληθείας φασὶ τὴν καταληπτικὴν φαντασίαν, τουτέστι τὴν ἀπὸ
ὑπάρχοντος, καθά φησι Χρύσιππος καὶ Ἀντίπατρος καὶ Ἀπολλόδωρος Diog. L. vii 54.
This view is attributed to Zeno himself: 'visum [Zeno ita definiit] ex eo, quod
esset, sicut esset, impressum et signatum et effictum' Cic. Ac. ii 24, 77.

[85] οἱ δὲ νεώτεροι προσετίθεσαν καὶ τὸ μηδὲν ἔχουσαν ἔνστημα Sext. math. vii 253.

[86] φαντασία πιθανὴ καὶ ἀπερίσπαστος καὶ περιωδευμένη Sext. math. vii 181. Such
was the definition of Carneades (Schmekel, p. 344).

[87] Diog. L. vii 54 (see § 80, note 68).

[88] 'posse eum [sapientem] falsa a veris distinguere' Cic. Ac. ii 21, 67.

theory of reason may be said to be a criterion; thus Chrysippus again said that 'the criteria are sensation and preconception,' and Boethus set up many criteria, as mind, sense, science, and (in practical matters) appetite[89].

158. Seeing that the full assurance of truth is not at every moment attainable, it is necessary to be contented from time to time with something less complete. Amongst such tests the 'general consent of mankind' plays an important part, especially in connexion with the dogma 'that gods exist.' We may indeed well believe that this criterion was not originally suggested by revolutionary philosophers, but rather by conservative advocates of an established religion; and therefore we are not surprised to see it emphasized first by Posidonius and afterwards by Seneca[90]. General consent is however by itself no proof of truth, but at most an indication of the presence of a 'common notion' in its rough shape. If however we see that the 'common notion' grows stronger and more clear every day, and if it is the more firmly held as men approach the standard of wisdom, it becomes a strong support[91].

General consent.

159. From a very early period, as we have already indicated, Stoic teachers accepted probability as the guide of life in its details, being perhaps aided by the happy ambiguity of the expression 'reasonableness' (τὸ εὔλογον), which suggests formally the pursuit of reason, but in practice is a justification of every course of which a plausible defence can be brought forward. Ptolemy Philopator, we are told, jestingly put wax fruit before Sphaerus at his table, and when Sphaerus tried to eat it cried out that he was giving his assent to a false mind-picture. Sphaerus replied that he had not assented to the picture 'this is fruit,' but only to the picture 'this is probably fruit[92].' Antipater of Tarsus, when he explained

Probability the guide of life.

---

[89] Diog. L. vii 54. See on this point Hicks, *Stoic and Epicurean*, p. 70.

[90] 'multum dare solemus praesumptioni omnium hominum, et apud nos veritatis argumentum est aliquid omnibus videri; tanquam deos esse inter alia hoc colligimus, quod omnibus insita de dis opinio est...neminem invenies, qui non putet et sapientiam bonum et sapere bonum' Sen. *Ep.* 117, 6.

[91] 'opinionum commenta delet dies, naturae iudicia confirmat' Cic. *N. D.* ii 2, 5.

[92] Diog. L. vii 177.

that the very essence of virtue lay in the choice of natural ends upon probable grounds[93], was felt to be giving way to Carneades[94]. Panaetius justified the maintaining of that which is plausible by the advocate, and Cicero, whose own conscience was not at ease in the matter, was glad enough to quote so respectable an authority on his own behalf[95]. In the Roman imperial period a growing spirit of humility and pessimism led to a general disparagement of human knowledge, centring in attacks on the trustworthiness of the senses. So Seneca speaks of the 'usual weakness' of the sense of sight[96], and Marcus Aurelius feels that 'the organs of sense are dim and easily imposed upon[97].' The older Stoics had admitted the frequent errors of the senses[98], but they had been confident they could surmount this difficulty. Their latest disciples had lost the courage to do this, and in consequence the practice of 'suspension of judgment,' which before had been the exception[99], became with them the rule. Nevertheless Epictetus, who alone amongst these later Stoics was an ardent student of dialectics, held fast to the main principle that certainty is attainable. 'How indeed' he said 'perception is effected, whether through the whole body or any part, perhaps I cannot explain, for both opinions perplex me. But that you and I are not the same, I know with perfect certainty[100].'

160. Having now dealt with the theory of knowledge, we may consider briefly the subordinate sciences (or rather 'arts') of Grammar, Logic (in the narrower sense), and Style. Here we may leave the technical divisions and sub-divisions of the Stoics; for these matters are substantially independent of the main lines upon which the ancient

Grammar.

---

[93] οὐσίαν τἀγαθοῦ τίθενται τὴν εὐλόγιστον ἐκλογὴν τῶν κατὰ φύσιν Plut. *comm. not.* 27, 9.

[94] ἐκεῖνον [τὸν Ἀντίπατρον] ὑπὸ Καρνεάδου πιεζόμενον, εἰς ταύτας καταδύεσθαι τὰς εὑρεσιλογίας *ib.* 27, 15.

[95] 'iudicis est semper in causis verum sequi; patroni nonnunquam verisimile, etiam si minus sit verum, defendere ; quod scribere...non auderem, nisi idem placeret gravissimo Stoicorum Panaetio' Cic. *Off.* ii 14, 51.

[96] 'visus noster solita imbecillitate deceptus' Sen. *N. Q.* i 2, 3.

[97] *To himself*, v 33.   [98] See above, §§ 146, 147.

[99] 'sapientem aliquando sustinere adsensionem' Cic. *Ac.* ii 17, 53.

[100] Epict. *Disc.* i 27, 17.

philosophies parted company, and have for us only a secondary
and historical interest. The Stoics distinguish five parts of
speech: 'name' (ὄνομα, *nomen*), as 'Diogenes'; 'class-name'
(προσηγορία, *appellatio*), as 'man, horse'[101]; 'verb' (ῥῆμα, *verbum*);
'conjunction' (σύνδεσμος, *coniunctio*); and 'article' (ἄρθρον, *ar-
ticulus*). The last they define naïvely as a little word which is
all ending, and serves to distinguish the cases and numbers[102].
To the list of the parts of speech Antipater added the 'mixed
part' or participle (μεσότης). The noun has four cases (πτώσεις),
the 'upright case' (πτῶσις εὐθεῖα, *casus rectus*; this is of course
a contradiction in terms); and the 'oblique' cases (πλάγιαι),
that is the 'class' case (γενική), the 'dative' (δοτική), and the
'effect' case (αἰτιατική). The ῥῆμα or verb is identical with
the κατηγόρημα or 'predicate,' and may take the 'active' form
(ὀρθά), the 'passive' (ὕπτια), or the 'neuter' (οὐδέτερα); some
verbs also express action and reaction, and are called 'reflexive'
(ἀντιπεπονθότα). The Stoics also distinguished the tenses.
Time (χρόνος) being of three kinds, past (παρῳχημένος), present (ἐνεστώς), and future (μέλλων), we have the following tenses
which are 'definite' (ὡρισμένοι): the 'present imperfect' (ἐνεστὼς
ἀτελής), the 'past imperfect' (παρῳχημένος ἀτελής), the 'present
perfect' (ἐνεστὼς τέλειος), and the 'past perfect' (παρῳχημένος
τέλειος); in addition to these we have the 'indefinite' tenses, the
future (μέλλων), and the past indefinite, called simply indefinite
(ἀόριστος)[103].

161. So far we find in the Stoic system the general framework of the grammar of the period, much of it
adapted with modifications from Aristotle. In
some other details points of real grammatical or philosophical
interest are raised. Such is the controversy between 'anomaly,'
the recognition of the individuality of each word in its flexion,
and 'analogy,' in which the validity of the rules of declension
and conjugation is insisted upon. Two Stoic masters, Chrysippus

Theories of speech.

[101] The distinction between 'name' and 'class-name' was due to Chrysippus:
see Sandys, *Classical Scholarship*, i p. 144.
[102] Diog. L. vii 58.
[103] For these and further particulars see Sandys, *Classical Scholarship*, i ch. ix;
R. Schmidt, *Stoicorum Grammatica*, pp. 18 sqq.

A.   10

and Crates of Mallos, took up the cause of 'anomaly[104].' Further
the Stoics held that all correct language exists by nature (φύσει),
and not by convention (θέσει), as Aristotle had maintained;
the elements of language being imitations of natural sounds[105].
Further, they held that the natural relation between 'things'
(σημαινόμενα, *significata*) and the words that express them
(σημαίνοντα, *significantia*) can frequently be determined by
etymology; for instance φωνή 'voice' is φῶς νοῦ 'the mind's
lamp,' αἰών 'age' is ἀεὶ ὄν 'enduring for ever[106].' Like Heraclitus and Aristotle, the Stoics distinguished between 'thought'
(λόγος ἐνδιάθετος, *ratio*) and 'speech' (λόγος προφορικός, *oratio*),
which the Greek word λόγος tends to confuse[107]; thought is im-
material, but speech, as consisting of air in motion, is body[108].
Young children and animals do not possess real speech, but only
'a sort of speech[109].'

162. Words in combination form statements, questions,
wishes, syllogisms, and so forth[110]; there is therefore no clear line drawn between what we call
syntax and logic respectively. Whenever we have
a complete combination of words expressing that which must
either be false or true, as 'Hannibal was a Carthaginian,' 'Scipio
destroyed Numantia,' we call it a 'statement' or 'proposition'
(ἀξίωμα)[111]; for phrases of all kinds we have the more general
term 'phrase' (λεκτόν, *id quod dicitur*)[112]. Of special interest is

Propositions and Syllo-gisms.

---

[104] 'Crates, nobilis grammaticus, fretus Chrysippo, homine acutissimo, qui reliquit
περὶ ἀνωμαλίας III libros, contra analogiam atque Aristarchum est nixus' Varro *L. L.*
ix I (Arnim ii 151).

[105] Orig. *cont. Celsum* i 24 (Arnim ii 146).

[106] Varr. *L. L.* vi II (Arnim ii 163).

[107] See Zeller, *Stoics* etc., p. 73, n. 2; Aristotle's distinction is between τὸν ἐν
τῇ ψυχῇ λόγον and τὸν ἔξω λόγον.

[108] 'vocem Stoici corpus esse contendunt eamque esse dicunt ictum aera'
A. Gellius, *N. A.* v 15, 6.

[109] 'hunc [qui primo dicitur iam fari] Chrysippus negat loqui, sed ut loqui;...
sic in corvis, cornicibus, pueris primitus incipientibus fari, verba non esse verba'
Varro *L. L.* vi 56 (Arnim ii 143).

[110] Diog. L. vii 63 to 78.

[111] Varro translates this by 'proloquium' (Gell. *N. A.* xvi 8, 8), Cicero pro-
visionally by 'pronuntiatum' (*Tusc. disp.* i 7, 14).

[112] A statement or proposition is therefore a phrase 'complete in itself' (λεκτὸν
αὐτοτελές) A. Gellius *N. A.* xvi 8, 4.

the conditional sentence (συνημμένον), which has two parts, the conditional clause (ἡγούμενον) and the contingent clause (λῆγον). The conditional or leading clause always contains a sign (σημεῖον), by means of which we reach proof: thus in saying 'if it is day, it is light' we mean that 'day' is a sign of light. Proof is 'speech on every subject gathering what is less clear from that which is more clear[113].' Its most important form is the syllogism, of which Chrysippus recognises five forms:

   (i) if A, then B; but A, therefore B.

   (ii) if A, then B; but not B, therefore not A.

   (iii) not A and B together; but A, therefore not B.

   (iv) either A or B; but A, therefore not B.

   (v) either A or B; but not A, therefore B[114].

All these matters admit of endless qualifications, subdivisions, and developments, and were therefore serviceable to those Stoics who were before all things makers of books[115]. Examples of Stoic syllogisms have been given above[116].

163. Closely connected with the theory of the syllogism is the enticing subject of the 'resolution of fallacies' (σοφισμάτων λύσις), which the Megarians had brought within the range of philosophy. To this subject the Stoics gave much attention[117]. The most famous fallacy is that of the 'heap' (σωρίτης, *acervus*); 'if two are few, so are three; if three, then four; and so forth.' In this Chrysippus took a special interest[118]; his reply was to keep still[119]. Another is the 'liar' (ψευδόμενος, *mentiens*); 'when a man says "I lie," does he lie or not? if he lies, he speaks the truth; if he speaks the truth, he lies[120].' On this subject Chrysippus wrote a treatise, which

Fallacies.

---

[113] Diog. L. vii 45. [114] *ib.* 80 and 81.

[115] 'ex iis modis conclusiones innumerabiles nascuntur' Cic. *Top.* 14, 57.

[116] § 83.

[117] Ἔλυε δὲ [Ζήνων] σοφίσματα, καὶ τὴν διαλεκτικήν, ὡς τοῦτο ποιεῖν δυναμένην, ἐκέλευε παραλαμβάνειν τοὺς μαθητάς Plut. *Sto. rep.* 8, 2.

[118] 'inventus, Chrysippe, tui finitor acervi' Pers. *Sat.* vi 80.

[119] 'placet enim Chrysippo, cum gradatim interrogetur, tria pauca sint anne multa, aliquanto prius quam ad multa perveniat, quiescere' Cic. *Ac.* ii 29, 93. Cf. Sext. *math.* vii 416.

[120] 'si te mentiri dicis idque verum dicis, mentiris an verum dicis?' Cic. *Ac.* ii 29, 95.

Epictetus thought not worth reading[121]. Seneca gives us examples of other fallacies, which also are verbal quibbles[122]. Of an
altogether different kind are those problems in which the question
of determinism as opposed to moral choice is involved. Such is
the 'reaper,' which maintains 'either you will reap or you will
not reap; it is not correct to say "perhaps you will reap."'
Such again is the 'master-argument' of Diodorus the Megarian,
directly aimed against every moral philosophy[123]. These difficulties we shall discuss later as touching the supreme problems
which are presented to the human reason[124].

164. The scientific study of syllogisms and fallacies promises
at first sight to be a guide to truth and a way of
Definition.
escape from error, but experience shews it nevertheless to be barren. It has however an advantage in securing
a careful statement of teaching, and for this purpose was much
used by Zeno and Chrysippus. The later members of the school
realized that this advantage could be more simply gained by
the practice of careful definition (ὅρος, *definitio*). Antipater thus
defined definition itself: 'definition is an expression which ela-
borates in detail without falling short or going too far[125].' He
and all other Stoics of his time gave numerous definitions of the
most important terms used in the system, such as God, fate, providence, the supreme good, virtue, and so forth; and these are of
great value in giving precision to their doctrine.

165. In considering Style we first notice the distinction
between dialectic in the narrower sense, in which
Style.
statements are made in the shortest and most pre-
cise form, and rhetoric, in which they are expanded at length[126].
Zeno compared one to the closed fist, the other to the open
palm[127]. Both Cleanthes and Chrysippus wrote upon rhetoric,

---

[121] Epict. *Disc.* ii 17, 34.

[122] 'mus syllaba est. mus autem caseum rodit: syllaba ergo caseum rodit...o
pueriles ineptias!' Sen. *Ep.* 48, 6 and 7; 'quod non perdidisti, habes; cornua autem
non perdidisti; cornua ergo habes' *ib.* 49, 8.

[123] Epict. *Disc.* ii 19, 1 sqq.   [124] See below, §§ 220, 221.

[125] Diog. L. vii 60.

[126] 'omnis oratio aut continua est aut inter respondentem et interrogantem discissa;
hanc διαλεκτικήν, illam ῥητορικήν placuit vocari' Sen. *Ep.* 89, 17.

[127] Cic. *Orator* 32, 113.

and it appears to have become a tradition to ridicule their teaching, chiefly on the ground of the novel terms which the Stoics introduced, as προηγμένα, κοσμόπολις[128]. But it is exactly in these new-fangled words that we observe one of the chief aims of the Stoic theory of style, namely the use of words which precisely and exclusively correspond to the objects described (κυριολογία, *proprietas verborum*), and which therefore lead up to transparent clearness of speech (σαφήνεια, *pellucida oratio*)[129]. To this clearness the study of grammar is contributory; 'barbarisms' (faults in spelling and pronunciation) must be avoided, with proper help from the doctrines of 'anomaly' and 'analogy'; for the Stoics learnt in time that neither of these is exclusively true. Equally important is the avoidance of 'solecisms,' or faults in syntax. In this way a pure use of language (Ἑλληνισμός, *Latinitas*) is attained; this is largely based upon the example of older writers, such as Homer in Greek, and Cato the elder in Latin[130], but not to such an extent as to employ words not commonly intelligible. But little more is needed; the Stoic will say what he has to say with 'brevity' (συντομία, *brevitas*); the graces of style will be represented by 'becomingness' (πρέπον, *decorum*) and 'neatness' (κατασκευή), the latter including euphony. These virtues of speech are sufficient for speaking well, which is neither more nor less than speaking truthfully[131]; for the Stoic needs only to instruct his hearer, and will not lower himself either to amuse him or to excite his emotions[132]. Style has three varieties, according as it is employed in the council, in the law-courts, or in praise of goodness and good men[133]; in the last there was no

[128] 'scripsit artem rhetoricam Cleanthes. Chrysippus etiam; sed sic, ut si quis obmutescere cupierit, nihil aliud legere debeat. itaque vides quo modo loquantur; nova verba fingunt, deserunt usitata' Cic. *Fin.* iv 3, 7.

[129] Diog. L. vii 59.

[130] 'uni M. Porcio me dedicavi atque despondi atque delegavi' Front. et Aur. *Ep.* ii 13.

[131] οἱ Στωϊκοὶ δὲ τὸ εὖ λέγειν ἔλεγον τὸ ἀληθῆ λέγειν Anon. *ad Herm. Rhet. Gr.* vii 8. Hence speech was a virtue; '[Stoicis] hanc habeo gratiam, quod soli ex omnibus eloquentiam virtutem ac sapientiam esse dixerunt' Cic. *de Or.* iii 18, 65.

[132] 'fuerunt et clari quidam auctores, quibus solum videretur oratoris officium docere; namque et effectus duplici ratione excludendos putabant, primum quia vitium esset omnis animi perturbatio, deinde quia iudicem a veritate pelli misericordia gratia similibusque non oporteret, et voluptatem audientium petere...vix etiam viro dignum arbitrabantur' Quint. *Inst. or.* v Prooem.   [133] Diog. L. vii 42.

doubt greater room allowed for that expansiveness of speech which the Stoics specially designated as 'rhetoric.'

166. The 'Stoic style' was a severe intellectual and moral The Stoic discipline. The speaker was called upon under all orator. circumstances to speak the truth, the whole truth, and nothing but the truth. He could hold back nothing from his audience, even though his words might be offensive to their religious opinions, their patriotic feelings, or their sense of decency; he could add no word which would touch their sympathies or kindle their indignation in the direction he himself might wish. He had always before his eyes the example of Socrates' defence before the Athenian jury and its result. The Stoic appeared before his audience as a brave, sane, and rather rugged speaker, painfully ill-equipped in all those arts which the circumstances demanded[134]. Even the Stoics of the transition period, in spite of their Academic leanings and their literary acquirements, made this impression at Rome. Diogenes, who had himself done much to elaborate the theory of style, was noted as a quiet and self-restrained speaker[135]. The influence of Panaetius may be traced in his friend Lucilius, who in his book on style is never tired of ridiculing the artifices of rhetoricians. Then followed a succession of these reserved speakers, which we shall trace in another chapter, leading up to Cato of Utica, by far the best-known and the most ridiculed of them all[136].

It is not easy to form a fair judgment of the merits of the Stoic style. It must be admitted that the works of Chrysippus are not readable; but on the other hand Antipater, Panaetius, Posidonius, Musonius Rufus, and Epictetus were all writers or speakers of great attractiveness[137].

167. In connexion with style we may call attention to the Paradox. important function of paradoxes ($\pi\alpha\rho\acute{\alpha}\delta o\xi\alpha$, *inopinata*), that is, propositions contrary to common

---

[134] 'orationis genus habent [Stoici] fortasse subtile et certe acutum; sed, ut in oratore, exile, inusitatum, abhorrens ab auribus vulgi, obscurum, inane, ieiunum, attamen eiusmodi quo uti ad vulgus nullo modo possit' Cic. *de Or.* iii 18, 66.

[135] 'dicebat modesta Diogenes et sobria' A. Gellius, *N. A.* vi 14, 10.

[136] See below, chap. xvi.   [137] See Smiley, *Latinitas* and Ἑλληνισμός.

opinion. Since all philosophies conflict with common opinion, they must necessarily include many paradoxes[138]. The chief Stoic paradoxes are those which were borrowed directly from the Cynic school, and indirectly from the teaching of Socrates[139]: and Cicero devotes a special work to their defence. He includes the following: (i) that only what is honourable is good; (ii) that virtue is sufficient for happiness; (iii) that right actions and offences are equal; (iv) that all foolish men are mad; (v) that the wise man alone is free and every foolish man a slave; (vi) that the wise man alone is rich. These of course include the very pith and marrow of Stoic ethics; and the form is calculated to arrest the attention of the crowd and to challenge defiantly its cherished opinions. The Stoics of literary taste and social position usually shew some distaste for paradoxes, and prefer to state their teaching in ways more obviously reasonable. But it should hardly be necessary to explain that no paradox is complete in itself, but each needs to be interpreted according to the principles of the school which propounds it. In proportion as the doctrines of any school win general recognition, its paradoxes tend to find ready acceptance, and may ultimately become truisms[140].

The treatment of myths as allegories[141] may also be considered as the use of a kind of paradox; this we shall find it most convenient to discuss in connexion with Stoic views upon the nature of the gods.

168. The study of logic is at first sight dismal and repulsive; when progress has been made in it, it seems illuminating; in the end it becomes so alluring, that the would-be philosopher may easily be lost for ever in its mazes[142]. The early Stoics had pressed this discipline upon

Dangers of logic.

---

[138] 'Philosophers utter words which are contrary to common opinion, as Cleanthes also said, but not words contrary to reason' Epict. *Disc.* iv 1, 173; 'where is the wonder if in philosophy many things which are true appear paradoxical to the inexperienced?' *ib.* i 25, 33.

[139] 'ista παράδοξα quae appellant, maxime videntur esse Socratica' Cic. *Parad.* Prooem. 4.

[140] 'nihil est tam incredibile, quod non dicendo fiat probabile' Cic. *Parad.* Prooem. 3; 'Stoica paradoxa, quorum nullum esse falsum nec tam mirabile quam prima facie videtur, adprobabo' Sen. *Ep.* 87, 1.

[141] Zeller, *Stoics* etc., pp. 354-370.

[142] A. Gellius, *N. A.* xvi 8, 16 and 17.

their pupils; those of the Roman period, themselves (with the exception of Epictetus) weak dialecticians, never cease to warn their hearers against its fascinations. So Seneca tells us that many logical inquiries have nothing to do with real life[143]; and that the older Stoics had wasted much time over them[144]; Epictetus complains that his hearers never get beyond the resolving of syllogisms[145], and M. Aurelius thanks the gods that he never wasted his time in this way[146].

169. It was a favourite contention of Cicero, adopted from Stoic and Academic logic. his teacher Antiochus, that the Stoic dialectic was no original system, but only a modification of the views of the old Academy[147]. Such a conclusion seems partly due to the fact that the Stoics of his own time had largely borrowed from the Academic system in detail; and partly to the overlooking by Antiochus of an essential difference of spirit between the two schools. Plato is speculative, Zeno positive; Plato plays with a dozen theories, Zeno consistently adheres to one. Plato ranks the mind high, Zeno the will; Plato bases his system on the general concept, Zeno on the individual person or object. It would seem that no contrast could be more complete. Nor does Zeno's theory agree with that of Epicurus. Both indeed are positive teachers, and hold that the senses are messengers of truth. But here Epicurus stops, whilst Zeno goes on. We have to understand rightly the functions and limitations of the senses, or we shall quickly glide into error; we have also to learn that the senses are but servants, and that the mind rules them as a monarch by divine right, coordinating the messages

[143] 'quaedam exercendi tantum ingenii causa quaeruntur, et semper extra vitam iacent' Sen. *Ben.* vi 1, 1.

[144] 'multum illis temporis verborum cavillatio eripuit et captiosae disputationes, quae acumen inritum exercent' *Ep.* 45, 5.

[145] 'We terminate in this, in learning what is said, and in being able to expound it to another, in resolving a syllogism, and in handling the hypothetical syllogism' Epict. *Disc.* iv 4, 14.

[146] 'Thanks [to the gods] too that, in spite of my ardour for philosophy, I did not fall into the hands of any sophist, or sit poring over essays or syllogisms, or become engrossed in scientific speculation' M. Aurelius *To himself* i 17.

[147] 'verum esse arbitror, ut Antiocho nostro familiari placebat, correctionem veteris Academiae potius quam aliquam novam disciplinam putandam [Stoicorum rationem]' Cic. *Ac.* i 12, 43.

they bring, shaping them according to its own creative capacity, even adding to them from the material it has derived from its source. The Stoic theory is in fact a bold survey of the results of the reflection of the human mind upon its own operations; it has, as we might expect, many gaps, a good deal of over-lapping description, and some inconsistencies. To sceptical objections it is of course unable to give answers which are logically satisfactory; but its general position proved accept-able to men who sought in philosophy a guide to practical life.

170. In the approximation between Stoicism and the Academy which characterizes the first century B.C., the Stoic logic obtained in the end the upper hand; and the logic of the so-called 'old Academy' founded by Antiochus is in all essentials that of the Stoics. Nevertheless the objections urged against it by Cicero represent not only his reason but also his sentiments. The positive system appears at its best in the education of children; and even at the present day the theory of knowledge which is tacitly adopted in schools is substantially that of the Stoics. It leads to careful observa-tion, earnest inquiry, and resolute choice; and thus lays the foundation of solidity of character. But it must be admitted that it also works in the direction of a certain roughness and harshness of disposition. Not only is the Stoically-minded man lacking in sympathy for beliefs different from his own, which he is bound to regard as both foolish and wicked; but he is also blind to that whole side of the universe which cannot be reduced to syllogistic shape. Thus we may account for the indifference or hostility with which most Stoics regarded both literature and art[148]. The Academic, on the other hand, even if he lacked moral firmness and saw too clearly both sides of every question, was saved by his critical powers from extreme

Questions of temperament.

[148] 'tunc intellegere nobis licebit, quam contemnenda miremur, simillimi pueris, quibus omne ludicrum in pretio est. quid ergo inter nos et illos interest, ut Ariston ait, nisi quod nos circa tabulas et statuas insanimus, carius inepti? illos reperti in litore calculi leves delectant, nos ingentium maculae columnarum' Sen. *Ep.* 115, 8. This tone is clearly derived from Cynism, as the reference to Aristo indicates. A modern Cynic is still more sweeping in his condemnation : 'all the nastiness and stupidity which you call science and art' (Count Leo Tolstoy in the *Westminster Gazette*, Sept. 3, 1910).

assertions and harsh personal judgments, and had a delicate appreciation of the finer shadings of life. Thus behind the formal differences of the two schools there lies a difference of character. We have long since learnt that the fundamental questions between the two schools are incapable of solution by the human mind, and we can therefore appreciate the one without condemning the other. In practical life each theory has its appropriate sphere; but the Romans were hardly in the wrong when in matters of doubt they leaned towards the Stoic side.

CHAPTER VII.

THE FOUNDATIONS OF PHYSICS.

171. UNDER the general heading of Physics the ancients
included a number of subjects which in modern
Physics. times form independent branches of philosophy.
Cleanthes subdivided the subject into Physics proper and
Theology[1]. Here it will be convenient to make a larger
number of subdivisions, so as to treat separately of (i) the
Foundations of Physics, generally called (after Aristotle's
treatise) 'Metaphysics'; (ii) Physics proper, that is, the account
of the Universe and its history; (iii) the final problems involved
in the history of the Universe, such as its government by Divine
Providence, the Existence of Evil, Free-will, and Chance;
(iv) the problems of Religion, such as the existence of gods,
their number, character, and claims on mankind; and (v) the
nature of Man, including the modern subjects of Psychology
and Physiology, and to some extent of Anthropology also,
treated by the Stoics as a Kingdom governed by the Soul.
According to Stoic principles these subjects cannot be separated
one from the other, or from the other parts of philosophy; and
therefore in treating each one we shall, as before, assume a
general knowledge of all the others. The Stoics laid great
stress upon the study of Physics, as the only sound basis for
a scientific rule of human conduct; and some of them (beginning
with Chrysippus), having especial regard to the elevated dignity
of the study of Theology, were disposed to rank this branch of
philosophy as the highest and last of its three principal divisions[2].
We shall however, in accordance with a view more generally
held, reserve the last place for Ethics[3].

[1] Diog. L. vii 41.   [2] Arnim ii 42 and 44.   [3] Diog. L. vii 40.

172. To the earlier Greek philosophers, as we have already
Fundamental seen, it appeared that a single bold intuition was
Conceptions. enough, or almost enough, to discover a sufficient
foundation upon which to construct a reasoned account of all
things. Thus the Ionic philosophers took up as such a foundation one or more of the elements of air, fire, and water. But
as soon as these three, together with earth, were recognized as
'elements' existing side by side, it became necessary to dig
deeper, so as to secure a foundation for these as well. Thus
Democritus resolved all four into 'atoms' and 'void'; his theory
was taken over by Epicurus, and remains to this day not only
the most popular solution of the problem, but also that which
(till quite recently) was tacitly assumed as the basis of all
scientific investigation. Anaxagoras, working on different lines,
began his account of the universe with 'mind' on the one hand
and a primal conglomerate 'matter' on the other; a doctrine
evidently based upon the popular dualism of soul and body,
and still the basis of all transcendental philosophy and established
religious conceptions. This Aristotle varied by assuming rather
an 'active' and a 'passive' principle, force which works and
matter upon which it works. Besides these conceptions many
others need to be considered, which if not absolutely fundamental, are nevertheless matters of discussion in all philosophical
schools, as those of motion, space, time, soul, body, God, the
universe, cause, effect, will and necessity. In this way the
original inquiry into the foundation of the universe developes
into a general study of fundamental conceptions; and it is at
this stage that it is taken over and dealt with by Stoicism,
which adds to the list certain conceptions on which it lays
a special stress and to which it gives a characteristic colour;
such are those of 'body,' 'spirit,' and 'tone.'

173. The fact that the Stoics use from time to time the
The Stoic language of other schools or of popular speculation
monism. does not necessarily imply that this language is
an adequate statement of their doctrine; and we frequently[4]
find that the discussion of particular problems seems to be

[4] Perhaps necessarily: on the definition of monism, see above, § 35, note 22.

based on dualisms, though these are in the end subordinated to monistic statements. Thus in logic we have already noticed the sharp contrast between the perceiving mind and the external object of perception (αἰσθητόν, ὑπάρχον); nevertheless mind and object are ultimately declared to be akin[5]. So in particular the popular dualism of 'soul' and 'body' is often accepted by the Stoics, and yet as steadily superseded by the paradox that 'soul is body.' The reason given for this is that 'body is that which acts and is acted upon[6]'; and this statement in the end overrides the Aristotelian distinction of force and matter, active principle and passive principle. 'Body,' as conceived by the Stoics, is the one ultimate element, the foundation and beginning of the universe; it contains within itself the capacity of action, and nothing but 'body' has this capacity. Body, and nothing but body, exists in the true sense; that certain other things have a quasi-existence (as we shall see later in this chapter) is an embarrassment which only brings into clearer relief this distinctive feature of the system. The Stoic 'body,' though it is also called 'matter' (ὕλη, materia), must not be confused with the 'matter' of modern philosophy, which has derived from Aristotle the implication of passivity[7]; much more closely it corresponds with the 'stuff' by which modern monistic philosophers denote the substratum of mind and body alike. To call the Stoics 'materialists' will generally prove misleading; it is the Epicurean system, to which the Stoics were sharply opposed, which (as we have seen)[8] corresponds to modern materialism.

174. The conception of 'body' therefore replaces in the Stoic system the various elements which the Ionic philosophers assumed as the basis of the universe, and combines both parts of such dualistic elements as were assumed by Democritus, Anaxagoras and Aristotle. Since it is the foundation of all things it must be capable of taking very various shapes. In logic we have met with it under the name

The nature of 'body.'

---

[5] See above, §§ 149, 153.

[6] '[Zeno] nullo modo arbitrabatur quicquam effici posse ab ea [natura], quae expers esset corporis...nec vero aut quod efficeret aliquid aut quod efficeretur, posse esse non corpus' Cic. Ac. i 11, 39; 'cui tanta vis est, ut impellat et cogat et retineat et iubeat, corpus est' Sen. Ep. 106, 9.

[7] See above, § 67.   [8] § 43.

of the 'substratum' (τὸ ὑπάρχον, *id quod est*)[9], but it none the less includes the 'subject' or feeling and reasoning mind. In the universe as a whole it is 'essence' (οὐσία, *essentia*); in its parts it is 'matter' (ὕλη, *silva*)[10]; but it also appears, possessed of intelligence, as the deity[11], and again is identified with 'breath' or 'spirit[12],' and through this with the human soul[13]. Even in ethics it has its place; for all causes are bodily, and not least 'the good' and the respective virtues, all of which are bodies, for they act upon body[14]; similarly the emotions such as anger and melancholy, are of the nature of body[15].

175. The Stoic 'body' in all its transformations is active and alert. It contains in itself the principle or power of movement; for though we observe that one body is set in motion by another, yet this could not be the case unless in the beginning there had been a body which had movement of itself[16]. As to the nature of the primal movement, the Stoics agree with Anaximenes that it may be described as alternate rarefaction and condensation. Rarefaction is a wave or 'spirit' spreading from the centre to the extremities; condensation is a contrary movement from the extremities to the centre[17]. The extension of body is 'space,' which therefore does

Motion, space and time.

---

[9] See above, § 157, note 84.

[10] ταὐτὸν σῶμα καὶ οὐσίαν ὁριζόμενοι Clem. Alex. *Strom.* ii p. 436 (Arnim ii 359); διδόασι δὲ καὶ σῶμα αὐτῇ [τῇ ὕλῃ] Plot. *Enn.* ii 4, 1 (Arnim ii 320). οὐσία in this sense is also called πρώτη ὕλη, see § 182, note 52.

[11] τὸν θεὸν...σῶμα νοερὸν...ποιοῦντες Plut. *comm. not.* 48, 2.

[12] 'vides autem tanto spiritum esse faciliorem omni alia materia, quanto tenuior est' Sen. *Ep.* 50, 6.

[13] 'et hoc [animus] corpus est' *ib.* 106, 4.

[14] οἱ Στωϊκοὶ πάντα τὰ αἴτια σωματικά· πνεύματα γάρ Aët. *plac.* i 11, 5; 'placet nostris quod bonum est, corpus esse' Sen. *Ep.* 117, 2; 'quaeris, bonum an corpus sit. bonum facit, prodest enim. quod facit, corpus est' *ib.* 106, 4.

[15] 'non puto te dubitaturum, an adfectus corpora sint, tanquam ira, amor, tristitia. si dubitas, vide an voltum nobis mutent, an frontem adstringant, an faciem diffundant, an ruborem evocent, an fugent sanguinem. quid ergo? tam manifestas notas corpori credis imprimi nisi a corpore?' *ib.* 106, 5.

[16] 'dicimus non posse quicquam ab alio moveri, nisi aliquid fuerit mobile ex semet' Sen. *N. Q.* ii 8; 'is ardor, qui est mundi, non agitatus ab alio, neque externo pulsu, sed per se ipse ac sua sponte [movetur]' Cic. *N. D.* ii 11, 31.

[17] οἱ δὲ Στωϊκοὶ...κίνησιν τὴν μανωτικὴν καὶ πυκνωτικὴν τίθενται, τὴν μὲν (sc. πυκνω-τικὴν) ἐπὶ τὰ ἔσω, τὴν δὲ ἐπὶ τὰ ἔξω Simpl. *Arist. cat.* p. 74; 'tenorem, qui rarescente materia a medio tendat ad summum, eadem concrescente rursus a summo referatur ad medium' Censorinus *de die nat.* p. 75 (Zeller, p. 128).

not exist of itself, but only as a function of body[18]. Where there is no body (and body is limited), there is no space, but only the 'boundless void' beyond the universe[19]; of this we cannot say that it 'exists'; rather it 'not exists.' Time also does not exist of itself, but only in the movement of body[20]. Neither space nor time existed before the universe, but have been all along bound up with it[21].

176. In almost every particular we find a sharp contrast between the Stoic conception of 'body' and the Epicurean 'atom.' The atom is extremely small and entirely unchangeable; 'body' is immensely large and in a high degree plastic. Atoms alternate with void; but 'body' spreads continuously throughout the entire universe; it can never be torn apart or show a gap[22]. Atoms move downwards in parallel straight lines; 'body' moves from the centre to the circumference, and thence returns to the centre. Two atoms can never occupy the same space; but 'body' everywhere moves through body, penetrating it and combining with it throughout its whole extent[23]. The atom is a convenient hypothesis within the range of modern physical and chemical science; the conception of 'body' gains force as we enter the region of biology. For life also is a movement which proceeds from a warm centre (and warmth is body rarefied), and extends towards a circum-

Body comprises life and thought.

---

[18] τόπον δ' εἶναι ὁ Χρύσιππος ἀπεφαίνετο τὸ κατεχόμενον δι' ὅλου ὑπὸ ὄντος Ar. Did. fr. 25 Diels (Arnim ii 503).

[19] κενὸν μὲν εἶναι φασι τὸ οἶόν τε ὑπὸ ὄντος κατέχεσθαι, μὴ κατεχόμενον δὲ Sext. math. x. 3 (Arnim ii 505); τὸ μὲν οὖν κενὸν ἄπειρον εἶναι λέγεσθαι· τὸ γὰρ ἐκτὸς τοῦ κόσμου τοιοῦτ' εἶναι, τὸν δὲ τόπον πεπερασμένον διὰ τὸ μηδὲν σῶμα ἄπειρον εἶναι Ar. Did. (as note 18).

[20] Χρύσιππος διάστημα [τὸν χρόνον εἶπε] τῆς τοῦ κόσμου κινήσεως Simpl. *Arist. cat.* p. 88 l (Arnim ii 510); οἱ πλείους τῶν Στωικῶν [χρόνου οὐσίαν] αὐτὴν τὴν κίνησιν Aët. *plac.* i 22, 7.

[21] χρόνος γὰρ οὐκ ἦν πρὸ κόσμου ἀλλ' ἢ σὺν αὐτῷ γέγονεν ἢ μετ' αὐτόν Philo *de mundi op.* § 26 (Arnim ii 511).

[22] The question is thus stated by Seneca: '[quaeramus] continua sit omnis et plena materia...an diducta, et solidis inane permixtum sit' Sen. *Dial.* viii 4, 2; and answered as follows 'nihil usquam inane est' *N. Q.* iii 16, 5. Cf. Arnim i 95 and ii 425.

[23] σώματα δὲ πάντα ὑπέθεντο καὶ σῶμα διὰ σώματος χωρεῖν Hipp. *Phil.* 21 (Arnim ii 469).

ference which is in comparison gross and cold[24]. Going further, we find that 'body' and its functions are so interpreted as to provide a key to the activities of the human reason and will.

177.   To the central conception of body are attached in the

Tone or tension.

Stoic system various supplementary conceptions, which serve to bring into clearer view its nature and powers.   Of these the most characteristic is that of 'tone' or 'strain' (τόνος, *intentio*).   This term appears originally to have expressed muscular activity[25], and was next used by the Cynics to denote that active condition of the soul which is the true end of life; 'no labour,' said Diogenes, 'is noble, unless its end is tone of soul[26].'   Although we cannot trace the term 'tone' directly to Zeno, we find that he explains sleep as a relaxation of the soul, substantially agreeing with later writers who call it a 'relaxation of the sensory tone around the soul[27].'   With Cleanthes the word becomes fairly common, first in the ethical application, in which 'tone' is 'a shock of fire, which if it be strong enough to stir the soul to fulfil its duties is called strength and force[28],' and then in physics to explain the unceasing activity of the universe[29], personified by Hercules in Stoic allegorical theology[30].   In later writers tone becomes constantly associated with the 'spirit' or 'thrill' which explains both the unity and the movement of all things[31], so that 'tone of spirit' or 'thrill-tone'

[24] 'animus ex inflammata anima constat, ut potissimum videri video Panaetio' Cic. *Tusc. disp.* i 18, 42.   The principle is however not carried out in the Stoic universe, in which the heat resides in the periphery, and the central earth is cold.

[25] νέων τι δρᾶν μὲν εὐτονώτεραι χέρες Eur. fr. 291 quoted by Corn. 31 (Arnim i 514); ὁμοίως ὥσπερ ἰσχὺς τοῦ σώματος τόνος ἐστὶν ἱκανὸς ἐν νευροῖς, οὕτω καὶ ἡ τῆς ψυχῆς ἰσχὺς τόνος ἐστί Stob. ii 7, 5 b 4.

[26] Epict. *Fr.* 57.

[27] See below, § 290.

[28] ὁ δὲ Κλεάνθης...εἰπὼν ὅτι πληγὴ πυρὸς ὁ τόνος ἐστί, κἂν ἱκανὸς ἐν τῇ ψυχῇ γένηται πρὸς τὸ ἐπιτελεῖν τὰ ἐπιβάλλοντα ἰσχὺς καλεῖται καὶ κράτος Plut. *Sto. rep.* 7, 4.

[29] Κλεάνθης δὲ οὕτω πώς φησι...τὸν ἐν τῇ τῶν ὅλων οὐσίᾳ τόνον μὴ παύεσθαι Stob. i 17, 3.

[30] Ἡρακλῆς δ' ἐστὶν ὁ ἐν τοῖς ὅλοις τόνος, καθ' ὃν ἡ φύσις ἰσχυρὰ καὶ κραταιά ἐστι Cornutus 31.

[31] 'quid autem est, quod magis credatur ex se ipso habere intentionem quam spiritus?' Sen. *N. Q.* ii 8.

($\pi\nu\epsilon\nu\mu\alpha\tau\iota\kappa\grave{o}\varsigma$ $\tau\acute{o}\nu o\varsigma$, *intentio spiritus*) explains to us the operations of body and mind alike[32].

178. Body however is not only active but creative; there is

The seed power.

inherent in it a power, which is that of the 'seed' ($\sigma\pi\acute{\epsilon}\rho\mu\alpha$, *semen*), and which is most conspicuously illustrated in the seed of animals and plants. It is the characteristic of seed that from a small beginning it developes a great plan, and that this plan never changes[33]. This plan or purpose is named by the Stoics its 'reason' or 'word' ($\lambda\acute{o}\gamma o\varsigma$), and at this point Stoicism incorporates the doctrine of the 'Word' or universal reason with which it became acquainted through Heraclitus. The 'Word' or 'seed-power' ($\lambda\acute{o}\gamma o\varsigma$ $\sigma\pi\epsilon\rho\mu\alpha\tau\iota\kappa\acute{o}\varsigma$) of the universe is one; it is the primal fire in its work of creation; it is Zeus the Creator who moulds gross matter into the things that are to be[34]; it is wisdom which plies matter as it will[35]. But there are also in individual objects, animate and inanimate, indestructible seed-powers, countless in number, displayed alike in growth, procreation, and purpose[36]; these seed-powers are, as it were, spirits or deities, spread throughout the universe, everywhere shaping, peopling, designing, multiplying; they are activities of fiery spirit working through tension[37] in its highest development. But the seed-power of the universe comprehends in itself all the individual seed-powers; they are begotten of it,

---

[32] 'quid est illi [animo] motus nisi intentio?' *ib.* ii 6, 6; 'quid cursus et motus omnis, nonne intenti spiritus operae sunt? hic facit vim nervis, velocitatem currentibus' *ib.* ii 6, 4.

[33] $\kappa\alpha\tau\alpha\beta\lambda\eta\theta\grave{\epsilon}\nu$ $\tau\grave{o}$ $\sigma\pi\acute{\epsilon}\rho\mu\alpha$ $\grave{\alpha}\nu\alpha\pi\lambda\eta\rho o\hat{\iota}$ $\tau o\grave{\nu}\varsigma$ $o\grave{\iota}\kappa\epsilon\acute{\iota}ov\varsigma$ $\lambda\acute{o}\gamma ov\varsigma$ $\kappa\alpha\grave{\iota}$ $\grave{\epsilon}\pi\iota\sigma\pi\hat{\alpha}\tau\alpha\iota$ $\tau\grave{\eta}\nu$ $\pi\alpha\rho\alpha\kappa\epsilon\iota$-$\mu\acute{\epsilon}\nu\eta\nu$ $\H{\upsilon}\lambda\eta\nu$ $\kappa\alpha\grave{\iota}$ $\delta\iota\alpha\mu o\rho\phi o\hat{\iota}$ Simpl. *Ar. cat.* O γ β.

[34] $o\H{\upsilon}\tau\omega$ $\kappa\alpha\grave{\iota}$ $\tauo\hat{\upsilon}\tau o\nu$ [$\tau\grave{o}\nu$ $\Delta\acute{\iota}\alpha$] $\sigma\pi\epsilon\rho\mu\alpha\tau\iota\kappa\grave{o}\nu$ $\lambda\acute{o}\gamma o\nu$ $\H{o}\nu\tau\alpha$ $\tauo\hat{\upsilon}$ $\kappa\acute{o}\sigma\mu ov$...$\epsilon\H{\upsilon}\epsilon\rho\gamma\grave{o}\nu$ $\alpha\grave{\upsilon}\tau\hat{\omega}$ $\pi o\iota o\hat{\upsilon}\nu\tau\alpha$ $\tau\grave{\eta}\nu$ $\H{\upsilon}\lambda\eta\nu$ $\pi\rho\grave{o}\varsigma$ $\tau\grave{\eta}\nu$ $\tau\hat{\omega}\nu$ $\grave{\epsilon}\xi\hat{\eta}\varsigma$ $\gamma\acute{\epsilon}\nu\epsilon\sigma\iota\nu$ Diog. L. vii 136; $\tau\grave{o}$ $\delta\grave{\epsilon}$ $\pi o\iota o\hat{\upsilon}\nu$ $\tau\grave{o}\nu$ $\grave{\epsilon}\nu$ $\alpha\grave{\upsilon}\tau\hat{\eta}$ $\lambda\acute{o}\gamma o\nu$ $\tau\grave{o}\nu$ $\theta\epsilon\acute{o}\nu$ *ib.* 134.

[35] 'ratio materiam format et quocunque vult versat' Sen. *Ep.* 65, 2. Cf. Tert. *Apol.* 21.

[36] $\grave{\alpha}\phi\theta\acute{\alpha}\rho\tau ov\varsigma$ [$\tau o\grave{\nu}\varsigma$ $\sigma\pi\epsilon\rho\mu\alpha\tau\iota\kappa o\grave{\nu}\varsigma$ $\lambda\acute{o}\gamma ov\varsigma$] $\grave{\epsilon}\pi o\acute{\iota}\eta\sigma\alpha\nu$, $\grave{\omega}\varsigma$ $o\grave{\iota}$ $\grave{\alpha}\pi\grave{o}$ $\tau\hat{\eta}\varsigma$ $\Sigma\tauo\hat{\alpha}\varsigma$ Proclus *in Parm.* iv 135. See further Stein, *Psychologie der Stoa*, i p. 49; Heinze, *Lehre vom Logos*, pp. 107–127.

[37] 'The original impulse of providence gave the origin and first momentum to the cosmic ordering of things, by selecting certain germs of future existences, and assigning to them productive capacities of realisation, change, and phenomenal succession.' M. Aurelius, *To himself* ix 1.

A.   11

and shall in the end return to it. Thus in the whole work of creation and re-absorption[38] we see the work of one Zeus, one divine Word, one all-pervading spirit[39].

179. Closely akin to the theory of 'seed-powers' and the

Cause.

Word is that of 'cause' (αἰτία, *causa*). Aristotle had already explained this term in connexion with cosmogony, laying down that, in order that a universe may come into being, three 'causes' are required; matter, without which nothing can be made; a workman, to make things; and the form or shape, which is imposed on every work as on a statue. To these may be added a fourth cause, the purpose of the work. Thus to produce a statue we need the bronze, the artist, the design, and the fee. Grammatically these causes may be expressed by the help of prepositions, as the *ex quo, a quo, in quo* and *propter quod*[40]. To this theory of multiple causes the Stoics oppose the doctrine of a single 'first cause,' the maker of the universe. This first cause can be none other than the primal creative fire in a new aspect; equally it is the creative Word.

It seems well to translate here in full the argument of Seneca on this point, for it stands almost alone as an example of his powers in continuous exposition :

The Stoic dogma is that there is one cause only, the maker. Aristotle holds that cause is threefold. 'The first cause,' he says, 'is the material itself, for without it nothing can be made. The second cause is the maker. The third is the design, which is impressed on every single work as on a statue ;' this Aristotle calls the εἶδος. I will now explain what he means.

The bronze is the first cause of a statue; for it could never have been made, had there not been stuff to be cast or wrought into shape. The second cause is the sculptor ; for the bronze could never have been brought into the shape of a statue without the artist's touch. The third cause is the

---

[38] 'ad initia deinde rerum redit [sapientia] aeternamque rationem [sc. τὸν λόγον] toti inditam, et vim omnium seminum [sc. τῶν σπερματικῶν λόγων] singula proprie figurantem' Sen. *Ep.* 90, 29. See also the interpretation of the picture of Samos, § 254, note 83.

[39] ὁ μὲν θεὸς πῦρ τεχνικὸν ὁδῷ βάδιζον ἐπὶ γενέσεις κόσμου ἐμπεριειληφὸς ἄπαντας τοὺς σπερματικοὺς λόγους, τὸ δὲ πνεῦμα αὐτοῦ διήκει δι' ὅλου τοῦ κόσμου Athen. *Supp.* 6, 7 B (Pearson Z. 45).

[40] See above, § 67.

design ; for the statue would not be called the 'javelin-man' or the 'crowned king' had not such a design been impressed upon it.

There is besides a fourth cause, the purpose. What is purpose? It is that which induced the sculptor to undertake the work, the aim that he had in view. It may have been money, if he intended to sell it; or glory, if he wished to make himself a name; or religious feeling, if he proposed to present it to a temple. That for the sake of which a thing is done is therefore also a cause ; for you cannot think it right in making up a list of causes to omit something, apart from which the thing would never have been made.

Thus Aristotle postulates a multiplicity of causes ; but we maintain that the list is either too long or too short.

If we hold that everything, apart from which the thing would never have been made, is a cause of its making, then the list is too short. We ought to reckon time as a cause, for nothing can be made without time. We ought to reckon space as a cause ; for if there is no room for a thing to be made, it will certainly not be made. Movement too should be placed in the list ; for without movement nothing can be produced or destroyed ; without movement there can be neither art nor change.

We Stoics look for a first and general cause. Such a cause must be single, for the stuff of the universe is single. We ask what that cause is, and reply that it is the creative reason, the deity. The various causes in the list that has been made are not a series of independent causes, but are all variations of a single cause, namely 'the maker[41].'

180. Although the 'first cause' and the 'Word' are thus

Causation and free-will.

formally identified, their associations in connexion with cosmogony are very different. For whereas the 'Word' suggests reason and purpose, and leads up to the dogma that the universe is governed by divine providence, the term 'cause' suggests the linking of cause and effect by an unending chain, the inevitable sequence of events which leaves no room for effort or hope. These terms therefore point to the supreme problems of Fate and divine Purpose, Determinism and Free-will, and as such will be discussed in a later chapter[42]. Here it is sufficient to note that the Stoics not only accept, but insist upon the use of terms suggesting both points of view, and look therefore beyond their immediate opposition to an ultimate reconciliation ; and that the importance attached to the doctrine of a 'single and general cause' by no means excludes a multiplicity of individual causes depending upon

[41] Sen. *Ep.* 65, 4 to 6, 11 and 12.
[42] See below, ch. ix.

it, and capable of classification according to their relative importance[43].

181. Thus the conception of 'body,' so simple to the plain
The cate-
gories. man, becomes to the philosopher manifold and
intricate. Its interpretation is to some extent
brought into harmony with common speech through the doctrine of the 'categories' based upon Aristotle's teaching[44]. But
whereas Aristotle endeavoured in his categories to classify the
various but independent classes of existences, the Stoics considered the different aspects in which the one primary body might
be studied. The first two categories, those of 'substance' ($\dot{v}\pi o$-
$\kappa \epsilon i\mu \epsilon \nu o\nu$) and of 'quality' ($\pi o\iota \acute{o}\nu$), agree with those of Aristotle[45],
and clearly correspond to the grammatical categories of noun
and adjective. The third category is that of 'disposition' ($\pi \grave{\omega}\varsigma$
$\check{\epsilon}\chi o\nu$), as 'lying down' or 'standing[46].' The fourth is that of
'relative position' ($\pi \rho \acute{o}\varsigma \tau \acute{\iota} \pi \omega\varsigma \check{\epsilon}\chi o\nu$), as 'right' and 'left,' 'son'
and 'father[47].' Some of the categories are further subdivided[48];
but enough is here stated to shew the object of the analysis,
which in practice may have been useful in securing some
completeness in the discussion of particular conceptions. Of
'substances' the Stoics, like others, say that they 'exist,' and
are 'bodies'; of qualities they boldly say the same[49]. But
they do not consistently apply the same terms to disposition
and relative position; in this direction they are at last led,
like other philosophers, to speak of things which 'do not exist.'
They could not take the modern view that all such discussions
are verbal entanglements, of which no solution is possible, because they believed that there was a natural harmony between
words and things. We on the other hand shall be little inclined
to follow their analysis into its manifold details[50].

[43] 'causarum enim,' inquit [Chrysippus], 'aliae sunt perfectae et principales, aliae
adiuvantes et proximae' Cic. *de Fato* 18, 41.

[44] See above, § 66.

[45] οἱ δέ γε Στωϊκοί...ποιοῦνται τὴν τομὴν εἰς τέσσαρα· εἰς ὑποκείμενα καὶ ποιὰ καὶ
πὼς ἔχοντα καὶ πρὸς τί πως ἔχοντα Simpl. *Arist. cat.* f 16 Δ (Arnim ii 369).

[46] Plotinus *Ennead.* vi¯1, 30 (Arnim ii 400).

[47] Simpl. *Arist. cat.* f 42 E (Arnim ii 403).

[48] For a fuller statement see Zeller, pp. 97–100.   [49] See § 183.

[50] For the position of 'things not existent' in the Stoic system see further below,
§ 187.

182. The analysis of the first two categories, those of
Substance and Quality, leads us at once to the
Substance. profoundest problems of Metaphysics; and even
if we allow that the difficulty is primarily grammatical, and
resolves itself into a discussion of the functions of Substantive
and Adjective, it is none the less inextricably interwoven with
all our habits of thought. It would be unreasonable to expect
from the Stoics perfectly clear and consistent language on this
point; they absorb into their system much from popular philosophy, and much from the teaching of Aristotle in particular.
The view which is distinctively Stoic is that Substance and
Quality are both body[51], but in two different aspects. The
terms 'body' and 'substance' refer to the same reality, but
do not describe it with the same fulness. Yet because the
very word 'substance' (οὐσία) suggests existence, the Stoics
are drawn also to speak of 'substance without quality' (ἄποιος
οὐσία), and seem to identify it with a dead 'matter' (ὕλη), or
'substratum' (ὑποκείμενον), as though life must be introduced
into it from without[52]. This is practically the view of Aristotle,
embodied in the phrase 'matter without quality is potentially
body'[53]; but just so far as terms of this kind imply a dualistic
explanation of the universe, they are not really reconcileable
with the fundamental principles of Stoicism, and they must
therefore be understood with reservations. It may often seem
that the three terms 'body,' 'substance,' 'matter,' are practically
interchangeable, but they are of different rank. For body exists
eternally of itself; whereas substance and matter, except when
loosely used as equivalents of body, do not exist of themselves,
but substance always in association with quality[54], and matter
always in association with force. Further we may distinguish
between 'substance' in general, or 'first matter,' which is a

[51] σῶμα δέ ἐστι κατ' αὐτοὺς ἡ οὐσία Diog. L. vii 150; ἔφησε δὲ ὁ Ποσειδώνιος τὴν
τῶν ὅλων οὐσίαν καὶ ὕλην ἄποιον καὶ ἄμορφον εἶναι Stob. i 11, 5 c.
[52] οὐσίαν δέ φασι τῶν ὄντων ἁπάντων τὴν πρώτην ὕλην· ὕλη δέ ἐστιν ἐξ ἧς ὁτιδηποτοῦν
γίνεται Diog. L. vii 150; ὕλην, σῶμα ὥς φασιν οὖσαν Plot. Enn. ii p. 114 (Arnim
ii 375).
[53] ἡ ἄποιος ὕλη, ἣν δυνάμει σῶμα Ἀριστοτέλης φησί Dexipp. Arist. cat. p. 23, 25
(Arnim ii 374).
[54] See Plutarch, comm. not. 50, 6.

'substratum' (ὑποκείμενον) to the universe, and the 'matter' of particular things[55]. The former never grows greater or less, the latter may alter in either direction[56].

183. Quality (ποιότης, τὸ ποιόν, *qualitas*) constitutes the

Quality.

second category. It is defined by the Stoics as a difference in a substance which cannot be detached from that substance, but makes it 'such and such,' as for instance 'sweet,' 'round,' 'red,' 'hot[57].' Qualities, say the Stoics, are bodies[58]. This paradoxical statement may be understood in two ways; first, in that qualities do not exist independently, but are aspects of 'body' which possesses quality; secondly, in that qualities are bodies in a secondary sense. We may consider it evidence of the second point of view that language describes the qualities by nouns, as 'sweetness,' 'rotundity,' 'redness,' 'heat'; and indeed it is not so long since our own chemists described heat as a 'substance' under the name of 'caloric.' This point of view is carried to an extreme when the Stoics say 'qualities are substances,' thus throwing the first two categories into one[59]. Much stronger is the tendency towards Aristotle's views, so that as substance becomes identified with dead matter, quality is explained as the movement, tension, or current which endows it with life. Hence the Stoics say 'the movement of rarefaction is the cause of quality[60]'; 'matter is a dull substratum, qualities are spirits and air-like tensions[61]'; 'quality is a spirit in a certain disposition[62]'; 'the air-current which keeps each thing together is the cause of its

---

[55] ἁπλῶς μὲν γὰρ ὑποκείμενον πᾶσιν ἡ πρώτη ὕλη, τισὶ δὲ ὑποκείμενον γιγνομένοις ἐπ' αὐτοῦ καὶ κατηγορουμένοις ὁ χαλκὸς καὶ ὁ Σωκράτης Dexippus *Arist. cat.* p. 23, 25 (Arnim ii 374).

[56] Diog. L. vii 150.

[57] Simplic. *Arist. cat.* p. 57 E (Arnim ii 378).

[58] ὁ περὶ τῶν ποιοτήτων λόγος καὶ τῶν συμβεβηκότων ἁπάντων, ἅ φασιν εἶναι Στωϊκῶν παῖδες σώματα Galen *qual. incorp.* I xix, p. 463 K (Arnim ii 377).

[59] τὰς δὲ ποιότητας αὖ πάλιν οὐσίας καὶ σώματα ποιοῦσι Plut. *comm. not.* 50, 1.

[60] οἱ δὲ Στωϊκοὶ κίνησιν [τὴν μανωτικήν see above, note 17] τοῦ ποιὸν εἶναι νομίζουσιν αἰτίαν Simpl. *Arist. cat.* p. 68 E (Arnim ii 452).

[61] τὴν ὕλην ἀργὸν ἐξ ἑαυτῆς καὶ ἀκίνητον ὑποκεῖσθαι ταῖς ποιότησιν ἀποφαίνουσι, τὰς δὲ ποιότητας πνεύματα οὔσας καὶ τόνους ἀερώδεις εἰδοποιεῖν ἕκαστα Plut. *Sto. rep.* 43, 4.

[62] ἀναιροῖτο ἂν τὸ τὴν ποιότητα εἶναι πνεῦμά πως ἔχον Alex. Aph. *Arist. Top.* iv p. 181 (Arnim ii 379).

quality[63].' All these expressions must however be interpreted in the light of the Stoic theory as a whole. Finally we notice that, corresponding to the two kinds of substance, general and particular, there are two kinds of quality, as shewn in the 'generically qualified' (κοινῶς ποιόν) and the 'individually qualified' (ἰδίως ποιόν); for instance, heat in the universe and heat in particular objects[64].

184. The third category is that of 'disposition' (πῶς
Disposition. ἔχοντα, res quodammodo se habens). It differs
from quality in its variableness; for a brave man is always brave, and fire is always hot; but a man is sometimes standing, sometimes lying; fire is sometimes lambent, sometimes still. Qualities therefore appear to correspond generally to the συμβεβηκότα (coniuncta) of Epicurus, in that they can never be separated from a body[65]; and dispositions rather with the συμπτώματα (eventa), which come and go[66]. The third category appears to be used by the Stoics in a very wide sense, and to correspond to several of the categories of Aristotle[67]. Disposition is attached to quality as quality is attached to substance[68]; and though dispositions are not expressly termed bodies, yet we must consider them to be, as the terms in the Greek and Latin sufficiently indicate, bodies in particular aspects.

In the further applications of Stoic theory disposition as defined above appears to be replaced in Greek by the term ἕξις. But this term is used in two different senses. In the first place it is the movement of rarefaction and condensation, by which a spirit or thrill passes from the centre of an object to the extremities, and returns from the extremities to the

[63] τοῦ ποιὸν ἕκαστον εἶναι αἴτιος ὁ συνέχων ἀήρ ἐστι Plut. Sto. rep. 43, 2.

[64] Zeller, pp. 103–107.

[65] 'pondus uti saxi, calor ignis, liquor aquaï, | tactus corporibus cunctis' Lucr. R. N. i 454, 455.

[66] 'servitium contra, paupertas, divitiaeque, | ...cetera quorum | adventu manet incolumis natura abituque, | haec soliti sumus, ut par est, eventa vocare' ib. 456–9.

[67] εἰ δέ τις εἰς τὸ πῶς ἔχον συντάττοι τὰς πλείστας κατηγορίας, ὥσπερ οἱ Στωϊκοί Dexipp. Arist. cat. p. 34, 19 (Arnim ii 399).

[68] τὰ μὲν ποιὰ περὶ τὴν ὕλην πῶς ἔχοντα, τὰ ἰδίως δὲ πῶς ἔχοντα περὶ τὰ ποιά Plot. Enn. vi 1, 30 (Arnim ii 400).

centre[69]; in this sense it is translated in Latin by *unitas*, and takes bodily form as an air-current[70]. This force, when it requires a further motive power in the direction of development, becomes the principle of growth (φύσις, *natura*), and is displayed not only in the vegetable world, but also in animals, as in particular in the hair and nails[71]. Growth when it takes to itself the further powers of sensation and impulse becomes soul (ψυχή, *anima*), and is the distinctive mark of the animal world[72].

In a rather different sense ἕξις or temporary condition is contrasted with διάθεσις or 'permanent disposition.' In this sense the virtues are permanent dispositions of the soul, because virtue is unchanging; the arts are temporary conditions. The virtues belong to the wise man only, the arts to the ordinary man. This distinction however does not hold its ground in the Roman period, the word *habitus* (representing ἕξις), our 'habit,' being used in both senses[73]. The virtues are bodies, being dispositions of the soul which is bodily[74].

185. The fourth category, that of 'relative position' (πρός

Relative position. τί πως ἔχον), appears to be of less importance than the others[75]. Its characteristic is that it may disappear without altering that to which it belongs. Thus that which is on the right hand may cease to be so by the disappearance of that which was on its left; a father may cease to be such on the death of his son[76]. It seems difficult to describe

[69] ἡ δὲ [ἕξις] ἐστι πνεῦμα ἀναστρέφον ἐφ᾽ ἑαυτό Philo *quod deus*, § 35 (Arnim ii 458).

[70] οὐδὲν ἄλλο τὰς ἕξεις πλὴν ἀέρας εἶναι [Χρύσιππός] φησιν· ὑπὸ τούτων γὰρ συνέχεται τὰ σώματα Plut. *Sto. rep.* 43, 2; 'esse autem unitatem in aere vel ex hoc intellegi potest, quod corpora nostra inter se cohaerent. quid est enim aliud quod teneret illa, quam spiritus?' Sen. *N. Q.* ii 6, 6.

[71] ἡ δὲ φύσις διατείνει καὶ ἐπὶ τὰ φυτά. καὶ ἐν ἡμῖν δέ ἐστιν ἐοικότα φυτοῖς, ὄνυχές τε καὶ τρίχες· ἐστι δὲ ἡ φύσις ἕξις ἤδη κινουμένη Philo *Leg. Alleg.* ii § 22 (Arnim ii 458).

[72] ψυχὴ δέ ἐστι φύσις προσειληφυῖα φαντασίαν καὶ ὁρμήν. αὕτη κοινὴ καὶ τῶν ἀλόγων ἐστίν ib.

[73] 'voluntas non erit recta, nisi habitus animi rectus fuerit; habitus porro animi non erit in optimo, nisi totius vitae leges perceperit' Sen. *Ep.* 95, 57.

[74] 'virtus autem nihil aliud est quam animus quodam modo se habens' *ib.* 113, 2.

[75] 'Relative position' must be distinguished from 'correlation' (πρός τι). Such terms as 'sweet' and 'bitter,' 'living' and 'dead' are said to be correlated. Simpl. *Arist. cat.* p. 42 e (Arnim ii 403).

[76] Simpl. as in last note.

the fourth category as one consisting of 'body,' but at least it is a function of body. Also it does not appear that 'relative position' can be predicated of the universe as a whole; it is peculiar to individual objects, but works towards their combination in a larger whole. The fourth category has an important application in practical ethics in the doctrine of daily duties, for these are largely determined by the relative positions ($\sigma\chi\acute{\epsilon}\sigma\epsilon\iota\varsigma$) of the parties concerned : such are the duties of a king to his people, a father to his son, a slave to his master[77].

186. Having fully considered bodies and their relationships, we proceed to consider their combination. In

Combination.

ordinary experience we meet with three kinds of combination; juxtaposition ($\pi\alpha\rho\acute{\alpha}\theta\epsilon\sigma\iota\varsigma$), as in a mixture of various kinds of grain; mixture ($\mu\hat{\iota}\xi\iota\varsigma$), when solid bodies are interfused, as fire and heat, or fusion ($\kappa\rho\hat{\alpha}\sigma\iota\varsigma$), when fluids are interfused, as wine poured into the sea; chemical mixture ($\sigma\acute{\upsilon}\gamma\chi\upsilon\sigma\iota\varsigma$), when each of the two bodies fused disappears[78]. Of these the second in its most completed form ($\kappa\rho\hat{\alpha}\sigma\iota\varsigma$ $\delta\iota'$ $\ddot{\delta}\lambda\omega\nu$, *universa fusio*) is of high importance. For in this way we find that soul is fused with body[79], quality with substance[80], light with air[81], God with the universe[82]. Aristotle admits that there is this mixture between substance and qualities; but as both of these are to the Stoics bodies, and so too are the members of the other pairs quoted, the Stoic doctrine must be summed up in the paradox 'body moves through body[83].' This also follows from the Stoic doctrine that there is no void in the universe. Correspondingly the sum total of body in its various aspects and

[77] See below, § 337.

[78] So Ar. Did. fr. 28, and, more exactly, Alex. Aph. *de mixt.* p. 216, 14 Br. (Arnim ii 473). Another division is as follows: 'quaedam continua esse corpora, ut hominem; quaedam esse composita, ut navem; quaedam ex distantibus, tanquam exercitus, populus, senatus' Sen. *Ep.* 102, 6.

[79] οἱ δὲ ἀπὸ τῆς Στοᾶς...διὰ παντὸς ὁρῶντες τοῦ σώματος καὶ τὴν ψυχὴν χωροῦσαν καὶ τὰς ποιότητας, ἐν ταῖς κράσεσι συνεχώρουν σῶμα διὰ σώματος χωρεῖν Simpl. *Arist. phys.* p. 530, 9 (Arnim ii 467).

[80] Arnim ii 411 and 467.

[81] τὸ φῶς δὲ τῷ ἀέρι ὁ Χρύσιππος κιρνᾶσθαι λέγει Alex. Aph. *de mixt.* p. 216, 14 (Arnim ii 473).

[82] 'Stoici enim volunt deum sic per materiam decucurrisse, quomodo mel per favos' Tertull. *adv. Hermog.* 44; and see below, § 207.

[83] Note 2 above.

170   ROMAN STOICISM

mixtures completes the whole (ὅλον), which is identical with
the 'world-order' or 'universe' (κόσμος)[84]. It seems likely that
this important conception had been reached in very early times
by the Chaldaean astronomers; it was definitely propounded
by Pythagoras[85], had been taken up by Socrates[86] and the
Sophists[87], and was in Stoic times generally accepted both in
popular philosophy and in scientific investigation.

187. Up to this point the Stoic system has been guided
by a determined monism. Body is; that which is
not body is not. Yet in the end the Stoics feel
compelled to speak of certain things which are not body
(ἀσώματα, *incorporalia*). In the first instance there is the void
beyond the universe[88]. It is possible to dispute as to whether
void may more correctly be said to exist or not to exist; but
at least it is a part of nature[89], and we need some term like
'the all' (τὸ πᾶν) to include both the universe and the void
beyond[90]. Next we have to deal with statements (λεκτά), and
mental conceptions of every kind, which stand as a class in
contrast with the real objects to which they may or may not
respectively correspond[91]. Lastly, the Stoics included space
and time, which they had previously explained as functions of
body, in the list of things not bodily[92]. Having thus reached
the two main classes of 'bodies,' and 'things not bodily,' the
monistic principle can only be saved by creating a supreme
class to include both. Let this then be called the existent
(τὸ ὄν, *quod est*)[93], or, if it be objected that things incorporeal

Quiddities.

---

[84] ὅλον μὲν γὰρ λέγουσι τὸν κόσμον Achill. *Is.* 5, p. 129 (Arnim ii 523).
[85] See Rendall, *M. Aurelius* Introd. p. xxix.
[86] ὁ τὸν ὅλον κόσμον συντάττων τε καὶ συνέχων Xen. *Mem.* iv 3, 13.
[87] *ib.* i 1, 11.   [88] See below, § 193.
[89] 'in rerum, inquiunt, natura quaedam sunt, quaedam non sunt; et haec autem,
quae non sunt, rerum natura complectitur' Sen. *Ep.* 58, 15.
[90] ὅλον μὲν γὰρ λέγουσι τὸν κόσμον· πᾶν δὲ μετὰ τοῦ κενοῦ Achill. *Isag.* 5, p. 129
(Arnim ii 523).
[91] Sen. as above.
[92] τῶν δὲ ἀσωμάτων τέσσαρα εἴδη καταριθμοῦνται, ὡς λεκτὸν καὶ κενὸν καὶ τόπον καὶ
χρόνον Sext. *math.* x 218 (Arnim ii 331).
[93] 'etiam nunc est aliquid superius quam corpus. dicimus enim quaedam
corporalia esse, quaedam incorporalia. quid ergo erit ex quo haec deducuntur?
illud, cui nomen modo parum proprium imposuimus, "quod est"' Sen. *Ep.* 58, 11.

do not exist[94], we may use the name 'quiddities' (τινά, *quid*)[95].
In this way the monistic theory, though a little damaged in
vitality, is again set on its feet so far as the ingenious use
of words can help.

188. The language of the Stoics with regard to the phenomena of speech and thought is not always easy to
follow, and perhaps not altogether consistent. On
the one hand, attaching high importance to the reasoning power,
they desire to include its operations in that which is real and
bodily. Thus the 'mind-pictures' and indeed all mental conceptions are bodily and even 'animal,' in the sense that they are
operations of body[96]; and truthfulness, ignorance, science and art
are all bodies in the sense that they are dispositions of the soul,
which is bodily[97]. But 'phrases' (λεκτά) are definitely incorporeal, and with them appear to be ranked all mental conceptions
and general ideas; about these there is a question, not merely
whether they exist or not, but whether they may even be classed
in the most general class of all as 'quiddities[98].' Nor can we call
general conceptions true or false[99]; though of some of them, as
of Centaurs, giants, and the like, we may say that they are formed
by false mental processes[100]. Finally statements are either true
or false, but are not to be called existent. The whole discussion

Statements.

---

[94] οἱ Στωϊκοί, ὡς οἱ περὶ τὸν Βασιλείδην, οἷς ἔδοξε μηδὲν εἶναι ἀσώματον Sext. *math.*
viii 258.

[95] ἐκεῖνοι [οἱ Στωϊκοὶ] νομοθετήσαντες αὑτοῖς τὸ ὂν κατὰ σωμάτων μόνων λέγεσθαι...
τὸ τὶ γενικώτερον αὐτοῦ φασιν εἶναι, κατηγορούμενον οὐ κατὰ σωμάτων μόνον, ἀλλὰ καὶ
κατὰ ἀσωμάτων Alex. Aphr. *Arist. Top.* iv p. 155 (Arnim ii 329); 'primum genus
Stoicis quibusdam videtur "quid"' Sen. *Ep.* 58, 15.

[96] 'animalia sunt omnia, quae cogitamus quaeque mente complectimur; sequitur
ut multa milia animalium habitent in his angustiis pectoris, et singuli multa simus
animalia. non sunt, inquit, multa, quia ex uno religata sunt et partes unius ac membra
sunt' Sen. *Ep.* 113, 3 and 9 (Seneca himself does not agree with this way of speaking).

[97] ἡ δὲ ἀλήθεια σῶμά ἐστιν παρ' ὅσον ἐπιστήμη πάντων ἀληθῶν ἀποφαντικὴ δοκεῖ
τυγχάνειν· πᾶσα δὲ ἐπιστήμη πὼς ἔχον ἐστὶν ἡγεμονικόν...τὸ δὲ ἡγεμονικὸν σῶμα κατὰ
τούτους ὑπῆρχε Sext. *math.* vii 38 (Zeller, p. 129).

[98] τὰ ἐννοήματά φασι μήτε τινὰ εἶναι μήτε ποιά, ὡσανεὶ δὲ τινὰ καὶ ὡσανεὶ ποιὰ
φαντάσματα ψυχῆς Ar. Did. fr. 40 (Diels).

[99] οὔτε ἀληθεῖς οὔτε ψευδεῖς εἰσιν αἱ γενικαὶ [φαντασίαι] Sext. *math.* vii 246.

[100] 'haec...quae animo succurrunt, tanquam Centauri, gigantes, et quicquid aliud
falsa cogitatione formatum habere aliquam imaginem coepit, quamvis non habeat
substantiam' Sen. *Ep.* 58, 15.

therefore ends with the broad distinction between the object, which may be real or 'existent,' and the predication which may be 'true'; and the attempt to unite these two conceptions is not persisted in[101].

189. Although the Stoics aim consistently at the monistic
Force and standard, they make frequent use of dualistic state-
matter. ments, some of which we have already noticed. The Latin writers often contrast soul and body from the standpoint of ethics[102]; and we meet in all the Stoic writers, and often in unguarded language, the favourite Aristotelian dualism of force and matter, or (what comes to the same thing) the active and passive principles. 'Zeno' (we are told) 'laid down that there are two principles in the universe, the active and the passive. The passive is matter, or essence without quality; the active is the Logos or deity within it[103].' So also Cleanthes and Chrysippus taught[104]; and in the Roman period Seneca regarded this as a well-understood dogma of the whole school[105]. But even if direct evidence were lacking, the whole bearing of the philosophy would shew that this dualism is also surmounted by an ultimate monism. God and matter are alike body; they cannot exist the one apart from the other[106]. Of this Cicero, speaking for the Stoics, gives a proof; matter could never have held together, without some

---

[101] οὐδὲν οὖν ἔτι δεῖ λέγειν τὸν χρόνον, τὸ κατηγόρημα, τὸ ἀξίωμα, τὸ συνημμένον, τὸ συμπεπλεγμένον· οἷς χρῶνται μὲν μάλιστα τῶν φιλοσόφων, ὄντα δὲ οὐ λέγουσιν εἶναι Plut. *comm. not.* 30, 12.

[102] See below, § 287.

[103] δοκεῖ δὲ αὐτοῖς ἀρχὰς εἶναι τῶν ὅλων δύο, τὸ ποιοῦν καὶ τὸ πάσχον, κ.τ.λ. Diog. L. vii 134.

[104] *ib.*; οἱ ἀπὸ τῆς Στοᾶς δύο λέγοντες ἀρχάς, θεὸν καὶ ἄποιον ὕλην Sext. *math.* ix 11 (Arnim ii 301).

[105] 'dicunt, ut scis, Stoici nostri, duo esse in rerum natura, ex quibus omnia fiant, causam et materiam. materia iacet iners, res ad omnia parata, cessatura si nemo moveat; causa autem, id est ratio, materiam format et quocunque vult versat' Sen. *Ep.* 65, 2; 'universa ex materia et ex deo constant. deus ista temperat, quae circumfusa rectorem sequuntur. potentius autem est ac pretiosius quod facit, quod est deus, quam materia patiens dei' *ib.* 23.

[106] ἄλλων δὲ καὶ ποιητικὴν μὲν αἰτίαν ἀπολειπόντων, ἀχώριστον δὲ ταύτην τῆς ὕλης, καθάπερ οἱ Στωϊκοί Syrianus *Arist. met.* (Arnim ii 308). 'Stoici naturam in duas partes dividunt, unam quae efficiat, alteram quae se ad faciendum tractabilem praebeat. in illa prima esse vim sentiendi, in hac materiam; nec alterum sine altero [esse] posse' Lact. *Div. inst.* vii 3.

force to bind it; nor force without matter[107]. We must not therefore be led by the term 'principles' (ἀρχαί, *principia*) to think of force and matter in any other way than as two aspects of primary body, separable as mental conceptions, inseparable as physical realities. The interpretation is essentially the same, whether the Stoics speak of God and the universe, matter and cause, body and tension, or substance and quality, and has been already discussed with some fulness under these separate headings.

190. The position of the four 'elements' (στοιχεῖα, *elementa*)
is similar; these are in the Stoic philosophy sub-divisions of the two principles just discussed. For fire and air are of the nature of cause and movement; water and earth of receptivity and passivity[108]. Body is therefore made up of the four elements mixed[109], or perhaps rather of the elementary qualities of heat and cold, dry and wet, which they represent[110]. The doctrine of primary or elemental qualities had been taught before, first by Anaximenes, then by Hippocrates the physician, and by Aristotle[111]; the list of the four elements is traced back to Empedocles. For Aristotle's 'fifth element' Zeno found no use[112].

The elements.

191. Such are the fundamental conceptions or postulates
with which the Stoics approach the problems of physics. It is not necessary for our purpose to compare their merit with those of Aristotle, or to set a value on the debt that Zeno and his successors owed to the founder of the Peripatetic school. Still less do we suggest that the

Conclusion.

[107] 'neque enim materiam ipsam cohaerere potuisse, si nulla vi contineretur, neque vim sine ulla materia' Cic. *Ac.* i 6, 24.

[108] Arnim ii 418; 'e quibus [elementis] aer et ignis movendi vim habent et efficiendi; reliquae partes accipiendi et quasi patiendi, aquam dico et terram' Cic. *Ac.* i 7, 26.

[109] κατὰ τοὺς Στωϊκούς, ἐκ τῆς τῶν τεσσάρων στοιχείων κράσεως γινομένου τοῦ σώματος Justin *de res.* 6 (Arnim ii 414).

[110] ὅσα τοίνυν σώματα πρῶτον τὰς τοιαύτας ἔχει ποιότητας, ἐκεῖνα στοιχεῖα τῶν ἄλλων ἁπάντων ἐστὶ καὶ τῆς σαρκός· ἔστι δὲ ταῦτα γῆ καὶ ὕδωρ καὶ ἀὴρ καὶ πῦρ Galen *const. art. med.* i p. 251 K (Arnim ii 405).

[111] Galen *meth. med.* i 2, X p. 15 K (Arnim ii 411).

[112] See below, § 196.

Stoics have perfectly analyzed the contents of the universe, or have even produced an orderly and rounded scheme. But at least it seems clear that their work shews intellectual power, and that speculation is not necessarily less profound because it is pursued with a practical aim[113]. The founders of the Stoic philosophy had a wide reach; they took all knowledge to be their province; and they worked persistently towards the harmonization of all its parts.

---

[113] Cf. Mahaffy's *Greek Life and Thought*; 'it is quite wrong to suppose that these thinkers [Zeno and Epicurus], busy as they were with practical life, despised or avoided speculation. Their philosophical theories demand hard reading and hard thinking' p. 137.

CHAPTER VIII.

THE UNIVERSE.

192. IN including in their system the study of the physical
Study of the heavens. universe the Stoics broke daringly with Socrates
and his faithful followers the Cynics. These had
joined with the ignorant and the prejudiced[1] in ridiculing those
whose eyes were always turned up towards the sky, whilst they
saw nothing of things that were nearer at hand and concerned
them more closely. But it was not for nothing that the most
highly civilised nations of antiquity, Egyptians, Chaldaeans, and
Babylonians, had studied the starry heavens, mapped out the
constellations, measured the paths of the wandering stars, predicted eclipses, reckoned with the tides, the seasons, and the
winds; with the result that their successors defied the common
opinion by declaring the earth to be a sphere, and to hold
inhabitants whom they called Antipodes, because they walk
with their feet turned up towards ours[2]. All this body of
knowledge, called generically the knowledge of the sky (though
it included the whole physical geography of the earth), had
impressed and fascinated the Eastern world. It seemed that
as the eyes were raised to the sky, so the mind of man was
elevated and made ampler and nobler[3], leaving behind it the
petty contentions and rivalries of common life; and further
that true knowledge had surely been reached, when the positions of the heavenly bodies and the eclipses of sun and moon

[1] As, for instance, Aristophanes in the *Clouds*.

[2] 'vos etiam dicitis esse e regione nobis, e contraria parte terrae, qui adversis
vestigiis stent contra nostra vestigia, quos Antipodas vocatis' Cic. *Ac.* ii 39, 123.

[3] 'cum tu, inter scabiem tantam et contagia lucri, | nil parvum sapias et adhuc
sublimia cures; | quae mare compescant causae; quid temperet annum; | stellae
sponte sua iussaene vagentur et errent' Hor. *Ep.* i 12, 14—17.

could be predicted so long before with unfailing accuracy. These feelings are now commonplaces of literature, and were fully shared by the Stoics. 'Is not the sun,' says Seneca, 'worthy of our gaze, the moon of our regard? When the sky displays its fires at night, and countless stars flash forth, who is not absorbed in contemplation of them? They glide past in their company, concealing swift motion under the outward appearance of immobility. We comprehend the movements of a few of them, but the greater number are beyond our ken. Their dignity fills all our thoughts⁴.' In the golden age which preceded our iron civilisation 'men lay at nights in the open fields, and watched the glorious spectacle of the heavens. It was their delight to note the stars that sank in one quarter and rose in another. The universe swept round them, performing its magnificent task in silence⁵.' 'Their order never changes, spring and autumn, winter and summer succeed according to fixed laws⁶.' And in the same tone writes the Stoic poet: 'unshaken the lights of heaven ever move onwards in their proper orbit⁷.' The emotion roused in the Stoic by the contemplation of the sky was thus identical with that expressed in Judaic poetry by the 'Song of the Three Holy Children⁸, and in more modern times by Addison's famous hymn⁹.

193. The phenomena of earth and heaven combined, in the general opinion of intelligent men, to show the existence of a 'world-order' or 'universe¹⁰.' The Stoics accepted this conception in their physics from

The world-order.

---

⁴ Sen. *Ben.* iv 23, 2 to 4.

⁵ 'in aperto iacentes sidera superlabebantur et insigne spectaculum noctium. mundus in praeceps agebatur silentio tantum opus ducens...libebat intueri signa ex media caeli parte vergentia, rursus ex occulto alia surgentia' *Ep.* 90, 42.

⁶ '[vides] ordinem rerum et naturam per constituta procedere. hiems nunquam aberravit. aestas suo tempore incaluit. autumni verisque, ut solet, facta mutatio est. tam solstitium quam aequinoctium suos dies rettulit' *N. Q.* iii 16, 3.

⁷ 'caelestia semper | inconcussa suo volvuntur sidera lapsu' Lucan *Phars.* ii 267, 8.

⁸ 'O all ye Works of the Lord, bless ye the Lord; praise and exalt him above all for ever' Daniel iii 57 to 82.

⁹ 'The spacious firmament on high, | with all the blue ethereal sky, | and spangled heavens, a shining frame, | their great Original proclaim,' etc. J. Addison (1728).

¹⁰ See above, § 186.

Heraclitus, who had declared that 'neither god nor man created this world-order,' as in their ethics from Diogenes, the 'citizen of the universe[11].' They therefore needed only to adjust an established notion to their own physical postulates. We observe at once that the very conception of an ordered whole differentiates that whole from the absolute totality of all things. The universe is indeed on the one hand identified with the substance of all things (οὐσία τῶν ὅλων), but only as a thing made individual by the possession of quality (ἰδίως ποιόν)[12], and necessarily one[13]. It is self-created; and it may therefore be identified with its creator, the deity[14]; it also includes all that is bodily[15]; but outside there remains the boundless void[16]. It is therefore defined by Chrysippus as 'the combination of heaven and earth and all natures that are in them,' or alternatively as 'the combination of gods and men and all that is created for their sake[17].'

194. The Stoic conception of the universe is therefore that of a continuous body, having a definite outline, and stationed in the boundless void. That the universe has shape the Stoics deduce from its having 'nature' (φύσις), that is, the principle of growth, displayed in the symmetry of its parts[18]; and its shape is the perfect shape of a sphere[19]. Within this sphere all things tend towards the middle[20]; and we use the terms 'down' meaning 'towards the middle,' and 'up' meaning

Its position.

---

[11] See below, § 303.

[12] καὶ ἔστι κόσμος ὁ ἰδίως ποιὸς τῆς τῶν ὅλων οὐσίας Diog. L. vii 138.

[13] ὅτι θ' εἷς ἐστιν [ὁ κόσμος] Ζήνων τέ φησιν ἐν τῷ περὶ τοῦ ὅλου καὶ Χρύσιππος ib. 143.

[14] λέγεται δὲ ἑτέρως κόσμος ὁ θεός Stob. i 21, 5.

[15] οἱ ἀπὸ τῆς Στοᾶς ἕνα κόσμον ἀπεφήναντο, ὃν δὴ τὸ πᾶν ἔφασαν εἶναι καὶ τὸ σωματικόν Aët. plac. i 5, 1.

[16] See § 187, note 90; Seneca however thinks there may be more outside the universe than void; 'illud scrutor, quod ultra mundum iacet, utrumne profunda vastilas sit an et hoc ipsum terminis suis cludatur; qualis sit habitus exclusus' Dial. viii 5, 6.

[17] Ar. Did. fr. 31.   [18] Arnim ii 534.

[19] Arnim ii 547.

[20] μέρη δέ ἐστιν αὐτοῦ γῆ, ὕδωρ, ἀήρ, πῦρ, ἃ πάντα νεύει ἐπὶ τὸ μέσον Achilles Isag. 9 (Arnim ii 554). But according to another view only earth and water, being naturally heavy, tend towards the middle; whereas air and fire, being naturally light, tend from it; ib. 4 (Arnim ii 555). See § 196.

thereby from the middle²¹. The Peripatetics are therefore need-
lessly alarmed, when they tell us that our universe will fall·down,
if it stands in the void; for, first, there is no 'up' or 'down' outside the universe; and, secondly, the universe possesses 'unity'
(ἕξις)²² which keeps it together²³. And here we see the folly of
Epicurus, who says that the atoms move downwards from
eternity in the boundless void; for there is no such thing as
'downwards' in that which is unlimited²⁴. Further, the universe
is divided into two parts, the earth (with the water and the air
surrounding it) which is stable in the middle, and the sky or
aether which revolves around it²⁵.

195. Thus early in their theory the Stoics were led to
make two assertions on questions of scientific fact,
in which they opposed the best scientific opinion
of their own time. For many authorities held that the earth
revolved on its axis, and that the revolution of the sky was
only apparent. Such were HICETAS of Syracuse²⁶, a Pythagorean philosopher, whose views were quoted with approval by
Theophrastus, and later ECPHANTUS the Pythagorean, and
HERACLIDES of Pontus²⁷. From the point of view of astronomical science this view seemed well worthy of consideration, as
Seneca in particular emphasizes²⁸. Other astronomers had gone

The heliocen-
tric theory.

²¹ Arnim ii 557.   ²² See above, § 184.
²³ Arnim ii 540. The universe, being 'body,' possesses 'up' and 'down,' 'front'
and 'back,' and all the other relations, according to the fourth category.
²⁴ Plut. *Sto. rep.* 44, 1.
²⁵ Ar. Did. fr. 31, quoting from Chrysippus. So Cornutus 1; ὁ οὐρανὸς περιέχει
κύκλῳ τὴν γῆν.
²⁶ 'Hicetas Syracosius caelum solem lunam stellas supera denique omnia stare
censet neque praeter terram rem ullam in mundo moveri, quae cum circum axem se
summa celeritate convertat et torqueat, eadem effici omnia, quae si stante terra
caelum moveretur' Cic. *Ac.* ii 39, 123, on which see Prof. Reid's note.
²⁷ Plut. *plac. phil.* iii 13, 3. The question of priority in the statement of this
theory has been much discussed in recent years; and it is contended that Hicetas and
Ecphantus never existed except as characters in dialogues composed by Heraclides of
Pontus, the true discoverer. See H. Steigmüller, *Archiv der Geschichte der Philosophie*, Berlin 1892; Otto Voss, *de Heraclidis Pontici vita et scriptis*, Rostock, 1896;
Tannery, *Pseudonymes antiques* (Revue des études grecques, 1897).
²⁸ 'pertinebit hoc excussisse, ut sciamus utrum mundus terra stante circumeat an
mundo stante terra vertatur. fuerunt enim qui dicerent nos esse, quos rerum natura
nescientes ferat' Sen. *N. Q.* vii 2, 3. Seneca however appears for himself to reject
the doctrine: 'scimus praeter terram nihil stare, cetera continua velocitate decurrere'
Ep. 93, 9.

further, declaring that the sun lay in the centre, and that the earth and other planets revolved round it. Theophrastus stated that Plato himself in his old age had felt regret that he had wrongly placed the earth in the centre of the universe; and the heliocentric view was put forward tentatively by ARISTARCHUS of Samos, and positively by the astronomer SELEUCUS, in connexion with the theory of the earth's rotation[29]. For this Cleanthes had said that the Greeks should have put Aristarchus on trial for impiety, as one who proposed to disturb 'the hearth of the universe[30].' This outburst of persecuting zeal, anticipating so remarkably the persecution of Galileo, was effective in preventing the spread of the novel doctrine. Posidonius was a great astronomer, and recognised the heliocentric doctrine as theoretically possible[31]; indeed, as one who had himself constructed an orrery, shewing the motion of all the planets[32], he must have been aware of its superior simplicity. Nevertheless he opposed it vigorously on theological grounds, and perhaps more than any other man was responsible for its being pushed aside for some 1500 years[33]. The precise ground of the objection is not made very clear to us, and probably it was instinctive rather than reasoned. It could hardly be deemed impious to place the sun, whom the Stoics acknowledged as a deity, in the centre of the universe; but that the earth should be reckoned merely as one of his attendant planets was humiliating to human self-esteem, and jeopardised the doctrine of Providence, in accordance with which the universe was created for the happiness of gods and men only.

196. Having determined that the earth is the centre of the universe, and the sun above it, the way is clear to incorporate in the system the doctrine of the four elements ($\sigma\tau\omicron\iota\chi\epsilon\hat{\iota}\alpha$, *naturae*)[34], which probably had its origin in

The elements.

---

[29] Plut. *qu. Plat.* viii 1, 2 and 3; Aët. *plac.* ii 24, 8 and iii 17, 9.

[30] Plut. *fac. lun.* 6, 3.   [31] Simplic. *Arist. phys.* p. 64.

[32] 'si in Scythiam aut in Britanniam sphaeram aliquis tulerit hanc, quam nuper familiaris noster effecit Posidonius, cuius singulae conversiones idem efficiunt in sole et in luna et in quinque stellis errantibus, quod efficitur in caelo singulis diebus et noctibus' Cic. *N. D.* ii 34, 88.

[33] Schmekel, p. 465.

[34] 'in rerum natura elementa sunt quattuor' Sen. *N. Q.* iii 12, 3.

a cruder form of physical speculation than the doctrine of the
heavenly bodies. As we have seen above[35], the elements are
not first principles of the Stoic physics, but hold an intermediate
position between the two principles of the active and the passive
on the one hand, and the organic and inorganic world on the
other. Earth is the lowest of the elements, and also the
grossest; above it is placed water, then air, then fire; and
these are in constant interchange, earth turning to water, this
into air, and this into aether, and so again in return. By this
interchange the unity of the universe is maintained[36]. The
transition from one element to the next is not abrupt, but
gradual; the lowest part of the aether is akin to air[37]; it is
therefore of no great importance whether we speak with Heraclitus of three elements, or with Empedocles of four. The two
grosser elements, earth and water, tend by nature downwards
and are passive; air and fire tend upwards and are active[38].
Zeno did not think it necessary to postulate a fifth element as
the substance of soul, for he held that fire was its substance[39].

197.   Fire, heat, and motion are ultimately identical, and are

Fire and   the source of all life[40]. Thus the elemental and
breath.   primary fire stands in contrast with the fire of
domestic use; the one creates and nourishes, the other destroys[41].

[35] See above, § 190.
[36] 'ex terra aqua, ex aqua oritur aer, ex aere aether; deinde retrorsum vicissim ex
aethere aer, ex aere aqua, ex aqua terra infima. sic naturis his, ex quibus omnia
constant, sursum deorsum ultro citro commeantibus, mundi partium coniunctio
continetur' Cic. *N. D.* ii 32, 84.
[37] 'necesse est ut et imus aether habeat aliquid aeri simile, et summus aer non sit
dissimilis imo aetheri, quia non fit statim in diversum ex diverso transitus; paulatim
ista in confinio vim suam miscent, ut dubitare possis an aer an hic iam aether sit'
Sen. *N. Q.* ii 14, 2; cf. iv 10.
[38] Arnim ii 555. But see above, § 194, note 20.
[39] 'de naturis autem sic [Zeno] sentiebat, ut in quattuor initiis rerum illis quintam
hanc naturam, ex qua superiores sensum et mentem effici rebantur, non adhiberet:
statuebat enim ignem esse ipsam naturam quae quidque gigneret, etiam mentem atque
sensus.' Cic. *Ac.* i 11, 39; cf. *Fin.* iv 5, 12.
[40] 'sic enim se res habet, ut omnia quae alantur et crescant, contineant in se vim
caloris : sine qua neque ali possent neque crescere.' *N. D.* ii 9, 23 and 24; 'caloris
[natura] vim [habet] in se vitalem, per omnem mundum pertinentem' *ib.*
[41] 'hic noster ignis, quem usus vitae requirit, confector est et consumptor omnium;
contra ille corporeus vitalis et salutaris omnia conservat alit auget sustinet sensuque
afficit' *ib.* ii 15, 41.   Cicero is quoting from Cleanthes (fr. 30 P); the teaching of Zeno
was the same (fr. 71 B).

It follows that fire, though it is one of the four elements, has from its divine nature a primacy amongst the elements[42], which corresponds to its lofty position in the universe[43]; and the other elements in turn all contain some proportion of fire. Thus although air has cold and darkness as primary and essential qualities[44], nevertheless it cannot exist without some share of warmth[45]. Hence air also may be associated with life, and it is possible to retain the popular term 'spirit' (πνεῦμα, spiritus) for the principle of life. In the development of the Stoic philosophy we seldom hear again of air in connexion with coldness; and between the 'warm breath' (anima inflammata) and the primary fire there is hardly a distinction; we may even say that 'spirit' has the highest possible tension[46].

198. Air on its downward path changes to water. This
God in change is described as due to loss of heat[47], and
the stone. yet water too has some heat and vitality[48]. Even
earth, the lowest and grossest of the elements, contains a share of the divine heat; otherwise it could not feed living plants and animals, much less send up exhalations with which to feed the sun and stars[49]. Thus we may say even of a stone that it has a part of the divinity in it[50]. Here then we see the reverse side of the so-called Stoic materialism. If it is true that God is body,

[42] τὸ δὲ [πῦρ καὶ] κατ᾽ ἐξοχὴν στοιχεῖον λέγεσθαι διὰ τὸ ἐξ αὐτοῦ πρῶτον τὰ λοιπὰ συνίστασθαι κατὰ μεταβολήν Ar. Did. fr. 21; 'Stoici ignem,...unum ex his quattuor elementis, et viventem et sapientem et ipsius mundi fabricatorem..., eumque omnino ignem deum esse putaverunt' Aug. Civ. De. viii 5.
[43] '[ignem] natura sursum vocat; in illo igne purissimo nihil est quod deprimatur' Sen. N. Q. ii 13, 1 and 2.
[44] οἱ μὲν Στωϊκοὶ τῷ ἀέρι τὸ πρώτως ψυχρὸν ἀποδιδόντες Plut. prim. frig. 9, 1; 'aer frigidus per se et obscurus' Sen. N. Q. ii 10.
[45] 'ipse vero aer, qui natura est maxime frigidus, minime est expers caloris' Cic. N. D. ii 10, 26; 'aer nunquam sine igne est. detrahe illi calorem; rigescet, stabit, durabitur' Sen. N. Q. iii 10, 4.
[46] 'quid autem est, quod magis credatur ex se ipso habere intentionem quam spiritus?' Sen. N. Q. ii 8. Aristotle held that air was warm (Arnim ii 431).
[47] 'detrahe [aeri] calorem; transiet in humorem' Sen. N. Q. iii 10, 4.
[48] 'est aliquid in aqua vitale' ib. v 5, 2.
[49] 'non esse terram sine spiritu palam est...illo dico vitali et vegeto et alente omnia. hunc nisi haberet, quomodo tot arbustis spiritum infunderet non aliunde viventibus, et tot satis?...totum hoc caelum,...omnes hae stellae..., hic tam prope a nobis agens cursum sol...alimentum ex terra trahunt' ib. vi 16, 1 and 2.
[50] Philod. de ira p. 77 Gomp.

and that the soul is body, it is equally true that even water, the
damp and cold element, and earth, the dry and cold element,
are both penetrated by the divinity, by the creative fire without
the operation of which both would fall in an instant into nothing-
ness[51].

199. We return to the consideration of the heavenly bodies.
The heavenly   These are set in spheres of various diameter, all
bodies.   alike revolving around the earth.   The succession
we find described in Plato's *Timaeus*[52]; the moon is nearest to
the earth, then comes the sun, then in order Venus, Mercury,
Mars, Jupiter and Saturn.   This theory was taken up by
Aristotle and after him by Eudoxus, from whom it passed to
Aratus and Chrysippus[53].   A tradition derived from Chaldaean
sources gave a different order, setting Venus and Mercury
nearer to the earth than the sun; and this order was accepted
by the middle Stoics, that is to say by Panaetius and Posidonius,
the latter placing Venus nearer to the earth, and therefore
further from the sun, than Mercury[54].   The moon, like the
earth, obtains her light from the sun, being crescent-shaped
when nearest to him, full-orbed when furthest away.   Her
distance from the earth is two million stadia (250,000 miles);
when she lies between the earth and the sun she eclipses his
light, but when she is on the side of the earth directly away
from the sun she is herself eclipsed[55].   Her phases are explained
by her position relative to the sun[56].   The sun is 60 millions of
miles from the earth[57]; his diameter is 37½ times as large as that
of the earth[58]; he appears larger when on the horizon because
his rays are refracted through the thick atmosphere[59].   The

[51] 'ex quo concluditur, calidum illud atque igneum in omni fusum esse natura'
Cic. *N. D.* ii 10, 28.

[52] cap. xi, p. 38 D.   [53] Schmekel, pp. 463, 4.   [54] *ib.* p. 464.

[55] Diog. L. vii 145 and 146; Posidonius is his general authority, but the theory
of the solar eclipse he refers to Zeno.

[56] '[lunae] tenuissimum lumen facit proximus accessus ad solem, digressus autem
longissimus quisque plenissimum' Cic. *N. D.* ii 19, 50.

[57] Pliny, *Nat. hist.* ii 21.

[58] Such was the calculation of Posidonius; see Mayor's note on Cic. *N. D.* ii 36, 92.
The sun's diameter is in fact three times as large as Posidonius thought.

[59] This explanation has so plausible a sound that it may not be superfluous to
remark that it is scientifically valueless.

planets, whether they revolve round the earth or the sun, are falsely called 'wandering stars,' since their orbits have been fixed from all eternity[60]. The fixed stars revolve round the earth at such a distance that the earth, when compared with it, is merely the central point[61]. All the heavenly bodies are, like the earth, of spherical form[62]. Finally Seneca, in advance of the school, declared the comets to be a regular part of the celestial world[62a].

200. Whilst the Stoics generally were in sympathy with

Cruder theories.

the best astronomical teaching of their time, they combined with it many views based on much cruder forms of observation. Even Seneca thinks it bold to suggest that the sun is not a little larger than the whole earth[63]; and it is commonly held that not only the sun and moon, but also the heavenly bodies generally, feed upon moist exhalations from the Ocean[64]. Cleanthes in particular seems to have viewed the astronomers with suspicion. He alone regarded the moon not as a sphere, but as a hemisphere with the flat side turned towards us[65]; the stars he considered to be conical[66]. These views, very probably derived from Heraclitus, seem to point to the conception of the sky or aether as a single fixed fiery sphere, in which the heavenly bodies only differ from the surrounding element by containing more closely packed masses of fiery matter[67]; a conception which harmonizes far more closely with the Stoic theory of the elements than the doctrines which

[60] Cic. *N. D.* ii 20, 51.

[61] 'persuadent enim mathematici terram in medio mundo sitam ad universi caeli complexum quasi puncti instar obtinere, quod κέντρον illi vocant.' *Tusc. disp.* i 17, 40.

[62] Diog. L. vii 144 and 145.

[62a] 'ego nostris non adsentior; non enim existimo cometen subitaneum ignem sed inter aeterna opera naturae' *N. Q.* vii 21, 1.

[63] 'omni terrarum ambitu non semel maior' Sen. *N. Q.* vi 16, 2.

[64] Ἡράκλειτος καὶ οἱ Στωϊκοὶ τρέφεσθαι τοὺς ἀστέρας ἐκ τῆς ἐπιγείου ἀναθυμιάσεως Aët. *plac.* ii 17, 4; '[sidera] marinis terrenisque umoribus longo intervallo extenuatis [aluntur]' Cic. *N. D.* ii 16, 43; 'totum hoc caelum ..halitu terrarum [sustinetur]' Sen. *N. Q.* vi 16, 2.

[65] Ar. Did. fr. 34; for the text and interpretation see Hirzel, pp. 121, 122.

[66] Aët. *plac.* ii 14, 1 and 2.

[67] 'solem quoque animantem esse oportet, et quidem reliqua astra, quae oriantur in ardore caelesti, qui aether vel caelum nominatur' Cic. *N. D.* ii 15, 41.

are astronomically more correct. Cleanthes also explained that
the sun could not venture to travel beyond his solstitial positions,
lest he should be out of reach of his terrestrial food[68]. And
Cleanthes and Posidonius agree that the sun keeps within the
'torrid zone' of the sky, because beneath it flows the Ocean,
from which the sun sucks up his nutriment[69].

201. From the relation of the heavenly bodies to the
Deity of   element of fire the Stoics draw the conclusion
the stars.   that they are animated, reasoning, self-determined,
and divine; in short, that they are gods[70]. This godhead per-
tains particularly to the sun[71]. Of this doctrine Cleanthes is
especially the upholder[72], deeming that the sun is the ruling
power in the universe, as reason in man[73]. It is not clear
whether the Stoics derived their theory of the divinity of the
heavenly bodies from logical deduction, or whether they were
here incorporating some Eastern worship. In favour of the
latter point of view is the consideration that at this time the
association of Mithra with the sun was probably making
some progress in the Persian religion, and that the popular
names of the seven days of the week, following the names
of the sun, moon, and five planets, must have been already
current.

202. But in the Stoic system this doctrine is overshadowed
Deity of the   by the paradox that the universe itself is a rational
universe.   animal, possessed of free-will and divine. This is
the teaching of all the masters of the school, beginning with
Zeno himself. It appeared to him to follow logically from two
principles, the first that the universe possesses a unity, the
second that the whole is greater than its parts. 'There cannot

---

[68] Cic. N. D. iii 14, 37.

[69] 'ideo enim, sicut et Posidonius et Cleanthes adfirmant, solis meatus a plaga,
quae usta dicitur, non recedit, quia sub ipsa currit Oceanus' Macrob. Sat. i 23, 2.

[70] 'hac mundi divinitate perspecta tribuenda est sideribus eadem divinitas, quae
ex mobilissima purissimaque aetheris parte gignuntur;...totaque sunt calida atque
perlucida, ut ea quoque rectissime animantia esse et sentire atque intellegere dicantur'
Cic. N. D. ii 15, 39.

[71] Sen. Ben. vii 31, 3.

[72] 'Cleanthes...solem dominari et rerum potiri putat' Cic. Ac. ii 41, 126.

[73] Diog. L. vii 139.

be a sentient part of a non-sentient whole. But the parts of the universe are sentient; therefore the universe is sentient[74].' 'The rational is better than the non-rational. But nothing is better than the universe; therefore the universe is rational[75].' 'The universe is one[76]'; we must not therefore think of it as of an army or a family, which comes into a kind of existence merely through the juxtaposition of its members. By the same reasoning the universe possesses divinity[77]. Upon this favourite Stoic text is based the frequent assertion of modern commentators that the philosophy is pantheistic[78]; but the more central position of Stoicism is that the deity bears the same relation to the universe as a man's soul to his body[79], and the universe is therefore no more all divine than a man is all soul. This view is expressed with great clearness by Varro, who says: 'As a man is called wise, being wise in mind, though he consists of mind and body; so the world is called God from its soul, though it consists of soul and body[80].' The Stoics are however in strong conflict with the Epicureans and all philosophers who hold that the world is fundamentally all matter, and that soul and mind are developments from matter. 'Nothing that is without mind can generate that which possesses mind,' says Cicero's Stoic[81],

[74] 'idemque [Zeno] hoc modo: "nullius sensu carentis pars aliqua potest esse sentiens. mundi autem partes sentientes sunt: non igitur caret sensu mundus"' Cic. *N. D.* ii 8, 22.

[75] 'quod ratione utitur, id melius est quam id, quod ratione non utitur. nihil autem mundo melius: ratione igitur mundus utitur' *ib.* 8, 21; see also § 83.

[76] Diog. L. vii 143; 'haec ita fieri omnibus inter se concinentibus mundi partibus profecto non possent, nisi ea uno divino et continuato spiritu continerentur' Cic. *N. D.* ii 7, 19. This unity of the universe is technically termed συμπάθεια τῶν ὅλων, 'consentiens conspirans continuata cognatio rerum' (Cic. as above). It was denied by Panaetius (Schmekel, pp. 191, 192).

[77] 'est ergo in eo virtus: sapiens est igitur et propterea deus' Cic. *N. D.* ii 14, 39; 'quid est autem, cur non existimes in eo divini aliquid existere, qui dei pars est? totum hoc, quo continemur, et unum est et deus; et socii sumus eius et membra' Sen. *Ep.* 92, 30.

[78] 'From what has been said it follows that the Stoics admitted no essential difference between God and the world. Their system was therefore strictly pantheistic' Zeller, p. 156.

[79] ὥσπερ δὲ ἡμεῖς ἀπὸ ψυχῆς διοικούμεθα, οὕτω καὶ ὁ κόσμος ψυχὴν ἔχει τὴν συνέχουσαν αὐτόν, καὶ αὕτη καλεῖται Ζεύς Cornutus 2.

[80] Varro Fr. i 27 b (Aug. *Civ. De.* vii 6).

[81] 'nihil quod animi quodque rationis est expers, id generare ex se potest animantem compotemque rationis' Cic. *N. D.* ii 8, 22.

in full opposition to modern popular theories of evolution.
Further, just as it may be questioned in the case of man
whether the soul is situated in the head or in the heart, so in
the case of the universe we may doubt whether its soul, or
rather its 'principate,' is in the sun, as Cleanthes held[82], or in
the sky generally, as Chrysippus and Posidonius maintain[83], or
in the aether, as Antipater of Tyre taught[84].

203.   In the study of the universe we are not called upon
merely to consider the earth as a member of the
The earth's
inhabitants. celestial company; we have to contemplate it as
the home of beings of various ranks, which also display to us
the principle of orderly arrangement.   Preëminent amongst the
inhabitants of the earth stands man, who is distinguished by
being the sole possessor of the faculty of reason, and in addition
owns all those capacities which are shewn in beings of lower
rank.   The nature of man constitutes so large a part of philosophy that we must reserve its full consideration for a special
chapter[85]; and must restrict ourselves here to treating of lower
beings, which fall into the three orders of animals, plants, and
inanimate beings.   But since each of the higher orders possesses
all the properties of every order that stands lower, the study of
the orders inferior to man is also the study of a large part of
human nature.   The number and classification of these orders
are not to be treated mechanically.   From one point of view
gods and men form one class, the rational, as opposed to every
kind of non-rational being.   On the other hand, from the standpoint with which we are rather concerned at this moment, gods,
men, and animals are subdivisions of the order of animate beings,
below which stand the plants, and lower still things without life.
Animals, as the name indicates, possess life or soul; the two
lower orders possess something corresponding to soul, but lower
in degree.   The general term which includes soul in the animal
and that which corresponds to it in the plants and in lifeless
bodies is 'spirit' ($\pi\nu\epsilon\hat{u}\mu\alpha$); soul therefore is the highest type
of 'spirit.'

[82] See above, § 101.   [83] Diog. L. vii 139.   [84] ib.
[85] See below, chap. xi.

204. To the dumb animals the Stoics consistently deny the
faculty of reason; and this position must have
The animals
have not   seemed to them self-evident, since the same word
reason   Logos expresses in the Greek both reason and
speech. In the Latin the point was no longer so clear; still
the words 'ratio' and 'oratio,' if not identical, appeared to be
connected by a natural association. Since the animals then are
necessarily unreasoning, those acts of animals which appear to
show reason must be explained in some other way. A dog
pursues a wild animal by its scent; it must therefore be admitted
that in a way the dog recognises that 'this scent is the sign of
the wild animal[86]'; still he is incapable of expressing this belief
in the form of a correct syllogism. The industry of the ant is
disposed of in a more summary way; this animal shows a 'rest-
less helplessness,' climbing up and down straws in meaningless
industry; many men however are no wiser[87]. For their young
the animals have a certain feeling, yet their grief at losing them
is comparatively shortlived[88]. In spite, however, of these limitations the animal world is one part of the wonders of nature, and
is deserving of our admiration; all animals have strong affection
for their young so long as these need their protection[89], and the
dog deserves special recognition both for his keen intelligence
and for his loyalty towards his master[90].

205. To define more accurately the nature of animals we
but a sort   must to some extent anticipate the discussion of
of reason.   human nature in a later chapter, which follows the
same general lines: for in every point the animals are like men,
but inferior. They possess soul, but without reason[91]; by soul
we here mean the twin powers of observation and of independent

---

[86] Sext. *math.* viii 270 (Arnim ii 727).

[87] 'inconsultus illis vanusque cursus est, qualis formicis per arbusta repentibus,
quae in summum cacumen, deinde in imum inanes aguntur. his plerique similem
vitam agunt, quorum non immerito quis "inquietam inertiam" dixerit' Sen. *Dial.*
ix 12, 3.

[88] *ib.* vi 7, 2.

[89] 'quid dicam, quantus amor bestiarum sit in educandis custodiendisque eis, quae
procreaverunt, usque ad eum finem, dum possint se ipsa defendere?' Cic. *N. D.* ii 51, 129.

[90] 'canum vero tam fida custodia,......quid significat?' *ib.* 63, 158.

[91] δῆλον ὅτι τὰ μὲν ἕξει διοικεῖται τὰ δὲ φύσει, τὰ δὲ ἀλόγῳ ψυχῇ Plut. *virt.
mor.* 12.

movement⁹². In a rough way the animals also possess a ruling part⁹³. Their power of observation enables them to distinguish what is healthful to them from that which is injurious; their power of movement shapes itself into pursuit of the healthful and avoidance of the injurious⁹⁴. They possess also properties which resemble the human feelings, such as anger, confidence, hope, fear; but they do not in a strict sense possess the same feelings as men⁹⁵. As they cannot attain to virtue, neither can they fall into vice⁹⁶.

206. From the animals we pass to the plants. These seem

Plant life.

to have soul, because they live and die⁹⁷; yet they have not soul in any strict sense of the word. It will therefore be better not to use this word, but to speak of the 'growth-power' (φύσις)⁹⁸. The governing part is situated in the root⁹⁹. The growth of plants both in size and in strength is very remarkable, inasmuch as little seeds, which at first find themselves place in crevices, attain such power that they split huge rocks and destroy noble monuments, thus illustrating what is meant by tone or tension; for it is a spirit which starts from the governing part (the root) and spreads to the trunk and branches,

---

⁹² τὴν τῆς αἰσθήσεώς τε καὶ ἐξ ἑαυτῆς κινήσεως [αἰτίαν ὀνομάζομεν] ψυχήν Galen adv. Iul. v (Arnim ii 718).

⁹³ ' omnem naturam necesse est...habere aliquem in se principatum, ut in homine mentem, in belua quiddam simile mentis' Cic. N. D. ii 11, 29; 'ipsum principale parum subtile, parum exactum. capit ergo visus speciesque rerum quibus ad impetus evocetur, sed turbidas et confusas' Sen. Dial. iii 3, 7 and 8.

⁹⁴ ' bestiis [natura] et sensum et motum dedit, et cum quodam appetitu accessum ad res salutares, a pestiferis recessum' Cic. N. D. ii 12, 34; and so again, ib. 47, 122.

⁹⁵ 'irasci quidem non magis sciunt quam ignoscere; muta animalia humanis adfectibus carent, habent autem similes illis quosdam impetus' Sen. Dial. iii 3, 5 and 6.

⁹⁶ '[ira], cum sit inimica rationi, nusquam nascitur, nisi ubi rationi locus est' ib. 3, 4.

⁹⁷ 'sunt quaedam quae animam habent nec sunt animalia. placet enim satis et arbustis animam inesse; itaque et vivere illa et mori dicimus' Sen. Ep. 58, 10; cf. N. Q. vi 16, 1.

⁹⁸ οἱ δὲ Στωϊκοὶ οὐδὲ ψυχὴν ὅλως ὀνομάζουσι τὴν τὰ φυτὰ διοικοῦσαν, ἀλλὰ φύσιν Galen de Hipp. et Plut. vi. 561 K (Arnim ii 710). Aristotle had used the term θρεπτικὴ ψυχή in the same sense. So too Cicero: 'iis quae [gignuntur] e terra natura nihil tribuit amplius quam ut ea alendo atque augendo tueretur' N. D. ii 12, 33.

⁹⁹ ib. ii 11, 29.

conveying a force equally strong to construct and to destroy[100]. From another point of view we may say that the seed contains the Logos or law of the fully developed plant, for under no possible circumstances can any other plant grow from that seed except the plant of its kind[101].

207. Lowest in the scale come inanimate objects, such as stones[102]. Yet even these have a property which

Cohesion.

corresponds to soul, and which keeps them together in a particular outward form or shape; this property we call 'cohesion' ($\xi\xi\iota$, *unitas*)[103]; like soul itself, it is a spirit pervading the whole[104], and again it is the Logos of the whole. An external force cannot impart this unity: so that the water contained in a glass is not an 'inanimate object' in this sense[105]. In this lowest grade of 'spirit' we read in Stoicism the antithesis of the materialism of Epicurus, who postulates for his 'atoms' the fundamental property of indivisibility, and can only account for the coherence of the bodies formed from them by supplying them with an elaborate system of 'hooks and eyes,' which was a frequent subject of derision to his critics. Epicurus makes the indivisibility of the smallest thing his starting-point, and from it constructs by degrees a compacted universe by arithmetical combination; the Stoics start from the indivisibility of the great whole, and working downwards explain its parts by a gradual shedding of primitive force. God is in fact in the stone by virtue of his power of universal penetration ($\kappa\rho\hat{\alpha}\sigma\iota\varsigma$ $\delta\iota$' $\ddot{o}\lambda\omega\nu$)[106].

---

[100] 'parvula admodum semina...in tantum convalescunt ut ingentia saxa disturbent et monumenta dissolvant. hoc quid est aliud quam intentio spiritus?' Sen. *N. Q.* ii 6, 5; and again 'quid aliud producit fruges et segetem imbecillam ac virentes exigit umbras ac distendit in ramos quam spiritus intentio et unitas?' *ib.* ii 6, 6. See also Cic. *N. D.* ii 32, 81.

[101] Arnim ii 713.

[102] 'quaedam anima carent, ut saxa; itaque erit aliquid animantibus antiquius, corpus scilicet' Sen. *Ep.* 58, 10.

[103] This use of $\xi\xi\iota\varsigma$ must be kept distinct from that which is contrasted with $\delta\iota\alpha\theta\epsilon\sigma\iota\varsigma$, as *habitus* from *dispositio*: see above, § 184.

[104] $\epsilon\kappa\tau\iota\kappa\grave{o}\nu$ $\mu\grave{e}\nu$ $o\grave{\upsilon}\nu$ $\epsilon\sigma\tau\iota$ $\pi\nu\epsilon\hat{\upsilon}\mu\alpha$ $\tau\grave{o}$ $\sigma\upsilon\nu\acute{e}\chi o\nu$ $\tau o\grave{\upsilon}\varsigma$ $\lambda\acute{\iota}\theta o\upsilon\varsigma$ Galen *introd. s. med.* xiv p. 726 K (Arnim ii 716).

[105] '[unitas corporum] ad naturam corporis [refert], nulla ope externa, sed unitate sua cohaerentis' Sen. *N. Q.* ii 2, 4.

[106] Alex. *de mixt.* p. 226, 24–30 Bruns (Arnim ii 1048); Lucian *Hermot.* 81. See above, § 186.

208.   No existing thing can possess one of the higher grades
Gradations   of spirit without also possessing all the lower.
of spirit.   Stones therefore have cohesion, plants growth
and cohesion, animals soul growth and cohesion; for these are
not different qualities which can be combined by addition, but
appearances of the same fundamental quality in varying intensity.
Man clearly possesses cohesion, for he has an outward shape;
there does not however seem to be any part of him which has
merely cohesion.   But in the bones, the nails, and the hair are
found growth and cohesion only, and these parts grow as the
plants do.   In the eyes, ears and nose, are sensation, as well as
growth and cohesion; that is, there is soul in the sense in which
the animals possess soul.   It is the intelligence only which in
man possesses soul in the highest grade[107].

209.   This universe, in spite of its majesty, beauty and
The con-   adaptation, in spite of its apparent equipoise and
flagration.   its essential divinity, is destined to perish.   'Where
the parts are perishable, so is the whole; but the parts of the
universe are perishable, for they change one into another; therefore the universe is perishable[108].'   Possibly this syllogism would
not have appeared so cogent to the Stoics, had they not long
before adopted from Heraclitus the impressive belief in the final
conflagration, familiar to us from its description in the 'second
epistle of Peter[109].'   According to this theory, the interchange
of the elements already described[110] is not evenly balanced, but
the upward movement is slightly in excess.   In the course of
long ages, therefore, all the water will have been converted into

---

[107] This gradation of soul-power is most clearly explained by Varro; 'idem Varro
tres esse adfirmat animae gradus in omni universaque natura; unum qui omnes partes
corporis, quae vivunt, transit et non habet sensum sed tantum ad vivendum valetudinem; hanc vim in nostro corpore permanare dicit in ossa ungues capillos, sicut in
mundo arbores sine sensu...crescunt et modo quodam suo vivunt; secundum gradum
animae, in quo sensus est; hanc vim pervenire in oculos aures nares os tactum; tertium
gradum esse animae summum, quod vocatur animus, in quo intellegentia praeminet;
hoc praeter hominem omnes carere mortales' Aug. *Civ. De.* vii 23.

[108] Diog. L. vii 141.

[109] 'The heavens shall pass away with a great noise, and the elements shall be
dissolved with fervent heat, and the earth and the works that are therein shall be
burned up.'   2 Peter iii 10.

[110] See above, § 196.

THE UNIVERSE 191

air and fire, and the universe will become hot with flame[111].
Then the earth and all upon it will become exhausted for want
of moisture, and the heavenly bodies themselves will lose their
vitality for want of the exhalations on which they feed. Rivers
will cease to flow, the earth will quake, great cities will be
swallowed up, star will collide with star. All living things will
die, and even the souls of the blest and the gods themselves
will once more be absorbed in the fire, which will thus regain
its primitive and essential unity[112]. Yet we may not say that
the universe dies, for it does not suffer the separation of soul
from body[113].

210. In connexion with the doctrine of the conflagration
the Stoics were called upon to take sides upon the
favourite philosophic problem whether the universe
is perishable, as Democritus and Epicurus hold, or
imperishable, as the Peripatetics say[114]. In replying to this
question, as in the theory as a whole, they relied on the
authority of Heraclitus[115]. The word universe is used in two
senses: there is an eternal universe (namely that already
described as the universal substance made individual by the
possession of quality[116]), which persists throughout an unending

Is the
universe
perishable?

[111] The theory of the conflagration appears to have been attached to the Stoic
system from without, and the logical contention is obviously weak. For if the
upward movement is in excess, the earth should disappear before the water. It
should also always be remembered that the fire that finally remains is not the
destructive, but a constructive element.

[112] 'ex quo eventurum nostri putant id,...ut ad extremum omnis mundus ignesceret,
cum humore consumpto neque terra ali posset neque remearet aer ; cuius ortus, aqua
omni exhausta, esse non posset : ita relinqui nihil praeter ignem, a quo rursum
animante ac deo renovatio mundi fieret, atque idem ornatus oriretur' Cic. *N. D.*
ii 46, 118. 'cum tempus advenerit, quo se mundus renovaturus extinguat, viribus
ista se suis caedent et sidera sideribus incurrent et omni flagrante materia uno igne
quicquid nunc ex disposito lucet ardebit. nos quoque felices animae atque aeterna
sortitae, parva ruinae ingentis accessio, in antiqua elementa vertemur' Sen. *Dial.*
vi 26, 6.

[113] οὐ ῥητέον ἀποθνήσκειν τὸν κόσμον Plut. *Sto. rep.* 39, 2.

[114] '[quaeramus] immortalis sit mundus, an inter caduca et ad tempus nata
numerandus' Sen. *Dial.* viii 4, 31.

[115] 'Heraclitus after all his speculations on the conflagration of the universe'
To himself (Rendall's transl.), iii 3. Aristotle interpreted Heraclitus in the same
way; thus he paraphrases fr. 26 (B), 66 (D); πάντα τὸ πῦρ ἐπελθὸν κρινέει καὶ καταλή-
ψεται as follows: Ἡράκλειτός φησιν ἅπαντα γίγνεσθαί ποτε πῦρ *Met.* xi 10.

[116] See above, § 193.

series of creations and conflagrations[117]. In another sense the universe, considered in relation to its present ordering, is perishable[118]. Just in the same way the word 'city' is used in two senses; and that which is a community of citizens may endure, even though the collection of temples and houses also called the 'city' is destroyed by fire[119].

211. The doctrine of the conflagration was not maintained Dissentient Stoics. by all Stoic teachers with equal conviction. Zeno treated it with fulness in his book 'on the universe[120]'; and Cleanthes and Chrysippus both assert that the whole universe is destined to change into fire, returning to that from which, as from a seed, it has sprung[121]. In the transition period, owing to the positive influence of Plato and Aristotle, and the critical acumen of Carneades, many leading Stoics abandoned the theory[122]. Posidonius however, though a pupil of Panaetius (the most conspicuous of the doubters[123]), was quite orthodox on this subject; though he pays to his master the tribute of asserting that the universe is the most permanent being imaginable[124], and that its existence will continue through an immense and *almost* unlimited period of time[125]. In the Roman period the conflagration is not only an accepted dogma, but one that makes a strong appeal to the feelings. For with the conflagration there comes to an end the struggle of the evil against the good; and the Deity may at last claim for himself a period of rest, during which he will contemplate with calmness

---

[117] Clem. Al. *Strom.* v 14 (Arnim ii 590) relying on fr. 20 (B), 30 (D). Philo *inc. mund.* p. 222, 2 (Arnim ii 620).

[118] Clem. Al. as before, relying on fr. 21 (B), 31 a (D); φθαρτὸς μὲν [ὁ κόσμος] ὁ κατὰ τὴν διακόσμησιν, Philo as above.

[119] Ar. Did. fr. 29.

[120] Diog. L. vii 142.

[121] Ζήνωνι καὶ Κλεάνθει καὶ Χρυσίππῳ ἀρέσκει τὴν οὐσίαν μεταβάλλειν οἷον εἰς σπέρμα τὸ πῦρ Ar. Did. fr. 36.

[122] See above, § 109.

[123] See above, § 115. For a full discussion of the motives of this change see Schmekel, pp. 304–318.

[124] 'ita stabilis mundus est atque ita cohaeret ad permanendum, ut nihil ne excogitari quidem possit aptius' Cic. *N. D.* ii 45, 115.

[125] '[mundi partium coniunctio] certe perdiuturna [est,] permanens ad longinquum et immensum paene tempus' *ib.* 33, 85.

the history of the universe that has passed away[126], and plan for himself a better one to follow[127].

212. Upon the conflagration will follow the reconstruction
The re- of the world (παλιγγενεσία, *renovatio*), which will
construction. lead again to a conflagration; the period between one conflagration and the next being termed a 'great year' (περίοδος, *magnus annus*). The conception of the 'great year' was borrowed by the Stoics from the Pythagoreans[128], and leads us back ultimately to astronomical calculations; for a great year is the period at the end of which sun, moon and planets all return to their original stations[129]. The phenomena of the sky recur in each new period in the same way as before; and hence we readily infer that all the phenomena of the universe, including the lives of individuals, will recur and take their course again. Although this doctrine appears only slightly connected with the general Stoic system, it was an accepted part of it: and Seneca expresses an instinctive and probably universal feeling when he says that few would willingly repeat their past histories, if they knew they were so doing[130].

213. We have put off till the end of this chapter the dis-
Creation. cussion of the Stoic theory of Creation, because it is in fact one of the least defined parts of the system. According to the theory of the great year creation is not a single work, but a recurring event; and therefore in one sense the history of the universe has neither beginning nor end. It would however be a mistake to suppose that this point of view was always present to the minds of Stoic teachers. The question of the beginning of things is of primary importance to

[126] '[Iuppiter,] resoluto mundo et dis in unum confusis paulisper cessante natura adquiescit sibi, cogitationibus suis traditus' Sen. *Ep.* 9, 16. On the relation of Ζεύς to the ἐκπύρωσις see Alex. *de mixt.* p. 226, 16 B; Philo *inc. mund.* c. 14, 15.

[127] '[conflagratio] fit, cum deo visum ordiri meliora, vetera finiri' *N. Q.* iii 28, 7.

[128] Zeller, p. 166.   [129] Cic. *N. D.* ii 20, 51: see also Schmekel, p. 241.

[130] 'veniet iterum, qui nos in lucem reponat dies; quem multi recusarent, nisi oblitos reduceret' Sen. *Ep.* 36, 10. Socrates and Plato will live again, their friends and fellow citizens will be the same, and they will be again treated as before; Nemes. *nat. hom.* p. 277 (Arnim ii 625). This theory is plainly not reconcileable with Seneca's hope of better things (see note 127). See also Hicks, *Stoic and Epicurean*, pp. 33 sqq.

every philosophy, and the Stoics approached it from many points of view, popular, scientific, mythological and theological, and gave a number of answers accordingly. To the orthodox Stoic all these answers are ultimately one, though the language in which they are expressed differs greatly; whilst the critic of Stoicism would assert that they are derived from different sources and are fundamentally irreconcileable. Seneca suggests four answers to the question 'Who made the universe?' It may be an omnipotent deity; or the impersonal Logos; or the divine Spirit working in all things by tension; or (lastly) destiny, that is, the unalterable succession of cause and result[131]. These answers we may examine in order.

214. The view that 'God made the world' is that of the

The golden age. theology which was now everywhere becoming popular; and it is usually associated, even when expounded by Stoic teachers, with dualistic views. Before the creation there existed a chaos, matter without shape, dark and damp[132]; the Deity formed a plan, and brought life order and light into the mass: from 'chaos' it became 'cosmos'[133]. This deity is the same that is commonly named Ζεύς[134] or Jove, and is called the 'father of gods and men.' The universe so created was at first happy and innocent, as is expressed in the tradition of the Golden Age. Men lived together in societies, willingly obeying the wisest and strongest of their number[135]; none were tempted to wrong their neighbours. They dwelt in natural grottos or in the stems of trees, and obtained nourishment from tame animals and wild fruits. Little by little they made progress in the arts, and learnt to build, to bake, and to make

[131] 'quisquis formator universi fuit, sive ille deus est potens omnium, sive incorporalis ratio ingentium operum artifex, sive divinus spiritus per omnia maxima et minima aequali intentione diffusus, sive fatum et immutabilis causarum inter se cohaerentium series' Sen. *Dial.* xii 8, 3.

[132] This chaos the Stoics identified with the watery stage which preceded the creation of earth in the history of the elements: see Pearson on Zeno fr. 112, 113.

[133] Seneca's writings are penetrated with this conception: 'hoc universum...dies aliquis dissipabit et in confusionem veterem tenebrasque demerget' *Dial.* xi 1, 2; cf. *Ep.* 65, 19.

[134] Δία δ' αὐτὸν καλοῦμεν, ὅτι δι' αὐτὸν γίνεται καὶ σώζεται τὰ πάντα Cornutus 2.

[135] 'illo ergo saeculo, quod aureum perhibent, penes sapientes fuisse regnum Posidonius iudicat' Sen. *Ep.* 90, 5.

use of metals. These views were especially developed by Posidonius, who believed that in the Mysians of his day, who lived on milk and honey, and abstained from flesh-meat, he could still trace the manners of this happy epoch[136]. It seems probable that it was from Posidonius, rather than from the Pythagoreans, that Varro derived his picture of the Golden Age, which has become familiar to us in turn through the version given by Ovid in his *Metamorphoses*[137].

215. These conceptions however are only familiar in the

Older Stoic theory. later forms of Stoicism. The teaching of the founders of Stoicism is on this matter monistic, and is based upon the teaching of Heraclitus that the world was in the beginning a creative fire, which was alike the creator and the material of creation. The process of creation (διακόσμησις) may be regarded as identical with that of the mutation of the elements on the downward path[138]; with the special note that when the stage of water is reached[139] the deity assumes the shape of the seed Logos (σπερματικὸς λόγος)[140], and begets in the first instance the four elements[141]; then, from a combination of these, trees and animals and all other things after their kind[142]. Yet even this statement is simplified if we regard the original fire as itself containing the seed Logoi of all things that are to be created[143]. To this is to be added that all this is well ordered, as in a duly constituted state[144]. From this point of view the

[136] Strabo vii 296. See generally Schmekel, pp. 288–290.
[137] Ov. *Met.* xv 96–142; Schmekel p. 288.
[138] κατ' ἀρχὰς μὲν οὖν καθ' αὑτὸν ὄντα [τὸν θεὸν] τρέπειν τὴν πᾶσαν οὐσίαν δι' ἀέρος εἰς ὕδωρ Diog. L. vii 136.
[139] This stage, at which the whole universe is water, even though the four elements have not yet been created, reflects the popular tradition as to Chaos as in the last section: see Pearson p. 102. For the process of creation as described by Cleanthes see Pearson p. 252.
[140] See above, § 178.
[141] καὶ ὥσπερ ἐν τῇ γονῇ τὸ σπέρμα περιέχεται, οὕτω καὶ τοῦτον, σπερματικὸν λόγον ὄντα τοῦ κόσμου......ἀπογεννᾶν πρῶτον τὰ τέσσαρα στοιχεῖα Diog. L. vii 136.
[142] εἶτα κατὰ μῖξιν ἐκ τούτων φυτά τε καὶ ζῷα καὶ τὰ ἄλλα γένη ib. 142.
[143] τὸ μέντοι πρῶτον πῦρ εἶναι καθαπερεί τι σπέρμα, τῶν ἀπάντων ἔχον τοὺς λόγους Arist. apud Euseb. *praep. ev.* xv (Arnim i 98).
[144] ταύτῃ δὲ πάντα διοικεῖσθαι τὰ κατὰ τὸν κόσμον ὑπέρευ,|καθάπερ ἐν εὐνομωτάτῃ τινὶ πολιτείᾳ ib.

Cosmos is a Cosmopolis, and we reach the border of the investigations which deal with the moral government of the universe, and the political organization of mankind.

216. We may sum up the history of the universe according
Summary. to the Stoics somewhat in the following way. Body is neither a burden on the soul nor its instrument, but all body is of itself instinct with motion, warmth, and life, which are essentially the same. This motion is not entirely that of contraction, or immobility would result; nor entirely that of expansion, else the universe would be scattered into the far distance[145]. One of these motions constantly succeeds the other, as Heraclitus says ' becoming extinguished by measure, and catching light by measure[146]'; as when a swimmer with all his strength can just hold his own against the force of the stream, or a bird straining its pinions appears to rest suspended in the air[147]. At the beginning of each world-period expansion or tension is supreme, and only the world-soul exists. Next the fiery breath begins to cool, the opposing principle of contraction asserts itself, the universe settles down and shrinks; the aether passes into air, and air in its turn to water. All this while tension is slackening, first in the centre, lastly even in the circumference; yet the vital force is not entirely quenched; beneath the covering of the waters lurks the promise of a new world. The fire still unextinguished within works upon the watery mass or chaos until it evolves from it the four elements as we know them. On its outer edge where it meets the expansive aether, the water rarefies until the belt of air is formed. All the while the outward and inward movements persist; particles of fire still pass into air, and thence into water and earth. Earth still in turn yields to water, water to air, and air to fire (ὁδὸς ἄνω κάτω). Thus by the interaction of conflicting tendencies an equilibrium (ἰσονομία) is established, and the result is the apparent permanence of the phenomenal world[148].

---

[145] Galen *de trem.* 6 VII, p. 616 K (Arnim ii 446).
[146] ἀπτόμενον μέτρα καὶ ἀποσβεννύμενον μέτρα Heracl. Fr. 20 (B), 30 (D).
[147] Galen *de musc.* i 7 and 8 (Arnim ii 450).
[148] ἐκπύρωσιν μὲν κατὰ τὴν τοῦ θεοῦ δυναστείαν τῶν ἄλλων ἐπικρατήσαντος, δια-

Finally the upward movement becomes slightly preponderant, water becomes absorbed in air and air transformed into fire, once more the conflagration results and all the world passes into the fiery breath from which it came[149].

κόσμησιν δὲ κατὰ τὴν τῶν τεττάρων στοιχείων ἰσονομίαν ἣν ἀντιδιδόασιν ἀλλήλοις Philo *an. sac.* II 242 M (Arnim ii 616).

[149] This concluding section is based upon a note, which was prepared by Mr A. C. Pearson for an edition of Chrysippus now abandoned, and which has been kindly placed by him at my disposal.

CHAPTER IX.

THE SUPREME PROBLEMS.

217. IN the preceding chapter we have discussed the uni-
*The
'mauvais pas.'* verse from the scientific standpoint. 'Such,' say
the Stoics, 'we find that the universe is ; such and
such it was in the beginning, and such it will be to the end.'
Their conclusions are reached by observation, classification, and
analysis ; and yet not entirely by these, for we must admit that
there is also employed that power of scientific imagination which
the ancients call 'divination.' Still on the whole the investigation has been that of the student, and the method that of
speculation or contemplation dissociated from any consideration
of the usefulness of the results attained. In the study we now
undertake all this is changed. Our philosophy proceeds to
assert that the universe is good, that it is directed by wise
purpose, and that it claims the reverence and obedience of
mankind. It calls upon its adherents to view the world with
moral approval, and to find in it an ethical standard. Such
conclusions cannot be reached by purely discursive reason ; but
they are such as are everywhere sought by practical men. They
appeal to a side of human nature different from that which
passes judgment on the conclusions previously reached. From
the first position 'the universe is' to the second 'the universe is
good' the step is slippery. We are on the dizzy heights of
philosophical speculation, where the most experienced climbers
find their way they know not how, and can hardly hold out a
hand to help those who are in distress. The Stoic teachers did
not perhaps always follow the same track, and now and again
they stumbled on the way. Reasoning often proved a weak
support, but resolution carried them through somehow to the
refuges on which their eyes were all along set.

218. To the problem of the meaning and government of the universe three answers were current in the epoch with which we are dealing. Either all things take place by fate; or the world is ruled by a divine providence; or else fortune is supreme[1]. These three terms are not always mutually exclusive: Virgil speaks commonly of the 'fates of the gods[2]'; and 'fortune' is frequently personified, not only in common speech, as when the Romans spoke of the 'fortune of the city,' but even by a philosopher like Lucretius, who speaks of 'Fortune the pilot[3],' with a half-humorous abandonment of exactitude. The Stoics have the merit of not only recognising fully these three powers, but also of using the terms with relative consistency. By fate then we mean an abstract necessity, an impersonal tendency, according to which events flow; by providence a personal will; by fortune the absence of both tendency and purpose, which results in a constant shifting to and fro, as when a man stands upon a ball, and is carried this way and that[4]. All explanations, both of general tendencies and of particular events, must ultimately resolve themselves into one or other of these three; every constructive system must necessarily aim at shewing that the three ultimately coincide, and that philosophy is the guardian and guide of mankind in the understanding of their relations one to another[5].

Fate, providence, and fortune.

219. The Stoics hold that 'all things happen by fate[6].' To this conclusion they are brought by the same reasoning that moved the Chaldaeans. The visible universe is, and has motion. The heavenly bodies move incessantly in their orbits; there is no force either within or without

Fate.

---

[1] The three explanations are very clearly stated by Seneca; 'dicet aliquis—quid mihi prodest philosophia, si fatum est? quid prodest, si deus rector est? quid prodest, si casus imperat?...quicquid est ex his, Lucili, vel si omnia haec sunt, philosophandum est; sive nos inexorabili lege fata constringunt, sive arbiter deus universi cuncta disponit, sive casus res humanas sine ordine impellit et iactat, philosophia nos tueri debet' Sen. *Ep.* 16, 4 and 5.

[2] e.g. *Aen.* vi 376.

[3] 'quod procul a nobis flectat Fortuna gubernans' *R. N.* v 108.

[4] 'vaga volubilisque Fortuna' Cic. *Milo* 26, 69; 'fortuna...amica varietati constantiam respuit' *N. D.* ii 16, 43.

[5] Seneca as in note 1.

[6] Diog. L. vii 149; '[Stoici] omnia fato fieri dicunt' Cic. *de Fato* 15, 33.

them that can turn them aside a hair's breadth, or make their
pace quicker or slower. No prayers of men, no prerogatives of
gods can make them change[7]. Without cause there is no effect;
and each effect is in its turn a new cause. Thus is constructed
an endless chain, in which all things living and inanimate are
alike bound. If a man knew all the causes that exist, he could
trace out all the consequences. What will be, will be; what will
not be, cannot be. This first Stoic interpretation of the universe
is that of Determinism; it reiterates and drives home the principle that is here our starting-point, 'the universe is.' 'Chrysippus,
Posidonius, and Zeno say that all things take place according to
fate; and fate is the linked cause of things that are, or the
system by which the universe is conducted[8].' This 'fate' is only
another name for 'necessity[9]'; fates cannot be changed[10].

220.   The doctrine of fate appears to contradict directly the
belief in human free will, and to lead up to the
practical doctrine of laziness (ἀργὸς λόγος, *ignava
ratio*). Once we allow it to be true that 'what will be,
will be,' it becomes useless to make any effort. As at the present
time, this argument was familiar in cases of sickness. One says
to the sick person, 'if it is your fate to recover, then you will
recover whether you call in the physician or not; and if it is
your fate not to recover, then you will not recover in either case.
But it is your fate either to recover or not to recover; therefore it will be useless to call in the physician.' To which another
will reply: 'you may as well argue that if it is your fate to beget
a son, you will beget one equally whether you consort with your
wife or not; therefore it will be useless to consort with your

The
'fallacies' of
determinism.

---

[7] 'et hoc secundum Stoicos, qui omnia dicunt fato regi et semel constituta nec
a numinibus posse mutari' Comment. in Lucan. ii 306 (Arnim ii 924).

[8] So Diog. L. vii 149. Cicero and Seneca describe with admirable clearness the
conception of fate: 'fieri omnia fato ratio cogit fateri. fatum autem id appello, quod
Graeci εἱμαρμένην, id est ordinem seriemque causarum, cum causa causae nexa rem ex
se gignat' Cic. *Div.* i 55, 125; 'quid enim intellegis fatum? existimo necessitatem
rerum omnium actionumque, quam nulla vis rumpat' Sen. *N. Q.* ii 36; cf. *Ep.* 19, 6
and *N. Q.* ii 35, 2.

[9] Χρύσιππος μὴ διαφέρειν [εἶπε] τοῦ εἱμαρμένου τὸ κατηναγκασμένον Aët. *plac.* i 27, 2.

[10] 'Stoicorum dogma [Vergilius] ostendit, nulla ratione posse fata mutari' Serv.
ad Verg. Aen. i 257 (Arnim ii 923).

wife[11].' With such verbal disputes Chrysippus delighted to deal; his reply to the 'lazy argument' was that certain things go together by fate (*iuncta fato, confatalia*)[12]. Thus in the above cases it may be determined by fate that you should both call in a physician and recover, both consort with your wife and beget a son.

So once more when Nestor says to the watchmen by his ships:

> Keep watch, my lads: let sleep seize no man's eyes,
> Lest foes, loud laughing, take us by surprize[13].

Some one then replies, 'No, they will not, even if we sleep, if it is predestined that the dock be not seized.' To such an objection any one can give the right answer: 'all these things are equally predestined, and go together by fate. There is no such thing as a watch kept by sleepers, a victory won by runaways, or a harvest reaped except after sowing good clean soil[14].'

221. The doctrine of fate also seems to conflict with some of the commonest forms of speech. For if it is *Logic of possibility.* correct to say 'Either this will happen, or it will not happen,' it seems incorrect to say 'it may happen'; and still more of the past, since we must admit of any event that 'it has happened' or 'it has not happened,' there seems no room for the statement 'it might have happened.' Chrysippus however maintains that the words 'may' and 'might' are correctly used, or (in other words) that we may assert that it is or was 'possible' for things to happen, whether or not they will happen or have happened. For example, the pearl here is breakable, and may be broken, though fate has ordained that it never will be broken. Cypselus might not have been tyrant of Corinth, though the oracle at Delphi declared a thousand years before the time that he would be[15]. This view had been sharply contested by Diodorus the Megarian; and the controversy was summed up in the 'master argument.' This is stated as follows: there are three propositions in conflict with one another in the sense that if any

[11] Orig. *cont. Cels.* ii 20 (Arnim ii 957).
[12] Cic. *de Fato* 12, 28 to 13, 30.
[13] Hom. *Il.* xi 192 and 193.
[14] Plut. fr. 15, 3 (Stob. ii 8, 25).
[15] Cic. *de Fato* 7, 13.

two of them are true, the third is false. They are these: (i) every
past event is necessary; (ii) the impossible cannot follow on the
possible; (iii) there are things possible that neither are nor will
be true. Diodorus accepted the first two; he therefore drew the
conclusion that there is nothing possible except that which is
or will be true; or in other words he denied the existence of any
category of 'things possible' distinct from that of facts past or
future. Cleanthes and Antipater accepted the second and third
propositions: Chrysippus accepted the first and third, but denied
the second[16]; that is he admitted that the possible thing (e.g. the
breaking of the pearl) might become the impossible because fate
had decided to the contrary. The choice intimates much; it
shows that the Stoics, however strongly they assert the rule
of fate or necessity, intend so to interpret these terms as to
reconcile them with the common use of words, that is, with the
inherited belief in divine and human will, breaking through the
chain of unending cause and effect[17].

222. The next step is professedly taken by way of definition
of the word 'fate' (εἱμαρμένη, *fatum*). Exactly as

Definitions
of fate.

the stuff of the universe, fire, has been explained
to be no mere passive or destructive element, but one possessed
of creative force and reason, so is fate declared to be no blind
or helpless sequence of events, but an active and wise power
which regulates the universe. Fate is in fact but another name
for the Logos or World-reason. On this point all Stoic teachers
are in the main agreed. 'Fate,' said Zeno, 'is a power which
stirs matter by the same laws and in the same way; it may
equally well be called providence or nature[18].' Chrysippus
gives us several alternative definitions: 'the essence of fate is
a spiritual force, duly ordering the universe[19]'; it is 'the Logos
of the universe[20],' or 'the law of events providentially ordered

---

[16] Epict. *Disc.* ii 19, 1 sqq.

[17] Cicero gives a humorous comment on this contention: 'περὶ δυνατῶν me scito
κατὰ Διόδωρον κρίνειν; quapropter si venturus es, scito necesse esse te venire: sin autem
non es, τῶν ἀδυνάτων est te venire. nunc vide, utra te κρίσις magis delectet, Χρυσιπ-
πείανε, an haec, quam noster Diodotus non concoquebat. sed de his etiam rebus,
otiosi cum erimus, loquemur; hoc etiam κατὰ Χρύσιππον δυνατόν est' *ad Fam.* ix 4.

[18] Aët. *plac.* i 27, 5.   [19] *ib.* i 28, 3.

[20] εἱμαρμένη ἐστὶν ὁ τοῦ κόσμου λόγος *ib.*

in the universe[21]'; or, 'the law by which things that have been have been, that are are, that will be will be[22].' But an important difference appears between the views of Cleanthes and Chrysippus. They are agreed that all that happens by providence also happens by fate. But Cleanthes will not allow, as Chrysippus is prepared to do, that all things that happen by fate happen providentially[23]. With Cleanthes the conception of fate is wider than that of providence, just as in Virgil the fates are more powerful than Jove. Cleanthes, being deeply conscious of the evil existing in the universe, refused to hold providence responsible for it. Chrysippus on the other hand identifies fate with the deity[24].

223. Providence (πρόνοια, *providentia*) differs from fate, if
Providence. at all, by including an element of personality. It
is a principal dogma of the Stoics that 'the universe is ruled by providence.' Cicero indeed assures us that the word 'providence' is merely an abbreviation for 'the providence of the gods,' and that the dogma really asserts that 'the universe is ruled by the gods with foresight'; and Balbus, the Stoic advocate, in his treatise, rebukes his opponent Cotta for having travestied the Stoic doctrine by speaking of providence as 'a fortune-telling hag,' as though she were some kind of goddess governing the world[25]. But the travesty is at least as instructive as the exposition. If 'providence' is on the one hand interpreted as God's providence[26], it is on the other hand equivalent to Nature[27], and again to the Mind of the universe; it is the Logos,

21 ἤ, λόγος τῶν ἐν τῷ κόσμῳ προνοίᾳ διοικουμένων Aët. *plac.* i 28, 3.
22 ἢ λόγος καθ᾽ ὃν τὰ μὲν γεγονότα γέγονε, τὰ δὲ γινόμενα γίνεται, τὰ δὲ γενησόμενα γενήσεται *ib.*
23 ' ex quo fieri, ut quae secundum fatum sunt etiam ex providentia sint, eodemque modo quae secundum providentiam ex fato, ut putat Chrysippus. alii vero, quae quidem ex providentiae auctoritate, fataliter quoque provenire, nec tamen quae fataliter ex providentia, ut Cleanthes' Chalc. *in Timaeum* 144 (Arnim ii 933).
24 'Chrysippus...deum dicit esse...fatalem vim et necessitatem rerum futurarum' Cic. *N. D.* i 15, 39.
25 'a te dictum est anum fatidicam πρόνοιαν a Stoicis induci, id est providentiam. quod eo errore dixisti, quod existimas ab his providentiam fingi quasi quandam deam singularem, quae mundum omnem gubernet et regat. plene autem et perfecte sic dici existimato, providentia deorum mundum administrari' *ib.* ii 29, 73 and 74.
26 Χρύσιππος καὶ Ζήνων ὑπέθεντο...διὰ πάντων διήκειν τὴν πρόνοιαν αὐτοῦ Hippolyt. *Philos.* 21, 1 (Arnim i 153).
27 ἥντινα [τὴν εἱμαρμένην] μὴ διαφέρειν πρόνοιαν καὶ φύσιν καλεῖν Aët. *plac.* i 27, 5.

the universal Law, the creative force[28]; not merely an attribute, but a manifestation and bodily presentment of deity. After the final conflagration three joining in one will be left, Zeus, providence, and the creative fire[29]. Lastly, if we consider the process of logical demonstration, it is from the reality of providence that the Stoics deduce the existence of the gods; only from the standpoint of dogmatic instruction is the order reversed.

224. The work and functions of Providence are open to our

Beauty of the universe.

view, for it has an aim and pathway of its own[30]. Its first aim is to create a universe capable of enduring; next, it makes that universe complete; thirdly, it endows it with every beauty and excellence[31]. The beauty of the world is a favourite theme upon which Stoic orators discourse at length; this is, in their view, the best world that could possibly have been created[32]. This sense of beauty appears to be derived from two sources, the admiration and awe felt in contemplating the sky, the sun moon and stars moving in it, lofty mountains, rushing rivers, and deep caves[33]; and the gentler delight stirred by the sight of the fertile field, the vine-clad hill, the river-pathway, the flocks and herds, which all subserve the convenience of man. Thus from beauty we pass to usefulness, and the Stoics now maintain that the world has been created and is maintained for the use of man[34]. In strict language, however, we must say that the universe is made for the use of rational beings, that is, for gods and men[35], that

[28] 'talis igitur mens mundi cum sit, ob eamque causam vel prudentia vel providentia appellari recte possit (Graece enim πρόνοια dicitur)...' Cic. N. D. ii 22, 58. The term 'nature' is used in the same sense by Epicurus also, though it does not harmonize very well with his theory; 'natura gubernans' R. N. v 78.

[29] ὅταν οὖν ἐκπύρωσις γένηται, μόνον ἄφθαρτον ὄντα τὸν Δία τῶν θεῶν ἀναχωρεῖν ἐπὶ τὴν πρόνοιαν, εἶτα ὁμοῦ γενομένους ἐπὶ μιᾶς τῆς τοῦ αἰθέρος οὐσίας διατελεῖν ἀμφοτέρους Plut. comm. not. 36, 5.

[30] 'habet quasi viam quandam et sectam, quam sequatur' Cic. N. D. ii 22, 57.

[31] ib. 22, 58.

[32] '[mundi] quidem administratio nihil habet in se, quod reprehendi possit; ex iis enim naturis, quae erant, quod effici optimum potuit, effectum est' ib. 34, 86.

[33] ib. 39, 98.

[34] 'omnia hominum causa facta esse et parata' ib. ii 61, 154.

[35] 'deorum et hominum causa factum esse mundum' ib. 53, 133.

it is a home or city in which gods and men alike have a share[36]. From the protection of providence the animals, according to the Stoic view, are in principle entirely excluded. Yet it did not escape notice that nature has often provided for their comfort in particulars, giving them instincts that enable them to maintain life, and an outward shape conformable to the conditions of their existence[37]. And Seneca especially found that man was apt to swell himself too greatly, as if that world were made for him, of which only a small part is adapted for him to dwell in, and where day and night, summer and winter would continue of themselves, even if no man observed them[38]. On the other hand zealots like Chrysippus worked out the detailed application of this theory in a way that provoked the amusement of their critics[39].

225. Providence cares for mankind in general, and therefore
Particular providence. for the parts of mankind, the various continents, nations, and cities. The Stoics are also inclined to hold that it cares for the individual[40]. The difficulty of this belief is great. Busy cities are overthrown by the earthquake; the crops of the careful farmer are blasted by the hailstorm; Socrates is condemned to death by the Athenians; Pythagoras, Zeno and Antiphon meet with violent ends. Yet we may not think that in any of these cases the sufferers were hated or neglected by the gods; it is rather an inevitable necessity that has worked their ruin. The gods who have great things in their charge, must sometimes overlook small matters; they must save the

[36] 'est enim mundus quasi communis deorum atque hominum domus aut urbs utrorumque' Cic. N. D. ii 62, 154; 'intraturus es urbem dis hominibusque communem' Sen. Dial. vi 18, 1.

[37] Cic. N. D. ii 47, 122.

[38] 'neque enim omnia deus homini fecit. quota pars operis tanti nobis committitur?' Sen. N. Q. vii 30, 3; 'nimis nos suspicimus, si digni nobis videmur propter quos tanta moveantur' Dial. iv 27, 2.

[39] Thus 'horses assist men in fighting, dogs in hunting: lions and leopards provide a discipline in courage: the sow is convenient for sacrifices to the gods, who have given her a soul to serve as salt, and keep the flesh from rotting. The peacock is created for his tail, and the peahen accompanies him for symmetry's sake. The flea is useful to wake us out of sleep, and the mouse to prevent us from being careless in leaving the cheese about.' All these particulars are attributed to Chrysippus (Arnim ii 1152, 1163).

[40] 'etiam singulis a dis immortalibus consuli et provideri solet' Cic. N. D. ii 65, 164.

community by sacrificing the individual[41]. The storm may rage
in the valley, yet there is peace on the mountain heights[42]. The
philosopher who is absorbed in contemplating the great whole
cannot even see the flaws in its details. 'If the gods care for
all men,' says Cicero's authority, 'it follows logically that they
care for each single man[43].' 'Nothing occurs on earth, nor in
the heaven above, nor in the sea, apart from thee, O God,' sings
Cleanthes[44]. 'It is impossible,' says Chrysippus, 'that even the
least of particulars can fall out otherwise than in accordance
with the will of God, with his Word, with law, with justice, and
with providence[45].'

226. The doctrine of providence, carried to a logical extreme,
Existence leads to the denial of the existence of evil. But
of evil.   the Stoics did not draw this conclusion; had they
done so, their whole treatment of ethics would have become
futile. We have therefore to scrutinize carefully the language
that they employ. If we meet with the paradox that 'this is
the best of all possible worlds,' we must remember that all
paradoxes need for their interpretation some sense of humour,
and that the 'best possible' is not the same as the 'best imaginable.' Somewhere or other there is, in a sense, a limitation to
the sphere of providence. If again in poetical passages we learn
that 'nothing occurs without God,' we must not forget the
doctrine that good and evil are alike brought in the end into
harmony with the divine nature. The most exact statement of
Stoic doctrine would seem to be that evil exists indeed, but is
not the equal of the good either in intensity or in duration; it
is an incident, not a first principle of the universe[46]. From this

[41] 'nec vero si segetibus aut vinetis cuiuspiam tempestas nocuerit,...eum, cui quid
horum acciderit, aut invisum deo aut neglectum a deo [iudicabimus]. magna di curant,
parva neglegunt' Cic. *N. D.* ii 66, 167; '[universorum] maior dis cura quam
singulorum est' Sen. *Dial.* i 3, 1. See also note 64.

[42] 'lege deum minimas rerum discordia turbat, | pacem magna tenent' Lucan
Phars. ii 273.

[43] 'licet contrahere universitatem generis humani eamque gradatim ad pauciores,
postremo deducere ad singulos' Cic. *N. D.* ii 65, 164.

[44] *Hymn,* vv. 15, 16.   [45] Plut. *comm. not.* 34, 5; *Sto. rep.* 34, 10.

[46] This appears to be the correct interpretation of the saying of Epictetus—'as
a mark is not set up for the purpose of missing the aim, so neither does the nature
of evil exist in the world' *Manual* 27 (Long's transl. ii p. 269, where see his note).

point of view it becomes possible to 'plead the cause of the gods,' to defend providence from the heavy accusations men bring forward against it[47]. Thus the Stoics set about to prove that, in spite of the existence of evil, the universe is ruled by the foresight of a beneficent deity.

227. The first argument for the defence is logical, and is
Logical
solutions. pressed by Chrysippus. Good implies its opposite, evil. 'There could be no justice, unless there were also injustice; no courage, unless there were cowardice; no truth, unless there were falsehood[48].' Just in the same way we find coarse wit in a comedy, which is objectionable in itself, and yet somehow contributes to the charm of the poem as a whole[49]. The second argument is based upon the doctrine of 'necessary consequence' ($\pi\alpha\rho\alpha\kappa o\lambda o\acute{v}\theta\eta\sigma\iota\varsigma$). The general design of the human head required that it should be compacted of small and delicate bones, accompanying which is the inevitable disadvantage that the head may easily be injured by blows[50]. War is an evil, but it turns to good by ridding the world of superfluous population[51].

In many other cases there may be explanations that are beyond our present knowledge, just as there are many kinds of animals of which we do not yet know the use[52].

228. More important are those arguments which introduce
Moral
solutions. moral considerations. In the first place the generous intentions of providence are often thwarted by the perverseness of wicked men[53], just as many a son uses his inheritance ill, and yet his father in bequeathing it to him did him a service[54]. The Deity treats good men as a Roman father his children, giving them a stern training, that they may grow in

---

[47] 'faciam rem non difficilem, causam deorum agam' Sen. *Dial.* i 1, 1.

[48] Gell. *N. A.* vii 1, 4 and 5 ; 'nulli vitium est, nisi cui virtus potest esse' Sen. *Ep.* 124, 19.

[49] Plut. *comm. not.* 14, 1 ; M. Ant. vi 42.   [50] A. Gellius, *N. A.* vii 1, 9 to 11.

[51] Plut. *Sto. rep.* 32, 2.   [52] Lactantius *de ira* 13 (Arnim ii 1172).

[53] πλὴν ὁπόσα ῥέζουσι κακοὶ σφετέρῃσιν ἀνοίαις Cleanthes *Hymn* 18.

[54] Cic. *N. D.* iii 28, 70.

virtue[55]; those that he loves, he hardens[56]. Earthquakes and conflagrations may occur on earth, and perhaps similar catastrophes in the sky, because the world needs to be purified from the wickedness that abounds[57]. The punishment of the wicked, for instance by pestilence and famine, stands for an example to other men, that they may learn to avoid a like disaster[58]. Often, if the wicked have gone unpunished, the penalty descends on their children, their grandchildren, and their descendants[59].

229. The very multiplicity of these explanations or excuses betrays the weakness of the case, and the Stoics are in the last resort driven to admit that the Deity is neither all-knowing nor all-powerful, and that the sphere of providence is limited by an all-encircling necessity. Thus Chrysippus explains blunders in divination by saying that 'the Deity cannot know everything[60],' and though he ascribes to the Deity all power, yet when hard pressed he admits that he cannot do everything, and that 'there is a good deal of necessity in the matter[61].' In this way he is forced back to the position which the shrewder Cleanthes had taken from the first[62]. After we have taken away from fate all that has life or meaning, there remains a residuum, which we can but vaguely assign to some 'natural necessity[63].' This point once granted, we realize that it includes many of the detailed explanations previously given. Thus it is by 'natural necessity' that good cannot exist without evil; that the past cannot be altered; that the one must suffer for the many[64]; that the good cannot always be

Divine power limited.

[55] 'patrium deus habet adversus bonos viros animum et illos fortiter amat; operibus, inquit, doloribus, damnis exagitentur, ut verum colligant robur' Sen. *Dial.* i 2, 6.

[56] 'deus quos probat, quos amat, indurat, recognoscit, exercet' *ib.* 4, 7; 'when a difficulty falls upon you, remember that God, like a trainer of wrestlers, has matched you with rough young men' Epict. *Disc.* i 24, 1.

[57] This view of Origen is conjecturally assigned to a Stoic source (Arnim ii 1174). See also Philo ap. Euseb. *praep. ev.* viii 13.

[58] Plut. *Sto. rep.* 15, 2.   [59] Cic. *N. D.* iii 38, 90; Sen. *Ben.* iv 32, 1.

[60] Arnim ii 1183.

[61] φησὶ δὲ πολὺ καὶ τὸ τῆς ἀνάγκης μεμῖχθαι Plut. *Sto. rep.* 37, 2.

[62] See above, § 222.

[63] Seneca uses the term 'law of mortality': 'minime dis [irascamur]: non enim illorum, sed lege mortalitatis patimur quicquid incommodi accidit' *Dial.* iv 28, 4.

[64] 'sciat illa ipsa, quibus laedi videtur, ad conservationem universi pertinere, et ex iis esse, quae cursum mundi officiumque consummant' *Ep.* 74, 20.

separated from the bad[65]; that character grows by the defiance of pain; that the individual is everywhere exposed to disaster from tyranny, war, pestilence, famine, and earthquake.

230. God and men allied. The recognition of the limitations of divine power creates a new tie between gods and men. Men are no longer the mere instruments of providence, they are its fellow-workers; we may even go further, and boldly call them its fellow-sufferers[66]. God has given man what he could, not what he would[67]; he could not change the stuff on which he had to work[68]; if anything has not been granted to us, it could not have been granted[69]. Under such circumstances a sensible man will not find fault with the gods, who have done their best[70]; nor will he make appeals to them to which they cannot respond[71]. Even less will he quarrel with a destiny that is both blind and deaf[72].

231. Fortune. In the Stoic explanation of the universe fortune plays no part; it has no existence in the absolute sense of the term[73]. But in practical life, and from the limited point of view of the individuals concerned, fortune is everywhere met with. Her actions are the same as we have

65 'di multa ingratis tribuunt. sed illa bonis paraverunt: contingunt etiam malis, quia separari non possunt. excerpere singulos non potuerunt' *Ben.* iv 28, 1.

66 'quicquid est quod nos sic vivere sic mori iussit, eadem necessitate et deos adligat' *Dial.* i 5, 8.

67 '[God] has given me the things which are in the power of the will. How was he able to make the earthly body free from hindrance? [He could not], and accordingly he has subjected to the revolution of the whole possessions, household things, house, children, wife' Epict. *Disc.* iv 1, 100. 'What says Zeus? since I was not able to do for you what I have mentioned, I have given you a small portion of us' *ib.* i 1, 10–12.

68 'non potest artifex mutare materiam' Sen. *Dial.* i 5, 9; see also Plut. *comm. not.* 34, and Mayor on Cic. *N. D.* ii 34, 86. In technical language, the gods cannot control the ἐπακολουθήματα and συναπτόμενα.

69 'quicquid nobis negatum est, dari non potuit' Sen. *Ben.* ii 29, 3.

70 'dementes itaque et ignari veritatis illis imputant saevitiam maris, immodicos imbres, pertinaciam hiemis' *Dial.* iv 27, 2.

71 'frustra vota ac studia sunt; habebit quisque quantum illi dies primus adscripsit' *ib.* vi 21, 6.

72 'accusare fata possumus, mutare non possumus: stant dura et inexorabilia' *ib.* xi 4, 1.

73 See above, § 226, note 46. Fortune only has ultimate existence if identified with fate or providence; 'sic nunc naturam voca, fatum, fortunam; omnia eiusdem dei nomina sunt varie utentis sua potestate' *Ben.* iv 8, 3.

just seen to be ascribed to 'natural necessity'; storms, ship-
wrecks, plagues, wars, and tyranny[74]. Fortune therefore by no
means excludes causality, but includes all events which are
without meaning from the point of view of the individual[75];
all advantages or disadvantages which he has not personally
merited, and which are not designed for his individual discipline.
So great is the sphere of Fortune, that it appears at first that she
is mistress of human life; and we may picture her as a tyrant,
mocking and merciless, without principle and without policy[76].
The further consideration of Fortune belongs to the department
of Ethics.

232. The supreme problems of philosophy, in their relation
to gods and men, the fellow-citizens of this universe,
centre in the question of free will. If we grant that
the divine power is to some extent less in range than
the power of necessity, does it still remain open to us to attribute
to it within that range some real choice between alternatives,
something of that individual power which common opinion
attributes to kings? or must we on the other hand regard the
divinity as a mere symbol of an unchanging law, girt with the
trappings of a royalty from which all real share in government
has been withdrawn? Is man again a mere puppet under the
control either of fate or of fortune, or has he too some share in
creating the destiny to which he must submit? Supposing him
to have this power of will, is it bound up with his privilege of
reason, or do the animals also possess it?

*Has God
or man
free will?*

233. To such questions the Stoics do not give the direct
answer 'Yes' or 'No.' The critics who wish to tie
them down to one or other of the opposing views
complain that they wriggle and grow flushed and

*The Stoics
incline
towards
free will.*

---

[74] 'fortuna ceteros casus rariores habet, primum ab inanimis procellas, tempestates,
naufragia, ruinas, incendia; deinde a bestiis ictus, morsus, impetus, etc.' Cic. *Off.* ii
6, 19; 'saepe...optimorum virorum segetem grando percussit. fert sortem suam
quisque' Sen. *Ben.* ii 28, 3.

[75] So Fortune is technically defined as 'a cause not discerned by human reason';
οἱ Στωϊκοὶ [τὴν τύχην] αἰτίαν ἄδηλον ἀνθρωπίνῳ λογισμῷ Aët. *plac.* i 29, 7.

[76] 'in regnum Fortunae et quidem durum atque invictum pervenimus, illius
arbitrio digna atque indigna passuri' Sen. *Dial.* vi 10, 6; 'hanc imaginem animo
tuo propone, ludos facere fortunam' *Ep.* 74, 7.

excited about their answer[77]. They accept apparently both views as dogmas, asserting that 'all things take place by destiny' and that 'something rests with us[78].' To the first dogma the whole of their treatment of physics points; but the second is required as a postulate for any science of ethics[78a]. The Stoics were in no way disposed to cut the knot by sacrificing one or the other of the principal parts of their philosophy. They go back upon the terms in which the questions are propounded, and endeavour by fresh investigation and more precise definition to do away with the obvious contradiction. In this work they were observed to have a bias in favour of free will[79]. The first sign of this bias we have already noticed in the vindication of the word 'possible[80].' If our eyes are fixed merely on the movement of the heavenly bodies, we shall hardly need a term which prints on future events a character which it denies to those that are past. The astronomer can describe to us with equal precision an eclipse taking place a thousand years before the battle of Salamis or a thousand years after. But the word 'possible' opens the door to the emotions of hope and fear, to the sense of right and wrong, with regard to the whole range of future events. However delicately the doctrine may be shaded, the main issue is determined when we say of gods and men that they 'can[81].'

[77] 'Chrysippus aestuans laboransque quonam pacto explicet et fato omnia fieri et esse aliquid in nobis, intricatur hoc modo' Gellius *N. A.* vii 2, 15.

[78] ἐκεῖνο γὰρ δὴ τὸ καταγελαστότατον ἁπάντων, τὸ μίγμα καὶ ἡ σύνοδος τοῦ καὶ ἐπὶ τοῖς ἀνθρώποις τι εἶναι, καὶ εἱρμὸν (seriem causarum) οὐδὲν ἧττον εἶναι Oenom. apud Euseb. *pr. ev.* vi p. 258 (Arnim ii 978); 'manente fato aliquid est in hominis arbitrio' Sen. *N. Q.* ii 38, 3.

[78a] 'ubi igitur virtus, si nihil situm est in nobis ipsis?' Cic. *Ac.* ii 12, 39.

[79] 'mihi quidem videtur, cum duae sententiae fuissent veterum philosophorum, una eorum qui censerent omnia ita fato fieri ut id fatum vim necessitatis adferret... altera eorum quibus viderentur sine ullo fato esse animorum motus voluntarii, Chrysippus tanquam arbiter honorarius medium ferire voluisse, sed adplicat se ad eos potius, qui necessitate motus animorum liberatos volunt' Cic. *de Fato* 17, 39.

[80] See above, § 221.

[81] It seems clear that so far as human thought goes 'possibility' is only an abstraction from that which 'a man can do,' reached by widening the subject 'man' so as to include both superhuman powers and half-personified unseen forces. In other words δυνατόν is derived from δύναται, *possibilitas* from *potest*. Such a combination as *fortuna potest*, though quite common, is really a contradiction in terms.

234. In order to reconcile the doctrines of causality and
possibility, we must first distinguish between outer
and inner compulsion, between 'proximate' and
'principal' causes. If a boy starts a cylinder
rolling down hill, he gives it an opportunity without which it
could not have rolled; this is the proximate cause (προκα-
ταρκτική, *proxima*). But the cylinder would not continue rolling
except by an inner compulsion, a law within itself, by which it
is the nature of cylinders to roll downwards[82]. This is the leading
or principal cause (προηγουμένη, *antecedens* or *principalis*). So
neither in thought nor in action can a man form a judgment,
unless there be a picture (φαντασία, *visum*) presented to his
mind. The picture is a proximate cause[83]. But assent to the
picture rests with the man himself; the man himself, his reason,
his will, is the principal cause. Here we touch on the dogma
which is the foundation of ethics: 'assent is in our power.'
Upon this rests the right of the philosopher to praise or blame,
the right of the lawgiver to reward and punish.

Proximate and principal causes.

235. We have to investigate further the inner compulsion,
the principal cause. With regard to the gods
their own disposition is a law to them, their character holds them to their purpose, their majesty
makes their decrees immutable[84]. This is the final answer of
philosophy, even though men cannot content themselves with it.
Even amongst those most disposed to accept Stoic principles,
there is a wish that the gods should be allowed a little *play*,
a choice at any rate in small matters not hampered by considerations of destiny and morality[85]; and upon this issue the poet

The divine nature immutable.

---

[82] 'qui protrusit cylindrum, dedit ei principium motionis, volubilitatem autem non dedit' Cic. *de Fato* 19, 43.

[83] 'quamquam adsensio non possit fieri nisi commota viso, tamen id visum proximam causam [habet], non principalem' *ib.* 18, 42.

[84] 'non externa cogunt deos, sed sua illis in legem aeterna voluntas est. statuerunt quae non mutarent,...nec unquam primi consilii deos paenitet. vis sua illos in pro-posito tenet' Sen. *Ben.* vi 23, 1 and 2; '[deus] scripsit quidem fata, sed sequitur. semper paret,,semel iussit' *Dial.* i 5, 8. So Lucan: 'qua cuncta coercet se quoque lege tenens' *Phars.* ii 9, 10.

[85] 'disco...liceat illi [sc. deo] hodieque decernere et ex lege fatorum aliquid derogare, an maiestatis diminutio sit et confessio erroris mutanda fecisse?' Sen. *N. Q.* i Prol. 3.

may deviate a little from the sterner creed of the philosopher[86]. Nor must we so interpret the wisdom and benevolence of the gods as to deny the efficacy of prayer[87].

236. In the case of men free will comes accompanied by a heavy burden of responsibility; for by its exercise men have defied the gods and brought evil into the world. In vain they accuse the gods and destiny, when their own perverseness has exaggerated their destiny, as Homer bears witness :

Man's wickedness.

'Lo you now, how vainly mortal men do blame the gods! For of us they say comes evil, whereas they even of themselves, through the blindness of their own hearts, have sorrows beyond that which is ordained[88].'

'Through the blindness of their own hearts they perished, fools[89].'

Equally in vain it is that they protest against the penalties prescribed by the lawgiver for acts to which they allege fate has drawn them[90]. Of their wrong-doing the 'principal cause' lies in their own natures ; if these are from the first wholesome, the blows of fate are deadened; if they are boorish and undisciplined, they rush of themselves into sin and error[91]. Into the further question, whether a man is responsible for his own nature, our authorities do not enter. It is sufficient that in ethics a way will be pointed out, by which all men, if only they consent to undergo the necessary training, may bring their wills into harmony with the will of the universe. As to the animals, they act upon impulse, but cannot be said in a strict sense to possess will, nor are they proper subjects for praise and blame.

[86] 'illud te, nulla fati quod lege tenetur, | pro Latio obtestor' Verg. *Aen.* xii 819, 820.

[87] 'nos quoque existimamus vota proficere, salva vi ac potestate fatorum' Sen. *N. Q.* ii 37, 2; 'deos quorum notitiam nulla res effugit, rogamus; et illos vota non exorant, sed admonent' *Ben.* v 25, 4.

[88] Hom. *Od.* i 32–34 (Butcher and Lang's translation). [89] *ib.* 7.

[90] 'propterea nocentium poenas legibus inique constitutas, si homines ad maleficia non sponte veniunt, sed fato trahuntur' A. Gellius *N. A.* vii 2, 5.

[91] 'contra ea Chrysippus argute disserit : ingenia, inquit, ipsa proinde sunt fato obnoxia, ut proprietas eorum est ipsa et qualitas. nam si sunt per naturam primitus salubriter utiliterque ficta, omnem illam vim quae de fato extrinsecus ingruit, inoffensius tractabiliusque transmittunt. sin vero sunt aspera et inscita et rudia...sua scaevitate et voluntario impetu in assidua delicta et in errores se ruunt' A. Gellius *N. A.* vii 2, 6 to 8.

237. Thus free will, which at first sight appears equivalent
to the negation of cause, is by the Stoics identified
with the highest type of cause. Action without
cause (τὸ ἀναίτιον), effect which is self-caused (τὸ
αὐτόματον), are totally denied[92]. Even if a man be given the
choice between two actions which appear exactly equivalent,
as when he must begin walking either with the right or with
the left foot, there is always a cause which determines between
them, though (as in all cases of 'chance') it is not discernible by
human reasoning[93]. In this way destiny, cause, will are all
brought into harmony; the dualism (which after all cannot be
entirely avoided) is thrust out of sight. 'All things take place
according to destiny, but not all things according to necessity[94]';
thus is saved the principle of free choice (τὸ ἐφ' ἡμῖν). In other
words, the Stoic fixes his attention on the pulsating, living, willing
powers of the universe, and refuses to dwell upon any blind non-
moral unbending 'necessity' of things, even whilst he admits that
such necessity is there.

No result without cause.

238. Now that the various steps have been decided upon,
by which our philosophy progresses from physics
to ethics, it remains to connect them by a pathway
in the form of a chain of reasoning. We cannot affirm that the
steps have been reached by any logical process, or that the show
of reasoning makes them any safer to tread in. But the logical
form is a convenient method of impressing dogmatic instruction
on the memory, and if it cannot remove difficulties inherent in
the subject-matter, it at least so distributes them that they may
be overlooked by the zealous and defied by the adventurous.
Thus then the argument runs :—

Pons Stoicus.

'If all things are determined by fate, then the ordering of the universe
must be smooth and unhindered; if this is so, there must be an ordered
universe; and if so, there must be gods. Now if there are gods, the gods
are good; and if they are good, goodness exists; and if goodness exists, so

---

[92] πρὸς τούτους ὁ Χρύσιππος ἀντιλέγων...[εἶπε] τὸ ἀναίτιον ὅλως ἀνύπαρκτον εἶναι καὶ
τὸ αὐτόματον Plut. *Sto. rep.* 23, 2 and 3.

[93] τί γὰρ ἄλλο ποιοῦσιν οἱ τὴν τύχην καὶ τὸ αὐτόματον ὁριζόμενοι αἰτίαν ἄδηλον
ἀνθρωπίνῳ λογισμῷ; Alex. Aph. *de fato* 8 (Arnim ii 970).

[94] *ib.* 10 (Arnim ii 960).

also does wisdom. And goodness and wisdom are the same for gods and for men[95]. If this is so, there must be a science of things to be done and to be avoided, that is of right actions and of sins. But right actions are praiseworthy, and sins blameable. Things praiseworthy deserve reward, and things blameable deserve punishment.

Therefore if all things are determined by fate, there must be rewards and punishments[96].'

All this chain of argument is convincing to the man who is already a Stoic; to his opponent it seems to display its weakness at every joint.

[95] ὁ ἐκ τῆς ποικίλης χορός, οἱ φάσκοντες εἶναι τὴν αὐτὴν ἀρετὴν καὶ ἀλήθειαν ἀνδρὸς καὶ θεοῦ Them. *Or.* ii p. 27 c (Arnim iii 251).

[96] Alex. Aphrod. *de fato* 37 (Arnim ii 1005).

CHAPTER X.

RELIGION.

239. WE now turn from the supreme problems of philosophy

Philosophy crystallized.

to the formulation of religious belief and practice. A complete change comes over the spirit of our study. Until now we have been reaching out to observe, to define in words, to coordinate in a monistic system every object, every statement, every generalisation of which the human mind can rightly take account. We have kept eyes and ears open to learn from the East and from the West, from the idealist and the materialist, from the poet and from the critic. At last we have reached our highest point in the dogmas of the providential ordering of the universe and the moral obligation of the individual man; dogmas which, as we have seen, are expounded in logical form, but are essentially such as logic can neither establish nor refute. Stoicism, having once breathed in the mountain air of supreme principles, now begins to descend to the plains of common life, and to find the due application of its theories in the ordering of practical affairs. The theory of religion is treated as the first stage in this downward path; it is the adaptation of philosophy to the language of social life and individual aspiration. By 'religion' we mean here the theory of the existence and character of the gods; the practice of ceremonies in their honour and of prayers for their favour; and further, the theory and practice of divination. Upon all these questions philosophy sits as the supreme judge: external authority, embodied in the traditions of Greece and Rome respectively, may claim consideration, but not submission, from the intellect.

240. In this attitude of the Stoics towards religion we can easily distinguish certain historical changes. Zeno represents in the main the critical temper; his tone is revolutionary and atheistic; he contemplates the entire subversion of existing religious practices to make room for a purer system. The principles of Cleanthes are the same, but find expression in a more cheerful spirit; he has no bitterness as to the present, and much confidence in the future. With Chrysippus there sets in a tide of reconciliation; the ingenuities of etymology and allegorical interpretation are set to work to prove that the old religion contains, at least in germ, the substance of the new. The practical dangers of this method are obvious, and have not escaped the notice of the critics of Stoicism. It may be well to smoothe the path of the convert by allowing him to use old formulas and practices with a new meaning; it is not so easy to excuse the acceptance of a purely formal conversion, by which philosophy enrols as its nominal adherents men who give it no real submission, and increases its numbers at the cost of its sincerity. Posidonius stands out as the type of this weakness; with him begins the subordination of philosophic principle to religious sentiment. In the first period of Roman Stoicism the struggle was acute; many of the Stoics had the courage to defy the inherited prejudices of their fellow-countrymen, others bowed before the storm. Those who condemn the Stoics in a body as having sacrificed their convictions, in order that they might hold the honoured and lucrative positions of defenders of the national religion[1], show a lack both of sympathy and of critical discernment. All through the Roman period the Stoics held in theory a definite and consistent position, which will be expounded in this chapter; in the application of their principles to practical problems they showed that variation of standard and temperament which history has always to record even of societies of honourable and intelligent men. But it must be admitted that as the Stoics increase in numbers, their devotion to vital principles grows weaker, till at last we recognise in Marcus Aurelius both the most critical of Stoic thinkers, and the man in whom the powers of thought are most definitely subjected to the play of old associations and prejudices.

Historical changes of view.

[1] e.g. Theodor Mommsen, *Roman History* iii 432 (Dickson's translation).

241. The theoretic teaching of the Stoics upon theology

Dogmas of natural religion. follows a very definite programme. Four dogmas need to be established : (i) that gods exist; (ii) that they are living, benevolent, and immortal; (iii) that they govern the universe; and (iv) that they seek the good of men. To each of these dogmas is attached a series of 'proofs,' such as are still in vogue as 'evidences of natural religion[2].' The whole of this body of teaching may be treated by us as an exposition in popular language of the central dogma that 'the universe is ordered by providence.' We have therefore first to consider whether the language used is really appropriate to the philosophic position, or whether it concedes too much to accepted beliefs. Secondly we have to consider whether the 'proofs' employed really correspond to the monistic point of view as understood by the Stoics, or whether dualisms abandoned in principle are regaining their old position in connexion with practical problems. Now the third and fourth dogmas, so far as they add to the first two, import nothing more than the general doctrine of providence. The first two dogmas, taken together, substitute for the abstract term 'providence' the more concrete, and (as we should phrase it) the more personal conception of a 'god' or 'gods.' The supreme question of the Stoic religion is therefore whether these terms are rightly used ; and it falls into two parts, the use of the singular 'god,' carrying with it associations derived from Persism and Judaism ; and the use of the plural 'gods,' which carries with it a qualified approval of the polytheism of the Greek and Roman pantheons. In accordance with the general principles of our philosophy, the wider question must be first determined.

242. The 'gods,' according to the Stoics, form a 'natura,' a

The 'nature' of gods. department of the universe, a category including one or more individuals. Hence the title of Cicero's work, 'de natura deorum'; that is, 'of the class of beings called gods.' Each department of philosophy, according to the Stoic interpretation, brings us in the end into touch with this world of deities. In dialectics we are led up to the supreme Reason,

[2] 'omnino dividunt nostri totam istam de dis immortalibus quaestionem in partes quattuor. primum docent esse deos; deinde quales sint; tum, mundum ab iis administrari ; postremo, consulere eos rebus humanis' Cic. *N. D.* ii 1, 3.

the Logos or Word, whose divine being permeates the universe[3].
Metaphysics points us to Body in its purest form[4]; to Spirit
which reaches from end to end of the universe[5]; to a first Cause,
a Cause of causes, the initial link in the unending chain of
events[6]. If we look to the elements in their unceasing interchange, we find deity in all things that shift and suffer meta-
morphosis, in water, in earth, and in air[7]; how much more then
in fire, which in one aspect is the purest of the elements, and in
another is the creative rational substance from which the whole
universe issues[8]? God is indeed the universe, and all that is in
it, though not in the pantheistic sense that he is evenly diffused
throughout all things[9]. Look towards this earth, which lies at
the centre of the world-order; even in its most repulsive contents, in its grossest matter, there is deity[10]. Lift up your eyes
to the heavens; God is the all-encircling sea of fire called
Aether[11]; he is sun[12] and stars[13]. Consider the universe in its
history; God is its creator[14], its ruler, its upholder[15]. Analyze

[3] 'λόγον, quem deum [Zeno] nuncupat' Lact. ver. sap. 9 (Arnim i 160) ; 'rationem deum vocat Zeno' Min. Felix 19, 10 (ib.); '[Zeno] rationem quandam, per omnem naturam rerum pertinentem, vi divina esse adfectam putat' Cic. N. D. i 14, 36.

[4] ἀρχὴν θεὸν τῶν πάντων, σῶμα ὄντα τὸ καθαρώτατον, ὑπέθεντο ὅ τε Χρύσιππος καὶ Ζήνων Hippol. Phil. 21 (Arnim ii 1029).

[5] τὸ δι' ὅλου κεχωρηκὸς πνεῦμα θεὸν δογματίζουσιν Theoph. Autol. i 4 (Arnim ii 1033).

[6] 'ille est prima omnium causa, ex qua ceterae pendent' Sen. Ben. iv 7, 2; 'hic est causa causarum' N. Q. ii 45, 2.

[7] '[Chrysippus ait] ea quae natura fluerent et manarent [divina esse], ut aquam et terram et aera' Cic N. D. i 15, 39.

[8] '[Chrysippus] deum ait ignem praeterea esse' ib. ; 'et deum ipsum ignem putavit [Zeno]' August. adv. Ac. iii 17, 38 (Arnim i 157); τὸν θεὸν πῦρ νοερὸν εἰπόντες Euseb. pr. ev. 15 (Arnim ii 1050).

[9] οὐσίαν δὲ θεοῦ Ζήνων μέν φησι τὸν ὅλον κόσμον καὶ τὸν οὐρανόν Diog. L. vii 148; 'Cleanthes ipsum mundum deum dicit esse' Cic. N. D. i 14, 37; 'vis illum vocare mundum? non falleris' Sen. N. Q. ii 45, 3; 'quid est deus? quod vides totum et quod non vides totum; solus est omnia' ib. i Prol. 13; 'Iuppiter est quodcunque vides quocunque moveris' Lucan Phars. ix 580.

[10] Arnim ii 1037 and 1039.

[11] 'Zenoni et reliquis fere Stoicis aether videtur summus deus' Cic. Ac. ii 41, 126.

[12] 'Cleanthes...solem dominari et rerum potiri putat' ib.

[13] '[Zeno] astris idem [sc. vim divinam] tribuit' N. D. i 14, 36; '[Cleanthes] divinitatem omnem tribuit astris' ib. 14, 37.

[14] 'tibi licet hunc auctorem rerum nostrarum compellare' Sen. Ben. iv 7, 1.

[15] 'rectorem custodemque universi' N. Q. ii 45, 1; 'stant beneficio eius omnia' Ben. iv 7, 1.

it; he is its soul[16], its mind[17]. Strain your sight to perceive the
meaning of all things: he is fate[18]; he is nature[19]; he is providence; he is necessity[20]. And if we look forward to the problems
of politics and ethics, we must say that God is the Universal Law
that calls for the reverence of gods and men as a community[21],
and equally demands, under the name of conscience, the unhesi-
tating obedience of the individual[22]. Lastly, in the history of
mankind, in its great men and useful discoveries, the Stoic
masters recognised the element of divinity[23]. In the language
of to-day, God is the pole in which all the parallels of human
inquiry merge, the x of the problem of the universe, the unknown
that is known in his works.

243. That God is one is a doctrine which the Stoics take
Unity of over from the Cynics[24] (who therein follow Socrates),
God. and from the general opinion; without making this
a formal dogma, they constantly assume it tacitly by using the
term 'God' (ὁ θεός, *deus*). With equal readiness they accept in
use plural and abstract nouns for the same conception, as *di immortales, vis divina*. The interpretation of this apparent conflict
of language must be found in the general principles of the Stoic
monism. Just as the elements are four, and yet are all the
creative fire in its changing shapes: just as the virtues are
many, and yet there is but one Virtue appearing under different
circumstances: so there is but one Deity, appearing under many

---

[16] Arnim i 532.

[17] '[Chrysippus] ait vim divinam esse positam in universae naturae animo atque
mente' Cic. *N. D.* i 15, 39; 'quid est deus? mens universi' Sen. *N. Q.* i Prol. 13;
cf. Arnim i 157.

[18] Arnim iii Ant. 35; 'hunc eundem et fatum si dixeris, non mentieris' Sen.
Ben. iv 7, 2.

[19] 'quid aliud est natura quam deus?' *ib.* 1.

[20] '[Chrysippus] deum dicit esse necessitatem rerum futurarum' Cic. *N. D.* i 15,
39; cf. Arnim ii 1076.

[21] οὔτε βροτοῖς γέρας ἄλλο τι μεῖζον | οὔτε θεοῖς, ἢ κοινὸν ἀεὶ νόμον ἐν δίκῃ ὑμνεῖν
Cleanthes *Hymn* 38, 39; 'naturalem legem [Zeno] divinam esse censet' Cic. *N. D.* i
14, 36.

[22] '[Chrysippus] legis perpetuae et aeternae vim, quae quasi dux vitae atque
magistra officiorum sit, Iovem dicit esse' *ib.* 15, 40.

[23] '[Chrysippus] homines etiam eos, qui immortalitatem essent consecuti [deos
dicit esse]' *ib.* 15, 39; 'Persaeus...inventa ipsa divina dicit' *ib.* 15, 38.

[24] 'Antisthenes populares deos multos, naturalem unum esse [dicit]' *ib.* i 13, 32.

names²⁵. This view the assailants of Stoicism reduce to the absurdity that some Stoic gods are created and mortal, whilst others are uncreated²⁶; and again that Zeus is worse than a Proteus, for the latter changed into a few shapes only and those seemly, whilst Zeus has a thousand metamorphoses, and there is nothing so foul that he does not in turn become²⁷. No one however who is familiar with the many points of view from which Greek philosophers approach the problem of 'the one and the many' will be readily disturbed by this rather superficial criticism.

244. In its practical application the belief in the one-ness of God assimilated itself to the worship of the Greek Ζεύς and the Latin Jove or Juppiter. It would be impossible within the limits of this work to trace the growth of monotheistic feeling in the Greco-Roman world in connexion with the names of these two deities, which in the mythologies are members of societies. We have already suggested that the most direct impulse came from Persism: but in connexion with Roman history it is important to notice that a similar impulse arrived through the Tuscan religion²⁸. The nature of the Stoic worship of Zeus is abundantly illustrated by the *Hymn* of Cleanthes²⁹; the intimate sense of companionship between Zeus and his worshipper comes to light, perhaps with a tinge of Cynic sentiment, in all the discourses of Epictetus. A special emphasis is laid on the fatherhood of Zeus. This attribute could be traced back to the poems of Homer, and is prominent throughout Virgil's *Aeneid*³⁰. It can be explained

Zeus.

²⁵ κύδιστ' ἀθανάτων, πολυώνυμε...Ζεῦ Cleanthes *Hymn* 1 and 2; 'Stoici dicunt non esse nisi unum deum et unam eandemque potestatem, quae pro ratione officiorum variis nominibus appellatur' Servius *ad Verg. Georg.* i 5 (Arnim ii 1070).
²⁶ οἱ μὲν γενητοὶ εἶναι καὶ φθαρτοὶ [λέγονται], οἱ δ' ἀγένητοι Plut. *Sto. rep.* 38, 5 (quoting from Chrysippus).
²⁷ Galen *qual. inc.* 6 (Arnim ii 1056).
²⁸ 'ne hoc quidem [illi altissimi viri] crediderunt, Iovem, qualem in Capitolio et in ceteris aedibus colimus, mittere manu fulmina, sed eundem quem nos Iovem intellegunt, rectorem custodemque universi, animum ac spiritum mundi, operis huius dominum et artificem, cui nomen omne convenit...idem Etruscis visum est' Sen. *N. Q.* ii 45, 1 and 3.
²⁹ See above, § 97.
³⁰ 'hominum sator atque deorum' *Aen.* i 254, and so *passim.*

in connexion with the growth of all living substances[31], but has a more lofty meaning in that man alone shares with the gods the inheritance of reason[32]. But the Homeric association of Zeus with mount Olympus entirely disappears in Stoicism in favour of the Persian conception of a god dwelling in heaven[33]. Further the Stoics agree with the Persians that this god must not be thought of as having the form of any animal or man[34]; he is without form[35], but capable of assuming all forms[36].

245. In the Stoic system the conception of godhead as one and supreme much exceeds in importance the con-

Definition of 'god.'

ception of a multiplicity of gods. We may therefore reasonably consider at this point the four dogmas of the Stoic theology. The first point to be examined is the definition of the word 'god.' As adopted by the Stoic school generally it runs thus: 'a rational and fiery spirit, having no shape, but changing to what it wills and made like to all things[37].' This definition corresponds satisfactorily to the Stoic system of physics; but even so we must notice that the statement 'God is necessity[38]' is an exaggeration, since 'necessity' is entirely devoid of the qualities of reasonableness and plasticity. We find a different definition in Antipater of Tarsus, which is emphasized by the Stoics of the transition period generally:—'God is a living being,

[31] ' tum pater omnipotens fecundis imbribus Aether | coniugis in gremium laetae descendit, et omnes | magnus alit, magno commixtus corpore, fetus' Virgil *Georg.* ii 325-327.

[32] This seems undoubtedly to be the meaning underlying the corrupt text of Cleanthes *Hymn* 4; Pearson well compares κοινωνίαν δ' ὑπάρχειν πρὸς ἀλλήλους (scil. θεοῦ καὶ ἀνθρώπων) διὰ τὸ λόγου μετέχειν Euseb. *praep. ev.* xv 15. See above, § 97.

[33] οὐρανὸς δέ ἐστιν ἡ ἐσχάτη περιφέρεια, ἐν ᾗ πᾶν ἵδρυται τὸ θεῖον Diog. L. vii 138 ; ......, ἐπεὶ ἐκεῖ ἐστι τὸ κυριώτατον μέρος τῆς τοῦ κόσμου ψυχῆς Corn. *N. D.* 8.

[34] [Χρύσιππός φησι] παιδαριωδῶς λέγεσθαι καὶ γράφεσθαι καὶ πλάττεσθαι θεοὺς ἀνθρωποειδεῖς, ὃν τρόπον καὶ πόλεις καὶ ποταμούς Philod. *de piet.* 11 (Arnim ii 1076) ; ' est aliquid in illo Stoici dei, iam video; nec cor nec caput habet' Sen. *Apoc.* 8, 1.

[35] ' Stoici negant habere ullam formam deum' Lact. *de ira* 18 (Arnim ii 1057).

[36] In connexion with the association of God with the universe we may say (but only in a secondary sense) that God has spherical form ; ἰδίαν ἔχει μορφὴν τὸ σφαιροειδές Frag. Herc. p. 250 (Arnim ii 1060) ; 'quae vero vita tribuitur isti rotundo deo?' Cic. *N. D.* i 10, 24.

[37] πνεῦμα νοερὸν καὶ πυρῶδες, οὐκ ἔχον μὲν μορφήν, μεταβάλλον δ' εἰς ὃ βούλεται καὶ συνεξομοιούμενον πᾶσιν Aët. *plac.* i 6, 1.

[38] See above, § 242, note 20.

blessed, imperishable, the benefactor of mankind[39].' This definition points clearly the way to the Stoic system of religion. The
difference between the two definitions marks then the step that
has here to be taken. There is an accentuation of the property
of personality; we pass from a 'rational spirit' to a 'living being.'
There is the addition of a moral quality; we pass from a plastic
substance to a beneficent will. The existence of deity in the
first sense has been displayed to us by our whole analysis of the
universe; it is with regard to the existence of deity in the second
sense that we need the constant support of the dogma of providence, expounded in the technical proofs which we now proceed
to examine.

246. The first Stoic dogma is 'that gods exist'; and of this
the first and most familiar 'proof' is that which
depends upon common consent. Amongst all men
and in all nations there is a fixed conviction that
gods exist; the conception is inborn, indeed we may say graven
on the minds of all men[40]. To this proof the Stoics attach the
highest possible importance; but its justification, as we have
seen, presents great difficulties[41]. Cleanthes, the most religiously
minded of the early Stoics, had not troubled to conceal his contempt for the opinions of the crowd[42]; and the ridiculous belief
in Tartarus[43] is as widespread as that in the gods. Here then
we must distinguish; it is not sufficient that a conception should
be universal, if it appeals most to foolish folk, and even so is de-
caying[44]. We must not however at this moment inquire into the

Gods exist: the proof from consent.

---

[39] θεὸν νοοῦμεν ζῷον μακάριον καὶ ἄφθαρτον καὶ εὐποιητικὸν ἀνθρώπων Plut. *Sto. rep.*
38, 3. A similar definition is given in Diog. L. vii 147 as indicating the view of the
Stoics generally.

[40] 'inter omnes omnium gentium sententia constat; omnibus enim innatum est et
in animo quasi insculptum, esse deos' Cic. *N. D.* ii 4, 12; 'nec ulla gens usquam est
adeo extra leges moresque proiecta, ut non aliquos deos credat' Sen. *Ep.* 117, 6.

[41] See above, § 158.

[42] οὐ γὰρ πλῆθος ἔχει συνετὴν κρίσιν οὔτε δικαίαν | οὔτε καλήν Cleanthes apud
Clem. Al. *Strom.* v 3 (Arnim i 559).

[43] See below, § 294.

[44] 'videmus ceteras opiniones fictas atque vanas diuturnitate extabuisse...quae
[enim] anus tam excors inveniri potest, quae illa quae quondam credebantur apud
inferos portenta, extimescat? opinionum enim commenta delet dies' Cic. *N. D.*
ii 2, 5.

causes of this belief[45]; for this is to pass from the question at issue to other proofs of the dogma. It seems clear that the value of this particular proof depends upon the Stoic doctrine of 'inborn conceptions,' which we have already discussed[46]. Without going over the whole ground again, the substance of the argument as applied to the present question may be thus stated. The mind of each individual man is by descent akin to the universal reason (κοινὸς λόγος, *universa ratio*)[47]. Therefore all men carry with them from their birth predispositions in favour of certain pre-conceptions; and the fact that these preconceptions are common to all is evidence of their divine origin. These predispositions by the growth and training of the individual on the one hand, by his contact with the outer world on the other hand through the organs of sense, ripen into reason. Now all men are born with a predisposition to explain what is beyond their own reasoning powers by the hypothesis of a living and reasoning agent. The belief in gods is therefore a 'preconception'; and if it is confirmed by growth and experience, it must be of divine origin and therefore self-proving. In the language of our own times, the belief in deity cannot be dispensed with as a working hypothesis; its omission lames human reason.

247. The second proof 'that gods exist' is particularly associated with the name of Chrysippus; it may be summed up by saying 'there must be a Being higher than man.' We begin by assuming that reason is the highest power in the universe[48]; an axiom which is always subject to limitation on account of the existence of 'natural necessity.' According to the Stoics, reason is common to gods and men; if, for the sake of argument, this is denied, then reason is possessed by men alone, for we can certainly find no better name than 'god' for higher reasoning beings[49]. If

The proof of the 'higher Being.'

---

[45] As for instance Cicero does (following Posidonius) *N. D.* ii 5, 13.

[46] See above, § 158.

[47] ἡ τῶν ὅλων φύσις ὑπὸ συγγενοῦς ὀφείλει καταλαμβάνεσθαι τοῦ λόγου Sext. *math.* ix 93, see § 149.

[48] See the next note.

[49] 'si di non sunt, quid esse potest in rerum natura homine melius? in eo enim solo ratio est, qua nihil potest esse praestantius' Cic. *N. D.* ii 6, 16.

then there exists something greater than human reason can produce, it must be the work of some reasoning being greater than man, that is, it must be the work of the gods. But the heavenly constellations are such a work; therefore they are the work of the gods, and therefore gods exist[50]. To this argument two others are supplementary. First, human reason itself must be derived from some source, and what other can we name but the deity[51]? Secondly, if there are no gods, man must be the supreme being; but such a claim is an arrogant infatuation[52]. The same arguments are attributed in substance to Zeno[53]; nay, so cogent are they that they are in part accepted even by Epicurus[54].

248. There follow two proofs connected with gradations in the scale of being. Earth and water are the two lower and grosser elements; and since temperament depends greatly upon climate, we find that men and the animals are all of somewhat heavy character. Air and fire are the higher and more refined elements; how then can we think otherwise than that they are the home of more lofty beings[55]? Then again the universe is either a simple or a composite body. That it is not composite is shown by the harmony ($\sigma\upsilon\mu\pi\acute{a}\theta\epsilon\iota a$, *concentus*) of its parts; it is therefore simple. A simple body must be held together by spirit in some

The proofs from the elements and the universe.

---

[50] 'si enim' inquit [Chrysippus] 'est aliquid in rerum natura, quod potestas humana efficere non possit; est certe id, quod illud efficit, homine melius. atqui res caelestes ab homine confici non possunt. est igitur id, quo illa conficiuntur, homine melius. id autem quid potius dixeris quam deum?' *ib.*

[51] 'et tamen ex ipsa hominum sollertia esse aliquam [mundi] mentem, et eam quidem acriorem et divinam, existimare debemus. unde enim haec homo arripuit? ut ait apud Xenophontem Socrates' *ib.* 18.

[52] 'esse autem hominem, qui nihil in omni mundo melius esse quam se putet, insipientis arrogantiae est' *ib.* 16.

[53] See above, § 83.

[54] 'placet enim illi [sc. Epicuro] esse deos, quia necesse sit praestantem esse aliquam naturam, qua nihil sit melius' Cic. *N. D.* ii 17, 46. See however Mayor's note.

[55] 'tantum vero ornatum mundi, tantam varietatem pulchritudinemque rerum caelestium...si non deorum immortalium domicilium putes, nonne plane desipere videare? an ne hoc quidem intellegimus, omnia supera esse meliora, terram autem esse infimam, quam crassissimus circumfundat aer?' etc. Cic. *N. D.* ii 6, 17. For the original argument of Chrysippus see Sext. *math.* ix 86 (Arnim ii 1014).

A. 15

one of its grades, either as unity, growth, or soul. Bodies held together merely by unity, like stones or logs, admit of very simple changes only ; but the universe admits of every kind of change and development, and yet keeps together ; it must therefore be held together by spirit in its highest grade, that is by soul and by reason. Being a whole, it must be greater than its parts, and include all that its parts possess. But a nature greater than man, and possessing soul and reason, is god[56].

249. The proof from the good gifts of providence has been already given in substance ; we may however notice the sharp reply given to Epicurus, who maintains that the wondrous contrivances of the Creator for the benefit of man result from the chance clashings of particles. ' As well contend,' replies the Stoic, ' that words and verses come from the chance shifting of the twenty-one letters of the alphabet, and that the poems of Ennius could be produced by shaking together a sufficient quantity of these in a box, and then pouring them out on the ground ! Chance would hardly produce a single verse[57].' The terrors of the universe, its storms, earthquakes, deluges, pestilences and wars, which seem to militate against this proof, are themselves turned into a fourth proof[58]. A further proof, which depends on the contemplation of the movements of the heavenly bodies[59], we have sufficiently considered in connexion with the influence of Chaldaean and Persian thought.

The proof from providence.

250. There remain two proofs, which at first sight may appear singular, but are nevertheless very strongly urged, the proofs from worship and divination ; which according to the Stoics are practices that must be justified, but cannot be justified without the

The proof from worship.

---

[56] 'haec ita fieri omnibus inter se concinentibus mundi partibus profecto non possent, nisi ea uno divino et continuato spiritu continerentur' Cic. *N. D.* ii 7, 19. Here cf. Sext. *math.* ix 78 to 85 (Arnim ii 1013).

[57] Cic. *N. D.* ii 37, 93.

[58] The third in the exposition of Cleanthes : 'tertiam [causam dixit Cleanthes esse], quae terreret animos fulminibus tempestatibus...pestilentia terrae motibus' *ib.* 5, 14.

[59] 'quartam causam esse, eamque vel maximam, conversionem caeli' *ib.* 5, 15.

postulate of the existence of gods. The proof from worship is best known in the paradoxical form, 'if there are altars, there are gods,' which is attributed to Chrysippus[60]. This proof is fused by Seneca with the proof from general consent[61]; but its true character seems to be different. 'Without gods there can be no piety, for piety is the right worship of the gods. Without gods there can be no holiness, for holiness is a right attitude towards the gods. Without gods there can be no wisdom, for wisdom is the knowledge of things human and divine[62]. But without piety, holiness, and wisdom a reasonable philosophy cannot be constructed. Therefore gods exist.' The argument in its simplest form is attributed to Zeno himself. 'It is reasonable to honour the gods. But it is not reasonable to honour the non-existent. Therefore gods exist[63].'

251. The final argument is that from divination; which is remarkable in view of the close association between divination and astrology, and the derivation of the latter from a scientific system which finds no place for divine interpositions. But both in Greece and Rome the forecasting of the future had long been reconciled with theology, upon the hypothesis that the gods warn men for their good of coming events. In accepting the truth of divination the Stoics were following the Socratic tradition[64]. This belief was accepted by all the great Stoic masters, and was a 'citadel' of their philosophy[65]. It is true that on this point Panaetius exercised the privilege of a suspense of judgment[66]; but all the more did his pupil, the pious Posidonius, lay stress upon the subject, on which he composed five books[66], of which the spirit is preserved to us in Cicero's books *de Divinatione*[67]. To Roman writers their

The proof from divination.

---

[60] Arnim ii 1019.

[61] '[non] in hunc furorem omnes mortales consensissent adloquendi surda numina et inefficaces deos, nisi nossemus illorum beneficia' Sen. *Ben.* iv 4, 2.

[62] Sext. *math.* ix 123 (Arnim ii 1017).

[63] *ib.* 133 (Arnim i 152). Pearson (Z. 108) describes the argument as a 'transparent sophistry'; but at the present time there is a widespread tendency towards its revival; see Höffding, *Philosophy of Religion*, ch. iii.

[64] Xen. *Mem.* i 1, 2.   [65] Cic. *Div.* i 5, 9 and 6, 10.

[66] *ib.* 3, 6; Diog. L. vii 149.

[67] Divination is based upon the συμπάθεια τῶν ὅλων (*continuatio coniunctioque naturae*), Cic. *Div.* ii 69, 142. See also Epict. *Disc.* i 14, and above, § 248.

inherited State practice of augury, with its elaborate though half-forgotten science, was long a motive for maintaining this belief[68]; but the ancient reputation of the oracle at Delphi maintained its hold still more persistently, and was abandoned with even greater reluctance[69]. Nevertheless the whole group of beliefs was quietly pushed aside by the Romans of the times of the empire, if we may judge from the words of Epictetus—'what need have I to consult the viscera of victims and the flight of birds, and why do I submit when he (the diviner) says "it is for your interest?" Have I not within me a diviner[70]?'

252. Our next enquiry is 'of what kind are the gods?'
Divine qualities. 'what are their qualities?' Here the Stoics break more decidedly with tradition. Antipater of Tarsus, as we have seen, defined the deity as 'a living being, happy, immortal and benevolent towards men[71].' It is clear that this description can only be applied in its fulness to the supreme deity, for all other gods are destined to pass away in the general conflagration[72]. That the supreme deity is possessed of life and of reason has already been assumed in the proofs of his existence; but we have here a reaffirmation of Stoic doctrine as against those that hold that the world is governed by blind destiny and chance. In stating that the gods are happy the Stoics agree with Epicurus; but according to them this happiness consists not in rest, but in activity. In this distinction the whole difference between the Stoic and Epicurean ideals of happiness, that is, between their ethical ends, comes into sight. The Stoics affirm that the gods are occupied, and that with matters of the greatest concern: and that any other conception is unworthy of them[73]. That the activity of the gods has for its aim the

---

[68] '[Tuscis] summa est fulgurum persequendorum scientia' Sen. *N. Q.* ii 32, 2.

[69] 'non ullo saecula dono | nostra carent maiore deum, quam Delphica sedes | quod siluit' Lucan *Phars.* v 111–113; cf. 86–96.

[70] Epict. *Disc.* ii 7, 3 and 4. The Stoic belief in divination is very severely criticized by Zeller: 'these vagaries show in Stoicism practical interests preponderating over science' *Stoics*, etc. p. 280. But the belief in μαντική is traced back to Zeno and Cleanthes, who were hardly 'practical' men in the sense in which Zeller seems to use the word.

[71] See above, § 245.   [72] See above, § 209.

[73] Cic. *N. D.* ii 30, 77.

happiness of men is plainly the doctrine of providence ; and in making benevolence an attribute of deity[74] the Stoics turn their backs for ever upon the belief in gods that are greedy, jealous, mischievous, and haughty ; that is, not merely on such deities as were still a part of the creed of the rustic[75], but also such as had provided the problems of the whole of Greek tragedy, and given the opportunity for the stinging attacks of Epicurus on religion[76]. In examining these attributes of the gods we have anticipated the enquiries which belong to the third and fourth categories ; namely as to the disposition and the relativity of the gods. Incidentally we have obtained an excellent illustration of the logical importance of definition and the four categories. Definition implies in advance what is contained in each of the categories, and each category contains implicitly what is contained in the other three ; but the logical mechanism enables us so to express the doctrine that it is for ever fixed on the memory. Nor can we easily imagine that the world will ever forget this conception of a Supreme God, in his essence a living all-wise Being ; in his attributes immortal, immutable[77], active and benevolent ; in his disposition occupied in contemplating and controlling his great work the universe, and in his relation to his creatures constantly concerned for their comfort and happiness.

253. It must by this time be plain that the whole atmosphere of Stoic religion was alien to that in which
the gods of the Greek and Roman mythology had
taken root. The nominal absorption of these gods
in the Stoic system has therefore no theoretical importance ; it was a work of political adaptation. The Stoics themselves doubtless believed that they were restoring the original meaning of the pantheon, and freeing it from corruptions for which the

Stoicism and the old mythology.

---

[74] '[di immortales] nec volunt obesse nec possunt. natura enim illis mitis et placida est' Sen. *Dial.* iv 27, 1 ; 'di aequali tenore bona sua per gentes populosque distribuunt, unam potentiam sortiti, prodesse' *Ben.* vii 31, 4.

[75] 'Faune, Nympharum fugientum amator, | per meos fines et aprica rura | lenis incedas, abeasque parvis | aequus alumnis' Hor. *C.* iii 18, 1–4.

[76] 'tantum relligio potuit suadere malorum' Lucr. *R. N.* i 102.

[77] 'Does the Zeus at Olympia lift up his brow ? No, his look is fixed as becomes him who is ready to say—Irrevocable is my word and shall not fail' Epict. *Disc.* ii 8, 26 (quoting from Hom. *Il.* i 526).

poets were responsible. The original meaning was also, in their judgment, the true meaning. Public opinion was already in revolt against the old theology, both on scientific and on moral grounds. The current tales of the gods were both incredible and revolting[78]; the worship of them too often an attempt to silence the voice of conscience[79]. The Stoics proposed to make the myths symbols of scientific truths, and the ritual an incentive to honest living. Their interpretation was in the main physical; the gods represent respectively the heavenly bodies, the elements, the plants; the amours of the gods represent the continuous work of the great creative forces of nature. To a lesser extent explanations are found in society and in history. These interpretations are greatly assisted by etymologies, according to the doctrine of dialectics that wisdom lies hid in words. The whole process may seem to the modern critic puerile, because the practical occasion for it has passed away; but there are still to be found thinkers who hold that by such processes alone it is possible for human thought to progress without civil society being disrupted.

254. According to this system Juppiter becomes the fiery heaven, the chief of the elements, the source of all life[80]; Juno is the softer air, into which the fire enters to become the germinating seed[81]. Thus she is called sister as a fellow-element[82], and wife as an instrument in the creative process. From a slightly different point of view Chrysippus interpreted Zeus as God, and Hera as matter; and their union as the commencement of the Creation, when God

The Stoic metamorphoses.

---

[78] 'sic vestras hallucinationes fero quemadmodum Iuppiter ineptias poetarum, quorum alius illi alas imposuit, alius cornua; alius adulterum illum induxit et abnoctantem, alius saevum in deos, alius iniquum in homines, alius parricidam et regni alieni paternique expugnatorem' Sen. *Dial.* vii 26, 6.

[79] This feeling finds expression at Rome as far back as the times of Hannibal; 'hoc scelesti illi in animum inducunt suum, | Iovem se placare posse donis, hostiis; | et operam et sumptum perdunt' Plaut. *Rud.* 22 to 24.

[80] '[Chrysippus] disputat aethera esse eum, quem homines Iovem appellarent' Cic. *N. D.* i 15, 40.

[81] 'aer autem, ut Stoici disputant, Iunonis nomine consecratur...effeminarunt autem eum Iunonique tribuerunt, quod nihil est eo mollius' *ib.* ii 26, 66.

[82] 'quoniam tenuitate haec elementa paria sunt, dixerunt esse germana' Serv. *ad Verg. Aen.* i 47 (Arnim ii 1066).

spread throughout matter the seed Logoi[83]. So again Hephaestus (Vulcan) represents fire ; Poseidon (Neptune) is the sea ; Dis (Pluto) and Rhea alike stand for the earth[84]. Demeter (Ceres) again is the corn-land[85], and Persephone (Proserpine) the growing crop ; as such she is lost to her mother and lamented by her for six months in every year[86]. Apollo is the sun, Luna or Diana the moon[87] ; Cronus, son of Earth and Heaven, is Chronos (χρόνος) or Time, and he is said to devour his children, because all that is begotten of time is in turn consumed by time[88]. Athene or Minerva is the daughter of Zeus, to whom he has given birth without a partner, because she is the divine Reason by which he made the universe[89]. Chrysippus wrote at length on the allegorical interpretation of the three Graces[90] ; and the work of Cornutus entirely consists of expositions of this system.

Other gods are recognised by the Stoics as personifications of actions or feelings ; Eros (Cupid), Aphrodite (Venus) and Pothos (regret) of feelings ; Hope ('Ελπίς, Spes), Justice (Δίκη, Iustitia), and Wise Law (Εὐνομία) of actions[91]. So in particular Ares (Mars) stands for war, or the setting of array against array.

255. We have already noticed that the gods that are bor-
Minor   rowed from the popular mythology do not possess
deities.   the divine attribute of immortality; and in some of

---

[83] Rival philosophers in the earlier times, and the church fathers later, concurred in reviling Chrysippus because he extended this principle of interpretation to a 'disgraceful' representation found in Argos or Samos, in which Hera receives the divine seed in her mouth ; yet Christian antiquity was about to absorb the similar notion of the conception of the Virgin Mary through the ear ('quae per aurem concepisti' in an old Latin hymn). Chrysippus of course rightly estimated the absurdity of criticising cosmic processes as if they were breaches of social decency, and by so doing relieved the pious souls of his own day from a real source of distress. See Arnim ii 1071–1074.

[84] Cic. *N. D.* ii 26, 66.   [85] *ib.* i 15, 40 and ii 26, 66.

[86] 'Proserpinam, quam frugum semen esse volunt absconditamque quaeri a matre fingunt' *ib.*   [87] *ib.* 27, 68.

[88] καὶ ὁ χρόνος δὲ τοιοῦτόν τί ἐστι· δαπανᾶται γὰρ ὑπ' αὐτοῦ τὰ γινόμενα ἐν αὐτῷ Cornutus *N. D.* 6. The castration of Uranus by Cronus is thus explained by the Stoics: 'caelestem naturam, id est igneam, quae per sese omnia gigneret, vacare voluerunt ea parte corporis, quae coniunctione alterius egeret ad procreandum" Cic. *N. D.* ii 24, 64.

[89] Justin *Apol.* i 64 (Arnim ii 1096).   [90] Sen. *Ben.* i 3, 9.

[91] Aët. *plac.* i 6, 13.

them the attribute of benevolence is not prominent. There was thus a constant tendency to assign them to an order of nature of lower rank than the deity. Such an order was already constituted by the popular belief, adopted by the Stoics, that the whole universe is full of spirits or daemons, some kindly, others mischievous. Highest in the former class stand the divine messengers, who everywhere throughout the universe keep watch over the affairs of men and bring report thereof to God[92]. This was a widespread belief, most in harmony with the principles of Persism, but also met with in the Rigveda[93] and in the poems of Hesiod[94]. These watchmen are however not the spies of a cruel tyrant, but the officers of a benevolent sovereign; we find them early in Roman literature identified with the stars[95], and this may account for the special recognition of the twins Castor and Pollux, as kindly daemons that protect sailors from shipwreck[96]. There are also spirits which are careless, idle, or mischievous[97]; these the deity may employ as his executioners[98]. A daemon which is solely the embodiment of an evil or mischievous principle, such as the Druh of Persism or the Satan of Judaism, is however not to be found in the Stoic system. Amongst daemons are also to be recognised the souls of men parted from their bodies, some good and some evil[99]. All beliefs of this kind are specially characteristic of the type of Stoicism introduced by Posidonius[100]. We may specially note the belief in the Genius which accompanies each man from his

[92] φασὶ δὲ εἶναι καί τινας δαίμονας ἀνθρώπων συμπάθειαν ἔχοντας, ἐπόπτας τῶν ἀνθρωπείων πραγμάτων Diog. L. vii 151.

[93] 'ásya [váruṇasya] spáśo ná ní miṣanti bhūrṇayaḥ' Rigv. ix 73, 4.

[94] τρὶς γὰρ μύριοι εἰσὶν ἐπὶ χθονὶ πουλυβοτείρῃ | ἀθάνατοι Ζηνὸς φύλακες θνητῶν ἀνθρώπων Hes. Op. et Di. 252, 253 ; see also § 33.

[95] 'et alia signa de caelo ad terram accidunt; | qui'st imperator divum atque hominum Iuppiter, | is nos per gentis hic alium alia disparat, | hominum qui facta mores pietatem et fidem | noscamus' Plaut. Rud. 8–12.

[96] καὶ τούτῳ συμφωνεῖ τὸ τοὺς Διοσκούρους ἀγαθούς τινας εἶναι δαίμονας "σωτῆρας εὐσέλμων νεῶν" Sext. math. ix 86 (Arnim ii 1014) ; 'clarum Tyndaridae sidus ab infimis | quassas eripiunt aequoribus rates' Hor. C. iv 8, 31 and 32.

[97] φαύλους δαίμονας ἀπέλιπε Χρύσιππος Plut. def. orac. 17.

[98] καθάπερ οἱ περὶ Χρύσιππον οἴονται φιλόσοφοι φαῦλα δαιμόνια περινοστεῖν, οἷς οἱ θεοὶ δημίοις χρῶνται κολασταῖς ἐπὶ τοὺς ἀνοσίους καὶ ἀδίκους ἀνθρώπους qu. Rom. 51.

[99] Arnim ii 1101.

[100] 'Posidonius censet homines somniare, quod plenus aer sit immortalium animorum' Cic. Div. i 30, 64.

birth to his death, (and which closely corresponds to the guardian angel of Persism,) because of the special vogue it obtained in the Roman world[101].

256. The Stoics never failed to close their list of deities with the recognition of men raised to the sky for their services to their fellow-men. Such were Hercules, who rid the earth of monsters; Castor and Pollux; Aesculapius the inventor of medicine; Liber the first cultivator of the vine, and (amongst the Romans) Romulus the founder of the city. These are deities established by the laws of each city[102]. The Stoics do not raise their own leaders to this position, but (as we shall see in dealing with the question of the 'wise man') they assign to them almost equal honours. This part of their theory appears to open the door to great practical abuses, since it might be used to justify the claims of the sovereigns of Egypt to be honoured as gods during their lifetime, and those of the Roman emperors that their predecessors should be worshipped as such after their death. But it does not seem that such an abuse actually occurred; and this part of the theory of gods always seems to have been regarded by the Stoics rather as an explanation of historical facts than as a principle of civic submission.

Deified men.

257. Questions as to the worship of the gods belong strictly to the department of politics, so far as public worship is concerned, and of ethics, so far as individuals are concerned. It may however be convenient to anticipate the discussion of them, since we cannot properly appreciate the Stoic views of religion apart from their practical application. We must therefore notice that Stoicism in its beginnings, in accordance with its Cynic origin, was revolutionary, unorthodox, in

Worship.

---

[101] ' Genius, natale comes qui temperat astrum | naturae deus humanae, mortalis in unum | quodque caput' Hor. *Ep.* ii 2, 187–189; 'sepone in praesentia, quae quibusdam placent, uni cuique nostrum paedagogum dari deum, ex eorum numero quos Ovidius ait "de plebe deos"' Sen. *Ep.* 110, 1; 'Zeus has placed by every man a guardian, every man's daemon, to whom he has committed the care of the man; a guardian who never sleeps, is never deceived' Epict. *Disc.* i 14, 12. M. Aurelius identifies this daemon with the principate (*To himself* v 27).

[102] Aët. *plac.* i 6, 9 and 15; Cic. *N. D.* ii 24, 62.

the popular language atheistic. Not only did it follow the principles of Persism in condemning altogether the worship of images, but it also poured scorn upon the building of temples and the offering of sacrifices. Thus Zeno in his book on 'the State' forbids the making of temples and images, because they are unworthy of the deity[103]; an idea which the Romans recognised as not altogether strange to their own history, seeing that for a hundred and seventy years (presumably during the Etruscan supremacy) no images had been known at Rome[104]. The Stoic condemnation of sacrifice is mostly expressed by silence, but it finds words in Seneca[105]. Although they thus denounced in principle the whole existing system of public worship, the Stoics did not feel themselves prevented from taking part in it as a seemly and ancient custom[106]; and the Roman Stoics took a special pride in the reputation of the city for attention to 'religion,' that is to say, to the ritual observances due to the gods[107].

258. Meanwhile the Stoics actively developed their own
Stoic   ideal of worship, namely the rendering of praise
hymnology.   and honour to the gods by means of hymns. 'It
is reasonable,' said Zeno, 'to honour the gods[108].' The hymn of Cleanthes shows the form in which this honour could find expression, and though in the main it is an outburst of individual conviction, yet it contains the germ of public hymnology[109]. The value of music in public worship was recognised by Diogenes of

[103] Arnim i 264. The feeling is reflected by Lucan : ' estne dei sedes, nisi terra et pontus et aër, | et caelum et virtus? superos quid quaerimus ultra?' *Phars.* ix 578-9.

[104] ' Varro dicit antiquos Romanos plus annos centum et septuaginta deos sine simulacro coluisse : "quod si adhuc mansisset, castius di observarentur"' August. *Civ. De.* iv 31.

[105] ' ne in victimis quidem deorum est honor ' Sen. *Ben.* i 6, 3.

[106] ' To make libations and to sacrifice and to offer first-fruits according to the custom of our fathers, purely and not meanly nor above our ability, is a thing which belongs to all to do' Epict. *Manual* 31, 5.

[107] ' si conferre volumus nostra cum externis; ceteris rebus aut pares aut etiam inferiores reperiemur, religione, id est cultu deorum, multum superiores ' Cic. *N. D.* ii 3, 8.

[108] See above, § 250.

[109] ὄφρ' ἂν τιμηθέντες ἀμειβώμεσθά σε τιμῇ, | ὑμνοῦντες τὰ σὰ ἔργα διηνεκές, ὡς ἐπέοικε *Hymn* 36, 37.

Babylon[110]. Posidonius laid it down that the best and most pious worship of the gods is to honour them with pure mind and voice[111]. Epictetus speaks continually in this spirit, and gives us examples of prose hymnology: 'great is God, who has given us implements with which we shall cultivate the earth[112]'; 'I give thee all thanks that thou hast allowed me to join in this thy assemblage of men, and to see thy works, and to comprehend this thy administration[113].' Thus ought we 'to sing hymns to the deity, and bless him, and tell of his benefits[114].'

259. Prayer to the gods may be taken as more characteristic of private and individual worship, though the paradox is worthy of attention that men should ask nothing of the gods that they cannot ask publicly[115]. The whole problem of prayer is so fully and admirably treated upon Stoic lines by Juvenal in his Tenth Satire, that nothing can be added to his exposition but the evidence that his teaching is in fact Stoic. Let us then enter the temples and listen to men's prayers. First they beg the doorkeeper for admission, though the deity is equally near to them outside; then they raise their hands to the sky, or press their mouths close to the ear of an image[116]. To the unlistening deity they pour out wishes so shameful that they could not let a fellow-man share their secret[117]. Decrepit old men babble prayers for long life, and make themselves out younger than they are[118]. Another prays for riches[119], or for some other thing that will do him harm[120]. Undertakers pray for a busy season[121]. Parents and nurses (and these are the nearest to innocence) pray for the success of their children in life[122]. They may be excused, but

Prayer.

---

[110] περὶ τοίνυν τῆς διὰ τ(ῶν μου)σικῶν (τ)οῦ θείου τει(μῆς εἴρη)ται μὲν αὐτάρκως καὶ πρότερον Philod. *mus.* iv 66 (Arnim iii Diog. 64).

[111] 'cultus autem deorum est optimus idemque castissimus atque sanctissimus plenissimusque pietatis, ut eos semper pura integra incorrupta et mente et voce veneremur' Cic. *N. D.* ii 28, 71.

[112] Epict. *Disc.* i 16, 17.   [113] *ib.* iii 5, 10.

[114] *ib.* i 16, 15.   [115] See above, § 121.

[116] 'non sunt ad caelum elevandae manus, nec exorandus aedituus, ut nos ad aurem simulacri admittat; prope est a te deus' Sen. *Ep.* 41, 1.

[117] 'turpissima vota dis insusurrant; si quis admoverit aurem, conticescent' *ib.* 10, 5.

[118] Sen. *Dial.* x 11, 1.   [119] *ib.* xi 4, 2.

[120] *Ben.* ii 14, 5.   [121] *ib.* vi 38, 1.   [122] *Ep.* 32, 4.

the thoughtful man should know that the advantages for which
friends have prayed have often in the end proved a man's destruction[123]. He should examine his own heart, and recognise
that his prayers till now have been unworthy and foolish[124].
Since the gods wish us well, let us leave it to them to choose
what is best for us[125]. 'Look up to God, and say:—deal with
me for the future as thou wilt: I am of the same mind as thou
art. I am thine, I refuse nothing that pleases thee[126].' 'Seek
not that the things which happen should happen as you wish;
but wish the things that happen to be as they are: and you will
have a tranquil flow of life[127].'

260. Prayer so regarded becomes not merely an act of
Self-
examination.
resignation, in which a man ceases to battle against
a destiny that is too strong for him; it is a daily
examination of his soul, to know whether it is in tune with the
purposes of the universe. This examination is a religious
exercise, never to be omitted before sleep. It is inculcated both
by Seneca and Epictetus. 'How beautiful' says Seneca, 'is this
custom of reviewing the whole day! how quiet a sleep follows
on self-examination! The mind takes its place on the judgment-
seat, investigates its own actions, and awards praise or blame
according as they are deserved[128].' And Epictetus adopts the
verses ascribed to Pythagoras:

'Let sleep not come upon thy languid eyes
Before each daily action thou hast scanned;
What's done amiss, what done, what left undone;
From first to last examine all, and then
Blame what is wrong, in what is right rejoice[129].'

[123] 'etiamnunc optas, quod tibi optavit nutrix tua aut paedagogus aut mater? o
quam inimica nobis sunt vota nostrorum!' Sen. *Ep.* 60, 1.
[124] 'se quisque consulat et in secretum pectoris sui redeat et inspiciat, quid tacitus
optaverit. quam multa sunt vota, quae etiam sibi fateri pudet! quam pauca, quae
facere coram teste possimus!' *Ben.* vi 38, 5.
[125] This sentiment we can trace back to the time of Plautus: 'stulti hau scimus
frustra ut simus, quom quid cupienter dari | petimus nobis: quasi quid in rem sit
possimus noscere' Plautus *Pseud.* 683–5.
[126] Epict. *Disc.* ii 16, 42. [127] *Manual* 8.
[128] Sen. *Dial.* v 36, 2. He describes his practice with naïve detail: 'cum
sublatum e conspectu lumen est et conticuit uxor moris mei iam conscia, totum
diem meum scrutor' *ib.* 3.
[129] Epict. *Disc.* iii 10, 2 and 3 (Long's transl.).

261. We are now in a position to sum up in technical

Religious duty. language[130] the obligations of religion freed from superstition[131]. Our duty towards the gods is rightly to believe in them, to acknowledge their greatness and benevolence, to submit to them as the creators and rulers of the universe[132]. We may not light lamps in their honour on sabbath-days, nor crowd round their temples in the early hours of the morning; we may not offer Jove a towel nor Juno a mirror[133]. Our service to them is to make ourselves like to them; he who would win their favour, must be a good man[134]. Wheresoever they call us, we must follow with gladness, for they are wiser than we[135]. Without God we must attempt nothing, but we must always reflect, examine ourselves, and seek to learn the divine will[136]. We came here when it pleased God, and we must depart when he shall please[137]. 'So live,' says the Stoic teacher, 'with your fellow-men, as believing that God sees you: so hold converse with God, as to be willing that all men should hear you[138].'

[130] 'quomodo sint di colendi, solet praecipi' Sen. *Ep.* 95, 47.

[131] 'non enim philosophi solum, verum etiam maiores nostri superstitionem a religione separaverunt' Cic. *N. D.* ii 28, 71.

[132] 'primus est deorum cultus deos credere, deinde reddere illis maiestatem suam, reddere bonitatem, sine qua nulla maiestas est; scire illos esse, qui praesident mundo' Sen. *Ep.* 95, 50.

[133] *ib.* 95, 47.

[134] 'vis deos propitiare? bonus esto. satis illos coluit, quisquis imitatus est *ib.* 95, 50.

[135] 'You must believe that you have been placed in the world to obey them, and to yield to them in everything which happens, and voluntarily to follow it as being accomplished by the wisest intelligence' Epict. *Manual* 31, 1.

[136] *Disc.* iii 22, 53 (compare Long's transl. ii p. 83).

[137] *ib.* iii 26, 30.

[138] 'sic vive cum hominibus, tanquam deus videat; sic loquere cum deo, tanquam homines audiant' Sen. *Ep.* 10, 5.

CHAPTER XI.

THE KINGDOM OF THE SOUL.

262. FROM the contemplation of the universe as a whole,

Man a part of the universe. both from the purely scientific standpoint in the study of physics, and from the more imaginative point of view in the dogmas of religion, we now pass on to the more intimate study of the individual man, consisting of body and soul. In its main outlines the Stoic theory has already been sketched. Thus it follows from the monistic standpoint that man is not ultimately an 'individual' or unit of the universe; for the universe itself is the only true unit, and a man is a part of it which cannot even for a moment break itself off completely from the whole. It is therefore only in a secondary and subordinate sense, and with special reference to the inculcation of ethics, that we can treat Zeno or Lucilius as separate and independent beings. Again, when we say that man 'consists of body and soul,' we are merely adopting popular language; for body and soul are ultimately one, and differ only in the gradation of spirit or tone which informs them. Then we have already learnt in dialectics that the highest power of man is that of 'assent' or free choice, which is displayed in every exercise of reason; and the same power, though in a different aspect, is at work in every moral act. The doctrine of the universe is based upon the postulate that it is a living rational being on the largest scale; and it follows that each man is a 'microcosm,' and contains in himself a complete representation of the universe in miniature. Lastly, we see that man takes his place in the universe, a little lower than gods and daemons, and as greatly higher than animals as these in their turn surpass plants and inanimate objects; and that his nature, considered as composite, includes all the varying gradations of spirit to which these orders correspond within the universe. In all his parts alike the divine element is immanent and it binds them together in a coherent unity (συμπάθεια τῶν μερῶν). It remains for us to put together from these and like points of departure a complete picture of human nature.

263. To indicate the general trend of Stoic thought on this subject we propose the title 'the kingdom of the soul.' Starting with the popular distinction between body and soul, we find that the biologist and the physician alike are preoccupied with the study of the body, that is, of physiology. Only as an afterthought and supplement to their work are the functions of soul considered; and they are treated as far as possible by the methods suggested by the study of the body. All this is reversed in the Stoic philosophy. The study of the soul stands in the front, and is treated by methods directly suggested by observation of the soul's functions. The body is not entirely ignored, but is considered of comparatively small importance. Further, the soul itself is manifold, and is likened to a State, in which all is well if the governing part have wisdom and benevolence proportionate to its power, and if the lower parts are content to fulfil their respective duties; but if the balance of the State is upset, all becomes disorder and misery[1]. Lastly, this kingdom is itself a part of a greater whole, namely of the Cosmopolis or universal State. By the comparison with a kingdom we are also directed towards right moral principle. For as the citizen of Corinth or Sparta ought not to repine because his city is of less grandeur than Athens, so no man should be anxious because his external opportunities are limited. He has a kingdom in his own mind and soul and heart. Let him be content to find his happiness in rightly administering it.

The soul's kingdom.

---

[1] 'rex noster est animus : hoc incolumi cetera manent in officio, parent, obtemperant ; cum ille paullum vacillavit, simul dubitant. ubi vero impotens, cupidus, delicatus est, fit tyrannus; tunc eum excipiunt adfectus impotentes' Sen. *Ep.* 114, 24.

264. The doctrine that man is a representation or reflection
of the universe is of unknown antiquity. It seems
to be clearly implied by the teaching of Heraclitus,
in so far as he lays it down that both the universe
and man are vivified and controlled by the Logos[2]. The
technical terms 'macrocosm' (μέγας κόσμος) and 'microcosm'
(μικρὸς κόσμος), are, as we have seen, employed by Aristotle[3].
But even if we suppose that this conception is a commonplace
of Greek philosophy, it is in Stoicism alone that it is of fundamental importance, and knit up with the whole framework of
the system. And accordingly we find that all the Stoic masters
laid stress upon this principle. The words of Zeno suggest to
Cicero that 'the universe displays all impulses of will and all
corresponding actions just like ourselves when we are stirred
through the mind and the senses[4].' Cleanthes used the dogma
of the soul of the universe to explain the existence of the
human soul as a part of it[5]. Chrysippus found a foundation
for ethics in the doctrine that man should study and imitate
the universe[6]. Diogenes of Babylon says boldly that God
penetrates the universe, as soul the man[7]; and Seneca that the
relation of God to matter is the same as that of the soul to
the body[8]. It is little wonder therefore if by Philo's time the
analogy had become a commonplace, and philosophers of more
than one school were accustomed to say that 'man is a little
universe, and the universe a big man[9].' God is therefore the
soul of the universe[10]; on the other hand the soul is God within
the human body[11], a self-moving force encased in relatively inert

Man a picture of the universe.

---

[2] See L. Stein *Psych.* i p. 206.   [3] See above, § 68.

[4] 'natura mundi omnes motus habet voluntarios conatusque et appetitiones, quas
ὁρμάς Graeci vocant, et his consentaneas actiones sic adhibet ut nosmetipsi, qui animis
movemur et sensibus' Cic. *N. D.* ii 22, 58.

[5] τὴν δὲ ψυχὴν δι' ὅλου τοῦ κόσμου διήκειν, ἧς μέρος μετέχοντας ἡμᾶς ἐμψυχοῦσθαι
Hermias *irris. gent. phil.* 7 (Arnim i 495).

[6] 'ipse autem homo ortus est ad mundum contemplandum et imitandum' Cic.
N. D. ii 14, 37.

[7] τὸν κόσμον περιέχειν τὸν Δία καθάπερ ἄνθρωπον ψυχήν Philod. *piet.* 15 (Arnim iii
Diog. 33).

[8] 'quem in hoc mundo locum deus obtinet, hunc in homine animus; quod est illic
materia, id in nobis corpus est' Sen. *Ep.* 65, 24.

[9] Philo *rer. div.* i 494 M (Stein *Psych.* i 207).   [10] See above, § 242.

[11] See below, § 274.

matter, providence at work within the limitations of natural necessity.

265. The dualism of body and soul appears in a sharply
Soul and body. defined shape in Persism, and upon it depends the popular dogma of the immortality of the soul, which (as we have already noticed) reached the Greco-Roman world from a Persian source[12]. It appears to be rooted in the more primitive ways of thinking termed 'Animism' and 'Spiritism,' in which men felt the presence both in natural objects and within themselves of forces which they conceived as distinct beings. According to this system a man's soul often assumes bodily shape, and quits his body even during life, either in sleep or during a swoon; sometimes indeed it may be seen to run away and return in the shape of a mouse or a hare. At death it is seen to leave the man as a breath of air, and to enter the atmosphere. But besides his soul a man possesses a shadow, a likeness, a double, a ghost, a name; and all these in varying degrees contribute to form what we should call his personality. In the animistic system the soul survives the man, and why not? But this survival is vaguely conceived, and only credited so far as the evidence of the senses supports it. Its formulation in the doctrine of immortality belongs to a more advanced stage of human thought[13].

266. This dualistic conception could be and was incor-
Soul and body are one. porated in the Stoic system to the same extent as the dualism of God and matter, but no further. Ultimately, as we have already learnt, soul and body are one; or, in the language of paradox, 'soul is body[14].' This follows not only from the general principles of our philosophy, but also specifically from observation of the facts of human life. 'The incorporeal,' argued Cleanthes, 'cannot be affected by the corporeal, nor the corporeal by the incorporeal, but only the corporeal by the corporeal. But the soul is affected

---

[12] See above, § 11.

[13] On the whole subject see Tylor, *Anthropology*, ch. xvi; *Primitive Culture*, chs. xi–xvii; Jevons, *Introd. to the history of Religion*, ch. v.

[14] See above, § 174.

by the body in disease and in mutilation, and the body by the
soul, for it reddens in shame and becomes pale in fear: therefore
the soul is body[15].' And similarly Chrysippus argues: 'death
is the separation of soul from body. Now the incorporeal
neither joins with nor is separated from body, but the soul
does both. The soul therefore is body[16].' This doctrine is
commonly adduced as evidence of the 'materialism' of the
Stoics: yet the Stoics do not say that 'soul is matter,' and (as
we shall see) they explain its workings upon principles quite
different to the laws of physics or chemistry. The essential
unity of body and soul follows also from the way in which we
acquire knowledge of them. For we perceive body by the
touch; and we learn the workings of the soul by a kind of touch,
called the inward touch (ἐντὸς ἁφή)[17].

267.   Having realised that the division of man into soul
Mind, soul   and body is not ultimate, we may more easily
and body.   prepare ourselves to make other divisions.   A
division into three parts, (i) body, (ii) soul or life (ψυχή, anima),
and (iii) mind (νοῦς, animus), was widely accepted in Stoic
times, and in particular by the school of Epicurus; the mind
being that which man has, and the animals have not[18]. The
Stoics develope this division by the principle of the microcosm.
Mind is that which man has in common with the deity; life
that which he has in common with the animals; growth (φύσις,
natura), that which he has in common with the plants, as for
instance is shown in the hair and nails[19]. Man also possesses

---

[15] Nemes. *nat. hom.* ii 85 and 86 (Arnim i 518).

[16] *ib.* 99 (Arnim ii 790).

[17] Here we come into close touch with modern ways of thinking. The soul is
the self as known subjectively and from within, as appealed to in the argument of
Descartes ' cogito, ergo sum.' The body is the self as known objectively and from
without, first in our neighbours who obstruct our efforts ('officium quod corporis
exstat, | officere atque obstare' Lucr. *R. N.* i 337, 8), and then by analogy in
ourselves. The Stoic theory then asserts that subjective and objective knowledge
are ultimately the same, both being activities of the same Logos. See above, § 149.

[18] The distinction is most clearly made by Juvenal: 'sensum a caelesti demissum
traximus arce, | cuius egent prona et terram spectantia. mundi | principio indulsit
communis conditor illis | tantum animas, nobis animum quoque, mutuus ut nos | ad-
fectus petere auxilium et praestare iuberet ' *Sat.* xv 146–150.

[19] See above, § 206.

cohesion (ἕξις, *unitas*) but never apart from higher powers. Further these four, mind, soul, growth, and cohesion, are not different in kind, but all are spirits (πνεύματα) which by their varying degrees of tension (τόνος, *intentio*) are, to a less or greater extent, removed from the divine being, the primal stuff. In this sense man is not one, nor two, but multiple, as the deity is multiple[20].

268. The soul in its substance or stuff is fire, identical with the creative fire which is the primal stuff of the universe[21]. But the popular conception, according to which the soul is air or breath, and is seen to leave the body at death, is also not without truth[22]. There is a very general opinion that the soul is a mixture of fire and air, or is hot air[23]. By this a Stoic would not mean that the soul was a compound of two different elements, but that it was a variety of fire in the first stage of the downward path, beginning to form air by relaxation of its tension : but even so this form of the doctrine was steadily subordinated to the older doctrine of Heraclitus, that the soul is identical with the divine fire. Formally the soul is defined, like the deity himself, as a 'fiery intelligent spirit[24]'; and in this definition it would seem that we have no right to emphasize the connexion between the word 'spirit' (πνεῦμα) and its original meaning 'breath,' since the word has in our philosophy many other associations. It is further a Stoic paradox that 'the soul is an animal,' just as God is an animal. But the soul and the man are not on that account two

The soul is fire and air.

---

[20] See above, § 203.

[21] 'Zenoni Stoico animus ignis videtur' Cic. *Tusc. disp.* i 10, 19.

[22] 'spiritum quippe animam esse Zenon quaerit hactenus; quo recedente a corpore moritur animal, hoc certe anima est. naturali porro spiritu recedente moritur animal; naturalis igitur spiritus anima est' Chalc. *in Tim.* 220 (Arnim i 138).

[23] 'probabilius enim videtur, tale quiddam esse animum, ut sit ex igni atque anima temperatum' Cic. *N. D.* iii 14, 36; cf. Arnim ii 786. This view was accepted by Panaetius: 'is animus...ex inflammata anima constat, ut potissimum videri video Panaetio' *Tusc. disp.* i 18, 42. The 'fire' and 'air' here referred to are not the ordinary elements: οὐ γὰρ πᾶν πῦρ οὐδὲ πᾶν πνεῦμα ταύτην ἔχει τὴν δύναμιν. μετά τινος οὖν ἔσται εἴδους ἰδίου καὶ λόγου καὶ δυνάμεως καί, ὡς αὐτοὶ λέγουσιν, τόνου Alex. Aphr. *de anima* p. 115, 6 (Arnim ii 785). See further Stein *Psychologie* i pp. 101 to 103.

[24] οἱ Στωϊκοὶ πνεῦμα νοερὸν θερμόν [τὴν ψυχήν] Aët. *plac.* iv 3, 3.

16—2

animals; all that is meant is that men and the brutes, by reason
of their being endowed with soul, become animals[25].

269. According to another theory, which is probably not
The tempera- specifically Stoic, but derived from the Greek
ments. physicians, the soul is compounded of all four
elements in varying proportion, and the character of each soul
(subject, in the Stoic theory, to the supreme control of reason[26])
is determined by the proportion or 'temperament' (κρᾶσις,
temperatura) of the four elements. There are accordingly four
temperaments, the fervid, the frigid, the dry, and the moist,
according to the preponderance of fire, air, earth, and water
respectively[27]. Dull and sleepy natures are those in which there
is an excess of the gross elements of earth and water[28]; whilst
an excess of cold air makes a man timorous, and an excess of
fire makes him passionate[29]. These characters are impressed
upon a man from birth and by his bodily conditions, and within
the limits indicated above are unalterable[30]. The 'temperaments'
have always been a favourite subject of discussion in popular
philosophy[31].

270. The characteristic attribute of the soul is that it is
The soul's self-moved (αὐτοκίνητον)[32]. Although in this point
parts. the Stoics agree with Plato, they do not go on to

[25] 'animum constat animal esse, cum ipse efficiat, ut simus animalia; et cum ab
illo animalia hoc nomen traxerint' Sen. *Ep.* 113, 2; 'et animus meus animal est et
ego animal sum; duo tamen non sumus. quare? quia animus mei pars est' *ib.* 5.

[26] Tertullian deals with this point as against Valentinian heretics; *de an.* 21.

[27] 'cum elementa sint quattuor, ignis aquae aeris terrae, potestates pares his sunt,
fervida frigida arida atque umida; eadem animalium hominumque discrimina sunt'
Sen. *Dial.* iv 19, 1 and 2; 'cuius [in homine] elementi portio praevalebit, inde mores
erunt' *ib.* 2.

[28] 'languida ingenia et in somnum itura inertibus nectuntur elementis' *ib.* i 5, 9.

[29] 'iracundos fervida animi natura faciet; frigidi mixtura timidos facit' *ib.* iv 19, 2.

[30] 'quaecunque adtribuit condicio nascendi et corporis temperatura, haerebunt'
Ep. 11, 6.

[31] For a treatment of the subject on modern lines see Ribot, *The emotions*,
chs. xii and xiii; and the works of Fouillée, Paulhan, and other French writers. For
the earlier history see Summers on Sen. *Ep.* 11, 3, and Stein *Psych.* i p. 175.

[32] ψυχή ἐστι κατὰ τοὺς Στωϊκοὺς σῶμα λεπτομερὲς ἐξ ἑαυτοῦ κινούμενον κατὰ σπερματικοὺς λόγους Galen *def. med.* 29 (Arnim ii 780); 'nosmetipsi qui animis movemur'
Cic. *N. D.* ii 22, 58; 'humanus animus agilis est et pronus ad motus' Sen. *Dial.*
ix 2, 11.

name life as another attribute, for they do not agree with the
argument of the *Phaedo* that the soul, having life as an inseparable attribute, is incapable of mortality. We pass on to
the dispositions of the soul, which correspond to its 'parts' in
other philosophies, and are indeed often called its parts. But
the soul has not in the strict sense parts[33]; what are so called
are its activities[34], which are usually reckoned as eight in
number, though the precise reckoning is of no importance[35].
The eight parts of the soul are the ruling part or 'principate[36],'
the five senses, and the powers of speech and generation. The
seven parts or powers other than the principate are subject to it
and do its bidding, so that the soul is, as we have called it, a
kingdom in itself. These seven parts are associated each with a
separate bodily organ, but at the same time each is connected
with the principate. They may therefore be identified with
'spirits which extend from the principate to the organs, like the
arms of an octopus[37],' where by a 'spirit' we mean a pulsation
or thrill, implying incessant motion and tension. The principate
itself, that is the mind, is also a spirit possessed of a still higher
tension; and the general agreement of the Stoics places its
throne conveniently at the heart and in the centre of the body[38].

[33] μία ἡ τῆς ψυχῆς δύναμις, ὡς τὴν αὐτήν πως ἔχουσαν ποτὲ μὲν διανοεῖσθαι, ποτὲ δὲ
ὀργίζεσθαι [qu. ὀρέγεσθαι ?] ποτὲ δ' ἐπιθυμεῖν παρὰ μέρος Alex. Aph. *de anima* p. 118
(Arnim ii 823).

[34] 'huiusmodi autem non tam partes animae habeantur quam vires et efficaciae
et operae' Tert. *de an.* 14. They may also be called the soul's qualities : οἱ ἀπὸ
Χρυσίππου καὶ Ζήνωνος φιλόσοφοι τὰς μὲν δυνάμεις ὡς ἐν τῷ ὑποκειμένῳ ποιότητας
συμβιβάζουσι, τὴν δὲ ψυχὴν ὡς οὐσίαν προϋποκειμένην ταῖς δυνάμεσι τιθέασι Stob. i
49, 33.

[35] See above, § 79; for other divisions Tert. *de an.* 14 (Arnim i 144), Cic. *Off.* i
28, 101, and generally Stein, *Psych.* i p. 123.

[36] On this translation see § 101, note 81.

[37] [ἀπὸ τοῦ ἡγεμονικοῦ] ταῦτα πάντα ἐπιτέταται διὰ τῶν οἰκείων ὀργάνων προσφερῶς
ταῖς τοῦ πολύποδος πλεκτάναις Aët. *plac.* iv 4, 4.

[38] Arnim ii 838. Since many philosophers think the mind seated in the head,
Chrysippus collects many arguments to the contrary ; for instance that women say,
when they don't agree with a statement, 'it won't go down,' pointing all the while to
the heart, Galen *plac. Hipp. et Plat.* iii 5, p. 323 K (Arnim ii 892). Further that
καρδία is derived from κράτησις, the heart being the seat of government *ib.* (Arnim ii
896). He could support his view by thousands of quotations from the poets. On
the other hand we find the suggestion that the principate resides in our spherical
heads, as in a universe (Aët. *plac.* iv 21, 4). This latter view may be due to
Academic influence (Schmekel, p. 259).

Accordingly Posidonius defined the soul's parts as 'powers of one substance seated at the heart[39].'

271. If we now fix our attention on the principate itself, we find it no more simple than the universe, the deity, the man, or the soul. In particular it resembles the deity in that, although essentially one, it is called by many names. It is the soul in its reasoning aspect, the reason, the intellect (λογικὴ ψυχή, νοῦς, διάνοια)[40]; it is also the 'ego,' that is, the will, the energy, the capacity for action[41]. It is in one aspect the divinity in us, world-wide, universal; in another the individual man with his special bent and character; so that we may even be said to have two souls in us, the world-soul and each man's particular soul[42]. The principate becomes also in turn each of the other functions or parts of the soul, for each of them is an aspect of the principate (ἡγεμονικόν πως ἔχον)[43]. In addition the principate has many titles of honour, as when Marcus Aurelius terms it the Pilot[44], the King and Lawgiver[45], the Controller and Governor[46], the God within[47].

Aspects of the principate.

272. Although for the purpose of discussion we may distinguish between reason and will, they are in fact everywhere intermingled. Thus the principate as the reasoning part of the soul includes the powers of perception, assent, comprehension, and of reason in the narrower sense, that is, the power of combining the various conceptions of the mind, so as ultimately to form a consistent

The principate as reason.

---

[39] δυνάμεις μιᾶς οὐσίας ἐκ τῆς καρδίας ὁρμωμένης Galen *plac. Hipp. et Plat.* p. 51 K.

[40] τὸ λογιστικὸν μόριον τῆς ψυχῆς, ὃ καὶ ἰδίως ἡγεμονικὸν καλεῖται Alex. Aphr. *de an.* p. 98, 24 (Arnim ii 839). In this direction Epictetus defines the rational faculty as 'that which contemplates both itself and all other things' *Disc.* i 1, 4.

[41] τὸ ἐγὼ λέγομεν κατὰ τοῦτο [τὸ ἡγεμονικὸν] δεικνύντες Galen *plac. Hipp. et Plat.* ii 2 p. 215 K.

[42] 'intellegendum est etiam, duabus quasi nos a natura indutos esse personis, quarum una communis est ex eo, quod omnes participes sumus rationis; altera autem, quae proprie singulis est tributa' Cic. *Off.* i 30, 107.

[43] Arnim ii 823.　　　　　　　　　　[44] *To himself* vii 64.

[45] *ib.* iv 12.　　　　　　　　　　　[46] *ib.* v 27.

[47] *ib.* iii 5, v 10, xii 1; so too Epictetus 'God is within, and your daemon is within' *Disc.* i 14, 14.

system[48]. But amongst these powers assent is equally an act of the will; and on the other hand the judgments formed by the reasoning mind are not purely speculative, but lead up to action; so that it is the reasoning power which must be kept pure, in order that it may duly control the soul's inclinations and aversions, its aims and shrinkings, its plans, interests and assents[49]. If in the Stoic theory the greater emphasis always appears to be laid on the reason, it is the more necessary in interpreting it to bear in mind that we are speaking of the reason of an active and social being.

273. The maintenance of the principate as will in a right

The principate as will.

condition is the problem of ethics; and it is important to understand what this right condition is. The answer is to be found in a series of analogies, drawn from all departments of philosophy. Thus from the standpoint of physics the right condition is a proper strain or tension, as opposed to slackness or unsteadiness[50]. In theology it is the agreement of the particular will with the divine or universal will[51]. From the point of view of the will itself it is the strength and force ($i\sigma\chi\dot{\upsilon}s$ $\kappa a\dot{\iota}$ $\kappa\rho\acute{a}\tau os$) of the will, the attitude that makes a man say 'I can[52].' Again it is that state of the soul which corresponds to health in the body[53]; and in a quiet mood the Stoic may describe it as a restful and calm condition[54]. Finally, if the soul as a whole is compared to a State, the principate in its function as the will may at its best be compared to a just and kind sovereign; but if this

---

[48] See above, §§ 146–156.

[49] ἔργα δὲ ψυχῆς ὁρμᾶν, ἀφορμᾶν, ὀρέγεσθαι, ἐκκλίνειν, παρασκευάζεσθαι, ἐπιβάλλεσθαι, συγκατατίθεσθαι. τί ποτ' οὖν ἐστι τὸ ἐν τούτοις τοῖς ἔργοις ῥυπαρὸν παρέχον αὐτὴν καὶ ἀκάθαρτον; οὐδὲν ἄλλο ἢ τὰ μοχθηρὰ κρίματα αὐτῆς Epict. Disc. iv 11, 6 and 7.

[50] ἡ τῆς ψυχῆς ἰσχὺς τόνος ἐστὶν ἱκανὸς ἐν τῷ κρίνειν καὶ πράττειν ἢ μή Stob. ii 7 5b 4; 'quaerimus quomodo animus semper secundo cursu eat' Sen. Dial. ix 2, 4; 'quidam se domi contrahunt, dilatant foris ac extendunt; vitium est haec diversitas et signum vacillantis animi ac nondum habentis tenorem suum' Ep. 20, 3.

[51] See above, § 96.

[52] 'satis natura homini dedit roboris, si illo utamur; nolle in causa est, non posse praetenditur' Sen. Ep. 116, 8.

[53] 'animi motus eos putemus sanissimos validissimosque, qui nostro arbitrio ibunt, non suo ferentur' Dial. iv 35, 2.

[54] 'hanc stabilem animi sedem Graeci εὐθυμίαν vocant, ego tranquillitatem voco' ib. ix 2, 3.

aim is missed, it may turn into a greedy and ungovernable tyrant[55].

274. The principate, as it is of divine origin[56], and destined, as we shall see, to be reabsorbed in the deity, may rightly be called god: it is a god making its settlement and home in a human body[57]: it keeps watch within over the moral principle[58]. In the language of paradox we may say to each man, 'You are a god[59].' Of this principle we see the proof in that man interests himself in things divine[60], and in it we find the first incentive to a lofty morality[61]. As however the deity is not conceived in human form, and is not subject to human weaknesses, there comes a point at which, in the study of the human principate, we part company with the divine; and this point we reach both when we consider the principate with regard to its seven distinctly human manifestations, and when we consider its possible degradation from the standard of health and virtue. We now turn to the seven parts or powers of the human soul which are subordinate to the reasoning faculty.

The principate, divine and human.

275. The first five powers of the principate are those which are recognised in popular philosophy as the 'five senses.' To materialistic philosophers nothing is plainer than that these are functions of the body;

Powers of the principate.

---

[55] *Ep.* 114, 24 (see above, § 263, note 1).

[56] 'non est [mens] ex terreno et gravi concreta corpore, ex illo caelesti spiritu descendit' *Dial.* xii 7, 7; 'ratio nihil aliud est quam in corpus humanum pars divini spiritus mersa' *Ep.* 66, 12.

[57] 'animus, sed hic rectus bonus magnus...quid aliud voces hunc quam deum in corpore humano hospitantem?' *ib.* 31, 11.

[58] 'sacer inter nos spiritus sedet, malorum bonorumque nostrorum observator [et] custos' *ib.* 41, 2.

[59] 'deum te igitur scito esse: si quidem deus est qui viget, qui sentit, qui meminit' Cic. *Rep.* vi (*Somn. Scip.*) 24, 26.

[60] Physics, and in particular astronomy, is meant: '[animus] hoc habet argumentum divinitatis suae, quod illum divina delectant; nec ut alienis sed ut suis interest' Sen. *N. Q.* i Prol. 12; cf. Horace *Ep.* i 12, 14–19.

[61] 'When you are in social intercourse, when you are exercising yourself, when you are engaged in discussion, know you not that you are nourishing a god, that you are exercising a god? Wretch, you are carrying about a god with you, and you know it not.' Epict. *Disc.* ii 8, 12.

is it not the eye which sees, and the ear which hears[62]? This
the Stoic denies. The eye does not see, but the soul sees
through the eye as through an open door. The ear does not
hear, but the soul hears through the ear. Sensation therefore is
an activity of the principate, acting in the manner already
described in the chapter on 'Reason and Speech[63].' The soul
is actively engaged, and sends forth its powers as water from a
fountain; the sense-organs are passively affected by the objects
perceived[64]. Subject to this general principle, sensation (αἴσθησις,
sensus) may be variously defined. It is 'a spirit which penetrates from the principate to the sensory processes'; it includes
alike the mind-picture (φαντασία, visum), that is, the first rough
sketch which the mind shapes when stimulated by the sense-
organ; the assent (συγκατάθεσις, adsensus), which the mind
gives or refuses to this sketch; and the final act of comprehension (κατάληψις, comprehensio) by which this assent is sealed
or ratified[65]. Of these the middle stage is the most important,
so that we may say paradoxically 'sense is assent[66].' Only in
a secondary and popular way can we use the word sensation
to denote the physical apparatus of the sensory organs
(αἰσθητήρια), as when we say of a blind man 'he has lost the
sense of sight[67].'

276. The nature of sensation is more particularly described
in the case of sight and hearing. In the first case
there proceed from the eyes rays, which cause
tension in the air, reaching towards the object seen[68]; this

The five
senses.

---

[62] 'dicere porro, oculos nullam rem cernere posse, | sed per eos animum ut foribus
spectare reclusis, | difficile est' Lucr. N. D. iii 360–362; cf. Arnim ii 862. See also
Cic. N. D. iii 4, 9, and Mayor's valuable note. Modern psychologists side with the Stoics.
[63] See above, § 146, note 18.
[64] τὰ μὲν πάθη ἐν τοῖς πεπονθόσι τόποις, τὰς δὲ αἰσθήσεις ἐν τῷ ἡγεμονικῷ Aët. plac.
iv 23, 1.
[65] See above, § 146, note 18.
[66] αἰσθητικῇ γὰρ φαντασίᾳ συγκατάθεσίς ἐστιν ἡ αἴσθησις Porph. de anima (Arnim
ii 74); 'dicunt Stoici sensus ipsos adsensus esse' Cic. Ac. ii 33, 108.
[67] αἴσθησις δὲ λέγεται...καὶ ἡ περὶ τὰ αἰσθητήρια κατασκευή, καθ' ἣν τινες πηροὶ
γίνονται Diog. L. vii 52.
[68] 'Stoici causas esse videndi dicunt radiorum ex oculis in ea, quae videri queunt,
emissionem aerisque simul intentionem' Gell. N. A. v 16, 2; 'Stoici videndi causam
in nativi spiritus intentione constituunt, cuius effigiem coni similem volunt' Chalc.
Tim. 237 (Arnim ii 863).

tension is cone-shaped, and as the distance from the pupil of the eye increases, the base of the cone is increased in size, whilst the vigour of the sight diminishes. This human activity effects vision of itself in one case; for we say 'darkness is visible,' when the eye shoots forth light at it, and correctly recognises that it is darkness[69]. But in complete vision there is an opposing wave-motion coming from the object, and the two waves become mutually absorbed: hence Posidonius called sight 'absorption' ($\sigma\acute{\nu}\mu\phi\nu\sigma\iota\varsigma$)[70]. Similarly, in the case of hearing, the pulsation (which, as we have seen, comes in the first instance from the principate) spreads from the ear to the speaker, and (as is now more distinctly specified) from the speaker to the hearer; this reverse pulsation being circular in shape, like the waves excited on the surface of a lake by throwing a stone into the water[71]. Of the sensations of smell, taste and touch we only hear that they are respectively (i) a spirit extending from the principate to the nostrils, (ii) a spirit extending from the principate to the tongue, and (iii) a spirit extending to the surface of the body and resulting in the easily-appreciated touch of an object[72].

277. The Stoic account of the functions of the soul dis-

Other activities.

played in the ordinary activities of life is either defective or mutilated; for even a slight outline of the subject should surely include at least breathing, eating (with drinking), speech, walking, and lifting. We need not however doubt that these, equally with the five senses, are all 'spirits stretching from the principate' to the bodily organs. This is expressly stated of walking[73]. Of all such activities we must consider voice to be typical, when it is described as the sixth function of the soul. Voice is described as 'pulsating air[74],' set in motion by the tongue[75]; but we can trace it back through the

---

[69] Arnim ii 869.

[70] Ποσειδώνιος γοῦν αὐτὴν (sc. τὴν ὄψιν) σύμφυσιν ὀνομάζει Aët. *plac.* iv 13, 3.

[71] Diog. L. vii 158.   [72] Arnim ii 836.

[73] 'Cleanthes [ambulationem] ait spiritum esse a principali usque in pedes permissum' Sen. *Ep.* 113, 23.

[74] 'vocem Stoici corpus esse contendunt, eamque esse dicunt ictum aera' Gellius *N. A.* v 15, 6.

[75] 'quid enim est vox nisi intentio aeris, ut audiatur, linguae formata percussu?' Sen. *N. Q.* ii 6, 3.

throat to some source below, which we can without difficulty
identify with the heart, the seat of the principate[76]. The
voice is indeed in a special relationship to the principate,
since the spoken word is but another aspect of the thought
which is expressed by it[77].

278. The seventh and last of the subordinate powers of the
soul, according to the Stoics, is that of procreation.
Procreation. This part of their system is of great importance,
not only for the study of human nature, but even in a higher
degree for its indirect bearing upon the question of the
development of the universe through 'procreative principles'
(σπερματικοὶ λόγοι), or, as we have termed them above, 'seed
powers[78].' That all things grow after their kind is of course
matter of common knowledge; no combination of circumstances,
no scientific arrangement of sustenance can make of an acorn
anything but an oak, or of a hen's egg anything but a chicken.
But in the common view this is, at least primarily, a corporeal
or material process; whereas the Stoics assert that it is not only
a property of the soul, but one so primary and fundamental that
it must be also assumed as a first principle of physical science.
Before approaching the subject from the Stoic standpoint, it
may be well to see how far materialistic theories, ancient and
modern, can carry us.

279. Lucretius finds this a very simple matter:

'Children often resemble not only their parents, but also their grand-
Heredity. parents and more remote ancestors. The explanation is that
the parents contain in their bodies a large number of atoms,
which they have received from their ancestors and pass on to their descendants.
In the chance clashing of atoms in procreation Venus produces all kinds of
effects, bringing about resemblances between children and their forebears, not
only in the face and person, but also in the look, the voice, and the hair[79].'

This account has a generally plausible sound until we bear
in mind that it is the fundamental property of atoms that,

---

[76] ὁ λόγος ἐκεῖθεν ἐκπέμπεται, ὅθεν καὶ ἡ φωνή. ἡ δὲ φωνὴ οὐκ ἐκ τῶν κατὰ τὴν
κεφαλὴν τόπων ἐκπέμπεται, ἀλλὰ φανερῶς ἐκ κάτωθεν μᾶλλον Galen. *plac. Hipp. et
Plat.* ii 5 p. 205 Müller.
[77] See above, § 161.
[78] See above, § 178.   [79] Lucr. *R. N.* iv 1214–1220.

though their own variety is limited, they can form things in infinite variety by changes in their combination and arrangement. They are like the letters out of which words, sentences, and poems are made up; and we can hardly expect to reproduce the voice or the spirit of an Aeschylus by a fresh shuffling of the letters contained in the *Agamemnon*. On the contrary, seeing that the atoms contained in the bodies of parents have largely been drawn from plants and animals, we could confidently reckon upon finding the complete fauna and flora of the neighbourhood amongst their offspring. Lucretius in effect postulates in his theory that particular atoms have a representative and creative character, passing from father to child in inseparable association with the marks of the human race, and endowed with a special capacity of combining with other like atoms to form the substratum of specifically human features. In giving his atoms these properties he is insensibly approximating to the Stoic standpoint.

280. Modern biologists deal with this subject with the minuteness of detail of which the microscope is the instrument, and with the wealth of illustration which results from the incessant accumulation of ascertained facts. But they are perhaps open to the criticism that where they reach the borders of their own science, they are apt to introduce references to the sciences of chemistry and physics as explaining all difficulties, even in regions to which these sciences do not apply. The following account is taken from one of the most eminent of them :

Modern theories.

'Hertwig discovered that the one essential occurrence in impregnation is the coalescence of the two sexual cells and their nuclei. Of the millions of male spermatozoa which swarm round a female egg-cell, only one forces its way into its plasmic substance. The nuclei of the two cells are drawn together by a mysterious force which we conceive as *a chemical sense-activity akin to smell*, approach each other and melt into one. So there arises through the sensitiveness of the two sexual nuclei, *as a result of erotic chemotropism*, a new cell which unites the inherited capacities of both parents; the spermatozoon contributes the paternal, the egg-cell the maternal characteristics to the primary-cell, from which the child is developed[80].'

[80] E. Haeckel, *Welträthsel* (Volksausg.) p. 30. The italics are those of the author of this book.

In another passage the same author sums up his results in bold language from which all qualifications and admissions of imperfect knowledge have disappeared:

'Physiology has proved that all *the phenomena of life may be reducēd to chemical and physical processes.* The cell-theory has shown us that all the complicated phenomena of the life of the higher plants and animals may be deduced from the simple physico-chemical processes in the elementary organism of the microscopic cells, and the material basis of them is the plasma of the cell-body[81].'

281. These utterances may be considered typical of modern materialistic philosophy in its extreme form. We may nevertheless infer from the references to a 'mysterious force,' 'chemical sense-activity akin to smell,' and 'erotic chemotropism,' that the analogies to biological facts which the writer finds in chemical science stand in need of further elucidation. We may notice further that the 'atom' has entirely disappeared from the discussion, and that the 'material basis' of the facts is a 'plasma' or 'plasmic substance,' something in fact which stands related to a 'protoplasm' of which the chemical and physical sciences know nothing, but which distinctly resembles the 'fiery creative body' which is the foundation of the Stoic physics. Further we must notice that the old problem of 'the one and the many' reappears in this modern description; for the cell and its nucleus are neither exactly one nor exactly two, but something which passes from two to one and from one to two; further the nuclei of the two cells, being drawn together, coalesce, and from their union is developed a 'new cell' which unites the capacities of its 'parents.' Modern science, therefore, although it has apparently simplified the history of generation by reducing it to the combination of two units out of many millions that are incessantly being produced by parent organisms, has left the philosophical problem of the manner of their combination entirely unchanged. In these microscopic cells is latent the whole physical and spiritual inheritance of the parents, whether men, animals or plants, from which they are derived; just as the atoms of Epicurus possess the germ of free

Their inadequacy.

---

[81] *ib. Anmerkungen*, p. 158.

will[82], so the cells of Haeckel smell and love, struggle for marriage union, melt away in each other's embrace, and lose their own individuality at the moment that a new being enters the universe.

282. If then the phenomena of reproduction are essentially

Creation and procreation.

the same, whether we consider the relations of two human beings or those of infinitesimal elements which seem to belong to another order of being, we are already prepared for the Stoic principle that the creation of the universe is repeated in miniature in the bringing into life of each individual amongst the millions of millions of organic beings which people it. From this standpoint we gain fresh light upon the Stoic theory of creation, and particularly of the relation of the eternal Logos to the infinite multitude of procreative principles or 'seed-powers.' Again, it is with the general theory of creation in our minds that we must revert to the Stoic explanation of ordinary generation. This is to him no humble or unclean function of the members of the body; it is the whole man, in his divine and human nature, that is concerned[83]. The 'procreative principle' in each man is a part of his soul[84]; 'the seed is a spirit' (or pulsation) 'extending from the principate to the parts of generation[85].' It is an emanation from the individual in which one becomes two, and two become one. Just as the human soul is a 'fragment' of the divine, so is the seed a fragment torn away, as it were, from the souls of parents and ancestors[86].

---

[82] Though Lucretius laughs at the idea of attributing laughter and tears to the elements ('hac ratione tibi pereunt primordia rerum: | fiet, uti risu tremulo concussa cachinnent, | et lacrumis salsis umectent ora genasque' *R. N.* i 917-919), yet he attributes to them the essential power of free-will: 'si...nec declinando faciunt primordia motus | principium quoddam, quod fati foedera rumpat, | unde est haec, inquam, fatis avolsa voluntas?' *R. N.* ii 253-257.

[83] οἱ Στωϊκοὶ ἀπὸ τοῦ σώματος ὅλου καὶ τῆς ψυχῆς φέρεσθαι τὰ σπέρματα Aët. *plac.* v. 11, 3; 'When you consort with your wife...you are carrying about a god with you' Epict. *Disc.* ii 8, 12.

[84] μέρη δὲ ψυχῆς λέγουσιν...τοὺς ἐν ἡμῖν σπερματικοὺς λόγους Diog. L. vii 157.

[85] τῶν δὲ λοιπῶν [μερῶν τῆς ψυχῆς] τὸ μὲν λέγεται σπέρμα, ὅπερ καὶ αὐτὸ πνεῦμά ἐστι διατεῖνον ἀπὸ τοῦ ἡγεμονικοῦ μέχρι τῶν παραστατῶν Aët. *plac.* iv 21, 4; cf. Diog. L. vii 159.

[86] τὸ δὲ σπέρμα φησὶν ὁ Ζήνων εἶναι ψυχῆς μέρος καὶ ἀπόσπασμα καὶ τοῦ σπέρματος

283. In the seed is contained the whole build of the man
that is to be[87]. It is therefore important to know
whether the procreative principle in the embryo
is derived from one or both parents, and if the latter, whether
in equal proportion. The Stoics do not appear to have kept
entirely free from the common prepossession, embodied in the
law of paternal descent, according to which the male element
is alone active in the development of the organism; and so they
allege that the female seed is lacking in tone and generative
power[88]. On the other hand observation appeared to them to
show that children inherit the psychical and bodily qualities of
both parents, and the general tendency of their philosophy was
towards the equalization of the sexes. On the whole the latter
considerations prevailed, so that the doctrine of Stoicism, as of
modern times, was that qualities, both of body and soul, are
inherited from the seed of both parents[89]; wherein the possibility
remains open, that in particular cases the debt to one parent
may be greater than to the other[90].

Motherhood.

284. The Stoic psychology is in its fundamental principles
wholly distinct from that of Plato; which does not
at all prevent its exponents, and least of all those
like Panaetius and Posidonius who were admirers of Plato, from
making use of his system as an auxiliary to their own. Plato
divided the soul into three parts; the rational part, the emotional
(and volitional) part, and the appetitive[91]. Both the two latter
parts need the control of the reason, but the emotional part

Impulses.

τοῦ τῶν προγόνων κέρασμα καὶ μῖγμα τῶν τῆς ψυχῆς μερῶν συνεληλυθός Euseb. *pr. ev.*
xv 20, 1 (Arnim i 128). That the separation or 'tearing away' (ἀπόσπασμα) is not
complete or absolute seems to follow from the general principles of Stoic physics : see
above § 262.

[87] 'in semine omnis futuri hominis ratio comprehensa est' Sen. *N. Q.* iii 29, 3.

[88] 'utrum ex patris tantummodo semine partus nascatur, ut...Stoici scripserunt'
Censor. *di. nat.* 5 ; cf. Diog. L. vii 159, Aët. *plac.* v 5, 2.

[89] The evidence for this is mainly indirect. [ὁ δὲ Κλεάνθης] οὐ μόνον, φησίν, ὅμοιοι
τοῖς γονεῦσι γινόμεθα κατὰ τὸ σῶμα ἀλλὰ κατὰ τὴν ψυχήν Nemes. *nat. hom.* ii 85
and 86 (Arnim i 518); 'quod declaret eorum similitudo, qui procreentur ; quae etiam
in ingeniis, non solum in corporibus appareat' Cic. *Tusc. disp.* i 32, 79.

[90] προίεσθαι δὲ καὶ τὴν γυναῖκα σπέρμα· κἂν μὲν ἐπικρατήσῃ τὸ τῆς γυναικός, ὅμοιον
εἶναι τὸ γεννώμενον τῇ μητρί, ἐὰν δὲ τὸ τοῦ ἀνδρός, τῷ πατρί Aët. *plac.* v 11, 4.

[91] See above, § 63.

inclines to virtue, the appetitive to vice[92]. The rational part, as with the Stoics, is peculiar to man; the other two are also possessed by the animals, and the appetitive soul even by plants. The Stoics do not however seriously allow any kinship between virtue and the emotions, and they deal with this part of the subject as follows. Nature has implanted in all living things certain impulses which are directed towards some object. An impulse towards an object is called 'appetite' (ὁρμή, *appetitus* or *impetus*); an impulse to avoid an object is called 'aversion' (ἀφορμή, *alienatio*)[93]. In man appetite should be governed by reason; if this is so, it becomes 'reasonable desire' (ὄρεξις εὔλογος, *recta appetitio*)[94]; if otherwise, it becomes 'unreasonable desire' (ὄρεξις ἀπειθὴς λόγῳ) or 'concupiscence' (ἐπιθυμία, *libido*). To living things lower in the scale than man terms that are related to reason can of course not apply.

285. Practical choice is, according to the Stoics, exactly analogous to intellectual decision. Just as the powers of sensation never deceive us[95], so also the impulses are never in themselves irrational[96]. An impulse is an adumbration of a course of action as proper to be pursued[97]; to this the will gives or refuses its assent[98]. It is the will, and the will only, which is liable to error, and this through want of proper tone and self-control. If there is this want, it appears in a false judgment, a weak assent, an exaggerated impulse; and this is what we call in ethics a perturbation[99]. A healthy assent

Will and responsibility.

[92] 'inrationalis pars animi duas habet partes, alteram animosam ambitiosam impotentem positam in adfectionibus, alteram humilem languidam voluptatibus deditam' Sen. *Ep.* 92, 8.

[93] 'appetitio (eam enim esse volumus ὁρμήν), qua ad agendum impellimur, et id appetimus quod est visum' Cic. *Ac.* ii 8, 24.

[94] This is termed by Panaetius ὄρεξις simply; the term ἐπιβολή is also used: see § 272, note 49.   [95] See above, § 146.

[96] Zeller (*Stoics*, p. 243) states that man has irrational as well as rational impulses. This seems to be incorrectly expressed.

[97] φαντασία ὁρμητικὴ τοῦ καθήκοντος Stob. ii 7, 9.

[98] 'omne rationale animal nihil agit, nisi primum specie alicuius rei inritatum est, deinde impetum cepit, deinde adsensio confirmavit hunc impetum. quid sit adsensio dicam. oportet me ambulare: tunc demum ambulo, cum hoc mihi dixi et adprobavi hanc opinionem meam' Sen. *Ep.* 113, 18.

[99] δοκεῖ δ' αὐτοῖς τὰ πάθη κρίσεις εἶναι, καθά φησι Χρύσιππος Diog. L. vii 111; 'omnes perturbationes iudicio censent fieri et opinione' Cic. *Tusc. disp.* iv 7, 14;

leads up to a right action: a false assent to a blunder or sin. Hence we hold to the Socratic paradox that 'no one sins willingly' (οὐδεὶς ἑκὼν ἁμαρτάνει); for the true and natural will cannot sin; it must first be warped to a false judgment and weakened by slackness of tone. We can equally use the paradox that 'every voluntary action is a judgment of the intellect,' or (in few words) that 'virtue is wisdom' (φρόνησις ἡ ἀρετή). In such views we find a starting-point for dealing with the problems of ethics, including those of the ethical ideal or supreme good, its application to daily duties, and its failure through ignorance or weakness of soul.

286. We pass on to consider the body, but at no great
The body.
length; partly because many functions often considered as bodily are by the Stoics treated as belonging to the soul (as sensations and impulses), partly because the study of the body is rather the task of the physician than of the philosopher. In the body we may notice separately (i) the bones, sinews, and joints, constituting the framework on which the whole is built up; (ii) the surface, including beauty of outline and features, and (iii) the complexion, which suffuses a glow over the surface and most attracts the attention[100]. No absolute distinction can be made between body and soul. Generally speaking, we may say that body is composed of the two grosser elements, earth and water, whilst soul (as we have seen) rests on the two higher elements of air and fire[101]; of the gradations of spirit body possesses distinctively (but not exclusively) that of coherence (ἕξις), whilst it shares with the soul the principle of growth (φύσις)[102]. Yet these contrasts are after all only secondary. As surely as soul is body so body is soul, and

ἀσθενῆ δὲ λέγουσι συγκατάθεσιν, ὅταν μηδέπω πεπεικότες ὦμεν ἡμᾶς αὐτούς Galen de peccatis ii 1 p. 59 K (Arnim iii 172); ἔστι δ' αὐτὸ τὸ πάθος κατὰ Ζήνωνα...ὁρμὴ πλεονάζουσα Diog. L. vii 110.

[100] 'in corpore nostro ossa nervique et articuli, firmamenta totius et vitalia, minime speciosa visu, prius ordinantur; deinde haec, ex quibus omnis in faciem adspectumque decor est. post haec omnia qui maxime oculos rapit, color, ultimus perfecto iam corpore adfunditur' Sen. Dial. iv 1, 2.

[101] See above, § 268.

[102] ἡ ψυχὴ πνεῦμά ἐστι σύμφυτον ἡμῖν Galen plac. Hipp. et Plat. iii 1 p. 251 M, quoting Chrysippus (Arnim ii 885).

A. 17

divinity penetrates into its humblest parts. In its practical applications Stoicism dwells so little on the body that the wise man seems hardly conscious of its existence.

287. Side by side with the strictly Stoic view of the body 'The flesh.' we find in all the Roman literature another conception which is strongly dualistic, and which we cannot but think to be drawn from some non-Stoic source[103]. According to this view the body, often called the 'flesh,' is essentially evil[104]; it is the prison-house of the soul[105], the source of corruption of the will[106], the hindrance to a clear insight of the intelligence. In the language picturesquely adopted in the *Pilgrim's Progress* (after St Paul), it is a burden which the enlightened man longs to shake off[107]. For the body so understood we find abusive names; it is the husk in which the grain is concealed[108], the ass from which the owner should be ready to part at any moment[109]. This language tends to be exaggerated and morbid, and leads in practice to asceticism[110]. It appealed in ancient as in modern times to a widespread sentiment, but is not reconcileable with the main teaching of the Stoic philosophy.

---

[103] Schmekel traces the introduction of this doctrine to Posidonius, and finds in it the starting-point of the later mysticism, *Philos. d. mittl. Stoa*, pp. 400 sqq. See also L. Stein, *Psych.* i 194.

[104] ''nos corpus tam putre sortiti' Sen. *Ep.* 120, 17; 'inutilis caro et fluida, receptandis tantum cibis habilis, ut ait Posidonius' *ib.* 92, 10.

[105] 'haec quae vides ossa circumiecta nobis, nervos et obductam cutem, voltumque et ministras manus, et cetera quibus involuti sumus, vincula animorum tenebraeque sunt. obruitur his animus, effocatur, inficitur, arcetur a veris et suis in falsa coniectus. omne illi cum hac carne grave certamen est' Sen. *Dial.* vi 24, 5; 'corpusculum hoc, custodia et vinculum animi' *ib.* xii 11, 7.

[106] 'What am I? a poor miserable man with my wretched bit of flesh. Through this kinship with the flesh, some of us become like wolves' Epict. *Disc.* i 3, 5 and 7.

[107] 'corpus hoc animi pondus et poena est' Sen. *Ep.* 65, 16; 'quantum per moras membrorum et hanc circumfusam gravem sarcinam licet' *Dial.* xii 11, 6; 'corporis velut oneris necessarii non amator sed procurator est' *Ep.* 92, 33.

[108] 'Epicurus placed the good in the husk' Epict. *Disc.* i 23, 1.

[109] 'You ought to possess your whole body as a poor ass loaded. When the body is an ass, all the other things are bits belonging to the ass, pack-saddles, shoes, barley, fodder' *ib.* iv 1, 79 and 80.

[110] In particular to the practice of self-mutilation, with which Seneca is disgusted: 'cottidie comminiscimur, per quae virilitati fiat iniuria...alius genitalia excidit' Sen. *N. Q.* vii 31, 3.

288. According to the true Stoic view, the body is a dwelling-place or temple inhabited for a time by the principate, its divinity[111]. Therefore the body as such is deserving of respect, even of veneration[112]. In particular the erect form of the human body is a mark of divine favour, by which it is hinted that man is fitted to contemplate the operations of the heavens[113]. The whole framework of the body, from the organs of sensation to those by which we breathe, swallow, and digest, is a masterpiece of divine skill, and an evidence of the care of providence for man[114]. And even as an architect provides that those parts of the house which are offensive to sight and smell should be out of sight, so has nature hidden away those parts of the body which are necessarily offensive, at a distance from the organs of sense[115]. The Stoic conception of the dignity of the body is symbolized in practical ethics by the culture of the beard, in which is latent the broad principle of attention to the cleanliness and healthy development of every part of the body.

Dignity of the body.

It is a mark of the Oriental associations of Stoicism that this respect for the body is never associated with the Hellenic cult of the body as displayed in art and gymnastics.

289. Having now studied man in all his parts, it is time to consider how those parts are compacted together, how man grows and decays, and what varieties of mankind exist. First then the principate is combined with the lower functions of the soul, and every part of the soul, by the process of interpenetration ($\sigma\hat{\omega}\mu\alpha$ $\delta\iota\grave{\alpha}$ $\sigma\acute{\omega}\mu\alpha\tau\sigma$

Junction of soul and body.

---

[111] 'nec domum esse hoc corpus, sed hospitium et quidem breve hospitium' Sen. *Ep.* 120, 14; 'hoc [corpus] natura ut quandam vestem animo circumdedit' *ib.* 92, 13.

[112] 'inter me teque conveniet corpus in honorem animi coli' *ib.* 92, 1. In the same spirit Seneca writes in condemnation of the gladiatorial conflicts 'homo sacra res homini' *ib.* 95, 33.

[113] '[natura] voltus nostros erexit ad caelum' *ib.* 94, 56; '[natura]...ut ab ortu sidera in occasum labentia prosequi posset, sublime fecit [homini] caput et collo flexili imposuit' *Dial.* viii 5, 4. See also Mayor on Juv. *Sat.* xv 147.

[114] Cic. *N. D.* ii 54 to 58.

[115] 'quae partes corporis, ad naturae necessitatem datae, adspectum essent deformem habiturae atque turpem, eas [natura] contexit atque abdidit' *Off.* i 35, 127.

χωρεῖ)[116]; or (from a slightly different point of view) upon body which has cohesion (ἕξις) is overlaid growth, on growth soul, and on soul reason ; so that the higher tension presupposes the lower, but not *vice versa*. In the act of generation the soul loses its higher tensions; and consequently the embryo possesses neither human nor animal soul, but only the principles of cohesion and growth. It is in fact a vegetable[117], but necessarily differs from other vegetables in having the potentiality of rising to a higher grade of spirit[118]. At the moment of birth its growth-power (φύσις) is brought into contact with the cold air, and through this chill it rises to the grade of animal life, and becomes soul (ψυχή from ψῦξις)[119]. This etymological theory provokes the ridicule of opponents, who do not fail to point out that soul, standing nearer to the divine fire than growth, ought to be produced by warmth rather than by coolness; but the Stoics probably had in mind that contact with either of the two higher elements must raise the gradation of spirit. The infant, according to this theory, is an animal, but not yet a man ; it has not the gift of reason[120]. To attain this higher stage there is need both of growth from within, and of association with reasonable beings without ; in these ways reason may be developed in or about the seventh year[121]. In the whole of its growth the soul needs continually to be refreshed by the inbreathing of air, and to be sustained by exhalations from the blood[122]. Here we touch upon one

[116] In the Epicurean system atoms of soul are dispersed amongst atoms of body, there being a mixture of the two, which however does not go beyond juxtaposition; in the Stoic system soul permeates body. The Stoic explanation is frequently referred to by opponents as a *reductio ad absurdum* : τῷ λέγοντι τὴν ψυχὴν σῶμα ἕπεται τὸ σῶμα διὰ σώματος χωρεῖν Alex. Aphr. *Arist. Top.* ii 93 (Arnim ii 798). The relation of the principate to the man as a whole is also called σύστασις (*constitutio*) ; ' constitutio est principale animi quodam modo se habens erga corpus' Sen. *Ep.* 121, 10.

[117] οἱ Στωϊκοὶ μέρος αὐτὸ [τὸ ἔμβρυον] τῆς γαστρός, οὐ ζῷον Aët. *plac.* v 14, 2 ; τὸ βρέφος ἐν τῇ γαστρὶ φύσει τρέφεσθαι [Χρύσιππος] νομίζει καθάπερ φυτόν Plut. *Sto. rep.* 41, 1.

[118] Stein, *Psych.* i p. 115.

[119] ὅταν δὲ τεχθῇ, ψυχούμενον ὑπὸ τοῦ ἀέρος τὸ πνεῦμα μεταβάλλειν καὶ γίνεσθαι ζῷον Plut. as above.

[120] ' infans nondum rationalis [est]' Sen. *Ep.* 121, 14; 'tu me expertem rationis genuisti, onus alienum' *Ben.* iii 31, 2.

[121] See above, § 153, note 66.

[122] διασῴζεσθαι λέγουσιν αὐτὴν [sc. τὴν ψυχὴν] ἔκ τε τῆς ἀναθυμιάσεως τοῦ αἵματος

of those fundamental doctrines of the system, derived by Zeno from Heraclitus[123], which bind together the great and the little world. Just as the heavenly bodies are maintained by exhalations from the Ocean[124], so the soul is dependent upon the body for its daily food. Hence follows the important consequence that weakness and disease of the body react upon the soul; the philosopher must keep his body in health for the soul's good, if for no other reason[125]. If the Stoics in discussing problems of ethics constantly maintain that the health of the soul is independent of that of the body, such statements are paradoxical and need qualification[126].

290. The mutual action of body and soul is most readily
Sleep and death. illustrated by sleep. The Stoics do not hold, as the Animists do, that the soul quits the body in sleep; nor do they agree with another popular view, that the soul then quits the extremities of the body and concentrates itself at the heart[127]. Sleep is due to a relaxation, contraction, or weakening of the spirit[128]; a lowering of its grade, which nevertheless is clearly no sign of ill health. In old age there is often an imperfection of the reason, and this is also seen in the sick, the tired, and the anaemic[129]. In death there is a

καὶ τοῦ κατὰ τὴν εἰσπνοὴν ἑλκομένου [ἀέρος] Galen *comm. Hipp.* 6 (Arnim ii 782); τρέφεσθαι ἐξ αἵματος τὴν ψυχήν, οὐσίαν δ' αὐτῆς ὑπάρχειν τὸ πνεῦμα *plac. Hipp. et Plat.* ii 8 (Arnim i 140); 'poor soul itself mere exhalation of the blood' M. Aurel. *To himself* v 33.

[123] Ζήνων τὴν ψυχὴν λέγει αἰσθητικὴν ἀναθυμίασιν, καθάπερ 'Ηράκλειτος'...' καὶ ψυχαὶ δὲ ἀπὸ τῶν ὑγρῶν ἀναθυμιῶνται.' ἀναθυμίασιν μὲν οὖν ὁμοίως τῷ 'Ηρακλείτῳ ἀποφαίνει Ζήνων Ar. Did. fr. 39, 2 and 3 (Diels); the reference to Heraclitus is not necessarily an exact quotation by Zeno, see Bywater's critical note on fr. 42; on the other side Diels' note on fr. 12. L. Stein is of opinion that the Stoics missed the meaning of Heraclitus whilst accepting his terminology; see *Psych.* i, note 182.

[124] See above, § 200.   [125] See § 316, note 100.

[126] καὶ τὴν ψυχὴν [οἱ Στωϊκοὶ] ἔφασαν μηδὲν ὑπὸ τοῦ σώματος ἢ ὠφελεῖσθαι ἢ βλάπτεσθαι Theod. *Gr. aff. cur.* 11; see generally the discussion by Stein, *Psych.* i pp. 139, 140.

[127] Plut. fr. (*de an.*) 6, 3.

[128] οἱ Στωϊκοὶ τὸν μὲν ὕπνον γίνεσθαι ἀνέσει τοῦ αἰσθητικοῦ πνεύματος Aët. *plac.* v 23, 4, cf. Plut. *Qu. conv.* iv ii 4, 6; 'contrahi autem animum Zeno et quasi labi putat atque concidere, et id ipsum esse dormire' Cic. *Div.* ii 58, 119. See also above, § 177.

[129] 'senes difficiles et queruli sunt, ut aegri et convalescentes, et quorum aut lassitudine aut detractione sanguinis exhaustus est calor' Sen. *Dial.* iv 19, 4.

complcte relaxation of tone in the breath that we can feel, that
is, in such spirit as belongs to the body[130]; there follows the
separation of soul from body.

291. We are thus brought to the critically important ques-

The beyond.   tion of the existence of the soul after death. On
this point we shall not expect to find that all Stoic
teachers agree in their language. In Zeno himself we shall be
sure to find that variety of suggestion which is accounted for by
his eagerness to learn from all sources; and later writers will
also differ according to their respective inclinations either to
draw strictly logical conclusions from the Stoic physics, or to
respect the common opinion of mankind and to draw from it
conclusions which may be a support to morality[131]. These
variations need not discourage us from the attempt to trace in
general outline the common teaching of the school. We have
already seen that the various parts of the Stoic system are
not bound together by strictly logical processes; where two
conclusions appear contradictory, and yet both recommend
themselves to the judgment, the Stoics are not prepared to
sacrifice either the one or the other, but always seek to lessen,
if they cannot altogether remove, the difficulties which stand in
the way of accepting both. On the other hand, we need not
too readily admit the charge of insincerity, whether it is found
in the candid admission of its temptations by Stoic teachers[132],
or in the less sympathetic criticisms of ancient or modern
exponents of the system[133].

[130] ὅταν δὲ παντελὴς γένηται ἡ ἄνεσις τοῦ αἰσθητικοῦ πνεύματος, τότε γίγνεσθαι
θάνατον Aët. *plac.* v 23, 4.

[131] 'cum animarum aeternitatem disserimus, non leve momentum apud nos habet
consensus hominum aut timentium inferos aut colentium' Sen. *Ep.* 117, 6.

[132] 'iuvabat de aeternitate animarum quaerere, immo mehercules credere. crede-
bam enim me facile opinionibus magnorum virorum rem gratissimam promittentium
magis quam probantium' Sen. *Ep.* 102, 2; cf. Cic. *Tusc. disp.* i 11, 24.

[133] So especially L. Stein: 'um nun ihre Philosophie populär und mundgerecht zu
machen, liessen sich die Stoiker zuweilen zu Äusserungen herbei, die dazu angethan
waren, ihr ganzes philosophisches System umzustossen' *Psych.* i 149. Further their
Scottish critic: 'thus did the later Stoicism try to meet the claims of the human heart,
which the earlier Stoicism had to a large extent ignored' W. L. Davidson, *The Stoic
creed*, p. 98; again 'die Lehre von der Fortdauer der Seele...war nur für die grosse
Menge berechnet' H. A. Winckler, *Stoicismus*, p. 50. Zeller is much more judicial,
Stoics, pp. 217–222.

292. On certain points all Stoic teachers seem to be agreed;
The Stoic first that the soul is, as regards its substance,
standpoint. imperishable; secondly, that the individual soul
cannot survive the general conflagration[134]; lastly, that it does
not of necessity perish with the body[135]. The first two dogmas
follow immediately from the fundamental principles of the Stoic
physics, and point out that every soul will find its last home by
being absorbed in the divine being. The third dogma leaves
play for ethical principles; subject to the monistic principle of
an ultimate reconciliation, there is room for some sharp distinction between the destiny of good and bad souls, such as
stands out in the Persian doctrine of rewards and punishments
after death. And so we find it generally held that the souls
of the good survive till the conflagration, whilst those of the
wicked have but a short separate existence, and those of the
lower and non-rational animals perish with their bodies[136]. If
this difference in duration will satisfy the moral sense, the nature
of the further existence of the soul may be determined on
physical principles.

293. In the living man the soul, as we have already seen
The released reason to suppose, derives its cohesion (ἕξις) and
soul. shape from its association with the body. Separated
from the body, it must assume a new shape, and what should
that be but the perfect shape of a sphere[137]? Again, the soul
being compounded of the elements of air and fire must by its
own nature, when freed from the body, pierce through this
murky atmosphere, and rise to a brighter region above, let us
say to that sphere which is just below the moon[138]. Here then

---

[134] ἔνιοι δὲ τὴν μὲν τοῦ ὅλου [ψυχὴν] ἀΐδιον, τὰς δὲ λοιπὰς συμμίγνυσθαι ἐπὶ τελευτῇ
εἰς ἐκείνην Ar. Did. fr. 39, 5.

[135] τὴν δὲ ψυχὴν γενητήν τε καὶ φθαρτὴν λέγουσιν· οὐκ εὐθὺς δὲ τοῦ σώματος ἀπαλ-
λαγεῖσαν φθείρεσθαι, ἀλλ' ἐπιμένειν τινὰς χρόνους καθ' ἑαυτήν ib. 6; 'Stoici...diu
mansuros aiunt animos, semper negant' Cic. *Tusc. disp.* i 31, 77.

[136] τὴν μὲν τῶν σπουδαίων [ψυχὴν διαμένειν] μέχρι τῆς εἰς πῦρ ἀναλύσεως τῶν
πάντων, τὴν δὲ τῶν ἀφρόνων πρὸς ποσούς τινας χρόνους·...τὰς δὲ τῶν ἀφρόνων καὶ
ἀλόγων ζῴων ψυχὰς συναπόλλυσθαι τοῖς σώμασι Ar. Did. fr. 39, 6 and 7.

[137] Arnim ii 815.

[138] [αἱ ψυχαὶ] λεπτομερεῖς οὖσαι καὶ οὐχ ἧττον πυρώδεις ἢ πνευματώδεις εἰς τοὺς ἄνω
μᾶλλον τόπους κουφοφοροῦσι...τὸν ὑπὸ σελήνην οἰκοῦσι τόπον Sext. *math.* ix 71 to 73
(Arnim ii 812); Ar. Did. fr. 39, 4; 'si [animae] permanent et conservant habitum

souls dwell like the stars, finding like them their food in exhalations from the earth[139]. Here they take rank as daemons or
heroes (of such the air is full), and as such are joined in the
fulfilment of the purposes of divine providence[140]. Yet it must
be admitted that this bright destiny, if substantiated by the laws
of physics, is also subject to physical difficulties. Suppose for
instance that a man is crushed by the fall of a heavy rock ; his
soul will not be able to escape in any direction, but will be at
once squeezed out of existence[141]. To fancies of this kind,
whether attractive or grotesque, we shall not be inclined to
pay serious attention.

294. In this general theory hope is perhaps held out before
the eyes of good souls, but there is little to terrify
the wicked, even if it be supposed that their souls

Tartarus.

neither survive so long, nor soar so high, as those of the good[142].
As against it we are told by a Church Father that Zeno
accepted the Persian doctrine of future rewards and punishments, and with it the primitive belief in an Inferno in its
crudest form[143]. We must agree with the first English editor
of the fragments of Zeno that 'it is hardly credible that Zeno
can have attached any philosophical importance to a theory stated
in these terms[144]'; they can at the best only have occurred in

suum,...necesse est ferantur ad caelum et ab his perrumpatur et dividatur crassus hic et
concretus aer ; calidior enim est vel potius ardentior animus, quam est hic aer'
Cic. *Tusc. disp.* i 18, 42 ; 'itaque sublimantur animae sapientes...apud Stoicos sub
lunam' Tert. *de an.* 54 (Arnim ii 814).

[139] τροφῇ τε χρῶνται οἰκείᾳ τῇ ἀπὸ γῆς ἀναθυμιάσει ὡς καὶ τὰ λοιπὰ ἄστρα Sext.
math. ix 73 ; 'fortium animas existimant in modum siderum vagari in aere' Comm.
in Lucan. ix 6 (Arnim ii 817).

[140] εἰ οὖν διαμένουσιν αἱ ψυχαί, δαίμοσιν αἱ αὐταὶ γίγνονται Sext. as in note 138 ;
φασὶ δὲ εἶναι καί τινας δαίμονας καὶ ἥρωας, τὰς ὑπολελειμμένας τῶν σπουδαίων ψυχάς
Diog. L. vii 151 ; 'plenus [est] aer immortalium animorum' Cic. *Div.* i 30, 64,
quoting from Posidonius.

[141] '[Stoici] existimant animam hominis magno pondere extriti permanere non
posse et statim spargi' Sen. *Ep.* 57, 7 ; Seneca himself rejects this opinion.

[142] Κλεάνθης μὲν οὖν πάσας [τὰς ψυχὰς] ἐπιδιαμένειν μέχρι τῆς ἐκπυρώσεως, Χρύσιππος
δὲ τὰς τῶν σοφῶν μόνον Diog. L. vii 157.

[143] 'esse inferos Zenon docuit et sedes piorum ab impiis esse discretas ; et illos
quidem quietas ac delectabiles incolere regiones, hos vero luere poenas in tenebrosis
locis atque in caeni voraginibus horrendis' Lactant. *Div. inst.* vii 7, 13 (Arnim i 147);
'reliquas animas ad inferos deiciunt' Tert. *de an.* 54. Cf. Cic. fr. 240, 6.

[144] Pearson, *Fragments*, p. 146.

some narration in the style of the Platonic myths, intended to illustrate a principle but not to convey a literal truth[145]. For just as the whole Hellenistic world, including the Stoics, stood aloof from the Persian doctrine of a spirit of evil, so it firmly rejected the dogma of a hell. Lucretius makes it a principal argument in favour of the philosophy of Epicurus that it drives out of men's hearts the fear of Tartarus[146]; but writers partly or wholly Stoic are not less emphatic. 'Ignorance of philosophy,' says Cicero, 'has produced the belief in hell and its terrors[147].' In the mouth of the representative of Stoicism he places the words 'Where can we find any old woman so silly as to believe the old stories of the horrors of the world below?[148]' 'Those tales' says Seneca 'which make the world below terrible to us, are poetic fictions. There is no black darkness awaiting the dead, no prison-house, no lake of fire or river of forgetfulness, no judgment-seat, no renewal of the rule of tyrants[149].'

295. Of far more importance to us is the theory of purgatory, familiar through the description in Virgil's *Aeneid*:

Purgatory of Virgil.

'In the beginning the earth and the sky, and the spaces of night,
Also the shining moon, and the sun Titanic and bright
Feed on an inward life, and, with all things mingled, a mind
Moves universal matter, with Nature's frame is combined.
Thence man's race, and the beast, and the feathered creature that flies, 5
All wild shapes that are hidden the gleaming waters beneath.
Each elemental seed has a fiery force from the skies,
Each its heavenly being, that no dull clay can disguise,
Bodies of earth ne'er deaden, nor limbs long destined to death.
Hence their fears and desires, their sorrows and joys; for their sight, 10
Blind with the gloom of a prison, discerns not the heavenly light.

---

[145] So Hirzel, *Untersuchungen* ii p. 29 note.

[146] 'et metus ille foras praeceps Acheruntis agendus, | funditus humanam qui vitam turbat ab imo, | omnia suffuscans mortis nigrore, neque ullam | esse voluptatem liquidam puramque relinquit' *R. N.* iii 37–40.

[147] Cic. *Tusc. disp.* i 16, 36.   [148] *N. D.* ii 2, 5.

[149] 'cogita illa, quae nobis inferos faciunt terribiles, fabulam esse; nullas imminere mortuis tenebras nec carcerem nec flumina igne flagrantia nec oblivionis amnem nec tribunalia...[nec] ullos iterum tyrannos. luserunt ista poetae et vanis nos agitavere terroribus' Sen. *Dial.* vi 19, 4. Here we have the opposite extreme to the statement in note 131.

Nor, when life at last leaves them, do all sad ills, that belong
Unto the sinful body, depart; still many survive
Lingering within them, alas! for it needs must be that the long
Growth should in wondrous fashion at full completion arrive.   15
So due vengeance racks them, for deeds of an earlier day
Suffering penance; and some to the winds hang viewless and thin,
Searched by the breezes; from others the deep infection of sin
Swirling water washes, or bright fire purges, away.
Each in his own sad ghost we endure; then, chastened aright,   20
Into Elysium pass. Few reach to the fields of delight
Till great time, when the cycles have run their courses on high,
Takes the inbred pollution, and leaves to us only the bright
Sense of the heaven's own ether, and fire from the springs of the sky[150].'

Although we cannot accept Virgil as a scientific exponent
of Stoic teaching, yet there is much reason to suppose that he
is here setting forth a belief which met with very general
acceptance in our school, and of which the principle is that the
sufferings of the disembodied are not a punishment for past
offences, but the necessary means for the purification of the
soul from a taint due to its long contact with the body.

296. The language in which Virgil first describes the
Probable   creation and life of the universe closely resembles
Stoic origin.   that of Stoicism; the phrases 'elemental seed,'
'fiery force,' 'heavenly being' might be used by any Stoic
teacher. The conception of the body as a 'prison-house,' even
though it does not express the most scientific aspect of Stoic
physics, was nevertheless, as we have seen, familiar to Stoics
of the later centuries. The ethical conception, again, of the
doctrine of purgatory is exactly that of which the Stoics felt a
need in order to reconcile the dualism of good and evil souls
with the ultimate prevalence of the divine will. Again, we can
have no difficulty in supposing that Virgil drew his material
from Stoic sources, seeing that he was characteristically a learned
poet, and reflects Stoic sentiment in many other passages of his
works[151]. We have also more direct evidence. The Church

---

[150] Virgil *Aen.* vi 724-747 (transl. by Lord Bowen). For the corresponding
description of Paradise, see *ib.* 638—644. The substance of this discussion is
drawn from Hirzel's full note in his *Untersuchungen* ii pp. 25-31.

[151] For instance *Georg.* iv 221 sqq. See also below, §§ 434, 435.

Father whom we have already quoted not only ascribes to the Stoics in another passage the doctrine of purgatory, but expressly quotes this passage from Virgil as an exposition of Stoic teaching. And here he is supported to some extent by Tertullian, who says that the Stoics held that the souls of the foolish after death receive instruction from the souls of the good[152]. Finally, we have the doctrine definitely accepted by Seneca[153].

297. We may now consider more particularly the views and feelings of individual Stoic teachers. It appears to us accordingly that Zeno left his followers room for considerable diversity of opinion, and quoted the Persian doctrine because of its suggestiveness rather than for its literal truth. Of Cleanthes we are told that he held that all souls survived till the conflagration, whilst Chrysippus believed this only of the souls of the wise[154]. Panaetius, although a great admirer of Plato, is nevertheless so strongly impressed by the scientific principle that 'all which is born must die,' that he is here again inclined to break away from Stoicism, and to suspend his judgment altogether as to the future existence of the soul[155]; the belief in a limited future existence was meaningless to a philosopher who disbelieved in the conflagration. Of the views of Posidonius we have the definite hint, that he taught that the 'air is full of immortal souls[156]';

Views of Greek Stoics.

[152] 'impias vero [animas Stoici dicunt]...habere aliquid imbecillitatis ex contagione carnis, cuius desideriis ac libidinibus addictae ineluibilem quendam fucum trahant labemque terrenam, quae cum temporis diuturnitate penitus inhaeserit, eius naturae reddi animas, ut...cruciabiles fiant per corporis maculam, quae peccatis inusta sensum doloris attribuit. quam sententiam poeta sic explicavit—"quin et supremo etc."' Lact. *Div. inst.* vii 20, 9 and 10 (Arnim ii 813); '[Stoicos] miror, quod † imprudentes animas circa terram prosternant, cum illas a sapientibus multo superioribus erudiri adfirment' Tert. *de an.* 54 (Arnim i 147, reading 'prudentes' on his own conjecture). On the other hand Augustine (*Civ. De.* xxi 13) ascribes the doctrine to 'Platonici quidam' and Comm. Luc. ix 9 (p. 291 Us.) to Pythagoras. See Schmekel, p. 105.

[153] 'facillimum ad superos iter est animis cito ab humana conversatione dimissis. facilius quicquid est illud obsoleti inlitique eluunt' Sen. *Dial.* vi 23, 1; '[filius tuus] paulum supra nos commoratus, dum expurgatur et inhaerentia vitia situmque omnem mortalis aevi excutit' *ib.* 25, 1.

[154] Diog. L. vii 157. [155] Cic. *Tusc. disp.* i 32, 79.

[156] See above, §§ 254, 293; for the teaching of Posidonius as to the pre-existence of the soul, see Schmekel, p. 250.

and this is in such harmony with the devout temper of this teacher that we may readily believe that he enriched the somewhat bare speculations of his predecessors by the help of an Oriental imagination, and that he introduced into Stoicism not only the doctrine of daemons but also that of purgatory, holding that souls were both pre-existent and post-existent.

298. In the period of the Roman principate the question
View of   of the future existence of the soul acquires special
Seneca.   prominence. Seneca is criticized on the ground that
he affects at times a belief which he does not sincerely entertain, partly in order to make his teaching more popular, partly to console his friends in times of mourning. The facts stand otherwise. At no time does Seneca exceed the limits of the accepted Stoic creed; he bids his friends look forward to the period of purgation[157], the life of pure souls in the regions of the aether, and the final union with the divine being. It is after purgation that the soul by the refinement of the elements of which it is built forces its way to higher regions[158]; it finds a quiet and peaceful home in the clear bright aether[159]; it has cast off the burden of the flesh[160]; it is parted by no mountains or seas from other happy souls[161]; it daily enjoys free converse with the great ones of the past[162]; it gazes on the human world below, and on the sublime company of the stars in its own neighbourhood[163]. At a later epoch all blessed souls will be re-absorbed in the primal elements[164], suffering change but not

[157] See above, § 296.
[158] 'animus beneficio subtilitatis suae erumpit' Sen. *Ep.* 57, 8.
[159] 'ibi illum aeterna requies manet e confusis crassisque pura et liquida visentem' *Dial.* vi 24, 5.
[160] 'emissis [animis] meliora restant onere detracto' *Ep.* 24, 18. So in the Burial Service 'the souls of the faithful, after they are delivered from the burden of the flesh, are in joy and felicity.'
[161] 'non illos interfusa maria discludunt nec altitudo montium; tramites omnium plani' *Dial.* vi 25, 3.
[162] 'ad excelsa sublatus inter felices currit animas, Scipiones Catonesque, interque contemptores vitae et mortis beneficio liberos' *ib.* 1.
[163] 'rerum naturae spectaculo fruitur et humana omnia ex superiore loco despicit, divina vero propius intuetur' *ib.* xi 9, 3.
[164] 'nos quoque, felices animae atque aeterna sortitae, parva ruinae ingentis accessio, in antiqua elementa vertemur' *ib.* vi 26, 7.

forfeiting their immortal nature[165]. The somewhat exuberant language of Seneca has frequently been adopted by Christian writers, to express a belief which is not necessarily identical[166]; but for the associations thus created Seneca must not be held responsible.

299. With the decay of interest in the Stoic physics there

Personality cannot survive.

begins a tendency to overlook the intermediate stage of the soul's life, and to dwell solely on its final absorption; whilst at the same time it is urged from the ethical standpoint that no possible opinion as to the soul's future should disturb the calm of the virtuous mind. On one further, but important, point the Stoic teaching becomes clearer. In no case is the soul that survives death to be identified with the man that once lived. Cut off from all human relations, from the body and its organs, and from its own subordinate powers[167], it is no longer 'you,' but is something else that takes your place in the due order of the universe. In all this the Stoic doctrine remains formally unchanged; but its expression is now so chastened that it seems only to give a negative reply to the inherited hope, and the chief comfort it offers is that 'death is the end of all troubles.' This change of tone begins in Seneca himself; it is he who says to the mourner 'your loved one has entered upon a great and never-ending rest[168]'; 'death is release from all pain and its end[169]'; 'death is not to be. I know all its meaning. As things were before I was born, so they will be after I am gone[170].' 'If we perish in death, nothing remains[171].' In Epictetus and Marcus Aurelius this new tone rings out much more clearly; if we like so to speak, more unrelentingly. To the characteristic passages from

---

[165] '[animus], si superstes est corpori, nullo genere [perire potest], quoniam nulla immortalitas cum exceptione est' *Ep.* 57, 9.

[166] See Winckler, *Der Stoicismus eine Wurzel des Christenthums*, p. 52.

[167] 'haec sunt ignorantis, cum de aeternitate animorum dicatur, de mente dici, non de partibus iis, in quibus aegritudines irae libidinesque versantur' Cic. *Tusc. disp.* i 33, 80.

[168] 'excepit illum magna et aeterna pax' Sen. *Dial.* vi 19, 6.

[169] 'mors dolorum omnium exsolutio est et finis' *ib.* 19, 5.

[170] 'mors est non esse. id quale sit, iam scio. hoc erit post me, quod ante me fuit' *Ep.* 54, 4.

[171] 'mors nos aut consumit aut exuit;...consumptis nihil restat' *ib.* 24, 18.

these writers which are quoted above[172] may be added the following, perhaps the most precise of all :

'If souls survive death, how can the air hold them from all eternity? How, we reply, does earth hold the bodies of generation after generation committed to the grave? Just as on earth, after a certain term of survival, change and dissolution of substance makes room for other dead bodies, so too the souls transmuted into air, after a period of survival, change by processes of diffusion and of ignition, and are resumed into the seminal principle of the universe, and in this way make room for others to take up their habitation in their stead. Such is the natural answer, assuming the survival of souls[173].'

Such are the last words of Stoicism, not wholly satisfying either to knowledge or to aspiration, but assuredly based on a wide outlook and a keen discrimination.

300. The whole nature of man, as discussed up to this
Men and point, is common to every individual born into the
women. world, with some exceptions dependent on age or temperament which have been explained incidentally. It remains to discuss shortly the important differences which result from sex, nationality, and location. There seems every reason to believe that the equality of men and women, though at the time seemingly paradoxical, was generally accepted by the earlier Stoics, and adopted as a practical principle in Stoic homes. The whole treatment of human nature by the Stoics applies equally to man and woman, and points to the conclusion that as moral agents they have the same capacities and the same responsibilities[174]. Seneca in writing to a great lady of philosophical sympathies states this as his firm conviction[175], and the lives of many Stoic wives and daughters (to whom we shall refer in a later chapter)[176] showed it to have a firm basis in fact. We need attach no great importance to those more distinctively masculine views which Seneca occasionally expresses, to the

[172] See above, §§ 140 and 141.   [173] M. Aurel. *To himself* iv 21.

[174] See below, § 306. Cleanthes wrote a book to show that 'virtue is the same in men and women'; see Diog. L. vii 103.

[175] 'quis dixit naturam maligne cum mulieribus ingeniis egisse, et virtutem illarum in artum retraxisse? par illis, mihi crede, vigor, par ad honesta, libeat, facultas est ; dolorem laboremque ex aequo, si consuevere, patiuntur' Sen. *Dial.* vi 16, 1.

[176] See below, §§ 431, 439, 444, 446.

effect that woman is hot-tempered, thoughtless, and lacking in self-control[177], or to the Peripatetic doctrine that man is born to rule, women to obey[178]; for these sentiments, however welcome to his individual correspondents, were not rooted in Stoic theory nor exemplified in the Roman society of his own days.

301. It follows with equal certainty from the early history
Class and of Stoicism, and in particular from the doctrine of
race. the Cosmopolis, that differences of class and race
were hardly perceived by its founders. For this there was further historical cause in the spread of Hellenistic civilisation, which was of an entirely catholic spirit and welcomed disciples from all nationalities[179]. The doctrine of Aristotle, that some nations are by nature fitted only for slavery, finds no echo in the Stoic world[180]. There we look in vain for any trace of that instinctive feeling of national difference, that sensitiveness to race and colour, which can easily be recognised in the early history of Greece and Rome, and which has become so acute in the development of modern world-politics. The Roman Stoics, as we shall see later, might individually be proud of advantages of birth, but they never associated this feeling with their philosophy. Here and there, however, we find signs of a scientific interest in the question of differences of national character, which are generally ascribed to the influences of climate. Seneca, for instance, remarks that the inhabitants of northern climates have characters as rude as their sky; hence they make good fighters, but poor rulers[181]. Yet when he contemplates the northern barbarians, his mind is mainly occupied by admiration ; and, like other pro-Germans of the period, he foresees with prophetic

[177] 'muliebre est furere in ira' Sen. *Clem.* i 5, 5; '[mulier] aeque imprudens [atque] animal est, et nisi scientia accessit et multa eruditio, ferum, cupiditatum incontinens' *Dial.* ii 14, 1.
[178] 'utraque turba [*i.e.* sexus] ad vitae societatem tantundem [confert], sed altera pars ad obsequendum, altera imperio nata [est]' *ib.* 1, 1.
[179] See below, § 303.　　　　　[180] See below, § 309.
[181] 'fere itaque imperia penes eos fuere populos, qui mitiore caelo utuntur. in frigora septentrionemque vergentibus immansueta ingenia sunt' Sen. *Dial.* iv 15, 5. So too Lucan: 'omnis in Arctois populus quicunque pruinis | nascitur, indomitus bellis et mortis amator' *Phars.* viii 363–6.

clearness a danger threatening the Roman empire. 'Should the
Germans once lay aside their fierce domestic quarrels, and add
to their courage reason and discipline, Rome will indeed have
cause to resume the virtues of its early history[182].' The roots
of true greatness of soul, then, lie deeper than in literary culture
or philosophic insight. It is a part of the irony of history that
Stoicism, which aimed above all things at being practical, should
diagnose so correctly the growing weakness of the Roman world,
and yet fail to suggest any remedy other than a reversion to an
epoch in which philosophy was unknown.

---

[182] 'agedum illis corporibus illis animis luxum opes ignorantibus da rationem, da
disciplinam : ut nihil amplius dicam, necesse erit certe nobis mores Romanos repetere'
Sen. *Dial.* iii 11, 4.

CHAPTER XII.

THE LAW FOR HUMANITY.

302. THE department of Ethics contains two divisions:
The Right Law. ethics (in the stricter sense) which is concerned with the action of the individual; and politics, which has to do with the order of the State. It has been maintained that in Stoicism the latter is altogether subordinated, and that the central aim of this philosophy is to erect a shelter for the individual[1]. The truth of this view is more than doubtful. Stoic ethics are not based on the needs of the individual, but on the demands of the supreme Law. 'If there is a universe, then there is a universal law, bidding us do this and refrain from that.' 'If there are gods, there is virtue[2].' We have already noticed that Zeno's earliest work was 'on the State[3],' and that it is an attempt to show how a state can be ordered by wise laws. The whole theory of the Logos leads up to the same point. The same eternal Wisdom through which the primal stuff took shape is, in another function, the Right Rule (ὀρθὸς λόγος, *vera ratio*) which commands and forbids[4]. Right Rule and Common Law (κοινὸς νόμος, *lex communis*) are terms of identical meaning, by which a standard of supreme authority is set up[5]; State law and

---

[1] e.g. Zeller, *Stoics* etc. pp. 16, 17; Stein *Psych.* ii p. 141.

[2] See Alex. Aph. *de fato*, chs. 35 and 37 (Arnim ii 1003 and 1005).

[3] See above, § 75.

[4] λόγος ὀρθὸς προστακτικὸς μὲν ὧν ποιητέον, ἀπαγορευτικὸς δὲ ὧν οὐ ποιητέον Alex. Aph. 35, p. 207, 8 B; cf. Diog. L. vii 88.

[5] 'Chrysippus sic incipit: ὁ νόμος πάντων ἐστὶ βασιλεὺς θείων τε καὶ ἀνθρωπίνων πραγμάτων· δεῖ δὲ αὐτὸν...κανόνα εἶναι δικαίων καὶ ἀδίκων' Marcianus i p. 11, 25 (Arnim iii 314); 'lex est ratio summa, insita in natura, quae iubet ea quae facienda sunt prohibetque contraria' Cic. *Leg.* i 6, 18.

conventional morality, though always of narrower range, and often of inferior purity, are yet a reflection of universal Law. The moral law must therefore first be studied in its bearings on man as a political and social animal.

303. The root-principle of the Stoic State is that it is world-wide, a cosmopolis. This title arose from the practice, attributed to Socrates and Diogenes (as well as others), of replying to the current question 'Of what city are you?' by the answer 'Of the universe[6].' We must therefore regard ourselves as members not of a clan or city, but of a world-wide society[7]. In this society all distinctions of race, caste and class are to be subordinated to the sense of kinship and brother-hood[8]. This principle is equally opposed to the nationalist prejudices which rank Hellene above barbarian, to philosophical theories (such as that of Aristotle) which distinguish intelligent peoples fitted by nature to rule and others only fitted to obey[9], and to ideal states (such as that of Plato) in which a ruling class is to be developed by artifice and schooling. Only the brute animals are excluded from this community, for they are not possessed of reason; they have therefore no rights, but exist for the service of men[10]. All human beings are capable of attaining to virtue, and as such are natural-born citizens of the Cosmopolis[11]. Loyalty to this state, however, in no wise hinders a due loyalty to existing states which may be regarded as partial

The Cosmopolis.

---

[6] 'Socrates cum rogaretur cuiatem se esse diceret, Mundanum, inquit. totius enim mundi se incolam et civem arbitrabatur' Cic. *Tusc. disp.* v 37, 108; [Διογένης] ἐρωτη-θεὶς πόθεν εἴη "κοσμοπολίτης" ἔφη Diog. L. vi 63; so Epict. *Disc.* i 9, 1.

[7] Arnim i 262; 'patriam meam esse mundum sciam' Sen. *Dial.* vii 20, 5.

[8] 'membra sumus corporis magni; natura nos cognatos edidit' *Ep.* 95, 52.

[9] 'quaecunque est hominis definitio, una in omnes valet. quod argumenti satis est, nullam dissimilitudinem esse in genere' Cic. *Leg.* i 10, 29 and 30.

[10] ἀρέσκει αὐτοῖς μηδὲν εἶναι ἡμῖν δίκαιον πρὸς τὰ ἄλλα ζῷα διὰ τὴν ἀνομοιότητα Diog. L. vii 129; 'quomodo hominum inter homines iuris esse vincula putant, sic homini nihil iuris esse cum bestiis' Cic. *Fin.* iii 20, 67. The honour of being the first to recognise the principle of consideration for our dumb partners belongs to the Hindus.

[11] 'nec est quisquam gentis ullius, qui ducem naturam nactus ad virtutem pervenire non possit' Cic. *Leg.* i 10, 31; 'if the mind-element is common to us all, so likewise is that reason which makes us rational; and therefore too that reason which bids us do or leave undone; and therefore the world-law; therefore we are fellow-citizens and share a common citizenship' M. Aurel. *To himself* iv 4.

realizations of it. Socrates submitted to the laws of Athens even when they bade him die; Zeno and Cleanthes declined the citizenship of that famous city, lest they should be thought to hold cheap the places of their birth[12]; and amongst the Romans Seneca frequently insists that every man is born into two communities, the cosmopolis and his native city[13].

304. The world-state is not held together either by force or by state-craft, but by goodwill. We must be able

The law of nature.

say 'Love is god there, and is a helpmate to make the city secure[14].' This feeling of love and friendship grows up naturally between wise men, because they partake in the reason of the universe; so that we may equally well say that the bond of the state is the Logos (*ratio atque oratio*)[15]. Since reason and the universal law exist in the community from the beginning, law does not need to be created; it exists of itself, and by natural growth ($\phi \dot{\upsilon} \sigma \epsilon \iota$)[16]. The writing down of laws is only a stage in their development[17].

305. The theory of the world-state, as first sketched by Zeno, found no place for any of the cherished in-

Zeno's revolutionary views.

stitutions of the Athens in which it was preached. In the heavenly city must be neither temples nor images[18]; so far the aims of the Persian invader are to be carried out. The reason given is far from flattering to the artistic pride of the

[12] Plut. *Sto. rep.* 4, 1.

[13] 'duas respublicas animo conplectamur, alteram magnam et vere publicam, qua di atque homines continentur;...alteram, cui nos adscripsit condicio nascendi' Sen. *Dial.* viii 4, 1. So too Epictetus: 'What is a man? a part of a state, of that first which consists of gods and men; then of that which is called next to it, which is a small image of the universal state' *Disc.* ii 5, 26.

[14] ἐν τῇ πολιτείᾳ ἔφη [ὁ Ζήνων] τὸν Ἔρωτα θεὸν εἶναι, συνεργὸν ὑπάρχοντα πρὸς τὴν τῆς πόλεως σωτηρίαν Athen. xiii 12 (Arnim i 263); 'salva autem esse societas nisi custodia et amore partium non potest' Sen. *Dial.* iv 31, 7.

[15] 'eius [societatis humanae] vinculum est ratio et oratio, quae conciliat inter se homines coniungitque naturali quadam societate' Cic. *Off.* i 16, 50.

[16] φύσει τε τὸ δίκαιον εἶναι καὶ μὴ θέσει, ὡς καὶ τὸν νόμον καὶ τὸν ὀρθὸν λόγον, καθά φησι Χρύσιππος Diog. L. vii 128; 'ius esse natura [Stoici censent]' Cic. *Fin.* iii 21, 71.

[17] 'non tum denique lex incipit esse, cum scripta est, sed tum cum orta est' Cic. *Leg.* ii 5, 10.

[18] ἱερὰ θεῶν μὴ οἰκοδομεῖν Plut. *Sto. rep.* 6, 1; ἀπαγορεύει ἀγάλματα τεκταίνειν Theod. *Aff.* iii 74 (Arnim i 264).

Athenians, for they are told that their magnificent buildings and statues of world-wide renown are only the work of common builders and workmen[19]. Nor must there be law-courts[20] or gymnasia. The practice of hearing both sides in a law-court is unreasonable, because if the plaintiff has proved his case it is useless to hear the defendant, and if he has not proved it, it is superfluous[21]. The training of the youth in grammar, music, and gymnastic is worthless[22], for the true education is in virtue. Coined money, as in modern communistic Utopias, should not be required either for commerce or for travel[23].

306. With regard to the position of women Zeno, agreeing
Women to be to some extent with Plato, asserted the startling
in common. doctrine that 'women should be in common, and men should mate with them as they pleased[24].' That Zeno was suggesting, even for an imaginary state, any sort of loose living, need not for a moment be supposed; his continence was notable[25]; he expressly approves of marriage[26]; and the members of his school were honourably known by their aversion to adultery[27]. But Zeno could not base his theory of the relation of the sexes merely upon established practice. We may assume that he observed that in the world of animals and of birds mating was free[28], whereas in human society it was encumbered by national prejudices, class privilege, and personal jealousy;

---

[19] Plut. *Sto. rep.* 6, 1.   [20] Diog. L. vii 33.

[21] Plutarch, in quoting this argument, makes the telling rejoinder that upon the same principle Zeno need not have published an answer to Plato's Republic; *Sto. rep.* 8, 1.

[22] Diog. L. vii 32. This particular condemnation was not uncongenial to the Stoics of the principate, and may partly account for the decay of literature in imperial Rome. But Chrysippus had meanwhile supplied the needed qualification that these studies are useful as a training preliminary to virtue; see Diog. L. vii 129, and cf. § 336.

[23] Diog. L. vii 33. Probably usury was also condemned by Zeno, as it was by Seneca: 'quid computationes et venale tempus et sanguinolentae centesimae?' Sen. *Ben.* vii 10, 4.

[24] Diog. L. vii 131.

[25] 'More continent than Zeno' became a proverb at Athens; *ib.* 27.

[26] *ib.* 121.

[27] ἐκκλίνουσι τὸ μοιχεύειν οἱ τὰ τοῦ Ζήνωνος φιλοσοφοῦντες Origen *cont. Celsum*, vii 63 (Arnim iii 729).

[28] This principle is stated by Chrysippus: πρὸς τὰ θηρία φησὶ δεῖν ἀποβλέπειν Plut. *Sto. rep.* 22, 1.

and in particular that woman was regarded as a chattel, contrary to the fundamental principle of his state[29]. By his doctrine of 'free mating' he aimed at the root of these evils. The gradual abolition at Rome of the restrictions on 'connubium' illustrates the application of his principle, just as the prohibition of 'miscegenation' in modern America illustrates its denial. Zeno may well have perceived how deeply the potentiality of marriage affects all social relations, and it is probable that the progress of Stoicism did much to break down the racial barriers that existed in Zeno's time, but which had almost completely disappeared five centuries later throughout the civilized world. Another application of his doctrine is found in the life of Cato of Utica[30]. But its general meaning is clear: marriage exists not by nature, but by institution (θέσει); its law is human and mutable, but nevertheless within proper limits is one that may not be transgressed. By the side of the text of Zeno we still have the authorized comment of Epictetus[31].

307. The Stoics did not shrink from insisting upon the abstract principle of the community of women even in an extreme case in which their doctrine encountered a violent prejudice. No natural law, they maintained, prohibits marriage relationship between near relatives[32]. The tale of Oedipus and Jocasta, which is so prominent a theme in the great Athenian tragedies, appears to Zeno to be a matter about which too much ado has been made[33]. For suppose the

Incest no abomination.

---

[29] The essential equality of the sexes in Stoic theory is illustrated in the development of Roman law: 'led by their theory of natural law, the [Roman] jurisconsults had evidently...assumed the equality of the sexes as a principle of their code of equity' Maine, *Ancient Law*, p. 154. Cf. on the whole subject Gomperz, *Greek Thinkers*, bk v ch. 13: e.g. 'to the common Greek sentiment exclusive personal appropriation [of women] and the resulting inequality in ownership was as yet very far from seeming so much of a law of nature, or meeting with such unconditional acceptance as...in modern times' (vol. iii p. 119).   [30] See § 431.

[31] 'What then, are not women common by nature? So I say also. Is not the theatre common to the citizens? When then they have taken their seats, come (if you think proper) and eject one of them!' Epict. *Disc.* ii 4, 8.

[32] καὶ μητράσι [Χρύσιππος] λέγει συνέρχεσθαι καὶ θυγατράσι καὶ υἱοῖς Diog. L. vii 188. A Church Father has caught the point better; εἶπον ὅτι τῷ ἰδίῳ λόγῳ θυγατράσι μίγνυσθαι ἀδιάφορόν ἐστι, εἰ καὶ μὴ χρὴ ἐν ταῖς καθεστώσαις πολιτείαις τὸ τοιοῦτον ποιεῖν Origen *cont. Cels.* iv 45 (Arnim iii 743). For the Persian view see Diog. L. Prol. 8.

[33] Arnim i 256.

case that all the world were destroyed by flood except one man
and his daughter; would it not be better that he should beget
children by her, and that the whole human race should not
perish[34]? In this reference to the traditional flood we may
readily trace one reason why the Stoics insisted on their principle. For at the beginning of human history we are compelled
to postulate an Adam and an Eve, a human pair related in their
birth and at the same time united as parents of the race[35]. Go
back to the beginnings of the universe; there too we must
postulate the same combination of relationships, and so only
can we understand the poets when they speak of Hera as 'wife
and sister of Zeus[36].'

308. Perhaps even more shocking to Hellenic feeling was
Burial a
convention.　　Zeno's indifference to the treatment of the dead.
Burial was to him no sacred duty to the departed
one; it was equally right to throw the body to the fire, as the
Indians, or to the vultures, as the Persians[37]. Nor is there any
need to condemn those nations amongst which the dead are
eaten by their own relatives[38], for all these things are matters
not of principle but of convenience, and to eat human flesh may
still be desirable if circumstances require it[39], as for instance in
shipwreck, or if a limb is amputated[40]. The problem of the
disposal of the dead became a favourite subject of discussion
in Stoic circles. Chrysippus wrote at length on the subject,
comparing the customs of various nations as well as the habits
of animals, in order to ascertain the law of nature. He reaches
the conclusion that dead bodies should be disposed of in the
simplest possible way, not being regarded as of more importance
than the hair or nail-parings from which we part in life[41]. Cicero
shortly sums up this discussion in the *Tusculan disputations*, and
draws the conclusion that whilst the living must consider what
it is fitting for them to do, to the dead man it is a matter totally

---

[34] Origen, as above.
[35] See below, § 478.
[36] See above, § 254.
[37] Arnim i 253.
[38] *ib.* i 254.
[39] Diog. L. vii 121.
[40] Arnim iii 748.
[41] Arnim iii 752. For the same view in earlier times see Gomperz, *Greek Thinkers*,
i p. 403.

indifferent[42]. In the imperial period this consideration is of importance as showing that the tyrant has no power after death[43].

309. The Stoic view of slavery can readily be inferred.

Slavery.

Without proposing the immediate abolition of this social institution, the Stoics treated it as essentially contrary to nature[44]. The earliest teachers seem to have passed over the subject in silence; Panaetius (as might be expected from his social position), justified slavery by the arguments of Plato and Aristotle in exceptional cases: 'all those who through the infirmity of their nature are unfit to govern themselves, are rightly made slaves'[45]. According to this theory we may speak of a 'natural slave' (φύσει δοῦλος), who as such can no more have rights in the community than the lower animals. The true Stoic theory appears however to be formulated by a definition of Chrysippus, who says that a slave is a 'labourer hired for life[46].' This definition makes of slavery a contract, to which there are two parties; and Seneca rightly uses this definition to argue that the relations of master to slave are those of man to man, and that as the master may wrong his slave, so the slave may do a service to his master[47]. All this is really implied in the dogma that 'women and slaves may become philosophers,' as is realized by the Church Father Lactantius[48].

[42] i 45, 108.

[43] 'ille divinus animus egressurus hominem, quo receptaculum suum conferatur, ignis illud exurat an terra contegat, an ferae distrahant, non magis ad se iudicat pertinere quam secundas ad editum infantem' Sen. *Ep.* 92, 34; 'But you will be cast out unburied...If the corpse is I, I shall be cast out; but if I am different from the corpse, speak more properly' Epict. *Disc.* iv 7, 31.

[44] For a plain statement to this effect we have to look to Philo: ἄνθρωπος γὰρ ἐκ φύσεως δοῦλος οὐδείς Sept. et fest. di. p. 283 M (Arnim iii 352).

[45] 'est genus iniustae servitutis, cum hi sunt alterius, qui sui possunt esse' Cic. *Rep.* iii 25, 37.

[46] 'servus, ut placet Chrysippo, perpetuus mercennarius est' Sen. *Ben.* iii 22, 1; 'non male praecipiunt, qui [servis] ita iubent uti, ut mercennariis: operam exigendam, iusta praebenda' Cic. *Off.* i 13, 41.

[47] 'potest [servus] dare beneficium domino, si a domino iniuriam accipere' Sen. *Ben.* iii 22, 3.

[48] 'quod si natura hominis sapientiae capax est, oportuit et opifices et rusticos et mulieres doceri, ut sapiant: populumque [sapientium] ex omni lingua et condicione et sexu et aetate conflari. senserunt hoc adeo Stoici, qui et servis et mulieribus philoso-phandum esse dixerunt' Lact. *Div. inst.* iii 25 (Arnim iii 253).

310. The Stoic principles of politics may be realized under
Constitutions. any form of government, and the theory of Constitutions, like that of grammar, belongs to a neutral
ground on which philosophers of different schools may work in
harmony. The Peripatetics appear first to have taken up this
study; of the Stoics Diogenes of Babylon[49], who himself acted
as a political representative of Athens, is stated to have shown
interest in this subject; and after him Panaetius developed a
complete theory, of which the substance is preserved for us in
Cicero's *de Re publica*[50]. According to this theory, which Cicero
puts in the mouth of Scipio Africanus, surrounded by Roman
Stoics of distinction such as Laelius, Tubero, and Furius Philo,
the best constitution is one in which the elements of monarchy,
aristocracy and democracy are combined, though a bias remains
in favour of monarchy[51]. This mixed constitution, according to
the teaching of Panaetius and his pupil Polybius, is best illustrated in the Roman state[52]; whereas tyranny, the perversion of
monarchy, is the worst of all governments. By such reasoning
the Roman nobles of the first century B.C. and the first century
A.D. alike persuaded themselves easily that Stoic teaching supported the position of the republican party. But in fact they
were maintaining Peripatetic theories of government, and the
real Stoic theory was far more in accord with that practice of
the principate, according to which all citizens are treated with
respect, and the government of them is placed in the hands of
men selected for their personal merit. We shall discuss the
whole question of the relation of Stoicism to Roman politics
in a later chapter[53]; but we may notice here that those Stoics
practically abandoned the theory of providence who looked
into the history of their own times with the intention of seeing
nowhere the 'king,' and everywhere the 'tyrant.' On the other

[49] See above, § 110.

[50] Schmekel, *Phil. d. mittleren Stoa*, pp. 63, 69.

[51] 'eorum nullum ipsum per se separatum probo; anteponoque singulis illud, quod
conflatum fuerit ex omnibus. sed si unum ac simplex probandum sit, regium probem
atque inprimis laudem' Cic. *Rep.* i 35, 54; 'optimus civitatis status sub rege iusto est'
Sen. *Ben.* ii 20, 2.

[52] 'memineram persaepe te cum Panaetio disserere solitum coram Polybio...
optimum longe statum civitatis esse eum, quem maiores nostri nobis reliquissent'
Cic. *Rep.* i 21, 34. [53] See below, ch. xvi.

hand the practical statesmen who set about to re-create Roman law on the principle of substituting everywhere human rights for class privileges were men thoroughly imbued with the Stoic spirit, whether or not they were avowed disciples of this philosophy.

311. We must therefore maintain that the true Stoic state,

The citizen. whether it be called monarchy or democracy, calls for a revolt against nationalism, antiquity, custom, pride, and prejudice; and a new construction based upon universal reason and individual liberty. For the realization of this state it is first necessary to build up the individual, to fill his mind with the conception of reason and love, to strengthen his will to a true independence: for it is not buying or selling that makes the slave, but the will within[54]. All are in truth slaves except the wise man; for freedom is the power of directing one's own actions[55]. Here then we pass from the community to the individual, from politics to ethics in the narrower sense.

312. For the individual man the ethical problem is to

The supreme good. bring himself, a part of nature, into harmony with the whole. Whether we think of destiny, of providence, of the gods, or of the state, success for the individual is to agree and to cooperate; to struggle and to rebel is to fail. This success is the end (τέλος) for which man exists, the supreme good (*summum bonum*), the ultimate good (*ultimum bonorum*), that towards which all other right action works, whilst it works itself for no other end[56]. Its name in the individual is virtue (ἀρετή, *virtus*), and it is an active and firmly-established disposition of the soul[57]. It follows from the monistic principle that the end for man is one, and that virtue is one; but nevertheless each is capable of being regarded in many aspects. The harmony of the ethical end with other parts of the Stoic philo-

---

[54] Arnim iii 354.

[55] Diog. L. vii 121.

[56] τέλος ἐστὶν οὗ ἕνεκα πάντα πράττεται καθηκόντως, αὐτὸ δὲ πράττεται οὐδενὸς ἕνεκα Stob. ii 7, 3 b.

[57] 'virtus nihil aliud est quam animus quodammodo se habens' Sen. *Ep.* 113, 2; 'virtus est adfectio animi constans conveniensque' Cic. *Tusc. disp.* iv 15, 34.

sophy is marked by such phrases as 'life according to nature⁵⁸,'
the rule 'keep company with God⁵⁹,' and the identification of
virtue and reason⁶⁰.

313. Because virtue is one thing and not many, it makes
a man's life one consistent whole, and stands in
sharp contrast to the changing and undecided
ways of the crowd. Virtue is therefore frequently defined as
consistency in life⁶¹, an even steady course of action⁶², self-con-
sistency⁶³, a principle in agreement with its applications⁶⁴. The
opposite of virtue is the unending restlessness and indecision of
the man in the crowd⁶⁵. Accordingly we are told that the earliest
Stoics thought it a sufficient definition of wisdom or virtue that
it was something simple⁶⁶; and similarly Zeno said that the end
of life was 'to live consistently⁶⁷.' To this short definition the
words 'with nature' were soon added⁶⁸, whereby the distinc-
tiveness of the original definition was diminished: for all the
philosophical schools are agreed that the right life must be
guided by nature (φύσει), not by convention (θέσει). From the
time of Chrysippus the relation of right living to nature was
further analyzed. Chrysippus defined the 'nature' referred to

Consistency with nature.

---

⁵⁸ In numerous variations: for the present it is sufficient to quote Cicero's phrase
'convenienter naturae vivere' *Fin.* iii 9, 31, etc., and from Seneca 'virtus secundum
naturam est; vitia inimica et infesta sunt' *Ep.* 50, 8. Cf. also 'we ought to go to be
instructed, in order that we may maintain our minds in harmony with the things that
happen' Epict. *Disc.* i 12, 17.

⁵⁹ '[virtus] habebit illud in animo vetus praeceptum: deum sequere' Sen. *Dial.*
vii 15, 5.

⁶⁰ 'ipsa virtus brevissime recta ratio dici potest' Cic. *Tusc. disp.* iv 15, 34.

⁶¹ 'virtutis definitio est—habitus consentiens vitae' Comm. *in Lucan.* ii 380
(Arnim iii 199).

⁶² 'perfecta virtus aequalitas [est] ac tenor vitae per omnia consonans sibi' Sen.
Ep. 31, 8.

⁶³ 'ante omnia hoc cura, ut constes tibi' *ib.* 35, 4.

⁶⁴ 'virtus convenientia constat: omnia opera eius cum ipsa concordant et congruunt' *ib.* 74, 30.

⁶⁵ '[stultitia] semper incipit vivere: quam foeda [est] hominum levitas cottidie
nova vitae fundamenta ponentium, novas spes in exitu incohantium! quid est turpius
quam senex vivere incipiens?' *ib.* 13, 16 and 17.

⁶⁶ 'Zeno is erat qui...id appellaret honestum, quod esset simplex quoddam et solum
et unum bonum' Cic. *Ac.* i 10, 36. So Seneca: 'quid est sapientia? semper idem
velle atque idem nolle' Sen. *Ep.* 20, 5. ⁶⁷ See above, § 81.

⁶⁸ Whether by Zeno (Diog. L. vii 87), or by Cleanthes (Stob. ii 7, 6 a: Arnim i
552) is a matter of no importance.

as 'universal and human nature[69],' thereby further approximating
to the teaching of rival schools; but on the other hand he gave
this new and more characteristic explanation 'to live virtuously
is to live according to scientific knowledge of the phenomena of
nature, doing nothing which the Universal Law forbids, which is
the Right Reason which pervades all things, and is the same
as Zeus, the Lord of the ordering of this world[70].' Diogenes of
Babylon introduced the words 'to take a reasonable course in
choosing or refusing things in accordance with nature[71].' Antipater's definition is 'to live with preference for what is natural,
and aversion to what is against nature[72],' thus throwing the stress
on the doctrine of the 'things of high degree[73].' Panaetius made
a distinct step forward when he admitted the claims of universal
nature to be supreme, but (subject to them) held that each man
should follow the pointings of his individual nature[74]; this
teaching however comes rather near to naming a twofold end.
Cicero follows Panaetius in his *de Officiis*[75], but in the *de Finibus*
adheres more closely to Chrysippus[76], and Seneca agrees with
him in laying stress on the need of scientific knowledge of
natural events[77]. In the main therefore 'life according to nature'
means to the Stoics life in accordance with the general movement
of the universe, to which the particular strivings of the individual
must be subordinated.

314. From the religious standpoint virtue is willing coopera-
Obedience tion with the deity, in preference to that unwilling
to God. cooperation to which even evil-doers are forced.
This conception, first set forth by Cleanthes in a poem that we

[69] See above, § 108. The emphasis on individual nature is sometimes still greater;
ἡ ἀρετὴ τελειότης ἐστὶ τῆς ἑκάστου φύσεως Galen *plac. Hipp. et Plat.* v 5, p. 468 K
(from Chrysippus).
[70] Diog. L. vii 87 and 88.   [71] Stob. ii 7, 6 a. See also above, § 258.
[72] Stob. ii 7, 6 a.   [73] See below, § 320.
[74] Παναίτιος τὸ ζῆν κατὰ τὰς δεδομένας ἡμῖν ἐκ φύσεως ἀφορμὰς τέλος ἀπεφήνατο
Clem. Al. *Strom.* ii 21, 129.
[75] 'sic est faciendum, ut contra universam naturam nihil contendamus; ea tamen
conservata, propriam naturam sequamur' *Off.* i 31, 110.
[76] 'vivere adhibentem scientiam earum rerum, quae natura evenirent' *Fin.*
iv 6, 14.
[77] 'huc et illud accedit, ut perfecta virtus sit aequalitas ac tenor vitae per omnia
consonans sibi, quod non potest esse nisi rerum scientia contingit et ars, per quam
humana ac divina noscantur; hoc est summum bonum' Sen. *Ep.* 31, 8.

have quoted above[78], is enforced by Seneca and Epictetus also in varying phrases. 'I do not obey God,' says Seneca, 'I agree with him. I go with him heart and soul, and not because I must[79].' With a slight change of language this leads us to the paradox that 'obedience to God is liberty[80].' 'I have placed my impulses,' says Epictetus, 'in obedience to God. Is it his will that I shall have fever? It is my will too. Is it his will that I should obtain anything? It is my wish also. Does he not wish it? I do not wish it[81].' The personal bent of Epictetus leads him to develope this idea in the direction of suffering rather than of acting. 'If the good man had foreknowledge of what would happen, he would cooperate towards his own sickness and death and mutilation, since he knows that these things are assigned to him in accordance with the universal arrangement[82].' The proof that this must be so rests on the unity of the Divine and individual purposes: 'Good cannot be one thing, and that at which we are rationally delighted another thing[83].'

315. It is not perhaps quite so clearly stated that the virtue of the individual is that disposition which will make him the best possible member of society, that is, the best possible citizen of the Cosmopolis. Yet this is everywhere implied. In the first place the wise man will take part in the life of the community[84], he will marry and bring up children[85]. In the second place the virtue of man differs first from the corresponding quality in the animals in that man is formed by nature for social union; hence his reason only comes into play simultaneously with the recognition that he is a member of a community, and as such bound to prefer the good of the whole to that of a part. 'Nature,' says Panaetius, 'through reason unites man to man, so that they have a common bond in con-

Social duty.

---

[78] See above, § 98.

[79] 'non pareo deo, sed adsentior. ex animo illum, non quia necesse est, sequor' Sen. *Ep.* 96, 2.

[80] 'deo parere libertas est' *Dial.* vii 15, 7.

[81] Epict. *Disc.* iv 1, 89 and 90.

[82] *ib.* ii 10, 5.   [83] *ib.* iii 7, 7.

[84] 'Zenon ait: accedet ad rempublicam sapiens, nisi si quid impedierit' Sen. *Dial.* viii 3, 2; πολιτεύσεσθαί φασι τὸν σοφόν, ὥς φησι Χρύσιππος Diog. L. vii 121.

[85] See § 306, note 26.

versation and life; it induces men to approve and take part in
public gatherings and festivals, and to collect the materials for
a social and cultivated life for themselves, their children, and all
whom they hold dear[86].'

316. Virtue, as a disposition of the soul[87], reflects all the
aspects in which the soul itself is regarded. Since

Health of soul. the principate is both wisdom and will, so virtue is
wisdom, according to the paradox of Socrates and the Cynics[88].
Because virtue is wisdom, it can be taught[89]; in fact, it can only
be acquired by teaching; and equally evil-doing can be cured
by teaching[90]. But no less virtue is will. Cleanthes emphasized
this aspect, and identified virtue both with the Socratic 'strength
of character' and with the Stoic 'tone[91].' In so far as virtue is
will, it is to be acquired by constant practice[92]. A true judgment
is endangered by hasty assent; a healthy will by slackness of
the soul's sinews. In the Stoic system vigour and strength
of mind is everywhere identified with the 'true tone' (εὐτονία)[93];
the possibility of overstrain is not considered. But in the development of the ideal we have two varying aspects of virtue
presented to us. At one moment we see the man of action,
engaged in the thick of the battle, sun-browned, dusty, horny-
handed[94]; with this model before him we find Musonius objecting
altogether to relaxation of moral tone as being equivalent to its

---

[86] Cic. *Off.* i 4, 12.

[87] τὴν ἀρετὴν διάθεσιν εἶναί φασι ψυχῆς σύμφωνον αὐτῇ περὶ ὅλον τὸν βίον Stob.
ii 7, 5 b 1.

[88] [ὁ Σωκράτης ἔφη] πᾶσαν ἀρετὴν σοφίαν εἶναι Xen. *Mem.* iii 9, 5; see also above,
§§ 48, 52.

[89] διδακτήν τε εἶναι τὴν ἀρετὴν καὶ Χρύσιππος καὶ Κλεάνθης καὶ Ποσειδώνιος Diog.
L. vii 91.

[90] 'They are thieves and robbers, you may say. What do you mean by thieves and
robbers? They are mistaken about good and evil. Show them their errors, and you
will see how they desist from their errors' Epict. *Disc.* i 18, 3 and 4.

[91] See above, § 177, note 28.

[92] 'If you would be a good reader, read; if a writer, write. Generally, if you
would make anything a habit, do it; if you would not make it a habit, do not do it'
Epict. *Disc.* ii 18, 2 and 4; 'nihil est quod non humana mens vincat, et in familiari-
tatem adducat adsidua meditatio' Sen. *Dial.* iv 12, 3.

[93] ὧν κατορθοῦσιν [ἄνθρωποι], ἡ ὀρθὴ κρίσις ἐξηγεῖται μετὰ τῆς κατὰ τὴν ψυχὴν
εὐτονίας Chrys. ap. Galen *plac. H. et Plat.* iv 6, p. 403 K (Arnim iii 473).

[94] 'virtutem convenies...pro muris stantem, pulverulentam, coloratam, callosas
habentem manus' Sen. *Dial.* vii 7, 3.

loss[95]. At another moment we see the man of quiet conviction, who goes his way unmoved in the face of the howls of the mob or the threats of the tyrant[96]; he is distinguished by a mental calm[97] which no storms can shake. Any discrepancy between these views is finally reconciled by introducing a comparison between the soul and the body. The philosophers had at all times been greatly influenced by the theories and practice of the physicians; and they were proud to call themselves 'physicians of the soul.' Chrysippus spent much time in comparing diseases of the soul to those of the body[98]. Equally there must be a healthy state of the soul corresponding to that of the body, in which all its parts are in harmony[99]. Hence in the Stoic prayer health of soul is asked for, side by side with health of body[100]; and Seneca bases a singularly complete statement of the Stoic conception of happiness upon a permanently healthy condition of the mind[101].

317. Virtue is a state of the mind, a disposition of the soul; it is not an act. Hence the bent of the mind
Virtue lies in intention. (*inclinatio*), its aim (*intentio*), its desire (βούλησις, *voluntas*) is everything; the performance through the organs of the body is nothing[102]. This Stoic dogma is to-day so familiar

[95] 'Saturnalia Athenis agitabamus hilare prorsum et modeste, non (ut dicitur) "remittentes animum," nam "remittere" inquit Musonius "animum quasi amittere est"' Gellius, *N. A.* xviii 2, 1.

[96] 'iustum ac tenacem propositi virum | non civium ardor prava iubentium, | non vultus instantis tyranni | mente quatit solida' Hor. *C.* iii 3, 1-4.

[97] 'hanc stabilem animi sedem Graeci εὐθυμίαν vocant; ego tranquillitatem voco' Sen. *Dial.* ix 2, 3.

[98] Cic. *Tusc. disp.* iv 10, 23.

[99] 'ut enim corporis temperatio, cum ea congruunt inter se ex quibus constamus, sanitas, sic animi dicitur, cum eius iudicia opinionesque concordant, eaque animi est virtus' *ib.* 13, 30.

[100] 'roga bonam mentem, bonam valetudinem animi, deinde tunc corporis' Sen. *Ep.* 10, 4; 'orandum est, ut sit mens sana in corpore sano' Juv. *Sat.* x 356.

[101] 'beata est vita conveniens naturae suae, quae non aliter contingere potest, quam si primum sana mens est et in perpetua possessione sanitatis suae, deinde fortis et vehemens, tum pulcherrima ac patiens, apta temporibus, corporis sui pertinentiumque ad id curiosa non anxie' Sen. *Dial.* vii 3, 3.

[102] 'actio recta non erit, nisi fuerit recta voluntas' Sen. *Ep.* 95, 57; 'gratus potest esse homo voluntate' *Ben.* ii 31, 1; 'sic timere, sic maerere, sic in libidine esse peccatum est, etiam sine effectu' Cic. *Fin.* iii 9, 32; 'The being of the good is a certain kind of will (προαίρεσις); the being of the bad is a certain kind of will. What then are externals? Material for the will' Epict. *Disc.* i 29, 1 and 2.

in divinity, law, and society that it is not easy to realize how paradoxical it seemed when first stated. By its proclamation the Stoics defied the whole system of *tabu* by which the ancient world prohibited certain acts as in themselves dangerous and detestable; a system still in force in many departments of life and theoretically defended by the 'intuitive system of morals.' The defenders of *tabu* were bitterly affronted, and indignantly asked questions which mostly concerned the sexual relations, with regard to which *tabu* appears to have been at the time most vigorous. 'Is there nothing wrong in cannibalism? in foul language? in incest? in the accursed relations with boy favourites (παιδικά)?' To these questions firm-minded Stoics were bound to give a negative answer, thereby laying themselves open to the charge of being defenders of immorality. This charge however is never to be taken seriously; the high practical morality of the Stoics placed them beyond reproach. But it was also easy to raise a laugh by quotations from these austere moralists which sounded like a defence of licentiousness. The solution of the difficulty in each individual case follows exactly the same lines as in politics; and there is the same divergence of method between the early Stoics, who assert their principles at all costs, and those of the transition period, who are intent upon adapting them to the existing conditions of society. Here we need only discuss the questions of principle, as we deal with questions affecting practical life in another chapter[103].

318. The principal *tabus* affecting the individual have to do with cannibalism, the sexual relations, nudity, and obscenity. Of the first we have already spoken; the other three appeared to the Stoics partly due to inherited prejudices, partly to the theory that the body is in itself vile and corrupt. Of neither point of view could the Stoics approve. Hence their repeated assertions that no sexual act, whether commonly described as natural or as unnatural, is *in itself* to be condemned, but only according as it is seemly or unseemly for the individual[104]. It was perhaps unnecessary to explain to Greeks that the naked body is in itself no offensive sight, but

Tabus.

---

[103] See below, § 383.   [104] Arnim i 250.

doubtless the Stoics had to make this clear to their Oriental pupils; Zeno at any rate laid down the principle when he said that men and women should wear the same clothes (meaning such as nature requires for warmth and not such as fashion prescribes), and hide no part of the body[105]. As to decency of language, it did not occur to the Stoics to discuss this question in connexion with the history of literature. Since truth is always good, and the very purpose of language is to express truth, a wise man will always say straight out what he needs to say[106].

319. Up to this point we find a broad resemblance between
Virtue in its
applications.
the ethical principles of the Stoics and the Cynics. Both assert the sole supremacy of virtue, ridicule traditional prejudices, and bid defiance to external circumstances. But there is at the same time divergence. To the Cynics virtue stands out as alone, needing no theory, and by itself in the universe. To the Stoics virtue is but one expression of that universal reason which is equally at work in the universe and in the human mind. The Stoics are therefore under the obligation of bringing virtue into touch with circumstances, the soul into harmony with the body. From this arises their doctrine that virtue is bound up with the study both of universal and of individual nature, and that amongst things indifferent there are some that the good man must seek, and others that he must avoid. The critics of Stoicism, both ancient and modern, regard this doctrine as an afterthought[107], suggested by practical difficulties, and alien from the original teaching of Zeno. This seems

---

[105] Diog. L. vii 33.

[106] 'placet Stoicis, suo quamque rem nomine appellare. sic enim disserunt, nihil esse obscenum, nihil turpe dictu' Cic. *Fam.* ix 22, 1. See further below, § 344.

[107] 'postea tuus ille Poenulus, causam non obtinens repugnante natura, verba versare coepit et primum rebus iis, quas non bonas dicimus, concessit ut haberentur †aestimabiles, et ad naturam accommodatae' *Fin.* iv 20, 56; 'the stricter Stoic theory of the good was modified by the admission of προηγμένα' Zeller, *Stoics*, p. 290. The true note is struck by Rendall, *Introd.* p. xlv: 'the course of Stoic ethics is, in fact, the progressive enlargement and clarification of the Cynic ideal of conduct, under the stress of that larger conception of "nature" which was inherent in Stoic monism. The full content and interpretation of the formula was only gradually realised. Its deeper implications unfolded themselves through life even more than through thought, and find their fullest exposition in the pages of the Roman Stoics.'

to be a misapprehension. Undoubtedly Zeno had said: 'some things are good, some are evil, some indifferent. Good are wisdom, temperance, justice, fortitude, everything that is virtue or an aspect of virtue; evil are folly, intemperance, injustice, cowardice, everything that is vice or an aspect of vice. Indifferent are life and death, glory and disgrace, pain and pleasure, riches and wealth, disease, health, and so forth [108].' But there is a difference between a principle and its application; and this very list of things indifferent indicates by its contrasts an underlying difference, though it is not the difference between good and evil. Zeno was therefore quite consistent in proceeding to examine the nature of this difference.

320. This secondary difference is termed by the Stoics a
Worth and   difference of worth (ἀξία, aestimatio)[109]. Health,
Unworth.   life, riches, have positive worth in greater or less
degree; disease, death, poverty, have negative worth (ἀπαξία, inaestimabile)[110]. Between these lie things that are absolutely indifferent, as, for example, whether the number of hairs on one's head is odd or even[111], or whether we take up one or the other of two coins that have the same general appearance and the same stamp[112]. Even here a slight distinction has to be made; as to whether the hairs on the head are odd or even in number we have not the slightest concern; but in the matter of the coins we must make a choice, and that quickly. Let us then settle the matter anyhow, by chance as common folk say; 'for a reason that is not clear to us,' as the Stoics say, not willing to admit an effect without a cause, and yet leaving the matter much where it was[113]. And now as to the things that have 'worth'; it is clear that in some sense they are 'according to nature,' and in

---

[108] Stob. ii 7, 5 a.

[109] 'aestimatio, quae ἀξία dicitur' Cic. *Fin.* iii 10, 34. Posidonius seems to have practically substituted ἀξίαν ἔχοντα for προηγμένα, but in strict usage the latter term is narrower, and includes only such things as have measurable worth.

[110] 'inter illa, quae nihil valerent ad beate misereve vivendum, aliquid tamen quo differrent esse voluerunt, ut essent eorum alia aestimabilia, alia contra, alia neutrum' *ib.* 15, 50; τῶν δὲ ἀξίαν ἐχόντων τὰ μὲν ἔχειν πολλὴν ἀξίαν, τὰ δὲ βραχεῖαν. ὁμοίως δὲ καὶ τῶν ἀπαξίαν ἐχόντων ἃ μὲν ἔχειν πολλὴν ἀπαξίαν, ἃ δὲ βραχεῖαν Stob. ii 7, 7 g; 'quae essent sumenda ex iis alia pluris esse aestimanda, alia minoris' Cic. *Ac.* i 10, 37.

[111] Stob. ii 7, 7.   [112] Arnim iii 122.

[113] Plut. *Sto. rep.* 23, 6.

A.   19

the same sense those things that have 'negative worth' are opposed to nature¹¹⁴; and the former in some way approximate to
the character of the good¹¹⁵. It is then necessary to describe
them by some term other than 'good.' Zeno selected the term
προηγμένον 'of high degree,' which Cicero translates variously
by *producta, promota, praecipua, praelata,* and *praeposita.* This
term, we are told, Zeno borrowed from court life: 'for no one
would think of calling a king "of high degree," but only those
who are of a rank next to his, though far below¹¹⁶.' The opposites were described as ἀποπροηγμένα (*remota, reiecta*) 'things
of low degree¹¹⁷.' Seneca, who states the theory with great
clearness¹¹⁸, commonly uses the handier terms *commoda* ('advantages') and *incommoda* ('disadvantages')¹¹⁹. In their treatment
of the separate matters which fall under these divisions the Stoics
were in close agreement with the Peripatetic theory of natural
ends (τὰ κατὰ φύσιν)¹²⁰: but their loyalty to their own school
came into question, if they actually termed them 'good' or
'evil,' as Chrysippus thought permissible if sufficient precautions
were taken¹²¹, and as Seneca often describes them in his less
careful moods¹²².

¹¹⁴ 'cetera autem, etsi nec bona nec mala essent, tamen alia secundum naturam
dicebat [Zeno], alia naturae esse contraria. his ipsis alia interiecta et media nume-
rabat' Cic. *Ac.* i 10, 36.
¹¹⁵ τὸ προηγμένον συνεγγίζειν πως τῇ τῶν ἀγαθῶν φύσει Stob. ii 7, 7 g.
¹¹⁶ '[hoc] Zeno προηγμένον nominavit, cum uteretur in lingua copiosa factis tamen
nominibus ac novis. "ut enim," inquit, "nemo dicit in regia regem ipsum quasi
productum esse ad dignitatem (id enim est προηγμένον), sed eos qui in aliquo honore
sint, quorum ordo proxime accedit, ut secundus sit, ad regium principatum"' Cic. *Fin.*
iii 15, 51.
¹¹⁷ 'quae pluris, ea praeposita appellabat; reiecta autem, quae minoris' *Ac.* i 10,
37; 'quae appellemus vel promota et remota, vel, ut dudum diximus, praeposita vel
praecipua, et illa reiecta' *Fin.* iii 16, 52.
¹¹⁸ 'quis porro sapientum, nostrorum dico, quibus unum est bonum virtus, negat
etiam haec, quae indifferentia vocamus, habere in se aliquid pretii et alia aliis esse
potiora? quibusdam ex iis tribuitur aliquid honoris, quibusdam multum' Sen. *Dial.*
vii 22, 4.
¹¹⁹ 'itaque commoda vocentur, et ut nostra lingua loquar, producta' *Ep.* 74, 17.
¹²⁰ See above, § 82.
¹²¹ 'bonum appello quidquid secundum naturam est; quod contra, malum; nec ego
solus, sed tu etiam, Chrysippe, in foro, domi; in schola desinis' Cic. *Fin.* v 29, 89;
cf. Arnim iii 137.
¹²² 'sunt animi bona, sunt corporis, sunt fortunae; illa animi bona a stulto ac
malo submoventur' Sen. *Ben.* v 13, 1.

321. The advocates of Stoicism maintain that the theory
The aim of 'advantages' is essential to their system, because
of virtue. without it virtue has no meaning, and practical
life no guide[123]; whereas as soon as this theory is established,
we can assign to virtue the permanent and distinctive character,
that it aims at securing 'advantages' and avoiding 'disadvantages[124].' Now we are able to enlarge, though we do not alter,
our definition of the supreme good; the 'consistent life,' the
'life consistent with nature,' is the 'life which is accompanied by
a true knowledge of the things that happen by nature'; to which
words we now add 'choosing those things which are in accordance with nature, and avoiding those things which are against
nature[125].' Nevertheless, virtue consists wholly in the aiming at
the mark, and not at all in the hitting it. As the true sportsman
finds all his pleasure in throwing his quoit according to the rules
of the game, and in aiming his arrow at the centre of the target,
but cares not in the least (so it would seem) whether he succeeds[126]; so the wise man, even though (by those circumstances
which he cannot control, and which in this connexion we call
'the play of fortune') he gain no 'advantage' at all, but suffer
dishonour, captivity, mutilation, and death, still possesses the
supreme good, still is as completely happy as though he enjoyed
all things. This is the Stoic doctrine of the 'sufficiency of virtue,'
expressed in the language of paradox, but nevertheless the central point of their whole ethical system; and its force is really

---

[123] 'deinceps explicatur differentia rerum; quam si non ullam esse diceremus, et confunderetur omnis vita, ut ab Aristone; neque ullum sapientiae munus aut opus inveniretur; cum inter res eas quae ad vitam degendam pertinerent, nihil omnino interesset, neque ullum delectum haberi oporteret' Cic. *Fin.* iii 15, 50.

[124] 'virtutis hoc proprium [est], earum rerum quae secundum naturam sint, habere delectum' *ib.* 4, 12.

[125] 'relinquitur ut summum bonum sit vivere scientiam adhibentem earum rerum quae natura eveniant, selegentem quae secundum naturam, et si quae contra naturam sunt, reicientem; id est, convenienter congruenterque naturae vivere' *ib.* 9, 31 (after Posidonius).

[126] 'ut si hoc fingamus esse quasi finem et ultimum, ita iacere talum, ut rectus assistat; qui ita talis erit iactus, ut cadat rectus, praepositum quiddam habebit ad finem; qui aliter, contra. neque tamen illa praepositio ad eum quem dixi finem perti-nebit: sic ea, quae sunt praeposita, referuntur illa quidem ad finem, sed ad eius vim naturamque nihil pertinent' *ib.* 16, 54; compare also 6, 22; 'non est turpe non consequi, dummodo sequaris' Sen. *Ben.* v 5, 3.

intensified by the doctrine of 'advantages,' which to a superficial
critic appears to relax it.

322. The doctrine of the sufficiency (αὐτάρκεια, *sufficientia*)
Sufficiency of virtue was consistently taught by the Stoics of
of virtue. all periods, though in ever-varying phraseology.
Zeno adopted the Cynic phrase 'virtue is sufficient for happiness,' or in other words 'virtue needs but herself for a happy
life[127].' Chrysippus maintains that there are only three logical
views as to the supreme good, that it is virtue or pleasure or
both[128], and for himself he chooses the first. Happiness therefore is not made greater if advantages are added to virtue; or
rather, virtue does not permit addition (*accessio*)[129]. In the transition period Antipater of Tarsus is said to have faltered, and to
have attributed a little importance, though very little, to external
advantages[130]; but, as we have seen above[131], his definition of the
supreme good is in full accord with the general teaching of the
school. Panaetius and Posidonius held to the orthodox doctrine
both in word and deed, if we may trust the direct statements of
Cicero[132]; nevertheless they were so anxious to assimilate their
expressions to those of ordinary life, that the conclusion could
easily be drawn that in their hearts they too attached importance
to external goods[133]. One authority indeed states that they held

[127] αὐτάρκη τε εἶναι αὐτὴν [τὴν ἀρετὴν] πρὸς εὐδαιμονίαν Diog. L. vii 127; 'a Zenone
hoc magnifice tanquam ex oraculo editur: virtus ad bene vivendum se ipsa contenta
est' Cic. *Fin.* v 27, 79; cf. Pearson, *Fragments*, p. 19.

[128] 'testatur saepe Chrysippus tres solas esse sententias, quae defendi possint, de
finibus bonorum; aut enim honestatem esse finem aut voluptatem aut utrumque' Cic.
Ac. ii 45, 138.

[129] 'crescere bonorum finem non putamus' Cic. *Fin.* iii 14, 48; 'honestum nullam
accessionem recipit' Sen. *Ep.* 66, 9; 'summum bonum nec infringitur nec augetur;
in suo modo permanet, utcunque se fortuna gessit. utrum maiorem an minorem
circulum scribas, ad spatium eius pertinet, non ad formam' *ib.* 74, 26 and 27.

[130] See above, § 110.   [131] See above, § 313.

[132] 'cum [Panaetius] sit is, qui id solum bonum iudicet, quod honestum sit' Cic.
Off. iii 3, 12; 'solebat narrare Pompeius se, cum Rhodum venisset decedens ex Syria,
audire voluisse Posidonium; sed cum audivisset eum graviter esse aegrum, quod vehementer eius artus laborarent, voluisse tamen nobilissimum philosophum visere...itaque
eum graviter et copiose de hoc ipso, nihil esse bonum, nisi quod honestum esset,
cubantem disputavisse: cumque quasi faces ei doloris admoverentur, saepe dixisse:
"nihil agis, dolor: quamvis sis molestus, nunquam te esse confitebor malum"' *Tusc.
disp.* ii 25, 61; cf. Sen. *Ep.* 87, 35.

[133] See above, § 114.

health, strength, and estate to be 'needful' for happiness, thus abandoning the sufficiency of virtue[134]; but in the absence of direct quotation we shall hardly be willing to accept this statement as implying anything different from the distinction of Chrysippus, viz. that 'the wise man *needs* nothing, but *has use* for everything[135].' But any faltering shown by the transition writers was more than made good by the zeal of the teachers under the principate. Seneca enforces the paradox in a score of phrases; in the form of a proverb 'virtue is its own reward[136]'; in rhetorical exuberance 'virtue can defy death, ill fortune, and tyranny[137]'; it is 'independent even of the deity[138]'; and 'no circumstances can increase or impair its perfection[139].' Epictetus often dwells on the same theme[140], and the whole work of Marcus Aurelius is a meditation upon it[141]. Nor is the dogma merely scholastic; the teachers of the Roman period lay special emphasis on the practical importance of upholding the ideal of virtue, as alike single and complete in itself[142].

323. But virtue, though single in its essence, is manifold in its applications; though it can only be possessed as a whole, it is attained by stages. By this amplification of the Stoic doctrine the way is prepared for that

Virtue and the virtues.

[134] Diog. L. vii 128.
[135] 'sapientem nulla re egere, et tamen multis ei rebus opus esse' Sen. *Ep.* 9, 14.
[136] '[virtus] ipsa pretium sui' *Dial.* vii 9, 4; 'recte factorum verus fructus [est] fecisse' *Clem.* i 1, 1; 'virtutum omnium pretium in ipsis est' *Ep.* 81, 20.
[137] 'sapienti non nocetur a paupertate, non a dolore, non ab aliis tempestatibus vitae; ipse semper in actu est; in effectu tunc maximus, cum illi fortuna se obposuit' *ib.* 85, 37.
[138] 'virtutem nemo unquam deo acceptam rettulit...iudicium hoc omnium mortalium est, fortunam a deo petendam, a se ipso sumendam esse sapientiam' Cic. *N. D.* iii 36, 86 and 88; 'aequum mi animum ipse parabo' Hor. *Ep.* i 18, 112; 'monstro, quod ipse tibi possis dare' Juv. *Sat.* x 363.
[139] See note 129.
[140] 'Do you seek a reward for a good man greater than doing what is good and just? Does it seem to you so small and worthless a thing to be good and happy?' Epict. *Disc.* iii 24, 51 and 52.
[141] 'What does not make the man himself worse, does not make his life worse either, nor injure him, without or within' *To himself* iv 8.
[142] 'nec summum bonum habebit sinceritatem suam, si aliquid in se viderit dissimile meliori' Sen. *Dial.* vii 15, 1; 'No man is able to make progress when he is wavering between opposite things; but if you have preferred this (one thing) to all things, if you choose to attend to this only, to work out this only, give up everything else' Epict. *Disc.* iv 2, 4.

adaptation of ethical doctrine to varieties of circumstance
which will be the special subject of our next chapter. By the
side of virtue stand 'the virtues,' sometimes conceived as virtue
herself endowed with various qualities[143], more often as virtue
at work in different spheres of action. In this way virtue assumes
in turn the shape of each one of the four virtues as commonly
understood, namely Wisdom, Justice, Courage, and Soberness[144];
we may, if we please, reckon with a smaller or greater number[145]; yet we must always remember that the virtues are so
knit together, that he who truly possesses one, possesses all[146].
Virtue again is displayed in single acts, each of which (whatever
its sphere) is a 'right action' ($\kappa\alpha\tau\delta\rho\theta\omega\mu\alpha$, *recte factum*)[147]. In
proportion as virtue is displayed in its various qualities and
spheres, and in successive right actions, it gains itself a larger
field; it cannot be said to increase, but it is in a way spread
out and broadened[148].

324. Virtue, as it is displayed in individual men, has also
a history. This follows clearly from Stoic principles, since virtue is an aspect of reason, and
children are not possessed of reason[149]. Virtue therefore comes
by training, not by birth[150]; by art, not by nature[151]. In the
period that precedes the attainment of virtue, there exist states
of the soul which are the semblances and the forerunners of
virtue; and he who is on his way towards wisdom, and whom
we call 'the probationer' ($\pi\rho\sigma\kappa\delta\pi\tau\omega\nu$, *proficiens*[152]), by learning
and practice comes daily nearer to his goal, till in the crowning
moment he wins it as a whole; for virtue is no sum of lesser

How virtue
is won.

[143] Chrysippus wrote a book $\pi\epsilon\rho\lambda$ $\tau o\hat{v}$ $\pi o\iota\grave{a}s$ $\epsilon\hat{\iota}\nu\alpha\iota$ $\tau\grave{a}s$ $\grave{a}\rho\epsilon\tau\acute{a}s$; see Arnim iii 256
[144] See below, §§ 335–350.   [145] Diog. L. vii 92.
[146] $\tau\grave{a}s$ $\grave{a}\rho\epsilon\tau\grave{a}s$ $\lambda\acute{\epsilon}\gamma o\upsilon\sigma\iota\nu$ $\grave{a}\nu\tau\alpha\kappa o\lambda o\upsilon\theta\epsilon\hat{\iota}\nu$ $\grave{a}\lambda\lambda\acute{\eta}\lambda\alpha\iota s$, $\kappa\alpha\grave{\iota}$ $\tau\grave{o}\nu$ $\mu\acute{\iota}\alpha\nu$ $\check{\epsilon}\chi o\nu\tau\alpha$ $\pi\acute{a}\sigma\alpha s$ $\check{\epsilon}\chi\epsilon\iota\nu$
Diog. L. vii 125; 'quicquid honeste fit, una virtus facit, sed ex consilii sententia' Sen.
Ep. 67, 10; 'virtutibus inter se concordia [est]' *Clem.* i 5, 3.
[147] 'videmus esse quiddam, quod recte factum appellemus; id autem est perfectum
officium' Cic. *Fin.* iii 18, 59; 'rectum, quod $\kappa\alpha\tau\delta\rho\theta\omega\mu\alpha$ dicebas' *ib.* iv 6, 15.
[148] 'quamquam negant nec virtutes nec vitia crescere; attamen utrumque eorum
fundi quodammodo et quasi dilatari putant' *ib.* iii 15, 48.
[149] See above, § 153, note 66.
[150] 'scit [sapiens] neminem nasci sapientem sed fieri' Sen. *Dial.* iv 10, 6.
[151] 'non dat natura virtutem; ars est bonum fieri' *Ep.* 90, 44.
[152] Zeno probably took over the term $\pi\rho o\kappa o\pi\acute{\eta}$ from the Peripatetics, see Diog. L.
vii 127; its implications he adapted to Stoic principles. See Plut. *prof. virt.* 12.

dispositions reached by a gradual addition of item to item, but a thing complete in itself[153]. Can virtue thus won be lost at a later time? Virtue, it may seem, is not really such, unless it is indestructible; and the Cynics and the earlier Stoics taught accordingly that virtue cannot be lost[154], that it is a 'possession for ever.' In this point, as in so many others, Chrysippus yielded to criticism, and admitted that virtue might be lost through intoxication or indigestion[155], to which causes might well be added the failure of the reason through insanity or old age[156]. But in spite of these difficulties the general feeling of the Stoic school held firmly to the doctrine that virtue once acquired is acquired for ever[157].

325. Virtue and vice are not mere theories of the philosopher; they exist and can be studied in human
Wise men. shape, in the wise and foolish men of myth, history,
and society. The lesson of virtue in particular can best be learnt by considering virtuous men[158]. Here the Stoics followed closely the teaching of their predecessors the Cynics[159]. As the best of models they accepted Hercules, the man rightly deemed a

---

[153] 'hoc autem ipsum bonum non accessione neque crescendo aut cum ceteris comparando, sed propria vi sua et sentimus et appellamus bonum' Cic. *Fin.* iii 10, 34.

[154] Stob. ii 7, 11 g; Diog. L. vii 127.

[155] τὴν ἀρετὴν Χρύσιππος ἀποβλητήν...διὰ μέθην καὶ μελαγχολίαν *ib.*

[156] See above, § 289.

[157] 'semel traditi nobis boni perpetua possessio est; non dediscitur virtus. contraria enim mala in alieno haerent, ideo depelli et exturbari possunt' Sen. *Ep.* 50, 8. Just in the same spirit we say that a new language or (say) the art of swimming, if once learnt, is learnt 'for good.'

[158] 'aliquis vir bonus nobis eligendus est, ac semper ante oculos habendus, ut sic tanquam illo spectante vivamus, et omnia tanquam illo vidente faciamus' Sen. *Ep.* 11, 8, quoting however from Epicurus.

[159] 'Heracles was the model whom [Antisthenes] and the other Cynics held up for imitation, the patron saint, so to speak, of the school. Antisthenes wrote a dialogue entitled "Heracles" and, with this for guidance, his followers delighted to tell again the story of the hero's laborious and militant life, identifying, by ingenious allegories, the foul monsters which he vanquished with the vices and lusts that beset the souls of men' Gomperz, *Greek Thinkers,* ii p. 151; 'the more generous Cynics aver that the great Heracles also, as he became the author of other blessings, so also left to mankind the chief pattern of this (Cynic) life' Julian, *Or.* vi p. 187, 3 (Mayor on Juv. *Sat.* x 361). So also in Buddhism: 'besides the ideal King, the personification of Power and Justice, another ideal has played an important part in the formation of early Buddhist ideas regarding their master. It was the ideal of a perfectly Wise Man, the personification of Wisdom, the Buddha' Rhys Davids, *Hibbert Lectures,* p. 141.

god[160], who travelled over all the world, purging it of every lawlessness, and bringing with him justice, holiness, and peace[161]. Next comes Ulysses, who like Hercules was untiring in his labours, triumphant over pain, and a conqueror throughout all the world[162]; an example to all men of endurance and vigour[163]. To barbarians Cyrus, king of Persia, was a like example to prove that suffering is a good[164]. Many such are counted amongst the philosophers; first Heraclitus, not for his insight into nature, but for his control over his passions[165]; then Socrates, who in life and death was equally a model as a man and as a citizen[166]. Diogenes the Cynic is worthy of special honour, for he was so filled with love for mankind and obedience to God, that he willingly undertook a life of labour and bodily suffering, and thus won himself the true freedom[167], and became truly happy, truly divine[168]. Zeno the most temperate of philosophers[169], and Cleanthes[170] the most enduring, were men of like type within the Stoic school itself.

[160] 'Herculem illum, quem hominum fama, beneficiorum memor, in concilio caelestium collocavit' Cic. *Off.* iii 5, 25.

[161] 'Hercules nihil sibi vicit: orbem terrarum transiit non concupiscendo sed vindicando, quid vinceret; malorum hostis, bonorum vindex, terrarum marisque pacator' Sen. *Ben.* i 13, 3. See also the brilliant descriptions in Epict. *Disc.* iii 24.

[162] 'Ulixen et Herculem...Stoici nostri sapientes pronuntiaverunt, invictos laboribus, contemptores voluptatis et victores omnium terrarum' Sen. *Dial.* ii 2, 1. Yet there is something to be said on the other side: 'Ulysses felt a desire for his wife, and wept as he sat on a rock...If Ulysses did weep and lament, he was not a good man' Epict. *Disc.* iii 24, 18.

[163] So Horace, quite in the Stoic spirit: 'rursus quid virtus et quid patientia possit, | utile proposuit nobis exemplar Ulixen' Hor. *Ep.* i 2, 17 and 18.

[164] Diog. L. vi 1, 2.

[165] 'By acting thus Heraclitus and those like him were deservedly divine, and were so called' Epict. *Manual* 15.

[166] 'praeclara est aequabilitas in omni vita, et idem semper vultus eademque frons, ut de Socrate accepimus' Cic. *Off.* i 26, 90; 'Socrates...violated nothing which was becoming to a good man, neither in making his defence nor by fixing a penalty on himself; nor even in the former part of his life when he was a senator or when he was a soldier' Epict. *Disc.* iii 24, 61.　　　　　　　[167] See above, § 17.

[168] 'si quis de felicitate Diogenis dubitat, potest idem dubitare et de deorum immortalium statu' Sen. *Dial.* ix 8, 5; 'By acting thus Diogenes...was deservedly divine, and was so called' Epict. *Manual* 15.

[169] See above, § 306, note 25.

[170] δεύτερος Ἡρακλῆς ὁ Κλεάνθης ἐκαλεῖτο Diog. L. vii 170; 'Learn how those live who are genuine philosophers: how Socrates lived, who had a wife and children; how Diogenes lived, and how Cleanthes, who attended to the school and drew water' Epict. *Disc.* iii 26, 23.

326. To the list of wise men recognised by the Greeks the
Romans were proud to add other names from their
own history, thereby associating their philosophic
principles with patriotic pride. From their mythology Aeneas
was selected, the man who crushes his desires that he may
loyally cooperate with the destiny of his people; from the times
of the republic Scipio Africanus minor and his gentle companion
Laelius[171]; whilst in Publius Rutilius Rufus a Roman could be
found who, like Socrates, would not when on his trial consent to
any other defence than a plain statement of the facts, in which
he neither exaggerated his own merits nor made any plea for
mercy[172]. But amongst all Romans Cato of Utica was pre-
eminent[173]. If Cicero, as a contemporary and a colleague in
political life, was little liable to illusions as to his character and
success, his testimony to Cato's sincerity is all the more valuable[174]; nor can we believe that Cato's voluntary death would so
soon and so greatly have stirred Roman feeling, had it not come
as the climax of a life worthily spent[175]. The period of the principate brought to the front both men and women whose fearless
lives and quiet self-approved deaths proved them to be worthy
successors to the heroes of the past; and at the same time we
notice a disposition to find some at least of the elements of the
heroic character in simple uneducated folk, as in the soldier, the
athlete, and the gladiator, so that these too serve in their degree
as models for those that seek wisdom[176].

327. The founders of Stoicism never doubted that wise men
had existed and did exist; they looked forward to
a time not far distant when there should be a Cos-

Wise Romans.

Wise men are few.

---

[171] 'aut Cato ille sit aut Scipio aut Laelius' Sen. *Ep.* 25, 6; 'elige remissioris
animi virum Laelium' *ib.* 11, 10.

[172] 'nam cum esset ille vir [P. Rutilius Rufus] exemplum, ut scitis, innocentiae,
cumque illo nemo neque integrior esset in civitate neque sanctior, non modo supplex
iudicibus esse noluit, sed ne ornatius quidem aut liberius causam dici suam, quam
simplex ratio veritatis ferebat' Cic. *de Or.* i 53, 229; cf. Sen. *Dial.* i 3, 4 and 7; and
see further, § 430.

[173] 'Catonem certius exemplar sapientis viri nobis deos immortales dedisse quam
Ulixen et Herculem prioribus saeculis' Sen. *Dial.* ii 2, 1.

[174] 'ego te [Cato] verissime dixerim peccare nihil' Cic. *Mur.* 29, 60.

[175] 'Catonis nobile letum' Hor. *C.* i 12, 35 and 36; and see below, § 430.

[176] 'nobis quoque militandum est' Sen. *Ep.* 51, 6; 'This is the true athlete. Great
is the combat, divine is the work' Epict. *Disc.* ii 18, 28. See also below, § 402.

mopolis in which every citizen should be wise. This robust belief
was not maintained by their successors. According to Chrysippus, only one or two wise men have ever existed[177]; and he
expressly denies that he himself or any of his acquaintance are
amongst the number[178]. The Stoics of the transition period
avoided the topic as troublesome[179]; and their opponents naturally pressed it on them all the more. Zeno had said 'It is
reasonable to honour the gods: it is not reasonable to honour
the non-existent: therefore the gods exist.' This was now
parodied: 'It is reasonable to honour wise men: it is not reasonable to honour the non-existent: therefore wise men exist.' If
this argument was unsatisfactory, as we are told[180], to the Stoics,
because they had not yet discovered their wise man anywhere,
we are not surprised to find that sometimes they refer him to
the golden age[181], at other times convert him into an ideal[182].
The Stoics under the Roman principate re-affirmed vigorously
the existence of the wise man[183]. Seneca however admits that
his appearance is as rare as that of the phoenix[184], and altogether
disclaims any such character for himself individually[185]. Epictetus is far more true to the spirit of the old doctrine, when he
not only abstains from any morbid depreciation of his own
character, but also urges his pupils never to give up the hope
of reaching perfection[186].

[177] Euseb. *pr. ev.* vi 8, 13; Alex. Aph. *de fato* 28, p. 199, 16 B.

[178] Plut. *Sto. rep.* 31, 5.

[179] 'qui sapiens sit aut fuerit, ne ipsi quidem solent dicere' Cic. *Ac.* ii 47, 145.
Thus Panaetius made no reference to the wise man; whilst Posidonius only defended
his possible existence in the future (Schmekel, pp. 213, 278).

[180] Sext. *math.* ix 133.   [181] See above, § 214.

[182] Even if Cicero is not the creator of the conception of an 'ideal character,' nowhere else can we find its meaning so clearly expressed. So of the wise man; 'iste
vir altus et excellens, magno animo, vere fortis, infra se omnia humana ducens, is,
inquam, quem efficere volumus, quem quaerimus certe, et confidere sibi debet, et
suae vitae et actae et consequenti, et bene de se iudicare' *Fin.* iii 8, 29.

[183] 'non est quod dicas hunc sapientem nostrum nusquam inveniri' Sen. *Dial.*
ii 7, 1.

[184] 'ille alter [sapiens primae notae] fortasse tanquam phoenix semel anno quin-
gentesimo nascitur' *Ep.* 42, 1, cf. Alex. Aphr. p. 34, n. 2; 'scit [sapiens] paucissimos
omni aevo sapientes evadere' Sen. *Dial.* iv 10, 6.

[185] See above, § 126.

[186] 'Socrates in this way became perfect, in all things improving himself, attending
to nothing except to reason. But you, though you are not yet a Socrates, ought to

328. Thus the Stoics founded their moral ideal on the triple

The glory of virtue. basis of the good citizen, the healthily-disposed soul, and the examples of wise men. In impressing this part of their system on their pupils, they made little use of definitions or syllogisms, but all the more they resorted to rhetorical description. As in their physics the Logos became almost a person, so here the picture of Virtue is drawn, as by Prodicus in the old allegory of the choice of Hercules, drawing men to her not by the pleasures she offers but by her majesty and beauty[187]. Cleanthes in particular heaps epithets of praise on virtue[188]; more usually it is sufficient to insist that virtue is good, praiseworthy, and expedient. That 'the wise man is a king[189]' almost ceases to be a paradox, since the soul is rightly compared to a kingdom; that he is rich, handsome, free, and invincible can equally be argued on Stoic principles[190]. To carry such statements further seems to savour of pedantry, to ridicule them at any stage is easy. Yet the statement that seems the boldest of all, that 'the wise man is happy even on the rack[191],' was many a time verified by the experience of individual Stoics[192]. That the wise man is a god, though subject to the limitations of mortality, is maintained without hesitation[193].

329. The Stoic morality differs not only in form and in its

Stoic ethics. reasoned basis, but in substance, both from the popular morality of the time and the ideals of rival philosophical schools. The Stoic heroes differ from those of Homer by a world-age; they possess what the Romans called

live as one who wishes to be a Socrates' Epict. *Manual* 50. Epictetus did not however ignore failures: 'we [Stoics] say one thing, but we do another; we talk of the things which are beautiful, but we do what is base' *Disc.* iii 7, 18.

[187] See above, § 42.
[188] See above, § 98.
[189] This is again a Socratic paradox: βασιλεῖς δὲ καὶ ἄρχοντας οὐ τοὺς τὰ σκῆπτρα ἔχοντας ἔφη εἶναι ἀλλὰ τοὺς ἐπισταμένους ἄρχειν Xen. *Mem.* iii 9, 10.
[190] Cic. *Fin.* iii 22, 75 and 76.
[191] 'eorum, qui dolorem in malis non habent, ratio certe cogit, uti in omnibus tormentis conservetur beata vita sapienti' *ib.* iii 13, 42; Arnim iii 585, 586; 'shew me a man who is sick and happy, in danger and happy, in exile and happy, in disgrace and happy. Shew him; I desire, by the gods, to see a Stoic' Epict. *Disc.* ii 19, 24.
[192] See below, §§ 431, 439.
[193] 'bonus tempore tantum a deo differt' Sen. *Dial.* i 1, 5; 'sapiens excepta mortalitate similis deo' *ib.* ii 8, 2; and see above, § 274.

humanitas, powers of reasoning and of sympathizing unknown to an age of warriors. The Epicurean sage was not, as popular criticism and that of many Stoics unjustly described him, a man of gross tastes and reckless selfishness; but he was essentially easy-going and a quietist, little inclined to risk his peace of mind by meddling with the troubles of others. To the Cynics the Stoics owed much in their principles, to the Academics (as we shall see) much in their application of them; they stood between the two, more reasonable and judicious than the former, firmer in principle than the latter, possessed of a breadth of outlook which neither of these schools could claim.

CHAPTER XIII.

DAILY DUTIES.

330. As in our study of the Stoic philosophy we turn aside

From principles to practice. from the supreme problems of the universe, such as gather round the questions of the divine purpose, the existence of evil, and unfettered choice, our way becomes easier. Our new problems, dealing with the constitution of the human soul, and the ideals of human life in the state and in the individual, are perhaps not simpler in themselves, but they are of narrower range, and in finding our way over the first rough ground we learn to tread with some assurance, so that we now feel ourselves, as it were, on a downward path. For all that, the problems of the universal law and the perfect man must still be compared to mountain tops, if not to the highest peaks of all. But from this point on we steadily descend towards the plains, to that common and practical life by which the worth of philosophy is tested. We no longer gaze on the same bright sunlight or breathe the same invigorating air; philosophy enters a region of mists and shadows, and even learns to adapt her language to new neighbours. But her meaning is the same as before, and the pathway to the heights is not closed behind her.

331. The region we have now reached is that of 'daily

The daily round. duties,' by which phrase we propose to translate here the Greek καθήκοντα and the Latin *officia*[1]. This word is defined by Zeno as meaning 'that which it comes

---

[1] The English term, like so many we have to use, is an imperfect translation; in discussing such questions as marriage and death we speak instead of 'ordinary' or 'simple' duties.

in one's way to do²,' and its quiet sound at once brings it into contrast with the proud claims of Virtue. The contrast is in fact great. Virtue, displaying itself in Right Action, is only possible for reasoning beings, that is, for gods and men; and within our view it is only attained, if at all, by the wise man. But daily duty is common to the wise and the unwise³; it not only extends to children, but also to the unreasoning animals⁴ and to plants⁵. Virtue always contemplates the Universal law; for daily duty it is sufficient to follow the individual nature⁶. Virtue cannot even be understood except by the trained philosopher, whilst the principles of daily duty may be explained to the simple. To use a comparison from mathematics, daily duty is the projection of virtue upon the plane of ordinary life. Between the two there always remains an assured correspondence. Each Right Action which Virtue achieves is at the same time the performance of a daily duty, and that in the most complete manner⁷; each daily duty performed by the unwise is a step by which he may in the end climb to Wisdom⁸.

332. The subject of 'daily duties' was treated both by Zeno⁹

First laws of nature.

and by Cleanthes¹⁰, and is implied in the theory of Stoic ethics as a whole; it has also a special relation to the doctrine of advantages and disadvantages. Nevertheless the Stoics do not directly say that daily duty consists in the seeking of advantages, but that it is based upon primary ends which nature sets up (πρῶτα κατὰ φύσιν, *principia naturae*)¹¹. This phrase indicates the source of this part of the Stoic philosophy; it marks teaching common to the Peripatetic school and the Academy, and accepted by Zeno from his teacher Polemo¹². We are not informed how Zeno and Cleanthes elaborated this

---

² κατωνομάσθαι δ' οὕτως ὑπὸ πρώτου Ζήνωνος τὸ καθῆκον, ἀπὸ τοῦ 'κατά τινας ἥκειν' τῆς προσονομασίας εἰλημμένης Diog. L. vii 108.

³ 'est quoddam commune officium sapientis et insipientis' Cic. *Fin.* iii 18, 59.

⁴ Stob. ii 7, 8.   ⁵ Diog. L. vii 107.   ⁶ Stob. ii 7, 8.

⁷ τῶν καθηκόντων τὰ μὲν εἶναί φασι τέλεια, ἃ δὴ καὶ κατορθώματα λέγεσθαι Stob. as above; '[sapiens] iudicat, cum agit, officium illud esse' Cic. *Fin.* iii 18, 59.

⁸ See below, §§ 357, 358.   ⁹ Diog. L. vii 4.   ¹⁰ *ib.* 175.

¹¹ 'omnia officia eo [referuntur], ut adipiscamur principia naturae' Cic. *Fin.* iii 6, 22.

¹² 'Zenonem cum Polemone disceptantem, a quo quae essent principia naturae acceperat' *ib.* iv 16, 45.

subject; and when we find it taken up in earnest, the spirit of the Academy is firmly established. Thus the Stoic demand for certain knowledge is here set aside; and we are told that the standard of daily duty is 'that which when done can reasonably be defended[13]'; which definition closely corresponds with the definition of the supreme good by Diogenes of Babylon 'to take a reasonable course in the choice of things according to nature[14].' Thus strong will and assured conviction are no longer required; the door is thrown open for convention, opportunism, and respectability. The daring moral theories and bold paradoxes of the founders of Stoicism tend to disappear from sight, and are replaced by shrewd good sense and worldly wisdom : in short, by the doctrine of 'making the best of both worlds.' The subject was therefore congenial to Panaetius, who was both a practical statesman and an admirer of Plato and Aristotle; and it was from this standpoint that Stoicism so rapidly won its way with the Roman nobility of the last century of the republic. Panaetius' book περὶ καθηκόντων was the basis of Cicero's work *de Officiis*, which is the only systematic treatise which we possess on Stoic ethics, and therefore generally the most convenient source of information. As however this work leans very strongly towards Peripatetic views, it will frequently be necessary to refer to other authorities, amongst which Cicero's *de Finibus* best represents the older Stoics, and Seneca and Epictetus the Stoics of the Roman principate.

333. It is no departure from the fundamental principles of Stoicism when we learn that the 'first lessons of nature' are those which are imprinted upon every animal at its birth[15]; Zeno himself had sought for the natural law of marriage by a like method[16]. The first natural

From the animals to man.

---

[13] καθῆκόν φασιν εἶναι ὃ πραχθὲν εὔλογόν τιν' ἴσχει ἀπολογισμόν Diog. L. vii 107; 'est autem officium, quod ita factum est, ut eius facti probabilis ratio reddi possit' Cic. *Fin.* iii 17, 58; 'ratio [non] debet agere quidquam, cuius non possit causam probabilem reddere' *Off.* i 29, 101; 'huic respondebimus, nunquam exspectare nos certissimam rerum comprehensionem, quoniam in arduo est veri exploratio; sed ea ire, qua ducit verisimilitudo. omne hac via procedit officium' Sen. *Ben.* iv 33, 2; and see above, § 159.

[14] See above, § 110.

[15] 'quod secundum naturam est, quod contigit protinus nato, non dico bonum sed initium boni' Sen. *Ep.* 124, 7.   [16] See above, § 306.

lesson is that each animal seeks, not indeed pleasure as the Epicureans hold, but its own preservation and the maintenance of its life in its completeness[17]. At a later stage is imparted the desire of sexual union for procreation's sake, and with it some kind of affection for each one's offspring[18]. But nature's best lessons are reserved for man; as to look into the future, and regard life as a whole[19]; to interest himself in his fellows, to attend public festivities, and to procure the amenities of a civilized life for himself and those dependent upon him[20]; in spare hours, to acquire information on points of historical or philosophical interest[21]; in riper life to claim freedom, and to refuse to submit to any arbitrary commands[22]; and finally, to perceive in all things harmony and beauty, and to avoid any disturbance of it by wilful action[23]. 'Such,' says Cicero, 'is the picture of a beautiful life; and could we see it with our eyes (as Plato says), great would be our desire to possess Wisdom for a bride[24].'

334. In this general sketch we miss a clear ethical standard.

Wavering as to the standard.

The first lessons of nature may easily be perverted, so far as they are common to men and animals, for they point towards the acts of eating, drinking, and sexual union, all of which are associated by the ordinary man with pleasure in a vicious sense. Hence arises a danger (from which many Stoics do not keep clear), that we may fall into the terrible error of the Epicureans, and hold that pleasure itself is a first law of nature[25]. It is therefore necessary to lay it down

---

[17] 'placet his, simul atque natum sit animal, ipsum sibi conciliari et commendari ad se conservandum, et ad suum statum eaque, quae conservantia sunt eius status, diligenda' Cic. *Fin.* iii 5, 16; the maintenance of a complete life is illustrated by the desire to avoid the loss of a limb or deformity, *ib.* 17. 'Universally (be not deceived) every animal is attached to nothing so much as to its own interest' Epict. *Disc.* ii 22, 15.

[18] 'commune autem animantium omnium est coniunctionis appetitus procreandi causa, et cura quaedam eorum, quae procreata sunt' Cic. *Off.* i 4, 11.

[19] *ib.*　　　　　　　　　　　　[20] *ib.* 12.

[21] Cic. *Off.* i 4, 13.　　　　[22] *ib.*　　　　　　　[23] *ib.* 14.

[24] 'formam quidem ipsam, Marce fili, et tanquam faciem honesti vides; quae si oculis cerneretur, mirabiles amores, ut ait Plato, excitaret sapientiae' *ib.* 5, 14.

[25] 'in principiis autem naturalibus plerique Stoici non putant voluptatem esse ponendam: quibus ego vehementer assentior, ne si voluptatem natura posuisse in iis rebus videatur, quae primae appetuntur, multa turpia sequantur' *Fin.* iii 5, 17. Yet Cicero, still writing as a Stoic, can say: '[beluae] nihil sentiunt nisi voluptatem, ad eamque feruntur omni impetu' *Off.* i 30, 105. See below, §§ 346, 347.

that man should aim specially at those results which are characteristic of human nature, that is at the development of powers
which he does not share with the lower animals. So far the
Academy and the Porch might travel together. But the only
higher capacities recognised by the Stoics are reason and the
political sense, which is an aspect of the universal reason; such
matters as antiquarian interests and the appreciation of beauty
could only be introduced under Academic influence. The last,
however, as we shall see, is to become with Panaetius the predominant consideration[26].

335. From the enunciation of general principles we pass on
The four
virtues.
to the separate virtues. Virtue in the strict sense
can only be possessed by the wise man; he there-
fore alone can practise the virtues; nevertheless we may use this
and like terms in a secondary sense to describe those adumbrations or reflections of virtue which fall within the reach of the
ordinary man[27]. The classification of the virtues varies. Panaetius divided virtue into two parts, theoretical and practical, and
Seneca follows him on this point[28]. It was perhaps Chrysippus
who distinguished between virtues that are 'arts' (τέχναι) and
which are based on theoretical principles, and those which are
'acquirements' (δυνάμεις), being attained by practice[29]. But
generally speaking the division of Virtue into the four cardinal
virtues of Wisdom, Justice, Courage, and Soberness is accepted
as sufficient; by subdivision the number of virtues may be increased to any extent; and in scholastic classifications of virtue
we find lists which have multiplicity for their direct aim[30].

[26] See below, §§ 343, 344.

[27] 'in iis, in quibus sapientia perfecta non est, ipsum illud quidem perfectum
honestum nullo modo, similitudines honesti esse possunt' Cic. *Off.* iii 3, 13; 'vivitur
cum iis, in quibus praeclare agitur, si sunt simulacra virtutis' *ib.* i 15, 46; 'est autem
quaedam animi sanitas, quae in insipientem etiam cadat, cum curatione medicorum
turbatio mentis aufertur' *Tusc. disp.* iv 13, 30.

[28] Diog. L. vii 92; 'in duas partes virtus dividitur, in contemplationem veri et
actionem' Sen. *Ep.* 94, 45.

[29] ταύτας μὲν οὖν τὰς ῥηθείσας ἀρετὰς τελείας (leg. τέχνας Hirz. ii 482) εἶναι λέγουσι
περὶ τὸν βίον καὶ συνεστηκέναι ἐκ θεωρημάτων· ἄλλας δὲ ἐπιγίνεσθαι ταύταις, οὐκ ἔτι
τέχνας οὔσας, ἀλλὰ δυνάμεις τινάς, ἐκ τῆς ἀσκήσεως περιγιγνομένας Stob. ii 7, 5 b 4.

[30] For the virtues recognised by Chrysippus and others see Arnim iii 262-293;
we find a sufficiently long list in Seneca: fortitudo, fides, temperantia, humanitas,

A. 20

336. Wisdom (φρόνησις, *prudentia*) is considered by Zeno
not only as the first of the virtues, but as the foundation of all; so that Courage is wisdom in suffering,
Justice is wisdom in distribution, and Soberness is wisdom in
enjoyment[31]. His successors treated Science (ἐπιστήμη, *scientia*)
as the parent virtue[32], thus placing Wisdom side by side with the
other cardinal virtues, yet losing the point of Zeno's genealogy.
The writers of the later periods desired to recognise separately
contemplative wisdom, and therefore introduced as a subdivision
of the first cardinal virtue 'Speculation' (σοφία, *sapientia*)[33]. But
the Stoics generally held that all wisdom must justify itself by
practical results. The study of the so-called 'liberal arts' has a
value for children, for it prepares the way for virtuous training[34].
Logic is needed to protect us against fallacious reasoning[35], and
physics that we may rightly understand the universe and its
providential government, upon which the conception of duty
depends[36]; in this sense we may speak of logic and physics as
virtues, that is, as subdivisions of the virtue of wisdom[37]. The
study of physics is also admirable because it elevates the soul[38].
Geometry, law, and astrology are useful in the several professions[39]. But study when carried to excess, as by antiquarians,

Wisdom.

simplicitas, modestia ac moderatio, frugalitas et parsimonia, clementia, *Ep.* 88, 29
and 30.

[31] Plut. *virt. mor.* 2; *de fort.* 2; *Sto. rep.* vii 1.

[32] Thus φρόνησις became ἐπιστήμη ὧν ποιητέον καὶ οὐ ποιητέον καὶ οὐδετέρων
Stob. ii 7 5 b 1, cf. Alex. Aph. *de fato* 37 (Arnim iii 283).

[33] 'omnis cogitatio motusque animi aut in consiliis capiendis de rebus honestis aut
in studiis scientiae cognitionisque versatur' Cic. *Off.* i 6, 19; 'natura nos ad utrumque
genuit, et contemplationi rerum et actioni' Sen. *Dial.* viii 5, 1.

[34] 'quid ergo? nihil nobis liberalia conferunt studia? ad alia multum, ad virtutem
nihil. quare ergo liberalibus studiis filios erudimus? quia animum ad accipiendam
virtutem praeparant' *Ep.* 88, 20.

[35] 'sine hac arte (sc. dialectica) quemvis arbitrantur a vero abduci fallique posse'
Cic. *Fin.* iii 21, 72.

[36] 'qui convenienter naturae victurus sit, ei proficiscendum est ab omni mundo
atque ab eius procuratione' *ib.* 22, 73.

[37] 'ad eas virtutes dialecticam etiam adiungunt et physicam, easque ambas virtutum
nomine appellant' *ib.* 21, 72.

[38] 'ad hoc nobis proderit inspicere rerum naturam. primo discedemus a sordidis;
deinde animum ipsum, quo summo magnoque opus est, seducemus a corpore; deinde
in occultis exercitata subtilitas non erit in aperta deterior' Sen. *N. Q.* iii Praef. 18.

[39] 'quae omnes artes [sc. astrologia, geometria, ius civile] in veri investigatione
versantur, cuius studio a rebus gerendis abduci contra officium est' Cic. *Off.* i 6, 19.

bookworms, and other learned time-wasters, is nothing but folly[40].

337. The second cardinal virtue is Justice (δικαιοσύνη, *ius-titia*), of which Chrysippus drew a striking allego-
Justice. rical picture. 'She is of virgin form, to show that she is incorruptible and does not give way to bad men;...of firm and fierce aspect,...inspiring fear in the wicked, confidence in the good; her eyes are keen-sighted, her bearing is at once sad and awe-inspiring[41].' Cicero distinguishes Justice in the narrower sense from 'Beneficence.' Justice proper is a political virtue, and consists in respect for the rights and property of individuals. By nature indeed all things are common; but since they have become private property by occupation, conquest, law, contract, and so forth, individuals may keep their own, provided they do not forget that they have always the duty of contributing to the common good[42], and that even slaves have reasonable claims upon them[43]. Beneficence needs the guidance of principle, and must be determined by considerations of person and occasion. The claims of persons upon us depend on propinquity; country, parents, wife and children must be first considered, then other relatives, then fellow-citizens, lastly men in general[44]. The consideration of the degrees of propinquity (σχέσεις) was a favourite subject with Epictetus, and a useful defence against those who maintained that the Stoic sage was lacking in natural affection[45]. The virtue of Justice appealed specially to the statesman in both its applications, and is dealt with fully by Panaetius, and by Cicero after him.

[40] 'est vitium, quod quidam nimis magnum studium...in res conferunt non necessarias' *ib.* 6, 18.
[41] A. Gellius, *N. A.* xiv 4, 4.
[42] Cic. *Off.* i 7, 21 and 22.   [43] *ib.* 13, 41.
[44] 'principes sint patria ac parentes; proximi liberi, totaque domus, quae spectat in nos solos; deinde bene convenientes propinqui' Cic. *Off.* i 17, 58.
[45] 'I ought not to be free from affections (ἀπαθής) like a statue, but I ought to maintain the relations (σχέσεις) natural and acquired, as a pious man, as a son, as a father, as a citizen' Epict. *Disc.* iii 2, 4; 'Duties are usually measured by relations (ταῖς σχέσεσι). Is a man a father? The precept is to take care of him, to yield to him in all things. Does a brother wrong you? Maintain then your own position towards him' *Manual* 30. All the duties of relationship on the one side imply corresponding duties on the other side; 'invicem ista, quantum exigunt, praestant, et parem desiderant regulam, quae (ut ait Hecaton) difficilis est' Sen. *Ben.* ii 18, 2.

338. The third cardinal virtue is Courage (ἀνδρεία, *fortitudo*),
which retains the tradition of the 'strength and
force' of Socrates. This again, according to Cicero,
has two parts, one passive, which consists in despising fortune
and its buffets, and is in harmony with the picture of the wise
man as usually drawn; the other part, which we may call Greatness of Soul (μεγαλοψυχία, *magnitudo animi*) is shown in the
undertaking of great enterprises. The virtue of Courage is characteristically Stoic, and may be considered, like its counterpart
Wisdom, as the foundation and source of all the virtues ; the
knowledge of good and evil can only be attained by the soul
that is duly strung to vigorous resolution[46]. The Stoics of the
principate perhaps insist most of all on this virtue, which alone
makes men independent of all that it lies with Fortune to give
and to take away. The man of courage will therefore detach
himself from fortune's gifts ; he will treat them as household
furniture lent to him which may be at any moment recalled[47].

339. Courage appears in its highest development in the
face of tyranny and death. It is the tyrant's boast
that he has men in his power : but the brave man
is an exception. His rank and his property may be taken away;
he may be subjected to the torture ; his life may be forfeited;
but the soul, that is the man himself, is beyond the tyrant's
reach[48]. To pain he answers 'if I can bear it, it will be light;
if I cannot bear it, it cannot be long[49].' Amidst all the extremities of fire and rack men have been found who never groaned,
never begged for mercy, never answered a question, and indeed

Courage. (margin note beside 338)

Death not to be feared. (margin note beside 339)

---

[46] '[fortitudo] scientia est distinguendi, quid sit malum et quid non sit' *Ep.* 85,
28; 'quomodo igitur Chrysippus? fortitudo est, inquit, scientia rerum perferendarum,
vel affectio animi in patiendo ac perferendo, summae legi parens sine timore' Cic.
Tusc. disp. iv 24, 53.

[47] 'quicquid est hoc, Marcia, quod circa nos ex adventicio fulget, liberi honores
opes, ampla atria et exclusorum clientium turba referta vestibula, clara nobilis aut
formosa coniunx ceteraque ex incerta et mobili sorte pendentia, alieni commodatique
adparatus sunt; nihil horum dono datur; collaticiis et ad dominos redituris instru-
mentis scena adornatur' Sen. *Dial.* vi 10, 1 ; 'victrix fortunae sapientia' Juv. *Sat.*
xiii 20.

[48] 'cum potentes et imperio editi nocere intendent, citra sapientiam omnes eorum
impetus deficient' Sen. *Dial.* ii 4, 1.

[49] 'levis est, si ferre possum ; brevis est, si ferre non possum' *Ep.* 24, 14.

laughed heartily[50]. Of death the Stoic has no fear; not only is it no evil, but it is to be welcomed as part of the course of nature[51]; it is the best of friends, for it offers a release from all troubles, and in particular from the oppression of the tyrant[52]. We do not indeed deny that normally life is an advantage, that nature's first lesson is self-preservation, and that death in itself is a thing terrible to contemplate[53]; but life is not the more desirable for its length[54]; and when old age begins to shatter the powers of the mind, and to degrade the man to the life of a vegetable, nature is calling him to quit his mortal body[55]. At no period is life worth purchasing at the cost of the loss of honour, without which it loses its savour[56]. The philosopher therefore will not merely see with calm confidence the approach of death; he will go forward to meet it of his own free will, if only he is assured that reasonable choice points that way.

340. The doctrine of 'reasonable departure' ($\epsilon\ddot{\upsilon}\lambda o\gamma o\varsigma$ $\dot{\epsilon}\xi a$-
Reasonable $\gamma\omega\gamma\dot{\eta}$, *rationalis e vita excessus*) plays a prominent
departure. part in the Stoic ethics. It cannot rightly be described as the recommendation of suicide; for the Stoics do not permit a man to pass sentence of death upon himself, but only to cooperate in carrying out the decree of a higher power. The doctrine is intended in the first instance to justify death gloriously met in fighting for one's country or one's friends; next when intolerable pain or incurable disease plainly indicates the

[50] 'inter haec tamen aliquis non gemuit. parum est, non rogavit. parum est, non respondit. parum est: risit, et quidem ex animo' *ib.* 78, 19.

[51] 'mors optimum inventum naturae' *Dial.* vi 20, 1; 'fortem posce animum, mortis terrore carentem, | qui spàtium vitae extremum inter munera ponat | naturae' Juv. *Sat.* x 357–9.

[52] 'caram te, vita, beneficio m̄ortis habeo' Sen. *Dial.* vi 20, 3; 'nullo nos invida tanto | armavit natura bono, quam ianua mortis | quod patet' Silius *Pun.* xi 186–8; 'adeo mors timenda non est, ut beneficio eius nihil timendum sit' Sen. *Ep.* 24, 11.

[53] '[mors] quin habeat aliquid in se terribile, ut et animos nostros, quos in amorem sui natura formavit, offendat, nemo dubitat' *ib.* 36, 8.

[54] So Heraclitus had said 'unus dies par omni est' *ib.* 12, 7; 'ut prorogetur tibi dies mortis, nihil proficitur ad felicitatem: quoniam mora non fit beatior vita, sed longior' *Ben.* v 17, 6.

[55] 'si [senectus] coeperit concutere mentem, si partes eius convellere, si mihi non vitam reliquerit sed animam, prosiliam ex aedificio putri ac ruenti' *Ep.* 58, 35.

[56] 'melius nos | Zenonis praecepta docent; nec enim omnia, quaedam | pro vita facienda putant' Juv. *Sat.* xv 106 to 108.

will of the deity[57]; in the development of Roman history a third reason was found in the loss of political freedom[58]. These reasons are not added to, but only systematized, when we are told that it is an 'ordinary duty' to quit life when a man's natural advantages (τὰ κατὰ φύσιν) are outweighed by the corresponding disadvantages[59]; for amongst 'natural advantages' are included in this connexion all those considerations of which an honourable man will rightly take account; and the calculation may equally lead him to the conclusion that, in spite of old age and suffering, and though he has never attained to true wisdom, his simple duty is to wait quietly in life[60].

341. The practice of 'reasonable departure' was largely recommended to the Stoics by the examples of

Its dangers.

Socrates (whose death they regarded as voluntary[61]) and of Cato[62]; and it was at first no small matter of pride to them to find that these examples found imitators, and that their system thus showed its power over the greatest of the terrors that beset humanity. But under the Roman principate 'free departure' soon became so common that it was a reproach rather than a glory to its advocates, a social disease pointing to morbidity of soul rather than to healthy resolution[63]. Hence

[57] Diog. L. vii 130. Ingenious members of the school found five good reasons for voluntarily quitting life, resembling the causes for breaking up a banquet. As the guests part, because of (i) a sudden need, such as the arrival of a friend, (ii) revellers breaking in and using violent language, (iii) the food turning bad, (iv) the food being eaten up, or (v) the company being drunk; so the wise man will depart, because of (i) a call to sacrifice himself for his country, (ii) tyrants doing him violence, (iii) disease hindering the use of the body, (iv) poverty, (v) madness, which is the drunkenness of the soul. See Arnim iii 768.

[58] Notably in the case of Cato.

[59] 'in quo plura sunt, quae secundum naturam sunt, huius officium est in vita manere; in quo autem aut sunt plura contraria, aut fore videntur, huius officium est e vita excedere' Cic. *Fin.* iii 18, 60.

[60] 'perspicuum est etiam stultorum, qui iidem miseri sint, officium esse manere in vita, si sint in maiore parte earum rerum, quas secundum naturam esse dicimus' *ib.* iii 18, 61.

[61] He might easily have obtained acquittal by a judicious defence: Xen. *Mem.* iv 4, 4.

[62] 'Catoni gladium adsertorem libertatis extorque: magnam partem detraxeris gloriae' Sen. *Ep.* 13, 14.

[63] 'ille adfectus multos occupavit, libido moriendi' *ib.* 24, 25; 'quid ergo? non multos spectavi abrumpentes vitam? ego vero vidi, sed plus momenti apud me habent qui ad mortem veniunt sine odio vitae, et admittunt illam, non adtrahunt' *ib.* 30, 15.

the philosophers turned from recommendation to reproof. 'A brave and wise man must not flee from life, but quit it,' says Seneca[64]; 'nothing is more disgraceful than to long for death'[65]. 'Friends,' says Epictetus, 'wait for God; when he shall give you the signal, then go to him[66].'

342. The 'free departure' is the most striking illustration *Courage is active.* of passive courage, but even before it was abused Cicero at least had perceived the attraction which this attitude of soul possesses, and its opposition to the spirit of active enterprise which he calls Greatness of Soul, and which he advocates perhaps more on Academic than on Stoic lines. Still the Stoics had already defined Courage as 'virtue fighting in the front rank in defence of justice[67].' A good man must indeed regard power and wealth as things indifferent; but he is to be blamed if he makes this an excuse for avoiding public life, and leaving to others magistracies at home or commands in the wars[68]. In the old world the love of glory and praise on the one hand, angry feeling against enemies on the other, has led men to seek these positions; but now they should seek them at home that they may have a wide field for the exercise of their virtues[69], and in the wars in order that all war may be brought to an end[70]. By the older Stoics this Greateartedness was advocated by precept and example: Zeno had said that the wise man should take part in public life[71], and his hearers Persaeus and Philonides had taken service under Antigonus Gonatas[72], and Sphaerus with Cleomenes III, king of Sparta[73]. We shall see later how large was the part played in Roman political life by men who were Stoics or inclined to Stoicism, in an age in which there was a strong current of fashion in favour of a quiet life. We must therefore recognise in Courage, fully as much as in Wisdom or Justice, a political as well as a private virtue.

---

[64] *ib.* 24, 25.   [65] *ib.* 117, 22.   [66] Epict. *Disc.* i 9, 16.

[67] 'probe definitur a Stoicis fortitudo, cum eam virtutem esse dicunt propugnantem pro aequitate' Cic. *Off.* i 19, 62.

[68] *ib.* 21, 71.   [69] *ib.* 26, 92.   [70] *ib.* 23, 80.

[71] 'Zenon ait; accedet ad rempublicam [sapiens], nisi si quid impedierit' Sen. *Dial.* viii 3, 2.

[72] See above, §§ 89, 90.   [73] See above, § 91.

343. The fourth cardinal virtue is Soberness (σωφροσύνη,

Soberness. *temperantia*). Of this there are various definitions, and amongst them that it is the principle which regulates our natural appetites so that they are neither in excess nor in defect[74]. From Cicero's point of view Soberness embraces all the virtues, for it is in the due regulation of the impulses that virtue consists. The standard to be attained is a healthy state of the soul; and this is to be judged, upon the analogy of the body, by the canon of that which is beautiful, symmetrical, and becoming (πρέπον, *decorum*)[75]. 'Just as bodily beauty is symmetry established between the limbs mutually, and also between each and the whole body, so beauty of the soul is symmetry between the reasoning power and its parts, and mutually between each of those parts[76].' Although this is in principle a doctrine accepted by the whole Stoic school, yet in its application we may easily find an entirely new departure, that is, if the appeal is made to an artistic standard which depends upon the taste of the individual. The door is then thrown open to an abandonment of the Cynico-Stoic theory of life according to reason, and to the acceptance of the standard of good feeling, which may easily be so stretched as to include existing prejudices and conventions. This danger is realized in Cicero's treatment of the virtue of 'decorum,' which in its distinctive sense is defined as having the element of 'gentlemanliness' in itself[77]. It begins with respect for the feelings and opinions of others[78]; it avoids all rough games and obscene jests[79]; it makes choice

[74] 'efficiendum autem est, ut appetitus rationi obediant, eamque neque praecurrant, nec propter pigritiam aut ignaviam deserant, sintque tranquilli atque omni perturbatione animi careant' Cic. *Off.* i 29, 102.
[75] 'hoc loco continetur id, quod dici Latine *decorum* potest; Graece enim πρέπον dicitur; huius vis ea est, ut ab honesto non queat separari' *ib.* i 27, 93.
[76] Stob. ii 7, 5 b 4; 'ut corporis est quaedam apta figura membrorum cum coloris quadam suavitate, ea quae dicitur pulchritudo; sic in animo opinionum iudiciorumque aequabilitas et constantia, cum firmitate quadam et stabilitate, pulchritudo vocatur' *Tusc. disp.* iv 13, 31.
[77] 'id decorum [volunt] esse, quod ita naturae consentaneum sit, ut in eo moderatio et temperantia appareat cum specie quadam liberali' *Off.* i 27, 96.
[78] 'adhibenda est igitur quaedam reverentia adversus homines, et optimi cuiusque et reliquorum' *ib.* 28, 99; 'to order myself lowly and reverently to all my betters' English Church Catechism.
[79] Cic. *Off.* i 29, 104.

of a profession adapted to the natural character of the individual[80]; it observes, as the actor does, the proprieties of youth
and age, rich and poor, citizen and foreigner[81]; it prescribes
dignity as fitting for men, gracefulness for women[82]. In particular decorum is displayed in modesty (*verecundia*). This is
shown by keeping out of sight those parts of the body which
nature, though she could not dispense with them, has concealed
and covered; in attending to their functions with the utmost
secrecy; and in referring both to these parts of the body and
to their uses by words that do not properly describe them[83].

344. Cicero's treatment of 'decorum' is so full of good sense
that his *de Officiis* was the most widely-known text-
book of Greco-Roman ethics in medieval schools,
and has retained its importance in the classical public schools
of the present day. But its logical justification on Stoic principles is far from easy. We are therefore not surprised to find
that, just as Zeno and the main body of his followers had proclaimed in advance that such doctrine was false in principle and
ridiculous in detail, so conversely the followers of Panaetius found
it necessary expressly to repudiate the teaching of a large number of Stoics[84]. We have in fact here a sharp conflict between
the cultured and Platonizing Stoics on the one side, and the
general feeling of the school on the other. Cicero elsewhere
treats it as an accepted Stoic doctrine that 'the wise man will
blurt things straight out[85]'; and the theory of 'gentlemanly

Cynism or 'decorum'?

[80] 'id enim maxime quemque decet, quod est cuiusque maxime suum. suum quisque igitur noscat ingenium' *ib.* 31, 113-4. Retail trading, and all the arts that
subserve luxury, are illiberal; agriculture is the most truly liberal: *ib.* 42, 150
and 151. [81] *ib.* 34, 122-124.
[82] 'venustatem muliebrem ducere debemus, dignitatem virilem' *ib.* 36, 130. In
the same spirit Epictetus says 'we ought not to confound the distinctions of the sexes'
Disc. i 16, 14.
[83] Cic. *Off.* i 35, 127.
[84] 'nec vero audiendi sunt Cynici, aut si qui fuerunt Stoici paene Cynici, qui
reprehendunt et irrident, quod ea quae re turpia non sint, verbis flagitiosa ducamus;
illa autem, quae turpia sint, nominibus appellemus suis' *ib.* i 35, 128; 'Cynicorum
autem rationem atque vitam alii cadere in sapientem dicunt, si quis eiusmodi forte
casus inciderit, ut id faciendum sit: alii nullo modo' *Fin.* iii 20, 68.
[85] 'habes scholam Stoicam, ὁ σοφὸς εὐθυρρημονήσει. ego servo et servabo (sic enim
adsuevi) Platonis verecundiam. itaque tectis verbis ea ad te scripsi, quae apertissimis
agunt Stoici' *Fam.* ix 22, 5. See also above, § 318.

professions' can never have appealed to any large social circle. In the period of the principate we find the theory of 'decorum,' as a whole, abandoned. Seneca, personally as sensitive as Cicero himself, recognises the absurdity of wasting time in hinting at a plain meaning[86], nor does he limit his choice of illustration even when addressing a lady of high social position[87]. We must look then in some other direction than the *de Officiis* for a duly proportioned exposition of the Stoic virtue of Soberness.

345. Reverting to the definitions of this virtue, we find, amongst those that are generally accepted, first, that it is 'the science of things that are to be sought or avoided or neither[88]'; secondly, that it is 'concerned with the human appetites[89].' Now the term 'appetite' or 'impulse' (ὁρμή, *appetitus*) includes in the Stoic philosophy all those first movements of the soul which draw us on towards some object, and which are adumbrations of right conduct requiring revision and control by reason. But it seems clear that Soberness has little to do with those higher impulses that are characteristic of man, such as the love of knowledge or of society, since other virtues are concerned with these. It remains that Soberness is the virtue which is concerned with the appetites common to men and the lower animals, which we may shortly call the 'lower appetites'; they are, as we have already stated, the desires of eating, drinking, and sexual union. It is just in this sphere that Pleasure arises, in the sense in which it is condemned by the Cynics and popular moralists[90]. We may therefore shortly define Soberness as a right disposition of soul in relation to Pleasure. Its peculiar characteristic is that it is in the main a negative virtue, displaying itself in abstinence from indulgence[91].

The appetites.

[86] 'rem ineptissimam fecero, si nunc verba quaesiero, quemadmodum dicam illum matelam sumpsisse' Sen. *Ben.* iii 26, 2.

[87] *Dial.* vi 20, 3.

[88] σωφροσύνην δ' εἶναι ἐπιστήμην αἱρετῶν καὶ φευκτῶν καὶ οὐδετέρων Stob. ii 7, 5 b 1.

[89] τὴν δὲ σωφροσύνην περὶ τὰς ὁρμὰς τοῦ ἀνθρώπου *ib.* 7, 5 b 2.

[90] μανείην μᾶλλον ἢ ἡσθείην was the expression of Antisthenes, see Diog. L. vi 3; 'voluptas est...res humilis, membrorum turpium aut vilium ministerio veniens' Sen. *Ben.* vii 2, 2.

[91] 'intelligitur appetitus omnes contrahendos sedandosque esse' Cic. *Off.* i 29, 103.

346. In order then rightly to understand the virtue of Sober-
Two views of Pleasure. ness, we need a clear idea of the attitude of the Stoics towards Pleasure. Zeno, as we have seen, whilst definitely placing Pleasure in the category of things indifferent, had nevertheless allowed it to be understood that it might be an advantage (προηγμένον), and the seeking after it natural (κατὰ φύσιν)[92]; and this is stated to have been the express teaching of Hecato, Apollodorus, and Chrysippus[93]. To other Stoics this appeared to be a disastrous concession to Epicurean views. Cleanthes, who had scornfully described the ideal of Epicurus by the picture of Pleasure enthroned as queen, with the Virtues submissively attending as her hand-maidens[94], interpreted the word 'indifferent' more strictly; he refused to admit that pleasure was 'natural' or possessed any worth[95]. In this view he was supported by a great many Stoics, and practically by Archedemus, when he said that pleasure was natural but valueless, like the hairs under the armpit[96]. Hence followed the acceptable conclusion that no sensible man would pay much attention to so trivial a matter[97]. Thus the one word

[92] See above, § 319. It does not seem possible to accept Pearson's view (on Z. fr. 128) that Zeno intended πόνος to be the προηγμένον, and ἡδονή the ἀποπροηγμένον; but both he and his successors undoubtedly recognised the value of πόνος (toil) as a discipline. The following remarks communicated to the writer by Mr Pearson throw much light on a really difficult question. 'Even the Cynics are forced to admit that not all "pleasure" is to be condemned (the evidence is in Zeller's *Socratics*, p. 308), but the only form of it which deserves consideration is that which is the result and after-effect of πόνος. In other words, it may be argued that true pleasure is the cessation of pain (Plat. *Phileb.* 44 B). The glorification of Heracles the toilsome hero corresponds; but pleasure as understood by the vulgar is unhesitatingly to be rejected. Zeno was the inheritor of all this, and, if he ever said that ἡδονή was προηγμένον, his remark can only have applied to the ἀπονία-ἡδονή; and such certainly was the view of Chrysippus (Plut. *Sto. rep.* 30, 2).' In the passage here referred to from Plutarch ἀπονία takes the place of ἡδονή as a προηγμένον; so also in Stob. ii 7, 7 e and Cic. *Fin.* iii 15, 51. See further §§ 347, 371.

[93] ἡδονή as an advantage is contrasted with πόνος (suffering) as a disadvantage in the list attributed to these writers in Diog. L. vii 102.

[94] Cic. *Fin.* ii 21, 69.

[95] Κλεάνθης μήτε κατὰ φύσιν αὐτὴν [ἡδονὴν] εἶναι μήτ' ἀξίαν ἔχειν ἐν τῷ βίῳ Sext. *math.* xi 74 (Arnim iii 155).

[96] Arnim iii 136, 155.

[97] 'sit impudens, si [voluptas] pluris esse contendat dulcedinem corporis, et titilla-tionem, ex eave natam laetitiam, quam gravitatem animi' Cic. *Fin.* iii 1, 1; 'quis mortalium per diem noctemque titillari velit?' Sen. *Dial.* vii 5, 4; 'quidni ista bene penset cum minutis et frivolis et non perseverantibus corpusculi motibus?' *ib.* 4, 4.

'indifferent' came to include two views which were substantially opposed, the one inclining to the Academic standpoint, and the other to Cynism.

347. From this contradiction an escape was sought by making a distinction. In one sense pleasure is an affection of the body, namely a tickling (*titillatio*) of the organs of sense, most readily illustrated in the eating of dainties. This kind of pleasure, even if it is not an advantage naturally sought, yet has some likeness to one; though it is not directly to be aimed at, yet it may be welcomed when nature grants it to us as an extra[98]. This new view practically coincides with that of Aristotle, who calls pleasure an 'aftergrowth' (ἐπιγέννημα, *accessio*), which of itself follows on virtuous action, and is attached to it as the scent to a flower[99]. But much more commonly, in ethical discussions, 'pleasure' denotes the excitement which is more strictly termed 'hilarity' (ἔπαρσις, *sublatio animi*), and is the unhealthy condition of the soul when it is unduly attracted to an object of choice[100]. For this mischief Cicero suggests the Latin term *laetitia*, which is perhaps not altogether adequate[101]. This 'pleasure' may be unreservedly condemned as not merely indifferent, but actually contrary to nature[102]; whilst the virtuous and natural disposition is that of the man who not only contemplates toil

Pleasure an aftergrowth, or an evil.

---

[98] 'voluptas habet quiddam simile naturali bono' Cic. *Leg.* i 11, 31; '[voluptas] condimenti fortasse nonnihil, utilitatis certe nihil habebit' *Off.* iii 33, 120; 'voluptatem natura necessariis rebus admiscuit, non ut illam peteremus, sed ut ea, sine quibus non possumus vivere, gratiora nobis illius faceret accessio' Sen. *Ep.* 116, 3; '[virtus voluptatem] non praestat, sed et hanc; nec huic laborat, sed labor eius, quamvis aliud petat, hoc quoque adsequetur' *Dial.* vii 9, 1. That this view was held by Chrysippus appears from Diog. L. vii 86 (cf. Arnim iii 229 a); see also above, notes 92 and 93.

[99] *Eth. N.* x 7.

[100] ἡδονὴ δέ ἐστιν ἄλογος ἔπαρσις ἐφ' αἱρετῷ δοκοῦντι ὑπάρχειν Diog. L. vii 114 (of Chrysippus); 'hoc interest, quod voluptas dicitur etiam in animo, vitiosa res, ut Stoici putant, qui eam sic definiunt; sublationem animi sine ratione, opinantis se magno bono frui' Cic. *Fin.* ii 4, 13; 'vitium esse voluptatem credimus' Sen. *Ep.* 59, 1.

[101] 'quam [perturbationem] Stoici ἡδονήν appellant, ego malo laetitiam appellare, quasi gestientis animi elationem voluptariam' Cic. *Fin.* iii 10, 35. Sometimes Cicero translates with more fulness by *laetitia gestiens* or *nimia*; *Tusc. disp.* iv 6, 13.

[102] Παναίτιος δὲ [ἡδονήν φησι] τινα μὲν κατὰ φύσιν ὑπάρχειν, τινὰ δὲ παρὰ φύσιν Sext. *math.* xi 73 (Arnim iii 155).

and pain with calm mind, but actually welcomes them as possible stepping stones towards his own true advantage[103].

348. Although the prevailing tendency in Stoic teaching
Active soberness. is to consider Soberness as a negative virtue, and as opposed to the perturbation of Hilarity, there is not wanting some recognition of its positive side. For Soberness also demands that there shall be a healthy activity of the soul in matters such as eating, drinking, and the relations of sex; abstinence is not in itself an end, and if pursued out of season is both a folly and a fault. But this point of view is not adequately treated by any Stoic writer. Panaetius in discussing daily duties omitted to consider the proper care of the body, as was afterwards noticed by Antipater of Tyre; and Cicero gets little further than a general recommendation of common sense and self-restraint in all the circumstances of life[104]. The Romans of the principate were disposed to leave the matter to the physician, suggesting only that food should suffice to allay hunger, drink to put an end to thirst, and clothing to keep away cold[105]; but it is probable that popular moral discourses stopped short of this, and favoured some amount of endurance as a discipline for the soul[106].

349. With regard to the relations of sex, the Socratic
Sober love. tradition was favourable to a more positive treatment. Accordingly the Stoics (not without some feeling that they are adopting a paradoxical position) assert that love (ἔρως, *amor*) is an essential, both for the maintenance of the State[107] and for the character of the good man. Zeno

---

[103] See below, §§ 371, 402, 403. On the whole subject see further Hicks, *Stoic and Epicurean*, pp. 110 to 112.

[104] 'Antipater Tyrius, Stoicus, qui Athenis nuper est mortuus, praeterit[am] censet a Panaetio valetudinis curationem. valetudo sustentatur notitia sui corporis et observatione, quae res aut prodesse soleant aut obesse, et continentia in victu omni atque cultu corporis tuendi causa, postremo arte eorum, quorum ad scientiam haec pertinent' Cic. *Off.* ii 24, 86.

[105] 'hanc sanam et salubrem formam vitae tenete, ut corpori tantum indulgeatis, quantum bonae valetudini satis est...cibus famem sedet, potio sitim extinguat, vestis arceat frigus, domus munimentum sit adversus infesta corporis' Sen. *Ep.* 8, 5; and so Musonius, below, § 381.

[106] Epict. *Disc.* iii 22 and 26.   [107] See above, § 304.

had laid it down that 'the wise man will love[108].' We must, however, make a sharp distinction between love as the desire of sexual union, and the higher Love (ἐρωτικὴ ἀρετή) which is defined anew as 'an effort to make friends suggested by a beautiful object[109].' Upon this impulse, which is natural in the widest sense, is based friendship in the young, and the more lasting tie between husband and wife. By imposing self-restraint on the man, and inviting the woman to share the lessons of philosophy, the Stoics introduced a new relation between husband and wife based upon equality and comradeship[110]. A notable precedent was furnished by the Cynic community, when the witty and learned Hipparchia joined Crates in the life of the beggar-preacher[111]; and Roman Stoicism supplies us with numerous instances of the same companionship[112]. Under such conditions marriage is no longer a matter of free choice; it is a civic duty incumbent on the young Stoic. The Stoics of the Roman principate well perceived the danger that threatened the society in which they lived through the growing practice of celibacy[113].

350. The Stoic attitude towards marriage is well illustrated by the following extract from a discourse by Anti-
Of marriage. pater of Tarsus :

'A youth of good family and noble soul, who has a sense of social duty, will feel that no life and no household is complete without wife and child. He will also bear in mind his duty towards the State, for how can that be maintained unless, as the fathers decay and fall away like the leaves of a fine tree, the sons marry in the flower of their age, and leave behind them fresh shoots to adorn the city, thereby providing for its protection against its enemies? He will look upon marriage also as a duty towards the gods ; for if the family dies out, who will perform the accustomed sacrifices?

[108] Diog. L. vii 129; 'Stoici sapientem amaturum esse dicunt' Cic. *Tusc. disp.* iv 34, 72.

[109] ἐπιβολὴν φιλοποιίας διὰ κάλλος ἐμφαινόμενον Diog. L. vii 130; '[Stoici] amorem ipsum conatum amicitiae faciendae ex pulchritudinis specie definiunt' Cic. as above. The ἐπιβολή or *conatus* is a variety of the ὁρμή or *appetitio*, Hirzel p. 390.

[110] Not of course new in any absolute sense; in the country at least such relations must always have been common.

[111] Diog. L. vi 96–98.

[112] See above, § 300, and § 306, note 29; and below, §§ 431, 439, 444, and 446.

[113] 'in consensu vidui caelibatus nemo uxorem duxit, nisi qui abduxit' Sen. *Ben.*
i 9, 4.

Besides this he who knows nothing of wife and child has not tasted the truest joys of affection. For other friendships are like platefuls of beans or other like mixtures of juxtaposition, but the union of man and wife is like the mixing of wine and water, or any other case of penetration (κρᾶσις δι' ὅλων); for they are united not only by the ties of substance and soul and the dearest bond of children, but also in body. Other alliances are for occasion, this is bound up with the whole purpose of life, so that the parents on each side gladly allow that the wife should be first in her husband's affection, and the husband in his wife's.

But in these days of dissolution and anarchy all things change for the worse and marriage is thought a hard thing; and men call the celibate life divine because it gives opportunity for licentiousness and varied pleasures, and they bar the door against a wife as against an enemy. Others have their fancy taken by beauty or dowry, and no longer look for a wife who is piously brought up and obedient and a good manager; nor do they trouble to instruct their wives in these matters. But if a man would attend to the warnings of philosophers, of all burdens a lawful wife would be the lightest and sweetest. Such a man would have four eyes instead of two, and four hands instead of two, to supply all his needs: and if he desired leisure to write books or take part in politics, he could hand over the whole business of housekeeping to his partner[114].'

351. The four cardinal virtues, however widely they are interpreted, do not exhaust the field of daily duties.

Advantages sought.

All objects that are 'advantages' (προηγμένα) are *prima facie* such that the good man aims at securing them; although if sufficient reason appears, he will entirely forego them. The advantages of the soul, good natural disposition, 'art,' and 'progress' are discussed elsewhere in this chapter; as advantages of the body are reckoned life, health, strength, good digestion, good proportions, and beauty; whilst external advantages are wealth, reputation, noble birth, and the like[115]. In all the details there is a lack of exactitude and of agreement amongst the teachers. According to Seneca, men may reasonably wish for tallness[116], and there is a kind of beauty (not dependent on youth) of which women may be proud without blame[117]. Fine clothes make no one the better man, but a certain degree of

---

[114] Stob. iv 22, 25; and see further, §§ 406, 407.

[115] Diog. L. vii 106.

[116] 'non contemnet se sapiens, etiamsi fuerit minimae staturae; esse tamen se procerum volet' Sen. *Dial.* vii 22, 2.

[117] 'unicum tibi ornamentum pulcherrima et nulli obnoxia aetati forma' *ib.* xii 16, 4.

neatness and cleanliness in dress is an advantage[118]. For nobility
the Stoics have little regard; all men are derived through an
equal number of degrees from the same divine origin; virtue
is the true nobility[119]. Good name (δόξα, *gloria*) is commonly
reckoned amongst 'advantages'[120]; but Chrysippus and Diogenes
are said to have taught that a good man need not move a finger
for the sake of reputation, unless some advantage can be
obtained by it. Later teachers, influenced (as we are told) by
the criticisms of Carneades, made it absolutely plain that they
reckoned good name (apart from anything attainable by it) as
an advantage, and they even considered it natural that a man
should think of posthumous reputation[121]. The general feeling
of the school seems to be that the approval of others is too
uncertain to be a fitting aim; its place is taken by the approval
of 'conscience.' This term, which originally expressed the
burden of a guilty secret, became in the Roman period modified
in meaning, and could thus express the approval awarded to a
man by his inner and personal consciousness, even when all the
world disapproves his acts: this self-approval is closely akin to
peace of mind[122].

352. On no subject would it be easier to find apparently
contradictory views amongst Stoic writers than on
Wealth.
that of wealth. To decry wealth and praise poverty
is to some extent a commonplace with all the philosophical
schools; and with Seneca in particular this was so frequent a

[118] 'contra naturam est, faciles odisse munditias' Sen. *Ep.* 5, 4; 'non splendeat
toga, ne sordeat quidem' *ib.* 5, 3.
[119] 'unus omnium parens mundus est: ad hunc prima cuiusque origo perducitur'
Ben. iii 28, 2; '[philosophia] stemma non inspicit...animus facit nobilem' *Ep.* 44, 1
and 5.
[120] Diog. L. vii 106; Cic. *Fin.* iii 15, 51.
[121] 'de bona autem fama...Chrysippus quidem et Diogenes, detracta utilitate, ne
digitum quidem eius causa porrigendum esse dicebant. qui autem, post eos fuerunt,
cum Carneadem sustinere non possent, hanc quam dixi bonam famam propter se prae-
positam et sumendam esse dixerunt' *ib.* 17, 57. Cicero and Seneca were both keenly
sensitive to the judgment of posterity: 'paucis natus est, qui populum aetatis suae
cogitat: multa annorum milia, multa populorum supervenient: ad illa respice. etiamsi
omnibus tecum viventibus silentium livor indixerit, venient qui sine offensa sine gratia
iudicent' Sen. *Ep.* 79, 17.
[122] 'pacem demus animo, quam dabit...intenta mens ad unius honesti cupiditatem.
conscientiae satis fiat; nil in famam laboremus' *Dial.* v 41, 2.

practice[123] that his hearers found some inconsistency between his words and his deeds; for he was, as is well known, a rich man. But the position of the school is clear. 'Riches are not a good' is a Stoic paradox, emphasized in a hundred forms, and by every teacher[124]; but nevertheless they are an 'advantage,' and thus are rightly aimed at by the good man[125]. To the wealthy Stoics generally, and to the Romans of the republican period especially, the maintenance of the family property (*res familiaris*) was a duty of high importance; and the wasting of it in wholesale largess, a serious misdeed[126]. The Stoic view was sufficiently summed up in a proverb borrowed from Epicurus or one of his followers: 'he who feels the need of wealth least, can make the best use of it[127].' Although Panaetius did not write a special chapter on the acquisition and use of wealth[128], yet his views on the latter point are made sufficiently plain in his treatment of the virtue of Justice[129]. The justification of wealth lies in the intention to use it well, and this was a favourite subject with Hecato of Rhodes[130]. As to its acquisition and investment, Cicero is content to refer us to the high-principled men who conduct the financial affairs of the capital[131].

[123] 'multis ad philosophandum obstitere divitiae; paupertas expedita est, secura est' *Ep.* 17, 3; 'transeamus ad patrimonia, maximam humanarum aerumnarum materiam' *Dial.* ix 8, 1.

[124] 'Posidonius sic interrogandum ait: quae neque magnitudinem animo dant nec fiduciam nec securitatem, non sunt bona. divitiae autem...nihil horum faciunt; ergo non sunt [bonum]' *Ep.* 87, 35.

[125] 'divitias nego bonum esse; nam si essent, bonos facerent. ceterum et habendas esse et utiles et magna commoda vitae adferentis fateor' *Dial.* vii 24, 5; '[sapiens] non amat divitias, sed mavult. maiorem virtuti suae materiem subministrari vult' *ib.* 21, 4.

[126] 'largitio quae fit ex re familiari, fontem ipsum benignitatis exhaurit' Cic. *Off.* ii 15, 52; 'mentitur prodigus liberalem, cum plurimum intersit utrum quis dare sciat an servare nesciat' Sen. *Ep.* 120, 8.

[127] 'is maxime divitiis fruitur, qui minime divitiis indiget' *ib.* 14, 17.

[128] Cic. *Off.* ii 24, 86.   [129] See above, § 337.

[130] 'Hecatonem quidem Rhodium, discipulum Panaeti, video in iis libris, quos de Officiis scripsit Q. Tuberoni, dicere "sapientis esse, nihil contra mores leges instituta facientem, habere rationem rei familiaris. neque enim solum nobis divites esse volumus, sed liberis propinquis amicis, maximeque reipublicae. singulorum enim facultates et copiae divitiae sunt civitatis"' Cic. *Off.* iii 15, 63.

[131] 'toto hoc de genere, de quaerenda, de collocanda pecunia, commodius a quibusdam optimis viris, ad Ianum medium sedentibus, quam ab ullis philosophis ulla in schola disputatur' *ib.* ii 25, 90; and see further, § 408.

353. Amongst those popular terms which hold an ambiguous

Liberty.

place in the Stoic philosophy we must reckon 'liberty' (ἐλευθερία, *libertas*). In one sense liberty is a condition of soul such as characterizes the free-born citizen in contrast to the slave; this liberty differs but little from the virtue of Greatness of Soul already described[132], and in its full meaning is a good, which the wise man alone can possess[133]. But in another sense liberty is an external advantage, sometimes defined as 'the power of living as you wish[134],' and as such eagerly desired by the slave; more often perhaps it is conceived as 'the right of saying what you please[135].' In this sense liberty is equivalent to the παρρησία which was the watchword of the democracy of Athens, and was the equally cherished privilege of the nobility of Rome[136]; in a slightly different sense it was the boast of the Cynic missionary. The Stoics take a middle position; whilst all recognise that some sort of liberty is a precious privilege[137], and are prepared on occasion to sacrifice life or position for its sake[138], there are not wanting voices to remind us that it is unreasonable to speak out one's mind without regard to persons or circumstances[139], that the wrath of tyrants ought not lightly to be provoked[140], and that the most terrible of all oppressors is the soul that has lost its self-control[141].

354. Just as virtue chooses advantages in accordance with

Disadvan-
tages.

natural laws, so it refuses disadvantages in accordance with a disinclination (ἔκκλισις, *alienatio*),

[132] See above, § 342.
[133] τὴν μὲν κατ' ἀλήθειαν ἐλευθερίαν ἀγαθόν,...δι' ὃ δὴ καὶ τὸν σπουδαῖον εἶναι μόνον ἐλεύθερον Stob. ii 7, 11 i.
[134] 'quid est enim libertas? potestas vivendi ut velis' Cic. *Par.* 5, 34.
[135] 'asperitas agrestis | vult libertas dici mera' Hor. *Ep.* i 18, 6 and 8.
[136] Juv. *Sat.* i 151-153.
[137] 'non potest gratis constare libertas; hanc si magno aestimas, omnia parvo aestimanda sunt' Sen. *Ep.* 104, 34, where the reference is to 'libertas' in both senses.
[138] 'nec civis erat, qui libera posset | verba animi proferre, et vitam impendere vero' Juv. *Sat.* iv 90 and 91.
[139] οὐ γὰρ ἀεὶ καὶ πανταχοῦ καὶ πρὸς ὁντινοῦν λεκτέον ἃ φρονοῦμεν Muson. apud Stob. iii 40, 9 (Hense, p. 754, 6).
[140] 'sapiens nunquam potentium iras provocabit; immo declinabit, non aliter quam in navigando procellam' Sen. *Ep.* 14, 7.
[141] 'Can we abolish the acropolis that is in us, and cast out the tyrant within us, whom we have daily over us?' Epict. *Disc.* iv 1, 86.

which is equally natural and right so long as it is controlled by reason[142]. Since to every advantage there is opposed a corresponding disadvantage, to choose the one is necessarily to refuse the other; and the doctrine of 'reasonable refusal' is that of reasonable choice in its negative form. It will therefore be sufficient to give a formal statement of the theory. Disadvantages, or things that have negative value (ἀπαξία), may be subdivided according as they are disadvantages in themselves, as an ungainly figure; or as they bring about other disadvantages, as shortness of ready money; or for both reasons, as bad memory or ill-health[143]. They may also be subdivided into three classes, according as they affect the soul, the body, or things external. Disadvantages of the soul are such things as inborn vulgarity or dulness of wit; of the body, ill-health, and dulness of the organs of sensation; of external things, poverty, loss of children, and the contempt of our neighbours[144].

355. Since the virtues are permanent dispositions (διαθέσεις)

Healthy affections. of the soul, rooted in firm principles in which the wise man never wavers, but to which none else can attain, some other name is required to describe those more passing but yet wholesome moods which stand in contrast with the evil 'affections' or perturbations of the soul which will be discussed in our next chapter. A beginning is made in this direction with the three 'good affections' (εὐπάθειαι, constantiae, sapientis affectiones). Here a new use of terms is introduced. Strictly speaking an 'affection' is an evil state of soul; but as we have no corresponding word for a good and calm condition, the use of the word 'affection' is extended in this direction[145]. Each of these 'good affections' is introduced to us in contrast with a perturbation to which it bears a superficial resemblance. Thus contrasted with Fear is 'Caution' (εὐλάβεια, cautio), which is right avoidance, and is entirely consistent with Courage

---

[142] Χρύσιππός φησι μαίνεσθαι τοὺς...τὴν ἀπονίαν ἐν μηδενὶ ποιουμένους Plut. Sto. rep. 30, 2; 'in aliis satis esse causae [Stoici voluerunt] quamobrem quibusdam anteponerentur, ut...in doloris vacuitate' Cic. Fin. iii.15, 51.

[143] Stob. ii 7, 7 b; Cic. Fin. iii 17, 56.   [144] Stob. as above.

[145] For a similar change in the meaning of the word 'conscience' see above, § 351; the new use of this word as of the word 'affection' is that now commonly understood in ethical discussion.

rightly understood. Subdivisions of Caution are (i) 'Shame' (αἰδώς, *verecundia*), the avoidance of deserved blame, and (ii) 'Sanctity' (ἁγνεία), the avoidance of offences against the gods[146]. Contrasted with Greed is 'Readiness' (βούλησις, *voluntas*), the reasonable stretching out after future advantages[147]; contrasted with Hilarity is Joy (χαρά, *gaudium*), the reasonable appreciation of present advantages[148]. Both Readiness and Joy are entirely consistent with Soberness rightly understood. To the perturbation of Grief no good affection is named as bearing any resemblance; but we need not for that reason question but that the wise man may entertain some quiet form of sympathy for the troubles of others, and of regret for the blows which fortune deals to him in political disappointment or personal bereavement[149].

The 'good affections' are possessed by the wise man only[150]; but not all wise men possess them, nor any at all times[151]. On the other hand it is a daily duty to approximate to them, so that on this ground the good citizen enters into competition with the wise man on not altogether uneven terms[152]. The whole doctrine of 'good affections' may be conceived as an answer to those who accuse the Stoic of lack of feeling[153]; for the much derided 'apathy' of the school is substituted the doctrine of 'eupathy.' Wisdom is not to be compared to the surface of a frozen sea, but to that of a rippling river. The lectures of Musonius and Epictetus bring out on every point the meaning of 'eupathy' in its various applications.

[146] Diog. L. vii 116; 'declinatio [malorum] si cum ratione fiet, cautio appelletur, eaque intellegatur in solo esse sapiente' Cic. *Tusc. disp.* iv 6, 13.

[147] 'eiusmodi appetitionem Stoici βούλησιν appellant, nos appellamus voluntatem: quam sic definiunt—voluntas est, quae quid cum ratione desiderat' *ib.* 6, 12.

[148] 'cum ratione animus movetur placide atque constanter, tum illud gaudium dicitur' *ib.* 6, 13.

[149] See below, §§ 374, 379.

[150] 'scio gaudium nisi sapienti non contingere. est enim animi elatio suis bonis verisque fidentis' Sen. *Ep.* 59, 1 and 2; 'sola virtus praestat gaudium perpetuum' *ib.* 27, 3.

[151] χαρὰν δὲ καὶ εὐφροσύνην καὶ φρόνιμον περιπάτησιν [λέγουσιν] οὔτε πᾶσι τοῖς φρονίμοις ὑπάρχειν οὔτε ἀεί Stob. ii 7, 5 c.

[152] 'in huius gaudii possessione esse te volo' Sen. *Ep.* 23, 4.

[153] 'ἀναλγησία enim atque ἀπάθεια quorundam etiam ex eadem porticu prudentiorum hominum, sicut iudicio Panaetii, inprobata abiectaque est' A. Gellius *N. A.* xii 5, 10.

356. We have now sketched the Stoic system of daily duties
The ethical motive. in its main features, and this sketch will be made
more complete in many particulars in the course
of the next two chapters. To the modern reader the question
here suggests itself—what compelling force has this system?
what motive is supplied to the ordinary man for thus planning
out his life? To this question the ancient philosophers did
not directly address themselves; nevertheless their answers are
implied in their teaching as a whole. Thus the Stoics would
doubtless reply, first, that daily duties are prescribed to us by
reason[154]; not perhaps always by reason in its highest sense,
to which we must not appeal in every individual action, but at
least by the spirit of reasonableness (εὐλογιστία). Secondly,
that the common opinion of mankind, growing daily stronger,
recommends them; they are, as we have seen from the beginning, things that it comes in our way to do, that every good
citizen and good man will be sure to do. As to future rewards
and punishments, though these are not excluded by Stoicism,
they are certainly never pressed as motives for right living.
But the strongest of all motives is undoubtedly the mental
picture of the wise man, the vision of that which is 'absolutely
good.' Critics may urge: 'it is a picture that never has been
or will be realized in men's lives, a vision of that which is very
far off and which you will never see or touch.' This the Stoics
hardly care to deny, but the difficulty does not disturb them.
The vision attracts by its own beauty, the hope of attainment
is cherished by all but the worst[155]. We have spoken of the
'ordinary man,' or, as the Stoics put it, of 'us who are not wise
men.' But, strictly speaking, there is no room for the ordinary
man in the system, but only for the 'probationer' (προκόπτων,
proficiens). It remains for us to trace the upward path from daily
duty to virtue, along which every good man is endeavouring to
advance.

---

[154] τὸ λογικὸν ζῷον ἀκολουθητικὸν φύσει ἐστι τῷ λόγῳ καὶ κατὰ τὸν λόγον ὡς ἂν
ἡγεμόνα πρακτικόν Galen *plac. Hipp. et Plat.* iv 2, p. 368 K.
[155] 'negat [Zenon] Platonem, si sapiens non sit, eadem esse in causa, qua tyrannum
Dionysium. huic mori optimum esse propter desperationem sapientiae; illi propter
spem vivere' Cic. *Fin.* iv 20, 56.

357. The doctrine of progress (προκοπή, *progressio*) is not

Progress.
peculiar to Stoicism, but it is nevertheless an essential feature of it[156]. Critics may indeed dispute as to whether virtue has ever been in practice attained; but the Stoic must hold fast to the ethical principles that 'virtue can be taught[157]' and that 'virtue is an art[158].' Every man has from birth a capacity for acquiring virtue[159], which varies in degree according to his natural disposition of soul[160]; on this foundation every man builds by concurrent learning and practice[161]. The child is greatly helped if he possesses the trait of 'modesty' (αἰδώς, *verecundia*), which is essentially a readiness to defer to others and to learn from those who are older and wiser[162]; though later it may turn to 'false shame,' which is a hindrance[163]. He will then learn to understand and perform his daily duties; and as his character ripens, this performance will daily become easier and more pleasurable to him[164], more certain and more steady in itself. And now daily duties come near to Right Actions, which are indeed daily duties perfected (τέλειον καθῆκον, *perfectum officium*), and complete in every point[165]. In order to rise to this higher standard the good man must first perform his duty in all particulars[166]; he must do

---

[156] See above, §§ 289, 324.

[157] For the Socratic paradox 'virtue can be taught,' see above, § 46, also Diog. L. vii 91; 'nemo est casu bonus. discenda virtus est' Sen. *Ep.* 123, 16.

[158] Arnim iii 214.

[159] 'omnibus natura fundamenta dedit semenque virtutum' Sen. *Ep.* 108, 8.

[160] The emphasis occasionally laid on εὐφυΐα (*bona indoles*) reflects aristocratic and Platonic influences, see Pearson, pp. 205, 206; 'those who have a good natural disposition (οἱ εὐφυεῖς), even if you try to turn them aside, cling still more to reason' Epict. *Disc.* iii 6, 9.

[161] 'Modest actions preserve the modest man, and immodest actions destroy him; actions of fidelity preserve the faithful man, and the contrary actions destroy him' *ib.* ii 9, 11; 'What then is progress? if any of you, withdrawing himself from externals, turns to his own will (προαίρεσις) to exercise it and to improve it by labour' *ib.* i 4, 18.

[162] Cic. *de Off.* i 28, 99 (§ 343 above); 'verecundiam, bonum in adulescente signum' Sen. *Ep.* 11, 1.

[163] '[obstitit] verecundia, quae multorum profectus silentio pressit' *Dial.* vi 24, 2; cf. *Ep.* 40, 14.

[164] 'paulatim voluptati sunt quae necessitate coeperunt' *Dial.* i 4, 15.

[165] Stob. iii 7, 8, 8 a, and 11 a; Cic. *Off.* i 3, 8 and iii 3, 14.

[166] ὁ δ᾽ ἐπ᾽ ἄκρον, φησὶ [Χρύσιππος], προκόπτων ἅπαντα πάντως ἀποδίδωσι τὰ καθήκοντα καὶ οὐδὲν παραλείπει Stob. iv (Flor.) 103, 22 M (Arnim iii 510).

so with regularity and in harmony with the order of nature[167];
he will then need only a certain fixity, conviction, and stability
to pass into the ranks of the wise[168].

358. The stages of progress are variously expounded by
Stoic writers[169]; but on one principle all are agreed.
Conversion. Progress is not a half-way stage between vice and
virtue, as the Peripatetics teach[170]; it is a long preparation, to be
followed by a change sudden and complete (μεταβολή, *con-
versio*)[171]. The final step, by which a foolish man becomes in
an instant wise, is different in kind to all that have gone before.
This position is a necessary consequence of the doctrine that
'the good is not constituted by addition[172],' and is enforced by
various illustrations. The probationer is like a man who has
long been under water; little by little he rises to the surface,
but all in a moment he finds himself able to breathe. He is
like a puppy in whom the organ of sight has been for days
past developing; all at once he gains the power of vision[173].
Just so when progress reaches the end there dawns upon the
eyes of the soul the complete and dazzling vision of the good,
of which till now only shadows and reflections have been perceived. For a moment he is wise, but does not even yet realize

---

[167] 'primum est officium, ut se conservet in naturae statu; deinceps ut ea teneat,
quae secundum naturam sint;...deinde ea [selectio] perpetua; tum ad extremum constans consentaneaque naturae; in qua primum inesse incipit et intellegi, quid sit, quod
vere bonum possit dici' Cic. *Fin.* iii 6, 20.

[168] ἐπιγίγνεσθαι [τῷ προκόπτοντι] τὴν εὐδαιμονίαν ὅταν αἱ μέσαι πράξεις αὗται
προσλάβωσι τὸ βέβαιον καὶ ἑκτικὸν καὶ ἰδίαν πῆξίν τινα λάβωσι Stob. as above; 'illud,
quod ultimum venit, ut fidem tibi habeas et recta ire te via credas' Sen. *Dial.* ix 2, 2.
Epictetus uses the technical term ἀμεταπτωσία 'unchangeable firmness of mind'
Disc. iii 2, 8.

[169] See especially Seneca, *Epp.* 75 and 95.

[170] Diog. L. vii 127.

[171] τὴν δὲ μεταστροφὴν τὴν ἐπὶ τὰ θεῖα οἱ μὲν Στωϊκοὶ ἐκ μεταβολῆς φασὶ γίνεσθαι,
μεταβαλλούσης τῆς ψυχῆς εἰς σοφίαν Clem. Al. *Strom.* iv 6, 28 (Arnim iii 221).

[172] Cic. *Fin.* iii 14, 45; and see above, § 322.

[173] 'ut qui demersi sunt in aqua, nihilo magis respirare possunt, si non longe absunt
a summo, ut iam iamque possint emergere, quam si etiam tum essent in profundo; nec
catulus ille, qui iam appropinquat ut videat, plus cernit quam is qui modo est natus;
item, qui processit aliquantum ad virtutis aditum, nihilominus in miseria est, quam ille
qui nihil processit' Cic. *Fin.* iii 14, 48.

his own wisdom; then again in a moment he passes on to the complete fruition of happiness[174].

359. Thus from the lowlier conception of 'daily duties' we have again climbed upwards to the supreme ethical end, to absolute goodness, which is Virtue in her full royalty and the Universal Law (κοινὸς νόμος) as it appeals to the individual man. In this connexion the ideal is familiar in modern times under the name of Duty. The ancient Stoics perhaps never quite reached to any such complete formulation of their ethical theory in a single word; but their general meaning is perfectly expressed by it. Just as the Socratic paradoxes mark the quarrel of philosophy with outworn ideas expressed in conventional language, so its reconciliation with the general opinion is marked by those newly-coined terms such as 'conscience' and 'affection' which are now familiar household words. We cannot indeed demonstrate that 'Duty exists,' any more than we can that deity or providence exists; but we may well say that without it ethical discussion would in our own day be hardly possible. The following stanzas from Wordsworth's 'Ode to Duty,' based upon a Stoic text[175], may be a useful reminder, not only of the dominant position of this conception in modern thought, but also of the continued tendency of the human mind to express its supreme convictions in anthropomorphic language.

> 'Stern daughter of the Voice of God!
> O Duty! if that name thou love
> Who art a light to guide, a rod
> To check the erring, and reprove:
> Thou who art victory and law
> When empty terrors overawe:
> From vain temptations dost set free;
> And calm'st the weary strife of frail humanity!
>
> Stern Lawgiver! yet thou dost wear
> The Godhead's most benignant grace;

---

[174] As to the man who is 'wise without knowing it' (διαλεληθὼς σοφός) see Arnim iii 539 to 542, and Plut. *Sto. rep.* 19, 3 and 4.

[175] 'iam non consilio bonus, sed more eo perductus, ut non tantum recte facere posset, sed nisi recte facere non posset' Sen. *Ep.* 120, 10.

Nor know we anything so fair
As is the smile upon thy face:
Flowers laugh before thee on thy beds
And fragrance in thy footing treads:
Thou dost preserve the stars from wrong;
And the most ancient heavens, through thee, are fresh and strong.

'To humbler functions, awful Power!
I call thee: I myself commend
Unto thy guidance from this hour;
O let my weakness have an end!
Give unto me, made lowly wise,
The spirit of self-sacrifice;
The confidence of Reason give;
And in the light of truth thy Bondman let me live!'[176]

[176] Written in 1805.

CHAPTER XIV.

SIN AND WEAKNESS.

360. THE Stoic view of the universe is coloured by opti-
mism. All comes from God, all works towards
good. None the less the Stoic morals are stern.
Men in the mass are both foolish and wicked; they defy God's
will and thwart his purpose. The world is full of sin, and all
sins (to use the Socratic paradox) are equal. What then is sin?
It is a missing of the mark at which virtue aims (ἁμάρτημα); it
is a stumbling on the road (*peccatum*); it is a transgressing of
the boundary line[1]. It is the child of ignorance, the outward
expression of ill health of the soul. Everywhere and in every
man it weakens, hampers, and delays the work of virtue. It
cannot however finally triumph, for it is at war with itself.
The Persians were wrong when they conceived an Evil Power,
a concentration of all the powers of mischief in one personality.
This cannot be, for sin lacks essential unity. It destroys but
does not build; it scatters but it does not sow. It is an earth-
born giant, whose unwieldy limbs will in the end be prostrated
by a combatant, small to the outward view, but inspired with
divine forcefulness. If we understand what sin is, we shall see
its repulsiveness; if we learn how it spreads, we shall seek protection against its infecting poison; if we attack it in detail, in
individual men and in their daily acts, we shall in the end lay it
low. Philosophy then proceeds to arm itself for its task.

---

[1] 'est peccare tanquam transilire lineas' Cic. *Par.* iii 20.

361. Sin is ignorance; more accurately, it is that which appears to be knowledge, but is not knowledge;

The four sin-ful conditions are errors. it is false judgment. If we follow the process by which knowledge is attained, we find that there is no error in the mind-picture (*visum*), whether it is sensory or partly sensory and partly rational; this is an adumbration automatically presented to the mind. But 'assent is in our power'; it is both an intellectual and a moral act. A too hasty assent to that which appears to be but is not is both an error and an offence; and most particularly so when it lies in the application of the general conceptions (προλήψεις) of 'good' and 'evil' to particular cases[2]. In this way we quickly reach four sinful conditions, which come about by mistaking things indifferent, that is, advantages and disadvantages, for things good or evil. These are:

(i) Fear (φόβος, *metus*), in which a future disadvantage is mistaken for a future evil;

(ii) Greed (ἐπιθυμία, *libido*), in which a future advantage is mistaken for a future good;

(iii) Grief (λύπη, *aegritudo*), in which a present disadvantage is mistaken for a present evil;

(iv) Hilarity (ἡδονή, *laetitia*), in which a present advantage is mistaken for a present good[3].

In the case of the last two evils the title presents difficulty in all languages; thus for Grief we might substitute any term such as Discontent, Vexation, Worry or Fretfulness; it is a lack of Courage in bearing pain or disappointment. Again for Hilarity we might substitute Elation, Exaltation, Excitement: it is a lack of Soberness in the moment of pleasure.

---

[2] 'Who among us does not speak of good and bad, of useful and not useful?... Adapt the preconception properly to the particular things' Epict. *Disc.* ii 17, 10 and 11.

[3] 'omnes [hae perturbationes] sunt genere quattuor, partibus plures; aegritudo, formido, libido, quamque Stoici communi nomine corporis et animi ἡδονήν appellant, ego malo laetitiam appellare, quasi gestientis animi elationem voluptariam' Cic. *Fin.* iii 10, 35; 'est igitur aegritudo opinio recens mali praesentis,...laetitia opinio recens boni praesentis;...metus opinio impendentis mali,...libido opinio venturi boni' *Tusc. disp.* iv 7, 14; 'hinc metuunt cupiuntque, dolent gaudentque' Verg. *Aen.* vi 733. See also Diog. L. vii 110 and Stob. ii 7, 10 b.

362. From another point of view all sin is due to a lack of
moral force, a want of tone in the moral sinews, an
unhealthy condition of the soul[4]. Ultimately this
point of view agrees with that just described : for it is the lack
of health and strength which leads to hasty and ill-judged
assent[5]. But for practical purposes we may use this distinction
to lead up to a difference of grade. Thus we may associate
ignorance with that rooted perversity of mind which is the
exact opposite of virtue, and which is therefore in the strictest
sense 'vice' (κακία, vitium)[5]; and want of tone with a passing
condition which we cannot deny to be an evil, but may
nevertheless describe by the gentler terms 'perturbation' and
'affection[6].' Such an evil is a disturbance of the soul's calm,
an 'infection' of its health. It may exist in three grades to
be hereafter described, as a 'ruffling,' a 'disturbance,' a 'disease';
and in both the latter forms it must be rooted out, for in both
grades it is an evil, and in the last it is a vice which threatens
to poison the man's whole nature. Hence we reach the Stoic
paradox that 'the affections must be extirpated[7].' But although
this is our only ethical standard, we are not debarred from
suggesting remedies which may alleviate the malady in particular
persons and under special circumstances.

They are also maladies. (margin note)

[4] Χρύσιππος ἀποδεικνύναι πειρᾶται, κρίσεις κενὰς εἶναι τοῦ λογιστικοῦ τὰ πάθη, Ζήνων δὲ οὐ τὰς κρίσεις αὐτάς, ἀλλὰ τὰς ἐπιγιγνομένας αὐταῖς συστολὰς καὶ χύσεις, ἐπάρσεις τε καὶ πτώσεις τῆς ψυχῆς ἐνόμιζεν εἶναι τὰ πάθη Galen *Hipp. et Plat.* v 1, p. 429 K; cf. *ib.* iv p. 387 K (Arnim i 461).

[5] In this sense there are four vices, each the precise opposite of one of the virtues; they are ἀφροσύνη (*insipientia*), ἀδικία (*iniustitia*), δειλία (*ignavia*) and ἀκολασία (*intemperantia*); and each of these is rooted in a fixed perverse judgment, so that he who has one vice has all (Stob. ii 7, 11 k, p. 106, 7 Wachsmuth).

[6] This view is summed up in the phrase that 'the perturbations are κακά, but not κακίαι' (Stob. ii 7, 5 b), which accords with the principle that only vice and what is akin to vice is evil. The Roman writers realized the difficulty in the use of words: 'morbi autem et aegrotationes partes sunt vitiositatis; sed perturbationes sintne eiusdem partes quaestio est. vitia enim adfectiones sunt manentes, perturbationes autem moventes, ut non possint adfectionum manentium partes esse' Cic. *Tusc. disp.* iv 13, 29 and 30.

[7] 'utrum satius sit modicos habere adfectus an nullos, saepe quaesitum est; nostri illos expellunt, Peripatetici temperant' Sen. *Ep.* 116, 1; 'vacandum omni est animi perturbatione, tum cupiditate et metu, tum etiam aegritudine et voluptate nimia et iracundia' Cic. *Off.* i 20, 69; 'contra adfectus impetu, non subtilitate pugnandum est' Sen. *Dial.* x 10, 1.

363. The evil of Fear (φόβος, *formido, metus*) is practically

opposed to the virtue of Courage. Here philosophy

Fear. builds upon the foundations of common opinion,

and its task is the easier. The youth who is brought up not

to regard suffering, poverty, exile, or death as evils, will never

be afraid. Since it is death that most alarms mankind by its

grim aspect, he who can face this giant without trembling will

not know fear, or at the most will only feel a slight ruffling of

the soul. In asserting that 'fear should be rooted out' the

Stoics cross no general sentiment; the tradition of the heroic

age is the same.

364. The treatment of Greed (ἐπιθυμία, *libido*) is similar.

This fault is opposed to the Soberness with which

Greed. men should aim at advantages; and when we have

determined the standard of Soberness every transgression of it

reveals Greed. But under this heading the Stoics include the

vices of Anger[8] and Cruelty, for which the heroic age had no

condemnation. In regard to the former they come into conflict

with the Peripatetics also, who maintain that Anger serves useful

ends, and should be controlled, not extirpated[9]. The considera-

tion of this condition of mind will therefore bring out the

divergence between the two schools.

365. The Peripatetics assign Anger to the passionate part

of the soul (τὸ ἐπιθυμητικόν); they admit that it

Anger. needs to be restrained by reason, but hold that

within proper limits it is both natural and necessary. In war

it is essential to heroic action; he who is filled with it despises

danger, and rushes on to great achievements[10]. It is no less

necessary in peace, in order that the wicked may not go un-

punished[11]. Aristotle says compendiously that 'anger is the

---

[8] ὀργὴ μὲν οὖν ἐστιν ἐπιθυμία τοῦ τιμωρήσασθαι τὸν δοκοῦντα ἠδικηκέναι Stob.
ii 7, 10 c; ὑπὸ τὴν ἐπιθυμίαν ὑπάγεται ὀργή *ib.* 10 b.

[9] Here Panaetius is faithful to the Stoic view: 'ira procul absit, cum qua nihil
recte fieri, nihil considerate potest' Cic. *Off.* i 38, 136.

[10] '[ira] extollit animos et incitat; nec quicquam sine illa magnificum in bello
fortitudo gerit' Sen. *Dial.* iii 7, 1.

[11] '"non potest" inquit "fieri" Theophrastus, "ut non vir bonus irascatur malis"'
ib. 14, 1; '"quid ergo?" inquit "vir bonus non irascitur, si caedi patrem suum viderit,
si rapi matrem?"' *ib.* 12, 1.

spur of virtue[12],' the armour of the man of high soul. To this point of view the Stoics are opposed alike on the ground of principle and of experience. We do not need disease as a means to health[13], or armour which sways instead of being swayed[14]. A good man will face danger unmoved, from the sense of duty; and will face it more firmly and more perseveringly than he whose passions are excited[15]. He will punish wrong-doers either for their amendment or for the protection of others, without being angry with them[16]. Fabius the Delayer conquered his own spirit before he overcame Hannibal[17]; and the very gladiators strike, not when their feelings move them, but when the opportunity has come[18].

366. Anger is technically defined as 'the greedy desire of

Degrees of anger;

avenging an injury,' or (more precisely) as 'the greedy desire to punish one whom you deem to have injured you unjustly[19].' That it is a temporary madness has always been held by the wise[20]; and this is indicated by the appearance of the angry, the threatening look, the heightened colour, the gnashing teeth, the stamp of the foot[21]; also by the fact that children are specially prone to anger, even for frivolous causes[22], and that anger is often directed against harmless persons or objects[23]. Nevertheless anger does not consist of a merely

[12] 'stat Aristoteles (fr. 80 Rose) defensor irae et vetat illam nobis exsecari; calcar ait esse virtutis' Sen. *Dial.* v 3, 1.

[13] 'abominandum remedii genus est sanitatem debere morbo' *ib.* iii 12, 6.

[14] 'haec arma quae Aristoteles virtuti dat, ipsa per se pugnant, non expectant manum, et habent non habentur' *ib.* 17, 1.

[15] 'adfectus cito cadit, aequalis est ratio' *ib.* 17, 5.

[16] 'corrigendus est qui peccat meliorque faciendus, non sine castigatione, sed sine ira' *ib.* 15, 1.

[17] '[Fabius] iram ante vicit quam Hannibalem' *ib.* 11, 5.

[18] 'nec [athletae] cum ira suadet, feriunt, sed cum occasio...ira enim perturbat artem' *ib.* iv 14, 2 and 3.

[19] ὀργὴ μὲν οὖν ἐστιν ἐπιθυμία [τοῦ] τιμωρήσασθαι τὸν δοκοῦντα ἠδικηκέναι παρὰ τὸ προσῆκον Stob. ii 7, 10 c; 'ira est cupiditas ulciscendae iniuriae, aut, ut ait Posidonius, cupiditas puniendi eius, a quo te inique putes laesum' Sen. *Dial.* iii 2, 4.

[20] 'ira furor brevis est' Hor. *Ep.* i 2, 62; 'quidam ex sapientibus viris iram dixerunt brevem insaniam' Sen. *Dial.* iii 1, 2.

[21] *ib.* 4.

[22] 'non pietas iram, sed infirmitas movet, sicut pueris, qui tam parentibus amissis flebunt quam nucibus' *ib.* 12, 4.

[23] 'nec in ea tantum, quae destinavit, sed in occurrentia obiter furit' *ib.* v 1, 3.

instinctive feeling, but implies the assent of the will[24]; so that
we can always trace the three stages, first the appearance of
an injury done (*species oblata iniuriae*), secondly the assent
(*animus adsentit atque adprobat*), thirdly the outbreak of anger

remedies   (*sequitur ira*)[25]. To check anger the first necessity
for it.   is time[26]: reflection will often show us that we have
not been injured at all, or not so much as we supposed[27]. Then
it is well to put ourselves in the place of the offender, and try to
look at the offence from his point of view[28]. Where anger has
become a disease (*iracundia*), more violent remedies must be used;
some have been cured by looking at themselves in a mirror[29];
others must apply the 'contrary twist[30],' and learn when struck
to turn quietly away[31].

367. Anger is an evil that has many varieties, and the pre-

Variations   cisians exercise their ingenuity in distinguishing the
of anger.   bitter-humoured (*amarus*), the fiery (*stomachosus*),
the fierce (*rabiosus*), the man who is hard to get on with (*difficilis*), and many other shades of character. But one variety
deserves special notice, because the evil disposition exists though
its expression is checked. The angry man of this type does not
allow himself to go beyond complaint and criticism, but he nurses
his feeling in the depths of his heart[32]. He would on no account
express himself in loud outcries, but his displeasure is easily
excited and persistent. This evil we call moroseness; it is a

---

[24] 'nobis placet nihil [iram] per se audere, sed animo adprobante' *ib.* iv 1, 4;
'nunquam impetus sine adsensu animi est' *ib.* 3, 4.

[25] *ib.* 3–5.

[26] 'maximum remedium irae mora est' *ib.* 29, 1; 'Keep quiet, and count the days
on which you have not been angry' Epict. *Disc.* ii 18, 12.

[27] 'pleraque eorum, propter quae irascimur, offendunt nos magis quam laedunt'
Sen. *Dial.* v 28, 4; 'contempt is that which putteth an edge upon anger, as much
or more than the hurt itself' Bacon, *Essay* 57.

[28] 'eo nos loco constituamus, quo ille est cui irascimur' Sen. *Dial.* 12, 3.

[29] 'quibusdam, ut ait Sextius, iratis profuit adspexisse speculum' *ib.* iv 36, 1.

[30] See below, § 403.

[31] 'percussit te: recede. referendo enim et occasionem saepius feriendi dabis et
excusationem' *ib.* 34, 5.

[32] 'quaedam [irae] ultra querelas et adversationes non exeunt. quaedam altae
gravesque sunt et introrsus versae' *ib.* iii 4, 3.

feeling characteristic of a decadent society[33], and (like all other kinds of anger) it calls for unsparing repression.

368. Cruelty, a tendency to excess in punishment[34], is an evil constantly attendant upon the possession of power,

Cruelty.

and directly opposed to the virtue of clemency. Roman history has exhibited many examples of it, beginning with Sulla who ordered seven thousand Roman citizens to be slain on one day[35], continuing with the many masters who are hated for cruelty to their slaves[36]. It cuts at the root of the ties of humanity and degrades man to the level of the beast[37]; in its extreme form it becomes a madness, when the slaying of a man is in itself a pleasure[38]. As a remedy for cruelty in its milder forms it is well to consider the true objects of punishment; first, to reform the offender; secondly, to make others better by a warning; thirdly, to give a sense of safety to the community by removing offenders[39]. All these objects are better effected if punishment is moderate and rare, and appears to be awarded with reluctance. When cruelty has become a disease it is necessary to remind the tyrant that his manner of life is a pitiable one[40], and that a complete cure can be worked by putting him to death[41].

369. In reckoning Grief in its countless varieties as an evil the Stoics did not altogether run counter to public

Grief.

opinion. In the heroic age grief was indeed not forbidden, but it was sharply limited; women might grieve, men

---

[33] 'inter hos morosum ponas licet, delicatum iracundiae genus. quaedam enim sunt irae, quae intra clamorem concidant, quaedam non minus pertinaces quam frequentes' Sen. *Dial.* 2 and 3.

[34] Defined as 'atrocitas animi in exigendis poenis' or 'inclinatio animi ad asperiora' Sen. *Clem.* ii 4, 1 and 3.

[35] *ib.* i 12, 1.

[36] 'domini crudeles tota civitate commonstrantur invisique et detestabiles sunt' *ib.* 18, 3.

[37] 'ferina ista rabies est sanguine gaudere et vulneribus' *ib.* 24, 3.

[38] 'tunc ille dirus animi morbus ad insaniam pervenit ultimam, cum crudelitas versa est in voluptatem et iam occidere hominem iuvat' *ib.* 25, 3.

[39] *ib.* 22, 1.

[40] 'puta tutam esse crudelitatem; quale eius regnum est?' *ib.* 26, 2.

[41] 'optimum est abire ei, qui ad se nunquam rediturus est' *Ben.* vii 20, 3.

should remember. But in prescribing the total extinction of this state of mind the Stoics appeared to pass the bounds of human nature; public feeling revolted against what seemed impossible of attainment. Our position to-day is not greatly altered; but we may notice that whereas in ordinary social life Grief is not only tolerated but approved, yet in battle, earthquake, flood, and pestilence our ideal of the hero is one which almost entirely excludes the indulgence of this emotion.

Grief takes many forms, as Fretfulness, Disappointment, Restlessness, Pity, and Mourning; we proceed to examine them in order.

370. The simplest form of Grief is fretfulness under bodily pain, the effect of depression of the soul and contraction of its sinews[42]. In all ages and under all philosophies the capacity of bearing pain without flinching is the primary test of virtue; and in the Cynic and Stoic schools alike the dogma 'pain is no evil' is of critical importance. In this matter correct doctrine needs to be strengthened by life-long discipline; but it is not required by Stoic principles that general principles should be forced upon the acceptance of individual sufferers. Panaetius therefore acted quite correctly when, in writing to Quintus Tubero on the subject of the endurance of pain, he abstained from pressing the usual paradox[43]. But all who see this trial awaiting them will do well to consider how much hardship men willingly endure for evil purposes, such as those of lust, money-making, or glory. Cocks and quails will fight to the death for victory: jugglers will risk their lives swallowing swords, walking on tight ropes, or flying like birds, when in each case a slip means death[44]. If we compose our minds long before to meet suffering, we shall have more courage when the time comes[45].

Fretfulness.

---

[42] λύπην δ' εἶναι συστολὴν ψυχῆς ἀπειθῆ λόγῳ Stob. ii 7, 10 b; 'est aegritudo opinio recens mali praesentis, in quo demitti contrahique animo rectum esse videatur' Cic. *Tusc. disp.* iv 7, 14.

[43] See above, § 114.

[44] Muson. ap. Stob. iii 29, 75.

[45] 'nemo non fortius ad id, cui se diu composuerat, accessit et duris quoque, si praemeditata erant, obstitit' Sen. *Ep.* 107, 4; and see further, § 339.

371.   Still more effective is active training[46]. Happy was the
Discipline of pain.   Spartan youth who came to Cleanthes to ask him whether pain was not a good; his education had
taught him that this was a more practical question than that
other, whether pain is an evil[47]. Recruits cry out at the slightest
wound, and are more afraid of the surgeon's touch than of the
sword; on the other hand veterans watch the life-blood draining
away without a sigh[48]. Some men groan at a box on the ear,
whilst others smile under the scourge[49]. Inexperience therefore
is the chief cause for weakness under pain; familiarity with it
brings strength[50].

372.   The Grief that gives way to pain of mind has very
Disappointed ambition.   various forms; but that which is due to disappointed ambition is perhaps the most typical.
Even men who had overcome the fear of death were known to
shudder at the bitterness of soul (*aegritudo animi*) which accompanies defeat in a contested election (*repulsa*) in a republic, or
displacement from the favour of the powerful under a monarchy[51].
For this malady the complete remedy is found in the paradox
that 'the wise man is king,' that virtue can never be unseated
from the curule chair[52]; temporary alleviations may be found,
even by philosophers, in biting sarcasms aimed at the incapacity
of one's fellow-citizens[53]. It may be in the abstract the duty of

[46] 'id in quoque solidissimum est quod exercuit. ad contemnendam malorum
potentiam animus patientia pervenit' Sen. *Dial.* i 4, 13.

[47] Stob. ii 31, 125 (Wachsmuth, p. 242, 30). The point is however complicated
by the ambiguity of the Greek word πόνος, which corresponds equally to *dolor* and
labor in Latin; see Cic. *Tusc. disp.* ii 15, 35.

[48] 'tirones leviter saucii tamen vociferantur et manus medicorum magis quam
ferrum horrent; at veterani, quamvis confossi, patienter ac sine gemitu velut aliena
corpora exsaniari patiuntur' *ib.* xii 3, 1.

[49] 'scio alios inter flagella ridere, alios gemere sub colapho' *Ep.* 13, 5.

[50] 'magna autem pars apud imperitos mali novitas; hoc ut scias, ea quae putaverant aspera, fortius, cum adsuevere, patiuntur' *ib.* 76, 34.

[51] 'quae maxima credis | esse mala, exiguum censum turpemque repulsam' Hor.
Ep. i 1, 43.

[52] 'virtus, repulsae nescia sordidae, | intaminatis fulget honoribus; | nec sumit aut
ponit secures | arbitrio popularis aurae' Hor. *C.* iii 2, 17–20.

[53] 'Chrysippus, when asked why he took no part in politics, replied: "because, if
a man is a bad politician, he is hateful to the gods; if a good politician, to his fellow-citizens' Stob. iv 4, 29.

a good man to take part in politics; but experience shows that the State has yet to be discovered which can tolerate a sage, or which a sage can tolerate[54]: Hence we find even Stoic teachers relapsing into practical Epicureanism, and bidding their followers to let the community go hang, and to reserve their energies for some nobler occupation[55]. To these lapses from sound principle we need not attach any serious importance; the individual Stoic did not always live up to his creed.

373. Restlessness is grief of mind without known cause; the unquiet soul rushes hither and thither, vainly seeking to be free from its own company[56]. The lesson that Horace had pressed a century earlier, that disquiet can only be cured by quiet, has not been learnt[57]. In Homer Achilles tosses on his bed in fever, lying first on his face, then on his back, never long at rest in any position; and so to-day our wealthy man first travels to luxurious Campania, then to the primitive district of the Bruttii; north and south are tried in turn, and alike disapproved, whilst after all the fault is not in the place, but in the man[58]. In this temper men come to hate leisure and complain that they have nothing to do[59]. This folly reaches an extreme when men trust themselves to the sea, take the chance of death without burial, and place themselves in positions in which human skill may avail nothing[60]. It even leads to great political disasters, as when Xerxes attacks Greece because he is weary of Asia, and Alexander invades India because the known world is too small for him[61]. The times will

Restlessness.

[54] 'si percensere singulas [res publicas] voluero, nullam inveniam, quae sapientem aut quam sapiens pati possit' Sen. *Dial.* viii 8, 3.

[55] 'si potes, subduc te istis occupationibus; si minus, eripe' *Ep.* 19, 1.

[56] 'mobilis et inquieta homini mens data est. nunquam se tenet, vaga et quietis impatiens, et novitate rerum laetissima' *ib.* xii 6, 6.

[57] 'ratio et prudentia curas | ...aufert; | caelum non animum mutant, qui trans mare currunt' Hor. *Ep.* i 11, 25-27.

[58] Sen. *Dial.* ix 12-15.

[59] 'inde ille adfectus otium suum detestantium querentiumque nihil ipsos habere quod agant' *ib.* 2, 10.

[60] 'incertam fortunam experimur, vim tempestatum nulla humana ope superabilem, mortem sine spe sepulturae. non erat tanti' *N. Q.* v 18, 6 and 7; 'non eadem est his et illis causa solvendi, sed iusta nulli' *ib.* 16; 'quid non potest mihi suaderi, cui persuasum est ut navigarem?' *Ep.* 53, 1.

[61] *N. Q.* v 18, 10.

come, when men will seek novelty by travelling through the air or under the sea; they will force their way through the cold of the poles and the damp heat of the forests of Africa. The remedy lies either in humbler submission to the will of the deity, or in a sense of humour which sees the absurdity of taking so much trouble for so little advantage[62].

374. Pity is that weakness of a feeble mind, which causes it to collapse at the sight of another man's troubles[63], wrongly believing them to be evils. Pity looks at the result, not at the cause, and it is most keenly felt by women of all ages, who are distressed by the tears even of the most abandoned criminals, and would gladly burst open the doors of the gaols to release them[64]. The cause of pity lies in a too rapid assent; we are caught napping by every sight that strikes on our senses. If we see a man weeping, we say 'he is undone': if we see a poor man, we say 'he is wretched; he has nothing to eat[65].' Now we Stoics have a bad name, as though we recommended to governors a system of harsh punishments[66]; but, on the contrary, none value more highly than we the royal virtue of clemency[67]. Only let it be considered that a wise man must keep a calm and untroubled mind, if only that he may be ready to give prompt help to those who need it; a saving hand to the shipwrecked, shelter to the exile, the dead body of her son to a mother's tears. The wise man will not pity, but help[68].

Pity.

375. Nearly akin to the evil of pity is that sensitiveness to the sufferings of others which leads men, contrary to reason, to turn the other way and avoid the

Sensibility.

[62] 'magis ridebis, cum cogitaveris vitae parari, in quae vita consumitur' Sen. *N. Q.* 16.

[63] 'misericordiam [boni viri] vitabunt; est enim vitium pusilli animi, ad speciem alienorum malorum succidentis' *Clem.* ii 5, 1.

[64] 'anus et mulierculae sunt, quae lacrimis nocentissimorum moventur, quae, si liceret, carcerem effringerent' *ib.*

[65] Epict. *Disc.* iii 3, 17.

[66] 'cum dicas esse pares res | furta latrociniis, et magnis parva mineris | falce recisurum simili te, si tibi regnum | permittant homines' Hor. *Sat.* i 3, 121–124; 'scio male audire apud imperitos sectam Stoicorum tanquam nimis duram et minime principibus regibusque bonum daturam consilium...sed nulla secta benignior leniorque est' Sen. *Clem.* ii 5, 2 and 3.

[67] See below, § 409.

[68] 'non miserebitur sapiens, sed succurret' Sen. *Clem.* ii 6, 3.

sight of them. Of this weakness Epictetus gives us a lively picture :

'When he was visited by one of the magistrates, Epictetus inquired of him about several particulars, and asked if he had children and a wife. The man replied that he had ; and Epictetus inquired further, how he felt under the circumstances. 'Miserable,' the man said. Then Epictetus asked ' In what respect? For men do not marry and beget children in order to be wretched, but rather to be happy.' 'But I,' the man replied, 'am so wretched about my children that lately, when my little daughter was sick and was supposed to be in danger, I could not endure to stay with her, but I left home till a person sent me news that she had reco- vered.' 'Well then,' said Epictetus, 'do you think that you acted right?' 'I acted naturally,' the man replied; 'this is the case with all or at least most fathers.' 'Let us be careful,' said Epictetus, 'to learn rightly the criterion of things according to nature. Does affection to those of your family appear to you to be according to nature and to be good?' 'Cer- tainly.' 'Is then that which is consistent with reason in contradiction with affection?' 'I think not.' 'Well then, to leave your sick child and to go away is not reasonable, and I suppose that you will not say that it is ; but it remains to inquire if it is consistent with affection.' 'Yes, let us consider.' 'Has the mother no affection for her child?' 'Certainly she has.' 'Ought then the mother to have left her, or ought she not?' 'She ought not.' 'And the nurse, does she love her?' 'She does.' 'Ought then she also to have left her?' 'By no means.' 'But if this is so, it results that your behaviour was not at all an affectionate act[69].''

Seneca draws for us the same picture of sentimental neglect of duty. ' Of our luxurious rich,' he says, 'no one sits by the side of his dying friend, no one watches the death of his own father, or joins in the last act of respect to the remains of any member of his family[70].'

376. Another form of the evil of Grief is that of undue sensitiveness to criticism and abuse. This mental weakness is illustrated by the case of Fidus Cor-
Sensitiveness.
nelius, who burst into tears because some one in the senate called him a 'plucked ostrich'; and in an earlier period Chry- sippus had been acquainted with a man who lost his temper merely because he was called a 'sea-calf[71].' Others are annoyed

[69] Epict. *Disc.* i 11.
[70] 'ex his nemo morienti amico adsidet, nemo videre mortem patris sui sustinet. quotusquisque funus domesticum ad rogum sequitur? fratrum propinquorumque extrema hora deseritur' Sen. *N. Q.* iii 18, 6.
[71] *Dial.* ii 17, 1.

by seeing their eccentricities imitated, or by reference to their poverty or old age. The remedy for all these things is humour; no one can be laughed at who turns the laugh against himself[72]. Another is to cease thinking about oneself[73].

377. The hardest to bear of all distresses is the loss of friends by death, and most particularly, the loss by parents of their children. To meet this trouble a special class of literature, called *consolationes*, grew up, not confined to any one school of philosophers. The treatise of Crantor the Academic was famous in Cicero's time[74]; and in the letter of Servius Sulpicius to Cicero upon his daughter's death we have an admirable example of the 'consolation' in private correspondence[75]. Sulpicius bids Cicero think of all the grief and trouble in the world, the loss of political liberty at Rome, the destruction of so many famous cities of antiquity, until he feels that man is born to sorrow, and that his own loss is but a drop in the ocean of the world's suffering. He also calls on the mourner to think of his own character, and to set an example of firmness to his household[76]. Cicero found his real comfort in none of these things, but in industrious authorship. We have unfortunately no example of a 'Consolation' by Musonius. Seneca has left us two treatises in this style, one a formal document addressed to the minister Polybius on the death of his brother, the other a more personal appeal to Marcia, a lady of an 'old Roman' family, on the death of a son. Besides the arguments already used by Sulpicius[77], he recommends to

Mourning.

---

[72] '[Vatinius] in pedes suos ipse plurima dicebat et in fauces concisas. sic inimicorum et in primis Ciceronis urbanitatem effugerat' Sen. *Dial.* ii 17, 3; ' nemo risum praebuit qui ex se cepit' *ib.* 2.

[73] 'cum primum te observare desieris, imago ista tristitiae discedet' *Ep.* 63, 3.

[74] Cicero wrote a treatise 'de Consolatione' based on this work, but only a few fragments remain. Plutarch's 'Consolation' for Apollonius was drawn from the same source (Schmekel, p. 150).

[75] Cic. *Fam.* iv 5.

[76] 'denique noli te oblivisci Ciceronem esse, et eum qui aliis consueris praecipere et dare consilium' *ib.* 5, 5.

[77] 'maximum ergo solatium est cogitare id sibi accidisse, quod ante se passi sunt omnes omnesque passuri' Sen. *Dial.* xi i, 4. On the other side 'malevoli solatii est turba miserorum' *ib.* vi 12, 5; '[cogita] fratribus te tuis exemplo esse debere' *ib.* xi 5, 4.

Polybius attention to the public service and the reading of Homer and Virgil[78]. Both to him and to Marcia he pictures the happiness of the soul now admitted to the company of the blest[79], or at any rate at peace and freed from all the pains of life[80]. In writing to Marcia he recalls with effect the examples of Octavia the sister, and Livia the wife of Augustus, each of whom lost a promising son in early manhood. Octavia gave herself up to her grief, never allowed her dead son to be mentioned in her presence, and wore mourning to the day of her death, though she was surrounded by her children and grandchildren. Livia, after paying the last tokens of respect, laid aside her grief, recalled with pleasure her son's achievements, and (advised so to act by her philosopher Areius) devoted herself to her social duties, refusing to make all Rome sad because one mother had lost a son[81].

378. The consolations of Epictetus include less philosophical speculation, and more religious resignation. To

Resignation.

begin with, preparation should be made for the loss of children. Parental affection should not pass the bounds of reason; every time that a father embraces his child, he should reflect 'this child is only lent to me,' 'this child is mortal[82].' If the child dies, his first thought should be 'he who has given takes away[83].' To others he will say 'I have restored the child[84].' His abiding mood will be that of resignation to the divine will. He will realize that in the course of a long life many and various things must happen; and that it is impossible to live to old age, without seeing the death of many whom we love[85].

---

[78] *ib.* 8, 2.   [79] *ib.* 9, 3; 'inter felices currit animas' *ib.* vi 5, 1.

[80] *ib.* xi 9, 4; 'excepit illum magna et aeterna pax' *ib.* vi 19, 6. See also above, §§ 298, 299.

[81] Sen. *Dial.* vi 3 to 5; above, § 123.

[82] 'If you are kissing your wife or child, say that it is a human being whom you are kissing; for when the wife or child dies, you will not be disturbed' Epict. *Manual* 3 (after Anaxagoras).

[83] *Disc.* iv 1, 101.

[84] 'Never say about anything, I have lost it, but say, I have restored it. Is your child dead? It has been restored. Is your wife dead? She has been restored' *Manual* 11.

[85] *Disc.* iii 24, 27.

379. All 'consolations' aim at diminishing the grief of
mourners, nature being inclined rather to excess
Comfort. than to defect in this matter. But the Stoics could
not altogether avoid the direct issue whether or not grief is a sin,
and weeping a weakness. The plain teaching of the school was
that 'death is no evil,' and therefore that grief for the dead is
against reason. And to this view the teachers give from time
to time formal adhesion, as being the better cause[86]. But in
individual cases they find that to a certain extent there is not
only excuse, but justification, for grief and tears; and thus they
come into touch with the common feelings of humanity[87], whilst
the plea of 'natural necessity' serves to ward off the criticism
of sterner philosophers[88]. From this concession emerges in the
Roman period the definite precept of a time-limit for grief[89];
and its undue continuance is sternly denounced as due to love
of ostentation[90], and the morbid enjoyment of sorrow by an ill-
balanced mind[91]. Grief in this shape is a dangerous disease;
there must be no trifling with it, but it must be totally destroyed[92].

380. Lastly, we include under the heading of Grief a weakness which often developes into serious disease; that
Misanthropy. general discontent, which is voiced in complaints
as to the wickedness of the age[93] and the degeneracy of young
Rome. Such discontent has always been characteristic of the
old[94]; but under the principate it has developed into a special

---

[86] 'illud, ut non doleas, vix audebo exigere; et esse melius scio. sed cui ista
firmitas animi contingat?' Sen. *Ep.* 63, 1.

[87] 'inhumanitas est ista, non virtus, funera suorum iisdem oculis, quibus ipsos,
videre' Sen. *Ep.* 99, 15; cf. *Dial.* xii 1, 2.

[88] 'cum primus nos nuntius acerbi funeris perculit, lacrimas naturalis necessitas
exprimit' *Ep.* 99, 18.

[89] 'nos quod praecipimus, honestum est; cum aliquid lacrimarum adfectus effuderit,
non esse tradendum animum dolori' *ib.* 27.

[90] 'at enim naturale desiderium suorum est. quis negat? sed plus est quod opinio
adicit quam quod natura imperavit' *Dial.* vi 7, 1.

[91] 'fit infelicis animi prava voluptas dolor' *ib.* 1, 7.

[92] 'non possum molliter adsequi tam durum dolorem; frangendus est' *ib.*

[93] 'obirascens fortunae animus et de seculo querens' Sen. *Dial.* ix 2, 11.

[94] 'difficilis, querulus, laudator temporis acti | se puero, censor castigatorque
minorum' Hor. *A. P.* 173, 174.

evil, the 'hatred of the human race' (*odium generis humani*). Of this fault even philosophers may be suspected; for it must be admitted that men are bad, have been bad, and always will be bad[95]; in short, that the whole human race is made up of mad-men[96]. But wise men will bear with this fact quietly and with a smile[97]. It is futile to bring accusations against the whole race[98], and a delusion to think our own times worse than those of our predecessors. The old Romans, to whom we look up as models of virtue, made just the same complaints of their own times; and as a matter of fact the standard of general morality never varies greatly from its average, either in an upward or a down-ward direction[99].

381. The fault of Hilarity (ἄλογος ἔπαρσις, *elatio animi*) is a departure from Soberness and cheerful Joy with
Eating. regard to the things that appeal to our appetites, and this in the direction of excess. With regard to food, it corresponds to 'greediness' in modern speech. The matter is but little discussed, but we have two interesting lectures by Musonius, which are chiefly concerned with this vice, from which we take the following extracts:

'Greediness is an unpleasant fault, making men to resemble pigs and dogs: but on the other hand healthy eating requires much supervision and practice (ἐπιμέλεια καὶ ἄσκησις). Of all pleasures that tempt men, greediness is the hardest to contend against; for it assails us twice every day. To eat too much is wrong; to eat too fast is wrong; so it is also to take too much pleasure in food, to prefer the sweet to the wholesome, or not to give your companions a fair share. Another fault is to let meals interfere with business. In all these points we should look chiefly to health. Now we observe that those who use the simplest foods are generally the strongest; servants are stronger than their masters, country-folk than townsmen, the poor than the rich. There is therefore good

[95] 'idem semper de nobis pronuntiare debebimus; malos esse nos, malos fuisse, invitus adiciam et futuros esse' Sen. *Ben.* i 10, 3; 'cupidi omnes et maligni omnes et timidi omnes' *ib.* v 17, 3.

[96] 'non est quod irascaris; omnes insaniunt' *ib.*

[97] 'satius est humana vitia placide accipere' *ib.* ix 15, 5; 'omnia vulgi vitia non invisa nobis, sed ridicula videantur' *ib.* 2.

[98] 'generi humano venia tribuenda est' *ib.* iv 10, 2.

[99] 'hoc maiores nostri questi sunt, hoc nos querimur, hoc posteri nostri querentur, eversos mores, regnare nequitiam, in deterius res humanas et omne nefas labi; at ista eodem stant loco stabuntque, paulum dumtaxat ultra aut citra mota' *Ben.* i 10, 1.

reason to prefer cheap food to that which is costly, and that which is
ready to hand to that which is only obtained with great trouble. Further,
some foods are more congenial than others to men's nature; as those
which grow from the earth, or can be obtained from animals without
killing them. Food that requires no cooking has an advantage, as ripe
fruit, some vegetables, milk, cheese, and honey. Flesh food is for many
reasons objectionable. It is heavy and impedes thought; the exhalations
from it are turbid and overshadow the soul. Men should imitate the
gods, who feed on the light exhalations of earth and water. But to-day
we have even worse corruptions. Many men are dainty and cannot eat
food without vinegar or some other seasoning. Also we call in art and
machinery to aid our pleasures, and actually have books written on
cookery. All this may serve to titillate the palate, but is mischievous to
health[100].'

The sarcasms of Seneca are aimed not so much against excess
in quantity or fastidiousness in quality, as against the collection
of dainties from all parts of the world[101].

382.   As to drinking, the Stoic period marks a great change
in feeling. In the times of Zeno, hard drinking had

Drinking.

almost the honour of a religious ceremony; and the
banquet (συμπόσιον) was the occasion of many a philosophical
discussion. Zeno began by laying it down as a principle that
'the wise man will not be drunken[102],' and Chrysippus went so
far as to name drunkenness as causing the loss of virtue[103]. But
the prohibition was carefully guarded. The earlier teachers
permitted 'wininess[104]'; and Seneca justifies this means of
banishing care, pointing out many instances of public men of
drinking habits who discharged their duties admirably[105]. Yet

[100] Stob. iii 17, 42 and 18, 37.

[101] 'ad vos deinde transeo, quorum profunda et insatiabilis gula hinc maria scru-
tatur, hinc terras. alia hamis, alia laqueis, alia retium variis generibus cum magno
labore persequitur. nullis animalibus nisi ex fastidio pax est' Sen. *Ep.* 89, 22.
Another form of luxury is in the eating of food extremely hot or extremely cold:
'quemadmodum nihil illis satis frigidum, sic nihil satis calidum est, sed ardentes
boletos demittunt' *N. Q.* iv 13, 10.

[102] See above, § 83, note 82.

[103] See above, § 324, note 155.

[104] καὶ οἰνωθήσεσθαι μὲν [τὸν σοφόν], οὐ μεθυσθήσεσθαι δέ Diog. L. vii 118. This
was the view of Chrysippus; see A. C. Pearson in *Journ. Phil.* xxx pp. 221 sqq.

[105] 'nonnunquam et usque ad ebrietatem veniendum [est], non ut mergat nos, sed
ut deprimat. eluit enim curas et ab imo animum movet' Sen. *Dial.* ix 17, 8; see
further *Ep.* 83, 14 and 15.

on the whole he inclines to a stricter view, finding that 'drunkenness is a voluntary madness,' and that it removes that sense of shame which most hinders men from wrongdoing[106]. Meanwhile a change in public taste, and perhaps the continual example of Cynic missionaries, had produced a tide of feeling in favour of simple living. The philosophical discussions sketched by Cicero take place at all times of the day, but most usually in the morning hours; they are never associated with riotous banqueting, but if necessary the meal is cut short to make room for the talk. Under the principate the fare is of the simplest; Seneca himself was a vegetarian in his youth[107]; his teacher Attalus was well content with porridge and water, and found an audience ready to approve his taste[108].

383. A similar but more profound change had taken place
Sexual indulgence. at the same time in regard to sexual relations. In the time of Socrates courtesans and boy-favourites played a large part in social life; associated with the banquet, they formed part of the accepted ideal of cultured enjoyment; even moralists approved of them as providing a satisfaction to natural desires and indirectly protecting the sanctity of the home[109]. The same attitude of mind is shown by Seneca under similar circumstances, when he recommends that princes be indulged with mistresses in order to make their character more gentle[110]. But little by little a more severe standard prevailed[111]. From the first the Stoics set themselves against the pursuit of other men's wives[112]. With regard to other relations, they did

---

[106] 'nihil aliud esse ebrietatem quam voluntariam insaniam' *Ep.* 83, 18; 'omne vitium ebrietas et incendit et detegit, obstantem malis conatibus verecundiam removet. plures enim pudore peccandi quam bona voluntate prohibitis abstinent' *ib.* 83, 19.

[107] See above, § 126.

[108] Sen. *Ep.* 110, 14 and 18.

[109] Xen. *Mem.* ii 1, 5.

[110] 'si pro magno petet munere artifices scenae et scorta et quae feritatem eius emolliant, libens offeram' Sen. *Ben:* vii 20, 3. The furthering of the amour of Nero with Acte was a practical application of this theory: 'tradit Cluvius...Senecam contra muliebres illecebras subsidium a femina petivisse, immissamque Acten libertam' Tac. *Ann.* xiv 2, 2.

[111] 'non est itaque quod credas nos plurimum libidini permisisse. longe enim frugalior haec iuventus quam illa est' Sen. *Ep.* 97, 9.

[112] See above, § 306, note 27.

not feel called upon to condemn them in other men[113]; they were indeed, in themselves, matters of indifference[114]; but they found it contrary to reason that a man's thoughts should be occupied with matters so low, or that he should bring himself into subjection to irregular habits and become a slave to a woman[115]. As the courtesan was gradually excluded by this rule[116], the general opinion fell back on the slave as the most accessible and least dangerous object of indulgence[117]. But the philosophers of the principate, following Zeno, who in these matters took the πρέπον (*decorum*) as his rule[118], find it in a high degree unfitting that the master, who should in all things be a model of self-control in his own household, should display so grave a weakness to his slaves.

384. Thus little by little there emerged the ideal of a strict chastity, to the principle of which not even the

Chastity.

marriage relation should form an exception[119]. Every falling off from this ideal is sin or transgression[120]; and it is especially true in this matter that each act of weakness leaves its trace on the character, and that he who yields becomes a feebler man[121]. The Socratic paradox, that the wise man will

---

[113] 'As to pleasure with women, abstain as far as you can before marriage; but if you do indulge in it, do it in the way which is conformable to custom. Do not however be disagreeable to those who indulge in these pleasures' Epict. *Manual* 33, 8.

[114] τὸ δὲ ἐρᾶν αὐτὸ μόνον ἀδιάφορον εἶναι Stob. ii 7, 5 b 9; cf. § 317.

[115] 'eleganter mihi videtur Panaetius respondisse adulescentulo cuidam quaerenti, an sapiens amaturus esset: "de sapiente" inquit "videbimus; mihi et tibi, qui adhuc a sapiente longe absumus, non est committendum ut incidamus in rem commotam, impotentem, alteri emancipatam, vilem sibi"' Sen. *Ep.* 116, 5; 'Did you never love any person, a young girl, slave or free?...have you never flattered your little slave? have you never kissed her feet? What then is slavery?' Epict. *Disc.* iv 1, 15 and 17.

[116] 'magno pudoris impendio dilecta scorta' Sen. *Dial.* ii 6, 7.

[117] Hor. *Sat.* i 2, 116-119.

[118] See above, § 318, note 104.

[119] 'Do not admire the beauty of your wife, and you will not be angry with the adulterer' Epict. *Disc.* i 18, 11. Ascetic principles were already practised in Seneca's time; 'vino quidam, alii Venere, quidam omni umore interdixere corporibus' *Dial.* iv 12, 4.

[120] 'lapsa est libido in muliere ignota...peccavit vero nihilominus, si quidem est peccare tanquam transilire lineas' Cic. *Par.* iii 1, 20.

[121] 'When you have been overcome in sexual intercourse with a person, do not reckon this single defeat only, but reckon that you have also increased your incontinence' Epict. *Disc.* ii 18, 6.

be a lover[122], is consistently maintained by the Stoics; but the practical limitations of this doctrine are well illustrated by the following striking passage from the lectures of the Stoic Musonius :—

'Men who do not wish to be licentious and bad should consider that sexual relations are only lawful in marriage, and for the begetting of children; such as aim at mere pleasure are lawless, even in marriage. Even apart from adultery and unnatural relations, all sexual connexions are disgraceful; for what sober-minded man would think of consorting with a courtesan, or with a free woman outside marriage? and least of all would he do so with his own slave. The lawlessness and foulness of such connexions is a disgrace to all who form them; as we may see that any man who is capable of a blush does his utmost to conceal them. Yet one argues: "in this case a man does no injustice; he does not wrong his neighbour or deprive him of the hope of lawful issue." I might reply that every one who sins injures himself, for he makes himself a worse and less honourable man. But at any rate he who gives way to foul pleasure and enjoys himself like a hog is an intemperate man; and not least he who consorts with his own slave-girl, a thing for which some people find excuse. To all this there is a simple answer; how would such a man approve of a mistress consorting with her own man-servant? Yet I presume he does not think men inferior to women, or less able to restrain their desires. If then men claim the supremacy over women, they must show themselves superior in self-control. To conclude; sexual connexion between a master and his female slave is nothing but licentiousness[123].'

385. Thus our detailed study of the four perturbations has
'Bear and forbear.'
led us to lay little stress on Fear and Greed, the weaknesses of the heroic period when men's minds were actively turned to the future, and to concentrate our attention on Grief and Hilarity, the two moods in which life's troubles and temptations are wrongly met with as they arrive. As we follow the history of Stoic philosophy through the times of the Roman principate, we find that this tendency to lay stress on the training of the passive character increases : till Epictetus tells us that of all the vices far the worst are 'lack of endurance' (*intolerantia*), which is the developed form of Grief, and 'lack of restraint' (*incontinentia*), which is the persistent inclination

---

[122] καὶ ἐρασθήσεσθαι δὲ τὸν σοφὸν τῶν νέων Diog. L. vii 129.
[123] Stob. iii 6, 23.

towards Hilarity[124]. Hence the cure for vice is summed up by him in the golden word, 'bear and forbear[125]'; that is, practise Courage and cast off Grief, practise Soberness and keep Hilarity far from you. 'A good rule,' a Peripatetic would reply, 'for women and slaves.'

386. This negative attitude is most strongly marked in Epictetus in connexion with the dangers of sexual passion. Thus his short advice to all young men with regard to the attractions of women is 'Flee at once[126]'; and even in this his advice was countenanced in advance by the more tolerant Seneca[127]. It would appear from both writers that the battle between the sexes had become unequal at this period, so often is the picture drawn of the promising and well-educated youth literally and hopelessly enslaved by a mistress presumably without birth, education, or honour[128]. It causes us some surprise to find that the distinction between heavenly and earthly love[129] is not brought in as a corrective of the latter. Only in a general way the suggestion is made that seductive attractions should be driven out by virtuous ideals:

Avoidance of temptation.

'Do not be hurried away by the appearance, but say: "Appearances, wait for me a little; let me see who you are and what you are about; let me put you to the test." And do not allow the appearance to lead you on and draw lively pictures of the things which will follow; for if you do, it will carry you off wherever it pleases. But rather bring in to oppose it some other beautiful and noble appearance and cast out this base appearance. And if you are accustomed to be exercised in this way, you will see what shoulders, what sinews, what strength you have....This is the true athlete....Stay, wretch, do not be carried away. Great is the

---

[124] 'idem ille Epictetus solitus dicere est duo esse vitia multo omnium gravissima ac taeterrima, intolerantiam et incontinentiam, cum aut iniurias, quae sunt ferendae, non toleramus neque ferimus, aut a quibus rebus voluptatibusque nos tenere debemus, non tenemus' A. Gellius, *N. A.* xvii 19, 5.

[125] 'verba haec duo dicebat: ἀνέχου et ἀπέχου *ib.* 6.

[126] 'At first fly far from that which is stronger than yourself; the contest is unequal between a charming young girl and a beginner in philosophy' Epict. *Disc.* iii 12, 12.

[127] 'id agere debemus, ut inritamenta vitiorum quam longissime profugiamus' Sen. *Ep.* 51, 5; 'ei, qui amorem exuere conatur, evitanda est omnis admonitio dilecti corporis' *ib.* 69, 3.

[128] Epict. *Disc.* iv 1, 15–21.

[129] See above, § 349.

combat, divine is the work; it is for kingship, for freedom, for happiness. Remember God; call on him as a helper and protector [130].'

387. From the study of the separate evils we revert to the general theory of Vice. And here we must recal the point that so far as vice is weakness or ill-health of the soul, it admits of gradations, which may conveniently be stated as three, namely (i) rufflings of the soul; (ii) commotions, infections, or illnesses; (iii) diseases or vices proper [131]. It is not quite easy to classify the rufflings or first slight disturbances of the soul (*prima agitatio animi*) under the four perturbations; but the bodily indications of them seem to be more marked in the weaknesses of the active or heroic character, namely Fear and Greed. Thus in the direction of Fear we meet with hair standing on end—pallor of complexion—trembling limbs—palpitation, and dizziness, all of which are bodily indications that fear is not far off; in the direction of Anger (a form of Greed) we meet with heightened colour, flashing eyes, and gnashing teeth [132]. In the direction of Grief we meet with tears and sighs, and in that of Hilarity the automatic sexual movements, amongst which we must perhaps include blushing.

Gradations of vice.

388. It does not appear that the early Stoic masters occupied themselves much with the gradations of vice; although a text can be taken from Zeno for a discourse on this subject. Neither does the earnest and cynically-minded Epictetus care to dwell on such details. On the other hand Seneca lays the greatest possible stress on the doctrine that 'rufflings' are not inconsistent with virtue. For this two arguments are available, which are perhaps not quite consistent. First, the bodily indications are beyond the control

Rufflings.

---

[130] Epict. *Disc.* ii 18, 24–29.

[131] The terms 'ruffling' (*levis motus*), and 'commotions' (*emotiones*) or 'perturbations' (*perturbationes*) are metaphors taken from the disturbance of a calm sea; the remaining terms properly describe bodily ill-health. The English words 'emotions,' 'affections' have almost entirely lost their original force, and are therefore no longer suitable as translations. The substitution of 'commotion' for 'emotion' has already been adopted by Maudsley, *Pathology of the Human Mind.*

[132] 'ad peiores nuntios subriguntur pili, et rubor ad improba verba subfunditur sequiturque vertigo praerupta cernentes' Sen. *Dial.* iv 2, 1; 'erubescunt pudici etiam loqui de pudicitia' Cic. *Leg.* i 19, 50. See also the following notes.

of the mind; they are necessary consequences of the union of body and soul, that is, of our mortal condition[133]. Secondly, the 'rufflings' correspond to the mind-pictures presented to the soul in thought, and therefore are neither moral nor immoral until the soul has given its assent to them[134]. From either point of view we arrive at a result congenial to this philosopher. The wise man is, in fact, subject to slight touches of such feelings as grief and fear[135]; he is a man, not a stone. Secondly, the sovereignty of the will remains unimpaired; give the mind but time to collect its forces, and it will restrain these feelings within their proper limits[136]. The doctrine is in reality, though not in form, a concession to the Peripatetic standpoint; it provides also a convenient means of defence against the mockers who observe that professors of philosophy often exhibit the outward signs of moral weakness.

389. If the soul gives way to any unreasoning impulse, it makes a false judgment and suffers relaxation of its tone: there takes place a 'commotion' or 'perturbation' (πάθος, *affectus*, *perturbatio*), which is a moral evil[137]. The Greek word πάθος admits of two interpretations; it may mean a passive state or a disease; we here use it in the milder sense. By an 'emotion' we mean that the soul is uprooted

'Commotions.'

[133] 'si quis pallorem et lacrimas procidentis et inritationem humoris obsceni altumve suspirium et oculos subito acriores aut quid his simile indicium adfectus animique signum putat, fallitur nec intellegit corporis hos esse pulsus' Sen. *Dial.* iv 3, 2; 'est primus motus non voluntarius quasi praeparatio adfectus et quaedam comminatio' *ib.* 4, 1.

[134] 'prima illa agitatio animi, quam species iniuriae incussit, non magis ira est quam ipsa iniuriae species' *ib.* 3, 5.

[135] '[sapiens] sentit levem quendam tenuemque motum, nam, ut dicit Zenon, in sapientis quoque animo, etiam cum vulnus sanatum est, cicatrix manet. sentiet itaque suspiciones quasdam et umbras adfectuum; ipsis carebit' *ib.* iii 16, 7; 'scio inveniri quosdam, qui negent doliturum esse sapientem; hi non videntur mihi unquam in eiusmodi casum incidisse' *ib.* xi 18, 5; 'nullo [dolore adfici] inhumana duritia est' *ib.* xii 16, 1.

[136] 'nec hoc dico, non sentit illa, sed vincit' *ib.* i 2, 2; 'invicti esse possumus, inconcussi non possumus' *N. Q.* ii 59, 3.

[137] 'adfectus est non ad oblatas rerum species moveri, sed permittere se illis et hunc fortuitum motum prosequi' *Dial.* iv 3, 1; '[Zeno] perturbationes voluntarias esse putabat opinionisque iudicio suscipi, et omnium perturbationum arbitrabatur matrem esse immoderatam quandam intemperantiam' Cic. *Ac.* i 10, 39; 'perturbationes autem nulla naturae vi commoventur, omniaque ea sunt opiniones et iudicia levitatis' *Fin.* iii 10, 35.

from its foundation, and begins as it were to toss on the sea; by 'affection' that it is seized or infected by some unwholesome condition[138]; by 'perturbation' that it has ceased to be an orderly whole, and is falling into confusion. When we regard these words in their true sense, and shake off the associations they carry with them in English, it is clear that all of them denote moral evils; nevertheless they cannot rightly be called 'diseases' of the soul[139]. The evils and weaknesses which have been discussed are commonly displayed in 'commotions' or 'perturbations,' and are normally equivalent to them.

390. The soul by giving way to perturbations becomes
Diseases of worse; it acquires habits of weakness in particular
the soul. directions. This weakness from a passing disposition (ἕξις) changes into a permanent disposition or habit (διάθεσις), and this is in the full sense a 'disease' of the soul[140] These diseases or vices are, strictly speaking, four in number[141]: but the Stoics run into great detail as regards their titles and subdivisions. Diseases in the ordinary sense (ἀρρωστήματα) display restlessness and want of self-control; such are ambition, avarice, greediness, drunkenness, running after women[142], passionate temper, obstinacy, and anxiety. An opposite class of maladies consists of unreasonable dislikes (κατὰ προσκοπὴν γινόμενα, offensiones); such are inhospitality, misogynism, and quarrelling with the world in general[143].

[138] 'neque enim sepositus est animus et extrinsecus speculatur adfectus, sed in adfectum ipse mutatur' Sen. *Dial.* iii 8, 2.

[139] 'perturbationes animorum, quas Graeci πάθη appellant, poteram ego verbum ipsum interpretans, morbos appellare: sed non conveniret ad omnia. quis enim misericordiam aut ipsam iracundiam morbum solet dicere? sed illi dicunt πάθος. sit igitur perturbatio, quae nomine ipso vitiosa declarari videtur' Cic. *Fin.* iii 10, 35.

[140] ὅταν εἰς μόνιμον ἀφίκηται διάθεσιν ἡ ἀλλοίωσις, ὀνομάζεται νόσημα Gal. *loc. aff.* i 3, p. 32 K (Arnim iii 429); on the other hand a νόσημα is called ἕξις Stob. vii 7, 10 e; 'adfectus sunt motus animi improbabiles, subiti et concitati, qui frequentes neglectique fecere morbum' Sen. *Ep.* 75, 12; 'morbi sunt inveterata vitia et dura; altius haec animum implicuerunt et perpetua eius mala esse coeperunt' *ib.* 11.

[141] For the technical terms see above, § 362, note 6.

[142] Cic. *Tusc. disp.* iv 11, 25.

[143] εἶναι δέ τινα [νοσήματα] κατὰ προσκοπὴν γινόμενα, οἷον μισογυνίαν, μισοινίαν, μισανθρωπίαν Stob. vii 7, 10 e; 'offensionum autem definitiones sunt eius modi, ut inhospitalitas sit opinio vehemens valde fugiendum esse hospitem, eaque inhaerens et penitus insita, et mulierum odium, ut Hippolyti, et ut Timonis generis humani' Cic. *Tusc. disp.* iv 11, 27.

A. 23

391. The study of vice in its various forms and gradations
Men are good or bad. leaves untouched the main positions of Stoic ethics, including the Socratic paradoxes. Men are of two classes only, the wise and the foolish, the good and the bad[144]. This bold dualism the Stoics hold in common with the Persians[145]; and though it is on the one hand tempered so as to meet the common opinion that most men are of middling character, and on the other hand subordinated to the monistic principle that good shall in the end prevail, it remains the key-stone of this department of philosophy. Virtue is a right state of mind; everything that falls short of it is therefore a wrong state of mind. Virtue and vice lie in the inward disposition, not in the outward act[146]; and one who has crossed the line is equally out of bounds whatever the distance to which he has travelled on the far side[147]. Each man has therefore an all-important choice to make. The great Stoic teachers were filled with a yearning after righteousness and reconciliation with the divine purpose and a disgust and horror of the condition of the man who is at variance with his Creator, his neighbour, and himself[148]. These convictions they encased as usual in paradoxes and syllogisms.

392. That 'the affections must be extirpated[149]' ceases to be
All sins are equal. a paradox, as soon as we have defined affections as states of mind contrary to reason, and have made room for the 'reasonable affections' of caution, good will, and joy[150]. That 'all sins are equal[151]' remains still, as of old, a

---

[144] ἀρέσκει γὰρ τῷ τε Ζήνωνι καὶ τοῖς ἀπ' αὐτοῦ Στωϊκοῖς φιλοσόφοις δύο γένη τῶν ἀνθρώπων εἶναι, τὸ μὲν τῶν σπουδαίων, τὸ δὲ τῶν φαύλων Stob. ii 7, 11 g.

[145] See above, § 8.

[146] See above, § 317.

[147] 'cum [lineam transilieris] culpa commissa est; quam longe progrediare, cum semel transieris, ad augendam culpam nihil pertinet' Cic. *Parad.* iii 20.

[148] Here we must altogether part company from Bishop Lightfoot, who writes 'the Stoic, so long as he was true to the tenets of his school, could have no real consciousness of sin' *Philippians*, p. 290. It may however be admitted that the feelings we ascribe to the Stoics are more forcibly expressed by Cleanthes, Antipater, Musonius and Epictetus than by Seneca.

[149] See above, § 362, note 7.   [150] See above, § 355.

[151] ἀρέσκει τε αὐτοῖς ἴσα ἡγεῖσθαι τὰ ἁμαρτήματα, καθά φησι Χρύσιππος καὶ Περσαῖος καὶ Ζήνων Diog. L. vii 120.

stumbling block[152]. Yet this Socratic paradox has a simple interpretation; it is a protest against the light-heartedness which tolerates 'petty' acts of wrong-doing, and is indifferent to the evil habits of mind thus acquired[153]. Two of the Stoic teachers of the transition period, Heraclides of Tarsus and Athenodorus, are said to have abandoned the paradox[154], and all Stoics were ready to admit that sins are 'unlike'[155]. But, as usual, the main body held firmly to a doctrine in which they had discovered a real practical value. Just the same principle is expressed by other paradoxes, as that 'he who has one vice has all, though he may not be equally inclined to all[156]'; and again that 'he who is not wise is a fool and a madman[157].'

393. In spite of the parallelism of virtue and vice the latter is destined to subordination, not only in the history of the universe, but also in the individual man. Even if sins are equal, vice as ill health of the soul has degrees. The first 'rufflings' of the soul are, as we have seen, not to be reckoned as real evils; its 'perturbations' give the hope of a coming calm; and grievous though its 'diseases' are, we have no suggestion of incurable sin, or of the hopeless offender. Even he who has most fallen retains the germs of virtue, and these may again ripen under a proper discipline[158].

Sin is curable.

---

[152] 'omne delictum scelus esse nefarium, nec minus delinquere eum qui gallum gallinaceum, cum opus non fuerit, quam eum qui patrem suffocaverit' Cic. *Mur.* 29, 61.

[153] 'parva, inquis, res est. at magna culpa. nec enim peccata rerum eventu, sed vitiis hominum metienda sunt' Cic. *Par.* iii 20; 'facilius est excludere perniciosa quam regere' Sen. *Dial.* iii 7, 2; 'optimum est ipsis repugnare seminibus' *ib.* 8, 1; 'si das aliquid iuris tristitiae timori cupiditati ceterisque motibus pravis, non erunt in nostra potestate' *Ep.* 85, 11.

[154] Diog. L. vii 121.

[155] ἴσα τε πάντα λέγουσιν εἶναι τὰ ἁμαρτήματα, οὐκέτι δ' ὅμοια Stob. ii 7, 11 l.

[156] 'stultus omnia vitia habet, sed non in omnia natura pronus est; alius in avaritiam, alius in luxuriam, alius in petulantiam inclinatur...' Sen. *Ben.* iv 27, 1; 'omnes stulti mali sunt; qui autem habet vitium unum, omnia habet' *ib.* v 15, 1.

[157] 'intellegendum est eos sensisse hoc idem, quod a Socrate acceptum diligenter Stoici retinuerunt, omnes insipientes esse non sanos' Cic. *Tusc. disp.* iii 5, 10.

[158] πάντας γὰρ ἀνθρώπους ἀφορμὰς ἔχειν ἐκ φύσεως πρὸς ἀρετήν· ὅθεν ἀτελεῖς μὲν ὄντας εἶναι φαύλους, τελειωθέντας δὲ σπουδαίους Cleanthes ap. Stob. ii 7, 5 b 8; 'in pessima ab optimis lapsus necesse est etiam in malo vestigia boni teneat. nunquam

394. The attitude of the Stoic school towards sin and
Stoic   weakness exposed it, as we have seen, to constant
austerity.   criticism and ridicule. To some extent this was
due to the profession of philosophy in itself: for every such
profes on implied some claim to clearer knowledge and more
consistent action than that of the crowd[159]. But the Stoics
also sought to be 'austere' with regard to social pleasures, and
thus it seemed that they neither offered others a share in their
own happiness nor sympathetically partook in that of others[160];
whilst at the same time they claimed exemption from the
weaknesses and failings of their neighbours. We have seen
both Seneca and Epictetus anxious to meet criticism on these
points by laying stress on those touches of natural feeling in
which wise and foolish alike share. But in addressing the
members of the sect their tone is very different; they hold
out, as a prize worth the winning, the prospect of attaining
to that calm and unchanging disposition of mind which has
for ever left behind the flutterings of fear and greed, of grief
and hilarity, and which is attuned to reason alone[161]. Epictetus
indeed often expresses elation and pride upon this theme :

'I will show the sinews of a philosopher. What are these? A desire
(ὄρεξις) never disappointed, an aversion (ἔκκλισις) which never meets with
that which it would avoid, a proper pursuit (ὁρμή), a diligent purpose
(πρόθεσις), an assent which is not rash. These you shall see[162].'

'Men, if you will attend to me, wherever you are, whatever you are
doing, you will not feel sorrow, nor anger, nor compulsion, nor hindrance,
but you will pass your time without perturbations and free from everything. When a man has this peace (not proclaimed by Caesar, for how
should he be able to proclaim it?) but by God through reason, is he not
content when he reflects—Now no evil can happen to me[163]?'

tantum virtus exstinguitur, ut non certiores animo notas imprimat, quam ut illas eradat
ulla mutatio' Sen. *Ben.* vii 19, 5; 'inest interim animis voluntas bona, sed torpet,
modo deliciis ac situ, modo officii inscitia' *ib.* v 25, 6.

[159] 'satis ipsum nomen philosophiae, etiamsi modice tractetur, invidiosum est'
Ep. 5, 2.

[160] αὐστηροὺς δέ φασιν εἶναι πάντας τοὺς σπουδαίους, τῷ μήτε αὐτοὺς πρὸς ἡδονὴν
ὁμιλεῖν μήτε παρ' ἄλλων τὰ πρὸς ἡδονὴν προσδέχεσθαι Diog. L. vii 117.

[161] '[sapiens] nec cupit nec timet beneficio rationis' Sen. *Dial.* vii 5, 1; 'erectus
laetusque est, inde continuo gaudio elatus' *ib.* ii 9, 3.

[162] Epict. *Disc.* ii 8, 29.   [163] *ib.* iii 13, 11 to 13.

CHAPTER XV.

COUNSELS OF PERFECTION.

395. WE have now set forth the Stoic theory of ethics,
both in its high philosophic framework and in its
Precepts. more detailed treatment, in which it prescribes
what is to be done and what is to be left undone, and how the soul
is to be disciplined in health and medicined in sickness. It
remains for us to study the application of the system to individual
cases, a matter which perhaps lies outside the scope of philosophy
as understood at the present day, but is an essential part of the
work of churches and social organizations. This department of
philosophy was termed by the ancients 'precepts,' or (more
fully) 'advice, dissuasion, admonition, exhortation, consolation,
warnings, praise, reproof' and so forth[1]; by some philosophers,
as for instance by Aristo of Chios, it was held in contempt, by
others (less inclined to Cynism) it was considered alone worthy
of pursuit[2]. But the steady conviction of the main body of Stoic
teachers was that theory and precept must go hand in hand[3];
that moral principles have no strength apart from their daily
application[4], and that practical suggestions apart from a sound
and reasoned system are like leaves cut from the bough, without

---

[1] 'omnia ista [monitiones, consolationes, dissuasiones, adhortationes, obiurgationes,
laudationes] monitionum genera sunt' Sen. *Ep.* 94, 39.

[2] 'eam partem philosophiae, quae dat propria cuique personae praecepta...
quidam solam receperunt, sed Ariston Stoicus e contrario hanc partem levem existimat' *ib.* 94, 1 and 2. The Cynics gave exhortations, but without having a system
for the purpose. See above, § 52.

[3] 'Posidonius non tantum praeceptionem, sed etiam suasionem et consolationem
et exhortationem necessariam iudicat' *ib.* 95, 65. Cf. Cic. *Off.* i 3, 7; Sen. *Ep.* 94, 34.

[4] 'ipsum de malis bonisque iudicium confirmatur officiorum exsecutione, ad quam
praecepta perducunt' *ib.*

lasting greenness[5]. Since precepts apply directly to individual
persons and particular circumstances, they presuppose some
relationship between teacher and hearer[6]; the latter must be
either a convert to the school or one who has grown up under its
influence. In the Roman period the department of precepts is
of increasing importance; we have something to learn from
Antipater, Panaetius and Cicero, but we find much more material
in the lectures (διατριβαί, 'diatribes') and letters of Musonius,
Seneca, Epictetus and other teachers of the period of the principate.

396. The 'precepts' which we find illustrated by our various
Training of
the young. authorities are not easily systematized, but they
have all the more the charm of personal intimacy;
through them we are admitted to the home life of the Stoics.
As Seneca wrote to Lucilius, so every day did Stoic fathers,
Stoic teachers, Stoic jurists, address those who came within
their influence. Believing every man to have the seed of
virtue in him, they had confidence that by their words it would
often be stirred to life[7]; and that in other cases, in which the
promising shoot had become overshadowed by ignorance or evil
habits, it would by the same means begin to grow again[8]. But
the full benefits of precepts could only be seen where they fell on
well-prepared ground, and formed part of a training extending
from infancy to the grave; where the instructor could daily
ensure their enforcement and observe their effect. This opportunity was necessarily found most often in the teaching of the
young; and the Stoic system of precepts, though not restricted
to one period of life, was to a large extent a foreshadowing of a
'Theory of Education.' It was under all circumstances guided
by the rule of 'little by little.' Precepts must be few[9], and must

---

[5] 'quemadmodum folia virere per se non possunt, ramum desiderant; sic ista
praecepta, si sola sunt, marcent; infigi volunt sectae' Sen. *Ep.* 95, 59.

[6] See below, § 397, note 21.   [7] Sen. *Ep.* 94, 29 and 108, 8.

[8] 'inest interim animis voluntas bona, sed torpet; modo deliciis et situ, modo
officii inscitia' *Ben.* v 25, 6.

[9] 'plus prodesse, si pauca praecepta sapientiae teneas, sed illa in promptu tibi et
in usu sint, quam si multa quidem didiceris, sed illa non habeas ad manum'
Ben. vii 1, 3; 'We ought to exercise ourselves in small things, and beginning with
them to proceed to the greater' Epict. *Disc.* i 18, 18.

be in themselves easy for the individual to carry out[10]; but by steady practice great things will be accomplished.

397. Since the value of precepts depends on the personal influence of the instructor, it is clear that his example will be of the greatest importance, and we may first ask what the discipline is to which he himself submits. Here the Cynic teacher seems to have the advantage, for he lives in the sight of all men; and the Indian, who allows himself to be scorched or burnt to show his contempt for pain, makes a still more forcible appeal[11]. The Stoic does not parade himself in this fashion, but neither does he lock the door of his private life against any who wish to examine it[12]. In the early morning he shakes off sleep, rousing himself to do the day's work of a man[13]. Having clothed himself, he turns his mind towards his Maker, and sings his praises; he resolves during the coming day to cooperate in his purposes, and to bear cheerfully any burden that may be placed upon him[14]. He will then give a short time to gymnastic exercises for the good of his health[15]; after which, if his strength allows it, he will take, winter or summer, a plunge into the cold bath[16]; next comes the slightest of meals[17]; then a short nap or reverie[18]. From this he is aroused by the stir around him, and he then applies himself to the day's studies, being careful to alternate reading and writing, so that his mind may be neither exhausted by the latter nor

The teacher's example.

[10] 'debet semper plus esse virium in actore quam in onere. necesse est opprimant onera, quae ferente maiora sunt' Sen. *Dial.* ix 6, 4.

[11] Arnim i 241.

[12] 'sic certe vivendum est, tanquam in conspectu vivamus' Sen. *Ep.* 83, 1.

[13] 'In the morning, when you feel loth to rise, fall back upon the thought "I am rising for man's work. Why make a grievance of setting about that for which I was born, and for sake of which I have been brought into the world? Is the end of my existence to lie snug in the blankets and keep warm?"' M. Aurel. *To himself* v 1.

[14] 'I obey, I follow, assenting to the words of the Commander, praising his acts; for I came when it pleased him, and I will also go away when it pleases him; and while I lived it was my duty to praise God' Epict. *Disc.* iii 26, 29 and 30. See also above, § 258.

[15] 'minimum exercitationi corporis datum' Sen. *Ep.* 83, 3.

[16] 'ab hac fatigatione magis quam exercitatione in frigidam descendi' *ib.* 5.

[17] 'panis deinde siccus et sine mensa prandium' *ib.* 6.

[18] 'brevissimo somno utor et quasi interiungo. satis est mihi vigilare desiisse. aliquando dormisse me scio, aliquando suspicor' *ib.*

relaxed by the former[19]. Later on he will consider his practical duties towards his relatives, his friends, and society in general. He will order his household and settle the disputes of his dependents. He will visit his friends, saying a word here and there in season[20], but not (like the Cynics) to all and sundry[21]. He will encourage those who are making progress in virtue, and sharply warn those who are in danger of a fall[22]. He advises a young mother to nurse her child at her own breast; and when he meets with objections, points out the wisdom and propriety of obeying the prescriptions of nature[23]. Returning home, he will again enjoy some slight bodily exercise, joining perhaps in a game of ball; his thoughts however will not always turn on success in the game, but he will consider how many principles in physics and ethics may be illustrated by it[24]. Now that evening comes on, he sits down to a meal (not over-elaborate) in the company of one or two favourite pupils[25]. Afterwards comes the temptation to burn the midnight oil in gathering seeds of wisdom for the morrow from the well-thumbed manuscript of Cleanthes or, it may be, of Epicurus[26]. Retiring to his chamber, he will examine his conscience, review the events of the past day, and be at peace with himself before he sleeps[27].

398. With the training of children the Stoic teacher is perhaps not altogether familiar, but he knows its importance[28]; it must be based on simplicity and austerity, for just at this time indulgence and luxury are

The child's life.

---

[19] 'nec scribere tantum nec tantum legere debemus; altera res contristabit, vires exhauriet (de stilo dico), altera solvet ac diluet' Sen. *Ep.* 84, 2.

[20] 'nulli enim nisi audituro dicendum est' *ib.* 29, 1.

[21] '[Diogenes et alii Cynici] libertate promiscua usi sunt et obvios monuerunt. hoc, mi Lucili, non existimo magno viro faciendum' *ib.* 29, 1 and 3.

[22] 'audebo illi mala sua ostendere' *ib.* 4.

[23] A. Gellius, *N. A.* xii 1. Favorinus, of whom this is related, was not himself a Stoic.

[24] Sen. *Ben.* ii 17, 3 to 5 and 32, 1 to 4.

[25] See above, § 125, note 90.

[26] 'at te nocturnis iuvat impallescere chartis; | cultor enim iuvenum purgatas inseris aures | fruge Cleanthea' Pers. *Sat.* v 62-64; 'quid est tamen, quare tu istas Epicuri voces putes esse, non publicas?' Sen. *Ep.* 8, 8.

[27] 'qualis ille somnus post recognitionem sui sequitur? quam tranquillus, quam altus ac liber!' *Dial.* v 36, 2.

[28] 'plurimum proderit pueros statim salubriter institui' *ib.* iv 21, 1.

most dangerous stimulants to the passions[29]. The child must learn to eat and drink in a mannerly way[30], to refrain from loud talking and laughing[31], to express himself in respectful and graceful words[32]. He must be taught to do right before he can understand the reason why[33], or else by doing wrong he will make it difficult for himself afterwards to do right; he must be ruled until he can rule himself[34]. For this reason we give children proverbs (*sententiae*) or anecdotes ($\chi\rho\epsilon\hat{\iota}\alpha\iota$) to write out and learn, such as 'honesty is the best policy' or 'Socrates being asked of what city he was...'; and these short pithy sayings sink deep[35]. But in the school life of children no attempt must be made to grapple with the real problems of life, because these are too hard for them, though parents often forget this objection[36]. Games and amusements may be permitted; for though in discussions on high principle the Stoics may be entirely opposed to 'relaxation of soul[37],' yet in practical life they freely admit its importance[38]. All dealings with children should be gentle; the discipline of the rod has long ago been abandoned by all sensible parents and teachers[39].

[29] 'tenuis ante omnia victus [sit] et non pretiosa vestis' *ib.* 11 ; 'nihil magis facit iracundos quam educatio mollis et blanda' *ib.* 6.

[30] 'if he...eats as a modest man, this is the man who truly progresses' Epict. *Disc.* i 4, 20 and 21.

[31] 'veritatis simplex oratio est' Sen. *Ep.* 49, 12 ; 'Let silence be the general rule, or let only what is necessary be said, and in a few words. Let not your laughter be much' Epict. *Manual* 33, 2 and 4.

[32] 'loquendum est pro magnitudine rei impensius et illa adicienda—pluris quam putas obligasti' Sen. *Ben.* ii 24, 4.

[33] 'inbecillioribus quidem ingeniis necesse est aliquem praeire—hoc vitabis, hoc facies' *Ep.* 94, 50.

[34] 'regi ergo debet, dum incipit posse se regere' *ib.* 51.

[35] 'facilius singula insidunt circumscripta et carminis modo inclusa. ideo pueris et sententias ediscendas damus et has quas Graeci chrias vocant' *ib.* 33, 6 and 7.

[36] 'He is ridiculous who says that he wishes to begin with the matters of real life, for it is not easy to begin with the more difficult things; and we ought to use this fact as an argument to parents' Epict. *Disc.* i 26, 4 and 5.

[37] See above, § 316.

[38] 'lusus quoque proderunt. modica enim voluptas laxat animos et temperat' Sen. *Dial.* iv 20, 3 ; 'danda est animis remissio' *ib.* ix 17, 5 ; 'mens ad iocos devocanda est' *ib.* 4.

[39] Chrysippus had approved of the rod : 'caedi discentis, quamlibet receptum sit et Chrysippus non improbet, minime velim' Quint. *Inst. Or.* i 3, 14. But Seneca writes quite otherwise: 'uter praeceptor dignior, qui excarnificabit discipulos, si memoria illis non constiterit...an qui monitionibus et verecundia emendare ac docere malit?' *Clem.* i 16, 2 and 3.

399.   Soft living is at all ages to be avoided[40]. It is in these
Harm of
soft living.   days a danger to the bodily health; for when a man is accustomed to be protected from a draught by glass windows, to have his feet kept warm by foot-warmers constantly renewed, and his dining-room kept at an even temperature by hot air, the slightest breeze may put him in danger of his life[41]. Those who envy men who 'live softly' forget that their character becomes soft thereby[42]. In particular clothing should not be such as altogether to protect the body from heat in summer, and from cold in winter. It is better to wear one shirt than two, best still to have only a coat. Then again, if you can bear it, it is better to go without shoes; for after all to be shod is not very different from being fettered, and runners do not use shoes[43]. So also avoid luxurious furniture; of what use is it that couches, tables and beds should be made of costly woods, and adorned with silver and gold? We eat, drink, and sleep better without these things. In all these matters the Spartans set us a good example; for while disease injures the body only, luxury corrupts both body and soul[44].

400.   Boys and girls must be educated alike. This nature
Training
of girls.   teaches us, for we train colts and puppies without any regard for the difference of sex. The true education of children is in the practice of the virtues, and these are the same for men and for women. Women need Wisdom to understand the ordering of a household, Justice to control the servants, Soberness that they may be modest and unselfish. But they also need Courage; in spite of the name 'manliness' ($\dot{a}\nu\delta\rho\epsilon\dot{i}a$), this is not a virtue reserved for men. Without it women may be led by threats into immodest acts. Females of all kinds fight to defend their young; the Amazons too were good fighters, and it is only for want of practice that

---

[40] 'fugite delicias, fugite enervatam felicitatem' Sen. *Dial.* i 4, 9.

[41] 'quem specularia semper ab adflatu vindicaverunt, cuius pedes inter fomenta subinde mutata tepuerunt, cuius cenationes subditus ac parietibus circumfusus calor temperavit, hunc levis aura non sine periculo stringet' *ib.*

[42] 'audire solemus sic quorundam vitam laudari, quibus invidetur—molliter vivit hoc dicunt—mollis est' *Ep.* 82, 2.

[43] Stob. iii 29, 78 (from Musonius).

[44] *ib.* 29, 75.

women cannot do the same to-day. That men, being the stronger, should do the heavier work, and women the lighter, is an arrangement which is often convenient, but circumstances may require the contrary. Girls at any rate must learn equally with boys to bear suffering, not to fear death, not to be in low spirits about anything that happens; to avoid grasping habits, to love equality and benevolence, and to do no harm to man or woman[45].

401. Children should obey their parents, but in the spirit of reason. We do not obey a father who gives orders for the treatment of a sick person contrary to those of the physician; nor one, who being himself ill, demands things that are not good for him; nor one who bids his son steal, or appropriate trust funds, or sacrifice his youthful bloom. We do not even obey him when he tells us to spell a word wrongly or strike a false note on the lyre. If your father forbids you to philosophize, show him by your manner of life, by prompt obedience, by good temper, by unselfishness, how good a thing philosophy is. But after all, the command of the universal Father is more urgent upon you; which is, to be just, kind, benevolent, sober, high-souled; above labours and above pleasures; pure from all envy and plotting. You need not assume the outward appearance of a philosopher; for the power of philosophy is in the innermost part of the soul, which the father can no more reach than the tyrant[46].

Obedience to parents.

402. The fancy of young men is easily attracted by the vision of virtue, but it is hard for them to persevere; they are like soft cheese which slips away from the hook by which it is taken up[47]. We must therefore put before them an ideal which appeals to them, and in which the advantages of fixed purpose and severe training are apparent to the eye. Such is the training of the athlete, the gladiator, and the soldier[48]. The teachers of wrestling bid the pupil try

Example of gladiators and soldiers.

---

[45] Muson. apud Stob. ii 31, 123.

[46] Muson. *ib.* iv 79, 25.

[47] 'It is not easy to exhort weak young men; for neither is it easy to hold soft cheese with a hook' Epict. *Disc.* iii 6, 9.

[48] See above, § 326.

again after each fall[49]; the trained boxer is eager to challenge the most formidable opponent[50]. The gladiator has learnt the lesson that pain is no evil, when he stands up wounded before a sympathetic crowd and makes a sign that it matters nothing[51]. But most of all the soldier's oath serves as an example, when he pledges himself to serve Caesar faithfully all his life: let the young philosopher pledge himself to serve his God as faithfully, to submit to the changes and chances of human life, and to obey willingly the command to act or to suffer[52]. Without effort, as Hesiod has taught us, no greatness can be attained[53].

403. In youth bad habits are apt to acquire some strength
The 'contrary twist.' before they can be rooted out, and it will be well to anticipate this evil by exercising body and soul in advance in a direction contrary to that of the most common temptations. The teacher will therefore give to his precepts an exaggerated character, reckoning upon human frailty to bring about a proper standard in practice[54]. Thus since luxury is a chief enemy of virtue, the body should at least occasionally be brought low. A practice approved by the example of eminent men is to mark out from time to time a few days for the exercise of the simple life; during this time life is to be maintained on coarse bread and water, in rough dress and all the surroundings of poverty[55]. Since Cynism

---

[49] 'See what the trainers of boys do. Has the boy fallen? Rise, they say, wrestle again till you are made strong' Epict. *Disc.* iv 9, 15.

[50] '[athletis] cura est, cum fortissimis quibusque confligere' Sen. *Dial.* i 2, 3.

[51] '[gladiator fortissimus] respiciens ad clamantem populum significat nihil esse et intercedi non patitur' *ib.* ii 16, 2.

[52] 'ad hoc sacramentum adacti sumus, ferre mortalia' *ib.* vii 15, 7; Epict. *Disc.* i 14, 15 and 16.

[53] See above, § 33; and compare Horace in his Stoic mood: 'nil sine magno | vita labore dedit mortalibus' *Sat.* i 9, 59 and 60.

[54] 'quaedam praecipimus ultra modum, ut ad verum et suum redeant' Sen. *Ben.* vii 22, 1; 'We ought to oppose to this habit a contrary habit, and where there is great slipperiness in the appearances, there to oppose the habit of exercise. I am rather inclined to pleasure; I will incline to the contrary side above measure for the sake of exercise' Epict. *Disc.* iii 12, 6 and 7.

[55] 'interponas aliquot dies, quibus contentus minimo ac vilissimo cibo, dura atque horrida veste, dicas tibi "hoc est quod timebatur?"...grabatus ille verus sit et sagum et panis durus ac sordidus—hoc triduo ac quatriduo fer' Sen. *Ep.* 18, 5 and 7; 'quod tibi scripsi magnos viros saepe fecisse' *ib.* 20, 13.

is a 'short cut to virtue[56],' philosophers may well employ the methods of Diogenes for short periods, as a corrective to any tendency to excess; rich people do as much for love of change[57].

404. On the question of personal appearance there is much to be said on both sides. Foppishness is a dis-
Personal appearance. agreeable vice, and it is contemptible that a young man should smell of perfumes. On the other hand a total disregard of appearances is not approved by the Stoics; 'it is against nature' says Seneca 'to be averse to neatness in appearance[58].' In these outward matters a sensible man will conform to fashion, nor will he wish to make the name of philosopher still more unpopular than it is[59]. The founders of Stoicism laid it down that men and women should wear the same dress; but the later teachers laid stress on the natural distinction of the sexes; and to men the beard should be an object of just pride, for it is more becoming than the cock's comb, or the lion's mane[60]. This is to the Stoic a point of honour; he should part with his head more readily than with his beard[61]. But the beard may be trimmed; for, as Zeno has observed, nature provides rather against the 'too little' than against the 'too much,' and reason must come to her help. Women do right to arrange their hair so as to make themselves more beautiful; but for men any kind of artistic hair-dressing is contemptible[62].

---

[56] Diog. L. vii 121.

[57] 'divites sumunt quosdam dies, quibus humi cenent, et remoto auro argentoque fictilibus utantur' Sen. *Dial.* xii 12, 3.

[58] 'contra naturam est faciles odisse munditias' Sen. *Ep.* 5, 4; 'I would rather that a young man, who is making his first movements towards philosophy, should come to me with his hair carefully trimmed' Epict. *Disc.* iv 11, 25.

[59] 'asperum cultum et intonsum caput et neglegentiorem barbam evita. intus omnia dissimilia sint, frons populo conveniat' Sen. *Ep.* 5, 2.

[60] 'We ought not to confound the distinctions of the sexes....How much more becoming is the beard than the cock's comb and the lion's mane! For this reason we ought to preserve the signs which God has given' Epict. *Disc.* i 16, 13 and 14.

[61] 'Come then, Epictetus, shave yourself.' If I am a philosopher, I answer, 'I will not shave myself.' 'But I will take off your head.' 'If that will do you any good, take it off' Epict. *Disc.* i 2, 29.　　　　[62] Stob. iii 6, 24 (from Musonius).

405. The young should train themselves alternately to bear
Solitude and society. solitude and to profit by society[63]: since the wise man is never dependent on his friends, though none can take better advantage of them[64]. In living alone a man follows the example of the deity, and comes to know his own heart[65]. But solitude must not be a screen for secret vices; a man only uses it rightly when he can without shame picture the whole world watching his hours of privacy[66]. The right choice of friends calls for true wisdom; for the soul cannot but be soiled by bad company[67]. The only true friendship is based on the mutual attraction of good folk[68]; therefore the wise are friends one to another even whilst they are unacquainted[69]. It is well to consider much before choosing a friend, but afterwards to give him implicit trust[70]; for a true friend is a second self[71]. Such friendship can only arise from the desire to love and be loved[72]; those who seek friends for their own advantage, will be abandoned by them in the day of trial[73]. In the companionship of well-chosen friends there grows up the 'common sense,' which is an instinctive contact with humanity as a whole, making each man a partner in the thoughts and needs of all around him. This feeling is a principal aim of

[63] 'miscenda tamen ista et alternanda [sunt], solitudo ac frequentia' Sen. *Dial.* ix 17, 3.

[64] 'ita sapiens se contentus est, non ut velit esse sine amico, sed ut possit' *Ep.* 9, 5.

[65] 'proderit per se ipsum secedere; meliores erimus singuli' *Dial.* viii 1, 1; 'A man ought to be prepared in a manner to be able to be sufficient for himself and to be his own companion. For Zeus dwells by himself and is tranquil by himself' Epict. *Disc.* iii 13, 6 and 7.

[66] 'tunc felicem esse te iudica, cum poteris vivere in publico; parietes plerumque circumdatos nobis iudicamus, non ut tutius vivamus sed ut peccemus occultius' Sen. *Ep.* 43, 3.

[67] 'It is impossible that a man can keep company with one who is covered with soot without being partaker of the soot himself' Epict. *Disc.* iii 16, 3.

[68] Diog. L. vii 124.

[69] 'Stoici censent sapientes sapientibus etiam ignotis esse amicos; nihil est enim virtute amabilius' Cic. *N. D.* i 44, 121; so Stob. ii 7 11 i.

[70] 'post amicitiam credendum est, ante amicitiam iudicandum' Sen. *Ep.* 3, 2.

[71] Ζήνων ἐρωτηθεὶς τί ἐστι φίλος "ἄλλος ἐγώ" ἔφη Diog. L. vii 23.

[72] 'Hecaton ait; ego tibi monstrabo amatorium: si vis amari, ama' Sen. *Ep.* 9, 6; 'multos tibi dabo, qui non amico sed amicitia caruerunt' *ib.* 6, 3.

[73] *ib.* 9, 8.

philosophy[74]. But the young philosopher should make no
enemies; he should be free from that dislike of others which so
often causes a man to be disliked, and should remember that he
who is an enemy to-day may be a friend to-morrow[75].

406. As the young Stoic passes from youth to manhood, he
will turn his mind towards marriage as a political
Comradeship in marriage. and social duty[76]; but if he is really touched by the
divine flame, he will also find in it that enlargement of his own
sympathies and opportunities of which the wise man is always
glad[77]. Under the Roman principate we observe a rapid development of personal sympathy between husband and wife;
and though in society girls who attended philosophers' classes
had an ill name as being self-willed and disputatious[78], yet it is
from this very circle that the ideal of a perfect harmony of mind
and purpose was developed most fully. Musonius often speaks
on this subject:

'Husband and wife enter upon a treaty to live and to earn together, and
to have all things in common, soul, body and property. Unlike the lower
animals, which mate at random, man cannot be content without perfect
community of thought and mutual affection. Marriage is for health and for
sickness alike, and each party will seek to outrun the other in love, not
seeking his own advantage, but that of his partner[79].'

'A man should look for a healthy body, of middle stature, capable of
hard work, and offering no attraction to the licentious. But the soul is far
more important; for as a crooked stick cannot be fitted with one that is
straight, so there can be no true agreement except between the good[80].'

Seneca is reticent as to marriage, but we have no reason to
doubt that his life with Paulina was typical of the best Stoic
marriages. Thus he excuses himself for taking more thought

[74] 'hoc primum philosophia promittit, sensum communem, humanitatem et
congregationem' *ib.* 5, 4; 'nullius boni sine socio iucunda possessio est' *ib.* 6, 4.

[75] 'monemus, ut ex inimico cogitet fieri posse amicum' *ib.* 95, 63.

[76] See above, § 349.

[77] '[sapiens]ducit uxorem se contentus, et liberos tollit se contentus' Sen. *Ep.* 9, 17;
'If indeed you had [this purpose], you would be content in sickness, in hunger, and
in death. If any among you has been in love with a charming girl, he knows that I
say what is true' Epict. *Disc.* iii 5, 18 and 19.

[78] ἀλλὰ νὴ Δία, φασί τινες, ὅτι αὐθάδεις ὡς ἐπὶ πολὺ καὶ θρασείας εἶναι ἀνάγκη τὰς
προσιούσας τοῖς φιλοσόφοις γυναῖκας Mus. apud Stob. ii 31, 126.

[79] Stob. iv 22, 90.

[80] Stob. iv 22, 104.

for his health than a philosopher should, by saying that the happiness of Paulina depends upon it. 'Her life is wrapped up in mine, for its sake I must take care of my own. What can be more delightful than to be so dear to one's wife, that for her sake one becomes dearer to himself[81]!'

407. On the question of marriage Epictetus strikes a contrary note, characteristic of his time, and of his bias towards Cynic practice:

Celibacy.

'In the present state of things, which is like that of an army placed in battle order, is it not fit that the Cynic should without any distraction be employed only on the ministration of God? To say nothing of other things, a father must have a heating apparatus for bathing the baby; wool for his wife when she is delivered, oil, a bed, a cup; and so the furniture of the house is increased. Where then now is that king, who devotes himself to the public interests,

> "The people's guardian and so full of cares[82]"

whose duty it is to look after others; to see who uses his wife well, who uses her badly, who quarrels, who administers his family well, and who does not? Consider what we are bringing the Cynic down to, how we are taking his royalty from him[83]!'

To this very definite conception of a celibate order of philosophers, devoting themselves to the good of humanity and entitled thereby to become the rulers of society, Musonius makes the following reply in advance from the true Stoic standpoint:

'Marriage was no hindrance to Pythagoras, Socrates or Crates; and who were better philosophers than they? Since marriage is natural, philosophers should set the example of it. Why else did the Creator separate the human race into two divisions, making the honourable parts of the body distinct for each, and implanting in each a yearning for the other, but that he wished them to live together and to propagate the race? He who would destroy marriage, destroys the family and the commonwealth. No relationship is so essential or so intimate; friend does not agree so well with friend, nor does a father feel so keenly separation from his son. And why should a philosopher be different from other men? Only that which is unbecoming is a hindrance to a philosopher; but by doing his daily duty as a man he will become kindlier in disposition and more social in his thoughts[84].'

[81] 'nam cum sciam spiritum illius [sc. Paulinae] in meo verti, incipio, ut illi consulam, mihi consulere. quid enim iucundius quam uxori tam carum esse, ut propter hoc tibi carior fias?' Sen. *Ep.* 104, 2 and 5.

[82] Hom. *Il.* ii 25.   [83] Epict. *Disc.* iii 22, 69 to 75.

[84] Stob. iv 22, 20.

408. The head of a household must have a means of living;

Means of livelihood.

and therefore the making of money ($\chi\rho\eta\mu\alpha\tau\iota\sigma\mu\acute{o}\varsigma$, *cura rei familiaris*) comes within the range of precepts. The Greek writers recognised three proper means of livelihood ; (i) from kingship, that is, to be either a king or a king's minister or general; (ii) from politics, that is, by acting as a magistrate or a judge; (iii) from sophistry, that is, by teaching philosophy to those who are wishing to learn[85]. To each profession there are obvious objections; indeed the sharp critic of Stoicism can see no reason why a wise man, who lacks nothing, should trouble himself about money-making. Each of the three professions named assumes the existence of men willing to be guided by philosophy, and these are not easily found. If pupils are taken, the question arises whether fees should be paid in advance or not. Now it is certainly more reasonable that a student should only pay if he profits by his teaching; but on the other hand no one can absolutely promise to make a man good in a year, and deferred payments are often found unsatisfactory[86]. Under the Roman principate we hear little of the professions connected with public life; but it is clear that the teacher and the physician are held in special regard[87]. Seneca has not the breadth of mind to respect the painter or the sculptor, any more than the wrestler or the stage-engineer[88]. Yet Chrysippus had suggested a bolder standpoint when he said that 'the wise man will turn three somersaults for a sufficient fee[89]'; and no rule can be laid down except that a man should earn his own living without injuring his neighbour[90]. Agriculture, as a calling favourable both to health of body and to innocence of soul, continued to be praised, but was seldom practised except as an amusement[91].

[85] Stob. ii 7, 11 m.

[86] Plut. *Sto. rep.* 20, 10.

[87] 'omnium horum [medicorum et praeceptorum] apud nos magna caritas, magna reverentia est' Sen. *Ben.* vi 15, 1; 'ex medico ac praeceptore in amicum transeunt' *ib.* 16, 1.

[88] *Ep.* 88, 18 and 22.

[89] Plut. *Sto. rep.* 30, 3.

[90] 'sic in vita sibi quemque petere quod pertineat ad usum, non iniquum est; alteri deripere ius non est' Cic. *Off.* iii 10, 42.

[91] See below, § 412.

A. 24

409. For every profession philosophy has appropriate pre-
Kingly duties. cepts, beginning with the king. There came one
day to Musonius a king of Syria, for in those times
there were kings subject to the Roman empire. Musonius
addressed him thus :

'You ought to be a philosopher as much as I. Your wish is to protect
and benefit your fellow-men ; to do that, you must know what is good and
what is evil. A king too must understand Justice ; for wars and revolts
come about because men quarrel about their rights. Also he must show
Soberness and Courage, that he may be an example to his subjects[92]. The
ancients thought that a king should be a living law (νόμος ἔμψυχος), and an
imitator of Zeus. Only a good man can be a good king.'

The king was highly pleased, and asked him to name any
boon he would. 'Abide by my words,' said Musonius, 'that
will be the best boon both for me and for you[93].'

Two precepts in particular are addressed to kings. The
first, that they should encourage friends who will speak the
truth to them. Even Augustus Caesar needed this lesson ;
bitterly as he lamented the deaths of Agrippa and Maecenas,
he would not have allowed them to speak frankly had they
lived[94]. The second, that they should practise clemency, following the example of Julius Caesar, who destroyed the evidence
upon which he might have punished his enemies[95]. None does
this virtue better become than kings and rulers[96].

410. To the man of high rank it is natural to desire to
Court life. move in the society of the great and the powerful.
Epictetus gives us a striking description of the
man who desires to be on the list of the 'Caesaris amici,' which
he thinks to be a good, though experience shows that it is not
such.

'Of whom shall we inquire ? What more trustworthy witness have we
than this very man who is become Caesar's friend ? "Come forward and tell
us, when did you sleep more quietly, now or before you became Caesar's

---

[92] So too Epictetus: 'To whose example should [the many] look except yours [the
governors']?' *Disc.* iii 4, 3.

[93] Stob. iv 7, 67.　　　　　　　　　[94] Sen. *Ben.* vi 32, 4.

[95] *Dial.* iv 23, 4.

[96] 'nullum tamen clementia ex omnibus magis quam regem aut principem decet'
Clem. i 3, 3.

friend?" Immediately you hear the answer, "Stop, I entreat you, and do not mock me; you know not what miseries I suffer, and sleep does not come to me; but one comes and says, Caesar is already awake, he is now going forth; then come troubles and cares." "Well, and did you sup with more pleasure, now or before?" Hear what he says about this also. He says that if he is not invited, he is pained; and if he is invited, he sups like a slave with his master, all the while being anxious that he does not say or do anything foolish. As befits so great a man, Caesar's friend, he is afraid that he may lose his head. I can swear that no man is so stupid as not to bewail his own misfortunes the nearer he is in friendship to Caesar[97].'

It is exactly under these circumstances that a thorough training in philosophy is of really practical value.

'When you are going in to any great personage, remember that another also from above sees what is going on, and that you ought to please him rather than that other. He then who sees from above asks you: "In the schools what used you to say about exile and bonds and death and disgrace?" "That they are things indifferent." "And the end of life, what is it?" "To follow thee." "Do you say this now also?" "I do." Then go in to the great personage boldly and remember these things: and you will see what a youth is who has studied these things, when he is among men who have not studied them. I imagine that you will have such thoughts as these; "Why do we make such great and so many preparations for nothing? Is this the thing which is named power? All this is nothing[98]."'

Yet a wise man will never challenge the anger of the powerful; he will turn aside from it, as a sailor from a storm[99]. The virtuous affection of caution must be called in to help him, so many are his dangers. An independence of look, a slight raising of the voice, an outspoken expression, an appeal to public opinion, even unsought popularity are enough to excite suspicion[100]. Perhaps after all the poet may be the wisest, who advises good men to stay away from court altogether, for it is a place where there is no room for them[101].

411. A common cause of moral corruption is the routine of city life. Here fashion dictates a round of occupa-
Life in the city. tions which are unnatural, but in which men and

---

[97] Epict. *Disc.* iv 1, 46 to 50.   [98] *ib.* i 30, 1 to 7.

[99] 'sapiens nunquam potentium iras provocabit, immo declinabit, non aliter quam in navigando procellam' Sen. *Ep.* 14, 7.

[100] *Dial.* iii 18, 2.

[101] 'exeat aula | qui volet esse pius. virtus et summa potestas | non coëunt: semper metuet, quem saeva pudebunt' Lucan *Phars.* viii 493 to 495.

women are alike absorbed[102]. Half of the morning is absorbed in sleep[103]; then follows the visit to the public shows, which are centres of demoralisation[104], and conversation with numerous friends, each one of whom suggests some abandonment of principle[105]. In the clubs all the most worthless members of society foregather[106]. The baths, which were at one time simply constructed, and for the purpose of cleanliness, are now instruments of luxury; and the water is now so hot as to be better fitted for torture than pleasure[107]. For the evening meal there must always be some novelty discovered, even if it is only to begin with the dessert and end with the eggs[108]; even the order of the seasons must be inverted, that roses may adorn the table in winter[109]. Upon the ill-spent day follows a disorderly night, and a heavy headache the next morning[110]. From the temptations of such a life the adherent of Stoicism will gladly escape.

412. A more real happiness is reserved for the man who gives up town life for that of the country. For it is most natural to win sustenance from the earth, which is our common mother, and liberally gives back many times over what is entrusted to her; and it is more healthy to live in the open than to be always sheltering in the shade. It matters little whether one works on one's own land or on that of another; for many industrious men have prospered on hired land. There is nothing disgraceful or unbecoming in any of the work of the farm; to plant trees, to reap, to tend the vine, to thrash out the corn, are all liberal occupations. Hesiod the poet tended sheep, and this did not hinder him from telling the story of the gods. And pasturage is (says Musonius) perhaps the best of all occupations; for even farm work, if it is exhausting, demands all the energies of the soul as well as of the body,

Life in the country.

---

[102] Sen. *Ep.* 77, 6, and 95, 20 and 21.

[103] 'turpis, qui alto sole semisomnus iacet, cuius vigilia medio die incipit' *ib.* 122, 1.

[104] 'nihil tam damnosum bonis moribus quam in aliquo spectaculo desidere' *ib.* 7, 2.

[105] 'inimica est multorum conversatio; nemo non aliquod nobis vitium aut commendat aut imprimit aut nescientibus adlinit' *ib.*

[106] 'vilissimus quisque tempus in aliquo circulo [terit]' *Dial.* i 5, 4.

[107] *Ep.* 86, 9 and 10.　　　　[108] *ib.* 114, 9.　　　　[109] *ib.* 122, 8.

[110] 'oculos hesterna graves crapula' *ib.* 122, 2.

whereas whilst tending sheep a man has some time for philoso-
phizing also.

It is true that our young men to-day are too sensitive and
too refined to live a country life ; but philosophy would be well
rid of these weaklings. A true lover of philosophy could find no
better discipline than to live with some wise and kindly man in
the country, associating with him in work and in relaxation, at
meals and in sleeping, and so 'learning goodness,' as Theognis
tells us to do, ' from the good [111].'

413. Within the household the head of it is a little king,
The house- and needs to display the kingly virtues of Justice
holder. and Soberness. In his dealings with the perverse
he must consider how far each man is capable of bearing the
truth[112]. Indeed, willingness to listen to reproof is no small
virtue ; few words are best, so that the wrongdoer may be left as
far as possible to correct his own ways[113]. Punishment must be
reserved for extreme cases, and is always to be administered
with calmness ; it is felt more keenly when it comes from a
merciful master[114]. Persistent kindness wins over even bad
men[115]. It is further the privilege of the head of a household to
distribute kindnesses to those below him. His wealth he must
regard as given him in trust ; he is only the steward of it, and
must neither hoard nor waste ; for he must give both a debit
and a credit account of all[116]. But if the right use of money
causes the possessor anxious thought, no trace of this should
appear to others ; giving should be without hesitation, and as a
delight[117]. The good citizen will pay his taxes with special

[111] Stob. iv 15, 18. Seneca gives a more qualified approval to country life : 'non
est per se magistra innocentiae solitudo, nec frugalitatem docent rura ; sed ubi testis
et spectator abscessit, vitia subsidunt, quorum monstrari et conspici fructus est'
Ep. 94, 69.

[112] 'de cetero vide, non tantum an verum sit quod dicis, sed an ille cui dicitur veri
patiens sit' *Dial.* v 36, 4.

[113] 'moneri velle ac posse secunda virtus est ; flectendus est paucis animus, sui
rector optimus' *Ben.* v 25, 4.

[114] 'gravior multo poena videtur, quae a miti viro constituitur' *Clem.* i 22, 3.

[115] 'vincit malos pertinax bonitas' *Ben.* vii 31, 1.

[116] 'quid tanquam tuo parcis ? procurator es, in depositi causa [divitiae] sunt'
Ben. vi 3, 2 ; 'donabit cum summo consilio dignissimos eligens, ut qui meminerit tam
expensorum quam acceptorum rationem esse reddendam' *ib.* 23, 5.

[117] 'demus ante omnia libenter, cito, sine ulla dubitatione' *Ben.* ii 1, 1.

pleasure, because in his eyes the welfare of the community stands higher than his own or that of his family[118]; but he will not refuse a kindness even to an enemy who is in need[119]; and in giving a farthing to a beggar, he will imply by his manner that he is only paying what the other is entitled to as his fellow-man[120]. In short, he will give as he would like to receive[121], and with the feeling that the chief pleasure of ownership is to share with another[122].

414. The good householder will associate on easy terms

Treatment of slaves.

with his slaves, remembering that they too are men, made of flesh and blood as he is himself[123]. It is however a difficult matter to decide whether a master should dine with his slave. Men of the old Roman type find this a disgraceful practice, but the philosopher should decide in its favour[124]. We do not need to inquire into a man's social position, if his character is attractive[125]. Plato has well said that we cannot find a king who is not descended from a slave, or a slave who is not descended from a king[126]; and in fact many a Roman slave was far better educated than his master[127]. Even if we do not suppose that Seneca's rule was commonly practised in great Roman houses, the suggestion itself throws a pleasing light on the position of a Roman slave. But if the master was thus called upon to ignore differences of social position, as much might be expected of the slave. With him it

---

[118] Cic. *Off.* i 17, 57.

[119] 'non desinemus opem ferre etiam inimicis' Sen. *Dial.* viii 1, 4.

[120] '[sapiens] dabit egenti stipem (non hanc contumeliosam, qua pars maior horum qui se misericordes videri volunt, abicit et fastidit quos adiuvat contingique ab his timet) sed ut homo homini ex communi dabit' *Clem.* ii 6, 2.

[121] 'sic demus, quomodo vellemus accipere' *Ben.* ii 1, 1.

[122] 'nullius boni sine socio iucunda possessio est' *Ep.* 6, 4.

[123] 'servi sunt? immo homines. servi sunt? immo humiles amici' *ib.* 47, 1; 'animas servorum et corpora nostra | materia constare putat paribusque elementis' Juv. *Sat.* xiv 16 and 17.

[124] 'cognovi familiariter te cum servis tuis vivere. hoc eruditionem decet. rideo istos, qui turpe putant cum servo suo cenare' Sen. *Ep.* 47, 1 and 2.

[125] 'refert cuius animi sit, non cuius status' *Ben.* iii 18, 2.

[126] *Ep.* 44, 4.

[127] '[Calvisius Sabinus] magna summa emit servos, unum qui Homerum teneret, unum qui Hesiodum. novem praeterea lyricis singulos adsignavit. magno emisse illum non est quod mireris: non invenerat, faciendos locavit' *Ep.* 27, 6.

was doubtless an instinct to prize liberty, 'the power of living as you like,' as the dearest of possessions. Yet many a slave who won this reward by years of faithful service found that liberty delusive, and would have been wiser to stay in the home where he was valued[128].

415. A question of pressing practical importance is that of large families (πολυπαιδία). Statesmen have always

Large families.

considered it best that the homes of citizens should be crowded with children; and for this reason the laws forbid abortion and the hindrance of conception; they demand fines for childlessness, and pay honours to those who bring up large families. Public opinion takes the same view; the father of many children is honoured as he goes about the city, and how charming is the sight of a mother surrounded by a swarm of children[129]! No religious procession is so imposing. For such parents every one feels sympathy, and every one is prepared to cooperate with them[130]. But nowadays even rich parents refuse to rear all their children, so that the first-born may be the richer. But it is better to have many brothers than few; and a brother is a richer legacy than a fortune. A fortune attracts enemies, but a brother helps to repel them[131].

416. We have now accompanied the man of mature years in his duties and his temptations: philosophy has

Comfort in poverty.

also a word to speak with regard to his trials. It is well indeed if he is convinced that the buffets of fortune are no real evils; but this doctrine can be supplemented by other consolations. Of the most bitter of all sufferings, bereavement by the death of friends and children, we have already spoken; we may now consider two other conditions usually held to be evil, namely poverty and exile. In poverty the first comfort is in the observation that poor men are usually stronger in body

---

[128] Epict. *Disc.* iv 1, 33 to 40.

[129] But hear Epictetus on the other side: 'Are those men greater benefactors to mankind who introduce into the world to occupy their own places two or three grunting children, or those who superintend as far as they can all mankind? Did Priamus who begat fifty worthless sons contribute more to the community than Homer?' *Disc.* iii 22, 77 and 78.

[130] Stob. iv 24, 15 (from Musonius). [131] *ib.* 27, 21.

than the rich[132], and quite as cheerful in mind[133]. Further the poor are free from many dangers which beset the rich; they can travel safely even when highwaymen are watching the road[134]. Poverty is an aid to philosophy, for a rich man, if he wishes to philosophize, must freely choose the life of the poor[135]. A poor man is not troubled by insincere friends[136]. In short, poverty is only hard for him who kicks against the pricks[137].

417. The subject of exile has the special interest that in
Comfort in fact so many philosophers endured this evil. To
exile. the Stoic there is in principle no such thing as exile, since the whole world is his country; but he does not for this reason disregard other sources of consolation. Cicero was plainly miserable, not only when he was formally exiled, but also when he was away from Rome in an honourable position; Seneca at least made the attempt to bear exile more bravely. Is it then so hard to be away from one's native place? Rome is crowded with strangers, who have come thither for pleasure or profit, study or novelty[138]. True, it is a beautiful town; but there is no place on earth so bare and unsightly, not even this Corsica to which Seneca is banished, but that some men choose it to reside in as a matter of taste[139]. Whole peoples have changed their abode, and we find Greek cities in the midst of barbarism, and the Macedonian language in India[140]; wherever he conquers the Roman dwells[141]. The exile has everywhere the company of the same stars above[142], of the same conscience within him[143]; even if he is separated from those near and dear

---

[132] See above, § 399.

[133] 'compara inter se pauperum et divitum voltus; saepius pauper et fidelius ridet' Sen. *Ep.* 80, 6.

[134] 'etiam in obsessa via pauperi pax est' *ib.* 14, 9.

[135] 'si vis vacare animo, aut pauper sis oportet aut pauperi similis' *ib.* 17, 5.

[136] '[paupertas] veros certosque amicos retinebit; discedet quisquis non te, sed aliud sequebatur. vel ob hoc unum amanda paupertas quod, a quibus ameris, ostendet' *ib.* 20, 7.

[137] 'paupertas nulli malum est nisi repugnanti' *ib.* 123, 16.

[138] *Dial.* xii 6, 2.

[139] 'usque eo commutatio ipsa locorum gravis non est, ut hic quoque locus a patria quosdam abduxerit' *ib.* 5.

[140] *ib.* 7, 1.   [141] 'ubicunque vicit Romanus habitat' *ib.* 7, 7.

[142] *ib.* 8, 6.

[143] 'licet in exilium euntibus virtutes suas secum ferre' *ib.* 8, 1.

to him, it is not for the first time, and he can still live with them in his thoughts and affections.

418. Free or slave, rich or poor, powerful or insignificant, wherever a man stands in the order of society, old age comes at last and imperiously stops all ambitions. It is, in the general opinion, a time of sadness[144]; to associate it with pleasure is not scandalous, only because it is paradoxical[145]. Cicero's work *de Senectute* shows how old age became attractive according to Roman tradition; Seneca is hardly so successful. With the fading of hope the stimulus to effort dies away in old age[146]; but though philosophy forbids idleness, nature cries out for rest. We cannot then approve when old men follow their professional occupations with undiminished zeal[147], and we must highly blame those who cannot quit their pleasures[148]. The great boon which old age brings is leisure; for this many great men, amongst them Augustus, have longed in vain[149]. This leisure gives the opportunity of making acquaintance with great men through their books, but better still, that of making acquaintance with our own selves.

Old age.

419. 'Give me,' said one to Musonius, 'a *viaticum* for old age.' He replied as follows:

Musonius' 'viaticum.'

'The rule is the same as for youth, to live methodically and according to nature[150]. Do not grieve because you are cut off from the pleasures of youth; for man is no more born for pleasure than any other animal: indeed man alone is an image of the deity[151], and has like excellences. And do not consider the divine excellences as beyond your reach; for we have no other

[144] 'subeunt morbi tristisque senectus' Verg. *G.* iii 67 quoted by Sen. *Ep.* 108, 29.

[145] 'plena est voluptatis [senectus], si illa scias uti' Sen. *Ep.* 12, 4.

[146] 'nihil magis cavendum est senectuti, quam ne languori se desidiaeque dedat' Cic. *Off.* i 34, 123; 'iuvenes possumus discere, possumus facilem animum et adhuc tractabilem ad meliora convertere' Sen. *Ep.* 108, 27.

[147] 'adeone iuvat occupatum mori?' Sen. *Dial.* x 20, 3. He instances an old gentleman of 90, who had consented to resign his official post at that age; but when the time came, he threw his whole household into mourning until he got his work back again.

[148] 'luxuria cum omni aetate turpis, tum senectuti foedissima est' Cic. *Off.* i 34, 123.

[149] Sen. *Dial.* x 4, 1 and 2. [150] τὸ ζῆν ὁδῷ καὶ κατὰ φύσιν.

[151] ἄνθρωπος μίμημα θεοῦ μόνον τῶν ἐπιγείων (see on hymn of Cleanthes, l. 5, in § 97).

notion of the gods than such as we derive from observing good men, whom therefore we call divine and godlike. He who has acquired in youth sound principles and systematic training will not be found to complain in old age of the loss of pleasures, of weakness of body, or because he is neglected by friends and acquaintance ; he will carry about with him a charm against all these evils, namely his own education. But if he has not been rightly educated, he will do well to go to a friend wiser than himself, and listen to his teaching and profit by it. And specially he will ponder over death, how it comes in nature's course to all, and therefore is no evil. With such thoughts he will be cheerful and contented, and so he will live a happy life. But let no one say that wealth brings happiness in old age ; that it does not bring a contented spirit is witnessed every day by a crowd of rich old men, who are in bad temper and low spirits, and feel deeply aggrieved[152].'

420. When we see death before us there remains a last act
Will-making.   to be performed. We look at the wealth which no longer belongs to us, and consider to whom it can most worthily be entrusted. We stand in the position of a judge who can no longer be bribed, and, with all the wisdom and good will that we have, we give this last verdict on those around us[153].

421. For death the whole of philosophy is a preparation ;
Death.   yet when it is no longer a matter of uncertain fear, but close at hand and sure, some last words are to be said. All this is in the course of nature, is according to the will of the Creator.

'God opens the door and says to you, "Go." "Go whither ?" To nothing terrible, but to the place from which you came, to your friends and kinsmen, to the elements[154]. What there was in you of fire goes to fire ; of earth, to earth ; of air, to air ; of water, to water. There is no Hades, nor Acheron, nor Cocytus, but all is full of gods and demons[155]. God has invited you ; be content when he calls others to the feast in your place.'

The philosopher does not look forward to renewing his personal life, or to meeting again with parent, wife, or child. But death is a release from all his pains and troubles ; and he

---

[152] Stob. *Flor.* 117, 8 (M).

[153] 'ubi mors interclusit omnia et ad ferendam sententiam incorruptum iudicem misit, quaerimus dignissimos quibus nostra tradamus ; nec quicquam cura sanctiore componimus quam quod ad nos non pertinet ' Sen. *Ben.* iv 11, 5.

[154] 'reverti unde veneris quid grave est ?' *Dial.* ix 11, 4.

[155] Epict. *Disc.* iii 13, 14 and 15; *ib.* iv 1, 106.

who has striven to live his life well will know how to meet death also at its due time[156]. If it come to him in the shipwreck, he will not scream nor blame God; if in the arena, he will not shrink from his enemy, whether man or beast. In this last short crisis he will bear witness that he accepts contentedly his mortal lot[157].

[156] 'male vivet quisquis nesciet bene mori' Sen. *Dial.* ix 11, 4; and see above, §§ 298, 299.

[157] 'quod tam cito fit, timetis diu?' Sen. *Dial.* i 6, 9; 'puto fortiorem eum esse, qui in ipsa morte est quam qui circa mortem. mors enim admota etiam imperitis animum dedit non vitandi inevitabilia ; sic gladiator tota pugna timidissimus iugulum adversario praestat et errantem gladium sibi adtemperat' *Ep.* 30, 8; 'the ship is sinking ! what then have I to do? I do the only thing that I can, not to be drowned full of fear, nor screaming nor blaming God, but knowing that what has been produced must also perish ; for I am not an immortal being' Epict. *Disc.* ii 5, 11 to 13.

CHAPTER XVI.

STOICISM IN ROMAN HISTORY AND LITERATURE.

422. ALTHOUGH up to this point it has been our main
Spread of   purpose to set forth the doctrines of Stoicism,
Stoicism.   we have seen incidentally that these came to
exercise a wide influence in Roman society, and that the later
teachers are far less occupied in the attainment of truth than in
the right guidance of disciples who lean upon them. In the
present chapter we propose to describe more particularly the
practical influence of Stoicism. Our information, whether drawn
from history or from poetry, refers generally to the upper classes
of Roman society; as to the influence of the sect amongst the
poor we have no sufficient record. But although it is very
generally held that the Stoics made no effort to reach the
working classes of Rome, or met with no success in that
direction[1], the evidence points rather to an opposite conclusion,
at any rate as regards all that development of the system which
was coloured by Cynism, the philosophy of the poor[2]. Our
actual records are therefore rather of the nature of side-lights
upon the system ; the main stream of Stoic influence may well
have flowed in courses with which we are imperfectly acquainted,
and its workings may perhaps come to light first in a period of
history which lies beyond our immediate scope.

---

[1] Lightfoot, *Philippians*, p. 319; Dill, *Roman Society*, p. 334; Warde Fowler,
Social Life at Rome, p. 27.

[2] The practice of street-preaching, as described by Horace and Epictetus, points
this way; and the world-wide diffusion of Stoicism, in more or less diluted forms, is
hardly reconcileable with its restriction to a single class of society.

423. Individual Romans who professed themselves disciples of the Porch owed their allegiance to the sect to two causes, in varying proportion. On the one hand they had attended lectures or private instruction given by eminent Stoic teachers, or had immersed themselves in Stoic literature. This influence was in almost all cases the influence of Greek upon Roman, and the friendship between the Stoic Panaetius and Scipio Aemilianus was the type of all subsequent discipleship. Scipio himself did not perhaps formally become a Stoic, but he introduced into Roman society the atmosphere of Stoicism, known to the Romans as *humanitas*: this included an aversion to war and civil strife, an eagerness to appreciate the art and literature of Greece, and an admiration for the ideals depicted by Xenophon, of the ruler in Cyrus, and of the citizen in Socrates[3]. All the Stoic nobles of the time of the republic are dominated by these feelings. On the other hand individuals were often attracted by the existence of a society which proclaimed itself independent of the will of rulers, and offered its members mutual support and consolation. Such men were often drawn into Stoicism by the persuasion of friends, without being necessarily well-grounded in philosophical principle; and in this way small groups or cliques might easily be formed in which social prejudice or political bias outweighed the formal doctrine of the school. Such a group was that of the 'old Romans' of the first century of the principate; and with the spread of Stoicism this indirect and imperfect method of attachment constantly grows in importance as compared with direct discipleship.

Conversion direct and indirect.

424. Of the first group of Roman Stoics the most notable was C. LAELIUS, the intimate friend of Scipio, who became consul in 140 B.C. In his youth he had listened to the teaching of Diogenes of Babylon, in later life he was the friend of Panaetius[4]. He was in his time· a

The Scipionic circle.

---

[3] 'semper Africanus Socraticum Xenophontem in manibus habebat' Cic. *Tusc. disp.* ii 26, 62; 'Cyrus ille a Xenophonte ad effigiem iusti imperi scriptus...quos quidem libros Africanus de manibus ponere non solebat' *ad Quint.* I i 8, 23.

[4] 'ille [Laelius] qui Diogenem Stoicum adulescens, post autem Panaetium audierat' *Fin.* ii 8, 24.

notable orator with a quiet flowing style[5]; his manners were cheerful[6], his temper was calm[7]; and, as we have seen[8], he seemed to many the nearest of all the Romans to the ideal of the Stoic sage. He is brought on as the chief speaker in Cicero's *de Amicitia*. Another close friend of Africanus was SP. MUMMIUS, the brother of the conqueror of Achaia; his oratory was marked by the ruggedness characteristic of the Stoic school[9]. Passing mention may be made of L. FURIUS PHILUS, consul in 136 B.C., and a member of the same group, though his philosophical views are not known to us[10].

425. From the 'humane' movement sprang the Gracchan reforms, which all alike aimed at deposing from power the class to which the reformers by birth belonged. To the temper of mind which made such a desire possible Stoic doctrine had largely contributed. The Greeks had taught their Roman pupils to see in the nascent Roman empire, bearing the watchword of the 'majesty of the Roman name' (*maiestas nominis Romani*), at least an approximation to the ideal Cosmopolis: and many Romans so far responded to this suggestion as to be not unfriendly towards plans for extending their citizenship and equalizing the privileges of those who enjoyed it. C. BLOSSIUS of Cumae, a pupil of Antipater of Tarsus, went so far as to instigate Tiberius Gracchus to the schemes which proved his destruction[11]; whilst other Stoics, equally sincere in their aims, disagreed with the violence shown by Tiberius in his choice of method. Amongst the latter was Q. AELIUS TUBERO, a nephew of Africanus[12], who became consul in 118 B.C. He devoted himself day and night to the

The Gracchan period.

---

[5] 'lenitatem Laelius habuit' Cic. *de Or.* iii 7, 28; 'C. Laelius et P. Africanus imprimis eloquentes' *Brut.* 21, 82.

[6] 'in C. Laelio multa hilaritas' *Off.* i 30, 108.

[7] 'praeclara est aequabilitas in omni vita et idem semper vultus eademque frons, ut de Socrate itemque de C. Laelio accepimus' *ib.* 26, 90.

[8] See above, § 326.

[9] 'Sp. [Mummius] nihilo ornatior, sed tamen astrictior; fuit enim doctus ex disciplina Stoicorum' Cic. *Brut.* 25, 94.

[10] 'non tulit ullos haec civitas humanitate politiores P. Africano, C. Laelio, L. Furio, qui secum eruditissimos homines ex Graecia palam semper habuerunt' *de Or.* ii 37, 154. [11] Cic. *Amic.* 11, 37.

[12] 'Ti. Gracchum a Q. Tuberone aequalibusque amicis derelictum videbamus' *ib.*

study of philosophy[13], and though of no mark as an orator, won himself respect by the strictness and consistency of his life[14]. Panaetius, Posidonius, and Hecato all addressed treatises to him[15]; and he is a leading speaker in Cicero's *Republic*.

426. After the fall of the Gracchi the Stoic nobles con-

Laelius to Lucilius.

tinued to play distinguished and honourable parts in public life. A family succession was maintained through two daughters of Laelius, so that here we may perhaps recognise the beginning of the deservedly famous 'Stoic marriages.' Of the two ladies the elder was married to Q. MUCIUS SCAEVOLA, known as 'the augur,' who was consul in 117 B.C. He was a devoted friend of Panaetius, and famous for his knowledge of civil law[16]. The younger daughter was married to C. FANNIUS, who obtained some distinction as a historian[17]. In C. LUCILIUS we find the Latin poet of Stoicism; the views which he expresses in his satires on religion and ethics are in the closest agreement with the teaching of Panaetius[18], and the large circulation of his poems must have diffused them through wide circles[19]. At the same time his attacks on the religious institutions of Numa and his ridicule of his own childish beliefs may well have brought philosophy into ill odour as atheistic and unpatriotic: and we find the statesmen of the next generation specially anxious to avoid any such imputations.

427. A dominating figure is that of Q. MUCIUS SCAEVOLA,

Scaevola 'the pontifex.'

commonly called 'the pontifex,' who was a nephew of his namesake mentioned above, and derived from him his interest in civil law; he was consul in 95 B.C. He overcame the difficulty about the popular religion by distin-

---

[13] *de Or.* iii 23, 87.

[14] 'quoniam Stoicorum est facta mentio, Q. Aelius Tubero fuit illo tempore, nullo in oratorum numero, sed vita severus et congruens cum ea disciplina quam colebat' *Brut.* 31, 117. [15] *Fin.* iv 9, 23; *Off.* iii 15, 63.

[16] 'Panaetii illius tui' Cic. *de Or.* i 11, 45; '[Mucius augur] oratorum in numero non fuit: iuris civilis intellegentia atque omni prudentiae genere praestitit' *Brut.* 26, 102.

[17] 'C. Fannius, C. Laeli gener,...instituto Laelii Panaetium audiverat. eius omnis in dicendo facultas ex historia ipsius non ineleganter scripta perspici potest' *ib.* 101.

[18] Schmekel, *Mittlere Stoa*, pp. 444, 445.

[19] See especially his praise of virtue, beginning 'virtus, Albine, est pretium persolvere verum | queis in versamur, queis vivimu' rebu' potesse' fr. 1.

guishing on Stoic lines three classes of deities, (i) mythical deities, celebrated by the poets with incredible and unworthy narrations[20]; (ii) philosophical deities, better suited for the schools than for the market-place; (iii) civic deities, whose ceremonies it is the duty of state officials to maintain[21], interpreting them so as to agree with the philosophers rather than with the poets[22]. In this spirit he filled the position of chief officer of the state religion. He was however no time-server; for being appointed after his consulship to be governor of Asia, he joined with his former quaestor P. RUTILIUS RUFUS in the design of repressing the extortion of the *publicani*. A decisive step taken by him was to declare all dishonourable contracts invalid[23]; and more than a generation later his just and sparing administration was gratefully remembered both at Rome and in the provinces[24]. The *equites* took their revenge not on Scaevola but on Rutilius[25], whom they brought to trial in 92 B.C., when Scaevola pleaded his cause in a simple and dignified way that became a Stoic, but did not exclude some traces of elegance[26]. He is regarded as the father of Roman law, for he was the first to codify it, which he did in eighteen volumes[27]. He also wrote a special work on definitions, which no doubt reflected the interest which the Stoics took in this part of logic.

428. It seems beyond dispute that the systematic study of law, which developed in later centuries into the science of Roman jurisprudence, and as such has exercised a weighty influence on the development of Western civilisation, had its beginnings amongst a group of men profoundly influenced by Stoic teaching. It does not

The Stoic lawyers.

---

[20] 'primum genus [poëticum] nugatorium dicit [Scaevola] esse, quod multa de dis fingantur indigna' Aug. *Civ. De.* iv 27, on the authority of Varro.

[21] 'tertium genus' inquit Varro 'quod in urbibus cives, maxime sacerdotes, nosse atque administrare debent' Aug. *Civ. De.* vi 5.

[22] 'maior societas nobis debet esse cum philosophis quam cum poetis' *ib.* 6.

[23] 'ego habeo [exceptionem] tectiorem ex Q. Mucii P. F. edicto Asiatico; *extra quam si ita negotium gestum est, ut eo stari non oporteat ex fide bona*; multaque sum secutus Scaevolae' Cic. *Att..* vi 1, 15..

[24] 'hanc gloriam iustitiae et abstinentiae fore inlustriorem spero.. quod Scaevolae contigit' *ib.* v 17, 5.   [25] See above, § 326.

[26] 'dixit causam illam quadam ex parte Q. Mucius, more suo, nullo adparatu, pure et dilucide' Cic. *de Or.* i 53, 229; 'Scaevola parcorum elegantissimus' *Brut.* 40, 148.

[27] 'Q. Mucius pontifex maximus ius civile primus constituit, generatim in libros XVIII redigendo' Pompon. *Dig.* i 2, 2, 41.

therefore follow that the fundamental ideas expressed by such terms as *ius gentium, lex naturae*, are exclusively Stoic in origin. The former phrase appears to have been in common use at this time to indicate the laws generally in force amongst the peoples that surrounded Rome; the latter is a philosophical term derived from the Greek, denoting an ideal law which ought to exist amongst men everywhere[28]. The principle of obedience to nature is not peculiar to the Stoic philosophy, but belongs to the common substratum of all philosophical thought. It does however seem to be the case that the Stoic theory of the 'common law' (κοινὸς νόμος) was in fact the stimulus which enabled the Romans to transform their system of 'rights,' gradually throwing over all that was of the nature of mechanical routine or caste privilege, and harmonizing contradictions by the principle of fairness. The successor of Scaevola was C. AQUILIUS GALLUS, praetor in 66 B.C. with Cicero, of whom it is specially noted that he guided his exposition of law by the principle of equity[29]; and after him S. SULPICIUS RUFUS, the contemporary and intimate friend of Cicero. We do not know that he was a Stoic, but he was a student of dialectic under L. LUCILIUS BALBUS, who as well as his brother belonged to this school[30]; and he followed Stoic principles in studying oratory just enough to make his exposition clear[31]. He was the acknowledged head of his profession, and compiled 180 books on law[32]. In the civil war he took sides with Caesar[33].

429. Amongst men of high rank definitely pledged to
Stoics of the   Stoicism in the generation preceding Cicero are
Sullan period.   further L. AELIUS STILO (circ. 145–75 B.C.)[34], who devoted himself to Roman grammar and antiquities, and was

---

[28] H. Nettleship, *Ius Gentium* (*Journal of Philology* xiii 26, pp. 169 sqq.).

[29] 'qui iuris civilis rationem nunquam ab aequitate seiunxerit' Cic. *Caec.* 27, 78.

[30] 'cum discendi causa duobus peritissimis operam dedisset, L. Lucilio Balbo et C. Aquilio Gallo' *Brut.* 42, 154; cf. *de Orat.* iii 21, 78.

[31] 'Servius [mihi videtur] eloquentiae tantum assumpsisse, ut ius civile facile possit tueri' *Brut.* 40, 150.

[32] '[Servius] longe omnium in iure civili princeps' *ib.* 41, 151: Pomp. *Dig.* i 2, 2, 43.

[33] For an interesting account of his career and death see Warde Fowler, *Social Life at Rome*, pp. 118–121.

[34] 'idem Aelius Stoicus esse voluit' Cic. *Brutus* 56, 206.

A.   25

the teacher of both Cicero and Varro; Q. LUCILIUS BALBUS, whose knowledge of this philosophy rivalled that of his Greek teachers[35], and who is the exponent of the Stoic view in Cicero's *de Natura Deorum*, the scene of which takes us back to about 76 B.C.; SEXTUS POMPEIUS, uncle of Pompey the Great, and distinguished both as a philosopher and as a jurist[36]; and more particularly P. RUTILIUS RUFUS, to whom we have already referred[37]. A pupil and devoted admirer of Panaetius[38], a trained philosopher[39], and a sound lawyer[40], he brought his career at Rome to an abrupt end by his firm resistance to the *publicani*, as already recounted[41]. With true cosmopolitanism he retired to Smyrna, and accepted the citizenship of that town. His stern principles did not prevent him from saving his life in the massacre ordered by Mithradates, by assuming Greek dress[42]; the massacre itself was the ripe fruit of the abuses which he had endeavoured to repress. He is one of the characters in Cicero's *de Republica*.

430. Of the Stoics of Cicero's time the most eminent was M. PORCIUS CATO (95–48 B.C.). In him Stoicism received a special colouring by association with the traditions of ancient Roman manners. In his early years he became a pupil of Antipater of Tyre[43], and so far adopted the Cynic ideal as to train himself for public life by freely submitting to hunger, cold, and hardship[44]. After a period of service in the army he made a journey to Asia to secure the companionship of Athenodorus the elder[45]. He became a practised speaker; and though he adhered firmly to the Stoic tradition of plain language and short sentences[46], yet could become eloquent on the great

---

[35] 'Q. Lucilius Balbus tantos progressus habebat in Stoicis, ut cum excellentibus in eo genere Graecis compararetur' *N. D.* i 6, 15.

[36] 'Sextus frater praestantissimum ingenium contulerat ad summam iuris civilis et rerum Stoicarum scientiam' *Brutus* 47, 175.　　　　　[37] See § 427.

[38] 'Posidonius scribit P. Rutilium dicere solere, quae Panaetius praetermisisset, propter eorum quae fecisset praestantiam neminem esse persecutum' Cic. *Off.* iii 2, 10.

[39] '[P. Rutilius], doctus vir et Graecis litteris eruditus, prope perfectus in Stoicis' *Brutus* 30, 114.

[40] 'multa praeclara de iure' *ib.*　　　　　[41] See above, § 326.

[42] Cic. *pro Rabir.* 10, 27.　　　　　[43] Plut. *Cato minor* 4, 1.

[44] *ib.* 5, 3.　　　　　[45] *ib.* 10, 1.

[46] 'Cato perfectus, mea sententia, Stoicus,...in ea est haeresi, quae nullum sequitur florem orationis neque dilatat argumentum; sed minutis interrogatiunculis, quasi punctis, quod proposuit efficit' Cic. *Par.* Pro. 2.

themes of his philosophy[47], and could win the approval of the people even for its paradoxes[48]. He was resolutely opposed to bribery and extortion. As quaestor in B.C. 66 he introduced reform into the public finances, and put an end to embezzlements by officials. His popularity became very great, and he was elected tribune of the plebs towards the end of the year 63 B.C., when his voice decided the senators to decree the death of the associates of Catiline. With his subsequent policy Cicero finds fault, because Cato refused to connive at the extortions of the *publicani*: and from Cicero's criticisms has arisen the accepted view that Cato was an unpractical statesman. On the other hand it may well be held that if the Roman aristocracy had included more men like Cato, the republic might have been saved: and towards the end of his life Cicero bitterly lamented that he had not sufficiently valued the sincere friendship which Cato offered him[49]. In the year 54 B.C. the candidates for the office of tribune paid him a singular compliment; each deposited with him a large sum of money, which he was to forfeit if in Cato's opinion he was guilty of bribery[50]. His whole political life was guided by the strictest moral principle[51]; even in so unimportant a matter as Cicero's request for a triumph he would do nothing to oblige a friend[52]. In private life he attempted to put into practice the principle of the community of women taught in Zeno's *Republic*. He had married Marcia, daughter of Philippus, and had three children by her: in 56 B.C. he gave her up to his friend C. Hortensius, whose family was in danger of becoming extinct: finally on the threatening of the civil war in B.C. 50 he took her back to his own home. At a time when the marriage bond was lightly treated by many of his contemporaries he at least rose above petty motives. In the civil

[47] 'Cato dumtaxat de magnitudine animi, de morte, de omni laude virtutis, Stoice solet, oratoriis ornamentis adhibitis, dicere' Cic. *Par.* Pro. 3.

[48] 'animadverti Catonem...dicendo consequi ut illa [=loci graves ex philosophia] populo probabilia viderentur' *ib.* 1.

[49] '[doleo] plus apud me simulationem aliorum quam [Catonis] fidem valuisse' *ad Att.* iii 15, 2 (in B.C. 48).

[50] *ib.* iv 15, 7.

[51] 'Catoni vitam ad certam rationis normam dirigenti et diligentissime perpendenti momenta officiorum omnium' *Mur.* 2, 3.

[52] Cato apud Cic. *ad Fam.* xv 5, 2.

war he took sides strongly against Caesar, his old political opponent. His self-sought death after Pharsalia won him a distinction which he had earned better by his life: and the unmeasured praise bestowed upon him a century later is perhaps due more to political bias than to philosophical respect[53]. The few words with which Virgil honours his memory are more effective, when he pictures Cato as chosen to be a judge in the world of the blest[54]. Cato represents the Stoic view as to the *summum bonum* in Cicero's *de Finibus*.

431. Contemporary with Cicero and Cato was M. TERENTIUS

Varro, Brutus and Porcia.
VARRO (B.C. 116–28). In his public career and political principles he was not unlike Cato; in his literary activity he more resembled Cicero. Both Varro and Cicero were deeply influenced by Stoic teaching, but as they were by no means professed adherents of this philosophy[55], they may be here passed by. In the next generation M. JUNIUS BRUTUS (85–42 B.C.) concerns us more: for by his marriage with PORCIA, Cato's daughter and an ardent Stoic, he came into a family connexion with the sect, with which his personal views, as we have seen, were not entirely in agreement[56]. Still Brutus was not altogether unfitted to play the part of Cato's successor; he was no mean orator[57], and wrote more than one philosophical treatise[58]; whilst Cicero dedicated several of his philosophical works to him[59]. But the practical Stoicism of Porcia, who stabbed herself in the thigh to show that she was fit to be trusted with a political secret, shines out more brightly than the speculations of her husband. In her honour Martial

[53] See for instance below, § 441, note 94.
[54] 'his [sc. piis] dantem iura Catonem' Verg. *Aen.* viii 670.
[55] 'illam Ἀκαδημικήν...ad Varronem transferamus: etenim sunt Ἀντιόχεια, quae iste valde probat' Cic. *Att.* xiii 12, 3; 'in iis quae erant contra ἀκαταληψίαν praeclare collecta ab Antiocho, Varroni dedi;...aptius esse nihil potuit ad id philosophiae genus, quo ille maxime mihi delectari videtur' *ib.* 19, 3 and 5.
[56] See above, § 123.
[57] 'tu, [Brute,] qui non linguam modo acuisses exercitatione dicendi, sed et ipsam eloquentiam locupletavisses graviorum artium instrumento' Cic. *Brutus* 97, 331.
[58] 'Brutus in eo libro quem de virtute composuit' Sen. *Dial.* xii 9, 4; 'Brutus in eo libro quem περὶ καθήκοντος inscripsit, dat multa praecepta' *Ep.* 95, 45. There was also a treatise *de patientia*.
[59] The *de Finibus*, *de Natura Deorum*, and *Tusculanae disputationes*.

has written one of the few epigrams in which he allows himself to be caught in a mood of admiration: yet his story of Porcia's death must be rejected as unhistorical[60].

432. After the death of Brutus Stoicism ceases for a while

Horace.

to play a prominent part in Roman history; but its indirect influence is very marked in the two great poets of the Augustan epoch, Horace and Virgil. Of these HORACE is in the main an Epicurean, and as such is quite entitled to use the Stoic paradoxes as matter for ridicule, and even to anticipate dangerous consequences from their practical application[61]. But in fact his works show a constantly increasing appreciation of the ethics of Stoicism. He recognises the high ideals and civic activity of its professors[62], and he draws a noble picture of the Stoic sage, confident in his convictions, and bidding defiance to the crowd and the tyrant alike[63]. Of that practical wisdom and genial criticism which has made Horace the favourite poet of so many men eminent in public life, no small part consists of Stoic principles deftly freed from the paradoxical form in which they were conveyed to professed adherents.

433. With this picture of Stoicism seen from without we

Virgil.

must contrast that given us by VIRGIL, who inherited the Stoic tradition from Aratus[64], his model for the *Georgics.* Virgil's mind is penetrated by Stoic feeling, and his works are an interpretation of the universe in the Stoic sense; but like so many of his contemporaries he holds aloof from formal adherence to the sect, and carefully avoids its technical language. Quite possibly too he incorporated in his system elements drawn from other philosophies. In physics he accepts the principle that the fiery aether is the source of all life[65]; it is identical with the divine spirit[66] and the all-informing mind[67]. From this standpoint he is led on to the doctrine of purgatory[68],

---

[60] Mart. *Ep.* i 42.   [61] See above, § 374, note 66.

[62] 'nunc agilis fio et mersor civilibus undis, | virtutis verae custos rigidusque satelles' *Ep.* i 1, 16 and 17.

[63] See above, § 316, note 96.   [64] See above, § 90.

[65] 'igneus est ollis vigor et caelestis origo | seminibus' *Aen.* vi 730, 731.

[66] 'caelum et terras | spiritus intus alit' *ib.* 724, 726.

[67] 'totamque infusa per artus | mens agitat molem' *ib.* 726, 727.

[68] See above, §§ 295 to 297.

and from that he looks forward to the time of the conflagration, when all creation will be reconciled by returning to its primitive unity in the primal fire-spirit[69]. Still Virgil's picture must be regarded rather as an adaptation than as an exposition of Stoicism ; it lacks the sharp outlines and the didactic tone of the poetry of Cleanthes or Lucretius, and other interpretations are by no means excluded.

434. With the problem of the government of the universe
Virgil's Virgil's mind is occupied throughout the *Aeneid*.
theology. He is constantly weighing the relative importance of the three forces, fate, the gods, and fortune, precisely as the philosophers do. To each of the three he assigns a part in the affairs of men ; but that taken by fate is unmistakably predominant. The individual gods have very little importance in the poem; they are to a large extent allegorical figures, representing human instincts and passions ; they cannot divert destiny from its path, though with their utmost effort they may slightly delay its work or change its incidence. Above all these little gods Jove towers aloft, a power magnificent and munificent; at his voice the gods shudder and the worlds obey. But the power of Jove rests upon his complete acceptance of the irrevocable decrees of fate[70]. The critic may even describe him as a puppet-king, who wears an outward semblance of royalty, but is really obedient to an incessant interference from a higher authority. Virgil however appears truly to hold the Stoic principle that Fate and Jove are one ; he thus takes us at once to the final problem of philosophy, the reconciliation of the conceptions of Law formed on the one hand by observing facts (the modern 'Laws of Nature') and on the other hand by recognising the moral instinct (the modern 'Moral Law'). As we have seen, a reconciliation of these two by logic is intrinsically impossible. Virgil however shows us how they may be in practice reconciled by a certain attitude of mind ; and because that attitude is one of resignation to and cooperation with the supreme power, it

---

[69] 'donec longa dies, perfecto temporis orbe, | concretam exemit labem, purumque reliquit | aetherium sensum atque aurai simplicis ignem' *Aen.* vi 745 to 747.
[70] 'desine fata deum flecti sperare precando' *ib.* 376.

would seem right to place Virgil by the side of Cleanthes as one of the religious poets of Stoicism.

435. Virgil's conception of ethics is displayed in the character

Virgil's ethics. of Aeneas. Much modern criticism revolts against the character of Aeneas exactly as it does against that of Cato, and for the same reason, that it is without sympathy for Stoic ethics. To understand Aeneas we must first picture a man whose whole soul is filled by a reverent regard for destiny and submission to Jove, who represents destiny on its personal side. He can therefore never play the part of the hero in revolt; but at the same time he is human, and liable to those petty weaknesses and aberrations from which even the sage is not exempt. He can hesitate or be hasty, can love or weep; but the sovereignty of his mind is never upset. In a happy phrase Virgil sums up the whole ethics of Stoicism :

'Calm in his soul he abides, and the tears roll down, but in vain[71].'

In contrast to Aeneas stands Dido, intensely human and passionate, and in full rebellion against her destiny. She is to him Eve the temptress, Cleopatra the seducer; but she is not destined to win a final triumph. A modern romance would doubtless have a different ending.

436. Amongst writers who adopted much of the formal

Ovid. teaching of Stoicism without imbibing its spirit we may reckon OVID (43 B.C.–18 A.D.). Not only does he accept the central idea of Stoicism, that it is the divine fire by virtue of which every man lives and moves[72], but he opens his greatest work by a description of the creation[73] which appears to follow Stoic lines, and in which the erect figure of man is specially recognised as the proof of the pre-eminence which Providence has assigned to him over all the other works of the Creator[74]. But the tales related in the *Metamorphoses* show no

---

[71] 'mens immota manet; lacrimae volvuntur inanes' *Aen.* iv 449; the 'lacrimae inanes' indicate the ruffling of the soul, in which the intelligence and will take no part.

[72] 'est deus in nobis: agitante calescimus illo' Ov. *F.* vi 5.

[73] 'ante mare et terras, et quod tegit omnia caelum, | unus erat toto Naturae vultus in orbe, | quem dixere Chaos, etc.' *Met.* i 5 to 88.

[74] 'os homini sublime dedit, caelumque tueri | iussit, et erectos ad sidera tollere vultus' *ib.* 85 and 86.

trace of the serious religious purpose of Virgil; and the society pictured in Ovid's love poems gives only a caricature of the Stoic doctrines of the community of women, the absence of jealousy, and outspokenness of speech. Finally the plaintive tone of the *Tristia* shows how little Ovid was in touch with Stoic self-control amidst the buffetings of fortune.

437. In the time of the next *princeps* we first find Cremutius Stoicism associated with an unsympathetic atti-
Cordus. tude towards the imperial government. There was nothing in Stoic principles to suggest this opposition. Tiberius himself had listened to the teaching of the Stoic Nestor, and the simplicity of his personal life and the gravity of his manners might well have won him the support of sincere philosophers. But if Stoicism did not create the spirit of opposition, it confirmed it where it already existed. The memory of Cato associated Stoic doctrines with republican views: vague idealisations of Brutus and Cassius suggested the glorification of tyrannicide. CREMUTIUS CORDUS (ob. A.D. 25) had offended Seianus by a sarcastic remark: for when Tiberius repaired the theatre of Pompey, and the senate voted that a statue of Seianus should be erected there, Cordus said that this meant really spoiling the theatre[75]. Seianus then dropped a hint to his client Satrius, who accused Cordus before the senate of writing a history in which he highly praised Brutus, and declared Cassius to have been 'the last of the Romans.' A word of apology would have saved the life of Cordus; he resolved to die by his own act[76], to the great annoyance of his prosecutors[77]. From this time on suicide became an object of political ambition. The Stoic tradition continued in the family of Cordus, and to his daughter Marcia, as a fellow-member of the sect, Seneca addressed the well-known *Consolatio*[78]; but the title of 'old Romans'

[75] 'exclamavit Cordus tunc vere theatrum perire' Sen. *Dial.* vi 22, 4.

[76] Tac. *Ann.* iv 34. Tacitus entirely ignores the personal motives underlying the story, and quite unnecessarily suggests that Tiberius was adopting the policy of repressing freedom of historical narration.

[77] 'accusatores queruntur mori Cordum' Sen. *Dial.* vi 22, 7.

[78] That Cremutius Cordus was a professed Stoic seems a fair inference from the story as a whole, and yet, as in several similar cases, is not expressly stated.

describes far better the true leanings of the men of whom Cordus
was the forerunner.

438. In the reign of Gaius (Caligula) we first find philoso-

Kanus
Iulius.
phers as such exposed to persecution; and we may
infer that, like the Jews, they resisted tacitly or
openly the claim of the emperor to be worshipped as a god.
IULIUS GRAECINUS, according to Seneca, was put to death for
no other reason than that he was a better man than a tyrant
liked to see alive[79]. KANUS IULIUS reproved the emperor to
his face, and heard with calmness his own doom pronounced.
During the ten days still left to him he went quietly on with his
daily occupations; he was engaged in a game of chess when the
centurion summoned him. 'After my death,' he said to his
opponent, 'do not boast that you won the game.' His philosopher
accompanied him, and inquired how his thoughts were occupied.
'I propose,' said Kanus, 'to observe whether at the last moment
the soul is conscious of its departure. Afterwards, if I discover
what the condition of departed souls is, I will come back and
inform my friends[80].'

439. In the reign of Claudius we find Stoics engaged in

Arria the
elder.
actual conspiracy against the emperor. The name
of PAETUS CAECINA introduces us to a famous
Stoic family, for his wife was ARRIA the elder. Pliny tells us,
on the authority of her granddaughter Fannia, how when her
husband and son both fell sick together, and the latter died, she
carried out the whole funeral without her husband's knowledge;
and each time that she entered his sick chamber, assumed a
cheerful smile and assured him that the boy was much better.
Whenever her grief became too strong, she would leave the
room for a few minutes to weep, and return once more calm.
When Scribonianus in Illyria rebelled against Claudius, Paetus
took his side; upon his fall he was brought a prisoner to Rome.
Arria was not allowed to accompany him, but she followed him
in a fishing boat. She encouraged him to face death by piercing

[79] 'quem [Graecinum Iulium] C. Caesar occidit ob hoc unum, quod melior vir erat
quam esse quemquam tyranno expedit' Sen. *Ben.* ii 21, 5.

[80] *Dial.* ix 14, 4-10.

her own breast with a dagger, declaring 'it doesn't hurt[81],' and
upon his death she determined not to survive him.   Thrasea,
her son-in-law, tried to dissuade her.   'If I were condemned,
would you,' said he, 'wish your daughter to die with me?'
'Yes,' said Arria, 'if she had lived with you as long and as
happily as I with Paetus.'   Here we have a deliberate justification
of the Hindu practice of the Satī.

440.   In the reign of Nero the Stoics are still more prominent, and almost always in opposition.   SENECA, of
course, the emperor's tutor and minister, is on the
government side; and from his life we can draw the truest
picture of the imperial civil servant in high office.   We shall
certainly not expect to find that Seneca illustrated in his own
life all the virtues that he preached; on the other hand we shall
not readily believe that the ardent disciple of Attalus[82] and
affectionate husband of Paulina was a man of dissolute life or of
avaricious passions.   Simple tastes, an endless capacity for hard
work, and scrupulous honesty were the ordinary marks of the
Roman official in those days, as they are of members of the
Civil Service of India to-day[83].   Seneca is often accused of
having been too supple as a minister; but he was carrying out
the principles of his sect better by taking an active part in
politics than if he had, like many others, held sullenly aloof[84].
He did not indeed imitate Cato or Rutilius Rufus, who had
carried firmness of principle to an extent that laid them open
to the charge of obstinacy; but in submitting frankly to power
greater than his own he still saw to it that his own influence
should count towards the better side.   For the story of his
political career we cannot do better than to refer to the latest

Seneca.

[81] 'casta suo gladium cum traderet Arria Paeto, | quem de visceribus traxerat ipsa
suis, | "si qua fides, vulnus quod feci non dolet," inquit, | "sed quod tu facies, hoc mihi,
Paete, dolet"' Martial *Ep.* i 14; 'praeclarum illud eiusdem, ferrum stringere, perfo-
dere pectus, extrahere pugionem, porrigere marito, addere vocem immortalem et
paene divinam "Paete, non dolet"' Pliny *Ep.* iii 16, 6.

[82] See above, § 126.

[83] 'non derunt et frugalitatis exactae homines et laboriosae operae' Sen. *Dial.* x
18, 4.   For the British official the authority of the author of *Tales from the Hills* will
suffice.

[84] See below, § 448, note 115.

historian of his times[85]; of his work as a philosopher, to which he himself attributed the greater importance, a general account has been given above[86] and more particular discussions form the central theme of this book.

441. From Seneca we pass naturally to some mention of
Persius and Lucan. the poets Persius and Lucan. A. PERSIUS FLACCUS (34–62 A.D.) became at 16 years of age the pupil and companion of the Stoic philosopher Cornutus: he was also a relative of the Arriae already mentioned. He gives us a charming picture of his teacher's ways of life, which were doubtless typical[87]: and his summary view of the scope of philosophy well indicates how its proportions had shrunk at this period. Dialectic is not mentioned, and physics has interest only in its bearing upon the position and duty of the individual.

> 'Go, study, hapless folk, and learn to know
> The end and object of our life—what are we;
> The purpose of our being here; the rank
> Assigned us at the start, and where and when
> The turn is smoothest round the perilous post;
> The bounds of wealth; life's lawful aims; the use
> Of hoards of coin new-minted; what the claims
> Of fatherland and kinsfolk near and dear;
> The will of God concerning thee, and where
> Thou standest in the commonwealth of man[88].'

His contemporary M. ANNAEUS LUCANUS (39–65 A.D.), a nephew of Seneca, plunged more deeply both into philosophy and into politics. In both he displayed ardour insufficiently tempered with discretion; he had a far keener sense of his personal grievances than became a Stoic, and was much more of a critic than of a reformer. Yet hardly any writer expresses more forcibly the characteristic doctrines of Stoicism, as they seized the imagination of young Romans of the upper classes.

[85] Henderson's *Nero*, pp. 31–38, 50–142, 257–288.
[86] See above, §§ 127–129.
[87] See above, § 125.
[88] Persius *Sat.* iii 66–72. The translations in this section are by Mr W. H. Porter.

Amongst such doctrines that of the conflagration was clearly prominent.

> 'So when this frame of things has been dissolved,
> And the world's many ages have received
> Their consummation in one final hour,
> Chaos recalled shall gain his utmost seat,
> The constellations in confusion dire
> Hurled each on each together clash; the stars
> Flaming shall fall into the deep; the earth
> No longer shall extend her barrier shores,
> And fling the waters from her; and the Moon
> Shall meet the Sun in fratricidal war[89].'

> 'One pyre awaits the Universe; in ruin
> 'Twill mix with bones of men the heavenly spheres[90].'

Lucan emphasizes the pantheistic interpretation of the divine nature;

> 'God is all eye can see or heart can feel[91].'

> 'The powers of heaven are round about us all;
> And though from out the temple come no voice,
> Nought can we do without the will of God[92].'

To the idealized Cato he addresses the noblest praises;

> 'For sure a consecrated life is thine,
> The laws of heaven thy pattern, God thy guide[93].'

> 'See the true Father of his country, worth
> The homage of thine altars, Rome; for they
> Who swear by him shall never be ashamed.
> If e'er the yoke is lifted from thy neck,
> Now or hereafter he shall be thy God[94].'

442. The careers of Seneca and Musonius, and the early years of Lucan himself, indicate sufficiently that there was no essential opposition between Stoic principles and the Roman principate; in other words, that Stoics as such were not 'republicans.' Rather the contrary; for nearly all the Greek philosophers had been inclined

Civil service and 'old Romans.'

---

[89] *Phars.* i 72 to 80.
[91] See above, § 242, note 9.
[93] *ib.* 556 and 557.
[90] *ib.* vii 814 and 815.
[92] *Phars.* ix 573 and 574.
[94] *ib.* 601 to 604. The force of this tribute is impaired by the similar praise given to Pompey (*Phars.* vii 682–689) and to Brutus (*ib.* 588 and 589).

to favour monarchy, and the Stoics had been conspicuous in the desire to abolish the distinctions of birth and class upon which the Roman aristocracy laid so much stress, and which the principate was disposed to ignore. But in fact Stoicism was the common mould in which the educated youth of Rome were shaped at this period; it produced honest, diligent, and simple-minded men, exactly suited to be instruments of the great imperial bureaucracy. Large numbers entered the service of the state, and were heard of no more; such an one (except for Seneca's incidental account of him) was C. LUCILIUS, Seneca's correspondent. The great work of Roman government was carried on in silence, just as that of India in the present day. This silence was probably on the whole beneficial to society, though it was often felt as a constraint by the individual. For this reason and many others there were at Rome (as everywhere and at all times) many able but disappointed men; they became the critics of the government, and from being critics they might at any time become conspirators; but at no period did they seriously aim at restoring the republican system. Their political creed was limited, and did not look beyond the interests of the class from which they sprang. They claimed for members of the senate at Rome their ancient personal privileges, and especially that of *libertas*, that is, freedom to criticize and even to insult the members of the government; they sang the praises of Cato, celebrated the birthdays of Brutus and Cassius[95], and practised a kind of 'passive resistance' based on Oriental methods, by quitting life without hesitation when they were baulked in their immediate wishes by the government. When the administration was carried on decently these men were ridiculous; when from time to time it became a scandal they were heroes.

443. The early years of Nero's reign show us plainly that the true spirit of Stoicism was far more developed on the side of the government than on that of the aristocracy. Nothing distinguishes Seneca more honourably than his humane attitude towards the slave population; and he

Republican
prejudices.

---

[95] 'quale coronati Thrasea Helvidiusque bibebant | Brutorum et Cassi natalibus' Juv. *Sat.* v 36 and 37. See also G. Boissier, *L'Opposition sous les Césars.*

was chief minister of the princeps when in the year A.D. 61 a 'notable case[96]' arose, in which the human rights of slaves were involved. The city prefect, Pedanius Secundus, was killed by one of his slaves. It was contended in the senate that by ancient custom the whole household, old and young, guilty and innocent, must be put to death alike; and this view prevailed and was carried into effect. Public opinion, according to Tacitus[97], was unanimous against such severity; it looked, not unreasonably, to the emperor and his minister to prevent it[97a]. They on the contrary left the decision to the free judgment of the senate. Where now were the men of philosophic principle, of world-wide sympathies, of outspoken utterance? The historian tells us that not one was found in the senate. The honourable men who could defy an emperor's death-sentence still lacked the courage to speak out against the prejudices of their own class; many indeed uttered exclamations, expressing pity for the women, the young, and the indubitably innocent, and even voted against the executions; but even in so simple a matter there was not a man to follow the lead of Catiline in Cicero's days, and take up as his own the cause of the oppressed. The leader of the merciless majority was C. Cassius Longinus, a celebrated jurist, and one who regularly celebrated the honours of Cassius the conspirator.

444. But although the administration of which Nero was the head was largely manned by professed Stoics, and stood as a whole for the better sympathies of the Roman people, the course of court intrigue brought about a fierce conflict between the government and a growing force of public opinion of which the 'old Roman' group of Stoics were sometimes the spokesmen, and at other times the silent representatives. To Nero the consideration of his own safety was predominant over every consideration of justice to individuals, and herein he stood condemned (and knew that it was so) by the judgment of all men of philosophic temper. The first of his

Nero and the Stoics.

---

[96] Henderson's *Nero*, pp. 90 sqq.　　　　　[97] *Annals* xiv 42, 2.

[97a] The government had in fact appointed an officer for the prevention of cruelty to slaves : 'de iniuriis dominorum in servos qui audiat positus est, qui et saevitiam et libidinem et in praebendis ad victum necessariis avaritiam compescat' Sen. *Ben.* iii 22, 3.

victims, and perhaps the most deserving of our admiration, was
RUBELLIUS PLAUTUS, accused by Tigellinus because he maintained the irritating cult of the 'tyrannicides,' and had joined the
disloyal sect of the Stoics[98]. The charge of disloyalty against
himself and his companions he disproved; for, advised by his
Stoic teachers Coeranus and Musonius, he declined to take part
in a rising which might have been successful, and calmly awaited
his fate (60 A.D.). In the conspiracy of Piso, which broke out a
few years later, PLAUTUS LATERANUS is named by the historian
as one of the few whose motives were honourable and whose
conduct was consistently courageous[99]. The later years of Nero's
reign are illuminated in the pages of Tacitus by the firmness of
men like THRASEA PAETUS, PACONIUS AGRIPPINUS, and BAREA
SORANUS, and the heroic devotion of women like the younger
ARRIA, Thrasea's wife, and SERVILIA, the daughter of Soranus[100].
In the persecution of this group the modern historian finds ex-
tenuating circumstances, but at Rome itself it appeared as though
the emperor were engaged in the attempt to extirpate virtue
itself[101].

445. Upon the fall of Nero the 'old Romans' came for a
short time into power under the principate of Galba,
and amongst others HELVIDIUS PRISCUS, Thrasea's
son-in-law, returned from exile. From the account of Tacitus
he appears to have been a very sincere adherent of the Stoic
school.

*Helvidius
Priscus.*

'He was not like others who adopt the name of philosopher in order to
cloak an idle disposition. He followed those teachers who maintain that
only the honourable is good, and only the base is evil; power, nobility, and
other things external to the soul being neither good nor evil. He designed
so to fortify himself thereby against the blows of fortune that he could play
his part in public affairs without flinching[102].'

His first act on returning to Rome was to commence a
prosecution of the accuser of Thrasea. The senate was divided
in opinion as to the wisdom of this step, and when Helvidius

---

[98] Tac. *Ann.* xiv 57.   [99] See Henderson's *Nero*, pp. 257-283.
[100] Tac. *Ann.* xvi 21-35.
[101] 'Nero virtutem ipsam exscindere concupivit' *ib.* 21.
[102] *Hist.* iv 5.

abandoned the suit some praised his charity, whilst others lamented his indecision[103]. He resumed his attempt, as we shall see, at a later time.

446. Vespasian was undoubtedly tolerant in his views : his reign began with the restitution of honours to the deceased Galba, and the much-respected Musonius[104]
His fall.
seized the opportunity to attack in the senate P. Egnatius Celer, whose treachery had brought about the fall of Soranus[105], for false evidence. The trial was postponed, but resulted a little later in the condemnation of Celer[106]. Public opinion took the side of Musonius: but the accused found a champion in Demetrius the Cynic philosopher, and at least defended himself with the ability and courage of his sect. Thereupon Helvidius resumed his prosecution of the accuser of Thrasea ; but the emperor, now anxious to let bygones be bygones, refused to approve[107]. This second failure appears to have embittered Helvidius: his opposition to Vespasian became open and insulting, and brought about his death[108]. The life of his wife FANNIA was worthy of the two Arriae, her grandmother and her mother. Twice she followed her husband into exile ; a third time she brought this punishment upon herself, by encouraging his friend Senecio to publish his biography, supplying him with the materials, and openly justifying her action. In her private life she had singular charm and affability ; and her death appeared to Pliny to close an era of noble women[109].

447. It seems probable that the Stoic nobles found the low birth of Vespasian as intolerable as the tyranny of Nero ; at any rate they soon resumed their attitude
Renewal of the Stoic opposition.
of opposition to the government, and the punishment of Helvidius, if intended as a warning, proved rather a provocation. It appears that he and the 'old Romans' began a systematic propaganda in favour of what they called 'democracy[110],' that is, the government of the Roman empire

---

[103] Tac. *Hist.* iv 6.   [104] See above, §§ 130, 131.   [105] See above, § 444.
[106] Tac. *Hist.* iv 40.   [107] *ib.* 43 and 44.
[108] Dill, *Roman Society*, p. 152.   [109] Pliny *Ep.* vii 19, 7.
[110] τῷ ὄχλῳ προσέκειτο, βασιλείας τε ἀεὶ κατηγόρει, καὶ δημοκρατίαν ἐπῄνει Dion Cassius lxvi 12.

by the senatorial class; and they probably involved many professed philosophers in this impracticable and reactionary movement. Vespasian resolved on expelling all the philosophers from Rome. From this general sentence the best known of all, Musonius, was excepted[111], and we must infer that he had shown the good sense to keep himself free from political entanglements. In spite of this act of Vespasian, Stoicism continued to gain ground, and during the greater part of the period of the Flavian dynasty met with little interference.

448. But towards the end of the reign of Domitian a more

Persecution by Domitian.

violent persecution broke out. ARULENUS RUSTICUS had been tribune of the plebs in 66 A.D., and had then proposed to use his veto in an attempt to save the life of Thrasea Paetus[112]. In 69 A.D. he was praetor, and as such headed an embassy sent by the senate to the soldiers under Petilius Cerealis. On this occasion he was roughly handled and wounded, and barely escaped with his life[113]. After many years of quiet, he was accused in 93 A.D., when Pliny was praetor, of having written and spoken in honour of Thrasea Paetus, Herennius Senecio, and Helvidius Priscus; he was condemned to death and his books were destroyed[114]. SENECIO was condemned at the same time for having written the biography of Helvidius Priscus, and for the further offence that since holding the quaestorship he had not become a candidate for any higher office[115]. About the same time were banished Artemidorus, the most single-minded and laborious of philosophers, whom Musonius had selected out of a crowd of competitors as the fittest to claim his daughter in marriage[116]; Junius Mauricus, brother of Arulenus Rusticus, who had joined Musonius in the attempt to secure the punishment of the *delatores* of Nero's time[117]; Demetrius, and Epictetus[118]; and further many distinguished ladies, including Arria and her daughter Fannia[119]. But from the time of the death of Domitian

[111] Dion Cassius lxvi 13.

[113] Tac. *Hist.* iii 80.

[115] Dion C. lxvii 13, Tac. *Agr.* 45.

[117] Tac. *Hist.* iv 40.

[118] A. Gellius *N. A.* xv 11, 5 (for Epictetus).

[119] Pliny *Ep.* iii 11, 3; 'tot nobilissimarum feminarum exilia et fugas' Tac. *Agr.* 45.

[112] See above, § 444.

[114] *Agr.* 2; Suetonius, *Dom.* 10.

[116] Pliny *Ep.* iii 11, 7.

in A.D. 96 the imperial government became finally reconciled with Stoicism, which was now the recognised creed of the great majority of the educated classes at Rome, of all ages and ranks. As such it appears in the writings of JUVENAL, who not only introduces into serious literature the Stoic principle of 'straight speaking,' but actually expounds much of the ethical teaching of Stoicism with more directness and force than any professed adherent of the system.

449. Stoicism, received into favour in the second century

Stoic reform of law.

A.D., won new opportunities and was exposed to new dangers. Its greatest achievement lay in the development of Roman law. As we have just seen[120], the 'old Romans' of Nero's day, in spite of their profession of Stoicism, were unbending upholders of the old law, with all its harshness and narrowness; and we have to go back a hundred years to the great lawyers of the times of Sulla and Cicero[121] to meet with men prepared to throw aside old traditions and build anew on the foundations of natural justice. But the larger view had not been lost sight of. It remained as the ideal of the more generous-minded members of the imperial civil service ; and in the times of the emperors Antoninus Pius (138–161 A.D.) and Marcus Aurelius (161–180 A.D.) it became the starting-point for a new development of Roman law, which is one of the great achievements of Roman history. The most eloquent of the historians of the origins of Christianity thus describes this movement.

'Le stoïcisme avait [déjà] pénétré le droit romain de ses larges maximes, et en avait fait le droit naturel, le droit philosophique, tel que la raison peut le concevoir pour tous les hommes. Le droit strict cède à l'équité ; la douceur l'emporte sur la sévérité ; la justice paraît inséparable de la bienfaisance. Les grands jurisconsultes d'Antonin continuèrent la même œuvre. Le dernier [Volusius Moecianus] fut le maître de Marc-Aurèle en fait de jurisprudence, et, à vrai dire, l'œuvre des deux saints empereurs ne saurait être séparée. C'est d'eux que datent la plupart de ces lois humaines et sensées qui fléchirent la rigueur du droit antique et firent, d'une législation primitivement étroite et implacable, un code susceptible d'être adopté par tous les peuples civilisés[122].'

[120] See above, § 443.
[121] See above, §§ 428, 429.
[122] Renan, *Marc-Aurèle*, pp. 22, 23; cf. Maine, *Ancient Law*, pp. 55, 56.

In the legislation of Antoninus and Aurelius the humane and cosmopolitan principles of Stoic politics at last triumph over Roman conservatism. The poor, the sick, the infant, and the famine-stricken are protected. The slave is treated as a human being ; to kill him becomes a crime, to injure him a misdemeanour ; his family and his property are protected by the tribunals. Slavery in fact is treated as a violation of the rights of nature ; manumission is in every way encouraged. The time is within sight when Ulpian will declare that 'all men, according to natural right, are born free and equal[123].' This legislation is not entirely the work of professed Stoics ; it is nevertheless the offspring of Stoicism.

450. There was in the second century, as there is still, a sharp antagonism between the manners of culti-
Repression of zeal.
vated society and the ardent profession of intellectual convictions. An anecdote related by Gellius well illustrates the social forces which were now constantly at work to check superfluous enthusiasm.

'There was with us at table a young student of philosophy who called himself a Stoic, but chiefly distinguished himself by an unwelcome loquacity. He was always bringing up in season and out of season recondite philosophical doctrines, and he looked upon all his neighbours as boors because they were unacquainted with them. His whole talk was strown with mention of syllogisms, fallacies, and the like, such as the "master-argument," the "quiescent," and the "heap" ; and he thought that he was the only man in the world who could solve them. Further he maintained that he had thoroughly studied the nature of the soul, the growth of virtue, the science of daily duties, and the cure of the weaknesses and diseases of the mind. Finally he considered he had attained to that state of perfect happiness which could be clouded by no disappointment, shaken by no pains of death[124].'

Such a man, we may think, might soon have become an apostle of sincere Stoicism, and might have left us a clear and systematic exposition of Stoic doctrine as refined by five centuries of experience. It was not to be. The polished Herodes Atticus crushed him with a quotation from the discourses of Epictetus. Not many offended in the same way. Even Seneca

---

[123] Renan, *Marc-Aurèle*, p. 30.
[124] Aulus Gellius *N. A.* i 2, 3 to 5.

had been severe on useless study in the regions of history and antiquity[125]; the new philosophers despised the study even of philosophy.

451. The Stoicism of the second century is therefore much less sharply defined than that of earlier times. Its doctrines, acquired in childhood, are accepted with ready acquiescence; but they are not accompanied by any firm repudiation of the opposing views of other schools. Once more, as in the time of Augustus, the 'philosopher' comes to the front; the particular colour of his philosophy seems of less importance[126]. It is philosophy in general which wins the patronage of the emperors. Nerva allowed the schools of the philosophers to be re-opened; Trajan interested himself in them as providing a useful training for the young. Hadrian went further, and endowed the teachers of philosophy at Rome; Antoninus Pius did the same throughout the provinces. Marcus Aurelius established representatives of each of the philosophic schools at Athens; and amongst later emperors Septimius Severus, aided by his wife Julia Domna, was conspicuous in the same direction. The philosophers, who had firmly resisted persecution, gradually sacrificed their independence under the influence of imperial favour. They still recited the dogmas of their respective founders, but unconsciously they became the partisans of the established forms of government and religion. Yet so gentle was the decay of philosophy that it might be regarded as progress if its true position were not illuminated by the attitude of Marcus Aurelius towards the Christians. For Marcus Aurelius was universally accepted as the most admirable practical representative of philosophy in its full ripeness, and no word of criticism of his policy was uttered by any teacher of Stoicism.

(margin) State establishment of philosophy.

[125] 'nam de illis nemo dubitabit, quin operose nihil agant, qui litterarum inutilium studiis detinentur, quae iam apud Romanos quoque magna manus est...ecce Romanos quoque invasit inane studium supervacua discendi,' etc. Sen. *Dial.* x 13, 1 and 3. The condemnation extends to the whole study of history, *N. Q.* iii Pr.
[126] 'In the purely moral sphere to which philosophy was now confined, the natural tendency of the different schools, not even excluding the Epicurean, was to assimilation and eclecticism' Dill, *Roman Society*, p. 343.

452. The decay of precise philosophic thought was accom-

The pagan revival. panied by a strong revival of pagan religious sentiment. The atmosphere in which Marcus Aurelius grew up, and by which his political actions were determined far more than by his philosophic profession, is thus sympathetically described by the latest editor of his Reflections.

'In house and town, the ancestral Penates of the hearth and the Lares of the streets guarded the intercourse of life ; in the individual breast, a minis-tering Genius shaped his destinies and responded to each mood of melancholy or of mirth. Thus all life lay under the regimen of spiritual powers, to be propitiated or appeased by appointed observances and ritual and forms of prayer. To this punctilious and devout form of Paganism Marcus was inured from childhood ; at the vintage festival he took his part in chant and sacrifice ; at eight years old he was admitted to the Salian priesthood ; " he was observed to perform all his sacerdotal functions with a constancy and exactness unusual at that age ; was soon a master of the sacred music ; and had all the forms and liturgies by heart." Our earliest statue depicts him as a youth offering incense ; and in his triumphal bas-reliefs he stands before the altar, a robed and sacrificing priest. To him "prayer and sacrifice, and all observances by which we own the presence and nearness of the gods," are "covenants and sacred ministries" admitting to "intimate communion with the divine[127]."'

The cult thus summarized is not that of the Greek mythology, much less that of the rationalized Stoic theology. It is the primitive ritualism of Italy, still dear to the hearts of the common people, and regaining its hold on the educated in proportion as they spared themselves the effort of individual criticism.

453. It was by no mere accident that Marcus Aurelius

State perse-cution. became the persecutor of the Christians. He was at heart no successor of the Zeno who held as essential the doctrine of a supreme deity, and absolutely rejected the use of temples and images. In the interval, official Stoicism had learnt first to tolerate superstition with a smile, next to become its advocate ; now it was to become a persecutor in its name. Pontius Pilatus is said to have recognised the innocence

---

[127] Rendall, *M. Aurelius to himself*, Introd. pp. cxxvii, cxxviii.

of the founder of Christianity, and might have protected him
had his instructions from Rome allowed him to stretch his
authority so-far; Gallio[128] was uninterested in the preaching of
Paul; but Aurelius was acquainted with the Christian profession
and its adherents[129], and opposed it as an obstinate resistance to
authority[130]. The popular antipathy to the new religion, and
the official distaste for all disturbing novelties, found in him a
willing supporter[131]. Thus began a new struggle between• the
power of the sword and that of inward conviction. Because
reason could not support the worship of the pagan deities,
violence must do so[132]. It became a triumph of the civil
authority and the popular will to extort a word of weakness by
two years of persistent torture[133]. No endowed professor or
enlightened magistrate raised his voice in protest; and in this
feeble acquiescence Stoicism perished.

454. For the consciences of the young revolted. Trained at
Revolt of the   home and in school to believe in providence, in duty,
young Stoics.   and in patient endurance of evil, they instinctively
recognised the Socratic force and example not in the magistrate
seated in his curule chair, nor in the rustic priest occupied in his
obsolete ritual, but in the teacher on the cross and the martyr on
the rack[134]. In ever increasing numbers men, who had from
their Stoic education imbibed the principles of the unity of the
Deity and the freedom of the will, came over to the new
society which professed the one without reservation, and dis-

---

[128] The connexion (if any) of Gallio the proconsul of Achaia (Acts xviii 12) with the
Junius Gallio who adopted Seneca's elder brother is uncertain.

[129] Renan, *Marc-Aurèle*, p. 55, note 2.

[130] M. Aurel. *To himself* xi 3.

[131] Renan *M.-A.* p. 329.

[132] 'quia ratione congredi non queunt, violentia premunt; incognita causa tanquam nocentissimos damnant' Lact. *Inst. Epit.* 47 (52), 4.

[133] 'vidi ego in Bithynia praesidem gaudio mirabiliter elatum tanquam barbarorum
gentem aliquam 'subegisset, quod unus qui per biennium magna virtute restiterat,
postremo cedere visus esset' *Div. inst.* v 11, 15.

[134] 'nam cum videat vulgus dilacerari homines et invictam tenere patientiam,
existimant nec perseverantiam morientium vanam esse nec ipsam patientiam sine deo
cruciatus tantos posse superare...dicit Horatius: "iustum ac tenacem..." quo nihil
verius dici potest, si ad eos referatur qui nullos cruciatus nullam mortem recusant'
ib. 13, 11 to 17.

played the other without flinching. With them they brought in large measure their philosophic habits of thought, and (in far more particulars than is generally recognised) the definite tenets which the Porch had always inculcated. Stoicism began a new history, which is not yet ended, within the Christian church; and we must now attempt to give some account of this after-growth of the philosophy.

CHAPTER XVII.

THE STOIC STRAIN IN CHRISTIANITY.

455. DURING the first century and a half of the Christian era

Neighbours, but strangers. Stoicism maintained an active and successful propaganda, without becoming conscious that meanwhile a new force was spreading in the Hellenic world which was soon to challenge its own supremacy. There is no evidence to show that any of the Stoic teachers with whom we have been concerned knew anything of Christianity beyond the bare name, until the two systems came into conflict in the time of Marcus Aurelius; and it is in the highest degree improbable that any of them were influenced in their opinions, directly or indirectly, by the preaching of Christianity[1]. On the other hand the apostles of the newer faith, as often as they entered any of the chief cities of the Roman empire, met at once not only with the professed adherents of Stoicism, but also with a still wider world of educated men and women which was penetrated by Stoic conceptions. From the first it was incumbent on Christian teachers to define their attitude towards this philosophy; and it is our purpose in this chapter to sketch shortly the manner in which they did so. This task belongs primarily to the historian of Christianity, but the present work would be incomplete without some adumbration of this important field of study. From the middle of the second century the relations between the two systems alter in character: there then sets in a steady stream of conversion by which the younger Stoics are drawn away from the older creed, and carry over to its rival not only their personal allegiance but also their intellectual equipment.

---

[1] As to supposed instances to the contrary see Winckler, *Stoicismus*, pp. 5 to 14.

456. It is necessarily a difficult task to estimate the influence
Common of Stoicism upon the historical development of
influences. Christianity, and it is impossible to do so without
trenching upon ground which is highly debateable. Upon
parallels between phrases used by Stoic and Christian writers
respectively not too much stress should be laid[2]. Many of these
can be traced back to common sources from which each religion
drew in turn. From Persism the Stoic creed inherited much
through Heraclitus, and Christianity through Judaism. The
kindred doctrines of Buddhism and Cynism present themselves
to our view in Christianity in the Sermon on the mount, and
in Stoicism through the discourses of Epictetus. Individuals in
either camp were also influenced in varying degrees by a wave
of feeling in favour of asceticism and resignation which spread
over the whole Greco-Roman world about this time, resulting
from exaggerated attention being paid to the individual consciousness at the cost of social and political life. We should therefore
endeavour to keep our eyes steadily fixed on the essential
features of Stoicism rather than on its details, and inquire how
these were regarded by Christian teachers in successive generations.

457. A starting-point is obviously afforded us by the speech
Progressive of St Paul upon Mars' hill, in which he accepts a
influence of verse from the Stoic poet Aratus[3] as a text upon
Stoicism. which to proclaim the fatherhood of God. This
Stoic doctrine (like many others to which he refers in his
writings) is treated by Paul as embodying an elementary truth,
and as a starting-point for fuller knowledge; from any other
point of view philosophy is regarded as a snare and an im-
posture[4]. A generation later we find that the editor of the
fourth gospel boldly places the Stoic version of the history of
creation in the fore-front of his work[5]. Later on in the second
century we find the doctrines of the double nature of the Christ
and of the variety inherent in the Deity becoming incorporated

---

[2] For material of this kind see Winckler's dissertation just quoted, and Lightfoot's *Philippians*, pp. 278–290.

[3] ' For we are also his offspring ' Acts xvii 28.

[4] 1 Cor. i 20–25.   [5] John i 1.

in technical Stoic forms as part of a defined Christian creed. From whatever point we regard the Stoic influence, it appears during this period as an increasing force. We shall speak of it here as the 'Stoic strain' in Christianity; meaning by this that a certain attitude of the intellect and sympathies, first developed in Stoicism, found for itself a home in early Christianity; that men, Stoics by inheritance or training, joined the church not simply as disciples, but to a large extent as teachers also. This point of view can perhaps best be explained by a sketch of the development of Christian doctrine as it might be regarded by fair-minded Stoics, attached to the principles of their philosophy but suspicious of its close relations with the religion of the State, and ready to welcome any new system which might appeal to their reason as well as to their moral sense.

458. A Stoic of the time of Vespasian (A.D. 69 to 79) might well be supposed to be made acquainted with the beginnings of Christianity by some Christian friend. The story he would hear would take the form of one of those 'oral gospels' which are now generally supposed to have preceded the shaping of the 'gospels' of our New Testament, and to have corresponded generally to the common parts of the first three gospels and some of the narratives of the fourth[6]. He would thus learn that the founder was a Jew named JESUS, the son of Joseph a carpenter of Nazareth[7]. This Jesus had in his childhood sat at the feet of the philosophic Rabbis of Jerusalem[8], and had learnt from them to interpret

Jesus from the Stoic stand-point.

[6] In the references to the New Testament books in this chapter no attempt is made to apply any precise critical theory of their origin or date. Since we suppose that all Christian doctrine was enunciated orally long before it was committed to writing, the date and circumstances of the written record become for the present purpose of secondary importance. Translations from the New Testament are, as a rule, taken from Dr R. F. Weymouth's *New Testament in Modern Speech* (London 1903). This admirable translation has for the present purpose the great negative advantage of keeping in the background the mass of associations which hinder the modern reader from taking the words of the writers in their simple and natural sense; but on the other hand, Dr Weymouth sometimes disguises the technical terms of ancient philosophy so far as to make them unrecognisable. In such cases the Revised Version is quoted, and occasionally the Greek text.

[7] Matt. xiii 55, Luke ii 48; and see below, § 482.

[8] Luke ii 46, 47. Such men would of course be typical of the spirit of 'Judaism,' see § 22 above.

the documents of Hebraism, 'the law and the prophets,' in the sense of the world-religions, and by the principle of allegorism to give a new and truer meaning to such parts of them as seemed obsolete or incredible[9]. Upon reaching manhood he had been shocked to find that the general body of the Pharisees, to which his teachers belonged, was far more interested in maintaining prejudices of race and class than in boldly proclaiming principles of world-wide application; and that whilst freely avowing their own opinions amongst friends, they held it indiscreet to reveal them to the crowd[10]. After a period of prolonged reflection and inward struggle[11] he resolved on coming forward as a teacher in his own name.

459. At this point our Stoic would assuredly be impressed
The wise man.   by the 'strength and force' of character displayed in the preaching of the young Jesus, and would so far be disposed to rank him with Socrates and with Zeno. In the content of Jesus' teaching he would at once recognise some of the prominent characteristics of Zeno's *Republic*. For Jesus too spoke of a model state, calling it the 'kingdom of heaven'; and in this state men of all nations were to find a place. Not only the ceremonies of the old Hebrew religion, its sacrifices and its sabbaths, were to be superseded[12]; the temple itself at Jerusalem was to cease to be a place of worship[13]; the social and economic system of the Jewish people was to be remodelled; the rich were to be swept away, and the poor to enter into their inheritance[14]. Men's prayers were no longer to be offered to the God of Abraham, but to the Father in heaven, surrounded by spirits like those of Persism, the Name, the Will, the Kingdom, the Glory and the Majesty[15]. That Jesus also spoke, after the Persian fashion, of rewards for the good and the wicked in a

[9] See the treatment of the Jonah myth (Matt. xii 40 and 41), and of the prophecy of the return of Elijah (Matt. xvii 10 to 13).

[10] Matt. xxiii 13.

[11] Matt. iv 1 to 11; Mark i 13; Luke iv 1 to 14.

[12] Matt. xii 1 to 13; Mark ii 23 to 28; Luke vi 1 to 10.

[13] John iv 21.   [14] Matt. v 5.

[15] Matt. vi 9 to 13; a doxology is first found in the MS of the *Teaching of the Apostles*, and it was probably not specifically connected with the prayer originally.

future existence might interest our Stoic less, but would not be inconsistent with the traditions of his own sect.

460. Whilst recognising this strength of character and sympathizing generally with the gospel message, our Stoic could not fail to observe that the Christian tradition did not claim for the Founder the imperturbable calm which the wise man should under all circumstances possess. From time to time his spirit was troubled[16]; sometimes by Anger, as when he denounced in turn the Pharisees, the scribes, and the traders in the temple; sometimes by Pity, as when he wept over Jerusalem; by Fear, as in the garden of Gethsemane[17]; then again by Shame, as in the meeting with the woman taken in adultery[18]; and even by Hilarity, as when he participated in the marriage revels at Cana. Yet perhaps, taking the character as a whole, a Stoic would not be surprised that the disciples should remember only the sweetness, the patience, and the perseverance of their master; that they should account him a perfect man[19], attributing his faults to the weakness of the body[20], and not to any taint of soul; and finally that they should accept him as their Lord and their God[21]. For all these points of view, without being specifically Stoic, find some kind of recognition within Stoicism itself.

The emotions in Jesus.

461. But as our inquirer proceeded to trace the history of Christianity after its Founder's death, he would soon find the beginnings of division within the Christian body. He would learn, for instance, that the Christians of Jerusalem, who even during their Master's lifetime had been puzzled by his condemnation of Hebrew traditions, had quickly relapsed upon his death into the ways of thinking to which in

Mythologic Christianity.

---

[16] John xiii 21.   [17] Luke xxii 44.
[18] John viii 6 and 8.   [19] Matt. v 48 ; Luke vi 40.
[20] Matt. xxvi 41 ; Mark xiv 38. The author of the *Epistle to the Hebrews* adopts the technical terms of Stoicism more completely. According to him Christ was touched with all the passions of weak men, but to a degree falling short of sin ; οὐ γὰρ ἔχομεν ἀρχιερέα μὴ δυνάμενον συμπαθῆσαι ταῖς ἀσθενείαις ἡμῶν...χωρὶς ἁμαρτίας Heb. iv 15. Thus the agony in the garden, though accompanied by loud cries and tears, did not pass the limits of the healthy affection of caution (εὐλάβεια), or (as we might say) 'anxiety' ; *ib.* v 7.
[21] John xx 28.

their childhood they had been accustomed. They had become once more Hebrews, and even ardent advocates of an obsolete ceremonialism ; and in this respect they seemed entirely to have forgotten the teaching of their Founder. But their allegiance to his person was unshakeable; and they cherished the conviction that during the lifetime of most of them he would rejoin them, and establish that earthly kingdom which in their hearts they had never ceased to covet. In view of this imminent revolution, quite as much as out of respect for the teaching of the Sermon on the mount, they encouraged their members to spend their savings on immediate necessities, and soon fell into dire poverty. To Christianity as an intellectual system they contributed nothing ; 'little children' at heart[22], they were content to live in a perfect affection one towards another, and their miserable circumstances were cheered by visions of angels and a sense of their master's continual presence[23]. From this company our Stoic might easily turn aside as from a band of ignorant fanatics, displaying the same simplicity and conservatism as the idol-worshippers of Rome, with the added mischief of being disloyal towards the majesty of the empire, and a possible danger to its security[24].

462. In startling contrast to this band of simple-minded
Philosophic brethren would appear the Christian propagandists
Christians. whose temper is revealed to us in the latter part of the book of Acts, in the epistles of Paul, the first epistle of Peter, and the epistle to the Hebrews. These fiery preachers, equally attached to the name of their Lord, might appear to have been singularly indifferent to his person and his history, and even to have paid little heed to the details of his teaching as recorded in the oral gospels[25]. But they were entirely possessed by his secret—the transmutation of Hebraism into a world-religion ; and they had an ardent desire to present it to the Roman world in a form that would win intellectual assent. Into this effort

---

[22] Mark x 15.   [23] Acts xii 15.

[24] This antipathy to the Roman government finds biting expression in the *Apocalypse of John.*

[25] There seems to be no definite reference even to the Lord's prayer, or to any of the parables, in the books named above.

they threw their whole personality; all the conceptions which filled their minds, some of them childish and common to them with uncivilised peoples, others derived from Jewish tradition or Hellenistic philosophy, were crudely but forcibly fused in the determination to present 'the Christ' to the world, as the solution of its difficulties and the centre of its hopes. The outpourings of these men were as unintelligible and unsympathetic to the fraternity at Jerusalem as they are to the average church-goer to-day; only breaking out here and there into the flame of clear expression when at last some long-sought conception had been grasped[26]. Of such preachers St Paul is for us the type, and we may describe them as the 'Paulists.' Paul himself is self-assertive in tone, as a man may be who feels himself misunderstood and misjudged in his own circle[27]. But an ardent Stoic might well have recognised in him a kindred spirit, an intellect grappling boldly with the supreme problems, and laying the foundations of a new philosophy of life.

463. PAUL was a man of Jewish descent, intensely proud of his nationality; but nevertheless brought up in the city of Tarsus, which had for centuries been a centre of Hellenistic philosophy of every type[28], and more especially of Stoicism[29]. This philosophy is to Paul's mind entirely inadequate and even dangerous; nevertheless he is steeped in Stoic ways of thinking, which are continually asserting themselves in his teaching without being formally recognised by him as such. Thus the 'universe' (κόσμος), which to the Stoic includes everything with which he is concerned, and in particular the subject-matter of religion, becomes with Paul the 'world,' that out of which and above which the Christian rises to the 'eternal' or

St Paul and Stoicism.

---

[26] For instance, that of 'love' in 1 Cor. xiii, and of 'faith' in Hebrews xi.

[27] For the conflict between St Paul and the church at Jerusalem, see below, § 480; for his tone towards those who differed from him, see Galatians i 8 and 9; Col. ii 4; 1 Tim. i 20, vi 3 to 5; Titus i 10. A gentle expostulation as to this style of controversy is found in the epistle of James, see note 39.

[28] 'With such zeal do the inhabitants [of Tarsus] study philosophy and literature, that they surpass Athens, Alexandria, and all other schools of learning....Rome knows well how many men of letters issue from this city, for her streets swarm with them' Strabo xiv p. 673.

[29] Juv. *Sat.* iii 117 and 118; and see above, § 25, note 65.

spiritual life.' Yet this contrast is not final[30]; and whether or not the Pauline 'spirit' is derived from the Stoic πνεῦμα, the Pauline system, as it is elaborated in detail, increasingly accommodates itself to that of the Stoics. Our supposed inquirer would examine the points both of likeness and of contrast.

464. The teaching of Paul was, like that of the Stoics,

The Paulist logic.

positive and dogmatic[31]. He accepted unquestion-ingly the evidence of the senses as trustworthy, without troubling himself as to the possibility of hallucinations, from which nevertheless his circle was not free[32]. He also accepted the theory of 'inborn ideas,' that is, of moral principles engraved upon the heart[33]; and for the faculty of the soul which realizes such principles he uses the special term 'conscience' (συνείδησις)[34]; conscience being described, with a correct sense of etymology and possibly a touch of humour, as that within a man which becomes a second witness to what the man says[35]. From another point of view the conscience is the divine spirit at work in the human spirit[36]. Closely associated with conscience in the Pauline system is 'faith' (πίστις), a faculty of the soul which properly has to do with things not as they are, but as we mean them to be[37]. The Stoic logic had failed to indicate clearly how from the knowledge of the universe as it is men could find a basis for their hopes and efforts for its future; the missing criterion is supplied by the Paulist doctrine of 'faith,' which may also be paradoxically described as the power always to say 'Yes[38].' The fraternity at Jerusalem appear to have been alarmed not so much at the principle of faith, as at the manner in which St Paul used it to enforce his own doctrines; we find them by way of

---

[30] Romans viii 20 and 21.   [31] Romans vi 17, 1 Cor. i 10.

[32] 2 Cor. xii 2 to 5.

[33] 'a knowledge of the conduct which the Law requires is engraven on the hearts [of the Gentiles]' Rom. ii 15.

[34] ib.   [35] 'my conscience adds its testimony to mine' Rom. ix 1.

[36] ib.

[37] 'Faith is a well-grounded assurance of that for which we hope' Heb. xi 1. Thus whilst sense-knowledge, and especially sight, calls for acceptance because it is 'objective,' and detached from personal bias, faith is essentially subjective, and suggests a power by which (in harmony with a divine source) personality dominates fact.

[38] 2 Cor. i 19.

contrast asserting the Academic position that 'none of us are
infallible[39].' We may here notice that the next generation of
Christians again brought the theory of faith into harmony with
Stoic principles, by explaining that the power of knowing the
right is strictly dependent upon right action[40].

465. In their metaphysical postulates the Paulists started,
Paulist
metaphysics. like all ancient philosophers, with the contrast
between soul and body, but this they transformed
into that between 'spirit' and 'flesh.' To them the 'spirit'
included the whole message of Christianity, the 'flesh' the
doctrine and practice of the Gentile world[41]. The terms themselves were in use in the oral gospel[42], but the Paulists developed
the content of 'spirit,' until it included a whole world of conceptions, encircling and interfused with the world of sense-
experience. But Paul did not desire that this spiritual world
should be regarded as wanting in reality, or as a mere product
of the imagination: and to express this objectivity of spirit he
adopted the Stoic term 'body.' Body then expresses the underlying monistic principle of all nature; and we may say 'spirit-
body' exists[43], with the same confidence with which we speak of
animal body or 'flesh-body.' There has been a flesh-body of
Jesus; with that we have no more concern[44]. There exists
eternally a spirit-body of Christ; from that his church draws its
life. The Christian feeds upon the spirit of his Master; but in
paradoxical phrase we may say that he eats his body and drinks
his blood[45]. What is not 'body' has no real existence at all[46].

[39] 'Do not be eager to become teachers; for we often stumble and fall, all of us'
James iii 1 and 2.
[40] 'He who does what is honest and right comes to the light' John iii 21; 'if any
one is willing to do His will, he shall know about the teaching' ib. vii 17.
[41] 'The cravings of the [flesh] are opposed to those of the spirit, and the cravings
of the spirit are opposed to those of the [flesh]' Gal. v 17; cf. Romans viii 12 and 13.
[42] See above, § 460, note 20.
[43] 'There are bodies which are celestial and there are bodies which are earthly'
1 Cor. xv 40; 'as surely as there is an animal body, so there is also a spiritual body'
ib. 44.
[44] 2 Cor. v 16.
[45] 1 Cor. xi 24, 25.
[46] 'which are a shadow of the things to come, but the body is Christ's' Col.
ii 17 (Revised Version).

466. St Paul in his letters appears entirely lacking in that
The Christian   reverent feeling towards the physical universe, that
universe.   admiration for sun, moon and stars, which marked
the earlier world-religions, and which he perhaps associated with
Babylonian idolatry. As we have seen, he only used the Stoic
term for universe in disapproval. And yet the conception of the
history of the universe was deeply impressed upon the Paulists,
and almost precisely in Stoic form. God, the Father, is the
beginning of all things; from him they come, and to him they
shall all return[47]. From the Father went forth an image of
him[48], his first-born Son[49], his word, the Christ; by this he
created the world, and for this the world exists[50]. By a further
outpouring of the divine spirit, men are created with the capacity
of becoming the 'images' or bodily representations of God and
his Son[51]. To this general doctrine individual Paulists add
special features; St Paul himself introduces 'woman' as a fourth
order of creation, an image or 'vessel' bearing the same relation
to man as man to Christ[52]; and a writer (of distinctly later date)
seems to refer not only to the creation of the elements[53], but also
to their coming destruction by the conflagration[54]. Of the
creation of the animals no notice is taken[55].

[47] 'The universe (τὰ πάντα) owes its origin to Him, was created by Him, and has
its aim and purpose in Him' Rom. xi 36 (Weymouth's translation); 'of him and
through him and unto him are all things' *ib.* (Revised Version); 'God, the Father,
who is the source of all things' 1 Cor. viii 6. See further *ib.* xv 24 and 28.

[48] 'Christ, who is the image of God' 2 Cor. iv 4; 'he brightly reflects God's
glory and is the exact representation of His being' Hebr. i 3.

[49] 'Christ is the visible representation of the invisible God, the First-born and
Lord of all creation' Col. i 15; 'it is in Christ that the fulness of God's nature dwells
embodied' *ib.* ii 9.

[50] 'in him were all things created...; all things have been created through him
and unto him' *ib.* i 16 (Revised Version); 'through whom [God] made the ages'
Hebrews i 2. Compare the discussion on the four causes above, § 179, and the phrase
of Marcus Aurelius: ἐκ σοῦ πάντα, εἰς σὲ πάντα, ἐν σοὶ πάντα *To himself*, iv 23.

[51] 'Those he has also predestined to bear the likeness of his Son' Rom. viii 29;
'a man is the image and glory of God' 1 Cor. xi 7.

[52] 'woman is the glory of man; woman takes her origin from man' 1 Cor. xi 7
and 8 (with special reference to Eve); cf. 1 Thess. iv 4 (R.V.), 1 Pet. iii 7.

[53] 'there were heavens which existed of old, and an earth, the latter arising out of
water by the [word] of God' 2 Pet. iii 5.

[54] 'the heavens will pass away with a rushing noise, the elements be destroyed in
the fierce heat, and the earth and all the works of man be utterly burnt up' *ib.* 10.
But compare 1 Cor. iii 13 to 15.

[55] The omission is due to contempt of dumb creatures, see 1 Cor. ix 9.

467. From this theory of creation it would seem to follow
The divine
immanence. as a consequence that the world is inhabited by
the Deity, and is essentially good. This is the
Stoic doctrine, and it is accepted boldly by Paul. God dwells
in the universe, and the universe in him; man is not in the strict
sense an individual, for apart from God he does not exist at all[56].
But there nevertheless remains the fact of the existence of evil,
both physical and moral, in apparent defiance of the divine will.
Here too the Paulists agree with Stoic teaching; they hold that
evil serves a moral purpose as a training in virtue[57]; that God
turns evil to his own purpose, so that in the final issue all things
are working together for good[58]; that God is active through his
Word in restoring a unity that has been for a time broken[59].
Neither can man shift on to his Maker the responsibility for
his own wrongdoing; that is (as Cleanthes had taught before)
the work of men following out their own ways in accordance
with some bias which is in conflict with their divine origin[60]. In
spite of all this common ground Paul maintains with at least
equal emphasis doctrines of a gloomier type. The universe, as
it is, is evil; its rulers are the powers of darkness[61]. St Paul by
no means put out of sight, as the Stoics did, the doctrine
of an Evil Spirit; on the contrary, this conception dominates
his mind and multiplies itself in it. Sin in particular is in
his eyes more widespread, more hideous, more dangerous than
it is to the Stoic philosopher. To this point we must revert
later.

[56] 'It is in closest union with Him that we live and move and have our being'
Acts xvii 28; 'one God and Father of all...rules over all, acts through all, and dwells
in all' Eph. iv 6.
[57] 'God is dealing with you as sons; for what son is there whom his father does
not discipline?' Heb. xii 7.
[58] 'for those who love God all things are working together for good' Rom. viii 28.
[59] 'God was in Christ reconciling the world to Himself' 2 Cor. v 19; cf.
Col. i 20.
[60] 'these men are without excuse, for...their senseless minds were darkened...
in accordance with their own depraved cravings' Romans i 20 to 24. The point
is brought out still more plainly by a writer of the opposite party, James i 13
to 15.
[61] 'ours is not a conflict with mere flesh and blood, but with the despotisms,
the empires, the forces that control and govern this dark world, the spiritual hosts of
evil arrayed against us in the heavenly warfare' Eph. vi 12.

468. With regard to religious belief and practice (we are here

Religion.

using the word 'religion' in the narrower sense, as in the previous chapter on this subject) Paul was in the first place a monotheist, and addresses his prayers and praises alike to the Father in heaven, and to him alone. At the same time he does not regard the Deity as dwelling in a world apart; he is to be worshipped in and through the Christ, who is the point of contact between him and humanity[62]. From the ceremonial practices of Hebraism all the Paulists break away completely. Its bloody sacrifices take away no sin[63]; the solemn rite of circumcision is nothing in itself[64], and in practice it is an impediment to the acceptance of Christ[65]. The disposition to observe days and seasons, sabbaths and new moons, is a matter for serious alarm[66]. In place of this ritualism is to be substituted 'a worship according to reason[67],' which is in close agreement with Stoic practice. To think rightly of the Deity[68], to give thanks to him[69], to honour him by an innocent life[70], is well pleasing to God; and the writings of Paul, like those of Epictetus, include many a hymn of praise, and show us the existence at this time of the beginnings of a great body of religious poetry[71].

469. In the analysis of human nature Paul again started

Human nature.

from the Stoic basis. In the first place he recognised the fundamental unity of the man as a compacted whole[72]; subject to this monism, he recognised three

---

[62] 'let your thanks to God the Father be presented in the name of our Lord Jesus Christ' *ib.* v 20.

[63] 'it is impossible for the blood of bulls and goats to take away sins' Hebr. x 4.

[64] 'in Christ Jesus neither circumcision nor uncircumcision is of any importance' Gal. v 6.

[65] 'if you receive circumcision Christ will avail you nothing' *ib.* v 2.

[66] 'you scrupulously observe days and months, special seasons, and years. I am alarmed about you' *ib.* iv 10 and 11; cf. Col. ii 16 to 19.

[67] παρακαλῶ οὖν ὑμᾶς παραστῆσαι τὰ σώματα ὑμῶν θυσίαν ζῶσαν ἁγίαν, τὴν λογικὴν λατρείαν ὑμῶν Rom. xii 1.

[68] 2 Cor. xiii 5.   [69] 1 Cor. xiv 15.   [70] 1 Tim. ii 8.

[71] Rom. xvi 25 to 27; 1 Cor. i 4; 2 Cor. i 3; Eph. i 3 to 14, iii 20 and 21; 1 Tim. i 17. Compare 1 Peter i 3 to 5.

[72] 'The whole body—its various parts closely fitting and firmly adhering to one another—grows by the aid of every contributory link, with power proportioned to the need of each individual part' Eph. iv 16; cf. Rom. xii 4 and 5.

parts, the spirit, the animal life, and the flesh[73]. Of these only
the two extremes, the spirit and the flesh, are usually mentioned; but these do not strictly correspond to the traditional
distinction of soul and body. The soul (ψυχή, *anima*) is that
which man has in common with the animals; the spirit (πνεῦμα,
spiritus) is that which he has in common with God. Where
therefore only two parts are mentioned, the soul and the flesh
must be considered both to be included under the name 'flesh.'
Soul and flesh are peculiar to the individual man; spirit is the
common possession of the Deity and of all men[74]. Thus God
and man share in the spiritual nature, and become partners in
an aspect of the universe from which animals, plants, and stones
are definitely excluded[75]. The 'spirit' of St Paul therefore
corresponds closely to the 'principate' of the Stoics, and though
the Christian apostle does not lay the same emphasis on its
intellectual aspect, he fully recognises that the spiritual life is
true wisdom, and its perversion folly and darkness[76].

470. From this analysis of human nature Paul approaches

Resurrection
and immor-
tality.

the central doctrine of the Christian community,
that of the resurrection of its Founder. To the
simple-minded fraternity at Jerusalem the resurrection of Jesus was a marvel, an interference with the orderly
course of divine providence, a proof of the truth of the gospel
message. Jesus has returned to his disciples in the body as he
lived; he has again departed, but before this generation has
passed away he will return to stay with them and establish his
kingdom. To St Paul all this is different. He accepts implicitly the fact of the resurrection, but as typical, not as abnormal.
As Christ has risen, so will his followers rise. But Christ lives
in the spirit; by their intrinsic nature neither the flesh-body
nor the soul-body can become immortal[77]. And in the spirit

---

[73] 1 Cor. xv 44.

[74] The point is continually emphasized that there is only one spirit. In English
translations the double printed form, Spirit and spirit, disguises the real meaning.
'if there is any common sharing of the spirit' Philipp. ii 1.

[75] 'You may, one and all, become sharers in the very nature of God' 2 Peter i 4.

[76] ἐσκοτίσθη ἡ ἀσύνετος αὐτῶν καρδία Rom. i 21.

[77] 'our mortal bodies cannot inherit the kingdom of God, nor will what is
perishable inherit what is imperishable' 1 Cor. xv 50; 'if we have known Christ
as a man (κατὰ σάρκα), yet now we do so no longer' 2 Cor. v 16. The Pauline

Christ's followers are joined with him, and will be more fully joined when they are rid of the burden of the flesh⁷⁸. This continued existence is no mere fancy; it is real, objective, and (in philosophical language) bodily. Though by the creation all men have some share in the divine spirit, yet immortality (at any rate in the full sense) is the privilege of the faithful only; it is won, not inherited. Paul does not venture to suggest that human individuality and personality are retained in the life beyond. He draws no picture of the reunion of preacher and disciple, of husband and wife, or of mother and child. It is enough for him to believe that he will be reunited with the glorified Christ, and be in some sense a member of the heavenly community⁷⁹.

471. On its philosophical side the Paulist view of immor-
The seed theory. tality is closely akin to the Stoic, and is exposed to the same charge of logical inconsistency. If the whole man is one, how can we cut off the flesh-body and the soul-body from this unity, and yet maintain that the spirit-body is not also destroyed? To meet this difficulty St Paul, in one of his grandest outbursts of conviction, propounds the doctrine of 'seeds,' closely connected with the Stoic doctrine of 'seed-powers' (σπερματικοὶ λόγοι)⁸⁰, and with the general principles of

doctrine of the spiritual resurrection, in spite of its place in the sacred canon, has never been recognised by popular Christianity, but it has found notable defenders in Origen in ancient times, and in Bishop Westcott recently. 'No one of [Origen's] opinions was more vehemently assailed than his teaching on the Resurrection. Even his early and later apologists were perplexed in their defence of him. Yet there is no point on which his insight was more conspicuous. By keeping strictly to the Apostolic language he anticipated results which we have hardly yet secured. He saw that it is the "spirit" which moulds the frame through which it is manifested; that the body is the same, not by any material continuity, but by the permanence of that which gives the law, the *ratio* as he calls it, of its constitution (Frag. *de res.* ii 1, p. 34). Our opponents say now that this idea is a late refinement of doctrine, forced upon us by the exigencies of controversy. The answer is that no exigencies of controversy brought Origen to his conclusion. It was, in his judgment, the clear teaching of St Paul' Westcott, *Religious Thought in the West*, p. 244.

⁷⁸ 'my earnest desire being to depart and to be with Christ' Philipp. i 23.

⁷⁹ 'We shall be with the Lord for ever' 1 Thess. iv 17. So another Paulist writer: 'we see them eager for a better land, that is to say, a heavenly one. For this reason God has now prepared a city for them' Heb. xi 16.

⁸⁰ The term used is κόκκος 'grain' in 1 Cor. xv 37, but σπέρμα 'seed' *ib.* 38. The Stoic term σπερματικὸς λόγος is found in Justin Martyr *Apol.* ii 8 and 13.

biological science as now understood. This seed is the true reality in man; it may throw off both soul and flesh, and assume to itself a new body, as a tree from which the branches are lopped off will throw out new branches. Thus, and not otherwise, was Christ raised; and as Christ was raised, so will his followers be raised[81]. Man is not in any final sense a unit; as the race is continued by the breaking off of the seed from the individual, so is the spirit-life won by the abandonment of soul and flesh.

472. At this point we are brought face to face with a very

Life and death.

old paradox, that life is death, and death is life. What is commonly called life is that of the soul and the flesh, which the animals share and which may mean the atrophy of man's higher part; on the other hand death has no power over the life of the spirit, which is therefore called 'eternal life' or 'life of the ages.' To enter upon this 'eternal life' is the very kernel of the gospel message[82]; in the language of philosophy it is the bridge between physics and ethics. Although the steps by which it is reached can be most clearly traced in the Pauline epistles, yet the general conclusion was accepted by the whole Christian church. From this point of view Abraham, Isaac, and Jacob, by virtue of their communion with God, are still alive[83]; he who holds his life dear, loses it; and he who makes it of no account keeps it to the life of the ages[84]; he who listens to the teaching of Jesus and believes in the Father who sent him, has passed over out of death into life[85].

473. From the doctrine of 'eternal life' follow the first

Moral principles.

principles of morals: eternal life is the moral end (τέλος) or *summum bonum*[86]. The spirit is everything, the act nothing; good lies in the intention, not in the

---

[81] 1 Cor. xv 16, 17.

[82] 'while we are at home in the body we are banished from the Lord; for we are living a life of faith, and not one of sight' 2 Cor. v 6; 'we by our baptism were buried with him in death, in order that we should also live an entirely new life' Rom. vi 4; 'surrender your very selves to God as living men who have risen from the dead' *ib.* 13.

[83] 'He is not the God of dead, but of living men' Matt. xxii 32.

[84] Matt. x 39, xvi 25, John xii 25. 		[85] John v 24.

[86] 'the end eternal life' Rom. vi 22 (Revised version); 'you have the Life of the ages as the final result' *ib.* (Weymouth).

performance[87]; we are saved by faith, not by works[88]. Therefore all *tabus* fall away; 'to the pure everything is pure[89]'; 'in
its own nature no food is impure; but if people regard any food
as impure, to them it is[90]'; 'our ungraceful parts come to have a
more abundant grace[91]'; 'everything that God has created is
good[92].' And because God and all men share in one spirit, all
men are fellow-citizens in the cosmopolis[93]. To this St Paul
sacrifices all personal advantages of which otherwise he might
be justly proud, his Hebrew descent, his free citizenship in the
Roman empire, and even his standing in sex above an inferior
part of the creation[94]. The spiritual condition is expressed in
terms of certain emotional attitudes which correspond to the
three Stoic 'constancies[95]'; the details vary, but love, joy, peace,
gentleness and sweet reasonableness[96] are frequently recurring
terms, whilst faith, hope and love are recommended in one
passage of the highest eloquence, love (ἀγαπή, *caritas*) being
given the highest place of all[97].

474. In the treatment of the virtues and vices we miss the
Virtues and familiar series of the four virtues, though three of
vices. them find a place here or there in some more
elaborate list[98]. The vices are treated with much more fulness.
Those connected with the sexual relations and functions are
invariably the first to be condemned; incest, adultery, harlotry,
foul conversation, are named in almost every list[99]. Next in
importance are ill-feeling and quarrelsomeness; heavy drinking
comes after these. More upon Stoic lines is the reproof of

---

[87] 'the end sought is the love which springs from a pure heart, a clear conscience, and a sincere faith' 1 Tim. i 5.

[88] 'it is as the result of faith that a man is held to be righteous, apart from actions done in obedience to Law' Rom. iii 28.

[89] Titus i 15.   [90] Romans xiv 14.   [91] 1 Cor. xii 23.

[92] 1 Tim. iv 4.   [93] Eph. ii 19.

[94] 'in Him the distinctions between Jew and Gentile, slave and free man, male and female, disappear' Gal. iii 28.

[95] See above, § 355.

[96] πραότης καὶ ἐπιείκεια 2 Cor. x 1.

[97] 1 Cor. xiii.   For the constancy of Caution see § 460, note 20.

[98] Justice (δικαιοσύνη) 1 Tim. vi 11; Courage (ὑπομονή) 1 Tim. vi 11, (δύναμις) 2 Tim. i 7; Soberness (ἐγκράτεια) Gal. v 23.

[99] Rom. i 26 to 30; Gal. v 19 and 20; Col. iii 5.

'excessive grief[100].' The necessity of steady progress is strongly pressed, and the term used (προκοπή) is that with which we are familiar in Greek philosophy[101]. In all the Paulist writers there is also incessant insistence upon the importance of the regular performance of daily duties[102]. Experience not only of the disasters which befel the church at Jerusalem, but also of similar tendencies nearer at hand, had impressed deeply on Paul the insufficiency of moral teaching which relied on general principles and emotional feeling only, especially if such teaching (as in the Sermon on the mount) was mainly negative. The Paulists at any rate set forth, almost in a fixed form, a body of instructions to serve the community as a whole, and social[103] rather than ethical in nature. This teaching follows closely the Stoic teaching of the same period, and is based upon the relationships (σχέσεις), such as those of king and subject, master and slave, husband and wife, parent and child[104]. It is conservative in character, advocating kindness, contentment, and zeal in social relations as they exist. Thus whilst we recognise the spirit of Zeno in the Sermon on the mount, we find that of Panaetius in the Paulist discourses.

475. As against the Stoic sage the Paulists set up as their
Sage and   ideal the saint, and used all the resources of
Saint.   eloquence in his commendation. He is the true king and priest[105]; even if he is a beggar, he is surpassingly rich[106]; he alone, though a slave, is free[107]. On the other hand the sinner is always a slave[108]; even his good acts are without

---

[100] 2 Cor. ii 7, vii 10.

[101] 'I shall go on working to promote your progress' Philipp. i 25; 'with my eyes fixed on the goal I push on' ib. iii 14. There is also (paradoxically) progress in wrongdoing; 'they will proceed from bad to worse in impiety' 2 Tim. ii 16.

[102] The technical term used is τὰ ἀνήκοντα (Eph. v 4, Philem. 8), once only (in negative form) καθήκοντα (Rom. i 28).

[103] In the sense in which the word 'political' is used above, §§ 302–311.

[104] Rom. xiii 1 to 9; Ephes. v and vi; Col. iii 18 to 25; Titus ii 1 to 10; 1 Peter ii and iii.

[105] 'You are a priesthood of kingly lineage' 1 Peter ii 9.

[106] 'as poor, but we bestow wealth on many; as having nothing, and yet we securely possess all things' 2 Cor. vi 10.

[107] 'where the spirit of the Lord is, freedom is enjoyed' 2 Cor. iii 17.

[108] 'every one who commits sin is the slave of sin' John viii 34.

real value[109]. All such phrases would be familiar to our Stoic inquirer; but perhaps he might be specially impressed by finding once more the doctrine of the 'sufficiency of virtue' amongst the Christians. The term is indeed altered[110], but it bears the same meaning as regards independence of wealth, health and liberty, though with more emphasis upon support from a divine source.

476. It is generally agreed that in the writings of St Paul

St Paul and sin.

there is displayed a special sense of shame and horror in speaking of sin[111], which entirely differentiates his teaching from that of the Stoics. This difference, however, cannot be due to St Paul treating sin as 'defiance towards a loving Father[112],' for this view was also that of Cleanthes and the Stoics generally; and Paul's horror of sin depends on no reasoning, but is felt by him as instinctive. It remains to add that our Stoic inquirer would find an apparent conflict between this instinct and Paul's reasoning. The sin of which St Paul finds it 'a shame even to speak[113]' is sexual; and so far as it consists in abnormal social habits, such as those relations between persons of the same sex which had found excuse in the classical world, the Stoic would at once agree that these practices were 'against nature[114]' and were unseemly. Again, the marriage of near relations, though not against nature in the sense in which nature is illustrated by the animal world, is still opposed to so deep-seated a social tradition as to merit instinctive condemnation[115]. But the instincts of St Paul go far deeper; the marriage relation is to him at the best a concession to human frailty, and falls short of the ideal[116]. Nor is this merely a personal view of Paul; it is deeply impressed upon

[109] 'if I am destitute of love, I am nothing' 1 Cor. xiii 2.

[110] It is ἱκανότης not αὐτάρκεια (2 Cor. iii 5 and 6), the latter word being used in a different sense, for which see § 480, note 135.

[111] The term (ἁμαρτία, peccatum) is Stoic.

[112] Lightfoot, *Philippians*, p. 296. This view has become familiar through Milton's treatment of the Fall of man in *Paradise Lost*. There the prohibition of the forbidden fruit is nothing but a test of readiness to obey. This point of view seems quite foreign to St Paul, who always speaks of sin as sinful in itself, not in consequence of the Creator's will.

[113] Eph. v 12 (R.V.).

[114] Rom. i 26.

[115] 1 Cor. v 1.

[116] 1 Cor. vii 1 to 8.

the consciousness of the whole Christian church. How, it would be asked, can this be reconciled with the abolition of the *tabu*, with the principle that all things are pure,' or even with the obvious purpose of the Creator when he created mankind male and female?

477.   It would seem that here we have touched a fundamental

The sex tabus. point in the historical development of the moral sentiments. The sexual *tabus* are the most primitive and deeply-seated in human history. From this point of view woman is by nature impure, the sex-functions which play so large a part in her mature life being to the savage both dangerous and abhorrent. Hence the view, so strongly held by St Paul, that woman as a part of the creation is inferior to man. But man too becomes by his sex-functions impure, though for shorter periods; and by union with woman lowers himself to her level. Hence the unconquerable repugnance of St Paul to the sexual relation under any conditions whatever[117]; a repugnance which reason and religion keep within limits[118], but which yet always breaks out afresh in his writings. Hence also he assumes as unquestionable the natural unseemliness of the sexual parts of the body; in all these points not going beyond feelings which are to-day as keen as ever, though no philosopher has found it easy to justify them. But in certain points St Paul outpaces the general feeling, and shows himself an extreme reactionary against the philosophic doctrines which he shared with the Stoic. He extends his dislike, in accordance with a most primitive *tabu*, to woman's hair[119]; he desires the subordination of woman to man to be marked in her outward appearance[120]; and he forbids women to speak in the general meetings of church members[121].

---

[117] ' It is well for a man to abstain altogether from marriage.   But because there is so much fornication every man should have a wife of his own ' 1 Cor. vii 1 and 2.

[118] ' If you marry, you have not sinned ' *ib.* 28.

[119] ' if a woman will not wear a veil, let her also cut off her hair ' 1 Cor. xi 6. For the savage tabu of women's hair see Jevons, *Introduction to the History of Religion*, p. 78.

[120] 1 Cor. xi 10.

[121] *ib.* xiv 34 and 35.

478. This intense feeling on the part of St Paul required,
Hebrew   as his writings assume, no justification; it was
feeling.   therefore an inherited feeling, as familiar to many
an Oriental as it is usually strange and unsympathetic to the
ancient and modern European. It appears also to be rooted in
Hebrew tradition; for if we are at liberty to interpret the myth
of Adam and Eve by the parallel of Yama and Yamī in the
Rigveda[122], the fall of man was nothing else than the first
marriage, in which Eve was the suitor and Adam the accomplice.
In the dramatic poem of the Rigveda Yama corresponds to the
Hebrew Adam, his sister Yamī to Eve[123]. Yamī yearns to
become the mother of the human race; Yama shudders at the
impiety of a sister's embrace. Zeno had already conceived the
world-problem in much the same shape[124]; but to the Oriental
it is more than a problem of cosmology; it is the fundamental
opposition of sex attitude, the woman who longs for the family
affections against the man who seeks an ideal purity. In
Genesis the prohibition of the apple appears at first sight
colourless, yet the meaning is hardly obscure. After touching
the forbidden fruit man and woman first feel the shame of
nakedness; and Eve is punished by the coming pains of child-
bearing, and a rank below her husband's. None the less she has
her wish, for she becomes the mother of all living. It is hard
to think that Paul, who always traces human sin back to the
offence of Adam, and finds it most shamelessly displayed in the
sex-relationships of his own time, could have conceived of the
Fall in any very different way.

479. According then to a point of view which we believe to
The taint in   be latent in all the teaching of Paul on the subject
procreation.   of sin, the original taint lay in procreation, and
through the begetting of children has passed on from one
generation of mankind to another; 'through the succession
from Adam all men become dead[125].' As an ethical standpoint

---

[122] Rigveda x 10.
[123] See the author's translation in his *Rigveda* (London, 1900).
[124] See above, § 307.
[125] 'just as through Adam all die, so also through Christ all will be made alive
again' 1 Cor. xv 22.

this position is very alien from Stoicism; with the Stoic it is
a first law of nature which bids all men seek for the continuance
of the race; with the Apostle the same yearning leads them to
enter the pathway of death.   It would lead us too far to attempt
here to discuss this profound moral problem, which has deeply
influenced the whole history of the Christian church.   We are
however greatly concerned with the influence of this sentiment
on Pauline doctrine.   For it follows that in order to attain to
a true moral or spiritual life man needs a new begetting and
a new birth[126]; he must become a son of God through the outpouring of his spirit[127].   This is one of the most familiar of
Pauline conceptions, and for us it is easy to link it on to the
Stoico-Pauline account of the creation, according to which man
was in the first instance created through the Word of God, and
endowed with his spirit.   But to the community at Jerusalem
all conceptions of this kind appear to have been hardly intelligible, and tended to aggravate the deep distrust of the
teachings and methods of St Paul and his companions, which
was rooted in his disregard of national tradition.

480.   This difference of mental attitude soon broke out into
an open quarrel.   So much was inevitable; and the
The quarrel.
fact that the quarrel is recorded at length in the
texts from which we are quoting is one of the strongest evidences
of their general accuracy.   The Christians at Jerusalem formed
themselves into a nationalist party; they claimed that all the
brothers should be in the first instance conformists to Hebrew
institutions.   Paul went up to Jerusalem[128], eager to argue the
matter with men of famous name.   He was disillusioned, as is
so often the traveller who returns after trying experiences and
much mental growth to the home to which his heart still clings.
Peter and the others had no arguments to meet Paul's; he could
learn nothing from them[129]; they had not even a consistent
practice[130].   At first Paul's moral sense was outraged; he
publicly rebuked Peter as double-faced.   After a little time he

---

[126] 'God in his great mercy has begotten us anew' 1 Peter i 3 ; 'you have been
begotten again from a germ not of perishable, but of imperishable life' *ib.* 23.

[127] 'you are all sons of God through faith' Gal. iii 26.

[128] Gal. ii 1.   [129] *ib.* 6.   [130] *ib.* 12.

realized that he had met with children; he remembered that he had once thought and acted in the same way[131]. Jews in heart, the home apostles still talked of marvels[132], still yearned for the return of Jesus in the flesh[133]. A philosophic religion was as much beyond their grasp as a consistent morality. Through a simple-minded application of the doctrines of the Sermon on the mount they had slipped into deep poverty[134]; they were ready to give Paul full recognition in return for charitable help. This was not refused them; but to his other teaching Paul now added a chapter on pecuniary independence[135]; and in his old age he left to his successors warnings against 'old wives' fables[136]' and 'Jewish legends[137].'

481. Thus for the first time the forces of mythology within The develop- the Christian church clashed with those of philo- ment of Christian sophy. For the moment Paul appeared to be the mythology. victor; he won the formal recognition of the church, with full authority to continue his preaching on the understanding that it was primarily directed to the Gentile world[138]. External events were also unfavourable to the Hebraists: the destruction of Jerusalem deprived them of their local centre; the failure of Jesus to reappear in the flesh within the lifetime of his companions disappointed them of their most cherished hope. But their sentiments and thoughts remained to a great extent unchanged. To Paul they gave their respect, to Peter their love; and the steady tradition of the Christian church has confirmed this judgment. No saint has been so loved as Peter; to none have so many churches been dedicated by the affectionate instinct of the many; whilst even the dominant position of Paul in the sacred canon has hardly secured him much more than formal recognition except by the learned. So again it was with Paul's teaching; formally recognised as orthodox, it remained misunderstood and unappreciated: it was even rapidly converted

[131] 1 Cor. xiii 11. [132] *ib.* i 22. [133] James v 8.
[134] James i 27, ii 15 to 17, v 1 to 3.
[135] 2 Cor. ix 8 (the technical term is αὐτάρκεια); 'if a man does not choose to work, neither shall he eat' 2 Thess. iii 10.
[136] 'worldly (i.e. materialistic) stories, fit only for credulous old women, have nothing to do with' 1 Tim. iv 7.
[137] Titus i 14. [138] Galatians ii 9.

into that mythological form to which Paul himself was so fiercely opposed.

482. This divergence of view is illustrated most strikingly
in the two doctrines which for both parties were
the cardinal points of Christian belief, the divine
nature of the Founder and his resurrection. On
the latter point the standpoint of the Hebraists is sufficiently
indicated by the tradition of the gospels, all of which emphatically
record as a decisive fact that the body of Jesus was not found in
his grave on the third day ; to the Paulists this point is entirely
irrelevant, and they pass it by unmentioned[139]. To Paul again
the man Jesus was of human and natural birth, born of the
posterity of David, born of a woman, born subject to the law[140] ;
in his aspect as the Christ he was, as his followers were to be,
begotten of the spirit and born anew[141]. His statement as to
descent from David (which hardly means more than that he was
of Jewish race) was crystallized by the mythologists in two
formal genealogies, which disagree so entirely in detail that they
have always been the despair of verbal apologists, but agree in
tracing the pedigree through Joseph to Jesus. The phrase
'begotten of the spirit' was interpreted with equal literalness ;
but the marvel-lovers were for a time puzzled to place the
'spirit' in the family relationship. In the first instance the
spirit seems to have been identified with the mother of Jesus[142] ;
but the misunderstanding of a Hebrew word which does not
necessarily connote physical virginity[143] assisted to fix the

The Virgin birth and the resurrection.

[139] '[Christ] was put to death in the flesh, but made alive in the spirit'
1 Peter iii 18.

[140] '[Jesus Christ] who, as regards His human descent, belonged to the posterity
of David, but as regards the holiness of His Spirit was decisively proved by the
Resurrection to be the Son of God' Romans i 4 ; 'God sent forth His Son, born of
a woman, born subject to Law' Gal. iv 4.

[141] 1 Peter i 3.

[142] In the account of the transfiguration in the *Gospel to the Hebrews* (p. 15,
36 Hilgenfeld ; Preuschen *Antileg.* 4) Jesus says 'Lately my mother, the holy spirit,
seized me by one of my hairs and carried me away to the great mountain of Thabor.'
Here Origen restores a philosophical interpretation by referring to Matt. xii 50 ;
'whoever shall do the will of my Father...is my mother' *Comm. in Joh.* ii 12,
p. 64 D. Modern writers find an identification of Mary with the Wisdom ($\sigma o \phi \iota a$) of
God. See Gruppe, *Griechische Mythologie und Religionsgeschichte*, vol. ii p. 1614.

[143] Matt. i 23.

function of fatherhood upon the divine parent. The antipathy to the natural process of procreation which we have traced in St Paul himself, and which was surely not less active amongst many of the Hebraists, has contributed to raise this materialisation of a philosophic tenet to a high place amongst the formal dogmas of historic Christianity.

483. But if the tendency to myth-making was still alive in the Christian church, that in the direction of philosophy had become self-confident and active. The Paulists had taken the measure of their former opponents; they felt themselves superior in intellectual and moral vigour, and they knew that they had won this superiority by contact with the Gentile world. More than before they applied themselves to plead the cause of the Christ before the Gentiles; but the storm and stress of the Pauline epistles gave way in time to a serener atmosphere, in which the truths of Stoicism were more generously acknowledged. A Stoic visitor of the reign of Trajan would meet in Christian circles the attitude represented to us by the fourth gospel, in which the problem of the Christ-nature stands to the front, and is treated on consistently Stoic lines. St Paul had spoken of Jesus as 'for us a wisdom which is from God[144]' and had asserted that 'from the beginning he had the nature of God[145]'; his successors declared frankly that Christ was the Logos, the Word[146]; and in place of the myth of the Virgin Birth they deliberately set in the beginning of their account of Christ the foundation-principles of Stoic physics and the Paulist account of the spiritual procreation of all Christians.

The doctrine of the Word.

'In the beginning was the Word, and the Word was with God, and the Word was God. He was in the beginning with God. All things came into being through him, and apart from him nothing that exists came into being[147].'

'To all who have received him, to them—that is, to those who trust in his name—he has given the privilege of becoming children of God; who were

[144] 1 Cor. i 30. [145] Philipp. ii 6.
[146] 'That which was from the beginning...concerning the Word of life' 1 John i 1; 'his name is the Word of God' Rev. xix 13.
[147] John i 1 to 3.

begotten as such not by human descent, nor through an impulse of their own nature, nor through the will of a human father, but from God.

'And the Word came in the flesh, and lived for a time in our midst, so that we saw his glory, the glory as of the Father's only Son, sent from his presence. He was full of grace and truth[148].'

The Stoic character of this teaching is no longer latent, but proclaimed; and the Church Fathers recognise this in no doubtful terms[149].

484. During the whole of the second century A.D. men trained in Stoic principles crowded into the Christian community. Within it they felt they had a special work to do in building up Christian doctrine so that it might face all storms of criticism. This effort gradually took the shape of schools modelled upon those of the philosophic sects. Such a school was founded by an ex-Stoic named PANTAENUS at Alexandria in 181 A.D.; and his successors CLEMENS of Alexandria (ob. c. 215 A.D.) and ORIGENES (c. 186–253 A.D.) specially devoted themselves to developing the theory of the divine nature upon Stoic lines. Not all the particulars they suggested were accepted by the general feeling of the Christian body, but from the discussion was developed gradually the ecclesiastical doctrine of the Trinity[150]. The elements of this doctrine have been already traced in St Paul's epistles, in which the dominating conceptions are those of God the Father, the Christ, and the divine spirit. For these in the next generation we find the Father, the Word, and the Spirit; and the last term of the triad becomes increasingly identified with the 'holy spirit' of Stoicism. But these three conceptions

The doctrine of the Trinity.

[148] John i 12 to 14.

[149] 'apud vestros quoque sapientes λόγον (id est sermonem atque rationem) constat artificem videri universitatis' Tert. *Apol.* 21; 'Zeno opificem universitatis λόγον praedicat, quem et fatum et necessitatem et animum Iovis nuncupat' Lact. *Div. inst.* iv 9. Naturally the Christian writers regard the Stoic doctrine of the Logos as an 'anticipation' of their own, exactly as in modern times the Darwinists, having borrowed from Epicurus the doctrine of atoms, regard the original doctrine as a 'marvellous anticipation' of modern science. Justin Martyr goes further, and concludes that all believers in the Logos were (by anticipation) Christians: οἱ μετὰ λόγου βιώσαντες Χριστιανοί εἰσι κἂν ἄθεοι ἐνομίσθησαν *Apol.* i 46.

[150] The term is first used by Theophilus (c. 180 A.D.), of God, his Word, and his Wisdom.

(with others) are in Stoic doctrine varying names or aspects of the divine unity. Seneca, for instance, had written in the following tone:

'To whatever country we are banished, two things go with us, our part in the starry heavens above and the world around, our sole right in the moral instincts of our own hearts. Such is the gift to us of the supreme power which shaped the universe. That power we sometimes call "the all-ruling God," sometimes "the incorporeal Wisdom" which is the creator of mighty works, sometimes the "divine spirit" which spreads through things great and small with duly strung tone, sometimes "destiny" or the changeless succession of causes linked one to another[151].'

Here the larger variety of terms used by the early Stoic teachers[152] is reduced to four aspects of the first cause, namely God, the Word, the divine spirit, and destiny. The Christian writers struck out from the series the fourth member, and the doctrine of the Trinity was there. Its stiff formulation for school purposes in the shape 'these three are one' has given it the appearance of a paradox; but to persons conversant with philosophic terminology such a phrase was almost commonplace, and is indeed found in various associations[153]. The subsequent conversion of the members of the triad into three 'persons' introduced a simplification which is only apparent, for the doctrine must always remain meaningless except as a typical solution of the old problem of 'the One and the many,' carried up to the level of ultimate Being[154].

485. In the ages that have since followed mythology and philosophy have been at work side by side within the Christian church. At no time had Christians of philosophic temperament entirely thrown off the belief in marvels, and this in increasing degree infected the whole

Subsequent history.

---

[151] In this passage an 'anticipation' of the doctrine of the Trinity has many times been discovered; for instance in the 18th century by the Jesuit Huet (Winckler, *der Stoicismus*, p. 9); in our own country by Dr Heberden (see Caesar Morgan, *An investigation of the Trinity of Plato*, Holden's edition, 1853, p. 155); and again recently by Amédée Fleury and others (Winckler, p. 8).

[152] See above, § 242.

[153] For instance in 1 John v 8, and (in substance) in 1 Cor. xiii 13.

[154] Whatever may be the ecclesiastical or legal sense of the word 'person,' in its original philosophical meaning it expresses an aspect of individuality, and not an individual: see Cicero's use of the term quoted above, § 271, note 42.

Hellenistic world from the second century onwards. But this spirit of concession proved no sure protection to men who, after all, were guilty of thinking. It was substantially on this ground that the first persecutions began within the church. Demetrius, bishop of Alexandria (circ. 230 A.D.), excommunicated Origen, and obtained the support of the great majority of the Christian churches for his action; still Origen steadily held his ground, and has found advocates in all ages of Christian history[155]. Throughout the 'dark ages' philosophical thought lay almost extinguished, and a childish credulity attained such monstrous dimensions as to threaten the very existence of social life. In the ecclesiastical chronicles of the middle ages miracles are so frequent that the orderly course of nature seems the exception; angels and devils are so many that men are almost forgotten. To these hallucinations and fictions of the monastery, so deservedly ridiculed in the *Ingoldsby Legends*[156], the practical experience of daily life must always have supplied some corrective; the swollen claim of 'faith' to say yes to every absurdity had to be met by the reassertion of criticism, the right to say 'no.' The Reformation, at the cost of infinite effort and sacrifice, swept away the miracles of the saints; modern criticism has spared none of the marvels of the Old Testament, and is beginning to lay its axe to the root of those of the New. Every day the conviction that 'miracles do not happen' gains ground amongst intelligent communities; that is (in philosophic language) the dualism of God and Nature is being absorbed in the wider monism according to which God and Nature are one.

486. As the credit of Christian mythology diminishes, the Christian philosophic content of the new religion is regaining philosophy. its authority. The doctrine of the 'spiritual life' has not yet lost its freshness or its power; but the more closely it is examined, the more clearly will it be seen that it is rooted in the fundamental Stoic conceptions of providence and duty, and that, in the history of the Christian church, it is specially bound up with the life and writings of the apostle Paul. It is

---

[155] See above, § 470, note 77.

[156] This book claims rank as a classic; amongst others of similar purpose may be mentioned R. Garnett's *Twilight of the gods* (New edition, London 1903).

not suggested that the sketch of Christian teaching contained in this chapter is in any way a complete or even a well-proportioned view of the Christian faith; for we have necessarily thrown into the background those elements of the new religion which are drawn from Judaism[157] or from the personality of the Founder. Nor have we found in Paul a Stoic philosopher: it remains for a more direct and profound study to determine which of the forces which stirred his complex intellect most exactly represents his true and final convictions.   No man at any rate ever admitted more frankly the conflict both of moral and of intellectual cravings within himself; no man ever cautioned his followers more carefully against accepting all his words as final.   With these reservations we may perhaps venture to join in the hopes of a recent writer who was endowed with no small prophetic insight:

'The doctrine of Paul will arise out of the tomb where for centuries it has lain buried.   It will edify the church of the future; it will have the consent of happier generations, the applause of less superstitious ages.   All will be too little to pay the debt which the church of God owes to this "least of the apostles, who was not fit to be called an apostle, because he persecuted the church of God[158]."'

487. When that day comes, it will be recognised that
Stoicism in   Stoicism is something more than what the Church
the present.   Fathers meant when they described it as part of
the 'preparation of the gospel'; that it may rather be regarded as forming an integral part of the Christian message, or (as it has been recently called) a 'root of Christianity[159].'   If this view is correct, Stoicism is not dead nor will it die; whether it is correct or not, the study of Stoicism is essential to the full understanding of the Christian religion, as also to that of many

---

[157] Amongst these elements we include all that Christianity has drawn from Persism through Judaism.   We have indeed referred to the Persian beliefs embodied in the 'Lord's prayer'; but it has lain outside our scope to discuss the Eschatology which figures so largely in popular conceptions of Christianity, but is now thought to be but slightly connected with its characteristic message.   On this point see especially Carl Clemen, *Religionsgeschichtliche Erklärung des Neuen Testaments* (Giessen, 1909), pp. 90-135.

[158] Matthew Arnold, *St Paul and Protestantism* (Popular edition, p. 80).

[159] The full title of Winckler's book from which we have often already quoted is *Der Stoicismus eine Wurzel des Christenthums*.

other fundamental conceptions of our modern life. Still the Christian churches celebrate yearly in quick succession the twin festivals of Pentecost and Trinity, in which the groundwork of the Stoic physics is set forth for acceptance by the faithful in its Christian garb; whilst the scientific world has lately in hot haste abandoned the atomic theory as a final explanation of the universe, and is busy in re-establishing in all its essentials the Stoic doctrine of an all-pervading aether. In the practical problems of statesmanship and private life we are at present too often drifting like a ship without a rudder, guided only by the mirages of convention, childishly alarmed at the least investigation of first principles; till the most numerous classes are in open revolt against a civilisation which makes no appeal to their reason, and a whole sex is fretting against a subordination which seems to subserve no clearly defined purpose. In this part of philosophy we may at least say that Stoicism has stated clearly the chief problems, and has begun to pave a road towards their solution. But that solution will not be found in the refinements of logical discussion : of supreme importance is the force of character which can at the right moment say 'yes' or say 'no.' In this sense also (and not by any more mechanical interpretation) we understand the words of the Founder of Christianity : 'let your language be "Yes, yes" or "No, no"; anything in excess of this comes from the Evil one[160].' To the simple and the straightforward, who trust themselves because they trust a power higher than themselves, the future belongs.

[160] Matt. v 37.

BIBLIOGRAPHY.

The numbers in brackets are those of the British Museum catalogue. The dates given are usually those of the latest available edition.

I. ANCIENT WRITERS AND PHILOSOPHERS.

Achilles (the astronomer). Isagoge ad Arati phaenomena. In Migne's Patrology. (2001 c.) A better text in E. Maass' Aratea ; see 'Aratus.'

Aëtius (1st cent. A.D.). Placita philosophiae. In 'Doxographi Graeci' ed. H. Diels, 1879. (2044 f.)

Alexander of Aphrodisias (circ. 200 A.D.). In Aristotelis metaphysica, ed. M. Hayduck (Ac. 855/9); in Arist. Top. ed. M. Wallies (Ac. 855/9) ; de anima, de fato, de mixtione, etc. ed. I. Bruns (2044 f).

Ammonius (the grammarian) of Alexandria. In Aristotelis analytica, ed. M. Wallies. (Ac. 855/9.)

Antigonus (of Carystus, circ. 250 B.C.). Mirae auscultationes, ed. A. Westermann, in 'Paradoxographi Graeci.' [His life of Zeno is the basis of that given by Diogenes Laertius.] Antigonus von Carystos, by Wilamowitz-Moellendorf, 1881. (12902 ee 25.)

Antipater (of Tarsus). Fragments in H. von Arnim 'Stoicorum veterum fragmenta.' (8460 k.)

Antoninus, M. Aur. See Aurelius.

Apollonius (of Tyana ; Neo-Pythagorean philosopher, ob. 97 A.D.). Ap. of T., a study of his life and times, by F. W. Groves Campbell, 1908. (10606 l 4.) See also Mead, G. R. S., and Whittaker, T.

Aratus. Phaenomena, ed. E. Maass, 1893. (11312 f 58.) Comm. in Aratum reliquiae, coll. E. Maass, 1898. (11313 gg 1.)
> *Maass, E.* Aratea. 1892.

Areius Didymus (time of Augustus). The presumed fragments collected by H. Diels in 'Doxographi Graeci.' 1879. (2044 f.)

Aristo. De Aristone Chio et Herillo Carthaginiensi Stoicis commentatio. N. Saal, 1852. (10605 e 33.) See also the article by H. von Arnim, in Pauly-Wissowa ii 957 sqq.

Aristotle. The commentaries on Aristotle are valuable authorities for Stoic teaching; new editions are in course of publication by the Royal Prussian Society of Science. The most important for our purpose are those of Alexander, Dexippus, Philoponus, Simplicius, and Themistius. (Ac. 855/9.)
> *Butcher, S. H.* Aristotle's Theory of Poetry and Fine Art. 1902. (2236 cc 9.) [Contains a discussion of the phrase κάθαρσις τῶν παθημάτων.]
> *Hicks, R. D.* Arist. de anima, 1907.
> *Wallace, Edwin.* Aristotle's Psychology in Greek and English, with introd. and notes. 1882. (2236 cc.)

Arrianus, Flavius (2nd cent. A.D.). Ed. A. G. Roos, in Bibl. Teub. (2047 c.)
Athenaeus. Ed. G. Kaibel, 3 vols., in Bibl. Teub. (2047 e.)
Augustinus (353—430 A.D.). In the Corpus Script. Eccles., vols. 25–28. (2003 d.)
Aurelius, M. Antoninus. Ed. with commentary by Gataker, 1652, with preface 'de Stoica disciplina cum sectis aliis collata.' Of this book G. Long says, 'it is a wonderful monument of learning, and certainly no Englishman has yet done anything like it.' (12205 ff 3.) Also ed. by J. Stich, in Bibl. Teub. (2047 e.) Also by J. H. Leopold, in Script. Cl. Bibl. Oxon. (2046 b.)

There are numerous translations. By M. Casaubon, 5th ed. 1692 (231 c 14), and edited with introd. by W. H. D. Rouse, 1899; by G. Long, 1862, and with an essay by Matthew Arnold attached, 1904 (12204 p 3 15); by J. Collier, revised by Alice Zimmern, 1891 (012207 l 3); by John Jackson, 1906 (8410 ee 23); and by G. H. Rendall, with introductory study on 'Stoicism and the last of the Stoics,' 1898 (08461 g 1).

Treatises by the following:
Alston, L. Stoic and Christian in the second century. 1906. (4532 de 6.)
Bach, N. De M. Aurelio Ant. Imperatore philosophante.
Bodek, Arn. M. Aur. Ant. als Freund und Zeitgenosse des Rabbi Jehuda ha-Nasi, 1868. (10605 ee 29.)
Braune, A. M. Aurel's Meditationen, 1878.
Crossley, Hastings. The fourth book, with translation, commentary, and appendix on C. Fronto, 1882. (8462 d 12.)
Dartigne-Peyrou, J. Marc-Aurèle dans ses rapports avec le christianisme, 1897. (4530 ee 30.)
Davis, C. H. S. Greek and Roman Stoicism and some of its disciples, 1903. (08461 g 11.)
Ellis, Robinson. The correspondence of Fronto and M. Aurelius. (11312 g 11/4.)
Königsbeck, Max. De Stoicismo M. Antonini, 1861. (8461 bbb 33.)
Pollock, Sir *Fred.* See *Mind,* 1st series, vol. iv, pp. 47–68.
Renan, J. E. Marc-Aurèle et la fin du monde antique. 1882. (A, B 35090.) Translated by W. Hutchinson, 1904. (012208 ee 120.)
Russell, E. W. Marcus Aurelius and the later Stoics. 1910.
Schuster, J. Ethices Stoicae apud M. Aur. Ant. fundamenta. 1869.
Smith, B. E. Selections from the original Greek, with introd. New York, 1899. (8411 de 4.)
Steinhauser, K. Filosofie stoicka a Cisar Mark Aurel. Caslau, 1892.
Suckau, M. E. Étude sur Marc-Aurèle, sa vie et sa doctrine, 1858. (8461 c. 10.)
des Vergers, M. Noel. Essai sur Marc-Aurèle, 1860. (10605 ee 19.)
Watson, P. B. M. Aurelius Ant. 1884.
Zeller, Ed. See his Vorträge und Abhandlungen, pp. 82–107.
Censorinus. De die natali liber, ed. F. Hultsch. (2047 g.)
Chalcidius. In Timaeum, ed. Wrobel. (8462 dd 2.)
Chrysippus. See Stoicorum veterum fragmenta, ed. Hans von Arnim. 3 vols., 1903-5. (8460 k.)
Baguet, F. N. G. De Chrysippi vita, etc. Louvain, 1822.
Bergk, Theodor. De Chrys. libris περὶ ἀποφατικῶν. Cassel, 1841.
Gercke, A. Chrysippea. 1885. (R. PP. 4986.)
Nicolai, R. De logicis Chrysippi libris. Quedlinburg, 1859.
Petersen, C. Philosophiae Chrysippeae fundamenta. 1827. (714 d 38.)

Cicero, M. Tullius. Philosophica omnia, ed. R. Klotz. 2 vols. 1840, 1.
Libros qui ad rempublicam et ad philosophiam spectant ed. Th. Schiche.
9 vols. Prag, 1881–1890. (11305 bb.)
> *Bernhardt, C. M.* De Cicerone graecae philosophiae interprete. 1865.
> *Brandis, C. A.* See Rheinisches Museum iii 541 sqq. (R. PP. 4980, 1.)
> *Gedike, Fr.* Zusammenstellung der auf die Geschichte der Philosophie bezüglichen Stellen des Cicero. Berlin, 1814.
> *Hirzel, Rudolf.* Untersuchungen zu Cicero's philosophischen Schriften. 3 vols., 1877–83. (8462 cc 12.)
> *Levin, T. W.* Six lectures introductory to the philosophical writings of Cicero. 1871. (8461 ee 19.)
> *Merguet, P. A. H.* Lexicon zu den philosophischen Schriften Cicero's. 3 vols. 1889–94. (12933 l 13.)
> *Thiaucourt, C.* Essai sur les traités philosophiques de Ciceron et leurs sources grecques. 1885. (8460 f 8.)
ACADEMICA. Edited with full commentary by J. S. Reid. Also translation. 2 vols. 1885. (2282 d 2.)
DE DIVINATIONE.
DE FATO.
DE FINIBUS. Ed. J. N. Madvig. 3rd ed., 1876. (8408 g 6.) Ed. with introd. and commentary by W. M. L. Hutchinson, 1909. (08407 f 26.)
DE LEGIBUS.
DE NATURA DEORUM. Ed. with introd. and comm. by J. B. Mayor. 3 vols. 1880–5. (2236 e 8.)
DE OFFICIIS. Ed. H. Holden, 7th ed. 1891. (2282 a 1.) Erklärende Ausgabe von C. F. W. Müller, 1882. Translated by G. B. Gardiner, 1899.
PARADOXA. Erklärt von Max Schneider, 1891.
DE REPUBLICA. La République de Ciceron traduite...avec un discours préliminaire, par A. F. Villemain. 1858. (12238 ee 2.)
TUSCULANAE DISPUTATIONES. Erk. von Otto Heine, 1896.
> *Corssen, P.* De Posidonio Rhodio M. Tulli Ciceronis in libro i Tusc. disp. et in Somnio Scipionis auctore. Rhein. Mus. xxxvi p. 505 sqq. (R. PP. 4980, 1.)
> *Zietschmann, G.* De Tusc. disp. fontibus. 1868.
Cleanthes. The fragments collected by A. C. Pearson, 1891 (2280 aa 3); and by H. von Arnim in ' Stoic. veterum fragm.' 1903–5. (8460 k.)
> *Mohnike, G. C. F.* Cleanthes der Stoiker. (832 b 14.)
> *Wachsmuth, C.* (i) Cleanthis physica; (ii) commentatio de Cleanthe Assio, 1874.
Clemens (of Alexandria, 150—211 A.D., and head of the Catecheten-school there), ed. G. Dindorf, 4 vols. 1869. (3805 bbb 22.) Protreptikos and Paidagogos ed. Otto Stählin, 1905.
> *de Faye, E.* Clém. d'Alexandrie. Études sur les rapports du Christianisme et de la philosophie grecque au II⁰ siècle, 1906. (R. Ac. 8929/7.)
Cornutus, Lucius Annaeus. De natura deorum I ed. Fr. Osann; adj. est J. de Volloison, de theologia physica Stoicorum commentatio. 1844. (1385 g 4.) Ed. G. Lang. 1881. (2048 a.)
> *de Martini, G. J.* Disp. de L. A. Cornuto, 1825. (8461 cc 12.)
> *Reppe, R.* De L. A. Cornuto. 1906.
Crates (of Mallos). De Cr. Mall. adiectis eius reliquiis. C. Wachsmuth, Leipzig, 1860.
Demetrius (of Magnesia, 1st cent. B.C.). D. Magnetis fragm. 1858. (11335 f 43.) He wrote a life of Zeno which is quoted by Themistius.

Dexippus (Platonist of 4th century A.D.) Ed. A. Busse. (Ac. 855/9.)

Diocles (of Magnesia). He wrote lives of the philosophers, from which Diogenes Laertius quotes freely.

Diogenes (of Seleucia or Babylon). See H. von Arnim 'Sto. vet. fragmenta.' (8460 k.)

Diogenes Laertius ('Laertius' is a nickname based on a verse of Homer; about 230 A.D.). Lives of the philosophers, in ten volumes, based upon earlier works. Our principal authority for Stoic doctrine. In Bibl. Teub., 2 vols. (10606 a 23.) English trans. by C. D. Yonge, 1848.

Dion Cassius. Historia Romana. Ed. J. Melber in Bibl. Teub. (2048 a.)

Dion of Prusa (popular philosopher, circ. 50 A.D.). Ed. J. de Arnim. (11391 ee 5.)

> *von Arnim, H.* Leben und Werke des Dio von Prusa, mit einer Einleitung 'Sophistik, Rhetorik, und Philosophie in ihrem Kampfe um die Jugendbildung.' 1898. (8460 g 20.)

Dionysius (of Halicarnassus). Ed. H. Usener and L. Radermacher. In Bibl. Teub. (2048 a.) Contains an account of Chrysippus.

Epictetus. Ep. diss. libri IV. Gr. et Lat. Ann. ill. J. Schweighäuser, 1799, 1800. (8459 g 4.) Ep. dissertationes, ed. H. Schenkl. In Bibl. Teub. (2278 k 5.) The references to the life of Epictetus are also collected here. A commentary exists dating from the 6th century A.D. See Simplicius. Translation with notes, a life of Epictetus, and a view of his philosophy, by G. Long, 1848. (8460 ccc 30.) Popular edition in 2 vols., 1891.

> *Asmus, R.* Quaestiones Epicteteae. Freiburg, 1888. (8463 i 6/2.)
> *Bernard, Edw. R.* Great Moral Teachers; Epictetus. (8410 p 29.)
> *Bonhöffer, A.* Epictet und die Stoa. 1890. (8460 g 11.) Die Ethik des Stoïker's Epictet. 1894.
> *Brandis, C. A.* Epictetus (Dict. of Greek and Roman Biography).
> *Braune, A.* Epictet und das Christenthum. Zeits. f. kirchl. Wiss., 1884-9.
> *Bruns, Ivo.* De schola Epicteti. Kiel, 1897.
> *Crossley, H.* Golden sayings of Epictetus, etc. 1903. (8462 de 8.)
> *Farrar, F. W.* Seekers after God: Epictetus. 1876. (3605 bb 3.)
> *Grosch, G.* Die Sittenlehre des Epictetus. Wernigerode, 1867.
> *Rouse, W. H. D.* Words of the ancient wise, from Epictetus. 1906. (8462 de 14.)
> *Schenkl, H.* Die epiktetischen Fragmente. Wien, 1888.
> *Schranka, E. M.* Der Stoïker Epictetus und seine Philosophie. Frankfurt, 1885.
> *Stuhrmann, J.* De vocabulis notionum philosophicarum ab Epicteto adhibitis. Neustadt, 1885.
> *Thurot, Charles.* Epictète, Manuel. 1892. (8460 aaa 37.)
> *Zahn, Theodor.* Der Stoïker Epiktet und sein Verhältniss zum Christenthum. Erlangen, 1895.

Epiphanius (Bishop of Constantia). Adversus haereses prooemium. (3627 c 19.)

Eusebius. Evangelica praeparatio, etc. Berlin, 1897. (2004 f.)

Fragmenta Herculaniensia. Ed. by Walter Scott. 1885. (7706 ee 13.)

Fronto. M. Cornelii Frontonis et M. Aurelii imperatoris epistulae. Ed. S. A. Naber. 1867. (10905 ccc 19.)

Galenus, Claudius (of Pergamus; circ. 131-200 A.D. He was a physician who attended the family of Marcus Aurelius, and he gives large extracts from Chrysippus' books *de anima* and *de affectibus*). Ed. C. G. Kuhn, 20 vols., 1821-3. (541 d 1 to 20.) This edition has a good index; its pages are referred to by the letter K. Also edited by Marquardt,

Müller, and others in Bibl. Teub. 1884–93. (2048 b.) Also an edition by Iw. Müller of the book *de placitis Hipp. et Plat.*, the pages of which are referred to by the letter M.

Gellius, Aulus (2nd cent. A.D.). Post M. Hertz ed. C. Hosius in Bibl. Teub. (2048 b.)

Hecataeus (a geographer of Miletus, circ. 500 B.C.). Fragm. Gr. et Lat. ed. C. et Th. Müller in 'Hist. Graec. fragmenta,' vol. i. Paris, 1878–85. (2053 b.)

Hecato (of Rhodes). Panaetii et Hecatonis fr. coll. H. N. Fowler. 1885.

Heracleides (of the Pontus; a pupil of Plato, and propounder of the heliocentric system). See Steigmüller, H. in the *Archiv f. d. Geschichte d. Philosophie* xv, pp. 141 sqq. (PP. 1253 ba.)

Heracleitus (of Ephesus). H. Ephesii reliquiae; rec. I. Bywater, 1877. (8460 ee 18.) H. Diels in 'die Fragmente der Vorsokratiker,' 1903. (2044 e.) H. von Ephesos, gr. und deutsch, von H. Diels, 1909.

> *Bernays, J.* Neue Bruchstücke des H. (4980, 1 and 204 g h); die Heraklitischen Briefe, 1869. (8461 dd 18.)
> *Campbell, Lewis.* Heraclitus and Parmenides, in his edition of Plato's *Theaetetus.* 1883. (12204 f 19.)
> *Diels, H.* Heraklit: eine Studie. 1904. (8461 ee 41.)
> *Drummond, James.* See his *Philo-Judaeus*, 1888. (8485 d f 18.)
> *Gladisch, A.* Herakleitos und Zoroaster. 1859. (4504 d 15.)
> *Gomperz, Th.* Zu Heraklit's Lehre. 1887.
> *Lassalle, F. J. G.* Die Philosophie H. 2 vols., 1858. (8461 e 22.) Also a new edition by Löwenthal in 4 vols.
> *Pfleiderer, Edmund.* Die Philosophie des H. im Lichte der Mysterienidee. 1886. (8485 e 28.)
> *Schäfer, G.* Die Philosophie d. Heraklit von Ephesus u. d. moderne Heraklitforschung. 1902.
> *Schultz, W.* Pythagoras und Heraklit. 1905.
> *Wendland, P.* Ein Wort des H. im neuen Testament. 1899.

Herillus. *Krug, W. T.* H. de summo bono sententia, 1822.

Hermias (perhaps 5th or 6th cent. A.D.). Irrisio gentilium philosophorum. Ed. J. C. Th. von Otto, Jena, 1872. Quoted in Diels' 'Doxographi Graeci.'

Herodotus. The history transl. into English by G. C. Macaulay. 2 vols. 1890. (2280 aa 2.)

Hierocles (Stoic). Ethische Elementarlehre, her. von H. von Arnim und Schubart. 1906.

> *Prächter, K.* Hierokles der Stoiker. 1901.

Hippolytus (Bishop in 2nd cent. A.D.). Ed. G. N. Bonwetsch and H. Achelis. 1897. (2004 f.)

Iamblichus (Neo-platonist philosopher, early in 4th cent. A.D.). Rec. G. Parthey, 1857.

Iulianus (the emperor). Ed. F. C. Hertlein, in Bibl. Teub. (2048 d); transl. by C. W. King (2500 f 13).

> *Gardner, Alice.* Julian the Philosopher. 1890. (10601 f 30.)
> *Rendall, G. H.* The Emperor Julian, Paganism and Christianity. 1879. (4534 cc 8.)

Iustinus (historian, circ. 4th cent. A.D.). Historiarum Philippicarum libri xliv. Ed. C. H. Frotscher. 3 vols., 1827. (9040 cc 12.)

Iustinus (the martyr: circ. 105–165 A.D.). Op. Gr. et Lat. ed. J. C. Th. von Otto. 3 vols. 1876–81. (3622 cc 3.)

Lactantius (3rd cent. A.D.). Ed. S. Brandt and G. Laubmann in Corpus Script. Eccl. Lat. (2003 d.)

Lucanus, M. Annaeus. Pharsalia, ed. C. E. Haskins. 1887. (2045 e.) Scholia in Lucanum. 1869. (11312 g 30.)

Diels, H. Seneca und Lucan. Abh. d. Ak. d. Wiss. z. Berlin, 1885. (Ac. 855/6.)

Lucianus (of Samosata, 130–200 A.D.). Ed. J. Sommerbrodt. 3 vols. 1886–99. Ed. Nils Nilén in Bibl. Teub. (2048 d.)

Bernays, J. Lucian und die Kyniker. 1879. (8462 cc 10.)

Lucilius, C. Rec. F. Marx. 2 vols. Leipzig, 1904–6.

Lucretius, T. Carus. Ed. H. A. J. Munro. 3 vols. 1893. (2045 h.)

Masson, J. Lucretius, Epicurean and Poet; with notes and comments by J. S. Reid. 2 vols. 1907–9. (2282 c 22.)

Macrobius. Ed. F. Eyssenhardt in Bibl. Teub. (2278 c 9.) On the λόγοι σπερματικοί see *Saturnalia* vii 16.

Marcellinus, Ammianus (historian, of 5th cent. A.D.). Ed. V. Gardthausen in Bibl. Teub. (2048 d.) Ed. C. U. Clark, Berlin, 1910.

Michael, H. De Amm. Marc. studiis Ciceronianis. Breslau, 1874.

Maximus (of Tyre: 2nd cent. A.D.). Ed. F. Dübner, Paris, 1840. (2046 e.) Ed. H. Hobein, 1910. Transl. by T. Taylor. 2 vols. 1804. (1385 g 3.)

Minucius, M. Felix (3rd cent. A.D.). Ed. H. Bönig in Bibl. Teub. 1903. (2047 a.)

Musonius, C. Rufus. Ed. O. Hense in Bibl. Teub. (2048 e.)

Baltzer, E. Musonius' Charakterbild aus der römischen Kaiserzeit. 1871.

Bernhardt, Otto. Zu Musonius Rufus. Sorau, 1866.

Pflieger, T. Musonius bei Stobaeus. Tauberbischofsheim, 1897.

Wendland, P. Quaestiones Musonianae. Berlin, 1886. (11312 dd 12/4.)

Nemesius (5th cent. A.D.). De natura hominis (in Greek). In Migne's Patrology. (2001 d.) Nemesius drew largely from Aëtius.

Origenes (185–254 A.D.). In Migne's Patrology. (2004 f.) Commentary on St John, ed. A. E. Brooke. 1896. Philosophumena: revised text with introd. etc., by J. A. Robinson, 1893.

Fairweather, W. Origen and Greek Patristic Theology. (10600 eee 7/13.)

Falconer, J. W. Origen and the return to Greek theology. Biblia Sacra liii, pp. 466 sqq.

Westcott, B. F. Origen and the beginnings of Christian philosophy. In his Essays in the history of religious thought in the West. 1891. (8486 aaa 1.)

Orphica. Ed. E. Abel. Prag, 1885.

Maass, E. Orpheus; Untersuchungen z. gr. röm. altchristl. Jenseitsdichtung und Religion. 1895.

Panaetius (180–110 A.D.). P. et Hecatonis librorum fragm. coll. H. N. Fowler, 1855. Disputatio hist. de P. Rhodio. F. van Lynden. Leyden, 1802. (8460 cc 16.)

Papiri Ercolanesi, ed. D. Comparetti. Turin, 1875. Contains an index to the Stoic philosophers.

Pausanias. Ed. H. Hitzig and H. Blümer, 1896–1910. (2044 f.) Transl. with comm. by J. G. Frazer, 1898. (2044 e.)

Persius, A. Flaccus. Ed. with transl. and comm. by J. Conington. Third edition by H. Nettleship, 1893.

Houck, M. E. De ratione stoica in Persii satiris conspicua. Daventriae, 1894.

Philo (of Alexandria, circ. 20 B.C. to 50 A.D.). Ed. T. Mangey, 1742. (691 k 78.) Ed. L. Cohn et P. Wendland, 1896–1906. (8459 h and 3623 de.)

Arnim, H. von. Quellenstudien z. P. von Al. 1888.

(Philo)

> *Drummond, James.* Philo Judaeus. 1888.
> *Freudenthal, J.* Die Erkenntnisslehre P.'s von Al. 1891.
> *Harnack, A.* De Phil. Jud. λόγῳ inquisitio. 1879.
> *Heinze, Max.* Die Lehre vom Logos in d. griech. Philosophie. 1872.
> *Lake, J. W.* Plato, Philo and Paul; or the pagan conception of a divine λόγος the basis of the Christian dogma. 1874. (4027 e 7/5.)
> *Mills, L, H.* Zarathustra, Philo, the Achaemenids, and Israel. 1905. (4506 ee 26.)
> *Wendland, P.* Die philos. Quellen des P. in s. Schrift über die Vorsehung. 1891. P.'s Schrift über die Vorsehung. 1892. (8460 f 4.)

Philodemus (of Gadara, 1st cent. B.C.). In Bibl. Teub. (2048 e.)

> *Gomperz, Th.* Zu Philodem's Büch. v. d. Musik. 1885.

Philoponus (Aristotelian commentator, 7th cent. A.D.). Ed. M. Hayduck and others for Royal Prussian Academy. 1887– . (Ac. 855/9.) The *comm. in Aristotelis physica* is of special value for its account of the Stoic logic.

Plotinus (Neo-platonist, 205–270 A.D.). Ed. R. Volkmann in Bibl. Teub. (2048 f.) He criticized specially the Stoic doctrine of categories.

Plutarchus (circ. 46–120 A.D.). Moralia, ed. G. N. Bernardakis in Bibl. Teub. (2047 a, etc.)

Posidonius. Pos. Rhodii rell. coll. J. Bake. 1810. (91 i 1.)

> *Corssen, P.* De Pos. R. Ciceronis in lib. i. Tusc. disp. et in somn. Scip. auctore. 1878. Rhein. Mus. xxxvi p. 505. (R. PP. 4980, 1 and 2049 h i.)
> *Hultsch, F.* Pos. über d. Grösse und Entfernung d. Sonne. 1897. (Ac. 6770.)
> *Scheppig, R.* De Pos. Apamensi. Berlin, 1870. (8367 f 7/12.)
> *Schühlein, F.* Zu Posidonius Rhodius. Freising, 1891. Über P.'s Schrift περὶ ὠκεανοῦ. 1900.
> *Töpelmann, V. E. P.* De Pos. Rhodio rerum scriptore. Bonn, 1867. (8363 b 7/13.)

Proclus Diadochus (Platonic commentator, 5th cent. A.D.). In Bibl. Teub.

Seneca, L. Annaeus. Opera, ed. by O. Hense and others, in Bibl. Teub. (2048 g 15, 16.) Quaestiones Naturales. Transl. by J. Clarke, with notes by Sir Archibald Geikie. 1910. (08709 c 2.)

> *Aubertin, C.* Sénèque et S. Paul. 1869. (4807 dd 3.)
> *Badstübner, E.* Beitr. z. Erkl. der philos. Schriften Sen.'s. Hamburg, 1901. (8460 l 5.)
> *Baumgarten, M. L. A.* Seneca u. d. Christenthum. 1895.
> *Baur, F. C.* Seneca und Paulus. 1858. In Zeitsch. f. wiss. Theologie, 1, 2 and 3. (PP. 88 c.)
> *Bernhardt, W.* Die Anschauung des Seneca vom Universum 1861. (8705 ee 15/5.)
> *Betzinger.* Weltfrohes u. Weltfreies aus S.'s Schriften. S. u. d. Christenthum. 1899.
> *Bock, F.* Aristoteles Theophrastus Seneca de matrimonio. Leipzig, 1898.
> *Burgmann, Rud.* S.'s Theologie in ihrem Verhältniss zum Stoicismus und zum Christenthum. 1872.
> *Diels, H.* Seneca und Lucan. Abh. d. Ak. d. Wiss. z. Berlin, 1885. (Ac. 855/6.)
> *Fleury, Amédée.* Saint Paul et Sénèque. 2 vols. 1853.

(Seneca, L. Annaeus)
> *Gercke, Alf.* Seneca-studien. 1895. (R.PP. 4986 Bd. 22, Heft 1.)
> *Heikel, J. A.* Seneca's Charakter und politische Thätigkeit. Helsingfors, 1888.
> *Hense, O. F.* Seneca und Athenodorus. Freiburg, 1893.
> *Lightfoot, J. B.* St Paul and Seneca. In his *Philippians*, 1879. (3266 ff 6.)
> *Martens, A.* De L. A. Sen. vita, etc. Altona 1871. (10605 ee 6.)
> *Martha, C.* Sénèque. C. R. Acad. d. Sci. mor. et pol., cxxxv, 1891.
> *Ribbeck, W.* L. A. Sen. der Philosoph, und sein Verhältniss zu Epikur, Plato, und dem Christenthum. Hannover, 1887. (8464 dd 34/9.)
> *Rubin, Sol.* Die Ethik S.'s in ihrem Verhältniss zur älteren und mittleren Stoa. München, 1901. (8409 m 15.)
> *Summers, W. C.* Select letters. 1910. (010910 e 35.)
> *Thomas, P.* Morceaux choisis. Extrait des lettres à Lucilius et des traités de morale. 1896.

Servius. Comm. ad Verg. Aen. (11312 i 35.)

Sextus Empiricus (3rd cent. A.D.). Ed. I. Bekker, 1842. (1385 i 3.)

Simplicius (Aristotelian commentator, 6th cent. A.D.). Ed. Heiberg and others for Royal Prussian Academy. (Ac. 855/9.)

Stobaeus, Johannes (4th or 5th cent. A.D.). A collector of extracts. His works were formerly divided into *Eclogae* and *Florilegium*. In the current edition by C. Wachsmuth and O. Hense, 4 vols., Berlin, 1884– (8462 ee), this distinction is dropped. This edition is not yet complete, and occasionally reference has to be made to A. Meineke's edition of the Florilegium, 6 vols., Leipzig, 1855–7. (2047 a.)

Strabo (geographer, circ. 54 B.C. to 24 A.D.). Ed. A. Meineke. 3 vols. Leipzig, 1877. Also in Didot's Script. Gr. Bibl. (2046 c.)

Suidas (lexicographer). Lexicon, ed. I. Bekker. 1854. (12923 ee 14.)

Tertullianus (160–220 A.D.). Ed. A. Reifferscheid et G. Wissowa, in the Corpus Script. Eccl. 1890–   (2003 d.)

Themistius (Aristotelian commentator, circ. 350 A.D.). Ed. R. Heinze and others for Royal Prussian Academy. (Ac. 855/9.)

Theodoretus (bishop of Cyrus, circ. 425 A.D.). Graecorum affectionum curatio, ed. J. Raeder in Bibl. Teub. (2049 a.) He has preserved long extracts from Aëtius.

Theophilus (bishop). Ed. J. G. Wolf, 1724. (3622 cc 3.)

Varro, M. Terentius. De lingua Latina quae supersunt ed. G. Goetz et Fr. Schöll. (12933 v 2.) Antiquitates divinae, ed. R. Agahd. In Bibl. Teub.

Xenocrates. Darstellung d. Lehre und Sammlung d. Fragmente, von R. Heinze. 1892.

Zeno. The fragments of Zeno and Cleanthes, by A. C. Pearson. 1891. (2280 aa 3.) Also in von Arnim's Stoicorum veterum fragmenta, 1903 to 1905. (8460 k.)
> *Meuleman.* Commentatio literaria de Zenone Stoico. Groningen, 1858.
> *Troost, K.* Z. Citiensis de rebus physicis doctrina. 1891. (PP. 4991 e.)
> *Wachsmuth, C.* Commentatio de Zenone Citiensi. 1874.
> *Wellmann, E.* Die Philosophie des Stoïker's Z. 1873.

Zoroaster. See article by Karl F. Geldner in the Encyclopaedia Britannica. Zoroaster the prophet of ancient Iran, by A. V. Williams-Jackson. New York, 1899. (4505 eee 9.) See also Philo (Mills).

II. MODERN WRITERS.

Aall, Anathon. Der Logos. Geschichte seiner Entwicklung in d. griech. Philosophie und in d. christlichen Literatur. 2 vols. 1896, 9. (08461 h 8.)

Adam, James. The religious teachers of Greece. 1908. (4506 i 7.)

Allard, P. Le Christianisme et l'Empire romain de Néron à Théodose. 2nd ed., 1897. (2208 a.)

Alston, L. Stoic and Christian in the second century. 1906. (4532 de 6.)

Apelt, O. Beiträge zur Geschichte d. gr. Philosophie. 1891. (8486 e 3.)

Archiv für Geschichte der Philosophie. Herausg. von Ludwig Stein. Berlin, 1888– (PP. 1253 ba.)

Arnim, Hans von. Stoicorum veterum fragmenta. 3 vols., 1903-5. (8460 k.) See also Aristo and Philo.

Arnold, Matthew. Essay attached to an edition of Long's Marcus Aurelius, 1904. (12204 p 3/15.) St Paul and Protestantism. Popular edition, 1887. (3266 bb 1.)

Aubertin, C. De sapientiae doctoribus, qui a Ciceronis morte ad Neronis principatum Romae viguerunt. Paris, 1857. (8461 bb 8.) See also Seneca.

Aust, E. Die Religion der Römer. Münster i. W., 1899. (4506 f 29.)

Avenel, J. d'. Le Stoïcisme et les Stoïciens. 1886.

Baldensperger, W. Das Selbstbewusstsein Jesu's im Lichte der messianischen Hoffnungen seiner Zeit. 2nd ed., 1892. (4226 h 2.)

Barth, Paul. Die Stoa. Stuttgart, 1908. (08464 f.)

Baumhauer, J. C. M. von. Veterum philosophorum, praecipue Stoicorum, doctrina de morte voluntaria. Bonn, 1842. (8460 e 13.)

Bäumker, Cl. Das Problem d. Materie in d. griech. Philosophie. Münster, 1890.

Baur, F. Ch. Zur Geschichte d. alten Philosophie und ihres Verhältnisses zum Christenthum. 1876.

Benn, A. W. The Greek Philosophers. 2 vols. 1882. (8461 dd 14.)

Bergson, Henri L. L'évolution créatrice. 1907. (7006 g 29.)

Bernays, J. Lucian und die Kyniker. 1879. (8462 cc 10.)

Bois, Henri. Essai sur les origines de la philosophie judéo-alexandrine. 1890. (8486 bbb 28.)

Boissier, Gaston. La fin du paganisme. 1891. (4530 Le 1.) L'opposition sous les Césars. 5th ed., 1905. (09039 bb 9.) La religion romaine d'Auguste jusqu'aux Antonins. 2 vols. 2nd ed., 1878. (2212 g.)

Bonhöffer, Adolf. Zur stoischen Psychologie. Philologus liv, 1895, pp. 4023-4429. (R. PP. 5043.) See also Epictetus.

Borchert, L. Num Antistius Labeo...Stoicae philosophiae fuerit addictus ? Breslau, 1869. (6006 e 11/2.)

Brandis, Christian August. Handbuch d. Gesch. d. gr-röm. Philosophie. 3 vols. 1835-66. (1386 d 20.) Gesch. d. Entwicklungen d. gr. Philosophie und ihrer Nachwirkungen im römischen Reiche. 2 vols. 1862-4. (2236 e 2.)

Bréheir, Émile. La théorie des incorporels dans l'ancien stoïcisme. Archiv f. d. Gesch. d. Philosophie xxi, pp. 115-125. (PP. 1253 ba.)

Brochard, Victor. Sur la logique des stoïciens. Archiv f. d. Gesch. d. Philosophie v, p. 449. (PP. 1253 ba.)

Bryant, J. H. The mutual influence of Christianity and the Stoic school. 1866. (8461 bbb 27.)

Burnet, J. Early Greek Philosophy. 1908. (2023 c.)

Caird, Edward. The Evolution of Theology in the Greek Philosophers. 2 vols., 1904. [On Stoicism see vol. ii, chs. xvi to xx.]

Caldecott, Alfred. The philosophy of religion. 1901. (4372 cc 29.)

Campbell, Lewis. Religion in Greek literature. See also Heracleitus. 1898. (4503 g 15.)

Capes, William Wolfe. Stoicism. 1882. (4421 f 64.)

Caspari, E. De Cynicis, qui fuerunt aetate imperatorum Romanorum. Chemnitz, 1896.

Cheyne, T. K. Zoroastrianism and Primitive Christianity. Hibbert Journal, 1903, 4. (R. PP. 324 ga.)

Clemen, Carl. Die religionsgeschichtliche Bedeutung des stoisch-christlichen Eudämonismus in Justin's Apologie. 1891. Religionsgeschichtliche Erklärung des neuen Testaments. 1909.

Collins, J. Churton. Studies in Shakespeare. 1904. [Gives parallels between Seneca's tragedies and Shakespeare.] (2300 b 9.)

Cruttwell, C. H. A literary history of early Christianity. 2 vols., 1893. (2208 b 3.)

Cumont, Fr. Textes et monum. fig. relatifs aux mystères de Mithra. 2 vols., 1899. La théologie solaire du paganisme romain. 1909. Les Religions Orientales dans le paganisme romain. 2nd ed., 1909.

Dähne, A. F. Geschichtliche Darstellung der jüdisch-alexandrinischen Religionsphilosophie. 2 vols. 1834. (1363 d 8.)

Davids, T. W. Rhys. Buddhism. 1901. (4505 cc 26.) Hibbert Lectures on some points in the history of Buddhism. 1881. (2217 aa 11.)

Davidson, William Leslie. The Stoic creed. 1907. (3605 i.)

Deussen, Paul. Allgemeine Geschichte der Philosophie, mit besonderer Rücksicht der Religionen. 1894. (8486 d.)

Dictionary of Philosophy and Psychology, ed. by J. M. Baldwin. 3 vols., 1905. (2023 h.)

Diderot, Denis. Essai sur les règnes de Claude et de Néron, et sur les mœurs et les écrits de Sénèque. 2 vols., 1782.

Diels, H. Über die Philosophenschulen der Griechen (Zeller-Aufsätze, 1887). Die Fragmente der Vorsokratiker, gr. und deutsch von H. D. 2nd ed., 1906–10. (2044 e.) Doxographi Graeci, 1879.

Dill, S. Roman Society from Nero to Marcus Aurelius. 1904. (09039 cc 3.)

Döring, A. Geschichte d. griech. Philosophie. 2 vols., 1903.

Dourif, J. Du Stoicisme et du Christianisme considerés dans leurs rapports. 1863. (8470 e 16.)

Drummond, James. Philo-Judaeus, or the Jewish-Alexandrian Philosophy in its development and completion. 1888. (8485 df 18.)

Dyroff, A. Die Ethik der alten Stoa. 1897, 8. (PP. 4991 e.)

Eisler, Rudolf. Geschichte der Philosophie im Grundriss. 1895. Wörterbuch der phil. Begriffe und Ausdrücke. 3rd ed., 1910. (2236 c 18.)

Eucken, Rudolph. Die Lebensanschauungen der grossen Denker. 1909. (8486 ee 6.) Geschichte der philos. Terminologie in Umriss. 1879. (8486 de 5.)

Ewald, P. Der Einfluss d. stoïsch-ciceronianischen Moral a. d. Darstellung d. Ethik bei Ambrosius. 1881. (8463 df 25/6.)

Fairweather, W. The Background of the Gospels; or Judaism in the period between the Old and New Testaments. 1908. (03225 h 15.)

Favre, Mme Jules. La morale stoïcienne. 1888. (8460 bb 27.)

Feine, —. Stoïcismus und Christenthum. Theol. Lit.-Blatt 1905, pp. 73 sqq.

Ferraz, —. De Stoica disciplina apud poetas Romanos. Paris, 1863.

Fischer, Kuno. Geschichte d. neueren Philosophie. Jubiläums-ausgabe, 1897–1901. (8486 ee.)

Fowler, W. Warde. Social life at Rome in the age of Cicero. 1908. (2382 e 10.)

Franke, Carl. Stoïcismus und Christenthum. Breslau, 1876. (4378 l 1.)

Freudenthal, Jakob. Ueber den Begriff des Wortes φαντασία bei Aristoteles. 1863. (11312 d 9.) Zur Geschichte d. Anschauungen über die jüdisch-hellenische Religionsphilosophie. 1869. (4034 dd 36/6.) Die Erkenntnisslehre Philo's von Alexandria. 1891.

Friedländer, L. Darstellungen aus d. Sittengeschichte Roms. 8th ed. 1910. (2258 b 2.) Authorized translation of 7th ed. by L. A. Magnus. 1908. (09039 dd.)

Friedländer, Moritz. Die religiösen Bewegungen innerhalb des Judaïsmus. 1905. (4516 eee 26.)

Geldner, K. See article 'Zoroaster' in Encyclopaedia Britannica.

Giesecke, Alfred. De philosophorum veterum quae ad exsilium spectant sententiis. 1891. (8460 dd 25.)

Giles, J. A. The writings of the early Christians of the second century. 1857. (3627 c 44.)

Girard, J. Le sentiment religieux en Grèce d'Homère à Eschyle. 1869–79.

Gladisch, A. Herakleitos und Zoroaster. 1859. (4504 d 15.) Die Religion und die Philosophie in ihrer weltgeschichtlichen Entwicklung. 1852. (4531 c 11.)

Glover, T. R. The conflict of religions in the Early Roman Empire. 3rd ed., 1909.

Gomperz, Theodor. Griechische Denker. 3 vols. 1903–8. (8486 dd.) English translation by Laurie Magnus and G. G. Berrie. 1905.

Göttling, O. W. Diogenes der Cyniker oder die Philosophie des griechischen Proletariats. Halle, 1851.

Grant, Sir **Alexander.** The Ancient Stoics. 1858. (PP. 6119 c.)

Gruppe, O. Griechische Mythologie und Religionsgeschichte. 2 vols., 1906. (2044 g.)

Haake, A. Die Gesellschaftslehre der Stoïker. 1887.

Häbler, A. Zur Kosmogonie der Stoïker. Jahrb. f. Phil. und Päd. cxlvii, 1893, pp. 298–300.

Haeckel, E. Die Welträthsel. 1899. English transl., 'The Riddle of the Universe,' by J. McCabe. 1908.

Hamelin, —. Sur la logique des stoïciens. Ann. philosophiques, 1902, p. 23.

Hardy, E. G. Christianity and the Roman Government. 1894. (4532 df 2.)

Harnack, A. Lehrbuch der Dogmengeschichte. 3 vols., 3rd ed., 1894–7. (3544 i.) History of Dogma, transl. by N. Buchanan, J. Millar, and W. McGilchrist. 7 vols. 1894–9. (2206 cc 3.)

Harrison, J. E. Prolegomena to the study of Greek Religion. 2nd ed., 1908.

Hatch, E. The influence of Greek ideas and usages upon the Christian church. 1890. (2217 aa 4.)

Heinze, Max. Die Lehre vom Logos in d. griechischen Philosophie. 1872. Zur Erkenntnisslehre der Stoïker. Leipziger Prog., 1879, 80. Stoicorum de fato doctrina. Stoicorum de affectibus doctrina. Stoicorum ethica ad origines suas relata. 1862.

Henderson, Bernard W. The life and principate of the Emperor Nero. 1903. (10606 e 12.)

Hepke, —. De philosophis qui Romae docuerunt usque ad Antoninos. Berlin, 1842.

Herford, O. C. The Stoics as teachers. 1889.

Hicks, E. Traces of Greek Philosophy and Roman Law in the New Testament. 1896. (4430 aaa 22.)

Hicks, R. D. Stoic and Epicurean. 1910.

Hirzel, Rudolf. De logica Stoicorum. 1879. (7006 c 17.) See also Cicero.

Höffding, H. Philosophy of Religion. Transl. by B. E. Meyer, 1906.

Hüber, N. Die Philosophie der Kirchenväter. 1859.

Jevons, Frank Byron. An Introduction to the History of Religion. 2nd ed., 1902. (2217 bb 9.)

Kaerst, J. Geschichte des hellenistischen Zeitalters. 1909.

Knauer, Vincenz. Die Hauptprobleme der Philosophie. 1892. (8462 g 2.)

Krische, A. B. Forschungen auf dem Gebiete der alten Philosophie. 1840. (1134 c 19.)
Laberthonnière, P. L. Essai de philosophie religieuse.
Laferrière, L. F. J. Mémoire concernant l'influence du Stoicisme sur la doctrine des Jurisconsultes romains. Mém. de l'acad. d. sciences morales, x, 1860, pp. 579–685. (5254 aaa 11.)
Le Blant, Edmond. Les persecutions et les martyrs aux premiers siècles de nôtre ère. 1893. (4530 ee 24.)
Lehmann, Edv. Die Perser. In de la Saussaye's Lehrbuch der Religionsgeschichte. 2nd ed., 1897. (3554 i.)
Lewes, G. H. History of Philosophy. New ed., 1897. (2023 a.)
Lightfoot, J. B. See Seneca.
Lindsay, James. Studies in European Philosophy. 1909. [Chap. IV deals with 'the ethical philosophy of Marcus Aurelius.']
Lodge, Sir Oliver J. Life and Matter. 2nd ed., 1909. (08461 f 40/1.)
Long, George. See Aurelius, Epictetus.
Luthe, Werner. Die Erkenntnisslehre der Stoiker. 1890. (08464 f 9/1.)
Mahaffy, J. P. Greek Life and Thought. 1896. (9026 bbb 3.) The progress of Hellenism in Alexander's Empire. 1905. (9025 bbb 28.) The empire of the Ptolemies. 1895. (2382 b 5.) A survey of Greek civilisation. 1897. (2258 b 19.)
Martha, C. Les moralistes sous l'empire romain. Philosophes et poètes. 1865. (8407 ff 17.) See also Seneca.
Masson, J. See Lucretius.
Mayor, J. B. A sketch of ancient philosophy from Thales to Cicero. 1881. (2322 b 57.)
Mead, G. R. S. Apollonius of Tyana. 1901. (10606 cc 8.)
Montée, P. Le Stoïcisme à Rome. 1865. (8461 aaa 6.)
Montefiore, Claude G. The Wisdom of Solomon. 1887. (Ac. 2076.)
Natorp, Paul. Forschungen zur Geschichte des Erkenntniss-problems im Alterthum. 1884. (8460 h 7.)
Naville, H. Adrien. Julian l'Apostat et la philosophie du polytheisme. 1877. (4504 bb 5.)
Neander, A. Vorlesungen über Geschichte d. christlichen Ethik. 1864. [On Stoicism see pp. 29—57.]
Nettleship, Henry. Jus Gentium. Journal of Philology xiii (1885), p. 26.
Neumann, C. J. Der römische Staat und die allg. Kirche bis auf Diocletian. 1890. (4534 d 16.)
Ogereau, F. Essai sur le système philosophique des stoïciens. 1885. (8460 ee 20.)
Oldenberg, H. Buddha; his life, his doctrine, his order. Transl. by W. Hoey. 1882. (759 d 4.)
Orttoff, Jo. Andr. Über den Einfluss d. stoïschen Philosophie auf die römische Jurisprudenz. 1797.
Pater, Walter H. Marius the Epicurean. 2 vols., 1892. (12620 dd 18.)
Pauly, A. F. von. Realencyclopädie d. klassischen Altertumswissenschaft. Neue Bearbeitung, herausg. von G. Wissowa. 1893– . (2046 f.)
Poussin, L. de la Vallée. Bouddhisme: opinions sur l'histoire de la Dogmatique. 1909.
Prächter, Karl. Hierocles der Stoïker. 1901. (8460 h 23.)
Prosopographia Imperii Romani Saec. I, II, III. Ed. E. Klebs and others. 1897– . [Gives the authorities for biographies of this period.]
Ramsay, Sir W. M. The Church in the Roman empire before A.D. 170. 7th ed. 1903. (2208 b 2.)
Rauch, G. Der Einfluss d. stoïschen Philosophie an d. Lehrbildung Tertullianus.
Ravaisson, F. Essai sur le Stoïcisme. 1856.

Renan, J. E. See Aurelius.

Rendall, G. H. The Emperor Julian, Paganism and Christianity. 1879. (4534 cc 8.) See also Aurelius.

Renouvier, C. B. Uchronie. [Deals with the secular importance of Stoicism.] (8008 g 1.)

Réville, Jean. La religion à Rome sous les Sévères. 1886. (4505 ee 19.)

Richter, D. Die Überlieferung der stoïschen Definitionen über die Affekte. 1873.

Sachau, C. E. Drei aramaïsche Papyrus-Urkunden aus Elephantine. 1907. Royal Prussian Society. (Ac. 855/6.)

Saussaye, P. D. C. de la. Lehrbuch der Religionsgeschichte. 3rd ed., 2 vols., 1905. (3554 i.)

Schiller, Hermann. Die stoïsche Opposition unter Nero. 1867, 8. (8485 bbb 28.)

Schmekel, August. Die Philosophie der mittleren Stoa in ihrem geschichtlichen Zusammenhange dargestellt. 1892. (8485 df 19.)

Schmidt, C. G. A. Essai historique sur la société civile dans le monde romain et sur sa transformation par le christianisme. 1853. (4531 c 25.) Trans. by Mrs Thorpe, 1907. (4532 de 10.)

Schmidt, R. T. Stoicorum Grammatica. 1839. (8462 b 1.)

Schulze, Vict. Geschichte des Untergangs der gr.-röm. Heidenthums. 2 vols. 1887-96. (4530 ee 8.)

Seeck, O. Geschichte des Untergangs der antiken Welt. 3rd ed., 1910– (09039 dd.)

Sidgwick, Henry. Outlines of the History of Ethics. 1886. [Ch. 11 deals with ' Greco-Roman Ethics.']

Smiley, C. N. Latinitas und Ἑλληνισμός. Wisconsin, 1906.

Sonnenschein, E. A. The new Stoicism. Hibbert Journal, April 1907. (R. PP. 324 ga.) Shakespeare and Stoicism. University Review, i 1. (PP. 1187 ief.)

Spiess, E. Logos Spermatikos. Parallelstellen z. neuen Test. aus d. Schriften d. alten Griechen. 1871. (3225 ee 29.)

Stein, Ludwig. Psychologie der Stoa. 2 vols., 1886-8. (PP. 4991 e.) Die Willensfreiheit etc. bei den jüdischen Philosophen. 1882. (8469 bbb 26.) Dualismus oder Monismus. 1909.

Steinthal, H. Geschichte der Sprachwissenschaft bei den Griechen und Römern. 2nd ed., 1890, 1. (12924 h 18.) [On the Stoic grammar see i pp. 265 sqq.]

Stern, J. Homerstudien der Stoïker. Lörrach, 1893.

Stock, St George W. J. Stoicism. (Phil. Ancient and Modern.) 1908. (8467 de.)

Striller, F. De Stoicorum studiis rhetoricis. Breslau, 1886. (12902 f 25.)

Susemihl, Fr. Geschichte der gr. Litteratur in d. Alexandrinerzeit. 2 vols., 1891, 2. (2045 g.)

Teuffel, W. S. History of Roman Literature. Translated by G. C. W. Warr. 2 vols., 1890. (2045 g.)

Thiersch, W. J. Politik und Philosophie in ihrem Verhältniss zur Religion unter Traianus, Hadrianus, und den beiden Antoninen. Marburg, 1853. (4573 e 37.)

Thomas, A. Rome et l'Empire aux deux premiers siècles de nôtre ère. 1897. (9039 d 9.) Transl.: Roman Life under the Caesars. 1899. (7701 aa 11.)

Thomson, Sir J. J. The corpuscular theory of matter. 1907. (08709 dd 16.)

Tiedemann, D. System der stoischen Philosophie. 1776.

Tucker, T. G. Life in the Roman World of Nero and St Paul. 1910.

Tylor, Edward B. Primitive culture. 4th ed., 2 vols., 1903. (2034 a.) Anthropology. 1881. (2024 b.)

A. 29

Überweg, Fr. Grundriss der Geschichte der Philosophie. Tenth ed. by K. Prächter, 1909– (8485 ff.) Translated from the 4th German edition by G. S. Morris. 2 vols. New York. 1872-4.

Usener, H. Épicurea. 1887. (8460 ee 36.) Religionsgeschichtliche Untersuchungen. 3 vols. 1889–99. (4532 dd 2.)

Vachereau, Étienne. Histoire critique de l'école d'Alexandrie. 3 vols., 1846–51. (2236 d 7–9.)

de Villoison, J. d'Ansse. De theologia physica Stoicorum commentatio. Göttingen, 1844. (1385 g 4.)

Voigt, M. Die Lehre vom *ius naturale, aequum et bonum,* und *ius gentium* der Römer. 4 vols., 1856–76. (5207 d 5.) Römische Rechtsgeschichte. 3 vols., 1892–1902. (5255 dd 1.)

Vollers, Charles. Die Weltreligionen in ihrem geschichtlichen Zusammenhange.

Vollman, F. Über das Verhältniss der späteren Stoa zur Sklaverei im römischen Reiche. Regensburg, 1890.

Wachsmuth, Curtius. Die Ansichten der Stoïker über Mantik und Dämonen, 1860. (8461 bb 44 (9).) De Cratete Mallota. 1860. (11312 g 40.)

Wadskin, S. E. Einfluss des Stoïcismus auf die christliche Lehrbildung. Theol. Stud. und Krit., 1880. (PP. 150.)

Wallace, William. Epicureanism. 1880. (4421 f 64.)

Walter, Julius. Die Lehre von der praktischen Vernunft in der griechischen Philosophie. 1874. (8462 cc 22.)

Weissenfels, C. O. De Platonicae et Stoicae doctrinae affinitate. Berlin, 1890.

Wellmann, Eduard. Die pneumatische Schule bis auf Archigenes in ihrer Entwicklung dargestellt. 1895. See also Fleckeisen's Jahrb. 1873, pp. 477 sqq.

Wendland, Paul. Die hellenisch-römische Kultur in ihren Beziehungen zu Judenthum und Christenthum. 1907.

Westcott, B. F. See Origenes.

Westermarck, Edward. The history of human marriage. 3rd ed. 1901. (2236 f 7.) The origin and development of the moral ideas. 2 vols. 1906-9. (08407 f 21.)

Wetzstein, O. Die Wandlung der stoïschen Lehre unter ihren späteren Vertretern. Neu-Strelitz, 1892-4.

Weygoldt, G. P. Die Philosophie der Stoa nach ihrem Wesen und ihren Schicksalen dargestellt. 1883. (8462 b 8.)

Whittaker, Thomas. Apollonius of Tyana and other essays. 1906. (012356 l 62.)

Winckler, H. A. Der Stoïcismus eine Wurzel des Christenthums. 1878.

Windelband, W. Geschichte der alten Philosophie. In the Handbuch d. klass. Alterthumswissenschaft. 1894. Translated by H. E. Cushmann, New York, 1899. (2236 cc 8.)

Winter, F. J. Stoicorum pantheismus et principia doctrinae ethicae. Leipzig, 1878.

Zeller, Eduard. Die Philosophie der Griechen in ihrer geschichtlichen Entwicklung. 5th ed. 1892– . (8486 h.) The Stoics, Epicureans and Sceptics. Translated from the German by O. J. Reichel. 1892. (2234 b 22.) Vorträge und Abhandlungen, 1875. (12250 i 13.) Philosophische Aufsätze, 1887. (8468 f 34.) Über eine Berührung des jüngeren Cynismus mit dem Christenthum. Sitzungsb. d. Akad. Wiss. z. Berlin, ix pp. 129-132. Kleine Schriften, unter Mitwirkung von H. Diels und K. Holl. Edited by Dr Otto Leuze. Berlin, 1910– . (12252 g.)

Zimmermann, D. Quae ratio philosophiae Stoicae sit cum religione Romana. Erlangen, 1858.

GENERAL INDEX.

The numbers refer to the pages and notes.

GREEK INDEX.